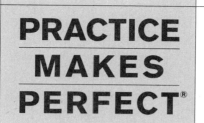

Complete French All-in-One

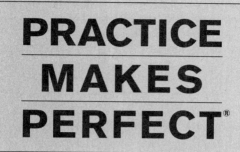

Complete French All-in-One

Premium Third Edition

Annie Heminway, Editor

New York Chicago San Francisco Athens London Madrid
Mexico City Milan New Delhi Singapore Sydney Toronto

Copyright © 2023, 2018, 2013 by McGraw Hill. All rights reserved. Printed in the United States of America. Except as permitted under the United States Copyright Act of 1976, no part of this publication may be reproduced or distributed in any form or by any means, or stored in a database or retrieval system, without the prior written permission of the publisher.

5 6 7 8 9 LBC 29 28 27 26 25

ISBN	978-1-264-28561-7
MHID	1-264-28561-2
e-ISBN	978-1-264-28562-4
e-MHID	1-264-28562-0

Portions of this book were previously published under the titles of *Practice Makes Perfect: Complete French Grammar*, *Practice Makes Perfect: French Nouns and Their Genders Up Close*, *Practice Makes Perfect: French Problem Solver*, *Practice Makes Perfect: French Pronouns and Prepositions*, *Practice Makes Perfect: French Verb Tenses*, *Practice Makes Perfect: French Vocabulary*, and *Practice Makes Perfect: French Sentence Builder*.

McGraw Hill, the McGraw Hill logo, Practice Makes Perfect, and related trade dress are trademarks or registered trademarks of McGraw Hill and/or its affiliates in the United States and other countries and may not be used without written permission. All other trademarks are the property of their respective owners. McGraw Hill is not associated with any product or vendor mentioned in this book.

Interior design by Village Bookworks, Inc.

McGraw Hill products are available at special quantity discounts to use as premiums and sales promotions or for use in corporate training programs. To contact a representative, please visit the Contact Us pages at www.mhprofessional.com.

McGraw Hill is committed to making our products accessible to all learners. To learn more about the available support and accommodations we offer, please contact us at accessibility@ mheducation.com. We also participate in the Access Text Network (www.accesstext.org), and ATN members may submit requests through ATN.

McGraw Hill Language Lab App

Extensive streaming audio recordings and vocabulary flashcards are available to support your study of this book. Go to mhlanguagelab.com to access the online version of this application or to locate links to the mobile app for iOS and Android devices. (Note: Internet access is required to access audio via the app.)

Contents

Preface ix

1 Articles 1

2 Basic gender endings: **Masculin** and **féminin** 13

3 More French nouns and their gender 37

4 Numbers 78

5 Vocabulary: Thoughts, feelings, communicating, home, travel, science, leisure, and technology 87

6 Building sentences 121

7 Asking questions 129

8 Exclamations and commands 149

9 Independent clauses and subordinate clauses 159

10 The present tense of **-er** verbs 174

11 The present of -ir and **-re** verbs 186

12 Être, **avoir,** and other irregular verbs 197

13 The immediate future, the immediate past, and the causative form 211

14 Pronominal verbs 221

15 The **passé composé** 227

v

16 The **imparfait** and the **plus-que-parfait** 237

17 The simple future and the past future 249

18 The present conditional and the past conditional 258

19 *Could, should, would?* 268

20 The present subjunctive and the past subjunctive 275

21 Prepositions 285

22 The infinitive mood 315

23 The imperative mood 328

24 The present participle and gerund 336

25 The simple past, the passive voice, and indirect speech 343

26 Pronouns 361

27 Relative pronouns 384

28 Adjectives 394

29 Adverbs 406

30 Written French: Making transitions and written correspondence 415

31 Verb transfers and confusing verbs 434

32 *Whatever, whenever, wherever*: French oddities and fun with prepositions 465

33 French in conversation: Meeting people 478

34 French in conversation: Making conversation and making plans 491

35 French in conversation: Discussing current events 510

36 French in conversation: Asking for help 525

37 A taste of French literature 537

Appendix A   French pronunciation   553
Appendix B   Grammatical terminology for verbs   557
Appendix C   French verb tables   561
Appendix D   French-English / English-French glossary   587
Answer key   611
Translations   641

Preface

The idea of a book containing all knowledge is probably as old as literacy. In one of his brilliant short fiction collections, *The Book of Sand*, Jorge Luis Borges describes the paradox of infinity contained between the covers of a book. As every student of French knows, there are always lacunae to fill—lexical, syntactic, orthographic, and so on. Despite any progress, the learner feels not only overwhelmed, but also stuck in quicksand, unable to reach solid ground. However, a solid foundation exists, and its title is *Practice Makes Perfect: Complete French All-in-One.*

This book provides a map of the French language—a cartographic representation, as it were—of the Empire of the French language, encompassing seven provinces. What makes this map self-sufficient is the fact that it contains numerous clues and indications to guide the wanderer through lesser-known, or even unmapped, labyrinths. Distilling the best content from seven *Practice Makes Perfect* titles, this book features hand-picked selections from the following:

- *Practice Makes Perfect: Complete French Grammar* may not include every grammatical rule conceivable to man or woman; nevertheless, it provides a general idea of French grammar, which you can use as a compass.
- *Practice Makes Perfect: French Nouns and Their Genders Up Close* entertains the quizzical world of French nouns, where words sometimes have two genders or even seem undecided. In this region, you will learn how to detect the correct gender of nouns on the basis of their context.
- *Practice Makes Perfect: French Vocabulary*, relying on its thematic structure, encourages the development of a rich vocabulary by starting from your own particular interests and naturally moving from a familiar context to lesser-known fields.
- In *Practice Makes Perfect: French Sentence Builder,* you'll assume the role of an architect, metaphorically speaking, of course. Nevertheless, you will learn, just as architects do, that a clear conception must precede the work of a building a structure. In this section, as in the others, engaging exercises and examples drawn from real life lead to a mastery of syntactic forms.
- It has been said that French prepositions are the Achilles' heel of highly proficient French students. Indeed, a wrong preposition can totally demolish an elegant French speaker's reputation. However, *Practice Makes Perfect: French Pronouns and Prepositions* provides a plethora of exercises, based on written French and everyday daily discourse, which will develop an ability to pick the right preposition and to grasp the preposition-pronoun synergy in French.

ix

- In the breathtaking province of *Practice Makes Perfect: French Verb Tenses,* the student learns to perceive time, particularly the past, in a new way. Grammar manuals may describe a tense, but a visit to this province teaches us the inimitable art of modulating tenses, from **passé composé** to **passé simple** to **imparfait** naturally and seamlessly as the narrative unfolds, just as a master of French prose would.
- *Practice Makes Perfect: French Problem Solver* tackles the many conundrums that haunt even the most accomplished learner. For example, a manual of grammar merely describes the dance of pronouns in a sentence with two pronouns; this section strives to explain the dance itself, thus encouraging you to look at what's behind grammatical rules.
- And accompanying this premium third edition are recordings of example sentences throughout the book, in addition to the answers to numerous exercises, available via the McGraw Hill Language Lab app. This streaming audio will help readers improve both listening and speaking skills.

Articles ·1·

The definite article with nouns

Let's first look at the definite article. All nouns in French have a gender: masculine or feminine, whether they refer to a person, an animal, a thing, or an abstract notion. While English has only one definite article *the*, French uses **le** for masculine nouns and **la** for feminine nouns. **Le** and **la** are shortened to **l'** before a singular noun or adjective that begins with a vowel sound. The plural **les** is used for both masculine and feminine.

Masculine

le village	*the village*
le pont	*the bridge*

Feminine

la ville	*the city*
la région	*the region*

Plural

les villages (*m.pl.*)	*the villages*
les villes (*f.pl.*)	*the cities*

Le and **la** become **l'** in front of singular nouns starting with a vowel or a mute **h**.

Masculine

l'océan	*the ocean*
l'ami	*the friend*

Feminine

l'île	*the island*
l'autoroute	*the highway*

Où se trouve **le pont** Alexandre III?	*Where is the Alexandre III bridge?*
La ville principale est à cent kilomètres d'ici.	*The main town is a hundred kilometers away.*
Prenez **le chemin** sur **la droite**.	*Take the path on the (your) right.*
Le réchauffement de **la planète** est **le sujet** de sa conférence.	*Global warming is the topic of his lecture.*
Les enfants jouent dans **le jardin**.	*The children are playing in the garden.*
L'ami de Sonia est japonais.	*Sonia's friend is Japanese.*

VOCABULAIRE

la terre	Earth	une plaine	a plain
une planète	a planet	une vallée	a valley
un pays	a country	une montagne	a mountain
un continent	a continent	une colline	a hill
une capitale	a capital	une île	an island
une ville	a city	un pont	a bridge
un village	a village	la mer	a sea
une rue	a street	un océan	an ocean
une ruelle	an alley, a lane	une rivière	a river (tributary)
une impasse	a dead end	un fleuve	a river (flowing into the sea)
un plan de la ville	a city map		
un arrondissement	a (city) district	un ruisseau	a brook, a stream
une région	a region	le nord	north
une province	a province	le sud	south
un état	a state	l'est (m.)	east
un royaume	a kingdom	l'ouest (m.)	west
le désert	the desert	un peuple	a people, a nation
une frontière	a border	une tribu	a tribe
une carte	a map	autochtone	native
une route	a road	étranger, étrangère	foreign
une autoroute	a highway	inconnu(e)	foreign, unknown
une côte	a coast(line)		

The indefinite and partitive articles with nouns

The indefinite articles are **un** (masculine singular) (*a*), **une** (feminine singular) (*a*), and **des** (both masculine and feminine plural) (*some*).

Masculine
un projet	*a project, a plan*
un bâtiment	*a building*
un immeuble	*an apartment building*

Feminine
une maison	*a house*
une lampe	*a lamp*
une avalanche	*an avalanche*
une aubergine	*an eggplant*

Masculine or feminine
un(e) architecte	*an architect*
un(e) artiste	*an artist*
un(e) journaliste	*a journalist*

Masculine and feminine plural
des murs (*m.pl.*)	*(some) walls*
des balcons (*m.pl.*)	*(some) balconies*
des fenêtres (*f.pl.*)	*(some) windows*
des amis (*m.pl.*)	*(some) friends (m.)*
des amies (*f.pl.*)	*(some) friends (f.)*

Est-ce qu'il y a **une piscine**?	*Is there a swimming pool?*
Elle a acheté **un vélo**.	*She bought a bike.*

2 PRACTICE MAKES PERFECT Complete French All-in-One

Nous avons vu **des lapins** dans le jardin.	We saw (some) rabbits in the garden.
Il a acheté **des rideaux** pour le salon.	He bought (some) curtains for the living room.
Il a **un nouveau chien**.	He has a new dog.
Tu veux emprunter **un de mes livres**?	Do you want to borrow one of my books?

The partitive article

The partitive article is used when the exact quantity of an item is unknown. In English, the partitive article is often omitted. We say, "I want bread" or "I want some bread." However, the partitive article is always required in French. It is formed by combining **de** and the definite article.

de + le = du
de + l' = de l'
de + la = de la
de + les = des

Je voudrais **du** pain.	I would like some bread.
Elle mange **du** chocolat.	She eats chocolate.
Nous buvons **de l'**eau minérale.	We drink mineral water.
Il achète **de la** viande.	He is buying meat.
Elle fait pousser **des** haricots verts.	She grows green beans.

When used in the negative, the **du**, **de la**, and **des** all become **de**, since the quantity of the item doesn't exist any longer.

Ce village a **du** charme.	This village has charm.
Ce village n'a pas **de** charme.	This village has no charm.
Il prête **de l'**argent à son ami.	He lends money to his friend.
Il ne prête pas **d'**argent à son ami.	He does not lend any money to his friend.
Elle a **des** amis à Paris.	She has friends in Paris.
Elle n'a pas **d'**amis à Paris.	She does not have any friends in Paris.
Nous avons **des** cartes routières.	We have road maps.
Nous n'avons pas **de** cartes routières.	We do not have any road maps.

One exception to this rule is when using the verb **être** (*to be*). In the negative, the partitive article is always used with **être**.

C'est **du** fromage de chèvre.	It's goat cheese.
Ce n'est pas **du** fromage de chèvre.	It's not goat cheese.
C'est **de la** porcelaine.	It's porcelain.
Ce n'est pas **de la** porcelaine.	It's not porcelain.
C'est **de l'**eau potable.	It's drinkable water.
Ce n'est pas **de l'**eau potable.	It's not drinking water.

EXERCICE
1·1

Compléter avec l'article partitif approprié.

1. Il prend _____ vacances.

2. Nous mangeons _____ pain.

3. Elle visite _____ monuments.

4. Elle a _____ chance.

Articles 3

5. Il met _____ ail dans la salade.

6. Vous choisissez _____ cadeaux pour vos amis.

7. Il boit _____ lait.

8. Nous envoyons _____ cartes postales en vacances.

9. Tu plantes _____ légumes.

10. Elle veut _____ crème fraîche.

Accent on accents

There is an annoying tendency, quite widespread in the English-speaking world, to dismiss French accents as another example of Gallic eccentricity. In fact, there are reference sources, whose publishers shall remain unnamed, containing thousands of titles, without accents, of French-language publications. French accents are a nuisance, these publishers maintain, and what counts is correct spelling. Indeed, but while we're talking about correct spelling, let us remind the anti-accent crowd that the result of removing a needed accent is a *typo*.

As we shall see, French accents, which by the way have nothing to do with stress, not only indicate the *correct pronunciation* of a vowel, but also act as *semantic markers*. For example, consider the following two exclamations:

> Vivre . . . ou . . . ?
> Vivre . . . où . . . ?

They may sound the same, but their meaning is completely different. The first phrase, which might remind us of the dilemma expressed in Hamlet's famous soliloquy, could be translated as: *To live . . . or to . . . ?*

Perhaps expressing some confusion, but definitely lacking any sinister overtones, the second phrase means: *To live . . . where . . . ?*

Or imagine getting a photograph of a friend at the Louvre Pyramid in Paris. Without the necessary accent, the caption would read:

> Marie a la pyramide du Louvre.

This literally means: *Marie has the Louvre Pyramid.*

Without the **accent grave**, **a** is the third-person singular of the verb **avoir**; when we add the **accent grave**, as in **à**, we get a preposition! Now you know why people who denigrate French accents are not to be trusted.

There are four accents in French for vowels and a cedilla for the consonant **c**. In most cases, their main purpose is to modify the pronunciation of a vowel, except for the cedilla, of course, which modifies the pronunciation of a consonant.

É

The **accent aigu** (*acute accent*) ´ is used only with the vowel **e**, as in **été** (*summer*), and it indicates that the vowel should be pronounced as a *closed e*. Think of the *e* in the English word *bed*. Here are other examples:

le café	*coffee*
le céléri	*celery*
le désir	*desire*

l'épaule	shoulder
gérer	to manage, to handle
le médecin	doctor
le mélange	mix
le musée	museum
la poésie	poetry
la sécheresse	drought

In some words the initial **é** replaces an initial **s** that figures in earlier Latin and Old French forms. Note that the Latin **s** is still alive in the English cognates. Let's look at a few examples:

l'éponge	sponge
l'état, l'État	state, condition
l'étudiant	student
étudier	to study

È, À, and Ù

The **accent grave** (*grave accent*) ` is used on the vowels **a**, **e**, and **u**, as in **à** (*at, in*) and **mère** (*mother*), and has a more open pronunciation. For example, **è** resembles the vowel sound in the English word *bad*. (If you ever meet someone from Geneva, Switzerland, ask him or her to pronounce the name of that city: Genève. You will hear a deliciously open vowel in the second syllable.) Let's look at other examples:

à	at, in
après	after
la/la collègue	colleague
le congrès	congress, conference
la crème	cream
la grève	strike
l'interprète	interpreter
là	here, there
où	where
le procès	lawsuit

Circumflex

The **accent circonflexe** ˆ (*circumflex*) can be found on **a**, **e**, **i**, **o**, and **u**:

Le chien s'amuse avec un bâton.	The dog plays with a stick.
Ils ramassent des champignons dans la forêt.	They pick mushrooms in the woods.
Un touriste finlandais est tombé dans un abîme dans les Alpes.	A Finnish tourist fell into an abyss in the Alps.
Les hôtes sont arrivés en retard.	The guests arrived late.
Cette pêche n'est pas mûre.	This peach is not ripe.

If the English cognate contains an **s** that is missing in the French word, you may assume that the French word will need a circumflex accent, which fills the space created by the disappearance of the **s** in French. Most of these words, as you may have guessed, are derived from Latin. For example:

| le coût | cost |
| la fête | feast |

Articles **5**

la forêt	*forest*
l'hôpital	*hospital*
l'hôte	*host*
l'intérêt	*interest*
la pâte	*pasta*

It is important to identify the meaning of words. Look at the examples:

- **a** versus **à**

| Il **a** un nouvel ordinateur. | He **has** a new computer. |
| Il habite **à** Strasbourg. | He lives **in** Strasbourg. |

- **de** versus **dé**

| Elle est revenue **de** Turquie. | She came back **from** Turkey. |
| Les enfants jouaient aux **dés** dans la rue. | The children played **dice** on the street. |

- **du** versus **dû**

| Tu veux du thé ou **du** café? | Do you want **some** tea or coffee? |
| Ils ont **dû** partir à six heures. | They **had to** leave at 6 o'clock. |

Diaeresis

Another accent is the **tréma**, or *diaeresis*. The diaeresis is used when two vowels are next to each other and the accented vowel represents a separate sound. In other words, both vowels in a diphthong must be articulated. For example:

aïe	*ouch*
ambiguïté	*ambiguity*
archaïque	*archaic*
bonsaï	*bonsai*
Caraïbe	*Caribbean*
coïncidence	*coincidence*
égoïste	*selfish*
faïence	*earthenware*
héroïne	*heroine*
laïc	*secular*
maïs	*corn*
mosaïque	*mosaic*
naïve	*naive*
Noël	*Christmas*

La cédille

There is also a graphic sign called **la cédille**, **ç**. The **cédille** (*cedilla*) is found only under the letter **c** before the vowels **a**, **o**, and **u**. It changes the hard sound of **catalogue** (*catalog*) (like a **k**) into a soft sound of **ça** (*this, that*). It is not used with the vowels **e** and **i**.

la balançoire	*swing*
le commerçant	*shopkeeper, merchant*
la façade	*façade, front*
la façon	*way, manner*
français	*French*
le garçon	*boy*
le glaçon	*ice cube*
la leçon	*lesson*
le reçu	*receipt*
le soupçon	*suspicion*

6 PRACTICE MAKES PERFECT Complete French All-in-One

It is important to remember to use the **cédille** when conjugating verbs in different tenses:

nous commençons	*we start*
elle a aperçu	*she noticed*
en remplaçant	*while replacing*
il menaçait	*he was threatening*
nous plaçons	*we are placing*
je soupçonne	*I suspect*
tu déplaçais	*you moved*
ils enfonçaient	*they pushed, hammered*
je conçois	*I conceive, imagine*
il pinça	*he pinched*

Choose the right form of the verb.

1. La journaliste annonçait/annoncait/annonssait les résultats de l'élection quand il y a eu une panne d'électricité.
2. Nous voyagons/voyageons/voyageeons en Sicile chaque automne.
3. Vous reconnaîssez/reconnaissez/reconnaiçez votre erreur.
4. Après la fête, mes amis rangèrent/rangerent/rangairent la maison très vite.
5. Élodie manga/mangai/mangea une crème brûlée.
6. Tu as été réveillé/reveillé/rêveillé par le chant du coq.
7. Je reconnaitrais/reconnaîtrais/reconnaîtrait la chanson si vous la chantiez.
8. Tous les étés, nous finançons/financons/finanssons une bibliothèque mobile.
9. J'ai enfin recu/ressu/reçu ma commande de livres.
10. Les associations écologiques empêchèrent/empecherent/empéchèrent le départ du vieux bateau.

Restore the accents or the graphic signs in the following passage. (See Translations *at the back of this book for the English.)*

La porte etroite, André Gide (1909)

—Tiens! Ma porte n'etait donc pas fermee? dit-elle.

—J'ai frappe; tu n'as pas repondu, Alissa, tu sais que je pars demain?

Elle ne repondit rien, mais posa sur la cheminee le collier qu'elle ne parvenait pas a agrafer. Le mot: fiancailles me paraissait trop nu, trop brutal, j'employai je ne sais quelle periphrase a la

place. Des qu'Alissa me comprit, il me parut qu'elle chancela, s'appuya contre la cheminee …
mais j'etais moi-meme si tremblant que craintivement j'evitais de regarder vers elle.

J'etais pres d'elle et, sans lever les yeux, lui pris la main; elle ne se degagea pas, mais,
inclinant un peu son visage et soulevant un peu ma main, elle y posa ses levres et murmura,
appuyee a demi contre moi:

—Non, Jerome, non; ne nous fiancons pas, je t'en prie … […]
—Pourquoi?
—Mais c'est moi qui peux te demander: pourquoi? pourquoi changer?
Je n'osais lui parler de la conversation de la veille, mais sans doute elle sentit que j'y
pensais, et, comme une reponse a ma pensee, dit en me regardant fixement:
—Tu te meprends, mon ami: je n'ai pas besoin de tant de bonheur. Ne sommes-nous pas
heureux ainsi?
Elle s'efforcait en vain a sourire.
—Non, puisque je dois te quitter.
—Ecoute, Jerome, je ne puis te parler ce soir … Ne gatons pas nos derniers instants …
Non, non. Je t'aime autant que jamais; rassure-toi. Je t'ecrirai; je t'expliquerai. Je te
promets de t'ecrire, des demain … des que tu seras parti. Va, maintenant!

The **h aspiré**

In the French language, about 1,500 words start with the letter **h**. And of these, three hundred of
them are called **h aspiré**.

You are acquainted with nouns like **l'habitant** (*inhabitant*), **l'habitude** (*habit*), **l'hélicoptère**
(*helicopter*), **l'heure** (*hour, time*), **l'histoire** (*history, story*), **l'hiver** (*winter*), **l'homme** (*man*), **l'hôpital** (*hospital*), **l'hôtel** (*hotel*), **l'huile** (*oil*), and so on. These nouns start with an **h** that is silent and
the article that precedes them needs an apostrophe.

The **h aspiré** is also silent, but the liaison between the article and the noun is not allowed, so
there is no apostrophe on the article. Here are some of the most important nouns with **h aspiré**:

la haie	*hedge*
la haine	*hatred*
le hamac	*hammock*
le hameau	*hamlet*
la hanche	*hip*
le handicap	*handicap*
le haricot	*bean*
le hasard	*chance*
le harcèlement	*harassment*
la hausse	*increase, rise*
le haut	*top, summit*
le héros	*hero*
la hiérarchie	*hierarchy*
le homard	*lobster*
la honte	*shame*
le hors-d'œuvre	*hors-d'oeuvre*

This is of the utmost importance, for you don't want the French laughing at you when they hear:
les héros de la Révolution, which when pronounced without the aspiration sounds like "The
zeros (dummies) of the Revolution"!

As we've seen before, rules can be unreliable, so it's better to remember words in context.

8 PRACTICE MAKES PERFECT Complete French All-in-One

EXERCICE 1·4

Using the preceding vocabulary list of **h aspiré** *words, translate the following sentences using the* **est-ce que** *form and* **tu** *when necessary.*

1. The hierarchy in this organization is a game of chance.

   _____

2. The hero of this new film is a man who lives in the hamlet next to our village.

   _____

3. The hatred between the two brothers is well-known.

   _____

4. Nora is surprised by the increase of the prices of the hotel's restaurant.

   _____

5. The hors-d'oeuvres they served were delicious.

   _____

6. Do you want to order the lobster on the menu?

   _____

7. Carole's father fractured his hip last week.

   _____

8. The hammock in the garden is a gift from Laurent.

   _____

9. The cold winter in this city is the main handicap for our grandparents.

   _____

10. The shame of his defeat is hard to accept.

   _____

Capitalization

In French, the capitalization of words differs quite a bit from English capitalization. After all this business of "rules but no rules," *one rule* is pretty solid: capitalization is more frequent in English than it is in French. Let's look at a few examples.

Nationalities

Adjectives that refer to nationalities are capitalized in English but not in French. Nouns that refer to nationalities are capitalized in both languages. For example:

Marie est **française**.   *Marie is* **French**.
Paolo est **brésilien**.   *Paolo is* **Brazilian**.

Son professeur est un **Français** de Lyon.	*Her teacher is a **Frenchman** from Lyon.*
Elle partage un appartement avec une **Italienne**.	*She shares her apartment with an **Italian woman**.*

Languages

Languages are capitalized in English but not in French. For example:

Ils apprennent l'**arabe**.	*They are learning **Arabic**.*
Nous parlons **espagnol** à la maison.	*We speak **Spanish** at home.*

Locations

When you write an address, the words for *street*, *avenue*, *place*, and other names for roads are not capitalized. For example:

25, rue de l'Université
55, avenue de Neuilly
110, boulevard des Capucines
37, quai Branly
1, place des Abbesses
7, impasse de la Tonnelle

Dates, time, days, months, and seasons

Such words are not capitalized. For example:

Son anniversaire est le 23 **août**.	*His birthday is on the 23rd of **August**.*
Nous partirons le 5 **décembre**.	*We'll leave on **December** 5.*
Paris, le 10 **mars** 2013	*Paris, **March** 10, 2013*
Il est 10**h**05.	*It is 10:05 **a.m.***

Religions

In French, the names of religions tend not to be capitalized except **l'Islam** (Islam):

le christianisme	*Christianity*
le judaïsme	*Judaism*
le bouddhisme	*Buddhism*
l'hindouisme	*Hinduism*

Geographical nouns

Geographic names, as we have seen at the beginning of this chapter, are capitalized: **l'Asie** (*Asia*), **l'Europe** (*Europe*), **les États-Unis** (*United States*), **la Loire** (*Loire River*), **La Nouvelle-Orléans** (*New Orleans*), **La Havane** (*Havana*), **Aix-en-Provence** (*Aix-en-Provence*).

If the geographic noun is composed of a generic name (*bay, cape, river, sea*, etc.) and a specific noun, only the specific noun is capitalized:

la mer Rouge	*the Red Sea*
la mer Noire	*the Black Sea*
la mer Morte	*the Dead Sea*
l'île Maurice	*Mauritius Island*
l'île de Ré	*Île de Ré*
la baie des Anges	*the Bay of Angels*

le cap Horn	Cape Horn
la péninsule Ibérique	the Iberian Peninsula
le désert d'Arabie	the Arabian Desert
l'océan Pacifique	the Pacific Ocean
le pôle Nord	the North Pole

You will run into many other cases like **l'Asie centrale** (*Central Asia*), **l'Asie Mineure** (*Asia Minor*), **l'Asie du Sud-Est** (*Southeast Asia*), **l'Arabie Saoudite** (*Saudi Arabia*), **le Moyen-Orient** (*the Middle East*), **l'Extrême-Orient** (*the Far East*), **les Grands Lacs** (*the Great Lakes*), so check your dictionary.

EXERCICE 1·5

*Translate the following sentences. Be aware of the capitalization of words, using **tu** when necessary.*

1. Jean is Belgian.

2. Isabella is Hungarian.

3. Bruno's children speak French with their friends and English with their parents.

4. In Greece, winter is mild.

5. Lucie was born on February 28.

6. The jazz festival takes place from July 1 to 4.

7. The Mediterranean Sea is less salty than the Dead Sea.

8. Spanish and Portuguese are the main languages in Latin America.

9. The South Pole is in the Antarctic.

10. When you are skiing in the Alps, you can go from France to Slovenia.

Addressing people

When writing to people in French, capitalize most titles:

Monsieur Verneuil
Madame Deneuve
Maître Didier Lebon
Monsieur le Recteur de l'académie de Poitiers
Monsieur le Premier ministre

Accents on capitals

An old topic for debate: are accents needed on capitals? Although there is still some disagreement, it is *absolutely necessary* to use accents on capitals to avoid misinterpretation. Here are a few examples of headlines in a newspaper. You'll see how including accents makes a significant difference!

A NANTES, UN ASSASSIN TUE.	*IN NANTES, A MURDERER KILLS.*
À NANTES, UN ASSASSIN TUÉ.	*IN NANTES, A MURDERER IS KILLED.*
PAUL EST INTERNE A L'HOPITAL.	*PAUL IS AN INTERN IN THE HOSPITAL.*
PAUL EST INTERNÉ À L'HÔPITAL.	*PAUL IS CONFINED IN THE MENTAL HOSPITAL.*

And for another reason, it is simply more elegant in prose. It's a question of pure aesthetics. Just take a look:

Étant donné la promotion d'Air France pour les vols à destination des États-Unis, Ève et Édouard ont décidé de passer une semaine à la Nouvelle-Orléans.
Given the Air France promotion for flights to the USA, Ève and Édouard have decided to spend a week in New Orleans.

So, all to your keyboards!

Basic gender endings: Masculin and féminin

Basic endings

As you already know, there are two genders in French: masculine and feminine, preceded by the definite article **le, la** or the indefinite article **un, une**. Since the purpose of this book is to forge a reliable method of identifying and learning French genders, we will learn the fundamental rules governing genders, starting with masculine nouns and then moving on the feminine nouns. Along with the rules, we will identify their exceptions. Indeed, exceptions to grammatical rules can be annoying, but this is a "flaw" of all natural languages. (Only constructed languages, such as Esperanto, contain rules without exceptions.)

While you may be tempted to say that French gender can sometimes be arbitrary, you do have some name endings to rely on. Memorization is crucial. Every new word must be learned in conjunction with its gender. This knowledge, as you will find out, quickly becomes tacit, internalized. After some practice, you will be able to identify the gender of a word by relying on your intuition, without even having to think in terms of rules and exceptions.

In your mind, each word will become like a short musical phrase. You won't have to think which key, major or minor, the musical phrase is in. You will simply know. When you study music, you learn scales. In French: **do, ré, mi, fa, sol, la, si, do**. Learning endings is similar. **Le train**, **le bateau**, and **le vin** will appear on your masculine scale, whereas **la beauté, la nature**, and **la culture** will register on your feminine scale. French is all about sounds. Gustave Flaubert used to isolate himself and shout his novels aloud in his **gueuloir**—more or less his screaming room—to make sure the words flowed beautifully. Think of endings as musical notes on a score.

In this chapter, you will learn how to connect a noun to its gender marker by studying the main endings of masculine nouns. Feminine nouns will follow. For example, nouns ending in a consonant or in any vowel but **e** tend to be masculine:

le bijou	*jewel*	**le gaz**	*gas*	**le sofa**	*sofa*
le cacao	*cocoa*	**le lieu**	*place*	**le tact**	*tact*
le carnaval	*carnival*	**le nez**	*nose*	**le zébu**	*zebu*
le gala	*gala*				

13

As we proceed, remember to focus on the endings and, at the same time, to memorize any exceptions that may crop up.

Basic masculine noun endings

The following endings tend to be masculine.

-age, -ige, -ège, -oge, -uge

l'éloge	praise	le prodige	prodigy, feat
le fromage	cheese	le refuge	refuge
le mariage	marriage	le sortilège	spell

Stéphane Audeguy a écrit un livre merveilleux, *Le petit éloge de la douceur.*
Les alpinistes ont dormi dans **un refuge**.
Félicie a offert un fauteuil art déco à sa cousine comme cadeau de **mariage**.

Stéphane Audeguy wrote a wonderful book, In **Praise** *of Sweetness.*
The climbers slept in **a refuge**.
Félicie gave her cousin an Art Deco armchair as a **wedding** *gift.*

However, there are a few exceptions:

la cage	cage	la Norvège	Norway
l'horloge	clock	la page	page
l'image	image	la plage	beach
la loge	dressing room/lodge	la rage	rage, fury, rabies
la luge	luge	la tige	stem
la nage	swimming		

Il manque **la** dernière **page** du livre.
Nous avons félicité **la diva** dans **sa loge**.

The last **page** *of the book is missing.*
We congratulated **the diva** *in* **her dressing room**.

-ail, -euil

l'épouvantail	scarecrow	le seuil	doorstep, threshold
le fauteuil	armchair	le travail	work
le recueil	collection, anthology	le vitrail	stained-glass window

Henri a mis **un épouvantail** dans son jardin.
Zoé lit **un recueil** de poèmes dans **son fauteuil**.

Henri has placed **a scarecrow** *in his garden.*
Zoé is reading **a poetry book** *in* **her armchair**.

-ain

le bain	bath, swim	le pain	bread
le grain	grain	le terrain	ground, land
le lendemain	following day	le train	train

There is one exception: **la main** (*hand*).

Samuel est arrivé le 3 mars et il est reparti **le lendemain**.
Va acheter **du pain** avant de prendre **ton bain**.

Samuel arrived on March 3rd and left **the following day**.
Go buy **some bread** *before taking* **a bath**.

-al

le cheval	*horse*	**le mal**	*harm, pain, evil*
le festival	*festival*	**le récital**	*recital*
le journal	*newspaper*	**le signal**	*signal*

Armelle a lu dans **le journal** qu'il y aurait **un récital** de musique baroque **au festival** de La Rochelle.
Le cheval d'Henri IV était-il vraiment blanc?

*Armelle read in **the paper** that there would be **a recital** of baroque music **at the** La Rochelle **festival**.*
*Was Henri IV's **horse** really white?*

-ament, -ement

le branchement	*connection*	**le médicament**	*medicine/medication*
le département	*department*	**le réchauffement**	*warming*
le jugement	*judgment/sentence*	**le testament**	*testament*

Ce médicament est recommandé pour l'hypertension.
Vu les problèmes dans la famille, il n'a pas encore fait **son testament**.

***This drug** is recommended for high blood pressure.*
*Given the family problems, he has not yet made out **his will**.*

-ard

le canard	*duck*	**le regard**	*look/gaze*
le guépard	*cheetah*	**le renard**	*fox*
le placard	*cupboard*	**le vieillard**	*old man*

Une famille de **canards** habite sur l'étang.
Son regard se posa sur elle.

*A family of **ducks** lives on the pond.*
***His eyes** came to rest on her.*

Some words ending in -**ard** may have a pejorative connotation, such as:

le bâtard	*bastard, illegitimate child*	**le fêtard**	*reveler*
le chauffard	*reckless driver*	**le vantard**	*boaster*
le clochard	*bum*		

-eau, -ou

le bateau	*boat*	**le chameau**	*camel*
le bijou	*jewel*	**le château**	*castle*
le cerveau	*brain*	**le chou**	*cabbage*

Patrick était **le cerveau** de l'affaire.
On lui a volé tous **ses bijoux**.

*Patrick was **the brains** behind the job.*
*All of **her jewelery** was stolen.*

Here are two exceptions: **la peau** (*skin*), **l'eau** (*water*). English and French share many nouns of Latin origin. It will come in handy to compare and deduce the meaning of words. For instance, these two particular exceptions are interesting, for they have retained the gender of their Latin ancestors: *pellis* (*skin*) and *aqua* (*water*).

Basic gender endings: **Masculin** and **féminin**   15

-el

l'appel	*call*	le matériel	*equipment, material*
le caramel	*caramel*	le sel	*salt*
le logiciel	*software*		

Ce logiciel vous permettra de créer un site web.
This software will help you create a website.

Passe-moi le sel, s'il te plaît.
Pass me the salt, please.

-ent, -ant

l'argent	*money*	le restaurant	*restaurant*
le chant	*singing, song*	le talent	*talent*
le diamant	*diamond*	le vent	*wind*

Here is one exception: la dent (tooth). And more Latin: dens (tooth) is feminine.

Églantine a emprunté de l'argent à sa mère.
Églantine borrowed money from her mother.

Puis elle s'est offert une bague en diamant.
Then she treated herself to a diamond ring.

-er

le boulanger	*baker*	le fer	*iron*
le danger	*danger*	le passager	*passenger*
le déjeuner	*lunch*	le verger	*orchard*

Ils ne produisent que des poires Williams dans ce verger.
They only produce Williams pears in this orchard.

Si on prenait du pain perdu au petit déjeuner?
What about having some French toast for breakfast?

-ier/yer

le calendrier	*calendar*	le loyer	*rent*
le clavier	*keyboard*	le tablier	*apron*
le fichier	*file*	le voilier	*sailboat*

Adèle n'a pas pu ouvrir ton fichier.
Adèle could not open your file.

Le loyer est-il cher pour ce studio?
Is the rent expensive for this studio?

-at, -et, -t

l'alphabet	*alphabet*	le débat	*debate*
le billet	*ticket*	le lit	*bed*
le circuit	*circuit, tour*	le perroquet	*parrot*

Nous regarderons le débat à la télé ce soir.
We'll watch the debate on TV tonight.

Ils dorment dans un lit à baldaquin.
They sleep in a four-poster bed.

Here are quite a few important exceptions:

la dot	*dowry*	la nuit	*night*
la forêt	*forest*	la part	*share*
la mort	*death*	la plupart	*most people/things*

The Latin word for *forest*, *silva*, although feminine, does not even resemble the French noun; however, it appears in words such as **sylviculture** (*forestry*). But look at the Latin roots of the other feminine words: *nox* (*night*), *mors* (*death*), *pars* (*part, share*), and *dos* (*dowry*).

La nuit, tous les chats sont gris.	*Everyone looks the same **in the dark**.*
De nombreuses espèces de perroquets se trouvent dans **la forêt** tropicale de l'île Maurice.	*Many species of parrot are to be found in **the** tropical **forest** of Mauritius Island.*

-eur

Nouns ending in -**eur** include names of professions as well as words denoting certain tools and machines.

l'aspirateur	*vacuum cleaner*	**le compositeur**	*composer*
le climatiseur	*air-conditioner*	**l'ordinateur**	*computer*
le cœur	*heart*	**le réfrigérateur**	*refrigerator*

Léa, tu devrais passer **l'aspirateur** dans le salon.	*Léa, you should **vacuum** the living room.*
Paul-Henri a **un cœur** de pierre.	*Paul-Henri has **a heart** of stone.*

Don't be intimidated by the references to Latin. No one expects a budding—or even competent—Francophone to become a Latinist. However, Latin is not only the direct ancestor of French but also a living presence. When a French-speaking person dips into the vast ocean of Latin vocabulary to create a handy neologism, he or she, as scholars have written, is not borrowing from a foreign language.

While English is a bit removed from Latin, let us not forget the Norman Conquest (1066), which imposed Norman French on England for more than three centuries. English was not accepted in the courts until 1386, becoming the fully accepted idiom only around 1400. As a result, modern English retains an enormous Latin vocabulary, acquired via Norman French. In fact, English is probably more French than any other non-Romance language, and English speakers use French in everyday life without even knowing it. For example, while *love* is a Germanic word, its adjective, *amorous,* is French. We are so used to our Romance vocabulary that we don't even notice our natural bilingualism when we alternate, depending on the context, between *friendly* (Germanic) and *amicable* (French). There are thousands of such examples—no surprise, since around 30 percent of our vocabulary is French. These affinities and similarities between English and French are good news for the learner.

In another example, we are all familiar with an elegant French word for *software*: **logiciel**. But the word for *gameware*, **ludiciel**, is equally elegant. Why **ludiciel**, you might wonder, since the word for *game* is **jeu**? But the Latin word for game is *ludus*, and the neologism sounds quite native to a French ear. Another interesting Latin-derived word is the French word for *computer*, **ordinateur**. It comes from the Latin *ordinator*, which not only means, literally, *the one who puts things in order*, but is also a synonym for *God*!

Basic gender endings: **Masculin** and **féminin**   **17**

-ien

le bien	*good*	**l'italien**	*Italian*
le chien	*dog*	**le lien**	*link, tie*
l'entretien	*interview, upkeep, maintenance*	**le végétarien**	*vegetarian*

Ludovic ne sait pas discerner **le bien** du mal.

*Ludovic is not able to tell **good** from evil.*

L'entretien de ces jardins coûte une fortune.

***The maintenance** of these gardens costs a fortune.*

-illon

le bouillon	*broth, bubble*	**le grillon**	*cricket*
le brouillon	*first draft, outline*	**le papillon**	*butterfly*
l'échantillon	*sample*	**le tourbillon**	*whirlwind, swirl*

Voudriez-vous **un échantillon** de ce tissu en lin?

*Would you like **a sample** of this linen fabric?*

La bibliothèque Mitterrand a organisé une exposition sur **les brouillons** des plus grands écrivains.

*The Mitterrand Library organized an exhibit on the greatest writers' **drafts**.*

-in

le chagrin	*grief*	**le moulin**	*mill*
le dessin	*drawing, design*	**le vin**	*wine*
le jardin	*garden*		

One exception is **la fin** (*end*).

Théo a fait **un** joli **dessin** dans **le jardin**.

*Théo did **a** nice **drawing** in **the garden**.*

Le meunier est mort de **chagrin** dans **son moulin**.

*The miller died of **sorrow** in **his mill**.*

-is

le compromis	*compromise*	**le fouillis**	*mess, jumble*
le croquis	*sketch*	**le taudis**	*slum*
le devis	*estimate*	**le tennis**	*tennis*

There are two exceptions: **la souris** (*mouse*) and **la vis** (*screw*).

Pourriez-vous nous donner **un devis** pour les réparations?

*Could you give us **an estimate** for the repairs?*

Quel fouillis! Je ne retrouve même plus **la souris** de mon ordinateur!

What a mess!** I can't even find **my** computer **mouse!

-isme

l'égoïsme	*selfishness*	**le romantisme**	*romanticism*
l'héroïsme	*heroism*	**le séisme**	*earthquake*
l'optimisme	*optimism*	**le socialisme**	*socialism*

Le **séisme** a fait de nombreuses victimes.		*The earthquake killed many people.*	
L'héroïsme de la population était inouï.		*The heroism of the people was unbelievable.*	

-oir, -oin

le besoin	*need*	le miroir	*mirror*
le coin	*corner, part*	le témoin	*witness*
le couloir	*hallway*	le trottoir	*sidewalk*

Sabrine a **besoin** d'**un** nouveau **miroir**.	*Sabrine **needs a** new **mirror**.*
Appelez **le témoin**!	*Call **the witness**!*

-on, -om

le cornichon	*gherkin*	le salon	*living room*
le nom	*name*	le torchon	*dish towel*
le prénom	*first name*	le violon	*violin*

Here are a few exceptions:

la boisson	*beverage*	la leçon	*lesson*
la chanson	*song*	la livraison	*delivery*
la cloison	*partition*	la rançon	*ransom*
la cuisson	*cooking*	la trahison	*betrayal*
la façon	*manner*		

Passe-moi **le torchon** jaune!	*Hand me **the** yellow **dish towel**!*
Quelle est l'origine de **ce prénom**?— Maylis? Je crois que c'est breton.	*What is the origin of **this first name**?— Maylis? I think it is Breton.*

Bear in mind that the -**on** ending often indicates Latin ancestry and that many feminine Latin words ending with -**tio** acquired -**tion** endings, which are also feminine in French. Thus the Latin *natio* became **nation**. In the same vein, **chanson** comes from *cantio* and **leçon** from *lectio*. It is safe to say that you have to be extra careful with -**on** words. For example, **son** (*sound*) retains the masculine gender of *sonus*, its Latin ancestor, whereas words like **nation** are feminine. It might be helpful to treat -**tion** as a separate ending, which always indicates a feminine word.

-phone

Nouns ending with -**phone** are masculine, often referring to machines and instruments connected to sound. This is a bit funny, because this ending stems from the Greek word for *voice*, *phōnē*, which is feminine, just as the French word **voix**, which comes from the equally feminine Latin *vox*. Yes, Greek, too, lurks behind the scenes, but there is no need for panic. In French, we get to enjoy the lexical opulence of the two classical languages without having to learn their respective grammars. That is a good thing, of course, since French grammar, as we know, is enough of a challenge.

le magnétophone	*tape recorder*	le saxophone	*saxophone*
le mégaphone	*megaphone*	le téléphone	*telephone*
le microphone	*microphone*	le xylophone	*xylophone*

Basic gender endings: **Masculin** and **féminin** 19

Leur téléphone est en dérangement.	**Their phone** is out of order.
Guillaume joue **du saxophone** dans un club le jeudi soir.	Guillaume plays **the saxophone** in a club on Thursday nights.

-scope

Nouns ending in -**scope** refer to optical instruments and related things, which makes sense, because the suffix comes from the Greek verb *skopeo*, which means *I look* and *I spy on someone*.

l'horoscope	*horoscope*	**le microscope**	*microscope*
le kaléidoscope	*kaleidoscope*	**le téléscope**	*telescope*
le magnétoscope	*videotape recorder*	**le trombinoscope**	*group photo*

Isabeau lit **son horoscope** tous les matins dans le journal.	Isabeau reads **her horoscope** every morning in the paper.
Nous avons observé Vénus grâce **au télescope** d'Alix.	We looked at Venus thanks to Alix's **telescope**.

As you have seen, there is some method in the madness of genders. True, there is no set of rules, free of exceptions, that one could memorize and thereby master French genders. If that were true, there would be no need for this book! However, by memorizing the principal ending types, you will make great strides toward mastery. You might even decide that incomplete mastery may be OK, because it leaves room for mystery.

Other masculine endings

You thought you were done with masculine endings? Not so fast. There are other interesting cases.

-a

Nouns ending with -**a** are usually masculine:

l'agenda	*agenda*	**le choléra**	*cholera*	**le pyjama**	*pyjamas*
le bégonia	*begonia*	**le cinéma**	*cinema*	**le visa**	*visa*
le brouhaha	*hubbub*	**l'opéra**	*opera*		

However, there are a few exceptions:

la diva	*diva*	**la saga**	*saga*	**la villa**	*villa*
la polka	*polka*	**la véranda**	*veranda*		

Le choléra sévit dans cette région.	**Cholera** is rampant in this region.
Il faut **un visa** pour entrer dans ce pays.	You need **a visa** to enter this country.

This may be quite confusing, since we know that -**a** is generally a feminine ending in Romance languages. Indeed, French can be a bit peculiar, but there is an explanation. Unlike the other Romance languages, French did not keep the -**a** ending in Latin-derived feminine nouns.

-as

Nouns ending with -**as** are generally masculine:

le bras	*arm*	**le fracas**	*crash, roar*	**le pas**	*step*
le cadenas	*padlock*	**le lilas**	*lilac*	**le repas**	*meal*
le cas	*case*	**le matelas**	*mattress*	**le verglas**	*glazed frost*
l'embarras	*embarrassment*				

J'ai besoin d'**un cadenas** pour ma valise.   *I need **a padlock** for my suitcase.*
Alice a fait **ses** premiers **pas** à huit mois.   *Alice made **her** first **steps** at the age of eight months.*

-ème, -me, -ome, -ôme, -aume, -rme, -sme

Nouns ending in **-ème**, **-me**, **-ome**, **-ôme**, **-aume**, **-rme**, and **-sme** tend to be masculine:

le dôme	*dome*	**le problème**	*problem*	**le spasme**	*spasm*
l'idiome	*idiom*	**le royaume**	*kingdom*	**le terme**	*term*
le poème	*poem*				

Mon royaume pour un cheval!   ***My kingdom** for a horse!*
C'est **le plus beau poème** qu'il m'ait jamais écrit.   *It is **the** most beautiful **poem** he ever wrote to me.*

-ble, -cle, -gle, -ple

Nouns ending in **-ble**, **-cle**, **-gle**, and **-ple** are often masculine:

l'angle	*angle*	**le sable**	*sand*
le câble	*cable*	**le spectacle**	*show*
le périple	*journey*	**le temple**	*temple*

Here are some interesting exceptions, all with a Latin pedigree, except for **la bible**, a Greek interloper. The Greek neuter plural (*ta biblia*), which means *the books*, having become feminine in Romance languages because of its deceptive **-a** ending, was bound to become **-e** in French. Back to our Latin-derived exceptions:

French	English	Latin
la boucle	*buckle*	*buccula* (meaning *little mouth*)
la fable	*fable*	*fabula*
la règle	*rule*	*regula*
la table	*table*	*tabula*

Le spectacle ne dura qu'une heure.   ***The show** lasted only an hour.*
La boucle est bouclée.   *We have come **full circle**.*

-ac, -ak, -ic, -oc, -uc

Nouns ending in **-ac**, **-ak**, **-ic**, **-oc**, and **-uc** tend to be masculine:

l'ammoniac	*ammonia*	**le croc**	*fang/hook*	**le public**	*public*
l'aqueduc	*aqueduct*	**le diagnostic**	*diagnosis*	**le stuc**	*stucco*
l'armagnac	*Armagnac*	**le duc**	*duke*	**le tabac**	*tobacco*
le basilic	*basil*	**le fric**	*money/cash*	**le trafic**	*traffic*
le bivouac	*bivouac*	**le hamac**	*hammock*	**le troc**	*barter*
le bloc	*block, writing pad*	**le kayak**	*kayak*	**le truc**	*trick/thing/gimmick*
le clic	*click*	**le lac**	*lake*	**le viaduc**	*viaduct*

Renaud vient de penser à **un truc**.   *Renaud just thought of **something**.*
Tu as **un bloc** de papier?   *Do you have a writing **pad**?*

Basic gender endings: **Masculin** and **féminin** 21

-g

Nouns ending in **-g** are generally masculine:

l'étang	*pond/lake*	**le joug**	*yoke*	**le sang**	*blood*
le faubourg	*suburb/ neighborhood*	**le rang**	*row/rank*		

Tristan a **du sang** sur sa chemise.	*Tristan has **blood** on his shirt.*
Célie est assise **au** troisième **rang**.	*Célie is sitting in **the** third **row**.*

-o, -op, -ort, -os, -ot, -ours, -us

Nouns ending in **-o**, **-op**, **-ort**, **-os**, **-ot**, **-ours**, and **-us** are usually masculine:

l'abricot	*apricot*	**l'escargot**	*snail*	**le numéro**	*number*
le cactus	*cactus*	**le jus**	*juice*	**l'ours**	*bear*
le coquelicot	*poppy*	**le lapsus**	*slip of the tongue*	**le paquebot**	*ocean liner*
le cours	*course*	**le lavabo**	*bathroom sink*	**le sirop**	*syrup*
le dos	*back*	**le mot**	*word*	**le sport**	*sport*
l'effort	*effort*	**le nimbus**	*nimbus cloud*	**le vélo**	*bicycle*

Quel numéro dois-je composer pour appeler Londres?	***What number** should I dial to call London?*
Vous devriez faire **un effort!**	*You should make **an effort!***

Remember that gender does not change when a word is abbreviated:

la météo	*weather forecast*	**la photo**	*photography*	**la stéréo**	*hi-fi/stereo system*
la philo	*philosophy*	**la psycho**	*psychology*	**la vidéo**	*video*

La photo que tu as prise est un peu floue.	***The picture** you took is a bit blurred.*
Comment il est, ton prof de **philo**?	*Your **philosophy** teacher, how is he?*

-ogue

Nouns ending in **-ogue** that refer to certain professionals may be masculine or feminine. For example, while Claude Lévi-Strauss was **un anthropologue** (*anthropologist*), we would call Margaret Mead **une anthropologue**.

Masculine nouns ending in -ogue

le catalogue	*catalog*	**l'épilogue**	*epilogue*
le dialogue	*dialogue*	**le prologue**	*prologue*

A hint: all these words are in some way derived from the Greek *logos*, a masculine noun that means *word*, and from many other words.

Feminine nouns ending in -ogue

la drogue	*drug*	**la synagogue**	*synagogue*
la morgue	*haughtiness/morgue*	**la vogue**	*fashion/vogue*
la pirogue	*pirogue, dug-out canoe*		

C'est **la** grande **vogue** maintenant.	*It's all **the rage** now.*
Les Gauthier ont descendu l'Amazone **en pirogue**.	*The Gauthiers went down the Amazon in **a pirogue**.*

-r, -er

Nouns ending in **-r** and **-er** are generally masculine:

l'avenir	*future*	**le cauchemar**	*nightmare*	**le jour**	*day*
le bar	*bar*	**le cuir**	*leather*	**le nénuphar**	*water lily*
le car	*bus/coach*	**le décor**	*décor*	**le tour**	*tour/trip/ride*
le castor	*beaver*	**le dollar**	*dollar*	**le trésor**	*treasure*

One exception to this rule is words ending in **-eur** when they do not denote a profession or a machine. Here are three additional exceptions:

la cour	*courtyard*
la star	*star, celebrity*
la tour	*tower*

C'était **le pire cauchemar** qu'on ait pu imaginer.	It was **the** worst **nightmare** we could have imagined.
Un sans-abri a découvert **un trésor** dans une grotte.	A homeless man discovered **a treasure** in a grotto.

-re

Nouns ending in **-re** are generally masculine:

le centre	*center*	**le lustre**	*luster/gloss*	**le mètre**	*meter*
le feutre	*felt*	**le maître**	*master/artist*	**le ventre**	*stomach, belly*
le filtre	*filter*				

These are some exceptions:

la fenêtre	*window*	**la lettre**	*letter*	**la vitre**	*window pane*
l'huître	*oyster*	**la montre**	*watch*		

Le centre culturel est juste à côté.	**The** cultural **center** is right next door.
Ne partez pas **le ventre** creux!	Don't leave with **an empty stomach**!

-x, -xe

For the most part, nouns ending in **-x** and **-xe** are masculine:

l'axe	*axis*	**le flux**	*flow, tide*	**le luxe**	*luxury*
le circonflexe	*circumflex*	**l'inox**	*stainless steel*	**le lynx**	*lynx*
le complexe	*complex*	**le juke-box**	*jukebox*	**le paradoxe**	*paradox*
l'équinoxe	*equinox*	**le larynx**	*larynx*	**le sexe**	*sex*

Here are some exceptions:

la boxe	*boxing*
la syntaxe	*syntax*
la taxe	*tax*

Interestingly, the word *syntax* is a derivation of the feminine Greek noun *taxis*, meaning *battle array*.

Tu oublies toujours **le circonflexe** sur « gâteau »!	You always forget **the circumflex** on gâteau!
Il vit dans **le luxe**.	He lives in **luxury**.

-e

Many nouns ending in **-e** are masculine, although there are some rather prominent feminine nouns in that category, such as **la gloire**. It is a mistake, however, to assume that the **-e** ending automatically defines a noun as feminine. Here are some examples:

l'ange	*angel*	**le groupe**	*group*	**le pouce**	*thumb*
le beurre	*butter*	**le palace**	*palace*	**le souffle**	*breath/blow*
le divorce	*divorce*	**le peigne**	*comb*	**le verbe**	*verb*
l'espace	*space*	**le poste**	*position/job*	**le verre**	*glass*

Tu préfères **le beurre salé** ou **le beurre doux?**	*Do you prefer **salted** or **unsalted** butter?*
Ce groupe est n'est pas compétent pour résoudre **ce problème**.	***This group** is not competent to solve **this problem**.*

Here we are, at the end of the masculine endings. Ouf!

To facilitate the memorization of gender, make up sentences or rhymes like this one:

Le soir, Lucas lis le journal dans son fauteuil et écoute le récital tandis que son chat joue avec le bouchon de la bouteille de son vin préféré.	*At night, Lucas reads the paper in his armchair and listens to the recital while his cat plays with the cork from a bottle of his favorite wine.*

Repeat this sentence a few times, and you'll have a few endings engraved in your mind. Then create new ones or extract some from French literature. Write them in a small notebook or make a "Gender" list on your computer. You'll see—it works!

Basic feminine noun endings

The following nouns tend to be feminine:

-ade

l'ambassade	*embassy*	**la limonade**	*lemonade*
la cascade	*waterfall, stunt, series*	**la promenade**	*walk, ride*
la grenade	*grenade/pomegranate*	**la salade**	*salad*

Here are a few exceptions:

le grade	*rank, degree*
le jade	*jade*
le stade	*stadium*

L'ambassade n'est pas ouverte aujourd'hui.	***The Embassy** is not open today.*
Moi, je prends **la salade** niçoise.	*I'm having **the salad** niçoise!*

-aie

la baie	*berry/bay/opening*	**la monnaie**	*change/currency*
la craie	*chalk*	**la palmeraie**	*palm grove*
la haie	*hedge/hurdle*	**la taie**	*pillowcase*

Leur jardin est entouré d'**une haie** d'aubépine.	*Their garden is surrounded with **a** hawthorn **hedge**.*
Auriez-vous de **la monnaie**?	*Could you give me **some change**?*

-aine

la douzaine	*dozen*	**la marraine**	*godmother*
la haine	*hatred*	**la migraine**	*migraine*
la laine	*wool*	**la semaine**	*week*

Here are a couple of exceptions:

le domaine	*estate, field/domain*
le Maine	*Maine*

Mathilde a acheté un tapis **de** haute **laine** à Marrakech.	*Mathilde bought a thick-pile **wool** rug in Marrakech.*
Offre-lui **une douzaine de** roses!	*Give her **a dozen** roses!*

-aison, -oison

la cloison	*partition, bulkhead, septum*	**la raison**	*reason, mind*
la conjugaison	*conjugation, union*	**la saison**	*season*
la maison	*house*	**la toison**	*fleece, mane*

Here are a few exceptions:

le poison	*poison*
le vison	*mink*

Connais-tu **la conjugaison** du verbe « s'asseoir »?	*Do you know **the conjugation** of the verb to sit?*
Jonathan se met en colère pour **une raison** ou une autre.	*Jonathan gets angry for **some reason** or other.*

-ence, -ance

la chance	*luck, chance*	**la puissance**	*power, authority*
l'indépendance	*independence*	**l'urgence**	*urgency, emergency*
la présidence	*presidency*	**la violence**	*violence, roughness*

Here is an exception: **le silence** (*silence*).

Vous avez de **la chance** d'aller en France demain.	*You are **lucky** to go to France tomorrow.*
Ils ont lutté pour **leur indépendance**.	*They fought for **their independence**.*

-ande

l'amande	*almond, kernel*	**la demande**	*request, application*
la bande	*band/bandage/group*	**la viande**	*meat*
la commande	*order, control*		

Julien a envoyé **sa demande** hier.	*Julien sent **his application** yesterday.*
Ma commande n'est pas encore arrivée.	*My order** has not arrived yet.*

-ée

l'année	*year*	**la durée**	*duration*
l'araignée	*spider*	**l'idée**	*idea*
la bouée	*rubber ring, buoy*	**la journée**	*day*

Basic gender endings: **Masculin** and **féminin**   **25**

Here are a few exceptions:

l'apogée	*apogee/peak*	**le mausolée**	*mausoleum*
l'athée	*atheist*	**le musée**	*museum*
le colisée	*coliseum*	**le rez-de-chaussée**	*main floor*
le lycée	*high school*	**le trophée**	*trophy*

Quelles idées folles!	*What crazy ideas!*
Quelle sera **la durée** du vol?	*What's the duration of the flight?*

Words indicating quantity are often feminine:

une assiettée	*plateful*	**une cuillerée**	*spoonful*
une bouchée	*mouthful*	**une pelletée**	*shovelful*
une brassée	*armful*	**une pincée**	*pinch*
une brouettée	*wheelbarrowful*	**une poignée**	*handful*

Sofia est arrivée avec **une brassée** de fleurs sauvages.	*Sofia arrived with an armful of wild flowers.*
Maheu m'a donné **une poignée** de cerises.	*Maheu gave me a handful of cherries.*

-esse, -osse, -ousse

la brosse	*brush*	**la politesse**	*politeness*
la housse	*cover*	**la sagesse**	*wisdom*
la jeunesse	*youth*	**la trousse**	*case*

Here are a couple of exceptions:

le carrosse	*coach*
le pamplemousse	*grapefruit*

Florin, c'est la voix de **la sagesse**.	*Florin, he is the voice of wisdom.*
J'ai perdu un bouton. Tu as **une trousse** à couture?	*I lost a button. Do you have a sewing kit?*

-ette

l'assiette	*plate, basis*	**la fourchette**	*fork/margin*
la dette	*debt*	**la noisette**	*hazelnut, small knob*
la devinette	*riddle*	**la serviette**	*towel/napkin*

Here are some interesting exceptions:

le bébé-éprouvette	*test-tube baby*	**le quartette**	*quartet*
le casse-noisette	*nutcracker*	**le quintette**	*quintet*
le porte-serviette	*napkin holder*	**le squelette**	*skeleton*

Diego a **une dette** de reconnaissance envers vous.	*Diego has a debt of gratitude toward you.*
Donne-moi **une** plus grande **asssiette**.	*Give me a larger plate.*

-eur (excluding nouns denoting professions and machines)

la chaleur	*heat*	**la lueur**	*glow, light*
la couleur	*color, light*	**la peur**	*fear*
la fleur	*flower*	**la tumeur**	*tumor*

Here are some exceptions:

le bonheur	*happiness*	**le labeur**	*labor/toil*
l'honneur	*honor*	**le malheur**	*misfortune/ordeal*

Margaux a **une peur** bleue des souris.
De **quelle couleur** allez-vous repeindre votre salle de bain?

*Margaux is **scared** to death of mice.*
***What color** are you going to repaint your bathroom?*

-ie, -rie

la magie	*magic*	**la thérapie**	*therapy*
la poésie	*poetry, poem*	**l'utopie**	*utopia*
la tapisserie	*tapestry, wallpaper*	**la vie**	*life*

More exceptions to add to the list include:

le génie	*genius*	**le parapluie**	*umbrella*
l'incendie	*fire*	**le sosie**	*double*
le messie	*messiah*	**le zombie**	*zombie*

Marie Laveau croit à **la magie**.
La thérapie de Lola a duré cinq ans.

*Marie Laveau believes in **magic**.*
*Lola's **therapy** lasted five years.*

-ise

la cerise	*cherry*	**la gourmandise**	*delicacy, greediness*
la chemise	*shirt, folder*	**la surprise**	*surprise*
la crise	*crisis, attack, fit*	**la valise**	*suitcase, bag*

La crise financière a eu un impact catastrophique sur cette province.
Je pense que **ta valise** est trop lourde.

***The** financial **crisis** had a terrible impact on this province.*
*I think **your suitcase** is too heavy.*

-aille

la bataille	*battle, fight*	**la médaille**	*medal, disk*
l'écaille	*scale, chip, flake*	**la paille**	*straw*
la faille	*flaw/fault (geology)*	**la taille**	*waist/size/height*

An exception is **le braille** (*Braille*). This exception could be explained by the fact that the Braille alphabet was named after its inventor, Louis Braille (1809–1852).

C'est trop serré à **la taille**.
Il y a **une faille** dans votre argument.

*It is too tight around **the waist**.*
*There is **a flaw** in your argument.*

-ille

la brindille	*twig*	**la lentille**	*lens/lentil*
la famille	*family*	**la myrtille**	*bilberry*
la fille	*girl, daughter*	**la vanille**	*vanilla*

Here is a trio of exceptions:

le gorille	*gorilla/bodyguard*
le quadrille	*quadrille*
le vaudeville	*vaudeville*

Manon ne veut pas de **lentilles** mais une glace à **la vanille**.
La famille d'Hadrien habite à Nîmes.

*Manon does not want **lentils** but a **vanilla** ice cream cone.*
*Hadrien's **family** lives in Nîmes.*

Basic gender endings: **Masculin** and **féminin**

-ouille

la brouille	*disagreement*	**la nouille**	*noodles*
la citrouille	*pumpkin*	**la patrouille**	*patrol*
la grenouille	*frog*	**la ratatouille**	*ratatouille*

La ratatouille de votre grand-mère est délicieuse.	*Your grandmother's **ratatouille** is delicious.*
La grenouille est assise sur **une citrouille** près du lac.	*The frog is sitting on **a pumpkin** near the lake.*

-ique

la botanique	*botany*	**la polémique**	*controversy*
la musique	*music*	**la politique**	*politics, policy*
la physique	*physics*	**la république**	*republic*

Here are quite a few exceptions:

l'antibiotique	*antibiotic*	**le plastique**	*plastic*
le lexique	*glossary*	**le portique**	*portico*
le moustique	*mosquito*	**le téléphérique**	*cable-car*
le pique-nique	*picnic*		

Quelle musique écoutez-vous?	*What music do you listen to?*
Cette politique est fort dangereuse.	*This policy is quite dangerous.*

Many **-ique** words come from Latin feminine nouns ending in *-ica*, such as *musica* and *res publica*. However, as we have seen, **-ique** words come to us from other languages as well, so one needs to tread gingerly.

-gion, -nion, -sion, -ssion

la compréhension	*understanding*	**l'opinion**	*opinion*
la décision	*decision*	**la passion**	*passion*
l'occasion	*chance/opportunity*	**la région**	*region*

Damien n'a **aucune compréhension** de la situation.	*Damien has **no understanding** of the situation.*
Antonin doit se faire **une opinion** sur la situation.	*Antonin must form **an opinion** on the situation.*

-tion, -xion

la connexion	*connection*	**la population**	*population*
la génération	*generation*	**la révolution**	*revolution*
l'information	*information, piece of news*	**la tradition**	*tradition, legend*

Here are a few exceptions:

l'avion	*airplane*
le champion	*champion*
le bastion	*bastion/stronghold*

Ils sont fidèles à **la tradition**.		*They are true to **tradition**.*	
La Révolution française a eu lieu en 1789.		*The French **Revolution** took place in 1789.*	

Why doesn't **avion**, you may ask, share the feminine gender of the other Latin-based words on this list, such as **population** or **tradition**? Well, **avion** is different because it is a neologism, an artificial construction, just like **logiciel**.

When the airplane was invented, people scrambled to find the right word. English speakers could not come up with anything better than the vaguely Latinate *aeroplane*, or *airplane*, which was less cumbersome than the German *das Flugzeug* but still far from perfect. Fortunately, French speakers know how to benefit from their visceral connection to Latin, which non-Romance languages can only dream about. In fact, **avion**, a construction based on the feminine Latin noun *avis*, which means *bird*, exemplifies the facility with which French incorporates the stupendously rich Latin vocabulary into its own lexicon. This proves the thesis, advanced by the great German literary scholar Ernst Robert Curtius, that Latin words in the French vocabulary are not loan words, since the source language is not foreign.

-ite

l'appendicite	*appendicitis*	**la limite**	*border, limit, edge*
la conduite	*behavior/conduct*	**la marguerite**	*daisy*
l'élite	*elite*	**la réussite**	*success*

Here is a list of exceptions:

l'anthracite	*anthracite*	**le satellite**	*satellite*
le gîte	*shelter/home*	**le site**	*area, site*
l'insolite	*unusual*	**le sulfite**	*sulphite*
le mérite	*merit*	**le termite**	*termite*
le rite	*rite*		

Au-delà de **cette limite**, votre billet n'est plus valable.		*Beyond **this limit**, your ticket is no longer valid.*
C'est un signe de **réussite sociale**.		*It's a sign of **social success**.*

-té, -tié

l'amitié	*friendship*	**la pitié**	*pity, mercy*
la cécité	*blindness*	**la santé**	*health*
la laïcité	*secularism*	**la virilité**	*virility*

Here are more exceptions to learn:

l'aparté	*private conversation/aside*	**l'été**	*summer*
l'arrêté	*decree*	**le karaté**	*karate*
le côté	*side*		

As mentioned earlier, some feminine nouns with these endings stem from Latin nouns ending in *-a*, such as *amicitia*.

La laïcité est un sujet controversé en France.		***Secularism** is a controversial topic in France.*
Leur **amitié** fut éternelle.		*Their **friendship** was eternal.*

Basic gender endings: **Masculin** and **féminin**   29

Here's a helpful hint: most feminine **-té** words have English cognates ending in *-ty*, a suffix that was stolen from French.

l'identité	*identity*	**la nationalité**	*nationality*
l'illégalité	*illegality*	**la propriété**	*property*
la liberté	*freedom/liberty*	**la vanité**	*vanity*

Quelle est **la nationalité** de Morgan?   *What's Morgan's **nationality**?*
Ulysse a agi en **toute liberté**.   *Ulysse acted with **complete freedom**.*

Here are three exceptions:

le comité	*committee*
le comté	*county*
le traité	*treaty*

Le traité aurait été signé pendant la nuit.   ***The treaty** was reportedly signed during the night.*

Le comité de soutien se réunira ce soir.   *The support **committee** will meet tonight.*

-ode

la commode	*chest of drawers*	**l'ode**	*ode*
la méthode	*method*	**la pagode**	*pagoda*
la mode	*fashion/style*	**la période**	*period/time*

Here some exceptions:

l'antipode	*antipode*	**l'exode**	*exodus*
le code	*code*	**le mode**	*mode, mood, method*
l'épisode	*episode/serial/phase*		

Quelle est **la meilleure méthode** pour mémoriser le genre des noms?   *What's **the best method** to memorize the gender of nouns?*
Plusieurs femmes priaient dans **la pagode**.   *Several women were praying in **the pagoda**.*

-tude

l'attitude	*attitude*	**l'inquiétude**	*anxiety, worry*
l'étude	*study*	**la longitude**	*longitude*
l'habitude	*habit*	**la solitude**	*solitude/loneliness*

Here are a couple of exceptions:

le prélude	*prelude*
l'interlude	*interlude*

Many French nouns with these endings come from feminine Latin words ending in *-tudo*, such as *solitudo*. The exceptions can be explained by the fact that these words are compounds containing the Latin word *ludus* (*game*), which is masculine.

Blaise, tu devrais te débarrasser de **cette** mauvaise **habitude**.   *Blaise, you should get rid of **this** bad **habit**.*
Ophélie aime **la solitude**.   *Ophélie loves being **by herself**.*

30   PRACTICE MAKES PERFECT   Complete French All-in-One

-ure

la censure	censorship, censure	**la nature**	nature
l'écriture	writing	**la peinture**	paint/painting
la lecture	reading	**la voiture**	car

You'll need to remember these exceptions:

l'augure	omen	**le murmure**	whisper/murmur
le cyanure	cyanide	**le parjure**	traitor

Cédric vient de vendre **une** autre **peinture** à l'huile.	Cédric just sold **another** oil **painting**.
La meilleure recette pour apprendre le français, c'est **la lecture** et **l'écriture**.	The best recipe for learning French is **reading** and **writing**.

Note: Just like **-tié**, which we have seen in **amitié**, the French ending **-re**, like in **nature**, stems from the Latin ending -ra, found in such eminently feminine words as natura. One of our exceptions, **l'augure**, also comes from Latin, but the original word is augurium, which is neuter. The only thing about the neuter we need to know is that Latin words in this gender automatically become masculine in French.

Incidentally, according to the Belgian philologist André Goosse, editor of the famed Bon usage, the fact that the masculine in French is a default gender for the Latin neuter undermines the notion that the masculine gender in French implies power. For example, the neuter medicamentum becomes **médicament**, a masculine noun in French. Whenever you think of English words ending in -um, more specifically the Latin words that seem to enjoy a green card status in English, words such as colloquium and opprobrium, you can be sure that their French equivalents, in this case **le colloque** and **l'opprobre**, are masculine.

Other cases

There are many other endings, and each must be studied case by case.

-ice

Nouns ending in **-ice**, except for the feminine forms of masculine words to denote people practicing particular professions, such as **rédactrice** (female editor) or **directrice** (female director), are often masculine:

le bénéfice	benefit	**l'exercice**	exercise	**le service**	service
le caprice	caprice	**l'indice**	clue	**le solstice**	solstice
le complice	accomplice	**le précipice**	precipice	**le vice**	vice
le dentifrice	toothpaste				

But watch out for the feminine nouns:

l'avarice	greed	**l'épice**	spice
la cicatrice	scar	**la malice**	malice, mischievousness

This looks like a rule that's not really a rule. However, we can get some help from an old friend, Latin. You see, as mentioned earlier, the French masculine nouns, in their old (i.e., Latin) form as neuter nouns ended in -um: beneficium (**le bénéfice**), indicium (**l'indice**), servitium (**le service**), solstitium (**le solstice**), and vitium (**le vice**).

Basic gender endings: **Masculin** and **féminin**   31

Now what about those pesky feminine nouns? Well, as we know, French likes to standardize noun endings, which explains why feminine Latin nouns such as *avaritia* (**l'avarice**), *cicatrix* (**la cicatrice**), and *malitia* (**la malice**), also ended up with **-ice** endings. Sometimes one has the impression (French is no exception) that languages have a mind of their own, often ignoring our wishes and desires. Frustrating, you may say, but a certain measure of unpredictability also makes languages fascinating and exciting.

La police a arrêté **le complice** du meurtrier.	*The police arrested **the murderer's accomplice**.*
Pourriez-vous me rendre **un service**?	*Could you do me **a favor**?*

-aire, -oire

We could try to make a rule for **-aire** and **-oire** being masculine:

l'anniversaire	*birthday*	**l'interrogatoire**	*questioning/cross-examination*
le dictionnaire	*dictionary*		
le formulaire	*form*	**le laboratoire**	*laboratory*
		le mémoire	*thesis/dissertation*

However, we cannot avoid the many androgynous words, such as **le/la stagiaire** (*intern*) and a very long list of exceptions. Here are a few of them:

l'affaire	*business, issue*	**la foire**	*fair*	**la moustiquaire**	*mosquito screen*
la baignoire	*bathtub*	**la grammaire**	*grammar*	**la victoire**	*victory*
la bouilloire	*kettle*	**la mémoire**	*memory*		

You might be better off making your own rhymes.

Le stagiaire, fatigué d'écrire **son mémoire** le jour de **son anniversaire**, a pris un bain dans **sa baignoire** avant d'aller à **la foire** artisanale.	*Tired of working on **his thesis** on **his birthday**, the intern took a bath in **his tub** and went to the arts and crafts **fair**.*
Quel interrogatoire! Ça a duré plus d'une semaine!	*What a **cross-examination!** It lasted more than a week!*
Remplissez d'abord **le formulaire**!	*Fill in **the form** first!*

-oi, -ois, -oix

The only feminine nouns ending in **-oi**, **-ois**, and **-oix** are:

la croix	*cross*	**la loi**	*law*	**la paroi**	*wall/partition*
la foi	*faith*	**la noix**	*nut*	**la voix**	*voice*

Elles parlaient à **voix basse**.	*They were talking in **low voices**.*
C'est **la loi** de la jungle.	*It's **the law** of the jungle.*

-f, -aim

The only feminine nouns ending in **-f** and **-aim** are:

la clef ou **la clé**	*key*	**la nef**	*nave*
la faim	*hunger*	**la soif**	*thirst*

La faim dans le monde empire chaque jour.	*World **hunger** gets worse every day.*
Où as-tu mis **la clé** du coffre-fort?	*Where did you put **the key** of the safe?*

32 PRACTICE MAKES PERFECT Complete French All-in-One

-ole, -ôle, -ule

Nouns ending in **-ole**, **-ôle**, or **-ule** seem willing to go either way. While Latin may provide some guidance, there is no foolproof method. Nevertheless, it helps to know that *symbolus*—**le symbole** (*symbol*)—is masculine in Latin and *crepusculum*—**le crépuscule** (*dusk*)—is neuter, while *schola*—**l'école** (*school*)—is feminine.

Masculine nouns ending in **-ole** or **-ôle**:

le contrôle	*control*	**le pactole**	*fortune/gold mine*	**le protocole**	*protocol*
le monopole	*monopoly*	**le pôle**	*pole*	**le symbole**	*symbol*

Feminine nouns ending in **-ole** or **-ôle**:

l'Acropole	*Acropolis*	**la console**	*console*	**l'idole**	*idol*
la banderole	*banner*	**l'école**	*school*	**la nécropole**	*necropolis*
la casserole	*pan*	**la gondole**	*gondola*	**la parole**	*speech*

Masculine nouns ending in **-ule**:

le crépuscule	*dusk*	**le préambule**	*preamble*	**le scrupule**	*scruple*
l'émule	*emulator*	**le ridicule**	*absurdity/*	**le véhicule**	*vehicle*
le funambule	*tightrope walker*		*ridiculousness*	**le vestibule**	*hall/lobby*

Feminine nouns ending in **-ule**:

la canicule	*heat wave*	**la majuscule**	*upper case/capital*	**la pilule**	*pill*
la cellule	*cell*	**la mule**	*mule*	**la spatule**	*spatula*
la formule	*formula*	**la pellicule**	*film/dandruff*	**la tentacule**	*tentacle*
la libellule	*dragonfly*	**la péninsule**	*peninsula*		

Ils ont fait le tour de Venise dans **une gondole** bleu nuit.	*They toured Venice in **a midnight blue gondola**.*
Une libellule voletait au-dessus d'un champ de maïs.	*A **dragonfly** was fluttering over a cornfield.*

-iste, -que

Nouns ending in **-iste** and **-que** that refer to persons can be either masculine or feminine:

le/la paysagiste	*landscape artist*	**le/la scientifique**	*scientist*	**le/la violoniste**	*violinist*
le/la scénariste	*scriptwriter*	**le/la spécialiste**	*specialist*		

Other nouns ending in **-iste** are feminine:

la liste	*list*
la piste	*track/path*

Agnès Varda est l'une **des** plus grandes **scénaristes** du cinéma français.	*Agnès Varda is one of **the** greatest **scriptwriters** of French cinema.*
Fais **une liste** de tout ce dont on a besoin d'acheter.	*Make **a list** of everything we need to buy.*

Nouns derived from past participles

Nouns derived from adjectives and the masculine forms of the past participle are masculine:

l'aîné	*the oldest*	**le favori**	*the favorite*	**le nu**	*naked*
le beau	*the handsome one*	**l'inconnu**	*the unknown*	**le vécu**	*lived experience*
le bien	*good*	**le mal**	*evil*	**le vieux**	*the old one*
le détenu	*prisoner*				

Basic gender endings: **Masculin** and **féminin** 33

Nouns derived from adjectives and the feminine forms of past participles are feminine:

la belle	*the beautiful*	**la mariée**	*the bride*	**la venue**	*the coming*
la crue	*flood*	**la petite**	*the little one*	**la vue**	*vision*
la disparue	*the vanished one*	**la retraitée**	*the retiree*		

Ce que le lecteur veut, c'est **du vécu**.

What the reader wants is ***real-life experience***.

La mariée était si belle dans sa robe d'organdi.

The bride was so beautiful in her organdy dress.

EXERCICE 2·1

Indicate the gender and definite article.

1. _____ tolérance
2. _____ pain
3. _____ compliment
4. _____ sapin
5. _____ présence
6. _____ courage
7. _____ agneau
8. _____ orangeraie
9. _____ chaîne
10. _____ plage

11. _____ ruisseau
12. _____ architecture
13. _____ classement
14. _____ symbolisme
15. _____ égalité
16. _____ odeur
17. _____ pudeur
18. _____ vignoble
19. _____ paille
20. _____ calepin

EXERCICE 2·2

Complete this nursery rhyme with the definite article, masculine or feminine, and translate the possessive adjectives.

J'aime _____ eau

J'aime _____ eau dans _____ (my) baignoire

Et sur _____ carrelage de _____ cuisine quand maman le nettoie

J'aime _____ eau sur _____ plage

J'aime les vaguelettes

Qui me chatouillent les doigts de pied

Et s'en vont avec _____ marée

J'aime _____ eau des flaques et des étangs

Des lacs et des barrages où elle se heurte en écumant

J'aime _____ pluie qui me mouille _____ langue

Et qui fait pousser les plantes dans _____ jardin

J'aime _____ eau des fleuves

_____ eau où pullulent les petits poissons

J'aime _____ eau quand elle est bien chaude

_____ matin dans _____ (my) lavabo

J'aime _____ eau quand elle est gelée

Quand je peux patiner sur les mares glacées.

EXERCICE 2·3

Indicate the gender of the nouns and the definite article.

1. _____ meuble
2. _____ soja
3. _____ référence
4. _____ cocktail
5. _____ rail
6. _____ fin
7. _____ attitude
8. _____ lainage
9. _____ parlement
10. _____ centaine
11. _____ sculpture
12. _____ libéralisme
13. _____ signal
14. _____ délicatesse
15. _____ horlogerie
16. _____ citadin
17. _____ tact
18. _____ orthographe
19. _____ clavecin
20. _____ fraternité

EXERCICE 2·4

Indicate the gender of the nouns and the definite article.

1. _____ acacia
2. _____ chanson
3. _____ portefeuille
4. _____ domino
5. _____ signature
6. _____ écaille
7. _____ millefeuille
8. _____ cinéma

Basic gender endings: **Masculin** and **féminin**   35

9. _____ tribu

10. _____ tracteur

11. _____ établissement

12. _____ altitude

13. _____ hamac

14. _____ ghetto

15. _____ confirmation

16. _____ noix

17. _____ main

18. _____ inclinaison

19. _____ soif

20. _____ faim

More French nouns and their gender

Naming people and animals

As a rule, professions are masculine when they refer to a man and feminine when they refer to a woman. You can just add a final **e**:

l'apprenti/ l'apprentie	*apprentice*	**l'avocat/ l'avocate**	*lawyer*
l'attaché/ l'attachée	*attaché*	**le magistrat/ la magistrate**	*magistrate, judge*

In the past, traditionally masculine professions, even if practiced by women, remained masculine:

le compositeur	*composer*	**le procureur**	*prosecutor*
le peintre	*painter*	**le professeur**	*professor/teacher*

In 1998, Lionel Jospin, the socialist prime minister, created a new commission to study the question. ***Femme, j'écris ton nom,*** the commission's resulting guide for the feminization of professions and titles, was published in 1999. If you are an insomniac, you may enjoy reading this hundred-page guide of some obscure professions in French or in English, which is available online. The guide had a major impact.

In addition, Quebec, at the cutting edge of feminization, played a key role, even if we, the French, won't admit it. . . . Over ten years ago, I started consulting and hosting workshops for the Blue Metropolis Montreal International Festival. I gasped when I saw myself listed in the festival's program as «**Annie Heminway, *professeure* à New York.**» I have to admit it took me some time to get used to it.

These days, you will read more frequently in the newspapers and magazines: **l'écrivaine** (*writer*), **l'ingénieure** (*engineer*), **la juge** (*judge*). Even the newspaper *Le Monde* talks about a famous writer as **l'écrivaine** Léonora Miano.

You have to use caution, though. Were you to send a letter to a minister of the government, you should ask the Chief of Protocol if she uses **Madame le ministre** or **Madame la ministre**. In a speech made by Roselyne Bachelot on January 2008, for example, the headline was: « **Discours de *Madame le ministre* de la santé, de la jeunesse et des sports**. » Then Roselyne Bachelot herself had written, a few lines down: « ***La ministre* de la qualité des soins que je veux être ne peut que reprendre à son compte de tels propos**. » As you can see, anything goes! The tendency today, however, is to use **Madame la ministre**.

37

Human beings

One way of identifying the nouns is to learn if they have identical or different root words.

Identical roots

In numerous cases, the noun of a profession is identical in the masculine and the feminine:

l'architecte/l'architecte	*architect*
le vétérinaire/la vétérinaire	*veterinarian*
le dentiste/la dentiste	*dentist*

In many instances, you add an **-e** at the end of the noun:

l'avocat/l'avocate	*lawyer*
le marchand/la marchande	*merchant*
l'associé/l'associée	*partner*

In other cases, there are many possible endings depending on the noun. Here are some examples, but always check in the dictionary.

l'ouvrier/l'ouvrière	*worker*
le conseiller/la conseillère	*adviser*
le chocolatier/la chocolatière	*chocolate maker*
l'acheteur/l'acheteuse	*buyer*
le vendeur/la vendeuse	*salesperson*
le coiffeur/la coiffeuse	*hairdresser*
le musicien/la musicienne	*musician*
le doyen/la doyenne	*dean, most senior member*
le pharmacien/la pharmacienne	*pharmacist*
le rédacteur/la rédactrice	*editor*
le concepteur/la conceptrice	*designer, project manager*
le spectateur/la spectatrice	*viewer, member of an audience*
le patron/la patronne	*boss*
le baron/la baronne	*baron*
le vigneron/la vigneronne	*wine grower*
le prince/la princesse	*prince/princess*
le maître/la maîtresse	*master/mistress*
le comte/la comtesse	*count/countess*

If there is an adjective, it will agree accordingly:

le directeur financier/la directrice financière	*financial director*

La coiffeuse d'Alice est aussi **musicienne**.	*Alice's **hairdresser** is also a **musician**.*
Les ouvriers ont demandé une augmentation à **leur patronne**.	*The workers asked **their boss** for a raise.*

EXERCICE 3·1

She has the same profession as her cousin, she is . . .

1. Il est directeur. Elle est _____.
2. Il est chanteur. Elle est _____.
3. Il est gardien. Elle est _____.
4. Il est commerçant. Elle est _____.
5. Il est pédiatre. Elle est _____.
6. Il est consultant. Elle est _____.
7. Il est traducteur. Elle est _____.
8. Il est agriculteur. Elle est _____.
9. Il est technicien. Elle est _____.
10. Il est psychologue. Elle est _____.
11. Il est assistant technique. Elle est _____.
12. Il est astrologue. Elle est _____.
13. Il est mécanicien. Elle est _____.
14. Il est boucher. Elle est _____.
15. Il est électricien. Elle est _____.
16. Il est archiduc. Elle est _____.
17. Il est dessinateur. Elle est _____.
18. Il est baron. Elle est _____.
19. Il est infirmier. Elle est _____.
20. Il est viticulteur. Elle est _____.

Different root words

Sometimes the basis for the masculine and the feminine is different or the root word happens to be different.

le beau-frère/la belle-sœur	*brother-in-law/sister-in-law*
le beau-père/la belle-mère	*father-in-law, stepfather/mother-in-law, stepmother*
le garçon/la fille	*boy/girl*
le gendre/la belle-fille	*son-in-law/daughter-in-law*
l'homme/la femme	*man/woman*
le mari/la femme	*husband/wife*
l'oncle/la tante	*uncle/aunt*
le parrain/la marraine	*godfather/godmother*

More French nouns and their gender 39

le père/la mère		father/mother	
le roi/la reine		king/queen	

Le cardinal de Mazarin fut **le parrain** de Louis XIV. — *Cardinal Mazarin was Louis XIV's **godfather**.*

C'est triste mais Corrine ne s'entend pas avec **son gendre**. — *It is sad but Corrine does not get along with **her son-in-law**.*

Some nouns follow no rule:

le barman/	*barman/*	**la couturière**	*seamstress*	
la barmaid	*barmaid*	**le steward/**	*flight attendant*	
le couturier	*couturier/*	**l'hôtesse de l'air**		
	fashion designer			

Coco Chanel était **un** grand **couturier**. — *Coco Chanel was **a great fashion designer**.*

As mentioned in the introduction, the feminization of nouns is widespread. And yet, the masculine form is still used by a lot of women. You may want to ask for the business card of the woman you are talking to so you'll have an answer as to which she prefers.

Here are more professions that are often feminized. But always ask to double-check.

l'acuponcteur/	*acupuncturist*	**l'inventeur/**	*inventor*
l'acuponctrice		**l'inventrice**	
le chirurgien/	*surgeon*	**le poète/**	*poet*
la chirurgienne		**la poétesse**	
le compositeur/	*composer*	**le sculpteur/**	*sculptor*
la compositrice		**la sculpteure**	
l'écrivain/l'écrivaine	*writer*	or **la sculptrice**	

Catherine a obtenu son diplôme d'**acuponctrice** à Paris. — *Catherine got her **acupuncture** diploma in Paris.*

Agnès Vincent est une talentueuse **compositrice** de musique de film. — *Agnès Vincent is a talented film **composer**.*

Masculine nouns for both men and women

Some nouns are always masculine whether referring to a man or a woman:

l'acolyte	*acolyte/associate*	**le chef**	*leader, boss*	**le mannequin**	*model*
l'agresseur	*attacker*	**le clerc**	*clerk*	**le monarque**	*monarch*
l'ange	*angel*	**le déserteur**	*deserter*	**le sauveur**	*savior*
l'apôtre	*apostle*	**le forçat**	*convict*	**le successeur**	*successor*
l'assassin	*murderer*	**le génie**	*genius*	**le témoin**	*witness*
le bandit	*bandit*	**le goinfre**	*glutton*	**le tyran**	*tyrant*
le brigand	*brigand*	**le gourmet**	*epicure*	**le vandale**	*vandal*
le charlatan	*charlatan, quack*	**l'imposteur**	*impostor*	**le voyou**	*hooligan, rascal*

Violène est **un beau mannequin**. — *Violène is **a beautiful model**.*

La femme de Louis est **un ange**. — *Louis's **wife** is **an angel**.*

Feminine nouns for both men and women

Some nouns are always feminine whether referring to a man or a woman:

l'Altesse	*Highness*	**l'étoile**	*star, leading dancer*	**la personne**	*person*
l'autorité	*authority*	**l'idole**	*idol*	**la star**	*star*
la célébrité	*celebrity*	**la Majesté**	*Majesty*	**la vedette**	*star*

Feminine nouns used only for men

Some feminine nouns are used only for men:

la brute	*bully, boor*	**la crapule**	*villain, crook*	**Son Éminence**	*His Eminence*
la canaille	*scoundrel*	**l'huile**	*big shot, bigwig*	**Sa Sainteté**	*His Holiness*

Ce type, c'est **une** véritable **crapule**.
Son Éminence Dzogchen Rinpoché a participé à une conférence avec le Dalai Lama à Toulouse.

__This guy__ is a real __crook__.
__His Eminence__ Dzogchen Rinpoché took part in a conference with the Dalai Lama in Toulouse.

In the army, some terms that were used only for men in the past are applicable for women today.

l'estafette	*courier*	**la recrue**	*recruit*	**la vigie**	*lookout/watch*
l'ordonnance	*orderly*	**la sentinelle**	*sentry/sentinel*		

EXERCICE
3·2

Complete with the indefinite article un *or* une.

1. Son cousin est _____ célébrité dans le monde du spectacle.

2. _____ altesse royale que nous n'avons pas vraiment reconnue, a fait halte dans notre village hier.

3. Ta tante est _____ ange!

4. Mathieu est _____ personne sur qui on peut compter.

5. Sandrine est _____ mannequin célèbre pour ses coiffures excentriques.

6. Monsieur Thibault est _____ génie en informatique.

7. Sa femme est _____ gourmet par excellence.

8. Ce chanteur, c'est _____ idole depuis des années.

9. Ce type, c'est _____ véritable crapule!

10. Julie est _____ témoin que le juge veut entendre.

More French nouns and their gender   **41**

EXERCICE 3·3

Put the possessive adjective son or sa before the noun.

1. L'impresario et _____ star prenaient un verre sur la Croisette.

2. Mélanie voudrait inviter _____ oncle et _____ tante pour son anniversaire.

3. La police n'a pas encore retrouvé _____ assassin.

4. Hervé est arrivé avec Anna, _____ successeur.

5. Alice, tu es _____ sauveur!

6. _____ parrain lui a offert un joli bracelet.

7. Lui et _____ acolyte, ils ne font que des bêtises!

8. Yan est venu nous voir avec _____ beau-frère et _____ belle-mère.

9. Ce pays ne peut pas se débarrasser de _____ tyran.

10. Quelle est _____ vedette préférée?

Animals

Since the animal kingdom, just like the human world, has genders, one usually has to learn two nouns for each species.

Animal couples with identical root words

Couples may be made of the male noun plus different suffixes:

agneau/agnelle	*lamb/ewe lamb*	**hérisson/hérissonne**	*hedgehog*
âne/ânesse	*donkey/she-donkey*	**héron/héronne**	*heron*
buffle/bufflonne	*buffalo*	**lapin/lapine**	*rabbit/doe rabbit*
chameau/chamelle	*camel/she-camel*	**lion/lionne**	*lion/lioness*
chat/chatte	*cat/she-cat*	**loup/louve**	*wolf/she-wolf*
chevreuil/chevrette	*roebuck/roe deer*	**ours/ourse**	*bear/she-bear*
chien/chienne	*dog/female dog*	**renard/renarde**	*fox/vixen*
éléphant/éléphante	*elephant/cow elephant*	**paon/paonne**	*peacock/peahen*
faisan/faisane	*pheasant/hen pheasant*	**tigre/tigresse**	*tiger/tigress*

Les enfants ont vu **une ourse polaire** et **un chameau** au zoo.

*The children saw **a polar she-bear** and **a camel** at the zoo.*

François, **le chat** de Michael, aime s'asseoir sur le clavier de l'ordinateur.

*François, Michael's **cat**, likes to sit on the computer keyboard.*

42 PRACTICE MAKES PERFECT Complete French All-in-One

Animal couples with different root words

Some male and female nouns of animals are totally different, just as in English:

bélier/brebis	*ram/ewe*	**dindon/dinde**	*turkey/turkey hen*
bouc/chèvre	*goat/she-goat*	**jars/oie**	*gander/goose*
canard/cane	*duck/female duck*	**porc/truie**	*hog/sow*
cerf/biche	*stag/doe*	**sanglier/laie**	*wild boar/wild sow*
cheval/jument	*horse/mare*	**singe/guenon**	*monkey/female monkey*
coq/poule	*rooster/hen*	**taureau/vache**	*bull/cow*

Épicène

Most names of animals are **épicène**. This strange-sounding word comes from the Greek *epikoinos*, meaning "common." **Épicène** nouns work with either gender. To differentiate between the two sexes, you add **mâle** or **femelle**. Here are some masculine names:

aigle	*eagle*	**faucon**	*falcon*	**mille-pattes**	*millipede*
blaireau	*badger*	**gorille**	*gorilla*	**oiseau**	*bird*
brochet	*pike*	**guépard**	*cheetah*	**panda**	*panda*
cachalot	*sperm whale*	**hanneton**	*cockchafer*	**papillon**	*butterfly*
canari	*canary*	**hibou**	*owl*	**perroquet**	*parrot*
castor	*beaver*	**hippocampe**	*sea horse*	**phoque**	*seal*
cochon	*pig*	**hippopotame**	*hippopotamus*	**pigeon**	*pigeon*
corbeau	*crow*	**homard**	*lobster*	**pingouin**	*penguin*
crapaud	*toad*	**jaguar**	*jaguar*	**requin**	*shark*
crocodile	*crocodile*	**kangourou**	*kangaroo*	**rhinocéros**	*rhinoceros*
cygne	*swan*	**koala**	*koala*	**saumon**	*salmon*
dauphin	*dolphin*	**lama**	*llama*	**scorpion**	*scorpion*
dromadaire	*dromedary*	**léopard**	*leopard*	**serpent**	*snake*
écureuil	*squirrel*	**lézard**	*lizard*	**vautour**	*vulture*
escargot	*snail*	**lynx**	*lynx*	**zèbre**	*zebra*

Here are some feminine names:

abeille	*bee*	**girafe**	*giraffe*	**mouche**	*fly*
autruche	*ostrich*	**grenouille**	*frog*	**mouette**	*gull*
baleine	*whale*	**grive**	*thrush*	**panthère**	*panther*
chauve-souris	*bat*	**guêpe**	*wasp*	**perruche**	*budgie*
chouette	*owl*	**hirondelle**	*swallow*	**pie**	*magpie*
cigale	*cicada*	**huître**	*oyster*	**souris**	*mouse*
cigogne	*stork*	**libellule**	*dragonfly*	**taupe**	*mole*
colombe	*dove*	**loutre**	*otter*	**tortue**	*turtle*
crevette	*shrimp*	**mante religieuse**	*praying mantis*	**tourterelle**	*turtledove*
fourmi	*ant*	**marmotte**	*woodchuck*	**truite**	*trout*
gazelle	*gazelle*	**méduse**	*jellyfish*	**vipère**	*viper*

Flaubert a emprunté **un perroquet** empaillé au musée de Rouen et l'a placé sur son bureau.	*Flaubert borrowed **a stuffed parrot** from the Rouen Museum and placed it on his desk.*
Tu commandes **le homard** ou **des huîtres**?	*Are you ordering **lobster** or **oysters**?*

EXERCICE 3·4

Complete with the definite article le *or* la.

1. _____ vache est agacée par _____ mouche qui tourne autour de sa tête.

2. En théorie, _____ lièvre court plus vite que _____ tortue.

3. _____ perroquet de _____ tante de Xavier répète sans cesse les mêmes mots.

4. Je veux choisir _____ chameau qui me plaît pour faire un tour dans le désert.

5. _____ louve et _____ ourse protègent farouchement leurs petits.

6. _____ cigale chante pendant que _____ fourmi travaille.

7. LÉO, _____ chat de Mademoiselle Gallatin est un magnifique Maine Coon.

8. _____ oiseau qui se perche sur notre balcon est un rouge-gorge.

9. As-tu mangé _____ saumon que tu as attrapé?

10. _____ guêpe qui était sur la table a fini par la piquer.

EXERCICE 3·5

Indicate the corresponding male animals.

1. la chamelle _____

2. la chèvre _____

3. la truie _____

4. la louve _____

5. l'oie _____

6. la chevrette _____

7. la jument _____

8. l'agnelle _____

9. la biche _____

10. la brebis _____

Places and the calendar

No, geography is not neutral either. There are rules—and exceptions. Let's start with cities.

Cities

The masculine is used more commonly for cities, but the feminine is still used in a more aesthetic or romantic sense. There is no set rule. You will find many examples in literature. Look at the following examples:

Le Paris populaire des années 1930	*The working-class **Paris** of the 1930s*
Paris est si **bruyant**; c'est **épuisant**.	*Paris is so **noisy**; it's **exhausting**.*
Paris, la magnifique	*Paris the magnificent*
Paris, traversée de fragrances **enivrantes**	*Paris, bathed in **intoxicating** fragrances*
Le Tout-Paris était **présent** pour l'inauguration du nouveau musée.	*Everybody who is anybody in Paris **attended** the inauguration of the new museum.*
Tout Venise souffrait des inondations.	*All of Venice suffered from the floods.*
Venise La Sérénissime	*Venice the Most Serene*
Venise, la belle, l'enchanteresse	*Venice, the beautiful, the bewitching*

Names of towns preceded by a masculine definite article are masculine:

Le Havre est **un grand port**.	*Le Havre is **a big harbor**.*
Le Caire est **connu** pour son musée de l'Antiquité Égyptienne.	*Cairo is **known** for its museum of Egyptian antiquity.*
Le Mans est **connu** pour sa course automobile.	*Le Mans is **known** for its car racing.*

Names of towns preceded by a feminine definite article are feminine:

La Rochelle est très **prisée** par les vacanciers.	*La Rochelle is highly **rated** by vacationers.*
La Havane est **fréquentée** par de merveilleux musiciens.	*Marvelous musicians are to be **found** in Havana.*
La Seyne-sur-Mer est **située** dans le Var.	*La Seyne-sur-Mer is **in** the Var.*

The gender of Italian cities varies:

La Florence des Médicis
Le Florence de James Ivory (in *Room with a View*)
La Venise de Casanova
Le Venise de Pasolini

It all depends on the context.

Usually, when the nouns of cities are preceded by the adjectives **grand**, **nouveau**, and **vieux**, they are used in the masculine form:

Le Grand Prague	**Le Vieux-Marseille**
Le Nouveau-Belleville	**Le Vieux-Québec**

More French nouns and their gender **45**

Departments, regions, and states

Now we are going to travel around the provinces and departments of France and states of America and try to figure out their genders.

Departments

Many departments take the gender of a river, a mountain, or a geographic site, like the coast.

l'Auvergne	la Dordogne	la Loire
le Cantal	le Finistère	la Manche

Le tunnel sous **la Manche** est ouvert
depuis 1994.
Dans **le Finistère**, Concarneau, ville
médiévale entourée de remparts, attire
de nombreux touristes.

The Chunnel has been open since 1994.

*In **the Finistère**, Concarneau, a medieval
walled town, attracts many tourists.*

Some departments are named after two rivers. If one river is masculine, it goes first and the noun is masculine. If both are feminine, the department is feminine.

l'Ille-et-Vilaine	le Maine-et-Loire	la Saône-et-Loire
l'Indre-et-Loire	la Meurthe-et-Moselle	le Tarn-et-Garonne
le Loir-et-Cher		

Chenonceau est l'un des plus beaux
châteaux de **l'Indre-et-Loire**.
La Meurthe-et-Moselle a l'une des
productions les plus élevées de
mirabelles de France.

*Chenonceau is one of the most beautiful
castles in **Indre-et-Loire**.*
***La Meurthe-et-Moselle** has one of the
highest productions of mirabelle
plums in France.*

Some departments are classified according to geographic parameters:

les Bouches-du-Rhône	les Hauts-de-Seine	la Seine-Saint-Denis
les Côtes-d'Armor	le Puy-de-Dôme	le Val-de-Marne
la Côte-d'Or		

Le Puy-de-Dôme porte le nom du volcan
endormi en Auvergne.
La Seine-Saint-Denis est le 93ème
département français. On l'appelle 9-3.

***Le Puy-de-Dôme** bears the name of the
dormant volcano in Auvergne.*
***La Seine-Saint-Denis** is the 93rd French
department. It is called 9-3.*

Others are determined by an adjective. Departments ending in **-e** tend to be feminine.

les Alpes-Maritimes	la Haute-Loire	la Haute-Vienne
le Bas-Rhin	la Haute-Savoie	les Pyrénées-Atlantiques

Le lac d'Annecy **en Haute-Savoie** est l'un
des plus grands de France.
Le festival du cinéma a lieu à Cannes dans
les **Alpes-Maritimes**.

*The Annecy Lake **in Haute-Savoie** is one
of the largest in France.*
*The film festival takes place in Cannes in
the **Alpes-Maritimes**.*

Many nouns of departments that do not end in **-e** tend to be masculine:

l'Ain	le Cantal	le Gers	le Loiret
l'Allier	le Cher	l'Hérault	le Nord
l'Aveyron	le Gard	le Jura	le Tarn
le Calvados			

46 PRACTICE MAKES PERFECT   Complete French All-in-One

L'Enfant sauvage de Truffaut est basé sur une histoire vraie dans **l'Aveyron** du dix huitième siècle.	The Wild Child *by Truffaut is based on a true story in the eighteenth-century **Aveyron** department.*
Le pont du **Gard** est un aqueduc romain qui enjambe le Gard.	*The Pont du **Gard** is a Roman aqueduct that crosses the Gard River.*

The overseas departments, called **les départements ultramarins**, are:

la Guadeloupe	**la Martinique**	**la Réunion**
la Guyane	**Mayotte**	

There are many ultramarine territories and collectives like:

la Nouvelle-Calédonie	**Saint-Pierre et Miquelon**
la Polynésie	**les Terres Australes et Antarctiques**

Le plus grand poète de **la Martinique** fut Aimé Césaire.	*The greatest poet in **Martinique** was Aimé Césaire.*
Mayotte est devenu le 101ème département français en mars 2011.	*As of March 2011, **Mayotte** has become the 101st French Department.*

If you are interested in the topic, visit the government website on the ultramarine departments and collectives: http://www.outre-mer.gouv.fr.

Regions and states

Regions, provinces, and states ending in **-e** tend to be feminine. The others tend to be masculine—with some exceptions, of course. Here are some examples in the masculine in France:

le Bordelais	**le Languedoc**	**le Midi**	**le Poitou**
le Jura	**le Limousin**	**le Nord-Pas-de-Calais**	**le Roussillon**

Les châteaux cathares **du Languedoc** sont remplis de mystère.	*The Cathar castles **in Languedoc** are full of mystery.*
La capitale **du Poitou** est Poitiers.	*The capital **of Poitou** is Poitiers.*

Here are some examples in the feminine in France:

l'Alsace	**la Bretagne**	**la Franche-Comté**	**la Picardie**
l'Aquitaine	**la Champagne**	**la Lorraine**	**la Provence**
l'Auvergne	**la Côte d'Azur**	**la Normandie**	**la Savoie**
la Bourgogne			

Un des personnages les plus célèbres **d'Aquitaine** est Aliénor d'Aquitaine qui fut reine de France puis d'Angleterre.	*One of most famous figures **of Aquitaine** was Eleanor of Aquitaine who was queen of France, then of England.*
La Picardie est composée de trois départements: l'Aisne, l'Oise et la Somme.	*The **Picardy region** is composed of three departments: l'Aisne, l'Oise, and la Somme.*

Here are some examples in the masculine in the United States:

le Colorado	**le Minnesota**	**le New-Hampshire**	**le Texas**
le Kansas	**le Mississippi**	**le Nouveau-Mexique**	**le Vermont**
le Maine	**le Nebraska**	**l'Ohio**	**le Wyoming**
le Michigan			

Here are some examples in the feminine in the United States:

la Californie	**la Floride**	**la Louisiane**	**la Virginie**
la Caroline-du-Sud	**la Géorgie**	**la Pennsylvanie**	

La Californie est l'un des États les plus visités par les Européens.
Napoléon vendit **la Louisiane** en 1803.

California is one of the states most visited by Europeans.
*Napoleon sold **Louisiana** in 1803.*

Note that you will say **l'État de New York** to avoid the confusion between New York State and New York City and **l'État de Washington** to distinguish between the state of Washington and Washington, D.C., the capital of the country. There are quite a few tricks to be aware of, so double-check the article and the preposition in the dictionary.

EXERCICE 3·6

Indicate the gender of the nouns by adding the definite article le, la, *or* les.

1. _____ Californie
2. _____ Seine-Saint-Denis
3. _____ Louisiane
4. _____ Bretagne
5. _____ Guadeloupe
6. _____ Caire
7. _____ Languedoc
8. _____ Dordogne
9. _____ Nebraska
10. _____ Vermont
11. _____ Maine
12. _____ Lorraine
13. _____ New Jersey
14. _____ Limousin
15. _____ Gard
16. _____ Poitou
17. _____ Missouri
18. _____ Provence
19. _____ Martinique
20. _____ Alpes-Maritimes

Countries

Like regions and states, the countries with an **-e** ending tend to be feminine. Other endings tend to be masculine, although you must watch out for the exceptions.

First, let's look at the feminine countries:

l'Albanie	*Albania*	**la Hongrie**	*Hungary*
l'Algérie	*Algeria*	**l'Inde**	*India*
l'Allemagne	*Germany*	**l'Irlande**	*Ireland*
l'Angleterre	*England*	**l'Italie**	*Italy*
l'Arabie saoudite	*Saudi Arabia*	**la Jordanie**	*Jordan*
l'Argentine	*Argentina*	**la Malaisie**	*Malaysia*
l'Australie	*Australia*	**la Mauritanie**	*Mauritania*
l'Autriche	*Austria*	**la Mongolie**	*Mongolia*
la Belgique	*Belgium*	**la Namibie**	*Namibia*
la Biélorussie	*Belarus*	**la Norvège**	*Norway*

48   PRACTICE MAKES PERFECT   Complete French All-in-One

la Bolivie	*Bolivia*	**la Pologne**	*Poland*
la Bulgarie	*Bulgaria*	**la Roumanie**	*Romania*
la Chine	*China*	**la Russie**	*Russia*
la Colombie	*Columbia*	**la Suède**	*Sweden*
la Côte d'Ivoire	*Ivory Coast*	**la Syrie**	*Syria*
l'Égypte	*Egypt*	**la Tanzanie**	*Tanzania*
l'Espagne	*Spain*	**la Thaïlande**	*Thailand*
l'Éthiopie	*Ethiopia*	**la Tunisie**	*Tunisia*
la Finlande	*Finland*	**la Turquie**	*Turkey*
la France	*France*	**la Sierra Leone**	*Sierra Leone*
la Grèce	*Greece*	**l'Ukraine**	*Ukraine*
la Guyane	*Guyana*	**la Zambie**	*Zambia*

Here are some exceptions. The following nouns end with an **-e** but are masculine:

le Cachemire	*Kashmir*	**le Mozambique***	*Mozambique*
le Cambodge	*Cambodia*	**le Zimbabwe****	*Zimbabwe*
le Mexique	*Mexico*		

*officially **la République du Mozambique**
or **la République du Zimbabwe

La Suède attribue les prix Nobel chaque année.	*Sweden awards Nobel prizes every year.*
Attiré par Istanbul, son frère s'est installé **en Turquie** l'an passé.	*Attracted by Istanbul, his brother settled in Turkey last year.*

Now let's look at some of the masculine countries:

l'Afghanistan	*Afghanistan*	**le Kenya**	*Kenya*
le Bangladesh	*Bangladesh*	**le Laos**	*Laos*
le Bénin	*Benin*	**le Liban**	*Lebanon*
le Bhoutan	*Bhutan*	**le Maroc**	*Morocco*
le Brésil	*Brazil*	**le Mali**	*Mali*
le Canada	*Canada*	**le Nigéria**	*Nigeria*
le Chili	*Chile*	**le Pakistan**	*Pakistan*
le Congo	*Congo*	**le Paraguay**	*Paraguay*
le Danemark	*Denmark*	**le Pérou**	*Peru*
l'Équateur	*Ecuador*	**le Portugal**	*Portugal*
le Gabon	*Gabon*	**le Sénégal**	*Senegal*
l'Iran	*Iran*	**le Tchad**	*Chad*
l'Irak	*Iraq*	**le Venezuela**	*Venezuela*
le Japon	*Japan*	**le Viêt-Nam**	*Vietnam*

Some countries do not have articles: **Israël, Oman**.

Le Viêt-Nam est l'un des plus grands producteurs de riz.	*Vietnam is one of the largest rice producers.*
Le Maroc a de nombreux sites protégés par l'UNESCO.	*Morocco has many sites protected by UNESCO.*

More French nouns and their gender **49**

EXERCICE 3·7

Indicate the gender of the nouns by adding the definite article le, la, *or* les.

1. _____ France
2. _____ Danemark
3. _____ Grèce
4. _____ Mexique
5. _____ Belgique
6. _____ Japon
7. _____ Chili
8. _____ Guatemala
9. _____ Brésil
10. _____ Cambodge
11. _____ Italie
12. _____ Portugal
13. _____ Chine
14. _____ Turquie
15. _____ Russie
16. _____ Bolivie
17. _____ Malaisie
18. _____ Nouvelle-Calédonie
19. _____ Costa Rica
20. _____ Philippines

EXERCICE 3·8

Indicate the gender of the country or province by adding the definite article le *or* la.

1. _____ Népal est un endroit idéal pour le trekking.
2. _____ Jordanie abrite l'ancienne cité de Pétra, patrimoine mondial de l'UNESCO.
3. En mars, Erwan visitera _____ Togo, _____ Bénin et _____ Sierra Leone.
4. _____ Nouvelle-Zélande attire Carla depuis longtemps.
5. _____ Guyane est un département ultramarin.
6. _____ Burkina Faso organise un gigantesque festival de cinéma tous les deux ans.
7. _____ Qatar a invité des architectes français pour construire des édifices.
8. _____ Viêt-Nam a fortement influencé l'écriture de Marguerite Duras.
9. _____ Pays-Bas sont de grands exportateurs de tulipes.
10. _____ Québec est traversé par le Saint-Laurent.

Islands, rivers, seas, and oceans

Now we are going to investigate the gender of islands and rivers. Could there be set rules?

Islands

The rules for the gender of isles are as fluid as their waters. You will find variations from one dictionary to the other, from one writer to the other. It remains a poetic enigma of islands . . . Even if the island is a state, the tendency is to use the feminine, referring to **l'île**, but not always. In fact, some islands do not even have articles:

Aruba	**Guernesey**	**Jersey**	**Samoa**
Bora, Bora	**Haïti**	**Madagascar**	**Terre-Neuve**
Chypre	**Hawaï**	**Malte**	**Taïwan**
Cuba	**Hong-Kong**	**Ouessant**	

Madagascar est situé dans l'océan Indien.	*Madagascar is in* the Indian Ocean.
Haïti chérie	*Darling Haiti* (political song, 1920)
Cuba, la belle	*Cuba, the beautiful*

Au quinzième siècle, **Cuba était peuplée** par les Taïnos.	*In the fifteenth century, **Cuba was inhabited** by the Taino Indians.*
Taïwan est située au centre de l'Asie.	*Taiwan is in* the center of Asia.

Some islands have a definite article, making things easy:

la Barbade	**la Grenade**	**l'Île de Sein**	**les Marquises**
le Cap-Vert	**la Guadeloupe**	**la Jamaïque**	**la Nouvelle-Guinée**
la Corse	**l'Île Maurice**	**les Maldives**	**les Seychelles**
la Crête	**l'Île de Ré**	**la Martinique**	**la Sicile**

La Corse est renommée pour **ses falaises**.	*Corsica is renowned for **its cliffs**.*
L'Île de Ré est l'île **favorite** des politiques français.	*The island of Ré is the **favorite** island of French politicians.*
Jacques Brel a passé de longues années **aux enchanteresses Marquises**.	*Jacques Brel spent many years on the enchanting Marquesas Islands.*

Rivers

In French, there is a difference between **un fleuve**, a river that flows into the sea or the ocean, and **une rivière**, which does not. Most **fleuves** not ending with **-e** are masculine. Watch out for exceptions! Here are a few examples from around the world:

Feminine

l'Amazone	**la Krishnâ**	**la Seine**	**la Volga**
la Garonne	**la Loire**	**la Vistule**	

Masculine

le Colorado	**le Mékong**	**le Rhin**	**la Tamise**
le Congo	**le Mississippi**	**le Rhône**	**le Tibre**
le Danube	**le Missouri**	**le Rio Grande**	**le Yangzy Jiang**
le Gange	**le Niger**	**le Saint-Laurent**	**le Yukon**
l'Hudson	**le Nil**	**le Sénégal**	**le Zambèze**

Le Mississippi est le plus long fleuve des États-Unis.	*The Mississipi is the longest river in the United States.*
Le Gange est le fleuve sacré de l'Inde.	*The Ganges is the sacred river of India.*

More French nouns and their gender **51**

Les rivières are either masculine or feminine. Here are a few examples in France:

le Cher	le Doubs	le Gers	la Mayenne
la Creuse	la Drôme	le Loir	la Moselle
la Dordogne	le Gard	le Lot	

La Dordogne est une rivière serpentine de presque 500 kilomètres.
Le château de Chenonceau est construit sur un pont qui enjambe **le Cher**.

The Dordogne is a serpentine river almost 500 kilometers long.
*The Chenonceau castle is built on a bridge across **the river Cher**.*

EXERCICE 3·9

Indicate the gender of the river by adding the definite article le *or* la.

1. _____ Rio Grande
2. _____ Somme
3. _____ Mékong
4. _____ Volga
5. _____ Loire
6. _____ Mississippi
7. _____ Têt
8. _____ Drâ
9. _____ Niger
10. _____ Rance

11. _____ Potomac
12. _____ Tumen
13. _____ Loir
14. _____ Seine
15. _____ Pô
16. _____ Drôme
17. _____ Nil
18. _____ Rhône
19. _____ Dordogne
20. _____ Vienne

Seas and oceans

La mer (*sea*) is feminine and **l'océan** (*ocean*) is masculine; that is fairly easy. The common mistakes have to do with capitalization. Always check in the dictionary.

le golfe de Californie	*the Gulf of California*	**la mer Noire**	*the Black Sea*
le golfe du Mexique	*the Gulf of Mexico*	**la mer du Nord**	*the North Sea*
le golfe Persique	*the Persian Gulf*	**l'océan Atlantique**	*the Atlantic Ocean*
la mer des Caraïbes	*the Caribbean Sea*	**l'océan Indien**	*the Indian Ocean*
la mer de Chine	*the China Sea*	**l'océan Pacifique**	*the Pacific Ocean*

L'Île Maurice, territoire ultramarin de la France, se trouve dans **l'océan Indien**.
Éric Tabarly a fait la traversée de **l'océan Atlantique** bien des fois.

*Mauritius Island, ultramarine territory of France is in **the Indian Ocean**.*
*Éric Tabarly crossed **the Atlantic Ocean** many times.*

Days, months, seasons, cardinal points

The days of the week are masculine:

le lundi	*Monday*
le mardi	*Tuesday*
le mercredi	*Wednesday*
le jeudi	*Thursday*
le vendredi	*Friday*
le samedi	*Saturday*
le dimanche	*Sunday*

The months of the year are also masculine:

janvier	*January*
février	*February*
mars	*March*
avril	*April*
mai	*May*
juin	*June*
juillet	*July*
août	*August*
septembre	*September*
octobre	*October*
novembre	*November*
décembre	*December*
un avril ensoleillé	*a sunny April*
un septembre venté	*a windy September*

The seasons are masculine:

un hiver froid	*a cold winter*
un printemps tardif	*a late spring*
un été pourri	*a rotten summer*
un automne pluvieux	*a rainy fall*

Cardinal points are also masculine:

le nord	*north*
le sud	*south*
l'est	*east*
l'ouest	*west*

Religious celebrations and holidays

Noël is usually used in the masculine form and without an article:

Nous serons chez notre grand-mère à **Noël**.	*We'll be at our grandmother's for **Christmas**.*

However, you may find an article when the day is qualified:

Nous avons eu **un Noël** sous la neige.	*We had **a snowy Christmas**.*

Do not be surprised if you find articles in front of the noun in old tales and literature:

Voici **la Noël** qui arrive.	***Christmas** is coming.*

More French nouns and their gender **53**

Some other holiday-related terms to keep in mind:

- **Pâque** used in the singular means *Passover*.
- **La Pâque orthodoxe** means *Orthodox Easter*.
- **Pâques** in the plural means *Easter*.
- **L'Ascension** (*Ascension Day*), **la Pentecôte** (*Pentecost*), and **la Toussaint** (*All Saints' Day*) are all feminine.
- **Le Ramadan** and **l'Aïd al Kébir** are masculine.
- **Thanksgiving** is masculine.

Now, let's see how to send holiday greetings:

Je vous souhaite...	*I wish you . . .*
...un Joyeux Noël	. . . *Merry Christmas*
...un bon Ramadan	. . . *Happy and Blessed Ramadan*
...un joyeux Thanksgiving	. . . *Happy Thanksgiving*
...de joyeuses Pâques	. . . *Happy Easter*
...une bonne et heureuse année	. . . *Happy New Year*
...une bonne année du singe	. . . *Happy Year of the Monkey*

EXERCICE 3·10

Indicate the gender of the noun by adding the definite article le *or* la.

_____ automne prochain, j'irai à l'Île Maurice dans _____ océan Indien. L'Île Maurice est merveilleuse car c'est une île volcanique. Puis _____ été suivant, mon amie Anne et moi envisageons de faire une croisière en Norvège. Anne connaît _____ mer Noire et _____ golfe du Mexique. En raison du travail de ses parents, elle a beaucoup voyagé. Elle rêve de voir _____ océan Pacifique. Nous irons sans doute ensemble un de ces jours.

Plants, wine, and cheese

We are going to explore the world of flowers, trees, and bushes and see if we can figure out a rule.

Flowers, tree, shrubs

Let's start with flowers. They play an important role in French life and also in art, especially in painting.

Flowers

One could think that flowers are feminine since flowers are delicate and feminine. That would be not only politically incorrect but also totally wrong. The truth is that most flowers not ending in -**e** tend to be masculine.

Hint: Try memorizing the gender of some flowers and connecting them with a person you know: Jérôme/**le tournesol**, Marie/**l'aubépine**, and so on.

Here are flowers with a masculine gender:

l'arum	*arum lily*	**le glaïeul**	*gladiola*
l'aster	*aster*	**l'hortensia**	*hydrangea*
le bégonia	*begonia*	**l'iris**	*iris*
le bouton d'or	*buttercup*	**le jasmin**	*jasmine*
le cactus	*cactus*	**le myosotis**	*forget-me-not*
le camélia	*camellia*	**le narcisse**	*narcissus*
le chrysanthème	*chrysanthemum*	**le nénuphar**	*water lily*
le coquelicot	*poppy*	**le nymphéa**	*white water lily*
le cyclamen	*cyclamen*		(Monet)
le freesia	*freesia*	**l'œillet**	*carnation*
le géranium	*geranium*	**le tournesol**	*sunflower*

Here are flowers with a feminine gender. Note that they all end with -**e**:

l'anémone	*anemone*	**la pivoine**	*peony*
l'angélique	*angelica*	**la primevère**	*primrose*
la capucine	*nasturtium*	**la rose**	*rose*
la colchique	*autumn crocus*	**la rue**	*rue*
la jacinthe	*hyacinth*	**la rose d'Inde**	*African marigold*
la jonquille	*daffodil*	**la rose pompon**	*button rose*
la marguerite	*daisy*	**la rose trémière**	*hollyhock*
l'orchidée	*orchid*	**la tulipe**	*tulip*
la patience	*patience dock*	**la véronique**	*speedwell/veronica*
la pensée	*pansy*	**la violette**	*violet*

Elle effeuillait **la marguerite**.

She was playing "**he loves me, he loves me not.**"

Le tournesol était une des fleurs favorites de Van Gogh.

The sunflower was one of Van Gogh's favorite flowers.

Trees and shrubs

Most trees and shrubs tend to be masculine:

l'abricotier	*apricot tree*	**l'érable**	*maple*	**le palmier**	*palm tree*
l'acacia	*acacia*	**l'eucalyptus**	*eucalyptus*	**le pêcher**	*peach tree*
l'acajou	*mahogany*	**le figuier**	*fig tree*	**le peuplier**	*poplar tree*
l'aulne	*alder*	**le frangipanier**	*frangipani tree*	**le pin**	*pine*
le bananier	*banana tree*	**le genévrier**	*juniper*	**le platane**	*plane tree*
le bambou	*bamboo*	**le groseillier**	*currant bush*	**le poirier**	*pear tree*
le bouleau	*birch*	**le hêtre**	*beech tree*	**le pommier**	*apple tree*
le cèdre	*cedar*	**l'hévéa**	*hevea*	**le prunier**	*plum tree*
le cerisier	*cherry tree*	**le houx**	*holly*	**le rhododendron**	*rhododendron*
le charme	*hornbeam*	**le laurier**	*laurel*	**le rosier**	*rosebush*
le châtaignier	*chestnut tree*	**le lilas**	*lilac tree*	**le sapin**	*fir tree*
le chêne	*oak*	**le marronnier**	*chestnut tree*	**le saule**	*willow*
le chèvrefeuille	*honeysuckle*	**le mélèze**	*larch*	**le séquoia**	*sequoia*
le citronnier	*lemon tree*	**l'olivier**	*olive tree*	**le tilleul**	*lime tree*
le cocotier	*coconut palm*	**l'orme**	*elm tree*	**le tremble**	*aspen*
le cyprès	*cypress*				

More French nouns and their gender   **55**

Here are a few exceptions:

l'aubépine	*hawthorn*	**la ronce**	*bramble*
la bruyère	*heather*	**la vigne**	*vine*

En France, de nombreuses routes sont bordées de **marronniers**.

In France, many roads are lined with chestnut trees.

Le bambou est très utilisé dans le décor moderne.

Bamboo is used a lot in modern décor.

EXERCICE 3·11

Complete with the definite or indefinite article un, une, le, *or* la.

1. Dans le jardin de Victoire, il y a _____ lilas et _____ laurier rose.

2. _____ rose sur ton chapeau est fanée.

3. Nous étions à la campagne et il a cueilli _____ bouton d'or.

4. Quand il était jeune, Bernard est tombé sur _____ cactus.

5. _____ chrysanthème est l'emblème national du Japon.

6. La mariée tenait _____ orchidée de la main gauche.

7. _____ séquoia que j'ai pris en photo faisait huit mètres de diamètre.

8. L'automobiliste s'est écrasé contre _____ platane.

9. Sur chaque table du restaurant, il y avait _____ rose rouge dans un vase noir.

10. _____ chêne dans le jardin de mon grand-père a près de 150 ans.

EXERCICE 3·12

Add the definite article le *or* la.

1. _____ pivoine rose signifie la sincérité. Vous pouvez compter sur moi.

2. _____ tournesol signifie que vous êtes mon soleil; je ne vois que vous.

3. _____ pensée signifie que je ne veux pas que vous m'oubliiez.

4. _____ mimosa signifie que je doute de votre amour.

5. _____ jacinthe signifie que je suis conscient de votre beauté.

6. _____ bégonia signifie que mon amitié pour vous est sincère.

7. _____ véronique signifie fidélité, âme sœur.

8. _____ bouton d'or signifie que vous vous moquez de moi.

9. _____ narcisse signifie l'égoïsme.

10. _____ rue signifie que j'aime l'indépendance.

Les fleurs ont leur langage. Check online sites for the meanings of flowers, and you will find quite a few versions of their significance. But never offer a chrysanthemum, as it is related to death. You will see them in the cemeteries **à la Toussaint**.

Fruit and vegetables

The names of fruit, nuts, and vegetables not ending in **-e** are usually masculine:

l'abricot	*apricot*	**le coing**	*quince*	**le navet**	*turnip*
l'ail	*garlic*	**le cornichon**	*gherkin*	**l'oignon**	*onion*
l'ananas	*pineapple*	**le cresson**	*cress*	**le piment**	*chili, pepper*
l'artichaut	*artichoke*	**l'épinard**	*spinach*	**le poireau**	*leek*
l'avocat	*avocado*	**le fenouil**	*fennel*	**le petit pois**	*garden pea*
le brocoli	*broccoli*	**le haricot**	*bean*	**le pois chiche**	*chickpea*
le brugnon	*white nectarine*	**le kiwi**	*kiwi*	**le poivron**	*sweet pepper*
le cassis	*black currant*	**le litchi**	*litchi*	**le potiron**	*pumpkin*
le céleri	*celery*	**le maïs**	*corn*	**le pruneau**	*prune*
le champignon	*mushroom*	**le manioc**	*manioc*	**le quinoa**	*quinoa*
le chou	*cabbage*	**le marron**	*chestnut*	**le radis**	*radish*
le chou-fleur	*cauliflower*	**le melon**	*melon*	**le raisin**	*grapes*
le citron	*lemon*				

Here are a few exceptions:

le concombre	*cucumber*	**le gingembre**	*ginger*	**le pamplemousse**	*grapefruit*

Here are some feminine nouns of fruit, nuts, and vegetables:

l'airelle	*cranberry*	**la courge**	*squash*	**l'olive**	*olive*
l'amande	*almond*	**la courgette**	*zucchini*	**l'orange**	*orange*
l'asperge	*asparagus*	**la datte**	*date*	**la pastèque**	*watermelon*
l'arachide	*peanut*	**l'échalote**	*shallot*	**la patate douce**	*sweet potato*
l'aubergine	*eggplant*	**l'endive**	*chicory*	**la pêche**	*peach*
la betterave	*beet*	**la fraise**	*strawberry*	**la pistache**	*pistachio*
la cacahouète	*peanut*	**la framboise**	*raspberry*	**la poire**	*pear*
la carotte	*carrot*	**la frisée**	*curly endive*	**la pomme**	*apple*
la châtaigne	*chestnut*	**la laitue**	*lettuce*	**la pomme de terre**	*potato*
la cerise	*cherry*	**la mirabelle**	*mirabelle*	**la prune**	*plum*
la ciboulette	*chives*	**la myrtille**	*blueberry*	**la tomate**	*tomato*
la citrouille	*pumpkin*	**la noisette**	*hazelnut*	**la truffe**	*truffle*
la clémentine	*clementine*	**la noix**	*nut*		

La glace à **la pistache** de chez Berthillon est la meilleure.
*Berthillon's **pistachio** ice cream is the best.*
Le citron est bon pour la peau.
***Lemon** is good for your skin.*

More French nouns and their gender **57**

EXERCICE 3·13

Complete by adding the indefinite article un *or* une.

C'est le vingtième anniversaire de Chloé. Sa cousine Lucie a invité une vingtaine de personnes. Chloé est végétarienne alors Lucie a fait un énorme gâteau et l'a décoré de toutes sortes de fruits et légumes.

Lucie a mis au milieu _____ demi-kiwi, puis _____ abricot, _____ petite poire. Ensuite, en forme de bouquet, _____ mirabelle, _____ cassis, _____ cerise, _____ myrtille, _____ framboise, _____ cassis. À chaque coin, elle a placé _____ marron et _____ cacahouète. Pour finir, elle a mis _____ truffe au chocolat pour chaque invité tout autour du gâteau.

Wine and cheese

Names of wines and other alcoholic beverages tend to be masculine:

l'armagnac	le chablis	le madère	le rhum
le beaujolais	le champagne	le margaux	le saint-Émilion
le bordeaux	le chinon	le médoc	le sake
le bourbon	le cognac	le muscadet	le saumur
le brandy	le côtes de Duras	le pernod	le sauternes
le cabernet	le côtes de Provence	le pouilly-fuissé	le vouvray
le calvados	le gin	le rosé d'Anjou	le whisky
le bourgogne			

Here are a few feminine exceptions:

l'anisette	la bénédictine	la mirabelle
la bière	l'eau de vie	la vodka

On utilise **le rhum** pour faire du punch.   *Rum is used to make punch.*
Le calvados est fait avec des pommes.   *Calvados is made from apples.*

Names of cheeses also tend to be masculine:

le beaufort	le chabichou	le gorgonzola	le pont-l'évêque
le bleu d'Auvergne	le chaumes	le gouda	le port-salut
le bleu des Causses	le cheddar	le gruyère	le raclette
le boursin	le chèvre	le livarot	le reblochon
le brie	le comté	le maroilles	le rocamadour
le brillat-savarin	le crottin de Chavignol	le mascarpone	le roquefort
le brin d'amour		le munster	le sainte-maure
le camembert	l'emmental	le parmesan	le vacherin
le cantal	l'époisse		

La raclette goes back to the Middle Ages and was consumed by Swiss peasants who were in need of a hot meal after a long day of labor and by herders who would cook **la raclette** on a campfire. Today in France, families and especially children enjoy it in the winter. It also has become trendy in upscale restaurants that have all the proper utensils.

Raclette comes from **racler** (*to scrape*). It is served with small potatoes and Savoy wine or Pinot Gris. It is definitely not **cuisine minceur** . . .

Here are a few feminine names of cheeses:

la faisselle	**la fourme**	**la mozzarella**	**la tome**
la feta	**la mimolette**	**la ricotta**	

Le roquefort est le fromage idéal pour la salade d'endives.

Achète **un chèvre** et **un camembert** au marché!

Roquefort is the ideal cheese for endive salad.

*Buy **a goat cheese** and **a camembert** at the market!*

EXERCICE
3·14

Add the indefinite article un *or* une.

Des copains sont réunis pour une soirée vin et fromage.

—Alex, qu'est-ce que tu prends? _____ médoc et _____ beaufort?

—Non, aujourd'hui, je voudrais _____ rosé d'Anjou et _____ gorgonzola.

—Et toi, Yves?

—_____ vodka et _____ vacherin.

—_____ vodka? En quel honneur? Tu prends toujours _____ saumur!

—Oui mais demain, on part pour Moscou. Je veux m'habituer.

—D'accord, _____ vodka pour Yves et _____ chablis pour Raoul?

—Exact. _____ chablis et _____ crottin de Chavignol.

—Tout le monde est servi?

—Non, Julien, tu m'as oublié. _____ pernod et _____ chabichou.

—Désolé. Ça arrive tout de suite.

Slang

What about learning some slang? The themes of this chapter are rich in idiomatic expressions. Learning them will help you memorize the gender.

Ce film est **un navet** (turnip).
Ton oncle est **une grosse légume** chez Renault?
C'est **la fin des haricots**!
Il était rouge comme **une tomate**.

*This film is **a flop**.*
*Your uncle is **a big shot** at Renault?*

*That's **the last straw**!*
*He was as red as **a beet**.*

More French nouns and their gender   **59**

Arrête de raconter **des salades**!	Stop telling **tall tales**!
Ce journal, c'est **une feuille de chou**!	*This paper is **a rag**!*
Je n'ai plus **un radis**.	*I haven't got **a penny** to my name.*
Zoé a fait **le poireau** une demi-heure.	*Zoé was left **cooling her heels** for half an hour.*
N'oublie pas **ta banane**!	*Don't forget **your fanny pack**!*
Ça permettra **de mettre du beurre dans les épinards**.	*That'll help you **make ends meet**.*
Jean **a failli tomber dans les pommes**.	*Jean **almost fainted**.*
Il est **haut comme trois pommes**.	*He is **knee-high to a grasshopper**.*
Il a **un cœur d'artichaut**.	*He **falls in love with every girl he meets**.*
Les carottes sont cuites.	*We've had it!*
J'ai **la tête comme une citrouille**.	*I feel **like my head is going to explode**.*
Occupez-vous de vos oignons!	*Mind your own business!*
Elle a **une peau de pêche**.	*She has **a peachlike complexion**.*
Ils ont **la pêche**.	*They are **in top form**.*
Il est **bonne poire**.	*He is **a real sucker**.*
Lucien est souvent **entre deux vins**.	*He is often **tipsy**.*
Elle a **le vin gai**.	*She gets **merry when she drinks**.*
Il faudra mettre **de l'eau dans ton vin**.	*You'll have **to make concessions**.*
Ce n'est pas la peine d'en faire **tout un fromage**.	*No need to make **a big fuss** about it.*

After this, I am sure a few correct genders will stick in your mind.

Colors and fabric, the elements, cars, and brands and acronyms

One could dream that some nouns would be neutral for a change. But this is not the case, even for stones or fabric.

Colors and fabric

Let's start with the palette of colors.

Colors

The word **couleur** (*color*) is feminine, as it ends with **-eur**. The colors themselves, however, are masculine:

l'ambre	*amber*	**l'indigo**	*indigo*	**l'orange**	*orange*
l'aubergine	*aubergine*	**l'ivoire**	*ivory*	**le rose**	*pink*
le beige	*beige*	**le jaune**	*yellow*	**le rouge**	*red*
le blanc	*white*	**le kaki**	*khaki*	**le safran**	*saffron*
le bleu	*blue*	**le marron**	*brown*	**le saumon**	*salmon*
le cramoisi	*crimson*	**le noir**	*black*	**le vert**	*green*
le gris	*gray*	**l'ocre**	*ochre*	**le violet**	*violet/purple*

Le bleu de sa robe est parfaitement assorti au **le jaune doré** de sa ceinture.	***The blue** of her dress coordinates perfectly with the **golden yellow** of her belt.*

60 PRACTICE MAKES PERFECT Complete French All-in-One

Pierre, **le vert** et **le bleu**... ça ne va pas dans cette pièce!

*Pierre, **green** and **blue** . . . it does not work in this room!*

Fabric

Most names of fabric are masculine:

l'acrylique	acrylic	l'écossais	plaid	l'organdi	organdy
l'alpaga	alpaca	le feutre	felt	le polyamide	polyamide
l'angora	angora	le Gore-tex	Gore-Tex	le polyester	polyester
le bambou	bamboo	le jacquard	jacquard	le prince	Prince of
le batik	batik	le jersey	jersey	de Galles	Wales suit
le brocard	brocade	le jute	jute	le raphia	raffia
le cachemire	cashmere	le lamé	lamé	le satin	satin
le coton	cotton	le lin	linen	le stretch	stretch
le crêpe de Chine	crêpe de Chine	le lycra	Lycra	le taffetas	taffeta
le crêpe de soie	silk crêpe	le madras	madras	le tulle	tulle
le cuir	leather	le mohair	mohair	le tweed	tweed
le damas	damask	le molleton	cotton fleece	le velours	velvet
le denim	denim	le nylon	nylon	le voile	voile

Here are some exceptions:

la dentelle	lace	la laine polaire	wool fleece	la serge	serge
la flanelle	flannel	la moire	moiré	la soie	silk
la gabardine	gabardine	la mousseline	muslin/ chiffon	la suédine	suedette
la gaze	gauze	la paille	straw	la viscose	viscose
la laine	wool	la popeline	poplin		

Le pantalon de Katia est en **lin beige**.
Le chapeau de M. Fillon est en **paille orange**.

*Katia's pants are made of **beige linen**.*
*Mr. Fillon's hat is made of **orange straw**.*

Precious and semiprecious stones

Stones can either be masculine or feminine. These are some masculine stones:

le corail	coral	le jade	jade	le quartz	quartz
le diamant	diamond	le lapis-lazuli	lapis lazuli	le rubis	ruby
le granit	granite	le marbre	marble	le saphir	sapphire
le grenat	garnet	l'onyx	onyx		

These are some feminine stones:

l'agate	agate	la citrine	citrine	l'opale	opal
l'aigue-marine	aquamarine	l'émeraude	emerald	la topaze	topaz
l'améthyste	amethyst	la kunzite	kunzite	la tourmaline	tourmaline
l'ardoise	slate				

Félix a offert **un rubis** à Marianne.
Ce granit rose sera idéal pour notre table.

*Felix gave **a ruby** to Marianne.*
***This** pink **granite** will be ideal for our table.*

More French nouns and their gender **61**

Metals, minerals, chemical elements

Most names of metals, minerals, and chemical elements tend to be masculine:

l'acier	steel	le cuivre	copper	l'oxygène	oxygen
l'aluminium	aluminum	l'étain	pewter	le platine	platinum
l'anthracite	anthracite	le fer	iron	le plomb	lead
l'argent	silver	le fluor	fluorine	le potassium	potassium
l'azote	nitrogen	l'hélium	helium	le plutonium	plutonium
le bronze	bronze	l'hydrogène	hydrogen	le radium	radium
le carbone	carbon	l'iode	iodine	le sel	salt
le calcium	calcium	le lithium	lithium	le soufre	sulfur
le charbon	coal	le magnesium	magnesium	le sulfite	sulfite
le chlore	chlorine	le manganèse	manganese	le titane	titanium
le chrome	chrome	le nickel	nickel	le zinc	zinc
le cobalt	cobalt	l'or	gold		

Here are a few feminine exceptions:

la bauxite	bauxite
la chaux	lime
la roche	rock

As-tu vu le film *La Ruée vers l'or*? *Have you seen the film* The **Gold** Rush?
Il y a **du fer** dans les épinards. *Spinach contains **iron**.*

EXERCICE 3·15

Indicate the gender of the nouns by adding the definite article le *or* la.

1. _____ émeraude
2. _____ diamant
3. _____ tourmaline
4. _____ étain
5. _____ potassium
6. _____ fer
7. _____ lithium
8. _____ marbre
9. _____ chaux
10. _____ charbon
11. _____ citrine
12. _____ quartz
13. _____ topaze
14. _____ bronze
15. _____ corail

16. _____ plomb

17. _____ bauxite

18. _____ sel

19. _____ jade

20. _____ rubis

Cars

In most cases, cars are used in the feminine form:

J'adore **ma nouvelle Citroën Picasso**.   *I love **my new Citroën Picasso**.*

However, as this list shows, some minivans or SUVs use the masculine form. It depends on the model:

la 206 (Peugeot)	**la Land Rover**	**la Panda** (Fiat)
le 4x4	**la Lexus**	**la Porsche**
la BMW	**la Mini** (BMW)	**la Renault Clio**
la Coccinelle (Beetle/Volkswagen)	**la Mondéo** (Ford)	**la Renault Scénic**
la Ferrari	**le monospace** (minivan)	**la Smart**
la Golf	**le** (ou **la**) **Kangoo**	**la Volvo familiale**
la jeep	**le Pajero** (Mitsubishi)	

Mon monospace est en panne. Peux-tu me prêter **ton Pajero**?   *My minivan has broken down. Can you lend me **your Mitsubishi**?*

Sa Volvo est parfaite pour son travail. Mais moi, je préfère **ma Coccinelle**.   *His Volvo is perfect for his job. But I prefer **my Beetle**.*

An anecdote from Quebec: In the past, a car was called **un véhicule automobile** and was little by little abbreviated to **un automobile**. The change was made in the 1940s. However, this is often described as **usage flottant** and you may hear:

Il s'est offert **un gros Chevrolet**.   *He treated himself **to a big Chevrolet**.*

instead of:

Il s'est offert **une grosse Chevrolet**.   *He treated himself **to a big Chevrolet**.*

We can use some of the many slang terms to talk about cars:

In France

la bagnole	*car/wheels*	**le tacot**	*clunker*
la caisse	*car/wheels*	**un tas de ferraille**	*pile of junk*
la guimbarde	*jalopy*	**la tire**	*old rattletrap*

In Quebec

le char	*car/wheels*	**la minoune**	*clunker*

Il a pris **sa caisse** pour aller faire un tour avec sa meuf.   *He took **his wheels** to go for a ride with his girlfriend.*

On va pas descendre sur la Côte avec **ton tas de ferraille**!   *We're not going to the Riviera with **your pile of junk**!*

More French nouns and their gender   **63**

EXERCICE 3·16

Complete with the possessive adjective son *or* sa.

Le père de mon copain Luc adore _____ BMW alors que sa femme préfère _____ Mini. Luc voudrait bien avoir _____ Pajero à lui tout seul mais ses parents ne sont pas d'accord. S'il passe le bac, il pourra rendre ses copains jaloux avec _____ Smart ou _____ Coccinelle.

Brands and acronyms

Like anything else, brands and acronyms follow a rule.

Brands

Brand names take the gender of the products they represent. For example, **une poupée** (*doll*) is feminine, so *Barbie* will be **une Barbie.**

Brand name	Derivation	
le bikini	le maillot de bain	*bathing suit*
le Bic	le stylo à bille	*pen*
le Botox	le comestique	*Botox*
le Canson	le papier dessin	*drawing paper*
la cellophane	la pellicule transparente	*cellophane*
le coca	le soda	*soda*
la cocotte minute	la marmite	*pressure cooker*
le digicode	le système	*door-entry system*
l'escalator	l'escalier roulant	*escalator*
le frigidaire/frigo	le réfrigérateur	*refrigerator*
le jacuzzi	le bain bouillonnant	*Jacuzzi*
le Kärcher	le nettoyeur haute pression	*high-pressure water cleaner*
le kleenex	le mouchoir	*Kleenex*
le K-way	le coupe-vent	*windbreaker*
l'Opinel	le couteau pliable	*folding knife*
le perfecto	le blouson en cuir	*leather jacket*
le polaroïd	l'appareil photo à développement instantané	*Polaroid camera*
le Post-it	le pense-bête autocollant	*Post-It*
la poubelle	le cuve	*garbage can*
le scotch	le ruban adhésif	*Scotch tape*
le spam	le courrier électronique non sollicité	*spam*
le Stabilo	le surligneur	*highlighter*
le taser	le pistolet électrique	*Taser gun*
la Téfal	une poêle anti-adhésive	*Teflon pan*
le ou la thermos	le récipient/la bouteille isolant	*Thermos*

La poubelle was introduced in 1884 by Eugène-René Poubelle, préfet de la Seine. All owners of buildings had to provide **une poubelle** to their tenants, a measure of public hygiene.

Dorothée ne fait jamais de randonnée sans **son Opinel**.	*Dorothée never goes hiking without **her Opinel knife**.*
C'est à toi de descendre **la poubelle**.	*It's your turn to take out **the garbage**.*

The name of Casanova, the famous and talented Venetian adventurer, writer, and musician, is often used as a "brand."

Son frère Fabrice, c'est un véritable **Casanova**.	*He is a real seducer.*

Acronyms

Acronyms take the gender of the nouns they represent:

la BBC	la radio/la chaîne de télévision	*BBC*
la BD	la bande dessinée	*comic strip*
la CIA	l'agence	*CIA*
la CNN	la chaîne de télé	*CNN*
le FBI	le bureau	*FBI*
le FMI	Fonds monétaire international	*IMF*
le GPS	le service de positionnement par satellite	*GPS*
l'HLM	l'habitation à loyer modéré	*public housing*
le KGB	le comité	*KGB*
la NASA	l'administration	*NASA*
l'OGM	l'organisme génétiquement modifié	*GMO*
l'OMS	L'organisation mondiale de la Santé	*WHO*
l'ONG	l'organisation non gouvernementale	*NGO*
l'ONU	l'organisation	*UN*
l'OTAN	l'organisation	*NATO*
l'OVNI	l'objet volant non-identifié	*UFO*
le PACS	le pacte civil de solidarité	*civil union between two people*
le/la PDG	le président directeur/trice général(e)	*CEO*
le RER	le réseau express régional	*suburban train that goes around Paris*
le TGV	le train à grande vitesse	*express train*
l'UE	l'Union européenne	*EU*
l'UNESCO	l'organisation	*UNESCO*

There are also acronyms without articles, as they refer to famous people:

BB	Brigitte Bardot
VGE	Valéry Giscard d'Estaing
DSK	Dominique Strauss-Kahn
PPDA	Patrick Poivre d'Arvor

Ils ont créé **une ONG** au Brésil.	*They set up **an NGO** in Brazil.*
Tout le monde attend la decision **du FMI** sur la fraude fiscale.	*Everyone is waiting for **the IMF**'s decision about tax evasion.*

More French nouns and their gender **65**

Other languages, parts of speech, and the sciences

In this chapter, we'll cover the gender of different languages, parts of speech, and also sciences. Do they have some mystery in store for us?

Names of languages

Nouns denoting particular languages are masculine. Note that, in French, the names of languages are in lowercase:

l'allemand	*German*	**le grec**	*Greek*	**le portugais**	*Portuguese*
l'anglais	*English*	**l'hindi**	*Hindi*	**le russe**	*Russian*
l'arabe	*Arabic*	**l'italien**	*Italian*	**le serbe**	*Serbian*
le bembé	*Bembe*	**le japonais**	*Japanese*	**le swahili**	*Swahili*
le chinois	*Chinese*	**le mandarin**	*Mandarin*	**le tamoul**	*Tamil*
l'espagnol	*Spanish*	**le polonais**	*Polish*	**le turc**	*Turkish*
le français	*French*				

Mai Hien a appris **le français** à Aix-en-Provence.
*Mai Hien learned **French** in Aix-en-Provence.*
Hervé a appris **le swahili** au Kenya.
*Hervé learned **Swahili** in Kenya.*

Nouns of foreign origin

Over the centuries, because of history, wars, colonialism, and the exploration of continents, the French language has absorbed words from all over the world. You will often hear that French is being contaminated by English. This is a backward approach to languages. During the Renaissance, for example, it was trendy and very chic to use Italian words in the French language. And it is a good thing, considering that French, even after borrowing words from many languages, has a much smaller vocabulary than does English, perhaps a half or a third of the English lexicon.

A large number of the nouns of foreign origin tend to be masculine. Let's look at a few examples, starting with words borrowed from English.

Nouns of English origin

Many nouns of English influence are masculine:

le baby-sitting	le camping	le flirt	le knock-out	le poker	le slogan
le badge	le cash	le footing	le know-how	le pressing	le smoking
le barman	le challenge	le freelance	le laser	le pull-over	le snack
le bermuda	le charter	le freezer	le leader	le puzzle	le snob
le best-seller	le chewing-	le gospel	le lifting	le rap	le sponsor
le blazer	gum	le hamburger	le listing	le reporter	le talkie-
le blues	le coach	le holding	le living-room	le ring	walkie (*in*
le boss	(*trainer*)	le hold-up	le lobby	(*boxing*)	*reverse*)
le boycott	le cocktail	le jackpot	(*political*)	le rock	le tank
le brainstorming	le crash	le jazz	le manager	le self-service	le thriller
le briefing	le dealer	le jean	le marketing	le shopping	le timing
le building	le fair-play	le job	l'outsider	le show	le training
le bulldozer	le fast-food	le jogging	le parking	le skateboard	le week-end
le business	le feeling	le kidnapping	le planning	le skipper	

66 PRACTICE MAKES PERFECT Complete French All-in-One

Here are a few feminine exceptions:

la barmaid	**l'overdose**	**la start-up**
la basket	**la rocking-chair**	**la superstar**
l'interview	**la snob**	

Trop de **snobs** fréquentent **ce bar**.	*Too many **snobs** go to **this bar**.*
Le boss a dit que **le briefing** aurait lieu **au snack-bar**.	*The boss said that the briefing would take place in the snackbar.*

It would be a mistake to think that the additions of English words to the French language are a sudden occurrence. When you hear the French complaining about the invasion of the English language, do not take it too seriously. As a French person, I'm giving myself permission to say it may be more a matter of "American envy."

Foreign words have enriched the French language for centuries. The word **camping**, for instance, has been in the French dictionary since 1903 when the concept of recreational activities started to flourish before World War I.

Also be aware of the origins of English words. For example, **flirter** was borrowed from the English but actually comes from the old French **fleureter**.

The origin of the word **gadget** is uncertain. Some sources say that in the 1850s it was similar to **gâchette**, a small tool. Other sources maintain that **gadget** comes from Gaget-Gauthier, the French company that designed miniatures of the Statue of Liberty to finance Frédéric Bartholdi's project. The name *Gaget* was written on the base of the miniatures, and the Americans started calling the statue *gadget*. Then the word crossed the Atlantic again and found its place in Le Robert's dictionary in 1946 under **gadget** with the English pronunciation. And then the French created a wonderful verb: **gadgétiser**.

Some new nouns, especially those connected to technology, are added on a regular basis.

le Bluetooth	**le geek**	**l'iPhone**	**le podcast**	**le texto**	**le Twitter**
le buzz	**l'internet**	**le mail**	**le podcasting**	**le tweet**	**le website**
le chat	**l'iPad**	**le multi-touch**	**le SMS**		

French has borrowed from many other languages you may identify, as they are similar or close to English. If you are not sure of the meaning of a word, check your dictionary at home or any bilingual dictionary online.

Nouns of Arabic origin

The influence of the Arabic language on the French language has been significant in many fields (mathematics, alchemy, botany, astronomy, medicine, philosophy, and mysticism). The Arab army came all the way to Poitiers in the eighth century and left quite a few words behind. Arabo-Andalusian music played an important role from the ninth to the fifteenth century, spreading gradually to Provence and becoming a source of inspiration for the French troubadours. Inevitably, words traveled back and forth from Spain to France, and many words were adopted by the French. For example, who does not like to rest on a **sofa**? Until the eighteenth century, Arab architects worked their way to England and left their mark, the arabesque. In addition, about two-thirds of the names of stars come from the Arabic language, such as **Al Bali**, **Aldébaran**, **Algol**, **Almanac**, **Altaïr**, **Mizar**, **Regulus**, **Rigel**, **Sadalmelek**, **Yad**, **Zaniah**, and so on.

At least five hundred Arabic words are used in the French language on a regular basis. Another factor in play is that the second, third, and fourth generations of immigrants from Tunisia, Algeria, Morocco, Egypt, Lebanon, and so on living in France have been so creative with the language through literature and music that the count keeps going up, and the French language enriches itself.

Here are a few examples, both masculine and feminine, of words of Arabic origin:

l'alambic	l'azimut	le couscous	le harem	le magasin	le taboulé
l'alcool	le baobab	le cramoisi	le hasard	la maroquinerie	le tambour
l'algèbre	le bled	l'élixir	le henné	le matelas	le tajine
l'almanach	le camaïeu	la gazelle	la jupe	le moucharabieh	le talc
l'amalgame	le camphre	le goudron	kif-kif	le sofa	le toubib
l'ambre	le carmin	le hammam	le luth	le sumac	le zénith
l'amiral					

Nouns from other languages

The French language, over the centuries, has borrowed words from numerous other languages as well.

Nouns of Chinese origin

le feng shui	le kung-fu	le tai-chi	le yang	le wok
le ginseng	le litchi	le Tao	le yin	

Nouns of German origin

le bretzel	l'ersatz	le kitsch	le putsch
le diktat	le hamster	le leitmotiv	

Nouns of Indian origin

l'atoll	le bouddha	le karma	le yoga
l'avatar	le gourou	le nirvana	

Nouns of Italian origin

le carnaval	le farniente	le graffiti	l'opéra	la pizzeria
le chianti	le ghetto	la loggia	le piano	la polenta
le crescendo	le gnocchi	la mezzanine	la pizza	

Nouns of Japanese origin

le bonsaï	l'ikébana	le karaoké	l'origami	le sushi
la geisha	le judo	le karaté	le saké	le tofu
le haïku	le kabuki	le kimono	le samouraï	le zen
le hara-kiri	le kamikaze	le manga	le sashimi	

Nouns of Russian origin

le blini	la datcha	le morse	la toundra
le bortsch	la douma	la steppe	la vodka
le cosaque	le mammouth	la taïga	

L'amiral a commandé **une pizza** et une bouteille de **saké**.

*The admiral ordered **a pizza** with a bottle of **sake**.*

En arrivant à Marrakech, elle a mangé **un couscous** avec du thé à la menthe puis elle s'est fait teindre les cheveux au **henné**.

*Upon arriving in Marrakech, she ate **couscous** with mint tea and she **hennaed** her hair.*

68 PRACTICE MAKES PERFECT Complete French All-in-One

EXERCICE 3·17

Complete with the definite article.

1. Antoine apprend _____ japonais car il veut aussi apprendre _____ karaté.
2. _____ marketing pour _____ vodka Van Gogh a bien réussi.
3. _____ tweet a été envoyé par _____ gourou de l'ashram d'Aurobindo.
4. _____ pizza et _____ polenta qu'elle a préparées étaient délicieuses.
5. Je cherche un interprète qui parle très bien _____ chinois et _____ russe.
6. _____ Carnaval de Venise a lieu en février.
7. Dans _____ datcha, cela sentait _____ bortsch et _____ vodka.
8. Akiko, aimez-vous _____ saké? Et _____ karaoké?
9. _____ nouveau manga de Yoshihiro Togashi connaît un grand succès.
10. Ils ont chevauché dans _____ steppe de Mongolie.

Compound nouns

After memorizing the genders of single nouns, could there be a trick to figure out the gender of compound ones?

Compound nouns composed of a verb derivative and a noun

Compound nouns composed of a verb derivative and a noun tend to be masculine:

l'abat-jour	*lamp shade*	**le faire-part**	*announcement*
l'aide-mémoire	*memorandum*	**le garde-fou**	*railing, parapet, safeguard*
l'allume-gaz	*gas lighter*		
l'amuse-gueule	*appetizer*	**le gratte-ciel**	*skyscraper*
le brise-glace	*icebreaker*	**le lave-vaisselle**	*dishwasher*
le cache-cache	*hide and seek*	**l'ouvre-boîte**	*can opener*
le casse-noisette	*nutcracker*	**le porte-clés**	*keychain*
le chasse-neige	*snowplow*	**le porte-monnaie**	*wallet*
le coupe-vent	*windbreaker*	**le porte-savon**	*soapdish*
le croque-monsieur	*toasted ham and cheese sandwich*	**le presse-papier**	*paper weight*
		le serre-livres	*bookends*
l'essuie-glace	*windshield wiper*	**le trompe-l'œil**	*trompe-l'œil*

One feminine exception is **la garde-robe** (*wardrobe*).

Elle vient d'acheter un **abat-jour** turquoise qui est parfait pour le vestibule.
*She just bought a turquoise **lamp shade** that is perfect for the foyer.*

Les **amuse-gueule** qu'ils ont servis étaient exquis.
***The appetizers** they served were exquisite.*

More French nouns and their gender **69**

Compound nouns composed of an adverb and a noun

Compound nouns composed of an adverb and a noun tend to take the gender of the noun. For example, **rasage** ends in **-age** so it is masculine. **L'après-rasage** is also masculine.

l'après-soleil	*after-sun lotion*	**l'avant-veille**	*two days before*
l'arrière-boutique	*back shop*	**la mini-jupe**	*mini-skirt*
l'avant-goût	*foretaste*	**le sous-bois**	*undergrowth, trees*
l'arrière-goût	*aftertaste*	**le sous-continent**	*subcontinent*
l'arrière-pensée	*ulterior motive*	**le sous emploi**	*underemployment*
l'arrière-plan	*background*	**la sous-estimation**	*underestimation*
l'avant-bras	*forearm*	**le sous-marin**	*submarine*
l'avant-première	*preview*	**la sous-traitance**	*subcontracting*

Here are a couple of exceptions: **l'avant-guerre** (*prewar years*) can be both masculine or feminine; **l'après-guerre** (*postwar years*) is only masculine.

Compound nouns composed of a noun plus a noun

Compound nouns composed of a noun and a noun tend to take the gender of the first noun:

l'appui-tête	*headrest*	**l'oiseau-mouche**	*hummingbird*
l'arc-en-ciel	*rainbow*	**la porte-fenêtre**	*French window*
le bébé-éprouvette	*test tube baby*	**le portrait-robot**	*identikit picture*
le drap-housse	*fitted sheet*	**le soutien-gorge**	*bra*
la langue-de-chat	*finger biscuit*	**le timbre-poste**	*postage stamp*
la main-d'œuvre	*workforce/labor*	**la voiture-restaurant**	*dining car*
la moissonneuse-batteuse	*combine harvester*		

Je n'ai pas trouvé de **drap-housse** assorti à ma couette.	*I have not found **the fitted sheet** that matches my duvet cover.*
Hier, nous avons vu **un** bel **arc-en-ciel** au-dessus de la mer.	*Yesterday we saw **a** beautiful **rainbow** over the sea.*

Nouns derived from verbs and adverbs

Nouns derived from verbs and adverbs tend to be masculine:

l'arrière	*back/rear*	**le derrière**	*bottom/behind*	**le manger**	*food*
l'avant	*front*	**le dessous**	*underside/back*	**le pourquoi**	*the why*
le boire	*drink*	**le dessus**	*top/right side*	**le rire**	*laugh*
le comment	*the how*	**le devant**	*front*	**le tout**	*the whole*

Tu vas t'asseoir à **l'avant** de la voiture.	*You'll sit in **the front** of the car.*
Je ne comprends pas **le pourquoi** de cette décision.	*I don't understand **why** this decision is being made.*

Abbreviated nouns

Abbreviated nouns keep the gender of the complete noun:

l'apéro/l'apéritif	*before lunch or dinner drink*	**la photo/la photographie**	*photography*
		le pseudo/le pseudonyme	*pseudonym*
le ciné/le cinéma	*cinema/movie theater*	**la radio/la radiodiffusion**	*radio*
la fac/la faculté	*school in a university, college, ability*	**le stylo/le stylographe**	*pen*
		le taxi/le taximètre	*taxi*
le métro/le métropolitain	*subway*	**la télé/la télévision**	*television*
la moto/la motocyclette	*motorbike*	**le vélo/le vélocipède**	*bicycle*
le petit dej/le petit déjeuner	*breakfast*		

Mon pseudo sur ton blog, c'est Cléopâtre.   *My pseudonym on your blog is Cleopatra.*
Et si on allait faire un tour en **vélo**?   *And what about taking a bike ride?*

Nouns of the sciences and academic disciplines

Names of sciences and disciplines are almost all feminine:

l'agronomie	*agronomy*	**l'électronique**	*electronics*	**la musicologie**	*musicology*
l'anatomie	*anatomy*	**la génétique**	*genetics*	**la nanoscience**	*nanoscience*
l'anthropologie	*anthropology*	**la géographie**	*geography*	**l'océanographie**	*oceanography*
l'archéologie	*archeology*	**la géologie**	*geology*	**la pédagogie**	*pedagogy*
l'astronomie	*astronomy*	**la géométrie**	*geometry*	**la philosophie**	*philosophy*
la biologie	*biology*	**l'histoire**	*history*	**la phonétique**	*phonetics*
la botanique	*botany*	**l'informatique**	*computer science*	**la physique**	*physics*
la chimie	*chemistry*	**la linguistique**	*linguistics*	**la psychologie**	*psychology*
la cosmologie	*cosmology*	**la logique**	*logics*	**la sociologie**	*sociology*
la criminologie	*criminology*	**les mathématiques**	*mathematics*	**la spéléologie**	*speleology*
l'écologie	*ecology*	**la mécanique**	*mechanics*	**les statistiques**	*statistics*
l'économie	*economics*	**la météorologie**	*meteorology*	**la théologie**	*theology*
l'éducation	*education*				

Here are a couple of masculine exceptions:

l'art	*art*
le droit	*law*

Ma meilleure amie étudie **l'anthropologie judiciaire** à Paris.   *My best friend studies **forensic anthropology** in Paris.*
Laura est professeur de **linguistique** à l'Université d'Angers.   *Laura is a **linguistics** professor at the University of Angers.*

EXERCICE 3·18

Complete with the definite article.

1. _____ nouvel abat-jour que tu as acheté est trop grand.
2. _____ devant de la maison a besoin de réparations.
3. Je ne peux pas trouver _____ casse-noisette. Où l'as-tu mis?
4. Thierry lui a offert _____ presse-papier en cristal dont elle rêvait.
5. Clara se demandait _____ pourquoi de toute chose.
6. Ils envisagent de construire _____ plus haut gratte-ciel du monde.
7. Quentin étudie _____ philosophie et _____ droit à la Sorbonne.
8. À quelle heure ouvre _____ voiture-restaurant?
9. _____ sous-marin *Le Redoutable* a fait une escale à Hawaï.
10. _____ lave-vaisselle est en panne. Allons au restaurant!

Épicène nouns: Nouns with two genders

Some nouns have their own idiosyncrasies: their gender varies for multiple reasons, and some are androgynous. This is just another twist to the never-ending story.

Some nouns can be either masculine or feminine. They are call **noms épicènes**. You encountered some earlier where, for example, **une tortue** can be either male or female.

The words that can be used with either gender are:

après-midi	*afternoon*	**oasis**	*oasis*
avant-guerre	*prewar years*	**palabres***	*never-ending discussions*
enzyme	*enzyme*	**parka**	*parka*
laque	*lacquer*	**perce-neige**	*snowdrop*
météorite	*meteorite*	**réglisse**	*licorice*

*Used in the plural.

Arnaud a photographié **une merveilleuse oasis** couverte de palmiers dattiers.	*Arnaud photographed **a wonderful oasis** covered with date palms.*
Une météorite de 150 kg est tombée dans un champ de blé à Ensisheim, Alsace en 1492.	*A 150-kilo **meteorite** fell in a wheatfield in Ensisheim, Alsace, in 1492.*

Nouns that are masculine in the singular and feminine in the plural

The gender of some nouns changes if an adjective follows or precedes them. We'll look at **amour**, **délice**, and **gens**. **Amour** is masculine in the common, singular usage:

L'amour fou est éternel.	***Being madly in love** is eternal.*
« Mais combien fait mal **un amour** qui meurt! » (Pierre Loti)	*"How **a dying love** is painful!"*

If the adjective precedes the noun when it is plural, the noun and the adjective are used in the feminine plural:

Dans son roman, il raconte **ses folles amours** avec la marquise.	*In his novel, he writes about **his mad love** for the marquise.*
Elle n'oubliera jamais **ses premières amours**.	*She'll never forget **her first romantic experiences**.*
« J'aspirais secrètement à de **belles amours**. » (Honoré de Balzac)	*"I was secretly longing for **beautiful love**."*

In the case of **délice**, it is more a matter of degree. In the masculine singular, **délice** means *joy, fun*:

Quel délice de manger ces mangues bien mûres!	***What a delight** to eat these very ripe mangoes!*

In the feminine plural, there is a sense of pleasure, intense transport of the mind and body:

Ils profitaient **des délices** de l'amour à Venise.	*They enjoyed **the pleasures** of love in Venice.*
Nous goûtions **les délices** de la vie.	*We enjoyed **the delights** of life.*

The noun **gens** is usually masculine plural. However, if an adjective precedes the noun, both the noun and the adjective become feminine and the meaning changes:

J'ai rencontré **des gens** très **distrayants**.	*I met very **entertaining people**.*
Ces vieilles gens vivent de très peu!	***These old people** live on very little!*
Quelles honnêtes gens!	***How honest these people are!***
Ce sont des **petites gens** sans ressources.	*They are **poor people** without resources.*
Leurs voisins, ce sont **des braves gens**.	*Their neighbors are **good folks**.*

However, **jeunes gens**, considered as a block, remains masculine:

De nombreux **jeunes gens** faisaient la queue devant le cinéma.	*Many **young people** were standing in line in front of the cinema.*

Homographic homonyms

A number of nouns are differentiated only by their gender. The spelling and the pronunciation are identical, but the meaning is different. It is very important to be aware of these *homographic homonyms*. Let's take an example from the hair salon:

Je voudrais **une mousse** de qualité pour ma croisière dans les îles des Caraïbes.	*I would like **a quality styling mousse** for my cruise in the Caribbean Islands.*

Versus:

Je voudrais **un mousse** de qualité pour ma croisière dans les îles des Caraïbes.	*I would like **a quality cabin boy** for my cruise in the Caribbean Islands.*

Memorize the gender of such words little by little, using them in full sentences and engraving them in your mind to keep out of trouble. Compare these masculine and feminine nouns:

Masculine		Feminine	
l'aide	*aide, assistant*	l'aide	*assistance, help*
l'aigle	*eagle*	l'aigle	*military insignia*
l'aria	*worry, problem*	l'aria	*aria*
l'aune	*alder*	l'aune	*measure/in term*
le barbe	*horse*	la barbe	*beard*
le boum	*boom*	la boum	*party*
le cache	*mask, cover*	la cache	*cache, hiding place*
le carpe	*carpus*	la carpe	*carp*
le champagne	*champagne*	la Champagne	*Champagne region*
le coche	*stage coach*	la coche	*notch, gash, groove*
le crêpe	*crêpe, fabric*	la crêpe	*pancake, crêpe*
le critique	*critic*	la critique	*review, criticism*
le garde	*guard, warden*	la garde	*guard, custody*
le gène	*gene*	la gêne	*embarrassment*
le gîte	*shelter, cottage*	la gîte	*bed of sunken ship*
le greffe	*clerk's office*	la greffe	*transplant, graft*
le laque	*lacquer*	la laque	*hairspray, shellac*
le légume	*vegetable*	la grosse légume	*big shot, bigwig*
le livre	*book*	la livre	*pound/pound sterling*
le manche	*handle*	la manche	*sleeve*
		la Manche	*the English Channel*
le/la manœuvre	*unskilled worker*	la manœuvre	*maneuver, operation*
le mémoire	*master's thesis*	la mémoire	*memory*
le mode	*mode, way*	la mode	*fashion*
le moule	*mold, pan*	la moule	*mussel*

More French nouns and their gender **73**

le mousse	cabin boy	la mousse	moss, foam, mousse
l'œuvre	shell of a building	l'œuvre	work, works
l'ombre	grayling	l'ombre	shade, shadow
le page	page (boy)	la page	page, episode
le parallèle	parallel	la parallèle	parallel line
le pendule	pendulum	la pendule	clock
le physique	physical appearance	la physique	physics
le platine	platinum	la platine	deck, turntable
le poêle	heating stove	la poêle	frying pan
le/la politique	politician	la politique	politics
le poste	job, extension	la poste	post office
le soi	self, oneself	la soie	silk
le solde	balance of an account, sale	la solde	soldier's pay
le somme	nap, snooze	la somme	sum, amount
le transat	deckchair	la transat	transatlantic race
le trompette	trumpet player	la trompette	trumpet
le vague	vagueness	la vague	wave
le vase	vase	la vase	slime, mud
le vapeur	steamship	la vapeur	steam, vapor
le voile	veil	la voile	sail, sailing

On lui a fait **une greffe** de la cornée. *He received **a corneal transplant**.*
Amina est contente de **son nouveau poste** chez Fauchon. *Amina is happy with **her new position** at Fauchon's.*

EXERCICE 3·19

Complete with the definite article le, la, *or* l'.

1. _____ livre qu'Éric a écrit est sur _____ mode en Italie.
2. Il a marché dans _____ vase et ses chaussures sont sales.
3. _____ seul légume que mon fils accepte de manger, c'est _____ brocoli chinois.
4. Elles m'ont suggéré _____ gîte dans le Lot où elles ont séjourné l'an passé.
5. _____ crêpe a collé à _____ poêle. Elle est immangeable!
6. Tu savais que Jean s'était laissé pousser _____ barbe?
7. Voudrais-tu faire de _____ voile au large de l'Île de Ré?
8. On doit lire le roman jusqu'à _____ page 150?
9. Xavier a oublié _____ mémoire qu'il doit remettre à son professeur.
10. _____ mousse pour le bain est parfumée à la lavande.

Homophonous homonyms

Homophonous homonyms are nouns that are pronounced in the same manner but have a different spelling and meaning. Some share the same gender. Others are either masculine or feminine. Let's start with the masculine.

Masculine homophonous homonyms

l'abîme	*abyss, gulf*	abyme (mise en abyme)	*story within a story*		
l'autel	*altar*	l'hôtel	*hotel*		
le baccara	*baccarat, casino*	le baccarat	*Baccarat crystal*		
le ban	*applause, banns*	le banc	*bench*		
le brocard	*brocket (deer), gibe*	le brocart	*brocade*		
le cahot	*jolt, bump*	le chaos	*chaos*		
le cep	*vine stock*	le cèpe	*porcini mushroom*		
le champ	*field, domain*	le chant	*song*		
le cœur	*heart*	le chœur	*choir, chorus*		
le compte	*count, account*	le comte	*count (nobility)*	le conte	*tale, story*
le cor	*horn*	le corps	*body, corpse*		
le crack	*ace, wizard*	le krach	*financial crash*		
le dessein	*goal, intention*	le dessin	*drawing, pattern*		
le différent	*the different person*	le différend	*disagreement*		
le filtre	*filter*	le philtre	*love potion*		
le flan	*custard flan*	le flanc	*flank, side, slope*		
le fond	*back, bottom*	le fonds	*fund, funds, capital*	le fonts	*baptismal font*
le galon	*piece of braid, stripe*	le gallon	*gallon*		
le golf	*golf*	le golfe	*gulf*		
le lac	*lake*	le laque	*lacquer*		
le Marocain	*Moroccan man*	le maroquin	*Morocco leather*		
le martyr	*martyr*	le martyre	*martyrdom, agony*		
le péché	*sin*	le pêcher	*peach tree*		
le plan	*plan, map*	le plant	*seedling, patch*		
le point	*period, dot, point*	le poing	*fist*		
le rancart	*scrap, heap*	le rancard	*rendezvous*		
le saint	*saint*	le sein	*breast, womb*	le seing	*signature (legal)*
le saut	*jump, leap*	le sceau	*seal/stamp*		
le seau	*bucket*	le sot	*fool*		
le ver	*worm*	le verre	*glass*		
le vers	*verse*	le vert	*green*		

Ce **dessin** de Matisse a été vendu aux enchères.	*This Matisse **drawing** was sold at auction.*
Leur maison est construite **à flanc** de colline.	*Their house is built **on** the hill**side**.*

More French nouns and their gender **75**

Feminine homophonous homonyms

Other homophonous homonyms are feminine:

l'amande	almond	**l'amende**	fine		
la balade	walk, drive, ride, trip	**la ballade**	ballad		
la cane	female duck	**la canne**	cane/stick		
la cession	transfer/abandon	**la session**	session		
la chair	flesh	**la chaire**	university chair	**la chère**	food
l'encre	ink	**l'ancre**	anchor		
la pause	pause, break	**la pose**	pose, posing		
la pensée	thought	**la pensée**	pansy		
la tache	spot, stain	**la tâche**	task		
la taule	jail	**la tôle**	sheet metal		
la voie	way/lane	**la voix**	voice		

Le capitaine a jeté **l'ancre** dans le port de Dakar. — The captain cast **the anchor** in the Dakar port.

Jean a dû payer **une amende** de 300 euros. — Jean had to pay a 300-euro **fine**.

Masculine and feminine homophonous homonyms

In the case of masculine and feminine homophonous homonyms, the gender and the spelling are different but the pronunciation is the same.

l'air	air/tune	**l'aire**	area/surface	**l'ère**	era
le bal	ball	**la balle**	ball, bullet		
le bamboula	tam-tam	**la bamboula**	African dance		
le bar	bar	**la barre**	rod, bar		
le bout	end, tip	**la boue**	mud		
le cerf	stag	**la serre**	greenhouse		
le chèvre	goat cheese	**la chèvre**	goat		
le col	collar, pass	**la colle**	glue		
le cours	course, rate	**la cour**	yard, the royal court, courting		
le court	tennis court	**la Cour suprême**	Supreme Court		
le chêne	oak tree	**la chaîne**	chain, channel		
le faîte	crest, ridge	**la fête**	holiday, party		
le faux	forgery, falsehood	**la faux**	scythe		
le foie	liver	**la foi**	faith	**la fois**	time, occurrence
le gaz	gas	**la gaze**	gauze		
le gril	broiler	**la grille**	gate, grid, scale		
le lit	bed	**la lie**	sediment, dregs		
le luth	lute	**la lutte**	struggle, wrestling		
le mal	evil	**la malle**	trunk		
le/la maire	mayor	**la mer**	sea	**la mère**	mother
le mythe	myth	**la mite**	moth		
le mort	dead man	**la mort**	death		
le mur	wall	**la mûre**	blackberry		
le pair	peer	**la paire**	pair		
le parti	party	**la partie**	part, game		
le poche	paperback	**la poche**	pocket, bag		
le pois	pea	**le poids**	weight		
le pot	pot/jar	**la peau**	skin		
le pouce	thumb	**la pousse**	sprout, shoot		
le racket	racketeering	**la raquette**	racket		

76 PRACTICE MAKES PERFECT Complete French All-in-One

le rai	*ray*	**la raie**	*line/hair part*			
le renne	*reindeer*	**la rêne**	*rein*	**la reine**	*queen*	
le repère	*landmark*	**le repaire**	*den, hideout*			
le roux	*roux, russet, redhead*	**la roue**	*wheel*			
le satyre	*satyr, maniac*	**la satire**	*satire*			
le sel	*salt*	**la selle**	*saddle*			
le sol	*ground, floor*	**la sole**	*sole*			
le tic	*tic, habit*	**la tique**	*tick*			
le tome	*tome, volume*	**la tome**	*Savoy cheese*			
le tout	*whole*	**la toux**	*cough*			
le tribut	*tribute*	**la tribu**	*tribe*			
le vice	*vice/defect*	**la vis**	*screw*			

Quels cours suis-tu cette session?   ***What courses** are you taking this session?*
Le château nous a servi de point de **repère**.   *We used the castle as **a landmark**.*

EXERCICE

3·20

Complete with the definite article le, la, *or* l'.

1. Je n'ai pas pu enlever _____ tache de vin sur ta chemise.

2. Le maître-nageur a mis _____ drapeau rouge car _____ mer est très agitée.

3. _____ diva a perdu _____ voix au beau milieu de _____ aria.

4. Vous aurez _____ peau lisse si vous utilisez cette crème hydratante.

5. La police a trouvé _____ repaire des trafiquants de drogue.

6. Attention! _____ sole jaune est tombée sur _____ sol.

7. Je ne connais pas _____ tribu dont elle a parlé lors de sa conférence.

8. Lucie a vu _____ plus vieux chêne de sa vie dans _____ forêt de Tronçais.

9. Prépare un bon repas. Bertrand aime _____ bonne chère.

10. _____ verre dans lequel tu bois est en cristal de Baccarat.

More French nouns and their gender   **77**

·4· Numbers

The numbers 0 to 50

Let's start with numbers from 0 to 50. Although consonants are generally silent in French, they are pronounced in the following numbers: **cinq**, **si<u>x</u>**, **sep<u>t</u>**, **hui<u>t</u>**, **neu<u>f</u>**, **di<u>x</u>**. With **sept**, the -**p**- is silent, but the final -**t** is pronounced. The final -**x** in **si<u>x</u>** and **di<u>x</u>** is pronounced like an **s**.

When the numbers **cinq**, **six**, **huit**, and **dix** are followed by a word beginning with a consonant, their final consonant is mute (silent).

zéro	*zero*	**vingt**	*twenty*
un	*one*	**vingt et un**	*twenty-one*
deux	*two*	**vingt-deux**	*twenty-two*
trois	*three*	**vingt-trois**	*twenty-three*
quatre	*four*	**vingt-quatre**	*twenty-four*
cinq	*five*	**vingt-cinq**	*twenty-five*
six	*six*	**vingt-six**	*twenty-six*
sept	*seven*	**vingt-sept**	*twenty-seven*
huit	*eight*	**vingt-huit**	*twenty-eight*
neuf	*nine*	**vingt-neuf**	*twenty-nine*
dix	*ten*	**trente**	*thirty*
onze	*eleven*	**trente et un**	*thirty-one*
douze	*twelve*	**trente-deux**	*thirty-two*
treize	*thirteen*	**trente-trois**	*thirty-three*
quatorze	*fourteen*	**quarante**	*forty*
quinze	*fifteen*	**quarante et un**	*forty-one*
seize	*sixteen*	**quarante-deux**	*forty-two*
dix-sept	*seventeen*	**quarante-trois**	*forty-three*
dix-huit	*eighteen*	**cinquante**	*fifty*
dix-neuf	*nineteen*		

EXERCICE

4·1

Écrire les nombres suivants en toutes lettres.

1. 6 _____

2. 14 _____

3. 23 _____

4. 28 _____

5. 35 _____
6. 39 _____
7. 41 _____
8. 46 _____
9. 49 _____
10. 52 _____

Ordinal numbers

Ordinal numbers, for the most part, follow a regular pattern, ending with **-ième**. **Premier/première** (*first*) and **dernier/dernière** (*last*) are the exceptions.

premier, première	*first*
deuxième	*second*
troisième	*third*
quatrième	*fourth*
cinquième	*fifth*
sixième	*sixth*
septième	*seventh*
huitième	*eighth*
neuvième	*ninth*
dixième	*tenth*
vingtième	*twentieth*
vingt et unième	*twenty-first*
vingt-deuxième	*twenty-second*
vingt-troisième	*twenty-third*
trentième	*thirtieth*
quarantième	*fortieth*
cinquantième	*fiftieth*

In France, **le premier étage** corresponds to the American second floor. The American first or ground floor is called **le rez-de-chaussée** in France. Note the following examples:

La première fois que j'ai pris l'avion, j'avais cinq ans.	*The first time I took the plane, I was five years old.*
L'appartement d'Olivier est **au dixième étage**.	*Olivier's apartment is on the eleventh floor.*

EXERCICE
4·2

Traduire en anglais les phrases suivantes.

1. Il a perdu pour la troisième fois.

2. J'habite au trente et unième étage.

Numbers 79

3. Elle a vendu sa deuxième voiture.

_____

4. C'est son cinquante-huitième anniversaire.

_____

5. Nous avons fait du ski pour la première fois.

_____

6. C'est la quatrième fois que nous nous croisons dans la rue.

_____

7. Il a obtenu la quarante-huitième place.

_____

8. J'adore la neuvième symphonie de Beethoven.

_____

9. Il habite au coin de la vingt-troisième rue et de la septième avenue.

_____

10. C'est sa deuxième année?

_____

The numbers 50 to 99

Last time we stopped counting at fifty, right? OK, let's keep going.

cinquante	*fifty*
cinquante et un	*fifty-one*
cinquante-deux	*fifty-two*
cinquante-trois	*fifty-three*
cinquante-quatre	*fifty-four*
cinquante-cinq	*fifty-five*
cinquante-six	*fifty-six*
cinquante-sept	*fifty-seven*
cinquante-huit	*fifty-eight*
cinquante-neuf	*fifty-nine*
soixante	*sixty*
soixante et un	*sixty-one*
soixante-deux	*sixty-two*
soixante-trois	*sixty-three*
soixante-quatre	*sixty-four*
soixante-cinq	*sixty-five*
soixante-six	*sixty-six*
soixante-sept	*sixty-seven*
soixante-huit	*sixty-eight*
soixante-neuf	*sixty-nine*
soixante-dix	*seventy*

From seventy-one to seventy-nine, you add the teen numbers.

soixante et onze	*seventy-one*
soixante-douze	*seventy-two*
soixante-treize	*seventy-three*
soixante-quatorze	*seventy-four*
soixante-quinze	*seventy-five*
soixante-seize	*seventy-six*
soixante-dix-sept	*seventy-seven*
soixante-dix-huit	*seventy-eight*
soixante-dix-neuf	*seventy-nine*

Eighty is really four times twenty. Therefore from eighty to ninety-nine, you'll keep adding to **quatre-vingts**. Note that **quatre-vingts** has an **-s**. But once you attach another number to **quatre-vingts**, the **-s** will drop.

quatre-vingts	*eighty*
quatre-vingt-un	*eighty-one*
quatre-vingt-deux	*eighty-two*
quatre-vingt-trois	*eighty-three*
quatre-vingt-quatre	*eighty-four*
quatre-vingt-cinq	*eighty-five*
quatre-vingt-six	*eighty-six*
quatre-vingt-sept	*eighty-seven*
quatre-vingt-huit	*eighty-eight*
quatre-vingt-neuf	*eighty-nine*
quatre-vingt-dix	*ninety*
quatre-vingt-onze	*ninety-one*
quatre-vingt-douze	*ninety-two*
quatre-vingt-treize	*ninety-three*
quatre-vingt-quatorze	*ninety-four*
quatre-vingt-quinze	*ninety-five*
quatre-vingt-seize	*ninety-six*
quatre-vingt-dix-sept	*ninety-seven*
quatre-vingt-dix-huit	*ninety-eight*
quatre-vingt-dix-neuf	*ninety-nine*

EXERCICE 4·3

Transcrire en chiffres les nombres suivants.

1. cinquante-trois _____

2. cinquante-neuf _____

3. soixante-deux _____

4. soixante-dix _____

5. soixante et onze _____

6. soixante-dix-huit _____

7. quatre-vingt-trois _____

8. quatre-vingt-sept _____

9. quatre-vingt-dix _____

10. quatre-vingt-treize _____

The numbers 100 to 999

Now we have reached one hundred! Let's keep going.

cent	*one hundred*
cent un	*one hundred one*
cent deux	*one hundred two*
cent trois	*one hundred three*
cent quatre	*one hundred four*
cent cinq	*one hundred five*
cent six	*one hundred six*
cent sept	*one hundred seven*
cent huit	*one hundred eight*
cent neuf	*one hundred nine*
cent dix	*one hundred ten*
cent onze	*one hundred eleven*
cent douze	*one hundred twelve*
cent treize	*one hundred thirteen*
cent quatorze	*one hundred fourteen*
cent quinze	*one hundred fifteen*
cent vingt	*one hundred twenty*
cent vingt et un	*one hundred twenty-one*
cent vingt-deux	*one hundred twenty-two*
cent trente	*one hundred thirty*
cent trente et un	*one hundred thirty-one*
cent trente-deux	*one hundred thirty-two*
cent quarante	*one hundred forty*
cent quarante et un	*one hundred forty-one*
cent quarante-deux	*one hundred forty-two*
cent cinquante	*one hundred fifty*
cent soixante	*one hundred sixty*
cent soixante-dix	*one hundred seventy*
cent soixante et onze	*one hundred seventy-one*
cent soixante-douze	*one hundred seventy-two*
cent quatre-vingts	*one hundred eighty*
cent quatre-vingt-un	*one hundred eighty-one*
cent quatre-vingt-dix	*one hundred ninety*
cent quatre-vingt-onze	*one hundred ninety-one*
cent quatre-vingt-douze	*one hundred ninety-two*

EXERCICE 4·4

Écrire les nombres suivants en toutes lettres.

1. 101 _____
2. 114 _____
3. 126 _____
4. 139 _____
5. 145 _____
6. 156 _____
7. 160 _____
8. 178 _____
9. 181 _____
10. 199 _____

Add an -s to **cent** greater than one hundred (**deux cents, trois cents**), except when **cent** is followed by another number.

deux cents	*two hundred*
trois cents	*three hundred*
quatre cents	*four hundred*
cinq cents	*five hundred*
six cents	*six hundred*
sept cents	*seven hundred*
huit cents	*eight hundred*
neuf cents	*nine hundred*

Note the following examples:

huit cent vingt-quatre	*eight hundred twenty-four*
deux cent quatre-vingt-trois	*two hundred eighty-three*

EXERCICE 4·5

Traduire (en toutes lettres) les nombres suivants.

1. two hundred twelve _____
2. three hundred fifteen _____
3. four hundred twenty _____
4. five hundred thirty-one _____
5. six hundred twenty-three _____
6. seven hundred ninety _____

7. eight hundred forty-eight _____

8. nine hundred four _____

9. six hundred forty-five _____

10. one hundred one _____

EXERCICE 4·6

Écrire les nombres suivants en toutes lettres.

1. 205 _____

2. 389 _____

3. 456 _____

4. 504 _____

5. 678 _____

6. 745 _____

7. 800 _____

8. 815 _____

9. 901 _____

10. 940 _____

The numbers 1,000 and greater

Never add an -s to **mille** (*one thousand*).

mille	*one thousand*
mille un	*one thousand one*
mille deux	*one thousand two*
mille dix	*one thousand ten*
mille vingt	*one thousand twenty*
mille trente	*one thousand thirty*
mille onze	*one thousand eleven*
mille vingt-trois	*one thousand twenty-three*
mille deux cents	*one thousand two hundred*
mille deux cent cinquante-trois	*one thousand two hundred fifty-three*
mille quatre cents	*one thousand four hundred*
deux mille	*two thousand*
deux mille cinq cents	*two thousand five hundred*
deux mille sept cent soixante-treize	*two thousand seven hundred seventy-three*
dix mille	*ten thousand*

84 PRACTICE MAKES PERFECT Complete French All-in-One

In French, an **-s** is added to **million** and **milliard** greater than **un** (*one*).

    un million   *a million*
    un milliard   *a billion*

    quatre millions trois cent mille quatre cent vingt-cinq   *four million three hundred thousand four hundred twenty-five*
    deux milliards quatre cent millions cinq cent mille   *two billion four hundred million five hundred thousand*

Years are written out as follows in French:

    1978   **mille neuf cent soixante-dix-huit**
                       or
              dix-neuf cent soixante-dix-huit
    2008   **deux mille huit**

EXERCICE 4·7

Écrire les nombres suivants en toutes lettres.

1. 1 005 _____
2. 2 456 _____
3. 3 021 _____
4. 4 789 _____
5. 10 450 _____
6. 24 008 _____
7. 170 890 _____
8. 1 230 000 _____
9. 30 030 000 _____
10. 1 600 000 000 _____

EXERCICE 4·8

Dans les phrases suivantes, transcrire les nombres.

1. Leur bibliothèque numérique sera prête en 2015.

_____

2. Cet appartement coûte 150 000 euros.

_____

Numbers   **85**

3. Hier, j'ai bu du Saint-Émilion 1978.

4. Le soixantième Festival de Cannes a lieu en mai 2007.

5. Il y a plus d'1 000 000 000 d'étoiles dans le ciel.

6. Il a remporté la médaille d'or du 1 500 mètres.

7. D'après une étude en 2006, plus d'1 000 000 de personnes écrivent un blog en France.

8. Victor Hugo est mort en 1885.

9. Cet administrateur de site gagne 5 000 euros par mois.

10. Nous sommes plus de 6 000 000 000 sur cette planète.

Vocabulary: Thoughts, feelings, communicating, home, travel, science, leisure, and technology

The vocabulary lists in this chapter are built to make learning both interesting and easy. The accompanying examples provide as much context as possible for you to understand the meaning of the vocabulary and how it is used in sentences.

Les états d'être (States of being)

The stages of development between birth and passing away are marked by stages such as growing up. Here are some verbs on that topic.

changer	*to change*
devenir	*to become*
être	*to be*
évoluer	*to evolve*
exister	*to exist*
grandir	*to grow*
mâturer	*to mature*
mourir	*to die*
naître	*to be born*
prendre de l'âge	*to grow old, get on in years*
rajeunir	*to grow, make younger*
s'épanouir	*to blossom*
survivre	*to survive*
vieillir	*grow old*
vivre	*live*

Le monde existe depuis longtemps.	*The world has existed for a long time.*
L'enfant s'épanouit quand il est aimé.	*A child blossoms when he is loved.*
On vieillit avec dignité.	*We grow old with dignity.*
On vit de plus en plus longtemps.	*People live longer and longer.*

EXERCICE 5·1

La biographie de Charles Perrault. **Charles Perrault's biography.** *Put the following sentences in chronological order, starting with the letter **A** and finishing with **H** to reconstitute this famous fairy tale writer's life.*

_____ 1. Il grandit à Paris.

_____ 2. Quand il prend de l'âge, il est l'auteur de beaucoup de contes comme «Le petit chaperon rouge» et «Cendrillon».

_____ 3. Il est brillant au lycée et à l'université.

_____ 4. Puis il devient membre de l'Académie française en 1671.

_____ 5. Il survit à la perte de l'amitié du roi.

_____ 6. Il vieillit et meurt à Paris en 1703.

_____ 7. Il veut d'abord devenir avocat.

_____ 8. Charles Perrault naît en 1628 à Paris.

Les états d'esprit (States of mind)

States of mind, such as *wondering* or *understanding,* vary according to favorable or adverse circumstances.

comprendre	*to understand*
croire	*to believe*
décider (de)	*to decide (to)*
désirer	*to desire*
devoir	*to have to, must*
douter	*to doubt*
espérer	*to hope*
oublier	*to forget*
penser	*to think*
réfléchir	*to think over*
renoncer à	*to give up*
rêver	*to dream*
s'analyser	*to analyze oneself*
s'imaginer	*to imagine*
s'interroger (sur)	*to ask oneself (about)*
savoir	*to know*
se demander	*to wonder*
se rappeler	*to remember*
se souvenir	*to remember*
se tromper	*to make a mistake*
songer à	*to think about*
souhaiter	*to wish*
supposer	*to suppose*
tenir à ce que (+ subjonctif)	*to want, to insist on*
vouloir	*to want*

Je me souviens de mes amis d'enfance.	*I remember my childhood friends.*
Je me trompe rarement.	*I am rarely mistaken.*
Je sais que de bons amis sont loyaux.	*I know that good friends are loyal.*
Je tiens à avoir de bonnes relations avec toi.	*I want to have good relations with you.*
Cela me semble raisonnable.	*That seems reasonable to me.*
Je rêve d'avoir une belle vie.	*I dream about having a beautiful life.*
Je n'oublierai jamais mes rêves.	*I will never forget my dreams.*

Many thought processes, such as remembering (**se rappeler** or **se souvenir**), are expressed with reflexive verbs. Verbs are reflexive when the action of the verb is reflected upon the subject. A reflexive verb is preceded by a reflexive pronoun regardless of tense or mode. In the following sentences, note how the reflexive pronoun changes with the subject.

je me souviens	I remember
tu te souviens	you remember
il/elle/on se souvient	he/she/one remembers
nous nous souvenons	we remember
vous vous souvenez	you remember
ils/elles se souviennent	they remember

Elle est célèbre. Tu t'imagines cela?	*She is famous. Can you imagine that?*
Nous nous rappelons bien cette comédie.	*We remember this comedy well.*
Il ne faut pas trop s'interroger.	*Better not ask yourself too many questions.*

EXERCICE
5·2

Un petit dialogue. **A little dialogue.** *Write the letter of the correct answer to each question.*

_____ 1. Qu'est-ce que tu souhaites pour la nouvelle année?

_____ 2. À quoi est-ce que tu tiens le plus en ce moment?

_____ 3. Tu te souviens de nos vacances en Italie?

_____ 4. Tu as renoncé à changer de travail?

_____ 5. Qu'est-ce que tu penses du nouveau film?

_____ 6. Tu crois que le prof est absent?

_____ 7. Tu es décidé à faire cette grosse dépense?

_____ 8. Tu songes souvent à ton avenir?

_____ 9. Tu crois que je pourrai devenir actrice?

_____ 10. Tu doutes de mon amitié?

a. Oui, j'ai décidé de garder le même job.

b. Il me semble plutôt intéressant.

c. J'ai confiance en toi. Vouloir c'est pouvoir.

d. Je voudrais faire un beau voyage en France.

e. Oui, bien sûr. Je m'imagine ce que ce sera dans dix ans.

f. Mais non, je sais très bien que tu es mon ami.

g. Ma petite amie est ce que j'ai de plus précieux.

h. Je me demande s'il n'est pas simplement en retard.

i. Oh oui. Je veux m'acheter cette voiture.

j. Je me rappelle très bien ce séjour à Rome.

Les états d'âme (Feelings)

Feelings and moods have many facets.

admirer	*to admire*
adorer	*to adore*
aimer	*to like, love*
avoir envie de	*to feel like*
avoir honte de	*to be ashamed*
craindre	*to fear*
détester	*to detest*
être dégoûté	*to be disgusted*
faire confiance à	*to trust*
jouir de	*to enjoy*
mépriser	*to despise*
préférer	*to prefer*
refouler	*to suppress*
ressentir	*to feel*
s'ennuyer de quelqu'un	*to miss someone*
s'inquiéter de	*to worry about*
se faire du souci	*to worry*
se méfier de	*to distrust*
se réjouir de	*to be delighted at*
souffrir	*to suffer*

Nous adorons les soirées en famille. — *We love family evenings.*
La région jouit d'un climat agréable. — *The region enjoys a pleasant climate.*
Mais nous avons envie d'être seuls. — *But we feel like being alone.*
Je m'ennuie de toi; je suis triste. — *I miss you; I am sad.*
Je préfère te voir heureux. — *I prefer seeing you happy.*
Je souffre de ton absence. — *I suffer because you are absent.*

EXERCICE 5·3

Vrai ou faux? **True or false?** *Write* **V** *for* **vrai** *or* **F** *for* **faux** *next to each statement, depending on whether you agree or disagree.*

_____ 1. Les parents s'inquiètent quand leurs enfants sont en retard.

_____ 2. Il est facile de refouler même les désirs les plus vifs.

_____ 3. On doit se réjouir du bonheur de ses amis.

_____ 4. On doit mépriser les gens qui ont du courage.

_____ 5. Il vaut mieux ne pas toujours faire confiance aux politiciens.

_____ 6. Il est naturel de s'ennuyer des gens qu'on aime.

_____ 7. Il faut craindre les gens honnêtes.

_____ 8. On ne doit pas détester son prochain.

_____ 9. Il faut jouir de la vie autant que possible.

_____ 10. On doit avoir honte quand on est jaloux de ses amis.

Communiquer (Communicating)

There are many forms of communication. We communicate information, feelings, opinions, advice, and orders on a regular basis.

Prendre un parti (Taking a position)

It is important to express one's point of view and take a stand.

accepter	*to accept*
admettre	*to admit*
affirmer	*to confirm, state*
agréer	*to agree*
avouer	*to confess*
persuader	*to persuade*
prendre le parti	*to take sides*
refuser	*to refuse*
rejeter	*to reject*

On l'a persuadé d'accepter le travail.	*They persuaded him to take the job.*
J'avoue que j'en suis bien content.	*I admit that it makes me happy.*
J'espère qu'il ne rejettera pas l'offre.	*I hope he will not reject the offer.*

Conseiller (Advising)

Giving advice or instructions is another form of communication.

apprendre	*to teach*
conseiller	*to advise*
corriger	*to correct*
expliquer	*to explain*
inculquer	*to instill*
insister	*to insist*
permettre	*to allow*
remarquer	*to notice, interject*
réviser	*to review*

Ils m'ont inculqué des principes moraux.	*They instilled moral values into me.*
Ils insistaient pour que j'écoute bien.	*They insisted that I listen well.*
Ils me corrigeaient fréquemment.	*They corrected me frequently.*
Ils m'ont appris à parler français.	*They taught me to speak French.*

Vocabulary: Thoughts, feelings, communicating, home, travel, science, leisure, and technology

Parler et écrire (Speaking and writing)

Knowing how to communicate in speaking and writing is a valuable skill.

annoncer	to announce
appeler	to call
bavarder	to chat
causer	to chat
constater	to observe
déclarer	to declare, state
demander à... de...	to ask
diffuser	to broadcast
dire	to say, tell
discuter	to discuss
écrire	to write
enseigner	to teach, instruct
être d'accord	to agree
exprimer	to express
faire suivre	to forward
parler	to speak
poser des questions	to ask questions
poster	to mail
publier	to publish
raconter	to tell
s'abonner à	to subscribe to
s'adresser à	to address oneself to
s'excuser	to apologize

On va publier sa lettre à le redacteur en chef.	They are going to publish his/her letter to the editor.
Il est libre d'exprimer ses opinions.	He is free to express his opinions.
Tu t'abonnes à des magazines?	Do you subscribe to magazines?

EXERCICE 5·4

M. Rapeau est journaliste. **Mr. Rapeau is a journalist.** *Complete each sentence with the appropriate word from the list provided.*

| discute | appelle | publie | inculque | annonce |
| comprend | révise | s'excuse | s'abonne | explique |

1. À la radio, on _____ du mauvais temps.
2. M. Rapeau _____ le journal pour annoncer qu'il arrivera en retard ce matin.
3. M. Rapeau _____ de son retard au rédacteur en chef.
4. Le rédacteur en chef _____ tous les articles.
5. Le rédacteur en chef _____ ses révisions à M. Rapeau.
6. M. Rapeau _____ les révisions avec le rédacteur en chef.
7. M. Rapeau _____ le point de vue du le rédacteur en chef.

8. Le journal de M. Rapeau _____ ses articles.

9. On _____ à ce journal en payant une cotisation mensuelle.

10. Ce genre de publication informative _____ le désir de lire et d'apprendre.

Forger des relations (Building relationships)

Socializing—being around people—is an important part of everyday life.

accompagner	to accompany
accueillir	to welcome
adopter	to adopt
avoir une relation	to have a relationship
charmer	to charm
embrasser	to kiss
faire la bise à, donner une bise à	to give a kiss to
faire la connaissance de	to make the acquaintance of
faire la cour à	to court
fonder une famille	to start a family
fréquenter	to keep company with
présenter	to present
respecter	to respect
revoir	to see again
s'intéresser à	to be interested in
se confier à	to confide in
se lier avec	to get close to
se marier avec	to get married to
(se) plaire	to be pleasing (to one another)
(se) rencontrer	to meet (each other)
(se) revoir	to see (each other) again
sortir avec	to go out with

Ginette a rencontré deux amis.	Ginette met two friends.
Ginette les présente à sa mère.	Ginette introduces them to her mother.
Leurs manières ne lui plaisent pas.	She does not like their manners.
Elle lui dit de ne pas les revoir.	She tells her not to see them again.
Ginette obéit car elle respecte sa mère.	Ginette obeys for she respects her mother.

EXERCICE 5·5

Quel conte de fée! What a fairy tale! *Put the following sentences in chronological order from to **A** through **J** to reconstitute this love story.*

_____ 1. Les parents de Gisèle l'accueillent chaleureusement.

_____ 2. Sa sœur Annie lui présente Gisèle.

_____ 3. David accompagne sa sœur Annie chez des amis.

_____ 4. Le jour du mariage David et Gisèle promettent de se protéger et de se respecter pour toute la vie.

_____ 5. David revoit Gisèle deux jours après chez elle.

_____ 6. Les deux jeunes gens se plaisent tout de suite.

_____ 7. David charme les parents de Gisèle: il serre la main au papa et fait la bise à la maman.

_____ 8. Les deux jeunes gens sortent alors régulièrement ensemble.

_____ 9. C'est ainsi qu'il fait la connaissance de Gisèle.

_____ 10. David et Gisèle décident de se marier et de fonder une famille.

Rompre des relations (Breaking up)

Some relationships disintegrate and break up.

décevoir	_to disappoint_
décourager	_to discourage_
déplaire	_to displease_
faire de la peine à	_to upset someone_
gêner	_to bother_
humilier	_to humiliate_
quitter	_to leave_
repousser	_to reject_
rompre	_to break_
se désintéresser de	_to lose interest_
se disputer	_to quarrel_
se perdre de vue	_to lose sight of each other_
se séparer	_to separate from each other_
soupçonner	_to suspect_
tromper	_to cheat, deceive_

Jojo et Mimi se disputent tout le temps.	_Jojo and Mimi quarrel all the time._
Jojo soupçonne Mimi de le tromper.	_Jojo suspects Mimi cheats on him._
Il se sent humilié.	_He feels humiliated._
Ce manque de confiance fait de la peine à Mimi.	_This lack of trust saddens Mimi._
Elle pense à se séparer de Jojo.	_She is thinking of separating from Jojo._
Elle voudrait le quitter.	_She would like to leave him._

EXERCICE
5·6

Le revers de la médaille! **The other side of the coin!** _For each verb, write the letter of its opposite._

_____ 1. attirer   a. humilier

_____ 2. soupçonner   b. déplaire

_____ 3. tromper   c. mettre à l'aise

_____ 4. respecter   d. quitter

_____ 5. rencontrer   e. repousser

_____	6. encourager	f.	faire confiance
_____	7. se lier	g.	décourager
_____	8. charmer	h.	être fidèle
_____	9. s'intéresser à	i.	se désintéresser de
_____	10. gêner	j.	se séparer

À l'aide des autres (Helping others)

An important aspect of the socialization process is having a social conscience and coming to other people's help by offering company, advice, gifts, or shelter.

abriter	_to shelter_
accompagner	_to accompany_
aider	_to help_
amuser	_to amuse_
apaiser	_to appease_
blaguer	_to kid, joke_
calmer	_to calm down_
caresser	_to caress_
conseiller	_to advise, council_
consoler	_to console_
divertir	_to entertain_
donner	_to give_
faire de bonnes actions	_to make charitable acts_
féliciter	_to congratulate_
inviter	_to invite_
libérer	_to liberate_
nourrir	_to feed_
offrir	_to offer_
plaisanter	_to joke_
pardonner	_to forgive_
prendre soin de	_to take care of_
réconforter	_to comfort_
s'occuper de	_to take care of_
soigner	_to provide care_
soulager	_to relieve_
soutenir	_to support_

Notre organisation accueille les sans-abris.	_Our organization welcomes the homeless._
On s'occupe d'eux et on les nourrit.	_We take care of them and feed them._
Ces jeunes amusent les personnes âgées.	_These youngsters entertain the old people._
La dame caresse le chien perdu.	_The lady caresses the lost dog._
Elle lui offre un os.	_She gives him a bone._

Vocabulary: Thoughts, feelings, communicating, home, travel, science, leisure, and technology **95**

EXERCICE 5·7

L'hôpital du docteur Poirot. Dr. Poirot's hospital. *Complete each sentence with the appropriate word from the list provided.*

divertir	aider	soulager	s'occuper	jouer
prendre soin	consoler	plaisanter	offrir	imiter

1. Le Dr. Poirot est devenu médecin pour _____ les autres gens.

2. Il peut généralement _____ les douleurs de ses patients.

3. L'infirmière est formée pour _____ des malades.

4. Si la patiente a faim, elle va _____ d'elle et lui donner à manger.

5. Des amis vont venir voir la patiente et lui _____ des fleurs.

6. Quelquefois il y a des groupes de jeunes qui viennent _____ les patients.

7. Ces jeunes aiment raconter des histoires drôles et _____.

8. Ils aiment aussi _____ des rôles et faire des petites pièces amusantes.

9. Par exemple ils savent bien _____ des célébrités.

10. Leur intention est de _____ les patients quand ils ont de la peine.

Agresser (Being aggressive)

Aggressive behavior is an unfortunate aspect of interactions between people.

agacer	*to pester*
attaquer	*to attack*
blesser	*to wound, injure*
calomnier	*to slander, libel*
cambrioler	*to rob*
contredire	*to contradict*
critiquer	*to criticize*
défendre de	*to forbid*
déranger	*to disturb*
donner un coup	*to hit*
écraser	*to squash*
effrayer	*to frighten*
éliminer	*to eliminate*
embêter	*to annoy*
emprisonner	*to put in jail*
enlever	*to kidnap*
ennuyer	*to annoy*
frapper	*to hit*
interdire de	*to forbid*
poignarder	*to stab*
punir	*to punish*
se fâcher contre	*to get mad at*

se mettre en colère contre	*to get mad, angry at*
surveiller	*to watch over*
taper	*to hit*
terroriser	*to terrorize*
tuer	*to kill*
voler	*to steal*

Il vaut mieux éviter de se fâcher.	*You better avoid getting mad.*
Les pirates de l'air ont terrorisé les passagers.	*The hijackers terrorized the passengers.*
Un voleur a cambriolé la maison du voisin.	*A thief robbed the neighbor's house.*
Il avait probablement surveillé le quartier.	*He had probably watched the neighborhood.*
Ces garçons se sont donné des coups de poing.	*These boys punched each other.*
Les lions effraient les enfants au zoo.	*The lions scare the children at the zoo.*

EXERCICE 5·8

***Faire et ne pas faire!* To do and not to do!** *Write the letter of the most appropriate opposite for each of the following verbs.*

_____ 1. donner   a. contredire

_____ 2. féliciter   b. blesser

_____ 3. apaiser   c. interdire

_____ 4. pardonner   d. éliminer

_____ 5. libérer   e. frapper

_____ 6. être d'accord   f. voler

_____ 7. permettre   g. déranger

_____ 8. caresser   h. emprisonner

_____ 9. soigner   i. punir

_____ 10. créer   j. calomnier

Entretenir un foyer (Housekeeping)

Taking care of a home is no easy task. It includes decorating, painting, fixing, furnishing, cleaning, and other such activities.

accrocher	*to hang*
aérer	*to air*
bricoler	*to tinker*
clouer	*to nail*
construire	*to construct*
décorer	*to decorate*

déménager	to move
démolir	to demolish
emménager	to move in
entretenir	to maintain
frotter	to scrub
habiter	to live, inhabit
loger	to live in
meubler	to furnish
nettoyer	to clean
peindre	to paint
ranger	to put in order
rénover	to renovate
réparer	to repair
s'habituer à	to get used to
s'installer	to settle in

Avant d'emménager, nous allons rénover.	*Before moving in, we are going to renovate.*
J'adore peindre les pièces en couleurs vives.	*I love painting rooms in bright colors.*
Le plombier va réparer le robinet.	*The plumber is going to repair the faucet.*
Moi, je vais frotter le parquet.	*I am going to scrub the parquet floor.*
Toi, tu vas accrocher ce tableau ici.	*You are going to hang this painting here.*
S'installer prend du temps!	*Settling in takes time!*

EXERCICE
5·9

Le nouvel appartement d'Aurore. **Aurore's new apartment.** *Complete each sentence with the appropriate verb from the list.*

| nettoyer | s'installer | ranger | clouer | s'habituer |
| meubler | peindre | accrocher | aérer | loger |

1. Aurore veut _____ dans un deux-pièces en ville.
2. Elle va le _____ avec des meubles très modernes.
3. Elle va _____ ses plus jolis tableaux impressionnistes dans le salon.
4. Elle va _____ ses vêtements dans le grand placard de la chambre à coucher.
5. Elle va _____ un porte-manteau au mur de l'entrée.
6. Elle va _____ le salon en jaune clair.
7. Elle va _____ son appartement tous les jours en ouvrant les fenêtres.
8. Elle va _____ toutes les fenêtres.
9. Elle va _____ dans l'appartement la semaine prochaine.
10. Il lui sera très facile de _____ à ce nouvel appartement.

Jardiner (Gardening)

A part of taking care of a home sometimes includes taking care of plants, flowers, and gardens—a favorite pastime for Parisians who leave the city is to tend their **jardins** in the country.

arroser	*to water*
bêcher	*to dig*
bouturer	*to cut and propagate*
creuser	*to dig*
cueillir	*to pick*
cultiver	*to cultivate*
déboiser	*to deforest*
défricher	*to clear land*
désherber	*to remove weeds*
entretenir	*to take care of*
faire pousser	*to (make) grow*
fertiliser	*to fertilize*
fleurir	*to blossom*
planter	*to plant*
pousser	*to grow*
râtisser	*to rake*
récolter	*to harvest*
semer	*to sow*
tailler	*to trim*
tondre	*to mow*

En automne, il faut râtisser les feuilles mortes.	*In the fall you have to rake the dead leaves.*
Il est amusant de bouturer les plantes.	*It is fun to take cuttings and start new plants.*
Tu vas bientôt tailler ces buissons?	*Are you going to trim those bushes soon?*
Ce fermier a déboisé un terrain.	*This farmer deforested a piece of land.*
Il va y faire pousser du blé.	*He is going to grow wheat there.*
Il faudra continuer de désherber ce champ.	*We will have to continue clearing weeds from this field.*

EXERCICE 5·10

***Que faut-il faire pour entretenir un beau jardin?* What must we do in order to keep a beautiful garden?** *Write **oui** or **non** for each question.*

_____ 1. Il faut râtisser les feuilles mortes?

_____ 2. Il faut planter des mauvaises herbes?

_____ 3. Il faut tailler les buissons et les arbres?

_____ 4. Il faut tondre les fleurs?

_____ 5. Il faut creuser de grands trous?

_____ 6. Il faut désherber régulièrement?

_____ 7. Il faut cueillir toutes les fleurs?

_____ 8. Il faut arroser seulement les feuilles des fleurs?

Vocabulary: Thoughts, feelings, communicating, home, travel, science, leisure, and technology

Conduire (Driving)

The car is one of the most frequently used means of transportation to get around.

accélérer	to speed up
démarrer	to start (car)
dépasser la limite	to go over the limit
déraper	to glide
doubler	to pass (a car)
freiner	to brake
heurter	to hit
mettre en marche	to start (engine)
passer le permis	to take the driver's license test
ralentir	to slow down
recevoir le permis	to receive a driver's license
respecter le code	to respect road rules
rester sur place	to stay in the same place
se garer	to park
se stationner	to park
stopper	to stop
tourner	to turn

Démarre! Le feu est vert.	Start! The light is green.
Ne se stationne surtout pas ici! C'est interdit!	Do not park here! It is forbidden!
Tu dois respecter le code de la route.	You must respect the rules of the road.
Tourne à gauche là-bas!	Turn left over there!
Il y a du verglas sur cette route. Tu dérapes!	There is ice on this road. The car is skidding!
Cherchons une place pour nous garer!	Let's look for a place to park!

EXERCICE 5·11

Êtes-vous raisonnable? Are you reasonable? Write **V** for **vrai** or **F** for **faux** for each of the following statements.

_____ 1. Au feu rouge, il faut accélérer.

_____ 2. Au feu vert, il faut rester sur place.

_____ 3. Quand un agent de police vous appréhende, il faut s'arrêter.

_____ 4. Quand il commence à y avoir de l'orage et des éclairs, il faut rentrer à la maison.

_____ 5. Quand il y a du verglas sur la route, il faut accélérer.

_____ 6. Avant de conduire une voiture, il faut passer le permis de conduire.

_____ 7. Quand on voit un accident devant nous, il faut freiner et ralentir.

_____ 8. Quand on voit un panneau «Stationnement interdit», il faut se stationner là.

_____ 9. Quand on voit une dispute entre conducteurs, il vaut mieux s'éloigner et appeler la police.

_____ 10. Quand on arrive à destination, il faut descendre.

Voyager (Traveling)

Travel requires certain preparations, planning, and choices.

accompagner	*to accompany*
arriver	*to arrive*
atterrir	*to land*
chercher	*to look for*
décoller	*to take off (by plane)*
faire des projets	*to plan*
faire escale	*to make a stopover*
faire la valise	*to pack*
faire les préparatifs	*to make preparations*
faire une excursion	*to go on a side trip*
faire un tour	*to go for a ride or stroll*
faire un voyage	*to go on a trip*
louer	*to rent*
partir	*to leave*
prendre congé	*to take a leave of absence*
prendre (l'avion, le bateau)	*to take (the plane, the boat)*
prolonger	*to prolong*
réserver	*to reserve*
s'arrêter	*to stop*
s'embarquer	*to embark*
s'informer	*to get information*
se rendre (quelque part)	*to go (somewhere)*
se renseigner	*to get information, inquire*
séjourner	*to stay*
trouver	*to find*
visiter	*to visit*

Elle voudrait faire un voyage au Canada.	*She would like to take a trip to Canada.*
Elle se renseigne sur les tarifs d'avion.	*She inquires about air fares.*
Elle aimerait séjourner au Québec.	*She would like to stay in Quebec.*
Trouvons-lui un hôtel à Québec!	*Let's find her a hotel in Quebec City!*
Elle veut faire escale à Montréal.	*She wants to make a stopover in Montreal.*
Moi, je compte l'accompagner.	*I intend to accompany her.*

EXERCICE 5·12

***Le voyage de Marie et de Paul à Paris.* Marie and Paul's trip to Paris.** *Put the following sentences in chronological order from **A** to **H** to reconstitute the story.*

_____ 1. Le vol doit être direct et l'hôtel doit être dans Le Quartier latin.

_____ 2. Il faudra peut-être prolonger le séjour, n'est-ce pas?

_____ 3. Il faut aussi se renseigner sur le prix des tours visites guidées et des excursions.

_____ 4. Marie et Paul ont décidé de faire un voyage en France cet été.

_____ 5. Deuxièmement, il faut s'informer sur le prix des voitures à louer.

_____ 6. Premièrement, il faut réserver les billets d'avion et une chambre d'hôtel.

_____ 7. Évidemment, on ne peut pas faire trop d'excursions quand le séjour ne dure qu'une semaine.

_____ 8. D'abord il faut faire tous les préparatifs nécessaires.

La science (Science)

Discoveries in science allow scientific progress in not only biology and medicine (e.g., antibiotics, vaccines) but also in technological fields (e.g., electric razors, iPods). From the early 1900s when Marie Curie followed by Frédéric Joliot and Irène Joliot-Curie won Nobel prizes in chemistry, to Claude Cohen-Tannoudji, a recent Nobel prize winner in physics, France has nurtured the sciences. Here are some frequently used verbs to discuss this topic.

analyser	to analyze
avertir	to warn
chercher	to look for
conclure	to conclude
découvrir	to discover
déduire	to deduce
diriger	to direct
essayer	to try
étudier	to study
évaluer	to evaluate
expérimenter	to experiment
faire des expériences	to conduct tests, experiments
faire un essai	to make an attempt, to make a test
observer	to observe
partager	to share
proposer	to propose
prouver	to prove
rassembler	to assemble
réaliser	to realize
recueillir (des données)	to collect (data)
réfléchir	to think over
remarquer	to notice
répéter	to repeat
répondre	to answer
résoudre	to resolve
réussir	to succeed
risquer	to risk
sélectionner	to select
signaler	to signal, warn
surveiller	to watch over
vérifier	to verify

Une approche scientifique consiste à analyser, déduire et conclure.	A scientific approach consists in analyzing, deducing, and concluding.
Il faut vérifier les résultats de l'expérience.	We must verify the results of the experiment.
Il faut répéter l'expérience pour être sûr.	You have to repeat the experiment to be sure.
Le savant observe les microbes sous le microscope.	The scientist observes the microbes under the microscope.
Les frères Montgolfier ont fait plusieurs essais avant de réussir.	The Montgolfier brothers made several attempts before succeeding.

EXERCICE 5·13

L'œuvre des Curie. *The accomplishments of the Curies. Complete each sentence with the appropriate verb from the list provided.*

observe	réussit	annonce	découvre	prouve
s'intéresse	partage	recueille	dirige	fait des expériences

1. Marie Curie, une Polonaise qui fait ses études à la Sorbonne, _____ aux découvertes de Wilhelm Roentgen sur les rayons X.
2. Elle épouse Pierre Curie qui _____ sur le magnétisme.
3. Pierre _____ les données nécessaires et il énonce la loi de Curie et définit le point de Curie.
4. Marie, elle _____ les rayonnements du pechblende, minerai d'uranium.
5. Elle _____ que ceux-ci sont plus intenses que ceux de l'uranium.
6. Bientôt elle _____ la découverte de deux nouveaux radioéléments: le polonium et le radium.
7. Elle _____ à extraire suffisamment de radium pour en déterminer la masse atomique.
8. Marie présente et _____ ses résultats dans sa thèse de doctorat en 1903.
9. Elle reçoit la même année le prix Nobel de physique qu'elle _____ avec son mari et Henri Becquerel.
10. Pendant la Première Guerre mondiale, elle _____ les services radiologiques de l'armée.

La médecine (Medicine)

Medical science is a field experiencing tremendous progress on a daily basis. New medications and treatments are constantly being introduced. **Médecins Sans Frontières** is an organization created by a group of French doctors to bring free medical care to developing countries.

accepter	*to accept*
administrer	*to administer*
analyser	*to analyze*
ausculter	*to examine by listening*
conseiller	*to advise, counsel*
découvrir	*to discover*
diagnostiquer	*to diagnose*
étudier	*to study*
examiner	*to examine*
gérer	*to manage*

greffer	*to transplant, graft*
guérir	*to heal, cure*
immuniser	*to immunize*
opérer	*to operate*
prescrire	*to prescribe*
radiographier	*to take x-rays*
recevoir	*to receive*
réanimer	*to resuscitate*
sauver	*to save*
soigner	*to take care*
traiter	*to treat*
transfuser	*to transfuse*
vacciner	*to vaccinate*
voir	*to see*

Le médecin prescrit un antibiotique.	*The doctor precribes an antibiotic.*
Le médecin a ressuscité le patient.	*The doctor resuscitated the patient.*
Il faut transfuser le sang d'un patient.	*They must transfuse the patient's blood.*
Pour greffer un rein, il faut des chirurgiens.	*To transplant a kidney, they need surgeons.*
Les enfants doivent être immunisés.	*Children must be immunized.*

EXERCICE 5·14

Le rôle des médecins de famille. **The role of family doctors.** *Write **V** for **vrai** or **F** for **faux** for each of the following statements.*

_____ 1. Un médecin de famille examine les personnes et les bêtes.

_____ 2. Il analyse les symptômes des patients.

_____ 3. Il diagnostique et traite les symptômes.

_____ 4. Il conseille aux patients de fumer.

_____ 5. Il immunise les enfants contre certaines maladies.

_____ 6. Il fait des opérations dans son cabinet.

_____ 7. Il sauve et transfuse tous ses patients.

_____ 8. Il gère les soins des patients.

_____ 9. Il prescrit des médicaments.

_____ 10. Il greffe des organes.

La santé (Health)

Progress in science and medicine helps make life easier and healthier. Here are a few frequently used verbs to discuss the topic of health and ailments.

aller (bien, mal, mieux)	*to feel (good, bad, better)*
attraper une maladie	*to catch a disease*

104 PRACTICE MAKES PERFECT Complete French All-in-One

avoir des vertiges	*to be dizzy*
brûler	*to burn*
se casser (un bras, une jambe)	*to break (an arm, a leg)*
éternuer	*to sneeze*
être en forme	*to be in shape*
être en bonne santé	*to be healthy*
faire une rechute	*to relapse*
frissonner	*to shiver*
garder le lit	*to stay in bed*
grossir	*to gain weight*
maigrir	*to lose weight*
perdre connaissance	*to faint, to lose consciousness*
reprendre des forces	*to regain strength*
s'améliorer	*to improve*
s'enrhumer	*to catch a cold*
se remettre	*to recover*
suer	*to sweat*
tomber malade	*to get sick*
tousser	*to cough*
transpirer	*to transpire, sweat*

Tu vas mieux aujourd'hui?	*Do you feel better today?*
Je vais vraiment mal.	*I feel really bad.*
Regarde comme je transpire.	*Look how I am sweating.*
Espérons que tu te remettras bientôt.	*Let's hope you recover soon.*
La fièvre vous fait frissonner.	*A fever makes you shiver.*
Voilà un sirop pour la toux.	*Here is a syrup for the cough.*
Tu t'es terriblement enrhumé.	*You got a terrible cold.*
Il vaut mieux que tu gardes le lit.	*You better stay in bed.*

EXERCICE 5·15

Annie, va-t-elle bien ou mal?* Does Annie feel good or bad?** *For each sentence, write* ***bien *or* ***mal*** *according to how Annie feels.*

_____ 1. Aujourd'hui Annie a de la fièvre et transpire intensément.

_____ 2. Annie est en forme et veut faire des courses.

_____ 3. Annie reprend des forces et retrouve son énergie habituelle.

_____ 4. Annie vient de se casser la jambe en tombant de cheval.

_____ 5. Annie éternue continuellement et elle frissonne.

_____ 6. Annie mange bien mais elle reste au lit.

_____ 7. Annie ne mange presque rien et maigrit rapidement.

_____ 8. Annie a des vertiges et perd connaissance.

Vocabulary: Thoughts, feelings, communicating, home, travel, science, leisure, and technology **105**

La technologie (Technology)

Science has proven effective in accelerating technological progress with ever-increasing speed. This progress is obvious in many areas such as transportation, information, communication, and multimedia. All of these contribute to the productivity of a country in a global economy.

afficher	*to post*
bloquer	*to block*
charger	*to load*
chatter	*to chat*
enrayer	*to lock, stop*
enregistrer	*to record*
filtrer	*to filter*
gérer	*to manage, organize*
informer	*to inform*
initier	*to initiate*
innover	*to innovate*
installer	*to install*
interdire	*to forbid*
inventer	*to invent*
mettre à jour	*to update*
naviguer	*to navigate*
optimiser	*to optimize*
organiser	*to organize*
perfectionner	*to perfect*
permettre	*to allow*
pirater	*to hack*
programmer	*to program*
(se) renseigner	*to inform (oneself)*
s'abonner	*to subscribe*
se connecter	*to connect*
sécuriser	*to ensure security*
simuler	*to simulate*
télécharger	*to download*
transmettre	*to transmit*
utiliser	*to use*

Le piratage informatique est sévèrement puni.	*Information hacking is severely punished.*
Je paie mes factures sur un site sécurisé.	*I pay my bills on a secure site.*
Tout le monde télécharge de la musique sur son iPod.	*Everybody downloads music onto his/her iPod.*
Tu peux afficher des annonces sur un site Internet.	*You can post announcements on an Internet site.*
Ce site doit être mis à jour.	*This site needs to be updated.*
Ce logiciel filtre mes messages.	*This software filters my messages.*
Je vais télécharger ce document et l'attacher à mon e-mail.	*I am going to download this document and attach it to my e-mail.*
Nous devons créer un nom pour ce fichier.	*We have to create a name for this file.*

106 PRACTICE MAKES PERFECT Complete French All-in-One

EXERCICE 5·16

Les ordinateurs. Quels en sont les avantages? Computers. What are their advantages? *Complete each sentence with the appropriate verb from the list provided.*

communiquer	afficher	initier	s'abonner	gérer
télécharger	transmettre	simuler	perfectionner	bloquer

1. On peut _____ des annonces sur des sites web.
2. On peut _____ toutes sortes d'informations très rapidement.
3. On peut _____ de la musique et des documents.
4. On peut _____ et chatter avec des personnes connues ou inconnues partout dans le monde.
5. On peut _____ à des programmes éducatifs.
6. On peut payer des factures et _____ ses finances.
7. On peut _____ toutes sortes d'actions et d'activités.
8. On peut _____ ses connaissances dans beaucoup de domaines.
9. On peut _____ le piratage.
10. On peut _____ des contacts, des échanges et des liens.

Les technologies de l'information et de la communication (Information and communication technologies)

Ever-increasing numbers of people with access to the Internet navigate it for personal and work use. In addition, new uses for the Internet are constantly emerging.

l'abonné(e) (*m./f.*)	subscriber
l'accès (libre) (*m.*)	(free) access
l'accès aux bases de données	access to databases
le chercheur, la chercheuse	user/researcher/searcher
la conversation en direct	direct conversation
le dictionnaire en ligne	online dictionary
le dictionnaire numérique	online dictionary
le diffuseur	broadcaster
le dossier	folder
l'espace web (*m.*)	Web space
le fichier	file
le forfait mensuel	(monthly) subscription fee
le fossé numérique	digital divide
l'inscription par e-mail/mèl/courriel (*f.*)	registration by e-mail
Internet (*m.*)	Internet
l'iPad (*m.*)	iPad

Vocabulary: Thoughts, feelings, communicating, home, travel, science, leisure, and technology

l'iPod (*m.*)	*iPod*
la librairie en ligne	*online bookstore*
le logiciel	*software*
le moteur de recherche	*search engine*
la page d'accueil	*home page*
le podcast	*podcast*
le podcaster	*podcaster*
le podcasting	*podcasting*
la requête	*request, search*
le réseau mondial	*World Wide Web*
le service sans fil	*wireless (service)*
le site web	*website*
le téléchargement	*uploading/downloading*
la téléconférence (vidéo/audio)	*teleconference*
l'utilisateur, l'utilisatrice (*m./f.*)	*user*

Whereas in Europe the English terms *podcast, podcaster,* and *podcasting* are more frequently used, in Canada the following terms are preferred: **baladodiffusion audio/vidéo/radio** (*audio/video/radio podcasting*). Abbreviated versions of the Canadian terms also exist: **balado audio/vidéo/radio/photo**.

There are several terms and spellings for the term *e-mail* in the French-speaking world. In France, the term **email** is favored, whereas **le courriel** is formal.

Une des missions des Nations Unies est de réduire **le fossé numérique** dans les pays en développement.	*One of the missions of the United Nations is to reduce the digital divide in developing countries.*
Grâce à mon **iPad**, j'ai **accès aux bases de données** de mon site universitaire à tout moment.	*Thanks to my iPad, I have access to the university's databases at any time.*
Je consulte Wikipedia pour obtenir un renseignement rapide sur l'histoire de France. Le service est gratuit, mais ils veulent bien accepter des dons.	*I check Wikipedia to get a quick fact about French history. The service is free, but they are happy to accept donations.*
Mon professeur nous donne accès à des **fichiers** sur son **espace web** universitaire.	*My professor gives us access to files on his university website.*
Mes camarades de classe et moi créons des **podcasts** vidéo et nous les diffusons sur YouTube.	*My classmates and I create video podcasts and we broadcast them on YouTube.*
Aucun résultat ne correspond à votre **requête**.	*No result corresponds to your search.*

108 PRACTICE MAKES PERFECT Complete French All-in-One

EXERCICE 5·17

Comment vous servez-vous des technologies de l'information? **How do you use information technologies?** *Complete each sentence with the appropriate noun from the list provided.*

| fichiers | fossé | dictionnaires | sites | utilisateurs |
| abonnés | requête | téléconférences | données | podcaster |

1. Il y a des _____ web qui vous procurent des clips vidéo pour vos cours de français.
2. Les _____ de ces sites paient un forfait mensuel.
3. Sur Internet, on trouve des _____ en ligne pour traduire des mots du français en anglais.
4. Sur un iPod, on peut télécharger des _____ audio ou vidéo de partout dans le monde.
5. Le _____ numérique existe malheureusement dans beaucoup de pays africains.
6. Le _____ doit suivre les règles et le protocole de l'Internet.
7. Les étudiants ont libre accès aux bases de _____ sur les sites de leur université.
8. Il faut simplement que les _____ d'un service s'identifient pour avoir accès à la page d'accueil.
9. Pour trouver un livre à acheter, il est facile de faire une _____ à des librairies en ligne.
10. Dans le monde des affaires et dans les cercles académiques, les _____ permettent la conversation en direct.

EXERCICE 5·18

Que savez-vous sur les technologies de l'information? **What do you know about information technologies?** *Show what you know about the information highway by writing **V** for **vrai** or **F** for **faux** for each statement.*

____ 1. L'iPad est automatiquement équipé de certains logiciels.
____ 2. Le diffuseur d'un podcast sur YouTube doit payer un forfait mensuel.
____ 3. La baladodiffusion est interdite aux étudiants.
____ 4. On peut souvent faire son inscription à des services électroniques par courriel.
____ 5. Le fossé numérique existe surtout en Amérique.

_____ 6. La page d'accueil du site est toujours accessible aux abonnés.

_____ 7. Les étudiants n'envoient jamais de fichiers électroniques à leurs professeurs.

_____ 8. Les requêtes d'un chercheur sont gratuites sur des sites comme Google ou Yahoo.

_____ 9. Les centres d'information des universités offrent généralement accès à Internet sans fil.

_____ 10. Le navigateur Internet bloque automatiquement le téléchargement de documents éducatifs.

Les instructions sur un site web (Instructions on a website)

When you navigate the Net using French-language functions or when you consult Francophone websites, you will encounter numerous instructions as you proceed. Here are some of them:

Accédez au site!	_Proceed to the site!_
Classez!	_Categorize!/Classify!_
Cliquez!	_Click!_
Créez un mot de passe!	_Create a password!_
Envoyez par mail!	_Send by e-mail!_
Fermez!	_Close!_
Gardez le contact!	_Keep in touch!_
Imprimez!	_Print!_
Inscrivez-vous!	_Sign up!/Register!/Enroll!_
Laissez un commentaire!	_Leave a comment!_
Lancez des recherches!	_Start a search!_
Mettez en réseau!	_Broadcast online!_
Partagez!	_Share!_
Publiez votre message!	_Publish your message!_
Réagissez!	_React!_
Recommandez!	_Recommend!_
Restez connectés!	_Stay connected!_
Tapez votre message!	_Type your message!_
Validez!	_Validate!_

Remember that in French instructions on a website may be expressed with infinitive forms in lieu of imperative forms: for example, **accéder** may replace **accédez**. Here are some verbal expressions that can be used for instructions:

ajouter	_add_
annuler	_cancel_
conserver le contenu	_keep/save the content_
éditer	_edit_
modifier	_modify_
afficher le billet	_post the entry_
rechercher	_search_
répondre	_answer_

signaler un abus	report abuse
supprimer	*delete*
terminer	*finish*
valider	*validate*

EXERCICE 5·19

***Que faire?* What should I do?** *Show that you will know what to do when instructed by matching the French and English instructions.*

_____ 1. Publier   a. Close
_____ 2. Rechercher   b. Cancel
_____ 3. Cliquer   c. Save
_____ 4. Ajouter   d. Search
_____ 5. Taper   e. Delete
_____ 6. Fermer   f. Print
_____ 7. Annuler   g. Click
_____ 8. Imprimer   h. Type
_____ 9. Supprimer   i. Add
_____ 10. Conserver   j. Publish

EXERCICE 5·20

***Dans quel ordre?* What is the right order?** *Write letters **A** through **F** on the lines provided to show in what order you are likely to encounter the following instructions on a website.*

_____ 1. Créez un mot de passe!
_____ 2. Publiez votre message!
_____ 3. Modifiez votre message!
_____ 4. Inscrivez-vous!
_____ 5. Terminez!
_____ 6. Tapez votre message!

Le langage Internet (Internet language)

The Internet serves millions of people all over the world and many websites can be accessed in a variety of languages, whereas others are accessed in the specific language of the broadcaster. To access a Francophone website that does not allow you to change the language, you need some key French vocabulary. Here are some frequently used terms related to the Internet:

l'abonné(e) (*m./f.*)	*subscriber*
l'abonnement (*m.*)	*subscription*
accéder	*to access*
l'adresse (*f.*)	*address*
l'archive (*f.*)	*archive*
l'application (*f.*)	*application*
l'arobase (*m./f.*)	*@ symbol*
la barre latérale	*tool bar*
le champ	*field*
cliquer	*to click*
le commentaire	*comment*
la chronologie	*timeline*
le compte de messagerie	*messaging account*
désabonner (se)	*to unsubscribe*
désactiver	*to deactivate*
le/la destinataire	*recipient, receiver*
en ligne	*online*
le favori	*favorite*
le fichier	*file*
le fournisseur Internet, le fournisseur d'accès	*(Internet) service provider*
l'hébergement (*m.*)	*hosting*
l'horodatage (*m.*)	*timestamping*
l'icône d'Internet (*f.*)	*Internet icon*
l'icône du son	*sound icon*
l'internaute (*m./f.*)	*Net surfer*
le lien	*link*
le livre numérique	*online/electronic book, e-book*
le logiciel (*m.*)	*software*
le média social	*social media*
le mot de passe	*password*
le navigateur	*browser*
le nom de domaine	*domain name*
le nom d'utilisateur	*(user) name*
le nombre de caractères	*number of characters*
la notification	*notification*
l'onglet (*m.*)	*thumbnail*
les outils (*m.pl.*)	*tools*
la page d'accueil	*home page*
le pirate	*hacker*
pirater	*to hack*
la police	*font*
la poubelle	*wastebasket/trash/recycle bin*
le prénom	*first name*
le profil	*profile*
sauvegarder	*to save*
le serveur	*server*
la souris	*mouse*
le sujet/le thème	*topic, theme*

la Toile	Web
le tweet	tweet
tweeter	to tweet
le tweeteur	tweet user
le twitto	tweet
l'utilisateur (*m.*)	user

Note that the French word for the @ symbol currently has several spellings (**arobase**, **arobas**, **arrobas**, **arobace**) and two pronunciations (with or without the final **s** sound). Although originally masculine, it is also used in the feminine.

Chaque **adresse** électronique comprend un **arobase**.	Every electronic address includes an at symbol.
Cherche les **outils** sur **la barre latérale**!	Find the tools on the tool bar!
Deux des caractères dans **le mot de passe** doivent être des chiffres.	Two of the characters in the password must be numbers.
Je lis un **livre numérique** sur mon iPad.	I'm reading an e-book on my iPad.
Écrivez votre prénom et votre nom dans les **champs** appropriés!	Write your first name and your last name in the appropriate fields!

EXERCICE
5·21

Reconnaissez-vous le langage Internet? **Do you recognize Internet language?** *Write* ***V*** *for* ***vrai*** *or* ***F*** *for* ***faux*** *for each statement.*

_____ 1. On ne peut jamais changer son nom d'utilisateur.

_____ 2. L'icône du son est un haut-parleur (*loudspeaker*).

_____ 3. Google, G-mail et AOL offrent des comptes de messagerie.

_____ 4. Le destinataire d'un message envoie le message.

_____ 5. Tous les mots de passe sont exclusivement des nombres.

_____ 6. Dans une adresse électronique, il y a une arobase.

_____ 7. Microsoft n'offre pas de choix de police aux utilisateurs.

_____ 8. Avant d'envoyer un mél, il faut absolument mettre le sujet du message dans le champ approprié.

_____ 9. Les services d'interaction sociale vous demandent généralement de publier votre profil.

_____ 10. Pour modifier la police, trouvez la barre latérale et les outils.

VOCABULAIRE

l'accès haut-débit (m.)	high-speed Internet access	une adresse IP	an Internet protocol address
un administrateur, une administratrice de site	a webmaster	les autoroutes de l'information (m.pl.)	information highways
une adresse URL	a URL	une bibliothèque numérique	a digital library
un blog	a blog	naviguer	to browse
un domaine	a domain	une page d'accueil	a home page
une fenêtre	a window	une page Web	a Web page
un fil RSS	an RSS feed	un pirate	a hacker
une foire aux questions (FAQ)	frequently asked questions (FAQ)	rechercher	to search
		un site Web	a website
un fournisseur d'accès	an access provider	un serveur	a server (Internet)
glisser-déposer	to drag and drop	un signet	a bookmark
un(e) internaute	a cybernaut, a Web user	surfer	to surf
		la Toile	the World Wide Web
un moteur de recherche	a search engine	le Web 2.0 (Web deux point zéro)	Web 2.0

EXERCICE 5·22

Je parle le langage Internet. **I speak the Internet language.** *Complete each sentence with one of the following words.*

la poubelle   la chronologie   caractères   l'arobase   archives

l'icône   fournisseur   numérique   prénom   d'utilisateur

1. Où est _____ du son? —Là, sur l'écran!
2. Cherche _____ sur ton clavier, en haut à gauche!
3. Tu ne veux pas ce fichier? Mets-le à _____ !
4. AOL est un grand _____ Internet.
5. Je veux voir mon document en format chronologique. Où est l'icône pour _____ ?
6. Cet auteur a publié un livre _____ .
7. Pour accéder à ce site, il faut un mot de passe de huit _____ .
8. Dans un profil, on met généralement son _____ , son nom et son adresse.
9. Ce nom _____ est déjà pris; il faut en choisir un autre.
10. Pour conserver ce dossier, mets-le aux _____ !

Les multifonctions d'un téléphone mobile (The many uses of a cell phone)

With the amazing evolution and integration of communication technologies, cell phones have assumed many different functions. In addition to receiving and making phone calls and text messages, they store data, text, pictures, and music; they are equipped with cameras and navigation software, and they can give you access to the Internet. Here are some frequently used terms:

l'accès aux cours de la Bourse (*m.*)	*access to stock exchange rates*
l'achat de billets (*m.*)	*ticket purchase*
l'appel téléphonique (*m.*)	*phone call*
l'application (*f.*)	*application/app*
le chat	*chat*
le clavier (virtuel)	*(virtual) keyboard*
un communiqué de presse (*m.*)	*news release*
la dépêche	*flash news/update*
l'envoi de messages (*m.*)	*messaging*
les horaires des séances de cinéma (*m.pl.*)	*movie schedules*
les horaires de transport	*transportation schedules*
l'innovation (*f.*)	*innovation*
les journaux télévisés (*m.pl.*)	*televised news*
le lien avec...	*link with . . .*
la liste de lectures	*playlist*
la messagerie (instantanée)	*instant messaging/IM*
le partage de documents	*document sharing*
la photographie, la photo	*photography, photo/photograph*
la réception de messages	*message reception/receiving*
le service météo	*weather report*
le smartphone	*smartphone*
SMS	*texting*
le système de navigation	*navigation (GPS) system*
le téléphone mobile/cellulaire/portable	*cell phone*
la touche virtuelle	*virtual key*
l'usage (*m.*)	*use*

Ma sœur m'envoie des **photos** électroniquement par son **ordiphone**.	*My sister sends me pictures electronically with her smartphone.*
Cherche **les horaires** de bus!	*Look for the bus schedules!*
Où est ce restaurant? Demande à ton **smartphone**!	*Where is this restaurant? Ask your smartphone!*
Quelles sont les chansons les plus récentes dans ta **liste de lecture**?	*What are the most recent songs in your playlist?*
Il y a **une dépêche** sur la grève à Paris!	*There is flash news/a news update about the strike in Paris!*

Vocabulary: Thoughts, feelings, communicating, home, travel, science, leisure, and technology **115**

EXERCICE 5·23

Que peut-on faire avec un ordiphone? What can you do with a smartphone?
Complete each sentence with a word from the following list.

innovation   chat   lectures   billets

virtuel   touche   photographie   applications

1. Un smartphone est équipé d'_____ pour avoir accès à toutes sortes de services comme la messagerie.

2. Le smartphone est une _____ du vingt et unième siècle.

3. Un smartphone a un clavier _____.

4. Le smartphone permet le _____ en ligne.

5. L'utilisateur de le smartphone peut acheter des _____ de cinéma en ligne.

6. Beaucoup d'utilisateurs de le smartphone ont une liste de _____ qui leur permet d'écouter leur musique.

7. La _____ est une autre application importante de le smartphone: elle permet de prendre et d'envoyer des photos.

8. La _____ virtuelle permet de passer d'une photo à l'autre ou d'une application à l'autre.

EXERCICE 5·24

Que peut-on et que ne peut-on PAS faire avec un ordiphone? What can you do and NOT do with a smartphone? *Write **V** for **vrai** or **F** for **faux** for each statement.*

_____ 1. On peut avoir des renseignements sur la météo.

_____ 2. On peut envoyer des messages et des photos à des amis.

_____ 3. On peut regarder les journaux télévisés.

_____ 4. On peut imprimer un document.

_____ 5. On peut faire des appels téléphoniques pendant le trajet en avion.

_____ 6. On peut regarder un film dans la salle d'attente de l'aéroport.

_____ 7. On peut naviguer sur Internet.

_____ 8. On peut trouver une adresse et des directions.

L'actualité et les nouvelles (Current events and news)

Current events and news broadcasts have been revolutionized by twenty-first-century technologies. Not only can we obtain news reports from major networks and newspapers online, but the Internet and integrated phone technologies make it possible for almost anyone to contribute to the reporting of current events and news by sending pictures or videos directly to television networks and Internet sites.

l'actualité locale (f.)	local news
l'actualité nationale	national news
le bulletin (mensuel/hebdomadaire)	(monthly/weekly) newsletter
la chaîne/la station (de télévision)	(television) station/channel
le citoyen (la citoyenne) reporter	citizen reporter
le contenu amateur	amateur content
le contenu télévisuel	television content
la dépêche	wire/flash news, news update
le forum (d'idées)	forum (of ideas)
l'heure de grande écoute (f.)	peak viewing/listening hours, prime time
l'internaute (m./f.)	Internet user
le journal en ligne	online newspaper
les médias (m.pl.)	media
la mise en ligne	broadcasting
le partage de documents	document sharing
la photo(graphie); la photographie	photo(graph); photography
le reportage (non-censuré)	(unedited) report
la soumission d'un fichier	file submission
le témoignage	testimony
le témoin	witness
la vidéo	video

L'actualité locale m'intéresse moins que l'actualité nationale.
Local news interests me less than national news.

Dans le train pour aller au travail, je lis le journal en ligne.
On the train on my way to work, I read online news.

Le témoin d'un cyclone envoie sa vidéo à la chaîne de télévision.
The witness of a cyclone sends his video film to the TV station.

Le contenu mis en ligne par ce citoyen reporter est excellent.
The material put online by this citizen reporter is excellent.

J'ai créé ce site web pour y afficher un forum d'idées.
I created this website to post a forum of ideas (on it).

EXERCICE 5·25

Les actualités. **Current events.** *Complete each sentence with a word from the following list.*

en ligne   reporter   témoins   bulletins   reportages   heures   fichier   partages

1. Un _____ audiovisuel est parfois accepté et mis en ligne par une chaîne de télévision.

2. Le témoignage d'un citoyen _____ peut être précieux s'il est authentique et validé.

3. Les médias invitent les _____ d'un accident à faire soumission de documents audiovisuels.

4. Les internautes font souvent des _____ de documents comme les podcasts et les photos.

5. Des groupes d'internautes se forment pour publier des _____ mensuels sur un sujet particulier.

6. Aux _____ de grande écoute, toutes les chaînes de télévision et les stations de radio diffusent des dépêches.

7. Sur Internet, on peut voir des _____ non-censurés.

8. Les photos du mariage du prince William ont été rapidement mises _____.

EXERCICE 5·26

Quelle est la définition? What is the definition? *Identify the definition of each phrase and write the corresponding letter on the line provided.*

_____ 1. une nouvelle récente	a. le partage
_____ 2. ce qui se passe dans la région	b. l'internaute
_____ 3. en ligne	c. les médias
_____ 4. chaque mois	d. amateur
_____ 5. celui/celle qui navigue sur Internet	e. l'actualité locale
_____ 6. non-professionnel	f. sur Internet
_____ 7. la télévision, les journaux, la presse	g. mensuel
_____ 8. l'acte de donner et de recevoir	h. la dépêche

La technologie et les médias sociaux (Technology and social media)

Terms related to social media are as new as the technologies from which they originate. To invite you to venture into the world of Francophone social media, we have gathered some frequently used terms encountered in Francophone magazine and newspaper articles as well as on websites and blogs.

Nouns

l'activité ludique (f.)	*fun (gamelike) activity*
l'affichage sur le web	*posting*
le billet/la note/l'article (m.)	*note (on a blog)*
le blog/le blogue	*blog*
le blogueur, la blogueuse	*blogger*
le commentaire	*comment*
la connaissance	*knowledge*
la conversation	*conversation*
la création	*creation*
le dialogue	*dialogue*
l'esprit de collaboration (m.)	*collaborative spirit*
le groupe	*group*
l'hyperlien (m.)	*hyperlink*
l'individu (m.)	*individual*
l'intelligence collective (f.)	*collective intelligence*
l'interaction sociale (f.)	*social networking*
la mise en page	*the page layout*
la modification	*modification*
le multimédia	*multimedia*
l'organisation (f.)	*organization*
le renseignement	*(piece of) information*

Pour certains **blogueurs**, **le blog** est un journal intime.

For certain bloggers, the blog is a diary.

Pour d'autres **individus**, **le blog** est un lieu de rencontre virtuel.

For other individuals, the blog is a virtual meeting place.

Le créateur d'un blog peut proposer un sujet de discussion et donner des **renseignements** à ce sujet.

The creator of a blog can propose a topic for discussion and give information on that topic.

Certains blogueurs postent **des billets** à longueur de journée. Ils sont en ordre chronologique.

Some bloggers post notes all day long. They are in chronological order.

Les blogues permettent à **l'intelligence collective** de résoudre des problèmes ou d'organiser des activités.

Blogs allow the collective intelligence to solve problems and organize activities.

Verbs

ajouter	*to add*
avertir	*to warn*
bloguer	*to blog*
créer	*to create*
demander conseil	*to ask for advice*
divertir	*to entertain*
donner conseil	*to give advice*
exposer un sujet	*to expose a topic*
interagir	*to interact*
modifier	*to modify*
poster	*to post*
publier	*to publish*
renseigner	*to inform*
résoudre un problème	*to solve a problem*
s'exprimer	*to express oneself*
soulever un problème	*to bring up a problem*

Les médias sociaux sont très populaires car **ils divertissent** les participants.	Social media are very popular because they entertain participants.
Sur un blog, on peut partager ses connaissances et **résoudre des problèmes**.	On a blog, we can share our knowledge and solve problems.
Un individu peut **demander conseil** à des milliers de gens.	An individual can ask the advice of thousands of people.
J'aime **interagir** avec beaucoup de gens pour résoudre des problèmes.	I like interacting with a lot of people in order to solve problems.
Les services d'interaction sociale Facebook et Twitter permettent **soulever des problèmes**.	The social network sites Facebook and Twitter allow us to bring up issues.

EXERCICE 5·27

Que savez-vous? **What do you know?** *Write **V** for **vrai** or **F** for **faux** for each statement.*

_____ 1. Un site d'interaction sociale permet à l'individu de rester en contact avec d'anciens et de nouveaux amis.

_____ 2. Sur un site d'interaction sociale, les gens peuvent s'exprimer librement.

_____ 3. On peut afficher seulement un message par jour sur un site comme Twitter.

_____ 4. Sur un site comme Facebook, on peut avoir des conversations avec beaucoup d'amis tous les jours.

_____ 5. Un blog est créé exclusivement pour demander conseil.

_____ 6. Un affichage d'un article n'est pas permis sur un blog.

_____ 7. La mise en page d'un blog peut être enrichie avec des photos et des hyperliens.

_____ 8. L'internaute qui visite un blog peut généralement modifier la mise en page du blog.

_____ 9. Beaucoup de créateurs de blog permettent que les visiteurs laissent des commentaires.

_____ 10. Les billets qu'on ajoute à un blog ne sont pas en ordre chronologique.

EXERCICE 5·28

Les sites d'interaction sociale. **Social networking sites.** *Write the letter of the appropriate completion for each blank space.*

a. photos   b. sociaux   c. sites   d. profil   e. virtuelle

Les réseaux (1) _____ sont des (2) _____ Internet. Ils forment une communauté (3) _____ pour des individus qui ont des intérêts en commun. Les membres d'un site doivent créer un (4) _____. Alors ils peuvent se connecter avec les autres membres par des courriels, des (5) _____ et des activités en ligne.

Building sentences ·6·

It is important to understand the difference between a phrase and a sentence. They are different in nature and serve different purposes. English and French have many similarities such as common vocabulary words derived from Latin. However, when it comes to word order, French and English sentences sometimes differ. Let's compare examples of the syntax of French and English sentences.

What is a phrase?

A phrase consists of more than one word but does not have the subject + verb organization of a sentence.

> one or more words excluding a verb → phrase
> subject + predicate (including verb) → sentence

Some phrases are formulas used frequently in social situations. Other phrases are common sayings or proverbs. Notice that they do not have a subject + verb structure:

À ce soir.	*See you tonight.*
Pas maintenant.	*Not now.*
la prunelle de mes yeux	*the apple of my eyes*

What is a sentence?

Unlike a phrase, a sentence is defined as a grammatical unit. To build this unit in French, you need nouns, verbal structures, object pronouns, adverbs, etc.—elements you may have previously learned. Think of these elements as the blocks that help you build a structure, the sum of the pieces of a whole that has a meaning of its own. A sentence includes a *subject*—a word or a group of words that tell you what or whom the sentence is about—and a *predicate*—a word or words that tell you something about the subject. Spelling and punctuation require a capital letter to start a sentence and a period to indicate the end of the message.

> On se verra ce soir. *We will see each other tonight.*

This is a sentence because there is a subject (**on**) and a predicate (**se verra ce soir**), as well as the verb **verra**.

> Elle surveille à ses enfants. *She watches her children.*

This is a sentence because there is a subject (**elle**) and a predicate (**surveille à ses enfants**), as well as the verb **surveille**.

In addition, in this sentence, the verb has an indirect object (**à ses enfants**).

121

Declarative sentences

According to the function they perform, sentences are classified in categories. First, we will study the category of *declarative sentences*. A declarative sentence (from the Latin ***declarare***) makes an affirmative or negative statement about a subject. A declarative sentence communicates information; it does not ask a question, it does not express exclamations, nor does it give a command. A declarative sentence consists of the following elements:

subject + predicate
Le pilote + atterrit sur la piste.
Le pilote atterrit sur la piste.   *The pilot lands (is landing) on the runway.*
Le pilote a atterri sur la piste.   *The pilot landed on the runway.*
Le pilote atterrira sur la piste.   *The pilot will land on the runway.*

All three of these examples are simple declarative sentences with one subject and one verb. Note that the tense of the verb in each example varies from one sentence to the next, using present, past, and future tenses. Now consider the following sentence and note how it meets the requirements of a declarative sentence:

Elle n'aime pas le bruit.   *She does not like noise.*

It is a sentence. It includes a subject: **elle**, and a predicate including the verb: **aime**. It makes a negative statement about the subject **elle**. It is not a question, nor is it a command.

Now consider the following sentences and note that they all meet the subject + verb requirements of a declarative sentence, that the verb in each sentence is either in the affirmative or negative form, and that the verb is in various tenses of the *indicative mood*:

Nous partons à quatre heures.   *We leave at four o'clock.*
Nous ne sommes pas partis hier.   *We did not leave yesterday.*
Nous partirons demain.   *We will leave tomorrow.*

partons   present tense *indicative mood*
ne sommes pas partis   passé composé of the *indicative mood*
partirons   future tense of the *indicative mood*

In a declarative sentence, the subject of the verb may be a *simple subject* as in the previous examples, or it may be a *compound subject*. A compound subject consists of two or more subjects. These subjects are joined by a coordinating conjunction such as **et** (*and*), and **ou** (*or*). They govern the same verb.

Jean, Paul **et** Raymond vont à Nice.   *Jean, Paul, **and** Raymond go to Nice.*
Gérard **ou** Arthur va venir me chercher.   *Gerard **or** Arthur is going to pick me up.*

EXERCICE
6·1

Translate the following sentences into French.

1. My brother is very young. _____
2. He is eighteen years old. _____
3. His name is Marc. _____

4. I called him yesterday. _____

5. He was not home. _____

6. He will answer me soon. _____

Underline the subject of each sentence and circle the verb.

1. Lili et Mélanie jouent ensemble.
2. Leur maman fait à manger.
3. Le papa travaille jusqu'à dix-huit heures.
4. Les dessins animés à la télé sont finis.
5. Le poulet rôtit dans le four.
6. Les petites filles se lavent les mains.

Word order in affirmative declarative sentences

The order of words within a simple French declarative sentence is often the same as the word order in an English sentence. However, it will differ when the sentence includes object pronouns, adjectives, adverbs, and adverbial phrases (see subsequent units).

Simple declarative sentences with direct object nouns

In English and in French alike, the natural word order of simple sentences (sentences limited to subject, verb, and object noun) is as follows:

subject + verb + object noun
Marie + loves + Paul.
Marie aime Paul.

Frequently, pronouns take the place of nouns. Just like nouns, they can play the role of subject or object in the sentence. (See Chapter 26 for more on personal pronouns.) In the following examples, the subjects are pronouns:

Tu appelles Jean.	*You call John.*
Elle lave la vaisselle.	*She washes the dishes.*

In the previous sentences, the following syntactical elements can be identified:

- **Tu** and **Elle** are the subjects of the verbs. They are personal pronouns and represent who completes the action of the verb.

- **Appelles** and **lave** are the verbs. They are in the present tense and represent the action that takes place.
- **Jean** and **la vaisselle** are the direct objects. They are the person or thing receiving the action of the verb.

Now consider the following sentence and note its syntactical elements:

Elise appellera Marie.   *Elise will call Marie.*

- **Elise** is the subject of the verb. The subject here is a noun and represents who completes the action of the verb.
- **Appellera** is the verb. It is in the future tense and represents the action that will take place.
- **Marie** is the direct object. She is the person who receives the action of the verb.

EXERCICE 6·3

Identify the subject in each sentence by writing S, the verb by writing V, and the object by writing O under each element, respectively.

EXAMPLE   Le chat attrape la souris.
                 S   V   O

1. Le contrôleur demande les billets.

2. Les passagers ont composté leurs billets.

3. Je lis mon livre.

4. J'admire les illustrations.

5. Mon voisin regarde le journal.

6. Il parle à sa femme.

EXERCICE 6·4

In the previous exercise, were the subjects nouns or pronouns? Write N for noun and P for pronoun on the lines provided.

1. _____   4. _____
2. _____   5. _____
3. _____   6. _____

Declarative sentences with direct and indirect object nouns

In every language, words must be arranged in the proper and logical order to avoid misunderstandings and to express ideas clearly. Consider the following declarative sentence that includes a *direct object* and an *indirect object*:

subject + verb + direct object + indirect object
Rémy + a acheté + un livre + à son père.
Rémy bought a book for his father.

Note in the previous sentences that the word order is the same in both the French and English. (*Father* is the object of a preposition.) Now consider this English variation: *Rémy bought his father a book.* The order of object nouns in this sentence has been reversed, which cannot be done in French. This demonstrates that word order is *more* flexible in the English sentence than in the French sentence when it comes to direct and indirect objects.

Is there a direct object in the following sentences? If there is, underline it; if not, write None.

1. Nous fêtons l'anniversaire de Viviane.
2. Ses amis ont organisé une fête chez Dorine.
3. Les invités vont arriver à dix-neuf heures.
4. Ils vont tous féliciter Viviane.
5. On servira le repas sur la terrace de Dorine.
6. Dorine allumera la chaîne hifi.

Complete each sentence with an appropriate direct object from the following list to find out what car this couple will buy.

son mari / des sièges de velours / les voitures confortables / un rêve / une voiture/
la performance de la voiture

1. Mimi et Jojo veulent _____
2. Mimi préfère _____
3. Mais Jojo a _____
4. Il imagine _____ sur l'autoroute.
5. Mimi, elle, imagine _____
6. Elle persuade _____ d'acheter un monospace.

EXERCICE 6·7

Complete each French sentence with the direct and/or indirect object(s).

1. *The teacher shows a movie to the students.*

   Le professeur montre _____.

2. *Mr. Dumont gives a grade to his students.*

   M. Dumont donne _____.

3. *The students do their assignment.*

   Les élèves font _____.

4. *The children bring their work to their parents.*

   Les enfants apportent _____.

5. *Some parents give a little gift to their children.*

   Certains parents donnent _____.

EXERCICE 6·8

Place the following sentence fragments in the appropriate order to find out a few facts about Jean and Lucie. Be sure to use the appropriate spelling and punctuation.

1. habite / Jean / la ville de Paris

   _____

2. est / Lucie / la femme / de Jean

   _____

3. à Jean et à Lucie / les parents de Jean / une maison / achètent

   _____

4. partent / Lucie et Jean / en lune de miel / aujourd'hui

   _____

5. l'annonce / nous avons lu / de leur mariage / dans le journal

   _____

6. vont passer / à Tahiti / une semaine / ils

   _____

EXERCICE 6·9

Translate the following sentences into French.

1. Today my friend Jean and I study French.

2. We already speak French.

3. We always finish our work.

4. We give our work to the teacher.

5. Sometimes I help my friend.

6. He helps me, too.

Word order in negative declarative sentences

Negative sentences must include negative words. To make an affirmative sentence negative, place the word **ne** (or **n'** before a vowel sound) directly before the verb and place the word **pas** directly after the verb.

Michelle joue au basket.	*Michelle plays basketball.*
Michelle **ne** joue **pas** au basket.	*Michelle does **not** play basketball.*
Marius habite à Marseille.	*Marius lives in Marseille.*
Marius **n'**habite **pas** à Marseille.	*Marius does **not** live in Marseille.*

Other negative words and phrases that are used to create negative declarative sentences are: **rien** (*nothing*), **plus** (*no longer*), **jamais** (*never*), **personne** (*nobody*), **ni** (*neither, nor*), and **nulle part** (*nowhere*). They are placed after the verb just like **pas** and also require **ne** or **n'** before the verb.

Je **ne** sais **rien**.	*I do **not** know **anything** (I know **nothing**).*
Nous **ne** partons **jamais** en hiver.	*We **never** leave in the winter.*
Il **ne** veut **plus** fumer.	*He does **not** want to smoke **anymore**.*

Unlike English, two or three negative words can be used in a single French sentence.

Je ne veux **plus jamais rien** faire de mal.	*I do **not ever** want to do **anything** bad **again**.*
Cela ne se fait **jamais nulle part**.	*This should **never** be done **anywhere**.*
Il n'y a **plus personne**.	*There is **nobody** left.*

Building sentences   **127**

EXERCICE 6·10

Write the following sentences in French making sure the negative word used is correct. Use only one negative construction in each sentence.

1. I never buy wine here. _____

2. The clerk is not very kind. _____

3. I do not like to pay high prices. _____

4. The owner never says hello. _____

5. We do not waste our time here. _____

EXERCICE 6·11

Add another negative word that makes sense in the following sentences:

1. Nous n'irons jamais _____ nager dans le lac quand il fera froid.

2. Nous ne ferons plus _____ d'aussi grosses bêtises.

3. Nous n'inviterons jamais _____ ici. C'est notre cachette.

4. Il n'y a plus _____ à voir. Il est tard.

5. Nous ne verrons plus _____ après que le soleil se couchera.

EXERCICE 6·12

Translate the following sentences into French.

1. I threw out my old phone because I did not want it anymore.

_____

2. But I cannot find my new cell phone anywhere.

_____

3. These days I do not remember anything anymore.

_____

4. Well, I cannot call anyone else tonight.

_____

5. I will never again forget to put it back into my purse.

_____

Asking questions

·7·

Interrogative sentences

An *interrogative* sentence serves to ask a question. We use interrogative sentences for different purposes: to obtain information, and to elicit confirmation or denial about something or someone.

Tu peux répondre, n'est-ce pas?	*You can answer, can't you?* (confirmation or denial)
Ginette n'est pas là?	*Is Ginette not there?* (confirmation or denial)
Quelle heure est-il?	*What time is it?* (information)
Où allons-nous?	*Where are we going?* (information)

To communicate effectively, you often must be able to ask precise questions in order to get the information you seek; furthermore you must understand a variety of questions in order to give others the information they seek from you. Consider the following sentence and the many questions that can be asked about it. Note the word order and the different question words used.

Chaque jour les fleurs devenaient de plus en plus belles grâce à l'attention diligente que papa leur accordait.	*Each day, the flowers grew more and more beautiful thanks to the diligent care Dad gave them.*
Est-ce que les fleurs devenaient de plus en plus belles?	*Did the flowers grow more and more beautiful?*
Les fleurs devenaient de plus en plus belles, n'est-ce pas?	*The flowers became more and more beautiful, did they not?*
Quand est-ce que les fleurs devenaient de plus en plus belles?	*When did the flowers grow more and more beautiful?*
Qu'est-ce qui devenait de plus en plus beau?	*What grew more and more beautiful?*
Pourquoi est-ce que les fleurs devenaient de plus en plus belles?	*Why did the flowers grow more and more beautiful?*
Grâce à qui est-ce que les fleurs devenaient de plus en plus belles?	*Thanks to whom did the flowers grow more and more beautiful?*

Interrogative sentences and intonation

In French the intonation or rising pitch at the end of a sentence signals for the listener that a question is being asked. This manner of asking a question is familiar and preferred in oral interactions. To transcribe this oral question into writing, a question mark helps identify an interrogative sentence. Sometimes a *yes* or *no* answer may suffice as is shown in the following examples:

129

Le train est arrivé? —Oui. / Non. *Did the train arrive? —Yes. / No.*
Tu passes un examen? —Oui. / Non. *Are you taking an exam? —Yes. / No.*
Elle ne viendra pas aujourd'hui? *Will she not come today? —Yes. / No.*
  —Oui. / Non.

Other times a question solicits specific information as in the following examples:

Qui a peint ce portrait? —Monet. *Who painted this portrait? —Monet.*
À quelle heure on dîne? —À huit heures. *At what time do we have dinner?*
    —At eight o'clock.
Où tu vas? —À la pharmacie. *Where are you going? —To the pharmacy.*

Affirmative interrogative sentences

There are several ways to communicate a question. One way to create an interrogative sentence is to use an affirmative sentence and end it with a rising inflection. The intonation alone communicates a question in spoken language; a question mark follows the interrogative sentence in written texts.

declarative sentence + ? → interrogative sentence

Note how the message of a straightforward declarative sentence changes when it becomes a question:

Le magasin est fermé. *The store is closed.*
Le magasin est fermé? *The store is closed?*

EXERCICE 7·1

Rewrite each statement, changing it to a question by using the appropriate punctuation.

1. Mon copain est en retard. _____
2. Tu as ma liste. _____
3. Le passager est patient. _____
4. Nous attendons. _____
5. Il y a un taxi au coin. _____
6. Il fait chaud ici. _____

EXERCICE 7·2

Using appropriate punctuation and capitalization, compose questions with the following sentence fragments, making sure to follow the word order of a declarative sentence.

1. les instructions / tu as compris
   _____
2. à ton avis / étaient claires / elles
   _____

3. à faire ce travail / on va / arriver

4. que ce ne sera pas trop difficile / certain / tu es

5. ce soir / commencer / tu veux

6. d'échouer / tu ne crains pas

Negative interrogative sentences

Another way of forming a question is to start with a negative declarative sentence. Add a question mark to a negative declarative sentence and as a result you have an interrogative sentence.

negative declarative sentence + ? → interrogative sentence

Vous ne travailliez pas pour nous.	*You were not working for us.*
Vous ne travailliez pas pour nous?	*Were you not working for us?*

This type of construction (**ne...pas**) is used when the questioner expects an affirmative answer or an affirmation. Consider the following sentences and note that a *yes* answer starts with **oui** when the interrogative sentence is affirmative; it starts with *si* when the interrogative sentence is negative.

affirmative interrogative sentence: oui (*yes*)

Ils **vont** au cours? —**Oui**, mais plus tard!	***Do*** *they* ***go*** *to class? —**Yes**, but later!*
Vous **avez** de l'argent? —**Oui**, un peu.	***Do*** *you* ***have*** *some money? —**Yes**, a little.*

negative interrogative sentence: si (*yes*)

Ils **ne vont pas** au cours? —**Si**, mais plus tard!	***Don't*** *they* ***go*** *to class? —**Yes**, but later!*
Vous **n'avez pas** d'argent? —**Si**, un peu.	*You* ***do not have*** *any money? —**Yes**, a little.*

Adverbs such as **encore** or **toujours** can be added to **pas** to build interrogative sentences.

pas encore	*not yet*
pas toujours	*not always*
pas ici	*not here*
pas bien	*not well*

And as always, by adding a question mark, the declarative sentence then becomes an interrogative sentence.

Ils **ne** sont **pas encore** ici.	*They are **not** here **yet**. (declarative)*
Ils **ne** sont **pas encore** ici?	*They are **not** here **yet**? (interrogative)*
Tu **n'**es **pas toujours** en forme.	*You are **not always** in shape. (declarative)*
Tu **n'**es **pas toujours** en forme?	*You are **not always** in shape? (interrogative)*
Cette montre **ne** marche **pas** bien.	*This watch does **not** work **well**. (declarative)*
Cette montre **ne** marche **pas** bien?	*This watch does **not** work **well**? (interrogative)*

As discussed in Chapter 6, other negative expressions can be used instead of **ne...pas** to build interrogative sentences. They are: **ne...plus** (*no longer*), **ne...rien** (*nothing/not anything*), **ne...jamais** (*never*), **ne...personne** (*nobody/not anybody*).

Asking questions **131**

Elle **ne** joue **plus** au piano?	She does **not** play the piano **anymore**?
Elle **ne** joue **jamais** au piano?	She **never** plays the piano?
Elle **ne** voit **rien**?	She does **not** see **anything**?
Elle **ne** voit **personne**?	She does **not** see **anyone**?

EXERCICE 7·3

*Answer each question with **oui, si, pas encore**, or **pas ici** as you see fit on the lines provided.*

1. Tu travailles? _____

2. Tu ne gagnes pas trop d'argent? _____

3. Tu n'as pas suivi de cours de français? _____

4. Tu vas être promu? _____

5. Tu es fiancé? _____

6. Tu ne vas pas te marier? _____

EXERCICE 7·4

Use one of the following negative expressions to complete each question.

pas / plus / personne / rien / jamais

1. Où est ton livre? Tu ne sais _____ ?

2. Tu as toujours tes affaires? Tu ne les oublies _____ ?

3. Tu voudrais rester ici? Tu ne peux _____ étudier? Tu es trop fatigué?

4. Tu sors avec des amis ce soir? Tu ne veux voir _____ ce soir? Tu restes à la maison?

5. Tu veux prendre un petit café avant de rentrer? Non, tu ne veux _____ ?

Interrogative sentences with est-ce que

There are several ways to communicate a simple question in French. We have previously seen that one way to create an interrogative sentence is to use an affirmative sentence and end it with a rising inflection. Another way to create an interrogative sentence in French is to place the phrase **est-ce que** before the declarative sentence.

est-ce que + declarative sentence → interrogative sentence

Le magasin est fermé.	The store is closed.
Est-ce que le magasin est fermé?	Is the store closed?

Compare the following French and English interrogative sentences and note that the structure in the French sentence is always the same. The structure in the English sentence varies depending on the tense used and depending on whether the verb *to be* or *to have* is a part of the structure.

est-ce que/qu' + subject + predicate   **verb** (*to be/to have*) + **subject** + **predicate**

Est-ce qu'il ne fait pas beau?   *Is the weather not nice?*
Est-ce que vous êtes triste?   *Are you sad?*
Est-ce qu'elle ne va pas se marier?   *Is she not going to get married?*
Est-ce que tu as mangé?   *Have you eaten?*

est-ce que/qu' + subject + predicate   **helping verb** (*do/does/did/will*) + **subject** + **predicate**

Est-ce que vous faites du ski?   *Do you ski?*
Est-ce que tu ne me dois pas d'argent?   *Don't you owe me money?*
Est-ce qu'ils ne sont pas arrivés?   *Did they not arrive?*
Est-ce que tu iras les chercheras ?   *Will you pick them up?*

EXERCICE 7·5

Translate each question into French using **est-ce que**.

1. Is the sun shining today?

2. Are we going to the beach?

3. Do you (**tu**) want to have breakfast on the terrace?

4. Will we go swim in the sea after breakfast?

5. Are you (**tu**) still a little sleepy?

6. Do you (**tu**) need a good shower?

Interrogative sentences with inversion

Another way to create interrogative sentences is to use the inversion method. The inverted interrogative structure is somewhat formal but is sometimes used in informal situations, for example, when asking for the time: **Quelle heure est-il?** To create such an interrogative structure, we will once again start with the declarative sentence. It will be important, however, to distinguish between a subject pronoun and a subject noun in the sentence when using this method.

When the subject is a pronoun

If the subject of the verb in the declarative sentence is a personal pronoun, it suffices to invert the subject and the verb while separating the two with a hyphen. The result is an interrogative sentence.

subject pronoun + verb → declarative sentence
verb + subject pronoun → interrogative sentence

Il est fermé.	*It is closed.*
Est-il fermé?	***Is it** closed?*
Elle chantera fort.	*She will sing loud.*
Chantera-t-elle fort?	***Will she sing** loud?*
Nous boirons à ta santé.	*We will drink to your health.*
Boirons-nous à ta santé?	***Will we drink** to your health?*
Vous êtes allés au cinéma.	*You went to the movies.*
Etes-vous allés au cinéma?	***Did you go** to the movies?*
On ne fait pas de bêtises.	*We are not doing anything silly.*
Ne fait-on pas des bêtises?	***Are we not being** silly?*
Il y a beaucoup de gens ici.	*There are a lot of people here.*
Y a-t-il beaucoup de gens ici?	***Are there** a lot of people here?*

You can always invert the subject pronoun and the verb except when the subject pronoun is **je**. The subject pronoun **je** and the verb are only inverted in very rare cases such as in **Puis-je?** (*May I?*) This phrase is commonly used, especially in the service business. **Puis** is a modified form of the verb **pouvoir** (*to be able*). In other cases, the inversion with the pronoun **je** can also be used but only to make an emphatic statement. Look at the following examples:

Puis-je vous aider, monsieur?	***May I** help you, sir?*
Ai-je autant de cheveux gris?	***Do I have** so much gray hair? (sense of humor)*
Vais-je y aller?	***Am I going** to go? (Should I?)*
Dois-je le faire?	***Must I do** it? (emphasis)*
Saurais-je le dire?	***Dare I say** it? (emphasis)*

When the subject is a noun

If the subject of the verb in the declarative sentence is a noun, the subject + verb structure of the declarative sentence will remain the same, but the appropriate subject pronoun that can replace the subject noun is added after the verb and is linked to the verb with a hyphen.

subject noun + verb → declarative sentence
subject noun + verb + - + pronoun → interrogative sentence

Le magasin est fermé.	*The store is closed.*
Le magasin **est-il** fermé?	***Is** the store closed?*

Compare the following declarative and interrogative sentences. Note that the pronoun to be added must have the same gender and number as the noun it completes; therefore it is either **il**, **ils**, **elle**, or **elles**. Also note that whenever a verb ends in a vowel, the letter **-t-** is inserted between the verb and the pronoun; the inserted **-t-** is wrapped between two hyphens.

La maison sera vendue.	*The house will be sold.*
La maison **sera-t-elle** vendue?	***Will** the house be sold?*
(la maison = elle)	
La petite fille va à l'école.	*The little girl goes to school.*
La petite fille **va-t-elle** à l'école?	***Will** the little girl **go** to school?*
(la fille = elle)	
Le marché aux fleurs n'existe plus.	*The flower market no longer exists.*
Le marché aux fleurs **n'existe-t-il** plus?	***Does** the flower market no longer **exist**?*
(le marché = il)	

Les personnes présentes voteront.
Les personnes présentes **voteront-elles**?
(les personnes = elles)

The people in attendance will vote.
***Will** the people in attendance **vote**?*

EXERCICE 7·6

Change the following declarative sentences into questions by using inversion.

1. Marie écoute bien les conseils de sa maman. _____

2. Elle est attentive. _____

3. Les frères jumeaux travaillent ensemble. _____

4. Ils sont inséparables. _____

5. Tu ne vois pas le bus. _____

6. Il faut se dépêcher. _____

Polite phrases in interrogative sentences

To demonstrate courtesy in asking a question, use a phrase such as **Pardon** or **Pardonnez-moi** (*Pardon, Pardon me*), **Excusez-moi** (*Excuse me*), **Excusez-moi de vous déranger** (*Forgive me for interrupting*), or **S'il vous plaît** (*Please*) before the question. Also be sure to use the appropriate title: **monsieur** (*sir*), **madame** (*madam*), or **mademoiselle** (*miss*). Consider the following examples and note the punctuation:

polite phrase + title + verb + subject pronoun + . . . ?

Pardonnez-moi, madame, avez-vous de la monnaie**?**

Pardon me, madam. Do you have change?

S'il vous plaît, monsieur, pouvez-vous ouvrir la porte**?**

Please, sir, could you open the door?

Excusez-moi, mademoiselle, êtes-vous la caissière**?**

Excuse me, miss. Are you the cashier?

EXERCICE 7·7

Play the role of a saleslady and write the following questions in French, in a very polite and formal manner.

1. Do you like this dress, miss? _____

2. Can I recommend a pair of shoes, miss? _____

3. Do you need a scarf, miss?

4. Are you ready to pay, miss?

5. Do you have a credit card, miss?

6. Would you like a bag, miss?

EXERCICE 7·8

Go back to the previous exercise and for each of those questions add one of the following polite phrases: **s'il vous plaît**, **excusez-moi**, **pardonnez-moi**, **pardon**, *or* **excusez-moi de vous déranger**.

1.

2.

3.

4.

5.

6.

EXERCICE 7·9

With the sentence fragments provided write a question using the inversion method and the present tense of the indicative mood.

1. préférer (tu) / un citron pressé / un coca / une bière

2. arriver (vous) cet après-midi / demain

3. désirer (ils) / aller à la plage / nager dans la piscine

4. acheter (nous) le parasol / la chaise-longue / une serviette

5. vouloir (elles) voir un film / dîner au restaurant

6. dormir (vous) dans le lit / sur le canapé

Tag questions

Another way of forming a question both in English and French is to add a "tag" at the end of a declarative sentence.

declarative sentence, + tag + ? → tag question

The tag phrase **n'est-ce pas** is used in all registers of the French language (familiar and formal), but it is more frequently used in formal situations.

Tu as mon sac, + n'est-ce pas + ? → tag question

Cette écharpe est chère, **n'est-ce pas?**	*This scarf is expensive, **isn't it?***
Elle a très bien parlé, **n'est-ce pas?**	*She spoke very well, **did she not?***
Tu nous rejoindras, **n'est-ce pas?**	*You will join us, **won't you?***

However, some other tags are only used in informal spoken communication. In any case, a questioner who poses a tag question expects agreement, not a *no* answer. In French, some common and familiar tags added to declarative sentences to create questions are: **non?** (*no?*), **pas vrai?** (*not true? / right?*), and **tu ne crois pas? / tu ne penses pas?** (*don't you think?*)

La gérante est intelligente, **non?**	*The manager is smart, **isn't she?***
Marc nage bien, **tu ne penses pas?**	*Marc swims very well, **don't you think?***
Cette fille a du talent, **pas vrai?**	*This girl has talent, **right?***

EXERCICE 7·10

Write the letter of the correct answer to each question on the lines provided.

1. Il est intelligent, non? _____
2. Il est grand, tu ne penses pas? _____
3. Tu veux une limonade, non? _____
4. Elles sont américaines, n'est-ce pas? _____
5. Tu viendras demain, pas vrai? _____

a. Non, un thé chaud.
b. Non, canadiennes.
c. Oui, mais le soir.
d. Oui, brillant même.
e. Non, au contraire, il est petit.

EXERCICE 7·11

*Translate the following questions into French using tag phrases. Use **tu** for you.*

1. You like this book, right?

2. You know who wrote it, don't you?

Asking questions **137**

3. This author is good, don't you think?

_____

4. He is a master of suspense, no?

_____

5. You have read his previous book, right?

_____

Complex questions

Questions in which you expect more specific information than a simple choice-answer or a straightforward *yes* or *no* response are referred to as complex questions. They start with an interrogative pronoun, an interrogative adverb, or any other interrogative word or phrase.

Questions with qui

There are several ways to create an interrogative sentence with the interrogative pronoun **qui**. The elements and word order in the sentence will vary according to the function performed by **qui**, which can be either *subject* or *direct object*. The various possible structures for an interrogative sentence introduced by **qui** are as follows:

Qui + verb

In this interrogative sentence, **qui** is the subject and is followed directly by the verb.

Qui était ce monsieur? (**qui** = subject of **était**)	*Who was that gentleman?*
Qui dit cela? (**qui** = subject of **dit**)	*Who says that?*
Qui a compris la leçon? (**qui** = subject of **a compris**)	*Who understood the lesson?*

Qui est-ce qui + verb

In this interrogative sentence, **qui** is the subject, but the word order is the one used in the **est-ce que** method with one difference: The phrase used is **est-ce qui**.

Qui est-ce qui dit cela?	*Who says that?*
Qui est-ce qui a compris?	*Who understood?*
Qui est-ce qui est le plus grand?	*Who is the tallest?*

Qui est-ce que + subject + verb

In this interrogative sentence structure, **qui** is the *direct object*, but the word order is the one used in the **est-ce que** method.

Qui est-ce que tu as vu?	*Whom did you see?*
Qui est-ce que nous inviterons?	*Whom will we invite?*
Qui est-ce que tu préfères?	*Whom do you prefer?*

138 PRACTICE MAKES PERFECT Complete French All-in-One

EXERCICE 7·12

*On the lines provided, write either **qui est-ce qui** or **qui est-ce que** as appropriate.*

1. _____ tu préfères, Rosie ou Chantal?
2. _____ tu inviteras à sortir?
3. _____ va accepter ton invitation?
4. _____ va nous la présenter?
5. _____ va s'asseoir à côté d'elle, toi ou moi?

Qui + interrogative sentence including inversion

In this interrogative sentence, **qui** is also the *direct object*, but the word order is the one used in the inversion method.

Qui Marielle a-t-elle épousé? (**qui** = direct object of **a épousé**)	**Whom** did Marielle marry?
Qui as-tu vu? (**qui** = direct object of **as vu**)	**Whom** did you see?
Qui inviterons-nous? (**qui** = direct object of **inviterons**)	**Whom** will we invite?
Qui avez-vous embauché? (**qui** = direct object of **avez embauché**)	**Whom** did you hire?
Qui aimez-vous le mieux ? (**qui** = direct object of **aimez**)	**Whom** do you love the most?

EXERCICE 7·13

Translate each question and answer into English.

1. Qui as-tu rencontré hier soir? —Un vieil ami.

2. Qui as-tu invité? —La famille.

3. Qui est-ce que Raymond va féliciter? —Son nouvel employé.

4. Qui cherchez-vous? —La vendeuse.

Asking questions   **139**

5. Qui est-ce que tes parents préfèrent? —Moi bien sûr.

6. Qui Suzanne embrasse-t-elle? —Son copain.

EXERCICE 7·14

Complete the following questions using **qui** *with an inversion. Use the formal pronoun* **vous** *for you.*

1. Whom are you calling? (appeler)
   Qui _____?

2. Whom are you inviting? (inviter)
   Qui _____?

3. Whom did you see? (voir)
   Qui _____?

4. Whom do you prefer? (préférer)
   Qui _____?

5. Whom are you going to pick up? (chercher)
   Qui _____?

6. Whom are you going to send back? (renvoyer)
   Qui _____?

Questions with qu'est-ce que and que

The phrase **qu'est-ce que/qu'** as well as the pronoun **que** express *what* and play the role of direct object in a sentence.

Qu'est-ce que/qu' + subject + verb

In this interrogative sentence, the phrase **qu'est-ce que** (*what*) is followed by a subject and a verb.

Qu'est-ce qu'Anne fait? *What is Anne doing?*
Qu'est-ce que tu désires? *What do you want?*
Qu'est-ce que nous allons manger? *What are we going to eat?*

Que/Qu' + verb + subject

In this interrogative sentence, **que** (*what*) is followed by a verb and a subject.

Que **fait** Anne? *What **is** Anne doing?*

(The noun, **Anne**, and the verb, **fait**, have been inverted.)

| Que **désires-tu**? | *What **would you like**?* |
| Qu'**allons-nous** manger? | *What **are we going** to eat?* |

EXERCICE 7·15

Write the letter of the phrase that completes each question on the lines provided.

1. _____ Qu'est-ce que...recevoir comme cadeaux?   a. vous dites
2. _____ Qu'est-ce que...vous offrent?   b. vous faites
3. _____ Qu'est-ce que...quand on vous donne un cadeau? c. vous aimez
4. _____ Qu'est-ce que...pour vous amuser?   d. vous n'aimez pas
5. _____ Qu'est-ce que...faire le jour de votre anniversaire? e. vos parents

EXERCICE 7·16

*Rewrite the questions from the previous exercise using **que/qu'** instead of **qu'est-ce que**.*

1. Qu' _____ ?
2. Que _____ ?
3. Que _____ ?
4. Que _____ ?
5. Que _____ ?

Questions with **qu'est-ce qui**

The phrase **qu'est-ce qui** is used to express *what*. It plays the role of *subject* in the sentence.

Qu'est-ce qui arrive?	***What** is happening?*
Qu'est-ce qui s'est passé?	***What** happened?*
Qu'est-ce qui prouve ce fait?	***What** proves this fact?*

EXERCICE 7·17

*Use **Que/Qu'**, **Qu'est-ce que**, or **Qu'est-ce qui** to complete each question.*

1. _____ regardes-tu?
2. _____ apportes-tu?
3. _____ Joseph aime faire?

Asking questions   141

4. _____ tu vas donner à ta mère?

5. _____ ne va pas?

6. _____ fait-il?

Questions with interrogative adverbs

With the interrogative adverbs **pourquoi** (*why*), **comment** (*how*), **quand** (*when*), **combien de** (*how many/how much*), and **où** (*where*), French uses the following methods to create interrogative sentences:

Interrogative adverb + **est-ce que** + word order of simple declarative sentence

In the following questions, the interrogative adverb is followed by the phrase **est-ce que**, the subject, and the verb.

Pourquoi **est-ce que Patrick n'aime pas** son travail?	*Why **doesn't Patrick like** his work?*
Comment **est-ce que tu vas**?	*How **are you**?*
Quand **est-ce que tu vas** au travail?	*When **are you going** to work?*
Combien de jours **est-ce que tu resteras**?	*How many days **will you stay**?*
Où **est-ce qu'Anne va** avec tous ces livres?	*Where **is Anne going** with all those books?*
Où **est-ce qu'elle habite**?	*Where **does she live**?*

Interrogative adverb + word order appropriate to inversion method

In using this method, apply what you have previously learned about the inversion method (remember not to invert a noun-subject with the verb; instead add a hyphen and a subject pronoun after the verb).

Pourquoi **Patrick n'aime-t-il pas** son travail?	*Why **doesn't Patrick like** his work?*
Comment **vas-tu**?	*How **are you**?*
Quand **vas-tu** au travail?	*When **do you go** to work?*
Combien de jours **resteras-tu**?	*How many days **will you stay**?*
Où **Anne va-t-elle** avec tous ces livres?	*Where **does Anne go** with all these books?*
Où **habite-t-elle**?	*Where **does she live**?*

Interrogative adverb + word order of simple declarative sentence

Using this method means simply adding the interrogative adverb to the declarative sentence and using a higher pitch intonation at the end of the sentence. This is used in very familiar settings only.

Pourquoi **Patrick n'aime pas** son travail?	*Why **doesn't Patrick like** his work?*

Note in the following sentences that the words **comment**, **quand**, **combien de jours**, and **où** can be placed at the head of the question or after the verb:

Comment tu vas?	*How **are you**?*
Tu vas **comment**?	*How **are you**?*
Quand tu vas au travail?	*When **do you go** to work?*
Tu vas au travail **quand**?	*When **do you go** to work?*
Combien de jours tu resteras?	*How many days **will you stay**?*

142 PRACTICE MAKES PERFECT Complete French All-in-One

EXERCICE 7·18

*Arranging the sentence fragments provided in the appropriate order, write questions to be used in familiar settings. Do not use **est-ce que**, and do not make an inversion, but remember to use a question mark.*

1. tu / vas / où / maintenant

2. vas / tu / comment / au travail

3. rentres / quand / tu / aujourd'hui

4. ne manges pas / pourquoi / tu

5. combien de cafés / veux / tu

6. ça / va / comment

EXERCICE 7·19

*Redo each question from the previous exercise, this time using the words provided with the **est-ce que** structure.*

1. tu / vas / où / maintenant

2. vas / tu / comment / au travail

3. rentres / quand / tu / aujourd'hui

4. ne manges pas / pourquoi / tu

5. combien de cafés / veux / tu

6. ça / va / comment

Asking questions

Questions with the adjective quel

Many very common interrogative questions include a form of the adjective **quel**. Here are a few. Note how the form of **quel** changes according to the gender (masculine or feminine) and the number (singular or plural) of the noun it accompanies. As previously seen, there are again three ways to create this type of question: the **est-ce que** method, the inversion method, and the voice pitch method.

Quel train **est-ce que tu prends**?	*Which train **are you taking**?*
Quel train **prends-tu**?	
Quel train **tu prends**?	
Quelle heure **est-ce qu'il est**?	*What time **is it**?*
Quelle heure **est-il**?	
Quelle heure **il est**?	
Quels livres **est-ce que tu as lus**?	*What books **have you read**?*
Quels livres **as-tu lus**?	
Quel livres **tu as lus**?	
Quelles dates **est-ce que tu préfères**?	*What dates **do you prefer**?*
Quelles dates **préfères-tu**?	
Quelles dates **tu préfères**?	

Now consider these examples in which **quel** does not directly precede the noun, and note the word order in this type of interrogative sentence:

Quel + être + subject

Quel + est + ton nom?	*What is your name?*
Quels sont tes numéros de téléphone?	*What are your phone numbers?*
Quelles sont les prévisions météorologiques?	*What is the weather forecast?*
Quelle est ton opinion?	*What is your opinion?*

EXERCICE
7·20

*Translate the following questions into French using the correct form of **quel**.*

1. What time is it? _____

2. What is his date of birth? _____

3. What is her telephone number? _____

4. What is the weather today? _____

5. What are his favorite colors? _____

6. What choice do I have? _____

EXERCICE 7·21

*Begin each question with the appropriate interrogative word **Qui, Quelle, Où, Comment, Que/Qu', Quand**. There may be more than one possible answer.*

1. _____ t'appelles-tu?
2. _____ habites-tu?
3. _____ est la date de ton anniversaire?
4. _____ fais-tu en fin de semaine?
5. _____ étudies-tu le français?
6. _____ utilises-tu l'ordinateur?
7. _____ sont tes amis?
8. _____ pars-tu en vacances?
9. _____ passes-tu tes vacances?
10. _____ t'accompagne?

EXERCICE 7·22

*Write either **où, qu', qu'est-ce qu'**, or **qu'est-ce qui** to complete the following questions.*

1. _____ est-ce que ton copain t'a emmenée hier soir pour ton anniversaire?
2. _____ avez-vous commandé à manger?
3. _____ il t'a offert comme cadeau?
4. _____ t'a plu le plus hier soir au restaurant?
5. Et après, _____ êtes-vous allés?
6. _____ avez-vous fait?

Questions with prepositions

Complex questions sometimes start with prepositions followed by question words; these are used to elicit concrete or fuller responses to a question. As previously seen, there are usually several ways to form a question: the **est-ce que** method, the inversion method, and using intonation in a declarative sentence. The word order in the complex interrogative sentence introduced by a preposition may be as follows:

preposition + interrogative word + est-ce que + declarative sentence

or

preposition + interrogative word + inversion method word order

Asking questions   145

or

preposition + interrogative word + declarative sentence (use of intonation in speaking, use of question mark in writing)

The following is a list of prepositions followed by an interrogative adverb often used to create complex questions:

À qui?	*To whom?*
Avec qui?	*With whom?*
De qui?	*From whom?*
Pour qui?	*For whom?*
D'où?	*From where? / Where from?*
Par où?	*Through where?*
Depuis quand?	*Since when?*
Jusqu'à quand?	*Until when?*
Pendant combien de temps?	*For how long?*
Dans combien de temps?	*When? / In how much time?*

Pour qui est-ce qu'elle achète le bijou?	*For whom does she buy the jewel?*
Pour qui achète-t-elle le bijou?	
Pour qui elle achète le bijou?	

Depuis quand est-ce qu'Anne habite Paris?	*Since when does Anne live in Paris?*
Depuis quand Anne habite-t-elle Paris?	
Depuis quand Anne habite Paris?	

Pendant combien de temps est-ce qu'ils ont attendu?	*For how long did they wait?*
Pendant combien de temps ont-ils attendu?	
Pendant combien de temps ils ont attendu?	

EXERCICE 7·23

*Using **tu** for you and the inversion method, translate the sentences into French.*

1. Where are you from? _____

2. Where are you going? _____

3. Since when do you study French? _____

4. When are you going to finish this exercise? _____

5. Until when are you going to wait? _____

6. To whom do you write most of your e-mails? _____

EXERCICE 7·24

*Complete the following questions for your favorite singer using **vous** to address him/her and the present indicative of the verbs in parentheses.*

1. Quel âge _____ ? (avoir)
2. _____ la couleur naturelle de vos cheveux? (être)
3. Où _____ ? (habiter)
4. _____ votre vrai nom? (être)
5. Pourquoi _____ à Paris? (ne pas venir)
6. Combien d'enfants _____ ? (avoir)

EXERCICE 7·25

*Translate the following questions into French, using **vous** for you and the inverted word order structure.*

1. Where would you like to go? _____
2. How much can you spend? _____
3. Who is traveling with you? _____
4. What airline do you prefer? _____
5. Why do you want to travel first class? _____

EXERCICE 7·26

Complete each of the following sentences with the appropriate interrogative term.

1. Pour _____ est-ce que tu vas voter?
2. D' _____ est-il? De Bretagne?
3. _____ est-ce que tu vas voter?
4. _____ est le slogan de sa campagne électorale?
5. _____ seront les élections?
6. _____ prendras-tu ta décision?

EXERCICE 7·27

Read the paragraph below and complete the following questions for each of the underlined sentences.

Aman Ary, à l'âge de dix-neuf ans, est un grand athlète. Comme enfant, il jouait déjà au foot et cette expérience l'a inspiré pour le reste de sa vie. Son père l'emmenait aussi régulièrement à des matchs de football. Aman voulait devenir célèbre, comme ses idoles, et il voulait jouer comme eux pour une équipe professionnelle aux États-Unis. Actuellement, Aman joue pour l'équipe nationale de France. Aman est très discipliné: il ne rate jamais l'entraînement et il maintient la forme. Son rêve s'est réalisé!

1. _____ a Aman Ary?

2. _____ faisait-il déjà comme enfant?

3. _____ est-ce que son père l'emmenait régulièrement?

4. _____ voulait devenir célèbre?

5. _____ voulait-il jouer un jour?

6. _____ est-ce qu'Aman joue actuellement?

7. _____ est Aman?

8. _____ il ne rate jamais?

9. _____ il maintient?

10. _____ s'est réalisé?

Limiting questions

Some interrogative terms are used to ask limiting or partial questions. Some elicit a specific answer about a noun such as the adverbial phrase **combien de** (*how much*) or the adjectives **lequel, laquelle, lesquels,** and **lesquelles** (*which one/which ones*).

Lequel de ces tableaux préfères-tu?   *Which one* of these paintings do you prefer?

(**Lequel** is in the masculine singular form; it refers to one **tableau**.)

Laquelle de ces serveuses est la plus serviable?   *Which one* of these waitresses is the most helpful?

(**Laquelle** is in the feminine singular form; it refers to one **serveuse**.)

Combien d'euros as-tu?   *How many* euros do you have?
Combien de temps avons-nous?   *How much* time do we have?

EXERCICE
7·28

*Complete the following questions with a form of **lequel** or with the phrase **combien de**.*

1. Regardez ces deux filles! _____ des deux est la plus grande?

2. Il y a deux bons films à la télé. _____ des deux veux-tu voir?

3. Nous pouvons acheter deux CD récents. _____ ?

4. Jacques a téléphoné? _____ fois?

5. _____ baguettes est-ce qu'il nous faut?

6. Les bananes sont mûres? _____ veux-tu?

148   PRACTICE MAKES PERFECT   Complete French All-in-One

Exclamations and commands

Basic exclamatory sentences

Exclamatory sentences communicate strong feelings. The speaker often adds voice modulation and facial expressions to stress emotions. Exclamatory sentences are more common in speech than in writing.

There are three basic ways of expressing yourself in an exclamatory manner in French. You may use a declarative sentence and add intonation (an exclamation mark in writing), or start a sentence with one of the conjunctions **que** or **comme** followed by the declarative sentence.

Ce souper est délicieux!	*Supper is delicious!* (intonation)
Que tu es gentil!	*How nice you are!*
Comme il fait froid!	*How cold it is!*

Declarative sentence with intonation or punctuation

With the appropriate punctuation you can use declarative sentences to express strong feelings. For some, a definition of an exclamatory sentence in English and in French alike is a forceful declarative sentence that shows strong emotion. In writing, an exclamation mark ends the sentence.

declarative sentence + ! → exclamatory sentence

The exclamation mark adds emphasis, an element of surprise, astonishment, admiration, or happiness to what was initially a simple declarative sentence (affirmative or negative).

Ce monsieur a gagné la loterie!	*This man won the lottery!*
Je suis la meilleure!	*I am the best!*
Il a du courage!	*He has courage!*
Tu n'as pas fait ton devoir!	*You did not do your homework!*
Regarde ma nouvelle voiture!	*Look at my new car!*
Bon, je ne dirai pas un mot!	*Fine, I will not say one word!*

EXERCICE 8·1

Fill in the blanks to complete the French translations of the following sentences.

1. *The moon is so beautiful!* Comme _____!

2. *We love the beach so much!* _____ tant la plage!

3. *It is hot outside!* Qu' _____!

4. *The lemonade is cold!* Que _____!

5. *Lucie is so tired!* _____

6. *Good! Now we* (fem.) *are ready!* _____
_____

EXERCICE
8·2

Express the following English statements in French as affirmative exclamations.

1. I am so cute! _____

2. I dance so well! _____

3. I have so many friends! _____

4. My boss loves me a lot! _____

5. I am very rich! _____

6. Everybody admires me! _____

Exclamatory sentences introduced by exclamatory conjunctions, adverbs, or adjectives

Exclamation words express the attitudes and emotions of the speaker. A definition of a formal exclamatory sentence (used in writing) is one that begins with an exclamation word.

Exclamations with que and comme

Some exclamatory sentences start with **que** (*how*) or **comme** (*how*). These words underscore the quality, nature, or intensity of the adjective or verb that follows them.

que + declarative sentence + ! → exclamatory sentence

Que c'est beau!	*How beautiful this is!*
Qu'il est grand!	*How tall he is!*
Que vous êtes polis!	*How polite you are!*
Que vous avez l'air content!	*How happy you look!*

comme + declarative sentence + ! → exclamatory sentence

Comme vous travaillez bien!	*How well you work!*
Comme ils sont mignons!	*How cute they are!*
Comme ils nagent vite!	*How fast they swim!*
Comme tu es amusante!	*How funny you are!*
Comme ils sont adorables!	*How adorable they are!*

Exclamations with combien, combien de/d', and que de/d'

Exclamatory sentences are also introduced by the exclamatory adverbs **combien** (*how much*), **combien de/d'**, and **que de/d'** (*how much/how many*). These words stress the quantity or intensity of the verb or noun that follows.

150 PRACTICE MAKES PERFECT   Complete French All-in-One

combien + declarative sentence + ! → exclamatory sentence

Combien j'aime ce pays!	*How I love this country!*
Combien j'ai attendu ce moment!	*How I waited for this moment!*

combien de + noun + ! → exclamatory phrase

Combien de roses!	*How many roses!*
Combien de compliments!	*How many compliments!*
Combien d'argent il a hérité!	*How much money he inherited!*

que de + noun + ! → exclamatory phrase

Que de cadeaux sous l'arbre de Noël!	*How many gifts under the Christmas tree!*
Que d'amour!	*How much love!*

que de + noun + declarative sentence + ! → exclamatory sentence

Que de confettis on jette dans les rues!	*How much confetti they throw into the streets!*
Que de papier vous gaspillez!	*How much paper you waste!*
Que de sucreries elle mange!	*How many sweets she eats!*

Exclamations with **quel**

Exclamations can also be introduced by a form of the adjective **quel** (*what*). This exclamation word underscores the quality, nature, or intensity of the noun or noun phrase it describes.

quel/quelle/quels/quelles + noun + ! → exclamatory phrase

Quel conducteur!	*What a driver!*
Quels sportifs!	*What athletes!*
Quelles magnifiques couleurs!	*What magnificent colors!*

quel/quelle/quels/quelles + noun + ! → exclamatory sentence

Quelle imagination elle a!	*What imagination she has!*
Quelle peur bleue j'ai eue hier soir!	*What horrible fright I had last night!*
Quelle force ils ont!	*What strength they have!*

These exclamations may have several meanings. For example, the exclamation **Quelle voiture!** (*What a car!*) could praise the size, value, performance, beauty, or other qualities of the car; or the context may suggest the car is ugly, old, or otherwise despicable.

Quel costume!	*What a cool (or awful) suit!*
Quelle maison il a achetée!	*What a great (or horrible) house he bought!*

EXERCICE

8·3

Translate the following sentences into English.

1. Que de plaisirs on trouve dans la vie!

_____

2. Combien de surprises elle nous réserve!

_____

3. Quelle innocence on voit dans les enfants!

_____

4. Combien nous sommes attachés à la vie!

_____

Exclamations and commands **151**

5. Comme nous sommes heureux!

_____

6. Quelle chance nous avons!

_____

EXERCICE
8·4

Place the sentence fragments provided in the right order to create exclamatory sentences about crazy drivers. Beware of capitalization and punctuation.

1. conduit vite / que / ce monsieur

_____

2. il y a / accidents / combien d' / sur les routes

_____

3. dangereux / comme / les chauffards / sont

_____

4. que d' / sur la route / obstacles / il y a

_____

5. les feux rouges / fous / combien de / brûlent

_____

Interjections and exclamatory sentences

Interjections are words or phrases used in an exclamation to add emotion. These utterances frequently appear in or with exclamatory sentences to express a reaction to what we perceive around us. Interjections end in an exclamation mark.

Tiens! Le temps s'éclaircit.	**Look at that!** *The weather is clearing up.*
Ah tiens! Voilà finalement l'autobus.	**Look at that!** *There is the bus finally!*

The following interjections are used to express pain or relief:

Aïe!	*Ouch!*	Ouïlle!	*Ouch!*
Dieu merci!	*Thank goodness!*	Ouf!	*Phew! (as in escaping a bad situation; sign of relief)*

The following interjections are used to express annoyance:

Zut!	*Darn!*	Zut alors!	*Darn!*
Oups!	*Oops!*	Bon sang!	*Good grief!*
Que diable!	*What in the dickens!*		

The following interjections are used to express spite, disgust, or indifference:

Bah!	*Nonsense!*	Hélas!	*Alas!*
Pouah!	*Yuck!*	Bof!	*So what!*

The following interjections are used to get somebody's attention:

Hé! Eh! Hep!	*Hey!*	Coucou!	*Hi!*
Allons!	*Come on!*	Attention!	*Watch out!*
Vite!	*Quick!*		

The following interjections are used to express helplessness or to call for help:

Ciel!	*Heavens!*	Mon Dieu!	*My goodness!*
Au secours!	*Help!*	À l'aide!	*Help!*

The following interjections are used to express surprise, disbelief, or cynicism:

Espérons!	*Let's hope!*	Tu parles!	*You bet!*
Quoi!	*What!*	Comment!	*What!*
Eh ben dis donc!	*You don't say!*	Sans blague!	*No kidding!*
Tiens!	*Look at that!*	Ah tiens!	*Look at that!*
Oh là là!	*Oh my!*		

The following interjections are used to express admiration, gratitude, and enthusiasm:

Chouette!	*Cool!*	Super!	*Great!*
Bravo!	*Great!*	Hourra!	*Hurrah!*
Pardi!	*For sure!*	Tant mieux!	*So much the better!*

The following interjections are used to ask for quiet:

Chut!	*Hush!*	Silence!	*Quiet!*

Some interjections are euphemisms, inoffensive expressions that replace those that may offend the listeners, or expressions that suggest something not pleasant. They are more common in speech.

Zut! Cet examen est difficile!	*Darn, this exam is hard!*
Eh ben dis donc! Je ne l'aurais jamais cru!	*You don't say! I would have never believed it!*
Tu vas au concert? —**Tu parles!**	*Are you going to the concert? —You bet!*
Ce poulet est atroce! **Pouah!**	*This chicken is awful. Yuck!*
Quoi! Ils n'ont pas encore fini?	*What! They have not yet finished?*
Sans blague! Tu vas faire le tour du monde?	*No kidding! You are going to take a trip around the world?*

EXERCICE
8·5

Write the letter of the word on the right that describes the emotion expressed in the following sentences. There may be more than one answer, depending on how you interpret the message.

1. _____ Zut! J'ai la migraine!

2. _____ Oh là là! Que j'ai peur!

3. _____ Ouf! J'ai retrouvé mes clefs!

    a. indifference

    b. relief

    c. impatience

Exclamations and commands **153**

4. _____ Pouah! Ce lait est aigre!   d.   disgust

5. _____ Bof! J'irai demain!   e.   fear

6. _____ Aïe! Je me suis fait mal au doigt!   f.   pain

EXERCICE 8·6

Write an interjection to respond to these statements. Remember, you need to express your feelings!

1. Ta voiture a un pneu crevé. _____

2. Tu appelles police-secours pour t'aider. _____

3. L'agent de police remplace ton pneu. _____

4. Ta voiture marche mais la route est mauvaise. _____

5. Tu arrives en retard à ton rendez-vous. _____

6. Tes amis t'attendent toujours. _____

EXERCICE 8·7

Translate the following sentences into French.

1. Hush! There is too much noise! _____

_____

2. Heavens! The conference starts at noon! _____

_____

3. Hey! We have arrived! _____

4. Alas! I have no time! _____

5. You (tu) want to win? Let's hope! _____

_____

6. Oh my! This watch is beautiful! _____

_____

154   PRACTICE MAKES PERFECT   Complete French All-in-One

Imperative clauses

Imperative clauses are used to give orders, commands, and sometimes instructions. This type of clause ends in an exclamation mark and excludes a subject of the verb.

The entire clause may consist of a single verb in the imperative mood, or it may consist of the predicate (verb in the imperative mood and complement). The imperative clause does not have an explicit subject. The subject of the verb is implied.

Imperative clause = verb in imperative mood

Consider the following examples of imperative clauses consisting of a single verb in the imperative mood. Note that the implied subject of each verb is **tu** (*you*) and that the conjugated form of the verb is in the second person of the present indicative (although -**s** has been dropped from the ending for regular -**er** verbs and for the irregular verb **aller**).

DECLARATIVE CLAUSE		IMPERATIVE CLAUSE		VERB GROUP
Tu écoutes.	*You listen.*	Écoute!	*Listen!*	-er verb
Tu choisis.	*You choose.*	Choisis!	*Choose!*	-ir verb
Tu réponds.	*You answer.*	Réponds!	*Answer!*	-re verb
Tu prends.	*You take.*	Prends!	*Take!*	irregular verb
Tu vas.	*You go.*	Va!	*Go!*	irregular verb and irregular imperative form

Imperative clause = verb in imperative mood + complement

Consider the following examples of imperative clauses consisting of a verb in the imperative mood and a complement.

Écoute cette nouvelle chanson!   *Listen to this new song!*
Choisis ta couleur préférée!   *Choose your favorite color!*
Réponds vite à la question!   *Quickly answer the question!*
Va à la maison!   *Go home!*

Note that the negative form of a verb in the imperative mood requires the use of **ne** and **pas** *hugging* the verb.

N'écoute pas cette nouvelle chanson!   ***Do not listen*** *to this new song!*
Ne choisis pas ta couleur préférée!   ***Do not choose*** *your favorite color!*
Ne réponds pas vite à la question!   ***Do not answer*** *the question quickly!*
Ne va pas à la maison!   ***Do not go*** *home!*

EXERCICE 8·8

Change each declarative sentence into an exclamatory imperative clause. Add appropriate punctuation.

1. Tu regardes un bon film. _____
2. Tu viens à onze heures. _____
3. Tu prends un café. _____

Exclamations and commands   **155**

4. Tu vas chez Paul. _____

5. Tu finis cet exercice. _____

6. Tu descends au premier étage. _____

EXERCICE 8·9

Answer each question with an affirmative or negative imperative clause.

1. Je pars maintenant? —Oui, _____ tout de suite!

2. Je fais la vaisselle d'abord? —Non, _____ la vaisselle!

3. Je prends la voiture? —Oui, _____ la voiture!

4. Je téléphone plus tard? —Non, _____ ! Ce n'est pas la peine.

5. Je rentre vers six heures? —Oui, _____ tôt!

Implied subject of the verb in the imperative clause

In English and French imperative clauses, the subject is implied. However, in the English clause, it may not always be clear whether one person or several persons are targeted in the command, whereas in the French sentence, the form of the verb makes it clear who is targeted in the command.

Va à la maison!	***Go*** *home!* (*you*, one person)
Cherche tes lunettes!	***Look*** *for your glasses!* (*you*, one person)
Allez à la maison!	***Go*** *home!* (*you*, several persons, or *you*, one person in formal address)
Finissez le diner!	***Finish*** *dinner!* (*you*, several persons, or *you*, one person in formal address)
Allons à la maison!	***Let's go*** *home!* (*both of us* or *all of us*)
Laissons nos affaires ici!	***Let's leave*** *our things here!* (*both of us* or *all of us*)

In an English imperative clause, there are two possible subjects that are implied:

- ◆ *You*, talking to one person or several people
- ◆ *We*, talking to at least one other person while including oneself

In a French imperative clause, however, there can be three implied subjects:

- ◆ **Tu**, talking to one person in a familiar situation
- ◆ **Vous**, talking to one person in a formal situation or talking to several people
- ◆ **Nous**, talking to at least one other person while including oneself

EXERCICE 8·10

For each of the following sentences, write 1 if Mr. Lemus addresses one student and + if he addresses more than one.

1. _____ Écris cette lettre!
2. _____ Finis ce rapport!
3. _____ Prenez des vacances!
4. _____ Fermez la porte!
5. _____ Approchez!
6. _____ Réponds!

EXERCICE 8·11

Instruct your little brother to do the following actions by translating each imperative clause into French.

1. Listen to your mommy! _____
2. Choose your movie! _____
3. Come down! _____
4. Finish your homework! _____
5. Do not look at your sister! _____
6. Go to your room! _____

EXERCICE 8·12

Instruct the children you are baby-sitting to do as you say by translating the following commands into French.

1. Do not scream! _____
2. Turn off the TV! _____
3. Go out into the garden! _____
4. Do not soil the couch! _____
5. Give me this towel! _____
6. Stay in your room! _____

Exclamations and commands

EXERCICE 8·13

You are among friends and make suggestions for weekend activities. Translate the following suggestions into French.

1. Let's eat at the restaurant! _____

2. Let's invite Jeanine! _____

3. Let's check the movie times! _____

4. Let's go! _____

5. Let's take a cab! _____

Independent clauses and subordinate clauses

Any structural group organized around a verbal nucleus is a clause. There are two types of clauses in English and in French: independent clauses and dependent clauses. If a clause can stand alone as a sentence—if it has at least a subject and a verb and expresses a complete thought—then it is an independent clause. In this chapter, we will see examples of independent clauses that exist by and for themselves (simple independent clauses) as well as independent clauses that give support to dependent clauses.

Simple independent clauses

Simple independent clauses constitute sentences. Their structure can be affirmative, negative, interrogative, or imperative. They express complete thoughts. They are made up of a subject and a verb, but can also include an adverb, a prepositional phrase, or various objects.

subject + verb (+ complement) → independent clause

Simple affirmative clauses

This type of clause is classified as simple because no other clause depends on it. And the clause is affirmative because it does not include any negative terms such as **pas**, **plus**, **jamais**, **personne**, **rien**, **aucun**, or **nul**. A simple affirmative clause is also independent as it expresses a complete thought and includes a subject as well as a verb. Here is an example of a simple affirmative independent clause:

Les Robert sont à l'hôtel aujourd'hui.   *The Roberts are at the hotel today.*

In this clause, we can identify the following elements:

- A subject: **les Robert**
- A predicate: **sont à l'hôtel aujourd'hui**

The predicate in this clause includes:

- The verb: **sont**
- A prepositional phrase: **à l'hôtel**
- An adverb: **aujourd'hui**

Additional characteristics of this clause are:

- The clause is simple: No other clause depends on it.
- The structure of the clause is affirmative: Look at the verb **sont**.
- The clause is independent: It expresses a complete thought and includes the structural elements of subject and verb.

159

Simple negative clauses

This type of clause is considered simple because no other clause depends on it. The clause is negative because it includes a negative term such as **pas**, **plus**, **jamais**, **personne**, **rien**, **aucun**, or **nul**. (To review negative structures, see Chapter 6 .) The clause is also independent because it expresses a complete thought and includes a subject as well as a verb. Here is an example of a simple negative independent clause:

Les Robert ne sont pas à la maison actuellement.   *The Roberts are not currently at home.*

In this clause, we can identify the same elements and characteristics as in the example of the simple affirmative clause in the previous section. The only difference in this clause is the negative structure of the verb. Here we can identify:

- A subject: **les Robert**
- A predicate: **ne sont pas à la maison**

The predicate in this clause includes:

- The verb: **ne sont pas**
- A prepositional phrase: **à la maison**
- An adverb: **actuellement**

Other characteristics of this clause to note are:

- The clause is simple: No other clause depends on it.
- The structure of the clause is negative: **ne sont pas**.
- The clause is independent: It expresses a complete thought and includes the structural elements of subject and verb.

Consider another example of a simple independent clause featuring a negative structure:

Je ne mange rien.   *I am not eating anything.*

Note once again that this clause expresses a complete thought and includes the necessary structural elements of an independent clause even though the clause is very short and includes nothing but the essential elements of a clause: the subject **Je** and the verb **mange**.

Consider a few more examples of simple negative independent clauses and note that these are all independent clauses including a subject and a verb:

Mon chat ne mange jamais de souris.	*My cat **never eats** any mice.*
Il ne les **attrape plus**.	*He **no longer catches** them.*
Je n'aime aucun de ces desserts.	*I **do not like any** of these desserts.*
Papa n'a nulle envie de faire la cuisine.	*Dad **has no desire** to do the cooking.*
Je n'ai invité personne ce weekend.	*I **did not invite anyone** this weekend.*

EXERCICE
9·1

Build simple affirmative clauses using the sentence fragments provided. Be sure to punctuate your sentences.

1. Jean / ce soir / va arriver

_____

2. préparons / nous / un bon repas

_____

3. content / tout le monde / est

4. était / absent / longtemps / il

5. il / dans sa chambre / va dormir

EXERCICE 9·2

With these sentence fragments, build simple negative clauses in the present tense using the negations provided and using proper punctuation.

1. Brigitte / dort / ne pas bien

2. Ginette / aime les gâteaux / ne plus

3. nous / voulons / ne rien / boire

4. vous / pouvez / ne pas / lire tout le roman

5. elles / ont / ne rien / à dire

6. vous / avez / ne pas encore / vingt ans

Simple interrogative clauses

This type of clause is simple because no other clause depends on it. The clause is interrogative because it asks a question. And the clause is independent because it expresses a complete thought and includes a subject as well as a verb. Now consider the following examples of simple independent clauses featuring an interrogative structure:

        subject + verb + ? → interrogative structure (using pitch of voice in oral expression)
        Elle mange?   *Does she eat?*

        est-ce que + subject + verb + ? → interrogative structure
        Est-ce qu'elle mange?   *Does she eat?*

        verb + subject + ? → interrogative structure
        Mange-t-elle?   *Does she eat?*

Although the interrogative structure varies from one sentence to another, each of these clauses expresses a complete thought and includes the necessary structural elements of an independent clause: the subject **elle** and the verb **mange**.

Now consider the following examples of simple interrogative clauses featuring the various interrogative structures and note that they are all independent clauses including a subject and a verb. (To review complex interrogative structures, see Chapter 7.)

On va au cinéma ce soir?	*Do we go* to the movies tonight?
Est-ce que **Marie-Claude veut** venir avec nous?	*Does Marie-Claude want* to come with us?
Est-elle à la maison en ce moment?	*Is she* home at this moment?

In addition, note that a verbal structure can be interrogative and negative at the same time, as shown in the following sentences. But as long as there is a subject and a verb and the sentence makes sense on its own, you are still building independent clauses.

Le cinéma des Arts n'est-il pas juste au coin?	*Isn't the Cinéma des Arts* just around the corner?
Est-ce qu'il n'a pas plu aujourd'hui?	*Did it not rain* today?
Tu n'as pas la monnaie exacte pour les billets?	*Don't you have* the exact change for the tickets?
Est-ce qu'ils ne coûtent pas trop cher?	*Don't they cost* too much?

EXERCICE 9·3

*Change each statement into a question, building simple interrogative clauses using the phrase **est-ce que**. Use proper punctuation.*

EXAMPLE   Les fleurs poussent bien.   Est-ce que les fleurs poussent bien?

1. Le ciel est bleu. _____
2. Les oiseaux chantent. _____
3. Le chien court derrière moi. _____
4. Je vais au parc. _____
5. Tu viens avec moi. _____

Simple imperative clauses

This type of clause is simple because no other clause depends on it. The clause is imperative because it serves to give commands, orders, or instructions. And the clause is independent because it expresses a complete thought and includes an *implicit* subject as well as a verb. This type of clause differs from previously mentioned independent clauses, because it lacks the explicit mention of the subject. In an imperative clause, the omitted and implied subject is *you* or *we*. (To study imperative structures, see Chapter 23.)

verb (+ complement) → simple imperative clause

Rentre chez toi! (tu)	*Go home!*
Répondez à la question! (vous)	***Answer** the question!*
N'ignorons pas la vérité! (nous)	***Let's not ignore** the truth!*
Conduis ta sœur au cinéma! (tu)	***Drive** your sister to the movie theater!*

EXERCICE 9·4

*Build simple affirmative imperative clauses using the words in parentheses. Use the familiar **tu** command only.*

1. Decorate your room! (décorer ta chambre)

2. Paint the walls! (peindre les murs)

3. Organize the closet! (organiser le placard)

4. Change the curtains! (changer les rideaux)

5. Hang some paintings! (accrocher des tableaux)

6. Move the bed! (déplacer le lit)

Main clauses

The examples of the previous section show us that an independent clause can be a complete sentence. Remember the definition of a sentence as a group of words including a subject and a predicate, and compare the following definitions of a sentence and an independent clause:

> subject + predicate → sentence
> subject + predicate → independent clause

You will notice that they are the same. One might then wonder why it is necessary to use the terminology *independent clause*. Why not simply call any structural grouping of a subject and predicate a *sentence*? The answer lies within the fact that a sentence is sometimes but not always limited to an independent clause. However, sometimes a sentence includes both an independent and a dependent clause.

> sentence = simple independent clause

or

> sentence = independent clause + dependent clause

Examine the following example of a sentence, which comprises both types of clauses: dependent and independent:

> Je mange en attendant ton arrivée.   *I eat while waiting for your arrival.*

In this sentence, one can identify the following clauses:

- An independent clause: **Je mange**
- A dependent clause: **en attendant ton arrivée**

We use the term *independent clause* to describe the subject + verb grouping: **Je mange**. It differentiates this type of clause, which can exist by itself and which makes sense by itself, from a dependent clause such as **en attendant ton arrivée**, which only makes sense in conjunction with the independent clause.

In a sentence such as **Je mange en attendant ton arrivée**, which includes both an independent and a dependent clause, the independent clause (the one which can stand alone and makes sense by itself) is also called the *main clause*.

main clause + dependent clause
Viens + faire tes devoirs!
Viens faire tes devoirs!
Come and do your homework!

Consider the following examples of sentences. They all include a boldfaced main clause and a dependent clause.

Dax rêvait de devenir pilote.	*Dax dreamed* of becoming a pilot.
Dara envoie des bises pour nous charmer.	*Dara gives kisses* to charm us.
Alex n'aime pas qu'on l'ignore.	*Alex does not like* to be ignored.
Sasha se fâche quand on l'ennuie.	*Sasha gets mad* when you bother him.
Amethyst adore s'occuper des enfants.	*Amethyst loves* taking care of children.
Barbara s'amuse à faire la cuisine.	*Barbara has fun* cooking.
Veux-tu que je t'aide?	*Do you want* me to help you?

In each of the previous sentences, the main clause is in itself an independent clause and supports a dependent clause. This dependent clause, by itself, does not express a complete thought. It depends on the main clause to provide the premise and the background for what is to be expressed.

Les Robert sont à l'hôtel bien que leur famille habite en ville.   *The Roberts are at the hotel* even though their family lives in town.

The clause **Les Robert sont à l'hôtel** is a main clause because it not only makes sense by itself (which makes it an independent clause) but it is also followed by the dependent clause **bien que leur famille habite en ville**. This last part of the sentence—*even though their family lives in town*—makes sense only if you understand the main idea that *the Roberts are at the hotel*.

EXERCICE 9·5

Ariane and Arlette are chatting. On the lines provided, write A *if the structure of the clause is affirmative,* N *if it is negative, and* IMP *if it is imperative.*

1. _____ Tu veux une glace, Arlette?

2. _____ Je ne mange jamais de glace, Ariane.

3. _____ Tu n'aimes pas ça, Arlette?

4. _____ Si, mais ça fait grossir.

5. _____ Oublie un peu ton régime, Arlette!

6. _____ Je suis trop stricte pour ça.

EXERCICE 9·6

Find the appropriate dependent clause in the right column for each main clause on the left, and write the letter on the line provided.

1. C'est très bizarre _____
2. On avait pourtant rendez-vous _____
3. Bon. Je vais me calmer _____
4. Tu finiras bien par appeler _____
5. J'entends la sonnette _____
6. J'avais bien tort _____

a. ou tu arriveras bientôt.
b. donc te voilà!
c. de me faire du souci.
d. que tu n'appelles pas.
e. car on devait aller danser ce soir.
f. et je vais attendre patiemment.

Compound sentences

A compound sentence includes two independent clauses. These clauses may be combined into a sentence by using punctuation (e.g., a semicolon).

independent clause + ; + independent clause
Lili ne mange pas + ; + elle n'a pas faim.
Lili does not eat; she is not hungry.

Tu pars; tu vas au concert. — *You are leaving; you are going to the concert.*
Elle joue; elle a le temps. — *She is playing; she has the time.*
Nous attendons; on va nous appeler. — *We are waiting; they are going to call us.*

More frequently, however, independent clauses are joined together with one of the following coordinating conjunctions: **et** (*and*), **ni** (*nor*), **ou** (*or*), **car** (*for*), **mais** (*but*), and **donc** (*so*).

independent clause + coordinating conjunction + independent clause
Je pense + donc + je suis.
I think therefore I am.

Josette est fatiguée **car** elle a travaillé très dur. — *Josette is tired **for** she worked hard.*
Elle n'est pas encore là **mais** elle est en route. — *She is not there yet, **but** she is on the way.*
Elle n'est pas encore arrivée **ni** Jean-Marc d'ailleurs. — *She has not yet arrived **nor** has Jean-Marc.*

In previous units you built *sentences*: affirmative and negative sentences, direct questions, imperatives, and exclamatory sentences. Some were similar to the examples below:

Je me réveille vers sept heures. — *I get up around seven o'clock.*
Je ne travaille pas le week-end. — *I do not work on weekends.*
Je fais des achats. — *I am going shopping.*
Je rentrerai vers midi. — *I will get back around noon.*
Je veux un nouveau pantalon. — *I want new pants.*
Je n'ai pas beaucoup d'argent. — *I do not have a lot of money.*
Donne-moi un peu d'argent. — *Give me a little money.*
Je ne pourrai pas l'acheter. — *I will not be able to buy it.*

In the next examples, see how the *coordinating conjunctions* join the simple sentences you just read.

Independent clauses and subordinate clauses **165**

Je me réveille vers sept heures **mais** je ne travaille pas le week-end.	I get up around seven o'clock, but I do not work on weekends.
Je fais des achats **et** je rentrerai vers midi.	I am going shopping, and I will get back around noon.
Je veux un nouveau pantalon **mais** je n'ai pas beaucoup d'argent.	I want new pants, but I do not have a lot of money.
Donne-moi un peu d'argent **sinon** je ne pourrai pas l'acheter.	Give me a little money, otherwise I will not be able to buy it.

Commonly used coordinating conjunctions are:

et	and	ou	or
soit...soit	either . . . or	ni	nor
ni...ni	neither . . . nor	mais	but
sinon	otherwise		

EXERCICE 9·7

Build new sentences by combining the two sentences provided with one of the conjunctions in parentheses as appropriate.

1. Toute la journée Mimi était chez ses grands-parents. Elle jouait avec leur chien Médor. (et, ni)

2. Je voulais déjeuner avec elle. Elle avait rendez-vous chez le dentiste. (et, mais)

3. Elle a dû aller à son rendez-vous. Elle n'aime pas aller chez le dentiste. (sinon, mais)

4. Mimi n'a pas mangé de toute la journée. Elle n'a pas mangé le soir. (ou, ni)

5. Aujourd'hui elle doit se sentir mieux. Elle doit retourner chez le dentiste. (ni, sinon)

6. Mimi est très gentille. Elle est aussi très indécise. (et, mais)

Omitting the subject and the verb in the second clause

In French, when the subject of the first and second clause is identical, it is frequently omitted. In English it can be omitted, too.

Beatrice a fermé les yeux et n'a pas vu l'accident.	Beatrice closed her eyes and did not see the accident.
Les détectives ont fait leur rapport et sont partis.	The detectives made their report and left.

It is also possible to omit the verb of the second clause for different reasons: for the sake of brevity, a balanced combination of sentences, or a simple matter of style.

Il n'a ni travail ni argent.   *He does not have a job nor money.*
Je vais préparer une omelette ou une salade.   *I will prepare an omelet or a salad.*

EXERCICE 9·8

In each of the following sentences, identify the subject and verb that can be omitted, and then rewrite the sentence using a coordinating conjunction.

1. Mes parents restent à la maison le samedi et ils restent à la maison le dimanche.

2. Papa ne mange pas de viande de bœuf et il ne mange pas de poulet.

3. Maman prépare la salade et elle prépare la vinaigrette.

4. Nous allons manger vers six heures ou nous allons manger vers sept heures.

5. Avant le dîner, nous buvons un verre de vin ou nous buvons un apéritif.

6. Après le dîner, nous faisons du thé ou nous faisons du café.

Coordinating conjunctions and their functions

Getting acquainted with coordinating conjunctions and focusing on the purpose each one communicates will help you choose the correct conjunction and build sentences in French.

CONJUNCTION	PURPOSE
et, ni Marise chante **et** moi, je danse.	adding a fact *Marise sings **and** I dance.*
ou, soit...soit J'irai **soit** à la piscine **soit** à la plage.	choosing one over another *I will go **either** to the pool **or** to the beach.*
donc Il pleut **donc** nous ne sortons pas.	expressing real consequences *It is raining, **so** we are not going out.*
mais Je suis fatigué **mais** je vais faire ce devoir.	expressing opposition/contrast *I am tired, **but** I am going to do this assignment.*
sinon Fais-le **sinon** ce sera trop tard!	expressing a possible consequence *Do it, **otherwise** it will be too late!*
ni Je ne fume **ni** bois.	adding two negative actions (verbs) *I neither smoke **nor** drink.*
ni...ni Tu n'as **ni** patience **ni** indulgence.	**ni** appears before both nouns *You have **neither** patience **nor** indulgence.*

Independent clauses and subordinate clauses

EXERCICE 9·9

Write complete and logical sentences using the sentence fragments provided.

1. d'écrire un roman / j'ai envie / au bureau / je vais / donc

2. le premier chapitre / j'écris / je ne l'aime pas / mais

3. le premier chapitre / je dois / récrire / la fin / sera / sinon / impossible

4. le début / changer / je peux / ou / la fin / du chapitre

5. donc / d'idées / je n'ai pas / je vais / me promener

6. dans un café / j'entre / je commande un expresso / et

EXERCICE 9·10

Combine each of the sentence pairs given, using a coordinating conjunction. There may be more than one possible answer.

1. Tu écris bien. Tu parles encore mieux.

2. Le pauvre n'entend pas. Il ne parle pas.

3. Tu es en retard. Dépêche-toi!

4. Tu arrives. Tu repars.

5. Ce manteau est cher. J'ai assez d'argent pour l'acheter.

6. Le magasin ne ferme pas à six heures. Il ne ferme pas à sept heures non plus.

Punctuation of sentences with more than two independent clauses

In French a comma is usually not needed with **et**, **mais**, **donc**, and **sinon**. However, when a sentence includes *more* than two independent clauses, the coordinating conjunction usually precedes the last sentence and a comma separates the other previous sentences.

independent clause 1 + , + independent clause 2 + conjunction + independent clause 3 → sentence

Nous prenons le petit déjeuner, allons au travail et rentrons.	We eat breakfast, go to work, and come back.
Je cours, je fais du vélo et de la natation.	I run, ride bike, and swim.

Note, in the following examples, that the expressions **ni...ni** and **soit...soit** do not require any punctuation:

Je ne veux **ni** soda **ni** jus.	I want **neither** soda **nor** juice.
J'irai au cinéma **soit** samedi **soit** dimanche.	I will go to the movies **either** on Saturday **or** on Sunday.

EXERCICE 9·11

Build sentences with the fragments provided, and use the correct punctuation.

1. s'habille / Zoé / se lève / se maquille / et

2. elle / ferme la porte à clef / sort / prend son sac / et

3. le métro / le bus / elle prend le vélo / ou

4. elle boit un verre de jus / ni thé / ni café / elle ne boit / mais

5. il fait de l'orage / elle se dépêche / et / il pleut fort / donc

EXERCICE 9·12

Translate the following sentences into French.

1. Sometimes I like to stay home and read a good book.

2. There are days when I do not want to go out nor talk to anybody.

3. I do answer the phone but only if it is family.

4. I can see my caller's name, so I know who calls.

5. I have neither scruples nor regrets.

Subordinate clauses

While studying this book, you will run into many different clauses. Let's summarize the categories so you can easily grasp their nature and their function. Generally speaking, the purpose of any subordinate clause is to explain or present a situation or a set of circumstances implied by the main clause.

The causal clause

The causal clause expresses the natural link between cause and effect. This clause is preceded by a conjunction such as the following: **car, parce que, plus... plus, moins... moins, puisque, étant donné que, vu que, du fait que, du moment que, dès l'instant que, dès lors que, d'autant (plus) que, surtout que, soit que... soit que, non que.**

J'ai réservé mes prochaines vacances sur Internet, **parce que** c'est beaucoup plus rapide.	*I made reservations for my next vacation online, because it is much faster.*

The completive or *that* clause

The *that* clause completes the main clause by adding an object, subject, attribute, and so on.

Que les enfants participent aux tâches ménagères me semble important.	*I think it's important that children participate in daily chores.*
Je suis déçu **qu'**il pleuve.	*I am disappointed that it's raining.*

There are various types of these clauses introduced by **que** or **ce que**.

Lucie ne s'attendait pas **à ce que** Paul cuisine si bien.	*Lucie didn't expect Paul to cook so well.*

The indirect interrogative clause

The hypothetical clause is often used in indirect speech.

Je me demande **si** elle aura son bac.	*I am wondering if she will graduate from high school.*
Nous nous demandons **quand** leur avion arrivera.	*We're wondering when their plane will arrive.*

170 PRACTICE MAKES PERFECT Complete French All-in-One

The infinitive clause

The infinitive clause is either used alone or follows a conjugated verb. As expected, this clause always contains an infinitive. It is important to note that the corresponding construction in English is the gerund clause.

Dîner dans ce restaurant est une experience inouïe.	*Dining in this restaurant is an extraordinary experience.*
Vous voulez **lire** vos mails?	*Do you want to read your e-mails?*

The concessive clause

Implying some kind of concession, from the Latin verb *concedo*, which among other things means *I allow* or *I concede*, this clause adds an element of surprise by introducing a somewhat unexpected main clause. Affecting the entire main clause, the concessive clause can either precede or follow it, sometimes appearing in the middle of the main clause.

Words introducing this clause are the following: **quoique, bien que, encore que, que... que, sans que, même si, quand, quand bien même.**

Bien que son ordinateur plante régulièrement, Nathan refuse d'en acheter un autre.	*Although Nathan's computer crashes on a regular basis, he refuses to buy a new one.*
Qu'il pleuve ou **qu**'il vente, tu sortiras ton chien!	*Whether it rains or blows, you will take your dog out for a walk!*

The consecutive clause

A consecutive clause can be introduced in two ways:

- ◆ Either by words illustrating a statement made in the main clause: **de façon que, de manière que, en sorte que, si bien que, sans que**.
- ◆ Or by words describing the intensity of an action presented in the main clause: **à tel/ce point que, à un tel point que, à un point que, si... que, tellement... que, tant que, tant/tellement de, tel que, assez/trop/suffisamment... pour que**.

Le site Internet de l'entreprise a été complètement remanie, **si bien que** je ne retrouve plus rien.	*The company's Internet site has been so thoroughly overhauled that I cannot find anything anymore.*
Ce pays est **si** endetté **que** son économie est fragilisée.	*This country is so much in debt that its economy has been weakened.*

The purpose clause

The purpose clause suggests the idea of the outcome of an action or situation. The following conjunctions are used: **pour que, afin que, à seule fin que, de peur que, de crainte que.**

J'ai encouragé Margot **pour qu**'elle obtienne son permis de conduire.	*I gave Margot a lot of encouragement so she would get her driver's license.*
Fabrice fermé la fenêtre **de peur que** le vent ne la brise.	*Fabrice closes the window, fearing the wind might shatter it.*

The hypothetical clause

This clause suggests the idea of an uncertain outcome. It is introduced by the following words: **si, sauf si, excepté si, même si, comme si, quand, quand même, quand bien même, à condition que,**

Independent clauses and subordinate clauses **171**

à supposer que, supposé que, pour peu que, à moins que, pourvu que, en admettant que, si tant est que, mettons que, soit que, soit que... soit que, selon que, suivant que, au cas où, pour le cas où.

> Mathilde ne viendra pas **sauf si** vous l'appelez.
> *Mathilde won't come unless you call her.*
>
> **Au cas où** nous devrions attendre au tribunal, emportons des journaux.
> *In case we have to wait in court, let's bring some newspapers.*

The relative clause

This clause is always introduced by words denoting relation, such as the following: **que, qui, quoi, dont, ou, lequel.**

> Manuel aime travailler avec des étudiants **qui** écoutent.
> *Manuel likes to work with students who listen.*
>
> La maison **où** ils sont tombés amoureux se trouve dans les Pyrénées.
> *The house where they fell in love is in the Pyrenees.*

The temporal clause

This clause establishes a temporal link with the main clause, suggesting the ideas of simultaneity, anteriority, or posteriority.

This clause is introduced by the following words: **lorsque, quand, comme, alors que, pendant que, tandis que, aussi longtemps que, tant que, au moment où, en même temps que, à présent que, maintenant que, à mesure que, à chaque fois que, toutes les fois que, avant que, jusqu'à ce que, jusqu'au moment où, en attendant que, après que, une fois que, dès que, sitôt que, depuis que.**

> Tu te seras endormi **avant qu**'il ne revienne.
> *You will have fallen asleep before he returns.*
>
> Le coureur No 36 menait le sprint jusqu'au **moment où** il a trébuché sur une pierre.
> *Sprinter No. 36 was leading the race when he stumbled on a stone.*

The comparative clause

This clause links two facts or actions by comparing them. It is introduced by the following words: **comme, ainsi que, autant que, de même que, tel que, autrement... que, plus/moins/aussi/autant... que, d'autant que, d'autant plus/moins que, dans la mesure où, selon que, à mesure que.**

> Elsa parle **plus qu**'elle ne chante.
> *Elsa talks more than she sings.*
>
> Ce tableau est exactement **comme** je l'avais imaginé.
> *This painting is exactly as I had imagined it.*

EXERCICE
9·13

Relier les deux propositions par l'élément qui convient: **afin que, avant que, bien que, car, de façon que, où, pendant que, plus... moins, quand bien même, que, trop... pour que....** *Plusieurs réponses sont parfois possibles.*

1. Victoire écoute toujours de la musique _____ elle fait du yoga.

2. Je suis heureux _____ vous me rendiez visite.

3. Les comédiens répètent souvent la pièce _____ la représentation soit parfaite.

4. Le musée _____ j'ai perdu ma montre est immense.

5. L'orateur se placera sur une estrade _____ tout le monde l'entende.

6. _____ on lui offrirait cette voiture, Joséphine n'en voudrait pas.

7. Tu voulais voir cette exposition _____ nous quittions la ville.

8. Les journalistes sont _____ nombreux _____ le ministre les reçoive tous.

9. _____ Héléna fait les magasins _____ elle a d'argent.

10. _____ le Cirque du Soleil arrive demain, je ne pourrai assister à aucune représentation, _____ je suis malade.

Independent clauses and subordinate clauses **173**

The present tense of -er verbs

Before studying the present tense in French, you need to be familiar with the grammatical terms in chapters presenting verbs. To conjugate a verb in the present tense, you'll need to find the *root* (or *stem*) of a verb to which you'll add the *ending* corresponding to the desired *tense*. The root of the verb is found in its *infinitive* form. In English, the infinitive is preceded by the preposition *to*: *to say, to wear*. Infinitives in French are not preceded by an equivalent of the preposition *to*. They are identified according to groups by their endings: **-er, -ir, -re, -oir**.

Regular -er verbs in the present

Let's start with the infinitives of verbs of the first group, ending in **-er**, such as **regarder** (*to look at*) and **chanter** (*to sing*). Most verbs that end in **-er** in the infinitive follow the same conjugation. The pattern is easy. You remove the **-er** ending of the verb to get the root: **parler** (*to speak*) → **parl-**. Then, you add the endings corresponding to the subject pronoun.

The endings for the **-er** regular verbs are: **-e, -es, -e, -ons, -ez, -ent**. The **-e, -es**, and **-ent** endings of the verbs are all silent. The final **-s** of **nous, vous, ils, elles** links with verbs beginning with a vowel sound, making a **z** sound. This is called a **liaison**.

Let's conjugate the verb **parler** (*to speak*). Note that, as in English, conjugated forms are preceded by a *subject pronoun*:

je parl**e**	*I speak*	nous parl**ons**	*we speak*
tu parl**es**	*you speak*	vous parl**ez**	*you speak*
il parl**e**	*he speaks*	ils parl**ent**	*they (m., m./f.) speak*
elle parl**e**	*she speaks*	elles parl**ent**	*they (f.) speak*
on parl**e**	*one/they/we speak*		

Here are some questions using **parler**:

Parlez-vous italien? *Do you speak Italian?*
Combien de langues **parles-tu**? *How many languages do you speak?*

Chanter (*to sing*) follows the same pattern:

je chant**e**	*I sing*	nous chant**ons**	*we sing*
tu chant**es**	*you sing*	vous chant**ez**	*you sing*
il chant**e**	*he sings*	ils chant**ent**	*they (m., m./f.) sing*
elle chant**e**	*she sings*	elles chant**ent**	*they (f.) sing*
on chant**e**	*one/they/we sing*		

To recapitulate, here are the subject pronouns with their English equivalents:

je	*I*
tu	*you* (singular familiar)
il	*he, it* (masculine)
elle	*she, it* (feminine)
on	*one, we, they*
nous	*we*
vous	*you* (singular formal and all plurals)
ils	*they* (masculine or mixed masculine and feminine)
elles	*they* (feminine)

There are two ways of saying *you* in French. Use **tu** to talk to friends, family members, children, and animals. Use **vous** when you are addressing a stranger, someone you don't know well, or to maintain a certain degree of distance or respect.

The pronoun **on** takes on different meanings. It may mean *one, we,* or *they* depending on how it is used. See the examples below.

Ici, **on parle** japonais.	*Japanese is spoken here.*
On ne devrait pas se comporter ainsi.	*One should not behave this way.*
On va au cinéma ce soir? (*familiar*)	*Shall we go to the movies tonight?*
En Espagne, **on mange** des tapas.	*In Spain, they eat tapas.*
On est tous d'accord. (*familiar*)	*We all agree.*

Here are some common regular **-er** verbs:

accepter	*to accept*
aimer	*to like, to love*
annuler	*to cancel*
apporter	*to bring*
attraper	*to catch*
augmenter	*to increase*
bavarder	*to chat*
casser	*to break*
chercher	*to look for*
commander	*to order*
couper	*to cut*
danser	*to dance*
déjeuner	*to have lunch*
demander	*to ask*
dessiner	*to draw*
donner	*to give*
emprunter	*to borrow*
enlever	*to remove*
étudier	*to study*
exprimer	*to express*
gagner	*to win, to earn*
garder	*to keep*
habiter	*to live*
laver	*to wash*
manger	*to eat*
mériter	*to deserve*
oublier	*to forget*
porter	*to carry*
prêter	*to lend*
refuser	*to refuse*

The present tense of **-er** verbs   **175**

regarder	*to watch*
saluer	*to greet*
sauter	*to jump*
tomber	*to fall*
travailler	*to work*
visiter	*to visit (a place)*

Mettre les verbes entre parenthèses au présent.

1. Lucie _____ (travailler) à Lyon.
2. Mon frère et moi, nous _____ (accepter) votre invitation.
3. M. et Mme Benoît _____ (chercher) un appartement.
4. Tu _____ (apporter) toujours des fleurs.
5. Vous _____ (bavarder) sur la terrasse.
6. Je _____ (commander) une soupe de légumes.
7. Ils _____ (habiter) en Normandie.
8. Elle _____ (déjeuner) avec sa belle-sœur.
9. Vous _____ (dessiner) très bien.
10. Nous _____ (visiter) le château de Fontainebleau.

Traduire en français.

1. We refuse the invitation.

2. She cancels the trip.

3. He speaks French.

4. You bring some flowers. (*formal*)

5. I cut the bread.

6. They are having lunch with Julie.

_____

7. He borrows ten euros.

_____

8. I order a dessert.

_____

9. You study Russian. (*informal*)

_____

10. They are looking for a good restaurant.

_____

VOCABULAIRE			
à midi	*at noon*	**le samedi,**	*on Saturdays, on*
à minuit	*at midnight*	**le dimanche**	*Sundays*
aujourd'hui	*today*	**cette semaine**	*this week*
demain	*tomorrow*	**le mois prochain**	*next month*
hier	*yesterday*	**le mois dernier**	*last month*
après-demain	*the day after tomorrow*	**à la fin du mois**	*at the end of the*
avant-hier	*the day before yesterday*		*month*
le matin	*in the morning*	**au début de l'année**	*at the beginning of*
l'après-midi	*in the afternoon*		*the year*
le soir	*in the evening*	**de temps en temps**	*from time to time*
toujours	*always*	**parfois**	*sometimes*
souvent	*often*		

-er verbs with spelling and stem changes

Some **-er** verbs, otherwise regular, show spelling or stem changes in the present tense, largely to maintain pronunciation. These can be learned according to their groups.

Verbs ending in -cer

Some spelling changes occur with some **-er** regular verbs. With verbs ending in **-cer**, such as **prononcer** (*to pronounce*) the **-c-** becomes **-ç-** before the letter **o**. The cedilla (**ç**) under the **c** is needed to keep the soft pronunciation of the **c** in the infinitive form.

je prononce	*I pronounce*	nous prononçons	*we pronounce*
tu prononces	*you pronounce*	vous prononcez	*you pronounce*
il/elle prononce	*he/she pronounces*	ils/elles prononcent	*they pronounce*

Here are a few examples of other **-cer** verbs:

nous annonçons   *we announce*
nous avançons   *we move forward*

The present tense of -er verbs   **177**

nous balançons	*we swing*
nous commençons	*we start*
nous défonçons	*we smash in*
nous déplaçons	*we move*
nous devançons	*we get ahead of*
nous effaçons	*we erase*
nous épiçons	*we spice*
nous façonnons	*we craft, we manufacture*
nous finançons	*we finance*
nous grimaçons	*we make faces*
nous influençons	*we influence*
nous laçons	*we lace up, we tie*
nous menaçons	*we threaten*
nous perçons	*we pierce*
nous plaçons	*we place*
nous ponçons	*we sand*
nous remplaçons	*we replace*
nous renonçons	*we give up*

EXERCICE 10·3

Mettre au présent les verbes entre parenthèses.

1. Nous _____ (commencer) à huit heures le matin.

2. Vous _____ (avancer) rapidement.

3. Je _____ (déplacer) les meubles du salon.

4. Nous _____ (devancer) nos concurrents.

5. Nous _____ (annoncer) une augmentation de salaire au début de l'année.

6. Tu _____ (effacer) le tableau.

7. Nous _____ (remplacer) toute l'équipe.

8. Ils _____ (exercer) une grande influence.

9. Nous _____ (financer) ce projet.

10. Elle _____ (menacer) de partir.

Verbs ending in -ger

With verbs ending in **-ger**, such as **voyager** (*to travel*), the **-g-** becomes **-ge-** before the letter **o**.

je voyage	*I travel*	nous voya**ge**ons	*we travel*
tu voyages	*you travel*	vous voyagez	*you travel*
il/elle voyage	*he/she travels*	ils/elles voyagent	*they travel*

Here are other common **-ger** verbs:

nous bougeons	*we move*
nous changeons	*we change*

178 PRACTICE MAKES PERFECT Complete French All-in-One

nous corrigeons	*we correct*
nous dégageons	*we release, we free*
nous déménageons	*we move (house)*
nous encourageons	*we encourage*
nous exigeons	*we demand*
nous hébergeons	*we host*
nous mangeons	*we eat*
nous mélangeons	*we mix*
nous nageons	*we swim*
nous négligeons	*we neglect*
nous partageons	*we share*
nous plongeons	*we dive*
nous protégeons	*we protect*
nous rangeons	*we put away*
nous vengeons	*we avenge*

EXERCICE 10·4

Mettre au présent les verbes entre parenthèses.

1. Vous _____ (mélanger) les ingrédients.

2. Je _____ (ranger) mes affaires.

3. Nous _____ (exiger) votre présence à la réunion.

4. Ils _____ (déménager) demain.

5. Elle _____ (héberger) ses amis.

6. Vous _____ (corriger) les exercices.

7. Nous _____ (manger) sur la terrasse à midi.

8. Tu _____ (nager) dans la piscine.

9. Nous _____ (encourager) ces jeunes talents.

10. Souvent, il _____ (changer) d'avis.

Verbs ending in -e + consonant + -er

With some verbs composed of **-e** + consonant + **-er**, such as **acheter** (*to buy*), some accent changes occur. An **accent grave** is added in all but the first- and the second-person plural.

j'ach**è**te	*I buy*	nous achetons	*we buy*
tu ach**è**tes	*you buy*	vous achetez	*you buy*
il/elle ach**è**te	*he/she buys*	ils/elles ach**è**tent	*they buy*

Here are a few other verbs following the same pattern:

achever	j'ach**è**ve	*I complete*
emmener	j'emm**è**ne	*I take along, I escort*
enlever	j'enl**è**ve	*I remove*
lever	je l**è**ve	*I raise*

The present tense of -**er** verbs **179**

mener	je mène	*I lead*
peser	je pèse	*I weigh*
semer	je sème	*I sow*

With some verbs composed of **-é** + consonant + **-er**, such as **répéter** (*to repeat*), changes may also occur. The **é aigu** changes to an **è grave** in all but the first- and second-person plural.

je répète	*I repeat*	nous répétons	*we repeat*
tu répètes	*you repeat*	vous répétez	*you repeat*
il/elle répète	*he/she repeats*	ils/elles répètent	*they repeat*

Here are a few other verbs following the same pattern:

céder	je cède	*I yield*
célébrer	je célèbre	*I celebrate*
considérer	je considère	*I consider*
déléguer	je délègue	*I delegate*
espérer	j'espère	*I hope*
exagérer	j'exagère	*I exaggerate*
gérer	je gère	*I manage*
lécher	je lèche	*I lick*
posséder	je possède	*I own*
préférer	je préfère	*I prefer*
révéler	je révèle	*I reveal*

Verbs ending in -e + l + -er

Some verbs composed of **-e** + **l** + **-er**, such as **épeler** (*to spell*), sometimes take two **l**s in all but the first- and second-person plural.

j'épelle	*I spell*	nous épelons	*we spell*
tu épelles	*you spell*	vous épelez	*you spell*
il/elle épelle	*he/she spells*	ils/elles épellent	*they spell*

Here are a few other verbs following the same pattern:

appeler	j'appelle	*I call*
ensorceler	j'ensorcelle	*I bewitch*
étinceler	j'étincelle	*I sparkle, I glitter*
ficeler	je ficelle	*I tie*
niveler	je nivelle	*I level*
rappeler	je rappelle	*I remind, I call back*
renouveler	je renouvelle	*I renew*

Mettre au présent les verbes entre parenthèses.

1. Il _____ (renouveler) son passeport.

2. Je _____ (emmener) ma nièce à l'opéra.

3. Vous _____ (acheter) un kilo de haricots.

4. Le sorcier _____ (ensorceler) le public.

5. Elle _____ (espérer) aller à Paris en mai.

6. Vous _____ (exagérer).

7. Elle _____ (s'appeler) Juliette.

8. Ces diamants _____ (étinceler) de mille feux.

9. Il _____ (répéter) mille fois la même chose.

10. Nous _____ (célébrer) son anniversaire.

EXERCICE 10·6

Mettre au présent les verbes entre parenthèses.

1. Aujourd'hui, il _____ (acheter) du poisson au marché.

2. Ils _____ (travailler) le samedi.

3. Vous _____ (emprunter) de l'argent à la banque.

4. Tu _____ (aimer) voyager en bateau.

5. Nous _____ (renoncer) à notre projet.

6. Je _____ (habiter) au dixième étage.

7. L'après-midi, elle _____ (préférer) aller dans le parc.

8. Comment _____ (s'appeler) sa sœur?

9. De temps en temps, nous _____ (bavarder) pendant la pause-café.

10. Il vous _____ (rappeler) avant midi.

EXERCICE 10·7

Faire correspondre les deux colonnes.

_____ 1. Il épelle		a. dans l'Atlantique
_____ 2. Je regarde		b. à midi et demi
_____ 3. Nous habitons		c. la comédienne malade
_____ 4. Tu aimes nager		d. Amélie
_____ 5. Ils déjeunent toujours		e. la télévision
_____ 6. Vous chantez		f. son voyage au Japon
_____ 7. Elle remplace		g. à la fin du mois

The present tense of **-er** verbs 181

_____	8. Je m'appelle	h. au troisième étage
_____	9. Elle annule	i. le mot
_____	10. Nous déménageons	j. une belle chanson

When is the present tense used in French?

The present indicative is used in a number of ways:

◆ To make a general statement and to describe ongoing actions in the present. It can be translated in three different ways.

Valérie **parle** à son ami Ludovic.	*Valérie is talking (talks, does talk) to her friend Ludovic.*
Il **regarde** les étoiles dans le ciel.	*He is looking (looks, does look) at the stars in the sky.*

◆ To express a close future

Il **part** demain soir.	*He'll leave tomorrow night.*
On **parle** de cela en fin de semaine.	*We'll discuss this at the end of the week.*

◆ To express a habitual action

Tous les jours, le soleil **se lève**.	*The sun rises every day.*
D'habitude, j'**achète** la viande dans cette boucherie.	*Usually I buy meat in this butcher shop.*

◆ To describe a past action closely connected to the present

Claude **revient** d'Asie et c'**est** la pagaille au bureau!	*Claude just returned from Asia and chaos started in the office!*
À peine rentrés et les problèmes **commencent** déjà.	*They have just come back and the problems have already started.*

◆ To express a historical fact

Flaubert **publie** *Madame Bovary* et c'**est** le scandale!	*Flaubert published* Madame Bovary *and the scandal broke out!*
Le président **arrive** en Chine et c'**est** la débâcle!	*The president arrived in China and it was a complete disaster!*

◆ To describe past events more dramatically

La reine **avance** vers le trône.	*The queen moved toward the throne.*
Et son pire ennemi **entre** dans la salle.	*And his worst enemy walked into the room.*

◆ To express an action in the process, **être en train de** + the infinitive form of the verb is used.

Un instant, s'il vous plaît, je **suis en train de parler** à Rémi.	*One moment, please, I am talking to Rémi.*
Qu'est-ce que tu **es en train de faire**?	*What are you doing?*

EXERCICE 10·8

*Reformuler les phrases en utilisant **être en train de** + infinitif.*

1. Nous chantons une chanson.

2. Elle dessine un mouton.

3. Je travaille dans la cuisine.

4. Tu effaces le tableau.

5. Vous étudiez l'histoire européenne.

6. Nous bavardons dans le jardin.

7. Il corrige les copies.

8. Tu laves la chemise.

9. Je range mes affaires.

10. Elle mange une omelette aux champignons.

One more use of the present tense: depuis

The present tense is used to express an action that began in the past and continues in the present. Note that in English, the past tense is used. There are different ways to formulate the questions, using either **depuis, il y a... que, cela (ça) fait... que**.

Let's start with **depuis**. To ask a question about the duration of an action, use **depuis quand** (*since when*) or **depuis combien de temps** (*how long*).

| **Depuis combien de temps** habites-tu à Nice? | *How long have you been living in Nice?* |
| —J'habite à Nice **depuis trois ans**. | *—I have been living in Nice for three years.* |

Depuis quand travaillez-vous chez L'Oréal?	*How long have you been working at L'Oréal?*
—Je travaille chez L'Oréal **depuis trois mois.**	*—I have been working at L'Oréal for three months.*
Il y a combien de temps que vous connaissez M. Blier?	*How long have you known Mr. Blier?*
—**Il y a quelques années que** je connais M. Blier.	*—I have known Mr. Blier for a few years.*
Ça fait combien de temps que vous avez ce dictionnaire?	*How long have you had this dictionary?*
—**Ça fait cinq ans que** j'ai ce dictionnaire.	*—I have had this dictionary for five years.*

EXERCICE
10·9

*Répondre aux questions en utilisant le présent et **depuis**.*

1. Depuis combien de temps chante-t-elle dans cette chorale? (trois ans)

_____

2. Depuis combien de temps partages-tu cet appartement? (six mois)

_____

3. Depuis combien de temps nage-t-il dans cette piscine? (un mois)

_____

4. Depuis quand habitez-vous à Montpellier? (2004)

_____

5. Depuis combien de temps possède-t-il cette propriété? (dix ans)

_____

6. Depuis combien de temps regardez-vous cette émission? (des années)

_____

7. Depuis quand travaille-t-il dans cette entreprise? (2002)

_____

8. Depuis combien de temps portez-vous des lunettes? (dix ans)

_____

9. Depuis quand est-il président? (2005)

_____

10. Depuis combien de temps ce magasin est-il fermé? (deux mois)

_____

EXERCICE 10·10

*Traduire les phrases suivantes en utilisant **vous** et l'inversion si nécessaire.*

1. I study French.

2. I spell my name.

3. They are moving tomorrow.

4. She likes to travel by boat.

5. How long have you been studying French?

6. You repeat the sentence. (*informal*)

7. We are financing the project.

8. She cancels the meeting.

9. How long have you been living in this house?

10. I weigh the vegetables.

The present tense of -ir and -re verbs

-ir verbs in the present

We studied the **-er** verbs in the previous chapter. Now, let's explore the **-ir** and **-re** verbs. The **-ir** verbs follow two different conjugation patterns.

Type 1 verbs drop the **-ir** of the infinitive, add an **-iss-** to the plural form, and then insert the appropriate ending.

choisir	to choose		
je chois**is**	I choose	nous chois**issons**	we choose
tu chois**is**	you choose	vous chois**issez**	you choose
il/elle chois**it**	he/she chooses	ils/elles chois**issent**	they choose

Many other verbs follow the same conjugation.

accomplir	to accomplish	nous accomplissons	we accomplish
adoucir	to soften, to mellow	nous adoucissons	we soften, we mellow
agrandir	to enlarge	nous agrandissons	we enlarge
applaudir	to applaud	nous applaudissons	we applaud
bâtir	to build	nous bâtissons	we build
bénir	to bless	nous bénissons	we bless
éclaircir	to lighten, to clear	nous éclaircissons	we lighten, we clear
s'épanouir	to bloom, to blossom	nous nous épanouissons	we bloom, we blossom
s'évanouir	to faint	nous nous évanouissons	we faint
finir	to finish	nous finissons	we finish
grandir	to grow up	nous grandissons	we grow up
grossir	to put on weight	nous grossissons	we put on weight
investir	to invest	nous investissons	we invest
maigrir	to lose weight	nous maigrissons	we lose weight
mincir	to slim down	nous mincissons	we slim down
obéir	to obey	nous obéissons	we obey
pâlir	to turn pale	nous pâlissons	we turn pale
rafraîchir	to refresh	nous rafraîchissons	we refresh
ralentir	to slow down	nous ralentissons	we slow down
réfléchir	to think, to reflect	nous réfléchissons	we think, we reflect
remplir	to fill	nous remplissons	we fill
réussir	to succeed	nous réussissons	we succeed
rougir	to blush	nous rougissons	we blush
saisir	to seize	nous saisissons	we seize
vieillir	to grow old	nous vieillissons	we grow old

Type 2 **-ir** verbs drop the **-ir** of the infinitive, then add the appropriate ending, *without* the **-iss-** in the **nous** and **vous** forms. These groups of **-ir** verbs can be termed irregular. Let's look at the examples below:

sortir *to go out*			
je **sors**	*I go out*	nous **sortons**	*we go out*
tu **sors**	*you go out*	vous **sortez**	*you go out*
il/elle **sort**	*he/she goes out*	ils/elles **sortent**	*they go out*

Study the first-person conjugations of the following **-ir** verbs.

bouillir	*to boil*	**je bous**	*I boil*	**nous bouillons**	*we boil*
courir	*to run*	**je cours**	*I run*	**nous courons**	*we run*
couvrir	*to cover*	**je couvre**	*I cover*	**nous couvrons**	*we cover*
cueillir	*to pick*	**je cueille**	*I pick*	**nous cueillons**	*we pick*
dormir	*to sleep*	**je dors**	*I sleep*	**nous dormons**	*we sleep*
fuir	*to flee*	**je fuis**	*I flee*	**nous fuyons**	*we flee*
mentir	*to lie*	**je mens**	*I lie*	**nous mentons**	*we lie*
mourir	*to die*	**je meurs**	*I die*	**nous mourons**	*we die*
obtenir	*to get*	**j'obtiens**	*I get*	**nous obtenons**	*we get*
offrir	*to offer*	**j'offre**	*I offer*	**nous offrons**	*we offer*
ouvrir	*to open*	**j'ouvre**	*I open*	**nous ouvrons**	*we open*
partir	*to leave*	**je pars**	*I leave*	**nous partons**	*we leave*
sentir	*to feel, to smell*	**je sens**	*I feel, I smell*	**nous sentons**	*we feel, we smell*
servir	*to serve*	**je sers**	*I serve*	**nous servons**	*we serve*
souffrir	*to suffer*	**je souffre**	*I suffer*	**nous souffrons**	*we suffer*

EXERCICE 11·1

Mettre les verbes entre parenthèses au présent.

1. Nous (cueillir) _____ des fleurs dans le jardin.

2. Ils (finir) _____ à dix-huit heures.

3. Je (remplir) _____ les verres des invités.

4. Nous (investir) _____ dans l'immobilier.

5. Ils (mentir) _____ à la police.

6. Tu (ouvrir) _____ les fenêtres du salon.

7. Vous (réfléchir) _____ à leur proposition.

8. Je (sentir) _____ les bonnes odeurs de la cuisine.

9. Ils (offrir) _____ toujours les mêmes fleurs.

10. Il (mourir) _____ de faim.

EXERCICE 11·2

Faire correspondre les deux colonnes.

_____ 1. Il agrandit

_____ 2. Le public applaudit

_____ 3. Nous choisissons

_____ 4. La voiture ralentit

_____ 5. Je vous offre

_____ 6. Tu ouvres

_____ 7. Ils dorment bien

_____ 8. Il bout

_____ 9. Vous réussissez

_____10. Je cours

a. un bon vin

b. la porte

c. très vite

d. la nuit

e. en voyant le gendarme

f. d'impatience

g. à l'examen

h. la photo

i. des chocolats pour votre anniversaire

j. l'artiste

EXERCICE 11·3

*Traduire les phrases suivantes en utilisant **vous** si nécessaire.*

1. We are leaving at ten.

_____

2. She opens the door.

_____

3. You pick some flowers in Florence's garden.

_____

4. The car is slowing down.

_____

5. We are going out tonight.

_____

6. She seizes the opportunity.

_____

7. She blushes easily.

_____

8. They run fast.

9. She solves the mystery.

10. They sleep in Sonia's bedroom.

VOCABULAIRE

Quelle langue parlez-vous?

l'allemand (*m.*)	*German*	**l'italien** (*m.*)	*Italian*
l'anglais (*m.*)	*English*	**le japonais**	*Japanese*
l'arabe (*m.*)	*Arabic*	**le polonais**	*Polish*
le chinois	*Chinese*	**le portugais**	*Portuguese*
le créole	*Creole*	**le russe**	*Russian*
l'espagnol (*m.*)	*Spanish*	**le swahili**	*Swahili*
le français	*French*	**le wolof**	*Wolof*
l'hindi (*m.*)	*Hindi*		

-re verbs in the present

For regular **-re** verbs, remove the **-re** ending and follow the pattern below.

vendre to sell			
je ven**ds**	*I sell*	nous vend**ons**	*we sell*
tu ven**ds**	*you sell*	vous vend**ez**	*you sell*
il/elle ven**d**	*he/she sells*	ils/elles vend**ent**	*they sell*

Here are other verbs that are conjugated in the same way:

attendre	*to wait*	**j'attends**	*I wait*
défendre	*to defend, to forbid*	**je défends**	*I defend, I forbid*
descendre	*to go down*	**je descends**	*I go down*
détendre	*to release, to relax*	**je détends**	*I release, I relax*
entendre	*to hear*	**j'entends**	*I hear*
étendre	*to spread out, to extend*	**j'étends**	*I spread out, I extend*
mordre	*to bite*	**je mords**	*I bite*
perdre	*to lose*	**je perds**	*I lose*
prétendre	*to claim*	**je prétends**	*I claim*
rendre	*to give back, to return*	**je rends**	*I give back, I return*
répandre	*to spread, to spill*	**je répands**	*I spread, I spill*
répondre	*to answer*	**je réponds**	*I answer*
tendre	*to stretch, to hold out*	**je tends**	*I stretch, I hold out*
tordre	*to twist*	**je tords**	*I twist*

The present tense of **-ir** and **-re** verbs **189**

EXERCICE 11·4

Mettre au présent les verbes entre parenthèses.

1. Nous (répondre) _____ aux questions du professeur de français.

2. La presse anglaise (répandre) _____ une rumeur inquiétante.

3. Vous (rendre) _____ les livres à la bibliothèque.

4. Ils (vendre) _____ des fruits et légumes au marché.

5. Je (descendre) _____ l'escalier à toute vitesse.

6. Tu (attendre) _____ l'autobus depuis dix minutes.

7. Il me (tendre) _____ la main pour me dire bonjour.

8. Elle (perdre) _____ toujours ses clés.

9. Il (prétendre) _____ être le plus intelligent.

10. Ils (étendre) _____ leur action à d'autres domaines.

EXERCICE 11·5

Faire correspondre les deux colonnes.

_____ 1. Le chat mord   a. le train

_____ 2. Je perds toujours   b. toutes sortes de marchandises

_____ 3. Elle prétend   c. au questionnaire

_____ 4. Nous entendons   d. leurs activités à l'étranger

_____ 5. Tu attends   e. mon parapluie

_____ 6. Je réponds   f. l'atmosphère

_____ 7. Ce magasin vend   g. être très riche

_____ 8. L'étudiant rend   h. la souris

_____ 9. Ils désirent étendre   i. du bruit dans la rue

_____ 10. Son humour détend un peu   j. trois livres à la bibliothèque

Irregular -re verbs

Some fairly common **-re** verbs are irregular. Let's look at **prendre** (*to take*):

je **prends**	*I take*	nous **prenons**	*we take*
tu **prends**	*you take*	vous **prenez**	*you take*
il/elle **prend**	*he/she takes*	ils/elles **prennent**	*they take*

And its variations:

apprendre	*to learn*	**j'apprends**	*I learn*
comprendre	*to understand*	**je comprends**	*I understand*
entreprendre	*to undertake*	**j'entreprends**	*I undertake*
surprendre	*to surprise, to discover*	**je surprends**	*I surprise, I discover*

EXERCICE 11·6

Mettre au présent les verbes entre parenthèses.

1. Nous (prendre) _____ le petit déjeuner à huit heures.
2. Il (entreprendre) _____ toujours des choses dangereuses.
3. Je (apprendre) _____ l'allemand.
4. Vous (comprendre) _____ son hésitation.
5. Ils (apprendre) _____ à conduire.
6. Il (surprendre) _____ le secret.
7. Vous (prendre) _____ de longues vacances.
8. Nous (comprendre) _____ le chinois.
9. Tu (prendre) _____ une autre direction.
10. Elle (comprendre) _____ tout.

EXERCICE 11·7

*Traduire les phrases suivantes en utilisant **vous** si nécessaire.*

1. He is learning Chinese.

2. She takes the subway every day.

3. He often loses his keys.

4. I can hear Pierre on the street.

5. He claims to be the king's brother.

6. You answer quickly.

_____

7. She sells flowers.

_____

8. We go down the Champs-Élysées.

_____

9. I am going down.

_____

10. We are waiting for an answer.

_____

The interrogative form

In French there are three ways of asking questions. You can do an inversion of the subject and the verb, use the **est-ce que** form, or simply use the affirmative form with an upward intonation. Let's start with the inversion:

Comprenez-vous la question?	*Do you understand the question?*
Parlez-vous espagnol?	*Do you speak Spanish?*

If the third-person singular of a verb ends with a vowel, a -**t**- is inserted to facilitate the pronunciation.

Parle-t-elle russe?	*Does she speak Russian?*
Voyage-t-il souvent en Europe?	*Does he often travel to Europe?*

A more colloquial way of asking a question is to use the **est-ce que** form in front of the *subject + verb.*

Est-ce que vous habitez à New York?	*Do you live in New York?*
Est-ce que tu sors ce soir?	*Are you going out tonight?*

Est-ce que becomes **est-ce qu'** before a vowel.

Est-ce que vous courez dans le parc?	*Do you run in the park?*
Est-ce qu'ils vendent des timbres?	*Do they sell stamps?*

A third way of asking a question, colloquially, is keeping the order *subject + verb* and speaking with an upward intonation.

Tu finis à cinq heures**?**	*You're finishing at five o'clock?*
Vous investissez en Asie**?**	*You're investing in Asia?*

192 PRACTICE MAKES PERFECT Complete French All-in-One

EXERCICE 11·8

Mettre les phrases suivantes à la forme interrogative en utilisant l'inversion.

1. Ils remplissent les formulaires.

2. Il réfléchit au problème.

3. Vous aimez aller au théâtre.

4. Elle préfère voyager en Italie.

5. Tu écoutes le discours du président.

6. Ils influencent le public.

7. Elle annule son voyage au Brésil.

8. Tu travailles le jeudi.

9. Vous apportez un nouveau livre.

10. Elle agrandit les photos.

EXERCICE 11·9

*Mettre les phrases suivantes à la forme interrogative en utilisant la forme **est-ce que**.*

1. Ils parlent de la nouvelle transaction.

2. Elle apprend le portugais.

3. Vous commandez une bouteille de vin blanc.

_____

4. Tu demandes une augmentation de salaire.

_____

5. Ils financent un grand projet.

_____

6. Vous choisissez une autre direction.

_____

7. Ils finissent tard.

_____

8. Il prétend être pauvre.

_____

9. Ils défendent cette théorie.

_____

10. Vous descendez par l'escalier.

_____

The negative form

To make a sentence negative, you simply place **ne... pas** around the verb.

Elle **travaille** le lundi.	_She works on Mondays._
Elle **ne travaille pas** le lundi.	_She does not work on Mondays._
Il **répond** à la lettre.	_He answers the letter._
Il **ne répond pas** à la lettre.	_He does not answer the letter._

If the **ne** precedes a verb starting with a vowel or a mute **h**, **ne** becomes **n'**.

J'**habite** à Strasbourg.	_I live in Strasbourg._
Je **n'habite pas** à Strasbourg.	_I do not live in Strasbourg._
Elle **aime** les marguerites.	_She likes daisies._
Elle **n'aime pas** les marguerites.	_She does not like daisies._

Aside from **ne... pas**, there are other negations, constructed in the same way.

Il **n'attend personne**.	_He is not waiting for anybody._
Tu **ne** voyages **jamais** en hiver.	_You never travel during the winter._
Il **n'a plus de** patience.	_He has no patience left._
Elle **ne** répond **rien**.	_She does not answer anything._
	(She answers nothing.)
Ce **n'est guère** raisonnable.	_It's hardly reasonable._

EXERCICE 11·10

Mettre les phrases suivantes à la forme négative.

1. Il encourage ses employés.

2. Ils visitent le musée.

3. Tu gagnes à la loterie.

4. Elle enlève son chapeau.

5. Vous exprimez vos opinions.

6. Tu pèses les fruits.

7. Il danse la valse.

8. Vous corrigez les copies des étudiants.

9. Nous étudions l'arabe.

10. Il maigrit en vacances.

The negation ni… ni…

The negation **ni… ni…** precedes each noun that it negates. In addition, the negative particle **ne** (**n'**) comes directly before the verb. When the definite article **le, la, l', les** is used before the noun, the definite article remains when the verb is negative.

Il aime **le** café et **le** chocolat.	*He likes coffee and chocolate.*
Il **n'**aime **ni le** café **ni le** chocolat.	*He likes neither coffee nor chocolate.*
Elle aime **le** bleu et **le** jaune.	*She likes blue and yellow.*
Elle **n'**aime **ni le** bleu **ni le** jaune.	*She likes neither blue nor yellow.*

When the indefinite or partitive article is used before the noun in the affirmative sentence, the article disappears when the verb is made negative.

Elle commande **de l'**eau et **du** vin.	*She orders water and wine.*
Elle **ne** commande **ni** eau **ni** vin.	*She orders neither water nor wine.*
Il vend **des** oranges et **des** mangues.	*He sells oranges and mangoes.*
Il **ne** vend **ni** oranges **ni** mangues.	*He sells neither oranges nor mangoes.*

EXERCICE 11·11

*Traduire les phrases suivantes en utilisant **vous** et l'inversion si nécessaire.*

1. I am learning Japanese.

2. He does not speak Italian.

3. She eats neither meat nor cheese.

4. They never listen to anybody.

5. You work late.

6. They like neither tea nor coffee.

7. Do you understand the question?

8. We pick flowers in the garden.

9. He never takes off his hat.

10. She never lies.

Être, avoir, and other irregular verbs

The verb être (to be)

The verbs **être** (*to be*) and **avoir** (*to have*) are essential verbs you need to memorize. They are both irregular. Let's start with **être**:

je **suis**	*I am*	nous **sommes**	*we are*
tu **es**	*you are* (familiar)	vous **êtes**	*you are*
il/elle **est**	*he/she is*	ils/elles **sont**	*they are*

Note that the **-s** of **vous** is pronounced as a **z** when followed by the vowel **ê-** in **êtes**.

Elle **est** américaine.	*She is American.*
Vous **êtes** brésilien?	*Are you Brazilian?*

VOCABULAIRE

agréable	*pleasant*	**heureux,**	*happy, content,*
amusant(e)	*funny*	**heureuse**	*glad*
beau, bel, belle	*beautiful*	**jeune**	*young*
bon, bonne	*good*	**libre**	*free*
charmant(e)	*charming*	**nouveau, nouvel,**	*new*
cher, chère	*expensive*	**nouvelle**	
créatif, créative	*creative*	**petit(e)**	*small*
efficace	*efficient*	**sec, sèche**	*dry*
frais, fraîche	*fresh, cool*	**sympathique**	*nice, friendly*
gentil(le)	*kind, nice*	**vieux, vieil, vieille**	*old*
grand(e)	*tall*		

EXERCICE 12·1

Mettre au présent les verbes entre parenthèses.

1. Le château (être) _____ vieux.

2. Nous (être) _____ libres demain soir.

3. Les produits (être) _____ beaucoup trop chers.

4. Tu (être) _____ plus jeune que lui?

5. Elles (être) _____ vraiment charmantes.

6. Vous (être) _____ occupé cet après-midi?

7. Ce (être) _____ un nouveau livre.

8. Leurs méthodes (ne pas être) _____ très efficaces.

9. Est-ce qu'il (être) _____ aussi amusant que son frère?

10. Je (être) _____ un peu en retard.

EXERCICE 12·2

Répondre aux questions à la forme affirmative.

1. Est-ce qu'ils sont en retard?

   _____

2. Le climat est sec?

   _____

3. Êtes-vous libre ce soir?

   _____

4. Est-il heureux?

   _____

5. Est-ce qu'elle est sympathique?

   _____

6. Ce restaurant français est cher?

   _____

7. Êtes-vous fatigué?

   _____

8. Est-ce que nous sommes à la bonne adresse?

   _____

9. Ce film est amusant?

   _____

10. Le musée est ouvert?

    _____

198 PRACTICE MAKES PERFECT Complete French All-in-One

The verb avoir (to have)

The verb **avoir** (*to have*) also has an irregular conjugation.

j'**ai**	*I have*	nous **avons**	*we have*
tu **as**	*you have*	vous **avez**	*you have*
il/elle **a**	*he/she has*	ils/elles **ont**	*they have*

Note that the **-s** of **nous, vous, ils, elles** is pronounced **z** when followed by a vowel.

Il**s ont** une belle maison. *They have a beautiful house.*
Vou**s avez** un instant? *Do you have a moment?*

Note that **un, une,** and **des** change to **de** or **d'** when the verb is in the negative form.

Tu as **des** amis à Paris? *Do you have friends in Paris?*
Non, je **n'**ai **pas d'**amis à Paris. *No, I do not have friends in Paris.*
Il a **des** enfants? *Does he have (any) children?*
Non, il **n'**a **pas d'**enfants. *No, he does not have (any) children.*

The verb **avoir** is used in many common idiomatic expressions. Here are a few examples:

j'ai de la chance	*I am lucky*
j'ai besoin de…	*I need…*
j'ai chaud	*I am hot, warm*
j'ai envie de…	*I feel like…*
j'ai faim	*I am hungry*
j'ai froid	*I am cold*
j'ai honte	*I am ashamed*
j'ai l'air de…	*I seem, I look…*
j'ai mal	*I have a pain, it hurts*
j'ai peur	*I am afraid*
j'ai (trente-cinq) ans	*I am (thirty-five) years old*
j'ai raison	*I am right*
j'ai soif	*I am thirsty*
j'ai tort	*I am wrong*

When referring to the state of one's body, French uses **avoir mal à** (*having an ache or pain*).

J'**ai mal à la tête**. *I have a headache.*
Il **a mal au bras**. *His arm hurts.*

When **avoir mal à** is followed by a verb, it means *to have trouble doing something*.

Nous **avons du mal à accepter** sa décision. *We have trouble accepting his decision.*
Elle **a du mal à monter** l'escalier. *She has trouble climbing the stairs.*

EXERCICE
12·3

Mettre au présent les verbes entre parenthèses.

1. Nous (avoir) _____ quelques minutes.
2. Tu (ne pas avoir) _____ assez d'arguments.
3. Je (avoir) _____ une grande estime pour lui.

4. Vous (avoir) _____ des amis à Londres?

5. Elle (avoir) _____ beaucoup de chance dans les affaires.

6. Ils (avoir) _____ une réunion à quinze heures.

7. Tu (avoir) _____ une maison à la campagne?

8. Nous (ne pas avoir) _____ besoin de son aide.

9. Vous (ne pas avoir) _____ toujours raison.

10. Je (avoir) _____ froid.

EXERCICE 12·4

Faire correspondre les deux colonnes.

_____ 1. J'ai faim, alors   a. au casino
_____ 2. Il a peur   b. à la tête
_____ 3. Ils ont de la chance   c. fatigué
_____ 4. L'étudiant de français a besoin   d. il ouvre la fenêtre
_____ 5. Tu as mal   e. de longues vacances
_____ 6. Il a tort, alors   f. elle boit un verre d'eau
_____ 7. Vous avez l'air   g. je mange quelque chose
_____ 8. Ils ont très envie   h. il présente ses excuses
_____ 9. Il a chaud, alors   i. d'un nouveau dictionnaire
_____ 10. Elle a soif, alors   j. des fantômes

EXERCICE 12·5

*Traduire les phrases suivantes en utilisant **vous** et l'inversion si nécessaire.*

1. I am tired.

2. He is very hungry.

3. They are always right.

4. Are they French?

5. Are you afraid of his reaction?

6. He is ashamed.

7. They have a dog.

8. She has a new hat.

9. It's very expensive.

10. Close the window. We are cold.

The -oir verbs

The **-oir** verbs do not all follow the same conjugation pattern. We'll start with the very useful verb **savoir** (*to know*). **Savoir** means *to know a fact, to know how to do something* from memory or study.

je **sais**	*I know*	nous **savons**	*we know*
tu **sais**	*you know*	vous **savez**	*you know*
il/elle **sait**	*he/she knows*	ils/elles **savent**	*they know*

Elle **sait jouer** du piano.   *She can play the piano.*
Il **sait** ce poème par cœur.   *He knows this poem by heart.*
Ils **savent gérer** leurs affaires.   *They know how to manage their business.*

Note that **savoir** is sometimes translated by *can*. Before a dependent clause or before an infinitive, only **savoir** can be used.

Je ne sais pas **où il est**.   *I don't know where he is.*
Il sait **qu'elle est occupée**.   *He knows she is busy.*

EXERCICE 12·6

Mettre au présent les verbes entre parenthèses.

1. Est-ce que vous (savoir) _____ jouer au poker?

2. Je (savoir) _____ que Laurent est un bon musicien.

3. Elle (ne pas savoir) _____ s'il travaille lundi.

4. Nous (savoir) _____ utiliser cet ordinateur.

5. Tu (savoir) _____ parler espagnol?

6. Est-ce que tu (savoir) _____ parler anglais?

7. Il (ne pas savoir) _____ faire la cuisine.

8. (Savoir) _____ -vous quand ils partent?

9. Tu (savoir) _____ si ce restaurant est cher?

10. Vous (savoir) _____ où se trouve la Bastille?

Connaître

When learning the verb **savoir**, you also need to become acquainted with the verb **connaître**, in order to understand when to use one or the other. **Connaître** means *to know, to be acquainted with, to be familiar with*. In a figurative way, it means *to enjoy, to experience*. It is always followed by a direct object; it is never followed by a dependent clause.

je **connais**	*I know*	nous **connaissons**	*we know*
tu **connais**	*you know*	vous **connaissez**	*you know*
il/elle **connaît**	*he/she knows*	ils/elles **connaissent**	*they know*

Elle **connaît** bien Paris. *She knows Paris well.*
Connaissez-vous les Tavernier? *Do you know the Taverniers?*
Son nouveau roman **connaît** un *His new novel is enjoying great success.*
grand succès.

EXERCICE
12·7

*Conjuguer le verbe **connaître** au présent.*

1. Ils _____ bien la Normandie.

2. Nous _____ Julien depuis trois ans.

3. Ce nouveau club _____ un grand succès.

4. Je _____ ce fait.

5. Cet artisan _____ son métier.

6. Vous _____ cette chanson?

7. Est-ce que vous _____ un bon restaurant italien?

8. Je _____ Paris comme ma poche.

9. Il _____ cette méthode à la perfection.

10. _____-vous l'œuvre de Victor Hugo?

EXERCICE
12·8

Connaître ou savoir?

1. Est-ce que tu _____ pourquoi il est absent?

2. Elle _____ cette chanson par cœur.

3. Tu _____ jouer au base-ball?

4. Nous _____ la fille de José.

5. Je ne _____ pas à quelle heure ouvre la banque.

6. Ils _____ un bon dentiste.

7. Ce nouveau produit _____ un grand succès sur le marché.

8. Vous _____ Bertrand?

9. Il _____ qu'il n'est pas qualifié pour ce travail.

10. Nous ne _____ pas ce quartier.

The verbs **pouvoir** and **vouloir**

Pouvoir (*can, may*) expresses ability and capability.

je **peux**	*I can*	nous **pouvons**	*we can*
tu **peux**	*you can*	vous **pouvez**	*you can*
il/elle **peut**	*he/she can*	ils/elles **peuvent**	*they can*

Elle ne **peut** pas **venir** aujourd'hui.	*She cannot come today.*
Est-ce que tu **peux** lui **téléphoner**?	*Can you call him?*
Je **peux** vous **donner** des renseignements?	*May I give you some information?*

When asking permission with inversion in formal style, the first-person singular of **pouvoir** takes a different form.

Puis-je vous aider?	*May I help you?*
Puis-je vous donner un conseil?	*May I give you a piece of advice?*

Another formal way of asking questions is to use the conditional form of **pouvoir**. We'll cover this in more depth in Chapter 19.

Pourriez-vous **résoudre** ce problème?	*Could you solve this problem?*
Pourriez-vous **annuler** notre vol?	*Could you cancel our flight?*

The verb **vouloir** (*to want*) is used to express wishes and desires. It is also used for a polite request in the conditional form.

je **veux**	*I want*	nous **voulons**	*we want*
tu **veux**	*you want*	vous **voulez**	*you want*
il/elle **veut**	*he/she wants*	ils/elles **veulent**	*they want*

Elle **veut** une augmentation.	*She wants a raise.*
Nous **voulons** une table près de la cheminée.	*We want a table by the fireplace.*
Je **voudrais** vous **parler**.	*I would like to speak with you.*

Être, avoir, and other irregular verbs   203

EXERCICE 12·9

Mettre au présent les verbes entre parenthèses.

1. Nous (vouloir) _____ une chambre qui donne sur le jardin.

2. Je (ne pas pouvoir) _____ assister à la réunion à quinze heures.

3. Je (vouloir) _____ vous parler avant jeudi.

4. Nous (pouvoir) _____ envoyer les documents par la poste.

5. Tu (vouloir) _____ venir ce soir?

6. Est-ce que vous (pouvoir) _____ écrire une lettre de recommandation?

7. Elle (pouvoir) _____ remplir ce formulaire.

8. Ils (vouloir) _____ partir avant midi.

9. Vous (vouloir) _____ prendre un verre?

10. Est-ce qu'ils (pouvoir) _____ arriver un peu plus tôt?

A number of other verbs ending in **-oir** are irregular. Let's look at a few examples in their first-person singular and plural forms:

apercevoir to see, to perceive			
j'aperçois	*I see, I perceive*	**nous apercevons**	*we see, we perceive*
décevoir to disappoint			
je déçois	*I disappoint*	**nous décevons**	*we disappoint*
devoir must, to have to			
je dois	*I must, I have to*	**nous devons**	*we must, we have to*
émouvoir to move, to stir			
j'émeus	*I move, I stir*	**nous émouvons**	*we move, we stir*
prévoir to foresee, to predict			
je prévois	*I foresee*	**nous prévoyons**	*we foresee*
promouvoir to promote			
je promeus	*I promote*	**nous promouvons**	*we promote*
recevoir to receive			
je reçois	*I receive*	**nous recevons**	*we receive*
valoir to be worth			
cela vaut	*it is worth*	**nous valons**	*we are worth*
voir to see			
je vois	*I see*	**nous voyons**	*we see*

Falloir and **pleuvoir** are used only in the third-person singular.

| falloir | to be necessary | il faut | it is necessary |
| pleuvoir | to rain | il pleut | it is raining |

EXERCICE 12·10

Mettre au présent les verbes entre parenthèses.

1. Je (apercevoir) _____ un château en haut de la colline.
2. Il (prévoir) _____ un avenir meilleur.
3. Il (pleuvoir) _____ toujours dans cette région.
4. Nous (voir) _____ une amélioration.
5. Tu (décevoir) _____ ton professeur.
6. Cette organisation (promouvoir) _____ la recherche scientifique.
7. Cela (valoir) _____ très cher.
8. Il (falloir) _____ apprendre les conjugaisons.
9. Cet écrivain (émouvoir) _____ le public.
10. Vous (recevoir) _____ nos félicitations.

EXERCICE 12·11

*Mettre au présent les verbes entre parenthèses en utilisant **tu** et la forme **est-ce que** si nécessaire.*

1. Can you swim?

___

2. Can he cook?

___

3. I don't know where he is.

___

4. Can she fill out this form?

___

5. She knows Caroline.

___

6. Do you know this French song by heart?

___

7. It is raining in France.

_____

8. You must arrive at noon.

_____

9. He foresees a great improvement.

_____

10. I see the castle.

_____

The verb **devoir** (*to have to, must*)

The verb **devoir** (*must, to have to*) is an irregular verb with various meanings.

je **dois**	*I must*	nous **devons**	*we must*
tu **dois**	*you must*	vous **devez**	*you must*
il/elle **doit**	*he/she must*	ils/elles **doivent**	*they must*

Let's start with the notion of *debt* in the literal and figurative meanings:

- **Devoir** as a *debt*:

Combien est-ce qu'on vous **doit**?	*How much do we owe you?*
Elle me **doit** mille euros.	*She owes me a thousand euros.*
Je vous **dois** quelque chose?	*Do I owe you anything?*
Il **doit** sa vie à son chirurgien.	*He owes his life to his surgeon.*

- **Devoir** as an *obligation*:

Vous **devez assister** à la réunion demain matin.	*You must attend the meeting tomorrow morning.*
L'enfant **doit obéir** à ses parents.	*The child must obey his parents.*
Vous **ne devez pas** y **aller**.	*You must not go there.*

- **Devoir** as a *probability*:

L'avion **doit atterrir** à dix heures.	*The plane is supposed to land at ten o'clock.*
Son livre **doit sortir** la semaine prochaine.	*Her book is supposed to be published next week.*

The voice intonation will often determine if **devoir** implies an obligation or a probability. For example, **il doit venir ce soir**, may mean *he is supposed to come tonight* or *he must come tonight*. Pay attention to intonation and gestures.

- **Devoir** as a *warning* and *suggestion*. When used in the conditional or the past conditional, **devoir** takes on the meaning of *should* or *should have*. We'll cover this aspect in depth in Chapter 19.

Tu **ne devrais pas** lui **prêter** d'argent.	*You should not lend him any money.*
Elles **devraient apprendre** une langue étrangère.	*They should learn a foreign language.*

206 PRACTICE MAKES PERFECT Complete French All-in-One

VOCABULAIRE			
une voiture	a car	atterrir	to land
un autobus	a bus	décoller	to take off (plane)
un taxi	a cab	manquer le train	to miss the train
un train	a train	conduire	to drive
un avion	a plane	tomber en panne	to break down
une navette	a shuttle	faire le plein	to fill up
la circulation	traffic	monter, descendre	to get on, to get off
embarquer	to go on board	voyager	to travel
débarquer	to get off		

EXERCICE 12·12

Mettre au présent les verbes entre parenthèses.

1. Elle (devoir) prévenir sa mère.

2. Tu (devoir) partir immédiatement.

3. Vous (devoir) refuser leur offre.

4. Elle (devoir) prendre une navette.

5. Ils (ne pas devoir) arriver avant dimanche.

6. Je (devoir) appeler Michel?

7. L'avion (devoir) décoller dans quelques minutes.

8. Les voitures (devoir) embarquer sur le ferry.

9. Je (devoir) préparer le dîner.

10. Tu (devoir) faire le plein sur l'autoroute.

EXERCICE 12·13

*Traduire les phrases suivantes en utilisant **vous** et la forme **est-ce que** si nécessaire.*

1. You must cook tonight.

2. She must not work today.

3. At what time is he supposed to arrive?

4. How much do I owe you?

5. Why must he sell his car?

6. She owes an excuse to Carole.

7. Are we supposed to know these verbs?

8. He owes two thousand dollars to the bank.

9. You should call Vincent.

10. You should not invite Pierre.

EXERCICE 12·14

Faire correspondre les deux colonnes.

_____ 1. Elle a des dettes.   a. Elle doit la vie à son médecin.

_____ 2. Elle n'est pas morte.   b. Elle doit être prudente.

_____ 3. Elle va peut-être voyager.   c. Elle doit faire la cuisine.

_____ 4. Elle a des invités.   d. Elle doit partir en vacances.

_____ 5. Elle hésite encore.   e. Elle doit de l'argent.

208 PRACTICE MAKES PERFECT Complete French All-in-One

Il y a (there is, there are)

Il y a is an impersonal expression that means both *there is* and *there are*.

Il y a un chat sur le canapé.	*There is a cat on the sofa.*
Il n'y a plus rien dans le frigo.	*There is nothing left in the fridge.*

Il y a is used in a variety of expressions.

Qu'est-ce qu'**il y a**?	*What's the matter?*
Il n'y a qu'à leur dire.	*Just tell them.*
Il y avait une fois...	*Once upon a time . . .*
Il y a cinquante kilomètres d'ici à Paris.	*It's fifty kilometers from here to Paris.*
Il y en a qui feraient mieux de se taire.	*Some people would do better to keep quiet.*

Il s'agit de (it is a matter of, it's about)

Il s'agit de (*it is a matter of, it's about*) is a fixed expression that introduces the subject of a work (book, film, etc.) or of a situation.

De quoi **s'agit-il**?	*What is it about?*
Dans ce film, **il s'agit d'**un crime.	*This film is about a crime.*
Dans ce roman, **il s'agit d'**une princesse.	*This novel is about a princess.*
Il s'agit de ton avenir.	*Your future is at stake.*
Il ne s'agit pas de plaisanter.	*This is no time for jokes.*
Il s'agit de faire vite.	*We must act quickly.*
Il ne s'agit pas de dettes.	*It is not a question of debts.*
Il s'agit d'amour.	*It is a matter of love.*

Verbs ending in -eindre and -aindre

Among the **-re** verbs, some verbs ending in **-eindre** or **-aindre** can be grouped together.

Verbs like **peindre** (*to paint*) include **teindre** (*to dye*), **ceindre** (*to encircle*), **feindre** (*to feign*), **craindre** (*to fear*), **plaindre** (*to pity*), and **se plaindre** (*to complain*).

Let's conjugate the verb **peindre**:

je **peins**	*I paint*	nous **peignons**	*we paint*
tu **peins**	*you paint*	vous **peignez**	*you paint*
il/elle **peint**	*he/she paints*	ils/elles **peignent**	*they paint*

Le peintre **peint** le plafond de l'opéra.	*The painter is painting the ceiling of the opera.*
Vous **peignez** un tableau abstrait.	*You are painting an abstract painting.*

Craindre follows a similar pattern.

je **crains**	*I fear*	nous **craignons**	*we fear*
tu **crains**	*you fear*	vous **craignez**	*you fear*
il/elle **craint**	*he/she fears*	ils/elles **craignent**	*they fear*

Ils **craignent** le pire.	*They fear the worst.*
Il ne **craint** pas la douleur.	*He is not afraid of pain.*

EXERCICE 12·15

Conjuguer au présent les verbes entre parenthèses.

1. Elle (craindre) _____ de profonds changements.

2. Il (feindre) _____ la tristesse.

3. Ils (plaindre) _____ la pauvre femme.

4. La muraille (ceindre) _____ la ville.

5. Vous (feindre) _____ l'indifférence.

6. Nous (craindre) _____ le ridicule.

7. Vous (peindre) _____ le mur en bleu.

8. Ils (craindre) _____ le froid.

9. Elle (teindre) _____ en blond les moustaches de l'acteur.

10. Elle (se plaindre) _____ tout le temps.

EXERCICE 12·16

*Traduire les phrases suivantes en utilisant **tu** et la forme **est-ce que** si nécessaire.*

1. She is painting the kitchen.

   _____

2. There is a dog in the car.

   _____

3. They pity the poor child.

   _____

4. This book is about the French president.

   _____

5. What is it about?

   _____

6. He fears the worst.

   _____

7. There are books on the table.

   _____

8. Is there a computer?

   _____

9. Are you painting the flowers?

   _____

10. It's a matter of passion.

    _____

The immediate future, the immediate past, and the causative form

The verb **aller** (*to go*)

Wherever you want to go, you'll need the verb **aller** (*to go*). It is an **-er** irregular verb, also used in many idiomatic expressions.

je **vais**	*I go*	nous **allons**	*we go*
tu **vas**	*you go*	vous **allez**	*you go*
il/elle **va**	*he/she goes*	ils/elles **vont**	*they go*

Ils **vont** à Paris à la fin du mois. — *They are going to Paris at the end of the month.*

Elle ne **va** pas à l'école demain. — *She is not going to school tomorrow.*

Use the preposition **à** (*to, at, in*) to say where you are going. Watch out for the contraction: **à** + **le** = **au** and **à** + **les** = **aux**.

Je vais **au** théâtre ce soir. — *I am going to the theater tonight.*
Elle va souvent **à l'**opéra. — *She often goes to the opera.*
Léa va **à la** bibliothèque. — *Léa is going to the library.*
Chloé veut aller **aux** États-Unis. — *Chloé wants to go to the United States.*

Aller is used in many common expressions.

Ça **va**? — *How are you? How are things going?*
Comment **allez**-vous? — *How are you?*
Ce tailleur vous **va** bien. — *This suit looks good on you.*
Comment **va** la famille? — *How is the family?*

VOCABULAIRE

lundi	*Monday*	**juin**	*June*
mardi	*Tuesday*	**juillet**	*July*
mercredi	*Wednesday*	**août**	*August*
jeudi	*Thursday*	**septembre**	*September*
vendredi	*Friday*	**octobre**	*October*
samedi	*Saturday*	**novembre**	*November*
dimanche	*Sunday*	**décembre**	*December*
janvier	*January*	**le printemps**	*spring*
février	*February*	**l'été** (*m.*)	*summer*
mars	*March*	**l'automne** (*m.*)	*fall*
avril	*April*	**l'hiver** (*m.*)	*winter*
mai	*May*		

The immediate future tense

Aller is also used to form the immediate future. So, to talk about what you are *going to do*, use **aller** in the present indicative followed immediately by a verb in the infinitive.

Je **vais acheter** une voiture en mai.	*I am going to buy a car in May.*
Nous **allons faire** un voyage en avril.	*We are going to go on a trip in April.*
Elle **va apprendre** le chinois.	*She is going to learn Chinese.*
Ils **vont** bientôt **déménager**.	*They're going to move soon.*

This construction can replace the present in colloquial speech.

Vous déjeunez avec nous?	*Are you having lunch with us?*
Vous **allez déjeuner** avec nous?	*Are you going to have lunch with us?*
Est-ce que tu acceptes leur offre?	*Are you accepting their offer?*
Est-ce que tu **vas accepter** leur offre?	*Are you going to accept their offer?*

And in everyday conversation, the immediate future is often used as a substitute for the future tense (*le futur simple*).

Vous **partirez** la semaine prochaine?	*You'll leave next week?*
Vous **allez partir** la semaine prochaine?	*You're going to leave next week?*
Vous **prendrez** des vacances?	*Will you take any vacation?*
Vous **allez prendre** des vacances?	*Are you going to take any vacation?*

EXERCICE 13·1

Mettre au présent les verbes entre parenthèses.

1. Nous (aller) _____ à la plage cet après-midi.
2. Ils (aller) _____ à Tahiti en décembre.
3. Je (aller) _____ chez le dentiste demain matin.
4. Le lundi, il (aller) _____ à son cours d'anglais.
5. Vous (aller) _____ en vacances à la fin de la semaine.
6. Ça (aller) _____ ?
7. Elle (aller) _____ à la banque cet après-midi.
8. Je (aller) _____ en Afrique avec mes amis.
9. Il (aller) _____ au match de base-ball ce soir.
10. Comment (aller) _____-vous?

EXERCICE 13·2

Mettre les phrases suivantes au futur immédiat.

1. Nous achetons une nouvelle machine à laver.

   _____

2. Il prend des vacances cet automne.

   _____

3. Vous investissez au Japon.

   _____

4. Elle a vingt ans.

   _____

5. Cette agence promeut cette marchandise.

   _____

6. Il est président.

   _____

7. Nous choisissons un cadeau.

   _____

8. Tu dînes au restaurant.

   _____

9. Ils déménagent en janvier.

   _____

10. Elle travaille au centre-ville.

    _____

The verb **venir** (*to come*)

The verb **venir** (*to come*) and its derivatives, **devenir** (*to become*), **prévenir** (*to warn, to inform*), **survenir** (*to occur*), are all commonly used verbs. First, let's look at the conjugation:

je **viens**	*I come*	nous **venons**	*we come*
tu **viens**	*you come*	vous **venez**	*you come*
il/elle **vient**	*he/she comes*	ils/elles **viennent**	*they come*

Vous **venez** à huit heures ce soir?	*Are you coming at eight this evening?*
D'où **viennent**-ils?	*Where are they coming from?*
N'oubliez pas de nous **prévenir**.	*Don't forget to inform us.*

The immediate future, the immediate past, and the causative form **213**

The immediate past

The verb **venir** (*to come*) in the present tense + **de**, combined with a verb in the infinitive, expresses an action that has just taken place. Although the construction **venir de** is in the present tense in French, it conveys an idea in the past in English.

Il **vient de partir**.   *He just left.*
Elle **vient de vendre** sa voiture.   *She just sold her car.*

Mettre au présent les verbes entre parenthèses.

1. Il (venir) _____ d'Espagne.
2. Est-ce qu'elles (venir) _____ ce midi?
3. Tu (venir) _____ avec nous?
4. Elle (venir) _____ du Canada.
5. Vous (revenir) _____ des Maldives?
6. Elle nous (prévenir) _____ toujours à la dernière minute.
7. Nous (venir) _____ tous ce soir.
8. Il (devenir) _____ fou avec tout ce travail.
9. Vous (revenir) _____ cet après-midi?
10. Je (venir) _____ de la contacter.

Mettre les phrases suivantes au passé immédiat.

1. Je téléphone à Bernard.
   _____

2. Il annule son vol.
   _____

3. Elle remplace tous ses meubles.
   _____

4. La police révèle le secret.
   _____

5. Vous commencez à travailler.
   _____

6. Elle manque le train.

_____

7. Tu as trente ans.

_____

8. Il achève ses études.

_____

9. Nous parlons à la directrice.

_____

10. Ils voient un bon film.

_____

_____

EXERCICE
13·5

*Traduire les phrases suivantes en utilisant **tu** et l'inversion si nécessaire.*

1. Are you going to the movies on Sunday?

_____

2. They are going to move soon.

_____

3. How are you doing?

_____

4. They are going to invest in Portugal.

_____

5. She's just started a new job.

_____

6. This hat looks good on you.

_____

7. They just canceled my flight.

_____

8. He goes to the library on Saturdays.

_____

9. She just called François.

_____

10. She is going to finish the book this afternoon.

_____

The immediate future, the immediate past, and the causative form   **215**

Tenir

Another verb conjugated like **ven**ir is **tenir** (*to hold*):

je **tiens**	*I hold*	nous **tenons**	*we hold*
tu **tiens**	*you hold*	vous **tenez**	*you hold*
il/elle **tient**	*he/she holds*	ils/elles **tiennent**	*they hold*

Il **tient** ses gants à la main. — *He holds his gloves in his hand.*
Tiens la porte! — *Hold the door!*

Tenir has several different meanings.

Le directeur ne **tient** jamais ses promesses. — *The manager never keeps his promises.*
Il **tient** son fils par la main. — *He is holding his son's hand.*
La caféine la **tient** éveillée. — *Caffeine keeps her awake.*
Ils **tiennent** un restaurant à Nice. — *They run a restaurant in Nice.*
Toutes ces affaires ne vont pas **tenir** dans ta valise. — *All these things won't fit in your suitcase.*
Ils **tiennent le rythme**. — *They are keeping up the pace.*
Elle **tient compte de** vos commentaires. — *She takes your comments into account.*
Tiens, tiens, c'est étrange... — *Well, well, this is strange . . .*
Tiens, prends ces trois livres. — *Here, take these three books.*

When used with the preposition **à** or **de**, **tenir** takes on another meaning.

Elle **tient à** ses bijoux. — *She is attached to her jewels.*
Ils **tiennent à** leurs habitudes. — *They are attached to their habits.*
Marc **tient à** vous voir. — *Marc insists on seeing you.*
De qui **tient**-elle? — *Whom does she take after?*
Elle **tient de** sa mère. — *She takes after her mother.*

EXERCICE
13·6

Faire correspondre les deux colonnes.

_____ 1. Il tient à sa voiture.   a. Il ressemble à sa parente.

_____ 2. Il ne tient compte de rien.   b. Il veut discuter avec toi.

_____ 3. Il ne tient pas ses promesses.   c. Il est attaché à cette chose.

_____ 4. Il tient de sa sœur.   d. Il ignore tout.

_____ 5. Il tient à te parler.   e. Il ne respecte pas ses engagements.

The verb **faire** (*to do, to make*)

Another verb you'll come across all the time is **faire** (*to do, to make*). Let's look at its conjugation:

je **fais**	*I do*	nous **faisons**	*we do*
tu **fais**	*you do*	vous **faites**	*you do*
il/elle **fait**	*he/she does*	ils/elles **font**	*they do*

Qu'est-ce que vous **faites** ce soir?	*What are you doing tonight?*
Nous **faisons** un gâteau.	*We're making a cake.*
Il ne sait pas quoi **faire**.	*He does not know what to do.*

Faire is also used in expressions relating to chores, activities, sports, etc.

Elle **fait les courses** ici.	*She shops here.*
Tu ne **fais** jamais **la cuisine**?	*You never cook?*
Il **fait le ménage** le samedi.	*He does the housecleaning on Saturdays.*
Viens **faire une promenade**!	*Come take a walk!*
L'enfant **fait la vaisselle**.	*The child is doing the dishes.*
Je ne veux pas **faire la queue**.	*I don't want to stand in line.*
Ça **fait combien**?	*How much does it cost?*
Tu **fais du vélo**?	*Do you ride a bike?*
Vous **faites du sport**?	*Do you play sports?*

Faire is used, with the impersonal third-person singular **il**, in most expressions relating to the weather.

Quel temps fait-il?	*What's the weather like?*
Il fait beau.	*It is nice.*
Il fait froid.	*It is cold.*
Il fait frais.	*It is cool.*
Il fait doux.	*It is mild.*
Il fait chaud.	*It is hot.*

A few verbs relating to the weather are used in the impersonal **il** form, without **faire**.

Il pleut.	*It is raining.*
Il neige.	*It is snowing.*
Il grêle.	*It is hailing.*
Il bruine.	*It is drizzling.*

EXERCICE
13·7

Mettre au présent les verbes entre parenthèses.

1. Qui (faire) _____ quoi dans cette entreprise?
2. Ils (faire) _____ un grand voyage chaque année.
3. Tu (faire) _____ la cuisine?
4. Quel temps (faire) _____-il à Rome aujourd'hui?
5. Nous (faire) _____ une promenade dans les jardins du Luxembourg.
6. Elle (faire) _____ le marché le samedi matin.
7. On (faire) _____ la queue depuis une demi-heure!
8. Ils (faire) _____ la sieste de trois à cinq heures.
9. Vous (faire) _____ de l'exercice pour rester en forme?
10. Il (faire) _____ des grimaces devant le miroir.

The causative form

The causative form is, in most cases, used to express the idea of *having something done by someone* or of *causing something to happen*. It is formed with the verb **faire** followed by an infinitive.

Elle **écrit** la lettre elle-même.	*She writes the letter herself.*
Elle **fait écrire** la lettre par sa secrétaire.	*She has the letter written by her secretary.*
Ils **envoient** le document.	*They send the document.*
Ils **font envoyer** le document.	*They have the document sent.*
Elle **fait** la robe.	*She is making the dress.*
Elle **fait faire** la robe.	*She is having the dress made.*

EXERCICE 13·8

Mettre les phrases suivantes à la forme causative.

1. Je lis le dossier.

2. Vous lavez la voiture.

3. Il répare la télévision.

4. Elle investit sa fortune.

5. J'envoie le paquet.

6. Il annule le voyage.

7. Tu remplaces l'employé malade.

8. Il visite l'entreprise.

9. Je corrige les copies des étudiants.

10. Je chante la chanson.

EXERCICE 13·9

*Traduire les phrases suivantes en utilisant **vous** et la forme **est-ce que** si nécessaire.*

1. They have the letter sent to Paris.

   _____

2. I have been standing in line for ten minutes.

   _____

3. They are attached to their friends.

   _____

4. He really wants to sing this song.

   _____

5. She is holding a vase.

   _____

6. He looks like his father.

   _____

7. It's raining.

   _____

8. Can you cook?

   _____

9. She has her car washed.

   _____

10. It's cold.

   _____

Other examples:

Je **nettoie** le sol.	I **clean** the floor.
Je **fais nettoyer** le sol.	I **have** the floor **cleaned**.
Amélia **désinstalle** son antivirus.	Amélia **is uninstalling** her antivirus software.
Amélia **a fait désinstaller** son antivirus.	Amélia **had** her antivirus software **uninstalled**.
Alain **coupe** du bois.	Alain **is cutting** some wood.
Alain **fait couper** du bois.	Alain **is having** some wood **cut**.
Nous **décorons** la salle avec des ballons pour la célébration.	We **are decorating** the room with balloons for the celebration.
Nous **faisons décorer** la salle avec des ballons pour la célébration.	We **are having** the room **decorated** with balloons for the celebration.

The immediate future, the immediate past, and the causative form   219

EXERCICE 13·10

Put the following sentences into the causative form. Pay attention to the tenses!

1. Je réparerai mon ordinateur.

   _____

2. Emmanuel remplacera toutes les lampes dans la bibliothèque.

   _____

3. J'ai visité les nouveaux bureaux de l'agence.

   _____

4. Shah Jahan a construit le Taj Mahal en mémoire de sa femme.

   _____

5. Envoie le paquet en express!

   _____

6. Victoria fera une robe pour le mariage de sa cousine.

   _____

7. Rédigez une demande de bourse de recherche!

   _____

8. Il livrera les fleurs à Madame de Guermantes avant midi.

   _____

9. Vous corrigerez les fautes d'orthographe dans votre essai.

   _____

10. Raphaël a lavé sa voiture avant de partir en vacances.

    _____

Pronominal verbs ·14·

Several different types of verbs are included in the pronominals: the *reflexive*, the *reciprocal*, the *passive*, and the *subjective*. Too many? Not at all! As you study the different types, you'll discover the subtleties of each. How to identify pronominal verbs? Pronominal verbs are verbs that are preceded in the infinitive and in conjugated forms by the pronouns **me**, **te**, **se**, **nous**, **vous**, **se**. Let's start with the reflexive verbs.

Reflexive verbs

The action of a reflexive verb is, for the most part, reflected back on the subject, the action being done to oneself. The pronouns **me**, **te**, **se** drop the **e** before mute **h** or a vowel.

je **me lève**	*I get up*	nous **nous levons**	*we get up*
tu **te lèves**	*you get up*	vous **vous levez**	*you get up*
il/elle **se lève**	*he/she gets up*	ils/elles **se lèvent**	*they get up*

Il **se lève** à sept heures.   *He gets up at seven.*
Je **me couche** à onze heures.   *I go to bed at eleven.*
Il **s'assoit** sur un banc.   *He sits down on a bench.*

In the negative form, the **ne** follows the subject pronoun and the **pas** follows the conjugated verb.

Elle **ne se réveille pas** avant huit heures.   *She does not wake up until eight o'clock.*
Tu **ne te reposes pas** assez.   *You do not rest enough.*

In the interrogative form, there are three ways of asking questions. You can always make a question with rising intonation (**Tu te couches déjà?**). When inversion is used, the reflexive pronoun remains in front of the verb.

Se rase-t-il tous les matins?   *Does he shave every morning?*
S'occupent-elles de ce dossier?   *Are they taking care of this case (file)?*
Vous maquillez-vous pour monter sur scène?   *Do you put on makeup to go on stage?*

Don't forget the simple interrogative with **est-ce que**:

Est-ce que vous vous préparez à partir?   *Are you getting ready to leave?*
Est-ce que tu t'habilles pour la soirée?   *Are you getting dressed for the party?*

VOCABULAIRE

la peau	*skin*	le coude	*elbow*
le visage	*face*	la main	*hand*
la tête	*head*	le doigt	*finger*
les cheveux (*m.pl.*)	*hair*	l'ongle (*m.*)	*nail*
les yeux (*m.pl.*)	*eyes*	la hanche	*hip*
le nez	*nose*	la taille	*waist*
la bouche	*mouth*	la jambe	*leg*
les lèvres (*f. pl.*)	*lips*	le genou	*knee*
l'oreille (*f.*)	*ear*	la cheville	*ankle*
le dos	*back*	le pied	*foot*
le bras	*arm*		

EXERCICE 14·1

Mettre au présent les verbes réfléchis entre parenthèses.

1. Je (s'habiller) _____ avant de prendre le petit déjeuner.

2. Nous (se lever) _____ tôt le matin.

3. Elle (se couper) _____ les cheveux elle-même.

4. Tu (se coucher) _____ trop tard tous les soirs.

5. Ils (se laver) _____ les mains.

6. Tu (se peigner) _____ avant de sortir.

7. Vous (se balader) _____ dans le parc.

8. Ils (se reposer) _____ le week-end.

9. Nous (s'amuser) _____ à la fête.

10. Elle (se détendre) _____ les jambes sur le canapé.

Reciprocal verbs

The second type of pronominal verb is called *reciprocal*. It describes an action two or more people perform with or for each other. Since two or more people are involved, reciprocal verbs can only be used in the plural (with **se**, **nous**, **vous**).

Ils **s'aiment** beaucoup.	*They love each other a lot.*
Nous **nous parlons** tous les jours.	*We talk to each other every day.*

EXERCICE 14·2

Mettre au présent les verbes réciproques entre parenthèses.

1. Ils (se marier) _____ la semaine prochaine.
2. Vous (s'embrasser) _____ sur le balcon.
3. Nous (s'écrire) _____ une fois par an.
4. Ils (se retrouver) _____ devant la brasserie.
5. Elles (se voir) _____ rarement.
6. Nous (se téléphoner) _____ chaque jour.
7. Vous (se quitter) _____ sur le quai de la gare.
8. Nous (se disputer) _____ assez souvent.
9. Ils (se détester) _____ depuis toujours.
10. Nous (se rencontrer) _____ toujours par hasard dans la rue.

Passive pronominals

A third type of pronominal verb is called *passive*. With the passive pronominal verbs, the subject is not a person or an animal. The subject does not perform the action of the verb but rather is subjected to it. It is in the third-person singular, with **se**.

Ça ne **se dit** pas.	*This is not said.*
Ça ne **se fait** pas.	*This is not done.*
Comment ça **se traduit**?	*How is it (that) translated?*
Ça **se voit**.	*It shows.*
Le vin rouge **se boit** chambré.	*Red wine is drunk at room temperature.*

Subjective pronominals

The last type of pronominal verb is called *subjective*. These verbs are neither reflexive nor reciprocal. For idiomatic or historical reasons, they just happen to use the pronominal forms. Try to learn their infinitives with the pronoun **se**.

Elle **s'en va**. (s'en aller)	*She is leaving.*
Il **se doute de** quelque chose. (se douter de)	*He suspects something.*
Ils **s'entendent** très bien. (s'entendre [avec])	*They get along very well.*

Here's a list of commonly used subjective verbs:

s'apercevoir	*to realize*	**je m'aperçois**	*I realize*
s'écrouler	*to collapse*	**je m'écroule**	*I am collapsing*
s'emparer	*to seize*	**je m'empare**	*I am seizing*
s'évanouir	*to faint*	**je m'évanouis**	*I am fainting*
se moquer	*to make fun*	**je me moque**	*I am making fun*

Pronominal verbs

se souvenir	to remember	je me souviens	I remember
s'en aller	to leave	je m'en vais	I am leaving
s'envoler	to vanish	je m'envole	I am vanishing
s'enfuir	to run away	je m'enfuis	I am running away

EXERCICE 14·3

Mettre au présent les verbes subjectifs entre parenthèses.

1. Elle (s'apercevoir) _____ de sa gaffe.
2. Ils (se dépêcher) _____ pour arriver à l'heure.
3. Tu (s'attendre) _____ à sa visite.
4. Qu'est-ce qui (se passer) _____ ?
5. Vous (se servir) _____ d'un nouvel appareil.
6. Je (se rendre compte) _____ de mon erreur.
7. Tu (se demander) _____ ce qui va se passer.
8. Elle (se dépêcher) _____ car elle est en retard.
9. Tu (se tromper) _____ de chemin.
10. L'oiseau (s'envoler) _____ dans le ciel.

Pronominals in the imperative and the infinitive

The pronominal verbs are often used in the imperative, to give commands (*Hurry up! Get up! Let's go!*). We'll study the imperative form in Chapter 23, but in the meantime, note how the imperative form is used with pronominal verbs. For the affirmative imperative, add the stressed pronoun **toi**, **nous**, or **vous** after the verb, connected with a hyphen.

Réveille-toi!	*Wake up!*
Reposons-nous sur un banc.	*Let's rest on a bench.*
Habillez-vous!	*Get dressed!*

For the negative imperative of pronominal verbs, use **ne** in front of the pronoun and **pas** after the verb. Note that in the negative the reflexive pronoun precedes the verb, as it would in a normal sentence.

Ne te couche pas si tard!	*Do not go to bed so late!*
Ne nous servons pas de cette machine!	*Let's not use this machine!*
Ne vous installez pas dans cette région!	*Do not settle in this region!*

When pronominal verbs are used in the infinitive, the reflexive pronoun is always in the same person and number as the subject, and it precedes the infinitive.

| **Vous** allez **vous apercevoir** de votre erreur. | *You are going to realize your mistake.* |
| **Tu** viens de **te marier**? | *Did you just get married?* |

EXERCICE 14·4

Conjuguer les verbes entre parenthèses.

1. J'aime (se promener) _____ le long de la Seine.

2. À quelle heure est-ce que tu vas (se lever) _____ ?

3. Nous venons de (se rendre compte) _____ des conséquences.

4. Elle ne peut pas (se souvenir) _____ de son nom.

5. Ils doivent (se marier) _____ au printemps.

6. Vous allez (se demander) _____ pourquoi il quitte Paris.

7. Nous voulons (s'écrire) _____ plus souvent.

8. Je dois (s'habiller) _____ pour aller au bal.

9. Vous allez (se voir) _____ pendant les vacances?

10. Nous ne pouvons pas (se plaindre) _____ de la situation.

EXERCICE 14·5

Faire correspondre les deux colonnes.

_____ 1. Ils sont toujours ensemble.   a. Ils s'écrivent.

_____ 2. Ils communiquent sans cesse.   b. Ils se détestent.

_____ 3. Ils s'attendent au pire.   c. Ils aiment marcher.

_____ 4. Ils se promènent.   d. Ils sont pessimistes.

_____ 5. Ils ne se parlent jamais.   e. Ils s'aiment.

EXERCICE 14·6

*Traduire les phrases suivantes en utilisant **tu** et l'inversion si nécessaire.*

1. Get up!

_____

2. She is getting dressed for the party.

_____

3. She cuts her hair.

_____

Pronominal verbs   225

4. We are walking in the park.

5. They rest because their legs are tired.

6. He is shaving.

7. They just got married.

8. They write to each other.

9. He is tired. He sits on a bench.

10. They love each other.

The passé composé

There are several forms that can be used to talk about the past in French. The most common is the **passé composé**, called in English the compound past or the present perfect. The **passé composé** is one of the tenses colloquially used in French to talk about past events. It refers to a single action in the past. It is built of two parts: the auxiliary or helping verb, **avoir** or **être**, + a past participle.

The past participle of regular verbs

The past participle is formed by adding an ending to the verb stem. Regular past participles take the following endings:

-**er** verbs take -**é**: **parler** (*to speak*) → **parlé** (*spoken*)
-**ir** verbs take -**i**: **choisir** (*to choose*) → **choisi** (*chosen*)
-**re** verbs take -**u**: **entendre** (*to hear*) → **entendu** (*heard*)

Note that the **passé composé** can be translated into English in different ways. Its English equivalent depends on the context.

Elle **a pris** une décision.
 She made a decision.
 She has made a decision.
 She did make a decision.

In the negative form, **ne (n')** is placed in front of **avoir** or **être**, and **pas** after **avoir** or **être**.

Il **a vendu** sa voiture.	*He sold his car.*
Il **n'a pas vendu** sa voiture.	*He did not sell his car.*
Ils **ont dîné** au restaurant.	*They had dinner at the restaurant.*
Ils **n'ont pas dîné** au restaurant.	*They did not have dinner at the restaurant.*

As in the present tense, there are three ways to make a question.

Rising intonation:	Vous avez aimé la pièce?	*Did you like the play?*
Inversion:	**Avez-vous** aimé la pièce?	*Did you like the play?*
With **est-ce que**:	**Est-ce que** vous avez aimé la pièce?	*Did you like the play?*

227

VOCABULAIRE			
le cinéma	cinema, movies	la vedette	star (film, sports)
le film	film	les coulisses (f.pl.)	backstage, wings
le documentaire	documentary (film)	les feux de la rampe (m.pl.)	footlights
le metteur en scène	director (film, theater)	l'éclairage (m.)	lighting
tourner un film	to shoot a movie	les décors (m.pl.)	sets
le tournage	shooting (film)	les accessoires (m.pl.)	props
le théâtre	theater	jouer	to play
la pièce de théâtre	play (theater)	un rôle	a part, a role
l'intrigue (f.)	plot	sous-titré(e)	subtitled
l'acteur, l'actrice	actor, actress	doublé(e)	dubbed
le comédien, la comédienne	actor, actress (theater)		

The passé composé with avoir

Most verbs in the **passé composé** are conjugated with **avoir**. Let's review the verb **avoir**:

j'**ai**	I have	nous **avons**	we have
tu **as**	you have	vous **avez**	you have
il/elle **a**	he/she has	ils/elles **ont**	they have

When **avoir** is used with the **passé composé**, with a few exceptions, the past participle *does not* agree in gender and number with the subject of the verb.

Let's briefly review the **passé composé** for -**er** verbs. It is formed with a conjugated form of **avoir** (or **être**) + the past participle. Drop the infinitive ending (-**er**) and add the participle ending -**é**.

voyager	*to travel*	**j'ai (tu as...) voyagé**	*I (you . . .) traveled*
marcher	*to walk*	**j'ai (tu as...) marché**	*I (you . . .) walked*
demander	*to ask*	**j'ai (tu as...) demandé**	*I (you . . .) asked*

EXERCICE 15·1

Mettre les verbes entre parenthèses au passé composé.

1. Il (inviter) _____ beaucoup de monde.

2. Nous (refuser) _____ leur invitation.

3. Tu (travailler) _____ hier matin?

4. Il (comprendre) _____ l'intrigue.

5. Elle (apporter) _____ un joli cadeau.

6. Je (voyager) _____ avec Rémi.

7. Vous (louer) _____ une voiture?

8. Elle (sous-titrer) _____ le film.

9. Vous (téléphoner) _____ à vos cousins.

10. Tu (assister) _____ à la pièce de théâtre.

Remember that the past participle of regular -**ir** and -**re** verbs is formed by dropping the infinitive endings -**ir** and -**re** and adding the appropriate ending -**i** or -**u**.

finir	*to finish*	**fin*i***	*finished*
choisir	*to choose*	**chois*i***	*chosen*
vendre	*to sell*	**vend*u***	*sold*
perdre	*to lose*	**perd*u***	*lost*

In the **passé composé** of verbs conjugated with **avoir**, the past participle agrees with the *direct object* of the verb, but only in sentences where the direct object noun or pronoun *precedes* the verb. For example:

Il a pris **la bonne décision**.	*He made the right decision.*
Il **l'**a pris**e**.	*He made it.*
Elle a compris **ses erreurs**.	*She understood her mistakes.*
Elle **les** a compris**es**.	*She understood them.*

EXERCICE 15·2

Mettre les verbes entre parenthèses au passé composé.

1. Ils (investir) _____ une grosse somme.

2. Le public (applaudir) _____ les comédiens.

3. Elles (réfléchir) _____ toute la journée.

4. La voiture (ralentir) _____ au carrefour.

5. Ils (attendre) _____ le train une demi-heure.

6. Nous (réussir) _____ à les convaincre.

7. Elle (perdre) _____ ses bijoux en vacances.

8. Tu (grandir) _____ en Europe?

9. Elle (sentir) _____ une bonne odeur venant de la cuisine.

10. Le théâtre (vendre) _____ beaucoup de billets.

EXERCICE 15·3

Traduire les phrases suivantes.

1. They sold the house in France.

2. I waited ten minutes.

3. He finished the novel.

4. She lost her dictionary.

5. I called Marc.

6. They served an elegant dinner.

7. He bought a car.

8. I chose a very good cheese.

9. We watched the film.

10. They applauded the actor.

Irregular past participles

Many verbs conjugated with **avoir** in the **passé composé** have irregular past participles that you simply have to learn by heart.

Il **a appris** le français à Strasbourg.	*He learned French in Strasbourg.*
Nous **avons compris** la situation.	*We understood the situation.*
Elle m'**a dit** bonjour.	*She said hello to me.*

Here is a sample list of irregular past participles:

acquérir	*to acquire*	**acquis**	*acquired*
apprendre	*to learn*	**appris**	*learned*
avoir	*to have*	**eu**	*had*

boire	*to drink*	**bu**	*drunk*
comprendre	*to understand*	**compris**	*understood*
conduire	*to drive*	**conduit**	*driven*
craindre	*to fear*	**craint**	*feared*
devoir	*must, to have to*	**dû**	*had to*
dire	*to say*	**dit**	*said*
écrire	*to write*	**écrit**	*written*
être	*to be*	**été**	*been, was*
faire	*to do, to make*	**fait**	*done, made*
falloir	*to have to*	**fallu**	*had to*
lire	*to read*	**lu**	*read*
mettre	*to put*	**mis**	*put*
mourir	*to die*	**mort**	*dead*
naître	*to be born*	**né**	*born*
offrir	*to offer*	**offert**	*offered*
ouvrir	*to open*	**ouvert**	*opened*
peindre	*to paint*	**peint**	*painted*
plaire	*to please*	**plu**	*pleased*
pleuvoir	*to rain*	**plu**	*rained*
pouvoir	*can, to be able to*	**pu**	*could*
prendre	*to take*	**pris**	*taken*
recevoir	*to receive*	**reçu**	*received*
rire	*to laugh*	**ri**	*laughed*
savoir	*to know*	**su**	*known*
suivre	*to follow*	**suivi**	*followed*
vivre	*to live*	**vécu**	*lived*
voir	*to see*	**vu**	*seen*
vouloir	*to want*	**voulu**	*wanted*

EXERCICE
15·4

Mettre les verbes entre parenthèses au passé composé.

1. Je (prendre) _____ le train à Lille.

2. Nous (ne pas pouvoir) _____ joindre les Quentin.

3. Ils (suivre) _____ un cours d'anglais en Angleterre.

4. Elle (peindre) _____ un paysage breton.

5. Il (pleuvoir) _____ tout l'après-midi.

6. Vous (recevoir) _____ beaucoup de compliments.

7. Nous (lire) _____ un roman de Zola.

8. Je (faire) _____ la cuisine pour toute la famille.

9. Il (mettre) _____ son chapeau gris.

10. Elle (ouvrir) _____ les fenêtres.

The **passé composé** 231

EXERCICE 15·5

Faire correspondre les deux colonnes.

_____ 1. Elle a conduit   a. le journal

_____ 2. Tu as compris   b. un accident

_____ 3. Vous avez lu   c. une promenade

_____ 4. Il a eu   d. les explications

_____ 5. Nous avons fait   e. à toute vitesse

The **passé composé** with **être**

Some verbs use **être** instead of **avoir** in the **passé composé**. It is very important to memorize the (finite) list of verbs conjugated with **être**. Many of these are intransitive verbs of movement (**aller, venir, monter**...). In addition, all pronominal (reflexive) verbs (see Chapter 14) are conjugated with **être** in the **passé composé**.

The past participle of verbs conjugated with **être** agrees in gender and number with the subject.

Il est arrivé en retard.	*He arrived late.*
Elle est arrivée en retard.	*She arrived late.*
Ils sont nés en Belgique.	*They (m.) were born in Belgium.*
Elles sont nées en Belgique.	*They (f.) were born in Belgium.*

Here are the verbs conjugated with **être** in the **passé composé**:

aller	*to go*
arriver	*to arrive*
descendre	*to go down*
devenir	*to become*
entrer	*to enter*
monter	*to go up, to climb*
mourir	*to die*
naître	*to be born*
partir	*to leave*
rentrer	*to return*
rester	*to stay*
retourner	*to return, to go back*
revenir	*to return*
sortir	*to go out*
tomber	*to fall*
venir	*to come, to arrive*

232   PRACTICE MAKES PERFECT   Complete French All-in-One

EXERCICE 15·6

Mettre les verbes entre parenthèses au passé composé en utilisant l'inversion si nécessaire.

1. À quel âge ce comédien (monter) _____ sur scène?
2. Nous (rentrer) _____ du théâtre à minuit.
3. La voiture (tomber) _____ en panne près de Madrid.
4. Ils (descendre) _____ par l'escalier.
5. Elles (revenir) _____ de vacances mardi.
6. Quel jour (partir) _____ ?
7. Elle (aller) _____ à l'opéra hier soir.
8. Luc (aller) _____ au Mexique l'hiver dernier.
9. Molière (mourir) _____ en 1673.
10. Le metteur en scène (rester) _____ dans les coulisses.

EXERCICE 15·7

Traduire les phrases suivantes.

1. She read the newspaper.
   _____

2. We went to Paris.
   _____

3. They left last night.
   _____

4. He had to leave at five o'clock.
   _____

5. They lived in Italy.
   _____

6. Zola died in 1902.
   _____

7. I wrote a long letter.
   _____

8. She has painted the wall white.

9. She stayed at home.

10. He took some vacation.

Pronominal verbs in the **passé composé**

As we mentioned earlier, all pronominal verbs are conjugated with **être**. The reflexive pronouns precede the auxiliary verb (**être**). In most cases, the past participle agrees in gender and number with the subject of the pronominal verb.

se réveiller to *wake up*			
je **me suis réveillé(e)**	*I woke up*	nous **nous sommes réveillé(e)s**	*we woke up*
tu **t'es réveillé(e)**	*you woke up*	vous **vous êtes réveillé(e)(s)**	*you woke up*
il/elle **s'est réveillé(e)**	*he/she woke up*	ils/elles **se sont réveillé(e)s**	*they woke up*

Elle **s'est promenée** sur la plage. — *She walked on the beach.*
Ils **se sont ennuyés** à la réception. — *They were (got) bored at the reception.*
Il **s'est évanoui** à cause de la chaleur. — *He fainted because of the heat.*

In the negative, the negation is placed around the auxiliary verb **être**.

Ils **ne** se sont **pas** couchés de bonne heure. — *They did not go to bed.*
Elle **ne** s'est **pas** promenée le long du canal. — *She did not take a walk along the canal.*

In the interrogative form, the reflexive pronoun is placed before **être**.

S'est-il rendu compte de son erreur? — *Did he realize his mistake?*
Vous êtes-vous bien amusés à la fête? — *Did you have a good time at the party?*

Note that the past participle does not agree with the subject of the pronominal verb when the verb is followed by a direct object or by another verb.

Elle s'est offert **une nouvelle moto**. — *She treated herself to a new motorbike.*
Elle s'est coupé **les ongles**. — *She trimmed her nails.*
Elle s'est fait **arracher** une dent. — *She had a tooth pulled.*

When reciprocal verbs take a *direct object*, the past participle agrees with the subject.

Ils **se sont rencontrés** à Venise. — *They met in Venice.*
Ils **se sont embrassés**. — *They kissed each other.*
Ils **se sont mariés** en mars. — *They got married in March.*

When reciprocal verbs take an *indirect object* in French, the past participle *does not* agree.

Ils **se sont téléphoné**.	*They called each other.*
Vous **vous êtes parlé** au téléphone.	*You talked to each other on the phone.*
Ils **se sont écrit** de longues lettres.	*They wrote each other long letters.*

Verbs conjugated with avoir or être

Six verbs among those conjugated with **être** in the **passé composé** (**sortir, rentrer, monter, descendre, passer, retourner**) are conjugated with **avoir** and follow the **avoir** agreement *when a direct object follows the verb*. In these cases, the meaning of the verb has changed.

Ils **sont montés** en haut de la Tour Eiffel.	*They went to the top of the Eiffel Tower.*
Ils **ont monté les malles** au grenier.	*They took the trunks up to the attic.*

Note above that **les malles** is the direct object of **monter**, thus it is conjugated with **avoir**.

Elle **est descendue** au rez-de-chaussée.	*She went down to the ground floor.*
Elle **a descendu les poubelles**.	*She took down the garbage cans.*
Elle **est sortie** avec des amis.	*She went out with some friends.*
Elle **a sorti la voiture** du garage.	*She took the car out of the garage.*
Elle **est rentrée** de vacances hier.	*She came back from vacation yesterday.*
Elle **a rentré les géraniums** dans le salon.	*She brought the geraniums into the living room.*
Je **suis passée** devant les Galeries Lafayette.	*I passed by the Galeries Lafayette.*
J'**ai passé trois semaines** à Tokyo.	*I spent three weeks in Tokyo.*
Je **suis retournée** à Venise pour la troisième fois.	*I went back to Venice for the third time.*
Elle **a retourné l'omelette**.	*She turned over the omelette.*

EXERCICE
15·8

Mettre au passé composé les verbes entre parenthèses.

1. Ils (se promener) _____ le long de la rivière.
2. Il (se douter) _____ de quelque chose.
3. Elles (se maquiller) _____ pour aller au bal.
4. Ils (s'écrire) _____ régulièrement.
5. Nous (s'arrêter) _____ au bord de la route.
6. Ils (s'occuper) _____ de tout.
7. Elles (se balader) _____ à la campagne.
8. Ils (se rencontrer) _____ à une conférence.
9. Tu (se couper) _____ le doigt.
10. Nous (se demander) _____ pourquoi il était absent.

EXERCICE 15·9

Faire correspondre les deux colonnes.

_____ 1. Elle a sorti   a. le bifteck

_____ 2. Il a retourné   b. devant le boulanger

_____ 3. Elle est rentrée   c. pour la cinquième fois

_____ 4. Je suis passée   d. très tard

_____ 5. Elle est retourné à Rome   e. les chaises de jardin

EXERCICE 15·10

Traduire les phrases suivantes.

1. They spent a month in China.

   _____

2. She fainted.

   _____

3. They kissed each other.

   _____

4. They had fun at the party.

   _____

5. She took the suitcases down.

   _____

6. He brushed his teeth.

   _____

7. He woke up tired.

   _____

8. They wrote each other regularly.

   _____

9. Anna stopped for ten minutes.

   _____

10. He flipped the omelette.

   _____

The **imparfait** and the plus-que-parfait

The **imparfait**

The uses of the **imparfait** (*imperfect*) are some of the most difficult aspects of French grammar to master. While the **passé composé** is used to talk about an action that took place on a specific occasion in the past, the **imparfait** plays a different role. It is used to describe a state of mind and being in the past as well as continuous, repeated, or habitual past actions.

To form the imperfect, take the **nous** form of the present tense and remove the -**ons** ending, which gives you the stem. Then add the **imparfait** endings (-**ais**, -**ais**, -**ait**, -**ions**, -**iez**, -**aient**) to this stem. For example:

parler *to speak*			
nous parlons →	**parl-**		
je parl**ais**	*I spoke*	nous parl**ions**	*we spoke*
tu parl**ais**	*you spoke*	vous parl**iez**	*you spoke*
il/elle parl**ait**	*he/she spoke*	ils/elles parl**aient**	*they spoke*

Note that the -**ais**, -**ait**, -**aient** endings are pronounced alike. Verbs with spelling changes in the present tense **nous** form, such as **manger** and **commencer** (see Chapter 10), retain the spelling change only for the **je**, **tu**, **il**, **elle**, **ils**, and **elles** subject pronouns.

j'**encourageais**	*I encouraged*
elle **exigeait**	*she demanded*
ils **partageaient**	*they shared*
il **avançait**	*he moved forward*
elle **remplaçait**	*she replaced*
elles **annonçaient**	*they announced*

The extra **e** or the **ç** are not needed in the **nous** and **vous** forms of the **imparfait**.

nous **nagions**	*we swam*
nous **protégions**	*we protected*
nous **commencions**	*we started*
vous **effaciez**	*you erased*

Depending on the context, the **imparfait** has several past equivalents in English.

Elle **faisait**... { *She was doing...* / *She used to do...* / *She did...* }

Note that the verb **être** has an irregular stem in the **imparfait**.

j'**étais**	*I was*	nous **étions**	*we were*
tu **étais**	*you were*	vous **étiez**	*you were*
il/elle **était**	*he/she was*	ils/elles **étaient**	*they were*

VOCABULAIRE

les vacances (*f.pl.*)	*vacation*	**escalader**	*to climb*
faire un voyage	*to go on a trip*	**une étape**	*a stopover (car travel)*
un voyage d'agrément	*a pleasure trip*	**explorer**	*to explore*
un voyage d'affaires	*a business trip*	**une expédition**	*an expedition*
un pèlerinage	*a pilgrimage*	**une visite guidée**	*a guided tour*
à la mer	*by the sea*	**visiter**	*to visit (a place)*
à la plage	*at the beach*	**rendre visite à**	*to visit (someone)*
à la campagne	*in the country*	**accueillir**	*to welcome*
à la montagne	*in the mountains*	**un festival**	*a festival*
le paysage	*landscape, countryside*	**un divertissement**	*an entertainment, an amusement*
dans le parc	*in the park*		
randonner	*to go hiking*	**les loisirs** (*m.pl.*)	*leisure time*

EXERCICE 16·1

Mettre les verbes entre parenthèses à l'imparfait.

1. Il (voyager) _____ chaque année en Australie.

2. Tu (faire) _____ du sport à l'école?

3. Nous (être) _____ enchantés de notre expédition.

4. Ils (boire) _____ du café noir le matin.

5. Je (être) _____ champion de tennis.

6. Nous (aimer) _____ faire la cuisine.

7. Elles (partager) _____ une chambre à l'université.

8. Il (prendre) _____ toujours une semaine de vacances en février.

9. Le guide (encourager) _____ les marcheurs.

10. Vous (aller) _____ au bord de la mer en été.

Let's look at the different uses of the **imparfait**. It is used for background and description. It describes a situation that existed in the past, a state of mind or being.

Les rues **étaient** embouteillées.	*The streets were jammed.*
La circulation **était** fluide.	*The traffic was flowing.*
Il **faisait** trop chaud.	*It was too hot.*

238 PRACTICE MAKES PERFECT Complete French All-in-One

| Il **avait** faim. | *He was hungry.* |
| Elle ne **savait** pas quoi faire. | *She did not know what to do.* |

The **imparfait** versus the **passé composé**

As they express a mental or physical state of being, some verbs tend to be used more often in the **imparfait** than in the **passé composé**. Among these verbs are: **être** (*to be*), **avoir** (*to have*), **penser** (*to think*), **croire** (*to believe*), **savoir** (*to know*), **espérer** (*to hope*), **sembler** (*to seem*), **paraître** (*to appear*). However, when these verbs are used in the **passé composé**, they may take on a different meaning.

Il **semblait** déprimé.	*He looked depressed.*
Tout à coup il **a semblé** comprendre la situation.	*Suddenly he seemed to understand the situation.*
Je **savais** qu'il avait raison.	*I knew he was right.*
Immédiatement, j'**ai su** qu'il était innocent.	*Immediately, I realized he was innocent.*

EXERCICE 16·2

Mettre les verbes entre parenthèses à l'imparfait.

1. Il (croire) _____ que tu ne voulais pas venir.

2. Je (être) _____ à la montagne.

3. Elle (penser) _____ à ses prochaines vacances.

4. Ils (espérer) _____ un miracle.

5. Elle (avoir) _____ très faim.

6. Je (savoir) _____ qu'il avait raison.

7. Nous (être) _____ réalistes.

8. Vous (paraître) _____ sceptique.

9. L'exposition (être) _____ fascinante.

10. Il (faire) _____ un temps glacial.

Another use of the **imparfait** is to express habitual, repetitive action. It describes past events that were repeated. *Used to* and *would* (meaning *habitually*) are translated into French by the **imparfait**.

Autrefois, elle **faisait** partie de la chorale.	*In the past, she used to belong to the choir.*
Ils **allaient** en Inde chaque année.	*They used to go (would go) to India every year.*
Il **jouait** au tennis le mardi.	*He used to (would) play tennis on Tuesdays.*

As you can see in the previous examples, some expressions of time or repetition may be an indication of the **imparfait**:

| **souvent** | *often* |
| **fréquemment** | *frequently* |

toujours	*always*
le mardi	*on Tuesdays*
le vendredi	*on Fridays*
chaque jour	*every day*
tous les jours	*every day*
chaque semaine	*every week*
chaque mois	*every month*
chaque année	*every year*
d'ordinaire	*ordinarily*
d'habitude	*usually*
habituellement	*usually*
régulièrement	*regularly*
comme à l'accoutumée	*as usual*
autrefois	*formerly*
jadis	*in times past*

EXERCICE 16·3

Mettre les verbes entre parenthèses à l'imparfait.

1. Nous (suivre) _____ des cours de danse tous les mardis.

2. Je (faire) _____ de la natation tous les jours.

3. La vie (être) _____ plus facile.

4. Nous (faire) _____ la grasse matinée tous les dimanches.

5. À cette époque, ils (habiter) _____ en banlieue.

6. Nous (boire) _____ du café.

7. Autrefois, ils (assister) _____ à tous les concerts.

8. Dans son enfance, elle (faire) _____ de l'équitation.

9. Dans le passé, vous (se voir) _____ plus souvent.

10. Elle (travailler) _____ chez Guerlain.

The **imparfait** is also used to describe a continuous action that was going on in the past when another action (expressed in the **passé composé**) interrupted it.

Elle **regardait** la télévision quand soudain elle **a entendu** un grand bruit.	*She was watching television when suddenly she heard a loud noise.*
Il **faisait** ses devoirs quand son frère **est arrivé**.	*He was doing his homework when his brother arrived.*

To express the idea that an action had been going on for a period of time before being interrupted, use the **imparfait** with **depuis**. This is the equivalent to the past of **depuis** + present tense you studied in Chapter 10.

240 PRACTICE MAKES PERFECT Complete French All-in-One

Ils **étaient** à la montagne **depuis une semaine** quand ils **ont décidé** d'aller au bord de la mer.	*They had been in the mountains for a week when they decided to go to the seashore.*
Il **randonnait depuis trois jours** quand il **a trouvé** cette belle auberge.	*He had been hiking for three days when he found this beautiful inn.*

EXERCICE 16·4

Mettre les verbes entre parenthèses à l'imparfait.

1. Il (faire) _____ un discours quand quelqu'un dans l'assistance l'a interrompu.
2. Je (dormir) _____ quand le chat a sauté sur mon lit.
3. Nous (bavarder) _____ depuis une heure quand il est arrivé.
4. Ils (se reposer) _____ quand une alarme a retenti.
5. Vous (parler) _____ depuis un moment quand soudain il s'est levé.
6. Elle (étudier) _____ l'architecture depuis un an quand elle a décidé de changer de filière.
7. Ils (danser) _____ quand la musique s'est arrêtée.
8. Il (réfléchir) _____ quand une idée lui a traversé l'esprit.
9. Elle (travailler) _____ dans son bureau quand ils ont frappé à la porte.
10. Je (attendre) _____ Roland depuis dix minutes quand enfin il est arrivé.

EXERCICE 16·5

*Traduire les phrases suivantes en utilisant la forme **tu** si nécessaire.*

1. I used to play tennis every Thursday.

2. You were studying when the phone rang.

3. We were sleeping when suddenly we heard a loud noise.

4. The restaurant was crowded.

5. It was cold in the mountains.

The **imparfait** and the **plus-que-parfait**   241

6. They looked tired.

_____

7. The play was fascinating.

_____

8. She used to work at the Galeries Lafayette.

_____

9. We were waiting for the bus when it started to rain.

_____

10. She knew they were wrong.

_____

The **imparfait** with special constructions

With a **si** + **on** construction, the **imparfait** is used to make a suggestion or to invite someone to do something. The informal **on** refers to two or more people and is conjugated in the third-person singular.

Si on allait en France cet été?	*What about going to France this summer?*
Si on achetait des billets?	*What about buying tickets?*
Si on allait nager dans le lac?	*What about going swimming in the lake?*
Si on allait rendre visite à Léo?	*What about paying a visit to Léo?*

EXERCICE 16·6

Mettre les verbes entre parenthèses à l'imparfait.

1. Si on (aller) _____ se promener dans la forêt?

2. Si on (déjeuner) _____ ensemble?

3. Si on (apporter) _____ une boîte de chocolats à Julie?

4. Si on (attendre) _____ encore quelques minutes?

5. Si on (commander) _____ un dessert?

6. Si on (faire) _____ un voyage en Grèce?

7. Si on (ouvrir) _____ un restaurant?

8. Si on (investir) _____ dans cette entreprise?

9. Si on (réfléchir) _____ avant de prendre une décision?

10. Si on (choisir) _____ une autre formule?

You will encounter the **imparfait** in other idiomatic constructions, for instance, preceded by **si seulement**, to express a wish or a regret.

Si seulement on pouvait prendre des vacances!	*If only we could take a vacation!*
Si seulement elle était à l'heure!	*If only she were on time!*
Si seulement ils habitaient plus près!	*If only they lived closer!*
Si seulement vous saviez!	*If only you knew!*

In Chapter 13, you studied the immediate past with the verb **venir** + **de** + infinitive. The immediate past can also be used in the **imparfait** to describe an action that *had just happened.*

Elle **vient de téléphoner**.	*She has just called.*
Elle **venait de téléphoner** quand il est entré.	*She had just called when he walked in.*
Il **vient d'accepter** ce poste.	*He just accepted this position.*
Il **venait d'acccepter** ce poste quand on lui en a proposé un autre.	*He had just accepted this position when he was offered another one.*

EXERCICE 16·7

Passé composé ou imparfait?

1. Je (aller) _____ chez le dentiste hier.
2. Quand il (être) _____ adolescent, il (jouer) _____ au football.
3. À cette époque-là, ils (tenir) _____ une brasserie place d'Italie.
4. Ils (randonner) _____ dans les Alpes le week-end passé.
5. Nous (dîner) _____ dans ce restaurant tous les samedis.
6. Si on (prendre) _____ un café?
7. Tu (avoir) _____ l'air fatigué.
8. Chaque jour, il (écrire) _____ une lettre à son amie.
9. Je (regarder) _____ un film quand elle (arriver) _____.
10. La campagne (être) _____ si belle.

The **plus-que-parfait**

The **plus-que-parfait** (*pluperfect*) indicates a past action that happened before another past action started (in English, *had done*). It can be seen as "past" past tense.

Formation of the **plus-que-parfait**

To form the **plus-que-parfait**, use the forms of **avoir** or **être** in the **imparfait** + the past participle of the main verb.

Let's review the **imparfait** of the auxiliaries **être** and **avoir**:

être *to be*

j'**étais**	*I was*	nous **étions**	*we were*
tu **étais**	*you were*	vous **étiez**	*you were*
il/elle **était**	*he/she was*	ils/elles **étaient**	*they were*

avoir *to have*

j'**avais**	*I had*	nous **avions**	*we had*
tu **avais**	*you had*	vous **aviez**	*you had*
il/elle **avait**	*he/she had*	ils/elles **avaient**	*they had*

Il **avait** toujours **fini** avant les autres.	*He had always finished before the others.*
Tu **avais oublié** l'anniversaire de ta meilleure amie.	*You had forgotten your best friend's birthday.*
Il n'**avait** pas **pu** les joindre.	*He had not been able to reach them.*
Elle **était partie** sans laisser d'adresse.	*She had departed without leaving an address.*

EXERCICE 16·8

Mettre au plus-que-parfait les verbes entre parenthèses.

1. Je (dîner) _____ place d'Italie.

2. Elle (expliquer) _____ la situation en détail.

3. Vous (investir) _____ dans leur entreprise.

4. Elles (arriver) _____ à la réception en retard.

5. Tu (décider) _____ d'aller en Russie.

6. Nous (rouler) _____ toute la nuit.

7. Il (échouer) _____ à son examen.

8. Tu (aller) _____ en vacances tout seul.

9. Je (obtenir) _____ un nouveau poste.

10. Il (boire) _____ un très bon vin.

VOCABULAIRE

une pharmacie	a pharmacy	une gélule	a capsule
un pharmacien, une pharmacienne	a pharmacist	un analgésique	a painkiller
une ordonnance	a prescription	une toux	a cough
un médicament	medicine, a medication	tousser	to cough
		avoir un rhume	to have a cold
		avoir la grippe	to have the flu
un remède	a remedy	avoir mal à la tête	to have a headache
un sirop	a syrup	avoir mal au dos	to have a backache
un traitement	a treatment	avoir mal au ventre	to have a stomachache
des contre-indications (f.pl.)	contraindications	être allergique	to be allergic
des effets secondaires (m.pl.)	side effects	une douleur	a pain, an ache
		souffrir	to suffer
un cachet d'aspirine	an aspirin tablet	conseiller	to advise

In the **plus-que-parfait**, all pronominal verbs are conjugated with **être** and agree in gender and number with the subject.

Je m'étais évanouie dans la pharmacie.	*I had fainted in the pharmacy.*
Vous vous étiez promenés le long du canal Saint-Martin.	*You had walked along the Saint-Martin canal.*
Nous nous étions embrassés sur le Pont-Neuf.	*We had kissed on the Pont-Neuf.*
Il s'était souvenu de cet incident avant de revoir son ancienne amie.	*He had remembered this incident before seeing his former girlfriend again.*

EXERCICE 16·9

Mettre au plus-que-parfait les verbes entre parenthèses.

1. Il (prendre) _____ un cachet d'aspirine.
2. Nous (se réveiller) _____ à l'aube
3. Tu (se demander) _____ s'il était allergique.
4. Elle (s'habiller) _____ pour la soirée.
5. Ils (se marier) _____ en septembre.
6. Louise et Julie (se coucher) _____ tard.
7. Il (se souvenir) _____ de cet homme.
8. Nous (se promener) _____ dans les jardins du Luxembourg.
9. Elle (se reposer) _____ sur un banc.
10. Elles (s'écrire) _____ pendant des années.

Use of the plus-que-parfait

As we mentioned earlier, the **plus-que-parfait** (*pluperfect*) indicates a past action that happened before another past action started. This anteriority can be implied or stated. Therefore, the **plus-que-parfait** is often combined with a dependent clause that states this clearly.

Je **ne m'étais pas rendu compte** que j'étais malade. *I had not realized I was sick.*

Elle avait faim parce qu'elle **n'avait pas eu** le temps de déjeuner. *She was hungry because she had not had time for lunch.*

EXERCICE 16·10

Mettre au plus-que-parfait les verbes entre parenthèses.

1. Il était en retard car sa voiture (tomber) _____ en panne sur l'autoroute.
2. Le médecin lui a demandé si elle (avoir) _____ la grippe.
3. Elle a pensé que je (ne pas expliquer) _____ la situation.
4. Il a refusé de prendre le médicament que le médecin (prescrire) _____ .
5. Elle était furieuse car il (oublier) _____ leur anniversaire de mariage.
6. Lorsque Lucie est arrivée, Paul (partir) _____ .
7. Je ne savais pas que Bertrand (inviter) _____ toute sa famille.
8. Elle ne se souvenait plus où elle (rencontrer) _____ le frère de Lucien.
9. Comme il n'avait pas d'analgésique, il (souffrir) _____ pendant des heures.
10. Il voulait savoir si elle (recevoir) _____ son bouquet de fleurs.

EXERCICE 16·11

Faire correspondre les deux colonnes.

_____ 1. Il avait commandé un sandwich   a. car il avait mal au dos
_____ 2. Il était arrivé en retard   b. car il n'avait pas assez étudié
_____ 3. Il avait perdu son carnet d'adresses   c. en raison d'une panne
_____ 4. Il avait échoué à son examen   d. parce qu'il avait faim
_____ 5. Il avait beaucoup souffert   e. et il n'avait pas pu nous téléphoner

Beware of the English language

Sometimes in English the French **plus-que-parfait** is translated as a simple tense. However, if there is any anteriority in a series of actions, the **plus-que-parfait** must be used in French.

Léa a dû prendre le médicament que le médecin lui **avait prescrit**.
*Léa had to take the medicine the doctor (had) **prescribed** for her.*

Elle a eu une réaction allergique au médicament qu'elle **avait pris**.
*She had an allergic reaction to the medicine she **took** (had taken).*

In Chapter 10, you studied **depuis** with the present tense. In this chapter, you studied **depuis** with the **imparfait** (where English uses the **plus-que-parfait**). Let's review a few examples.

Ils **dînent** dans ce restaurant thaïlandais **depuis des années**.
They have been dining at this Thai restaurant for years.

Ils **dînaient** dans ce restaurant thaïlandais **depuis des années** quand ils **ont décidé** d'essayer le restaurant d'en face.
They had been dining at this Thai restaurant for years when they decided to try the restaurant across the street.

Elle **prend** de la vitamine C **depuis des mois**.
She has been taking vitamin C for months.

Elle **prenait** de la vitamine C **depuis des mois** quand le médecin lui **a dit** de prendre aussi du calcium.
She had been taking vitamin C for months when the doctor told her to take calcium also.

The **plus-que-parfait**, when used with **si seulement**, expresses a wish or regret about past events.

Si seulement il n'avait pas attrapé un rhume!
If only he had not caught a cold!

Si seulement il était allé chez le médecin plus tôt!
If only he had gone to the doctor's earlier!

Si seulement elle n'avait pas raté son examen!
If only she had not failed her exam!

Si seulement vous aviez pu être parmi nous!
If only you had been able to be with us!

EXERCICE
16·12

*Commencer les phrases par **si seulement** et mettre au plus-que-parfait les verbes entre parenthèses.*

1. (vous) (ne pas être) en retard

2. (tu) (étudier) le français plus jeune

3. (nous) (savoir) la vérité

4. (elle) (rester) plus longtemps

5. (il) (rendre visite à) sa cousine Flore

6. (je) (prendre) une meilleure décision

7. (elle) (expliquer) la situation plus clairement

8. (vous) (pouvoir venir) à la réception

9. (tu) (comprendre) les problèmes

10. (il) (conseiller) autre chose

EXERCICE 16·13

Traduire les phrases suivantes.

1. He took the medicine the doctor had prescribed.

2. She knew they had made a mistake.

3. He was sick because he had eaten too much dessert.

4. I wondered why she had stayed three months in Vienna.

5. I thought they had understood the problem.

6. If only he had not been late!

7. She was tired because she had only slept five hours.

8. He was hungry because he had not eaten since seven A.M.

9. We thought he had seen this film.

10. He thought she had read the book.

The simple future and the past future

The **futur simple**

You have become acquainted with the future in Chapter 13 when you studied the **futur immédiat**. French has two other future constructions: the **futur simple** and the **futur antérieur**. To form the **futur simple** of most verbs, use the infinitive as the stem and add the endings -**ai**, -**as**, -**a**, -**ons**, -**ez**, -**ont**. For -**re** verbs, drop the **e** from the infinitive before adding the endings. Here are some examples:

décider to decide

je déciderai	I'll decide	nous déciderons	we'll decide
tu décideras	you'll decide	vous déciderez	you'll decide
il/elle décidera	he'll/she'll decide	ils/elles décideront	they'll decide

choisir to choose

je choisirai	I'll choose	nous choisirons	we'll choose
tu choisiras	you'll choose	vous choisirez	you'll choose
il/elle choisira	he'll/she'll choose	ils/elles choisiront	they'll choose

répondre to answer

je répondrai	I'll answer	nous répondrons	we'll answer
tu répondras	you'll answer	vous répondrez	you'll answer
il/elle répondra	he'll/she'll answer	ils/elles répondront	they'll answer

VOCABULAIRE

un(e) élève	a student (elementary school)	un brouillon	a first draft
		passer un examen	to take an exam
		réussir à un examen	to pass an exam
un étudiant, une étudiante	a student (university)	échouer à un examen	to fail an exam
		parler l'anglais couramment	to be fluent in English
un professeur	a teacher, a professor	être rouillé(e)	to be rusty
un cours	a course	un curriculum vitae (C.V.)	a résumé
un examen	an exam		
un stage	training, an internship	analyser	to analyze
		expliquer	to explain
apprendre	to learn	faire l'école buissonnière	to play hooky
enseigner	to teach		
étudier	to study	recevoir son diplôme	to get one's degree
suivre un cours	to take a class		
les devoirs (m.pl.)	homework	une note	a grade

EXERCICE 17·1

Mettre au futur simple les verbes entre parenthèses.

1. Vous (suivre) _____ un cours de français.
2. Nous (dîner) _____ chez Yann la semaine prochaine.
3. Tu (entendre) _____ de la belle musique.
4. Elle (chercher) _____ un autre emploi.
5. Ils (ne jamais oublier) _____ votre générosité.
6. Je (travailler) _____ samedi après-midi.
7. Nous (rendre visite) _____ à notre famille.
8. Il (finir) _____ le livre avant lundi.
9. On (remplacer) _____ tous les meubles.
10. Tu (partir) _____ avant nous.

The endings of the **futur simple** are the same for all verbs. However, some irregular verbs have irregular stems. You simply have to memorize them.

aller	*to go*	**j'irai**	*I'll go*
apercevoir	*to notice*	**j'apercevrai**	*I'll notice*
avoir	*to have*	**j'aurai**	*I'll have*
courir	*to run*	**je courrai**	*I'll run*
devenir	*to become*	**je deviendrai**	*I'll become*
devoir	*must, to have to*	**je devrai**	*I'll have to*
envoyer	*to send*	**j'enverrai**	*I'll send*
être	*to be*	**je serai**	*I'll be*
faire	*to do*	**je ferai**	*I'll do*
falloir	*to have to*	**il faudra**	*one will have to*
mourir	*to die*	**je mourrai**	*I'll die*
pleuvoir	*to rain*	**il pleuvra**	*it'll rain*
pouvoir	*can, to be able to*	**je pourrai**	*I'll be able to*
recevoir	*to receive*	**je recevrai**	*I'll receive*
revenir	*to return, to come back*	**je reviendrai**	*I'll return, I'll come back*
savoir	*to know*	**je saurai**	*I'll know*
tenir	*to hold*	**je tiendrai**	*I'll hold*
valoir	*to be worth*	**il vaudra**	*it will be worth*
venir	*to come*	**je viendrai**	*I'll come*
voir	*to see*	**je verrai**	*I'll see*
vouloir	*to want*	**je voudrai**	*I'll want*

Some slight spelling modifications occur with some verbs. These are seen throughout all persons of the future conjugation.

acheter	*to buy*	**j'achèterai**	*I'll buy*
appeler	*to call*	**j'appellerai**	*I'll call*
employer	*to hire*	**j'emploierai**	*I'll use, I'll hire*
essuyer	*to wipe*	**j'essuierai**	*I'll wipe*
jeter	*to throw*	**je jetterai**	*I'll throw*

nettoyer	*to clean*	**je nettoierai**	*I'll clean*
préférer	*to prefer*	**je préférerai**	*I'll prefer*

EXERCICE 17·2

Mettre au futur simple les verbes entre parenthèses.

1. Il (être) _____ déçu de ne pas vous voir.
2. L'étudiant (faire) _____ un stage à Nantes.
3. Tu (savoir) _____ demain si tu as réussi à ton examen.
4. Nous (avoir) _____ les résultats demain.
5. Le professeur (aller) _____ à Paris en juin.
6. Il (préférer) _____ suivre le cours d'histoire de l'art.
7. Nous (voir) _____ un bon film au cinéma.
8. Il (falloir) _____ remettre les devoirs jeudi.
9. Elle (pouvoir) _____ aller à la campagne avec nous.
10. Il (pleuvoir) _____ demain.

As in English, the French future tense is used to describe future events.

Les étudiants **passeront** leurs examens en mai.	*Students will take their exams in May.*
Les cours **recommenceront** en décembre.	*Courses will resume in December.*

In a compound sentence in French, if the main clause is in the **futur simple**, the dependent clause, introduced by some conjunctions, will also be in the **futur simple**. Note that in English, such a dependent clause will be in the present tense.

aussitôt que	*as soon as*
dès que	*as soon as*
lorsque	*when*
quand	*when*
tant que	*as long as*

Elle **ira** à Paris quand elle **aura** le temps.	*She'll go to Paris when she **has** time.*
Il nous **dira** lorsqu'il **faudra** parler.	*He'll tell us when we **have** to talk.*
Elle vous **préviendra** dès qu'elle **aura** les résultats.	*She'll inform you as soon as she **gets** the results.*
Aussitôt qu'il **arrivera**, nous **partirons**.	*As soon as he **arrives**, we'll leave.*
Elle vous **téléphonera** aussitôt qu'elle **atterrira** à Londres.	*She'll call you as soon as she **lands** in London.*
Tant qu'il y **aura** du soleil, nous **resterons** sur la terrasse.	*As long as the sun **is** out, we'll stay on the terrace.*

The future tense of **être** and **avoir** is sometimes used to express *probability* in the present, to indicate something that is likely or allegedly true.

The simple future and the past future

L'étudiant n'est pas en classe. Il **sera** encore endormi.
The student is not in class. He is probably still asleep.

Le professeur n'a pas demandé nos devoirs. Il **sera** distrait.
The teacher did not ask for our homework. He's probably distracted.

In a narration, the **futur simple** can be used to express a future idea from the standpoint of the past, as shown in the following examples. (Note that English uses a conditional form, *would*, in this case.)

Malheureusement, ses œuvres ne **seront** reconnues qu'après sa mort.
Unfortunately, her works would become recognized only after her death.

Un des génies du dix-huitième siècle et il **mourra** dans la misère.
One of the geniuses of the eighteenth century, and he would die in misery.

The **futur simple** can be used instead of an imperative (command form) to achieve a less peremptory tone.

Vous voudrez bien lui envoyer ma réponse. *Please send him my answer.*
Je vous demanderai de faire preuve de compassion. *Please show a little compassion.*
Vous voudrez bien nous excuser. *Please excuse us.*

EXERCICE 17·3

Mettre au futur simple les verbes entre parenthèses.

1. Vous (aller) _____ à l'opéra quand vos amis (être) _____ à Lyon.
2. Nous (prendre) _____ une décision dès que la presse (annoncer) _____ les résultats.
3. L'exposition (avoir lieu) _____ en janvier quand tous les tableaux (être) _____ réunis.
4. Le professeur (emmener) _____ les élèves au musée dès qu'il (pouvoir) _____ .
5. Il (devoir) _____ nous appeler dès qu'il (être) _____ en contact avec M. Clément.
6. Tant qu'il y (avoir) _____ des hommes, il y (avoir) _____ des guerres.
7. Elle (enseigner) _____ le français quand elle (habiter) _____ au Vietnam.
8. Nous (jouer) _____ au bridge quand nous (rendre visite) _____ à nos amis.
9. Elle (se reposer) _____ quand elle (avoir) _____ de longues vacances.
10. Dès qu'il (obtenir) _____ l'accord, il (partir) _____ .

EXERCICE 17·4

Changer les verbes du futur immédiat au futur simple.

1. L'avion va décoller à onze heures.

2. Tu vas apprendre à conduire.

3. Je vais peindre le salon.

4. Ils vont sortir avec des amis.

5. Vous allez recevoir une invitation.

6. Nous allons débarquer à midi.

7. Elle va écrire une lettre au président.

8. Tu vas mettre ton chapeau gris.

9. Ils vont aller en Bolivie.

10. Il va vivre jusqu'à cent ans.

EXERCICE 17·5

Faire correspondre les deux colonnes.

_____ 1. Elle recevra   a. le français
_____ 2. Tu courras   b. à un âge avancé
_____ 3. Il enseignera   c. son diplôme en juin
_____ 4. Elle mourra   d. pilote de ligne
_____ 5. Il deviendra   e. dans le parc

The **futur antérieur**

The **futur antérieur** (*future perfect*) describes an action that will take place and be completed before another future action. To form this compound tense, use the future tense of **avoir** or **être** + the past participle of the main verb. Agreement rules are the same as for the **passé composé**. Although it is rarely used in English, it must be used in French under certain circumstances.

écrire to write			
j'**aurai écrit**	*I'll have written*	nous **aurons écrit**	*we'll have written*
tu **auras écrit**	*you'll have written*	vous **aurez écrit**	*you'll have written*
il/elle **aura écrit**	*he/she will have written*	ils/elles **auront écrit**	*they'll have written*

devenir to become			
je **serai devenu(e)**	*I'll have become*	nous **serons devenu(e)s**	*we'll have become*
tu **seras devenu(e)**	*you'll have become*	vous **serez devenu(e)(s)**	*you'll have become*
il/elle **sera devenu(e)**	*he'll/she'll have become*	ils/elles **seront devenu(e)s**	*they'll have become*

Nous **aurons résolu** tous les problèmes d'ici la fin de l'année.	*We'll have solved all the problems by the end of the year.*
Il **aura enseigné** le français toute sa vie.	*He'll have taught French all his life.*

EXERCICE 17·6

Mettre les verbes entre parenthèses au futur antérieur.

1. Elle (apprendre) _____ le français au Laos.

2. Il (finir) _____ son roman avant la fin de l'année.

3. Nous (visiter) _____ tous les sites historiques de la région.

4. Les chercheurs (trouver) _____ un nouveau vaccin.

5. On (découvrir) _____ un remède plus efficace.

6. Je (répondre) _____ à toutes les questions.

7. Elle (se reposer) _____ des semaines au bord du lac.

8. Ils (compléter) _____ leur stage de formation.

9. Il (mourir) _____ depuis longtemps.

10. Je (voir) _____ l'essentiel.

Sometimes you have a choice between the **futur simple** and the **futur antérieur**. When both clauses use the **futur simple**, it is implied that both actions take place simultaneously.

Elle vous **téléphonera** dès qu'elle **finira** son roman.	*She'll call you as soon as she finishes her novel.*

254 PRACTICE MAKES PERFECT Complete French All-in-One

If you want to mark an anteriority, use the **futur antérieur**.

> Elle vous **téléphonera** dès qu'elle **aura fini** son roman.
> *She'll call you as soon as she finishes (will have finished) her novel.*
>
> Dès que vous **accepterez** cette théorie, on en **discutera** plus longuement.
> *As soon as you accept this theory, we'll discuss it at length.*
>
> Dès que vous **aurez accepté** cette théorie, on en **discutera** plus longuement.
> *As soon as you accept (will have accepted) this theory, we'll discuss it at length.*

The **futur antérieur** can also express the *probability* of a past action, in the same way that the **futur simple** can be used to express probability in the present.

> Elle **aura** encore **échoué** à ses examens!
> *She probably failed her exams again!*
>
> Il **aura** encore **brûlé** le gigot d'agneau!
> *He probably burnt the leg of lamb again!*
>
> Ils **auront manqué** leur train.
> *They probably missed their train.*
>
> Son fils **aura** encore **fait** des bêtises!
> *His son probably got in trouble again!*

The **futur antérieur** is also used after **si**, implying a completed action. **Si** means *whether* in this case.

> Je me demande **s'ils auront signé** le contrat.
> *I wonder whether they'll have signed the contract.*
>
> Je me demande **si** j'**aurai** tout **réglé** avant ce soir.
> *I am wondering whether I'll have resolved everything by tonight.*
>
> Il se demande **s'il aura terminé** à temps.
> *He wonders whether he'll have finished on time.*

In French, the **futur antérieur** is *never* used after **si** implying a future condition. Use the present instead.

> S'il **a** le temps, il passera vous voir.
> *If he has time, he'll stop by to see you.*
>
> Si vous **pouvez**, envoyez-moi votre CV avant lundi.
> *If you can, send me your résumé before Monday.*

EXERCICE 17·7

*Traduire les phrases suivantes en utilisant **vous** si nécessaire.*

1. We'll play tennis.

   _____

2. You'll need to buy a new car.

   _____

3. I'll take a history course.

   _____

4. We'll visit Venice when we are in Italy.

   _____

5. They'll go to Dakar.

   _____

6. We'll walk along the beach.

7. He'll study French when he is in Bordeaux.

8. They'll see the Picasso exhibition when they are in Paris.

9. She'll travel to Asia when she gets her degree.

10. He'll become a doctor.

Conjunctions used with the indicative mood

You have just seen examples of conjunctions frequently used with the **futur simple** and the **futur antérieur**. These include:

aussitôt que	*as soon as*
dès que	*as soon as*
lorsque	*when*
quand	*when*
tant que	*as long as*

Let's learn a few more conjunctions followed by the indicative mood. In Chapter 20 we'll study other conjunctions followed by the subjunctive mood.

alors que	*while, whereas*
après que	*after*
comme	*as, since*
étant donné que	*given, in view of*
maintenant que	*now that*
parce que	*because*
pendant que	*while*
puisque	*since*
si	*if*
sous prétexte que	*under the pretext that*
tandis que	*whereas*
vu que	*given, in view of*

As we saw earlier in this chapter, some conjunctions require the future tense in both the main and the dependent clauses. When using another tense, the balance of tenses is the same as with the other conjunctions.

Elle apprendra le russe **quand** elle sera en Russie.	*She'll learn Russian when she is in Russia.*
Je t'écrirai **dès que** je serai à Rio.	*I'll write to you as soon as I am in Rio.*
Dès qu'ils sortaient de l'école, ils allaient au stade.	*As soon as they left school, they used to go to the stadium.*

256 PRACTICE MAKES PERFECT Complete French All-in-One

Il a fondu en larmes **quand** il a appris qu'il avait raté l'examen.	*He burst into tears when he found out he had failed the exam.*
Puisque tu as le temps, aide-moi à finir mes devoirs.	*Since you have time, help me finish my homework.*
Il lisait pendant **qu'**elle écrivait.	*He was reading while she was writing.*
Étant donné que vous avez démissionné, nous ne pouvons rien faire pour vous.	*Given that you resigned, we cannot do anything for you.*
Il t'a fait ce cadeau **parce que** tu le mérites.	*He gave you this present because you deserve it.*
Comme il pleuvait, ils sont partis.	*Since it was raining, they left.*
Le téléphone a sonné **alors que** j'étais dans mon bain.	*The phone rang while I was in my bath.*
Si tu veux y aller, appelle-moi!	*If you want to go there, call me!*

EXERCICE 17·8

Mettre au futur simple les verbes entre parenthèses.

1. Puisqu'il a raté son examen, il (ne pas aller) _____ en vacances.

2. Étant donné qu'il est parti, la situation ne (faire) _____ qu'empirer.

3. Il devra trouver une excuse parce qu'elle (ne pas pouvoir) _____ assister à la réunion.

4. Il fera chaud chez elle alors que chez lui, on (geler) _____ .

5. Si nous avons le temps, nous (se promener) _____ au bord du lac.

6. Dès que j'aurai terminé l'enregistrement, je vous (envoyer) _____ un CD.

7. Elle dormira tandis que je (faire) _____ la vaisselle.

8. Tant qu'ils seront là, tout (aller) _____ bien.

9. Quand tu vivras à Paris, tu (découvrir) _____ beaucoup de nouvelles choses.

10. Aussitôt que le paquet sera arrivé, je vous (contacter) _____ .

The simple future and the past future **257**

The present conditional and the past conditional

The present conditional

The **présent du conditionnel** (*present conditional*) has many uses we'll explore in this chapter. It is formed by adding the endings of the imperfect to the future stem of the verb. For **-er** and **-ir** verbs, the future stem is the entire infinitive form. For **-re** verbs, drop the final **-e** from the infinitive before adding the conditional endings. As you saw in Chapter 17, a number of irregular verbs have an irregular future stem. This same stem is used to form the present conditional.

mettre *to put*

je **mettrais**	*I would put*	nous **mettrions**	*we would put*
tu **mettrais**	*you would put*	vous **mettriez**	*you would put*
il/elle **mettrait**	*he/she would put*	ils/elles **mettraient**	*they would put*

faire *to do*

je **ferais**	*I would do*	nous **ferions**	*we would do*
tu **ferais**	*you would do*	vous **feriez**	*you would do*
il/elle **ferait**	*he/she would do*	ils/elles **feraient**	*they would do*

VOCABULAIRE

un animal	*an animal*	**un dauphin**	*a dolphin*
un agneau	*a lamb*	**un écureuil**	*a squirrel*
un aigle	*an eagle*	**un éléphant**	*an elephant*
un âne	*a donkey*	**une girafe**	*a giraffe*
une baleine	*a whale*	**une grenouille**	*a frog*
un bœuf	*an ox*	**un hippopotame**	*a hippopotamus*
un canard	*a duck*	**un kangourou**	*a kangaroo*
un chameau	*a camel*	**un lapin**	*a rabbit*
un chat	*a cat*	**un lion**	*a lion*
un chaton	*a kitten*	**un loup**	*a wolf*
une chauve-souris	*a bat*	**un mouton**	*a sheep*
un cheval	*a horse*	**un oiseau**	*a bird*
une chèvre	*a goat*	**un ours**	*a bear*
un chien	*a dog*	**un pingouin**	*a penguin*
un cochon	*a pig*	**un poisson**	*a fish*
une colombe	*a dove*	**un poisson rouge**	*a goldfish*
un coq	*a rooster*	**une poule**	*a hen*
un crapaud	*a toad*	**un renard**	*a fox*
un crocodile	*a crocodile*	**un requin**	*a shark*

un rhinocéros	a rhinoceros	un tigre	a tiger
un serpent	a snake	une tortue	a tortoise
un singe	a monkey	une vache	a cow
une souris	a mouse	un veau	a calf
un taureau	a bull	un zèbre	a zebra

Ces animaux **auraient** plus à manger dans cette région.
These animals would have more to eat in this region.

Il **aimerait** avoir une tortue.
He would like to have a turtle.

Dans un monde idéal, il n'y **aurait** pas de guerres.
In an ideal world, there would be no war.

Dans de telles circonstances, que **feriez**-vous?
In such circumstances, what would you do?

EXERCICE 18·1

Mettre les verbes au présent du conditionnel.

1. aller (nous) _____
2. voyager (elle) _____
3. dire (nous) _____
4. avoir (je) _____
5. manger (ils) _____
6. prendre (elle) _____
7. être (tu) _____
8. demander (vous) _____
9. écrire (je) _____
10. savoir (tu) _____

Uses of the present conditional

The **présent du conditionnel** is used to express a wish or a suggestion. For example:

Je **voudrais finir** ce projet aussitôt que possible.
I would like to finish this project as soon as possible.

À ta place, je **parierais** sur ce cheval.
If I were you, I would bet on this horse.

Ce **serait** génial de pouvoir y aller ensemble.
It would be great to go together.

Il **aimerait rencontrer** la femme de sa vie.
He would like to meet the woman of his dreams.

The **présent du conditionnel** is used to make a statement or a request more polite.

Pourriez-vous nous **donner** votre avis?	*Could you give us your opinion?*
Voudriez-vous **dîner** avec nous ce soir?	*Would you like to have dinner with us this evening?*
Est-ce que tu **pourrais** me **donner** un coup de main?	*Could you give me a hand?*
Est-ce que tu **voudrais assister** à la réunion?	*Would you like to attend the meeting?*

EXERCICE 18·2

*Traduire les verbes entre parenthèses en utilisant **vous** et l'inversion.*

1. (*Would you*) aller au théâtre la semaine prochaine? _____
2. (*Could we*) passer chez vous après le spectacle? _____
3. (*Could you*) changer la date de votre départ? _____
4. (*Would you*) m'acheter le journal pendant mes vacances? _____
5. (*Would he*) signer cette pétition? _____
6. (*Could you*) nourrir mes poissons rouges? _____
7. (*Could she*) prendre un train plus tard? _____
8. (*Would you*) aller avec moi en Tanzanie? _____
9. (*Could we*) finir ce projet la semaine prochaine? _____
10. (*Would they*) accompagner Sonia à la gare? _____

The **présent du conditionnel** is used when a condition is implied. When the main clause is in the **présent du conditionnel**, the **si** clause is in the **imparfait**.

Nous **irions** à Rome **si** nous **pouvions**.	*We would go to Rome if we could.*
Régis **finirait** son roman **s'il pouvait** trouver une maison d'édition.	*Régis would finish his novel if he could find a publisher.*
Nous **aurions** un chien **si** notre appartement **était** plus grand.	*We would have a dog if our apartment were bigger.*
Nous **viendrions si** notre baby-sitter **était** disponible.	*We would come if our babysitter were available.*

The **présent du conditionnel** is also used to express unconfirmed or alleged information. In this case it is called the **conditionnel journalistique**, seen from time to time in the press or heard on news broadcasts.

La reine d'Angleterre **se rendrait** en Australie la semaine prochaine.	*The Queen of England is reportedly going to Australia next week.*
Son beau-frère **serait impliqué** dans une affaire de fraude fiscale.	*His (her) brother-in-law is allegedly involved in tax fraud.*
Le président **signerait** le traité en fin d'après-midi.	*The president will reportedly sign the treaty by the end of the afternoon.*

Un sous-marin hollandais **serait** au large des côtes bretonnes.

A Dutch submarine is reportedly off the coast of Brittany.

In formal French, **savoir** in the **présent du conditionnel** is the equivalent of **pouvoir** (*can, to be able to*) in the present or the simple future.

Je ne **saurais** vous dire combien j'apprécie votre geste.
Je ne **saurais** vous répondre.

I shall never be able to tell you how much I appreciate your gesture.
I am afraid I can't answer. (I wouldn't know how to answer you.)

EXERCICE 18·3

Mettre à l'imparfait les verbes dans la proposition si, et au conditionnel ceux de la proposition principale.

1. Si je (avoir) moins de travail, je (voyager) plus.

2. S'ils (attendre), ils (obtenir) un meilleur prix pour leur appartement.

3. Si nous (planter) plus de fleurs, nous (avoir) un plus beau jardin.

4. Si je (vendre) mon appartement, je (pouvoir) acheter cette maison.

5. S'il (pouvoir), il (déménager).

6. Si vous les (inviter), nous (être) ravis.

7. Si ma voiture (tomber) en panne, je (piquer) une crise.

8. Si elle (avoir) plus d'argent, elle (venir) avec nous.

9. Si vous (s'organiser) autrement, votre vie (être) plus facile.

10. Si tu (dormir) plus, tu (avoir) de meilleures notes à l'école.

EXERCICE 18·4

Conjuguer les verbes entre parenthèses en utilisant d'abord le présent du conditionnel, puis l'imparfait.

1. Elle (être) contente si tu (venir) ce soir.

2. Nous (faire) une promenade dans le parc s'il (faire) beau.

3. Ils (prendre) leur retraite s'ils (pouvoir).

4. Il (accompagner) Sophie à l'opéra s'il (ne pas être) occupé.

5. Il y (avoir) moins de problèmes si vous (suivre) mes conseils.

6. Elles (aller) au musée s'il (être) ouvert avant onze heures.

7. Vous (finir) plus tôt si vous (travailler) plus efficacement.

8. Nous vous (croire) si vous nous (dire) la vérité.

9. Elle (acheter) cette voiture si elle (être) moins chère.

10. Tu lui (offrir) ce poste si tu (avoir) confiance en lui.

EXERCICE 18·5

*Traduire les phrases suivantes en utilisant **tu** si nécessaire.*

1. He would go to Paris if he had more time.

2. She would buy this coat if it were less expensive.

3. We would be delighted if you came on Sunday.

4. I would write a letter if you needed it.

5. The president is reportedly in Brazil today.

6. It would be prettier if there were more flowers.

7. I would invite Chloé if I went to Paris.

8. The director will reportedly sign the contract.

9. She would eat the soup if she were hungry.

10. He would read the paper this morning if he could.

EXERCICE
18·6

Faire correspondre les deux colonnes.

_____ 1. Le chat serait content	a. s'il y faisait moins chaud
_____ 2. Le mouton dormirait tranquillement	b. si elle ne portait pas sa maison sur son dos
_____ 3. L'ours visiterait le désert	c. s'il attrapait une souris
_____ 4. La grenouille serait ravie	d. si le loup n'était pas dans la forêt
_____ 5. La tortue avancerait plus vite	e. si elle pouvait être aussi grosse qu'un bœuf

The past conditional

The **passé du conditionnel** (*past conditional*) expresses what would have happened if another event had taken place, or if certain conditions had or had not been present. It is formed with the present conditional of **être** or **avoir** and the past participle of the main verb. The rules of agreement common to all compound tenses still apply.

The present conditional and the past conditional   **263**

donner *to give*			
j'**aurais donné**	*I would have given*	nous **aurions donné**	*we would have given*
tu **aurais donné**	*you would have given*	vous **auriez donné**	*you would have given*
il/elle **aurait donné**	*he/she would have given*	ils/elles **auraient donné**	*they would have given*

venir *to come*			
je **serais venu(e)**	*I would have come*	nous **serions venu(e)s**	*we would have come*
tu **serais venu(e)**	*you would have come*	vous **seriez venu(e)(s)**	*you would have come*
il/elle **serait venu(e)**	*he/she would have come*	ils/elles **seraient venu(e)s**	*they would have come*

Elle **aurait accepté** votre offre.	*She would have accepted your offer.*
Nous **aurions été** déçus.	*We would have been disappointed.*
Tu **aurais ri**!	*You would have laughed!*
Ils **se seraient mis** en colère.	*They would have gotten angry.*

Uses of the past conditional

The **passé du conditionnel** can express regret or reproach.

Nous **aurions voulu** y assister.	*We would have liked to attend.*
Tu **aurais dû** arriver plus tôt.	*You should have arrived earlier.*
Elle **aurait aimé** le féliciter.	*She would have liked to congratulate him.*
Cela **aurait été** tellement plus facile.	*It would have been so much easier.*

The **passé du conditionnel** is usually found in sentences where the **si** (dependent) clause is in the **plus-que-parfait**.

Elle **aurait fini** plus tôt **si** vous l'**aviez aidée**.	*She would have finished earlier if you had helped her.*
Je **serais arrivé** à l'heure **s'il y avait eu** moins de circulation.	*I would have arrived on time if there had been less traffic.*
Si le patron **n'avait pas voté** la délocalisation, l'usine **serait restée** ouverte.	*If the boss had not opted for a relocation, the factory would have stayed open.*
Il n'aurait pas tant **gagné** d'argent **s'il était resté** à Bordeaux.	*He would not have made as much money if he had stayed in Bordeaux.*

The **passé du conditionnel** is used like the **present du conditionnel** as a **conditionnel journalistique** to express a statement not necessarily confirmed by authorities. In most cases that imply the English *allegedly* or *reportedly*, the conditional (past or present) will be used in French. See the following examples:

Le tremblement de terre **aurait fait** des milliers de victimes au Mexique.	*The earthquake reportedly killed thousands of people in Mexico.*
Le président l'**aurait gracié**.	*The president reportedly granted him his pardon.*
Ce célèbre chanteur français **se serait installé** en Suisse.	*This famous French singer reportedly moved to Switzerland.*
Il **aurait volé** la voiture de son voisin.	*He allegedly stole his neighbor's car.*

264 PRACTICE MAKES PERFECT Complete French All-in-One

EXERCICE 18·7

Conjuguer les verbes entre parenthèses en utilisant d'abord le passé du conditionnel, puis le plus-que-parfait.

1. Nous (dîner) avec vous si nous (pouvoir).

2. Elle (visiter) ce musée si elle (avoir) plus de temps.

3. Elle (voir) ce film s'il (être) sous-titré.

4. Ils (inviter) Charles s'il (ne pas travailler) ce soir-là.

5. Il (faire) un documentaire sur ce sujet s'il (trouver) le financement.

6. Ils (vendre) leur maison si leurs enfants (déménager).

7. Vous (arriver) à temps si votre voiture (ne pas tomber) en panne.

8. Le directeur (démissionner) si les ouvriers (ne pas faire) pression.

9. Cette pièce (avoir) du succès s'il y (avoir) plus de temps pour les répétitions.

10. Nous (venir) si nous (recevoir) votre invitation plus tôt.

EXERCICE 18·8

Conjuguer les verbes entre parenthèses en utilisant d'abord le plus-que-parfait, puis le passé du conditionnel.

1. S'il (finir) son projet, il (ne pas devoir) travailler le week-end.

2. Si je (mettre) mon manteau, je (ne pas avoir) si froid.

The present conditional and the past conditional 265

3. Si vous (pouvoir) témoigner au tribunal, la situation (être) différente.

_____

4. Si on (ne pas guillotiner) le roi, l'histoire du pays (prendre) une tournure différente.

_____

5. S'il (apprendre) sa grammaire, il (faire) moins de fautes.

_____

6. Si elle (se présenter) aux élections, elle (être élue).

_____

7. Si nous (commander) un couscous, nous (ne pas avoir) faim plus tard.

_____

8. Si elle (pouvoir), elle (être) danseuse.

_____

9. Si tu (être) plus pratique, nous (voyager) sans bagages.

_____

10. Si je (savoir), je (ne pas engager) Daniel.

_____

The **présent** or **passé du conditionnel** are also used with the expression **au cas où** (*in case*).

Au cas où le projet **ne serait pas fini** cet après-midi, appelez-moi.	*In case the project is not finished by this afternoon, call me.*
Au cas où ce cadeau **ne** vous **plairait pas**, dites-le-moi.	*In case you do not like this present, let me know.*
Au cas où il **aurait échoué** à l'examen, on lui donnera une autre chance.	*In case he failed the exam, we'll give him another chance.*
Au cas où tu **n'aurais pas retrouvé** tes clés, Christian s'occupera de toi.	*In case you did not find your keys, Christian will take care of you.*

EXERCICE
18·9

Traduire les phrases suivantes en utilisant le conditionnel journalistique, présent ou passé.

1. The prime minister reportedly went to China yesterday.

_____

2. The witness allegedly gave the police a different version.

_____

3. The cyclone reportedly killed two hundred people in this town.

_____

266 PRACTICE MAKES PERFECT Complete French All-in-One

4. The director reportedly resigned.

_____

5. The storm has reportedly destroyed a hundred houses.

_____

6. Unemployment is reportedly going to decline next year.

_____

7. The health minister reportedly signed the reform.

_____

8. Penguins are reportedly unable to reproduce because of global warming.

_____

9. His new neighbor allegedly stole his car.

_____

10. A French actor reportedly bought a house in California last week.

_____

EXERCICE 18·10

Faire correspondre les deux colonnes.

_____	1. Au cas où il pleuvrait	a. viens regarder le film chez moi
_____	2. Au cas où tu l'aurais oublié	b. elle pourrait se servir des miennes
_____	3. Au cas où ta télévision serait en panne	c. prends un parapluie
_____	4. Au cas où elle aurait perdu ses notes	d. prévenez la police
_____	5. Au cas où quelque chose aurait été volé	e. c'est mon anniversaire demain

The present conditional and the past conditional

Could, should, would?

Could, *should*, and *would* have different meanings in English and are translated in several ways in French. Each time you come across one of these verbs, try to consider its nuance in English.

Could

When *could* refers to a single, unique action in the past, the **passé composé** of **pouvoir** is used.

j'**ai pu**	*I could*	nous **avons pu**	*we could*
tu **as pu**	*you could*	vous **avez pu**	*you could*
il/elle **a pu**	*he/she could*	ils/elles **ont pu**	*they could*

Note the following examples:

Il n'**a** pas **pu** lui parler.	*He could not talk to him.*
J'**ai pu** la convaincre.	*I managed to convince her.*
Nous n'**avons** pas **pu** y aller.	*We could not go there.*
Il a **pu** obtenir les fonds.	*He succeeded in obtaining the funding.*

When *could* refers to a description or a habitual action, the **imparfait** of **pouvoir** is used.

je **pouvais**	*I could*	nous **pouvions**	*we could*
tu **pouvais**	*you could*	vous **pouviez**	*you could*
il/elle **pouvait**	*he/she could*	ils/elles **pouvaient**	*they could*

Note the following examples:

En ce temps-là, les femmes ne **pouvaient** pas voter.	*At that time, women could not vote.*
À cette époque, les voitures ne **pouvaient** pas traverser la ville.	*At that time, cars couldn't drive through the city.*
Si jeune, il **pouvait** quand même prendre une telle décision!	*So young, he was still able to make such a decision!*
Après la mort de sa femme, il ne **pouvait** plus écrire.	*After his wife's death, he could no longer write.*

When *could* refers to an idea of the future, a hypothesis, a suggestion, or a request, the **présent du conditionnel** of **pouvoir** is used.

je **pourrais**	*I could*	nous **pourrions**	*we could*
tu **pourrais**	*you could*	vous **pourriez**	*you could*
il/elle **pourrait**	*he/she could*	ils/elles **pourraient**	*they could*

Note the following examples:

Pourrais-tu me prêter le livre dont tu m'as parlé?	*Could you lend me the book you told me about?*
Pourriez-vous m'expliquer votre méthode de travail?	*Could you explain to me your working method?*
Je **pourrais** vous prêter ma voiture.	*I could lend you my car.*
Ils **pourraient** apprendre à jouer de la clarinette.	*They could learn how to play the clarinet.*

VOCABULAIRE

les instruments (*m.pl.*)	*instruments*	**l'harmonica** (*m.*)	*harmonica*
l'accordéon (*m.*)	*accordion*	**la harpe**	*harp*
l'alto (*m.*)	*viola*	**le hautbois**	*oboe*
la basse	*string bass; bass guitar*	**le piano**	*piano*
la batterie	*drums*	**le saxophone**	*saxophone*
les castagnettes (*f.pl.*)	*castanets*	**le synthétiseur**	*synthesizer*
la clarinette	*clarinet*	**le tambour**	*drum*
le clavecin	*harpsichord*	**le tambourin**	*tambourine*
le cor	*French horn*	**le trombone**	*trombone*
la contrebasse	*double bass* (= **la basse**)	**la trompette**	*trumpet*
la cymbale	*cymbal*	**le violon**	*violin*
la flûte	*flute*	**le violoncelle**	*cello*
la guitare	*guitar*	**le xylophone**	*xylophone*
la guitare électrique	*electric guitar*		

EXERCICE
19·1

*Traduire les phrases suivantes en utilisant **vous** et l'inversion si nécessaire.*

1. Could you help clean the house after the party?

   _____

2. We could not go on vacation.

   _____

3. I could buy her a new flute.

   _____

4. At that time, they could not understand.

   _____

5. Could we start eating?

6. We could go see a movie tonight.

7. Thanks to her rich aunt, she could pay for her studies.

8. I think she could do better.

9. When you were a kid, you would play with your dolls for hours.

10. Could you teach me how to play the guitar?

Should

When *should* means *ought to*, the **conditionnel** (**présent** or **passé**) is used.

je **devrais**	I should	j'**aurais dû**	I should have
tu **devrais**	you should	tu **aurais dû**	you should have
il/elle **devrait**	he/she should	il/elle **aurait dû**	he/she should have
nous **devrions**	we should	nous **aurions dû**	we should have
vous **devriez**	you should	vous **auriez dû**	you should have
ils/elles **devraient**	they should	ils/elles **auraient dû**	they should have

Note the following examples:

Elle **devrait se détendre** un peu.	She should relax a bit.
Vous **devriez aller** au concert.	You should go to the concert.
Tu **aurais dû** lui **demander** des explications.	You should have asked him for explanations.
Vous **auriez dû** l'**emmener** au festival de musique.	You should have taken him to the music festival.

EXERCICE
19·2

*Traduire les phrases suivantes en utilisant **vous** et l'inversion si nécessaire.*

1. You should learn to play the guitar.

2. They shouldn't have said that.

3. I should write to Pierre.

4. I should have talked to them.

5. Do you think Julien should have called you before coming?

6. I shouldn't have called so early.

7. We shouldn't take the car, it's too dangerous.

8. I think you should take a vacation.

9. You should rent a piano for the party.

10. Marie thinks her father should be present for this occasion.

Would

When *would* refers to a repeated action in the past, the **imparfait** is used. Note the following examples:

Quand j'étais étudiant, je **lisais** les journaux tous les jours.	*When I was a student, I would read the newspapers every day.*
Quand ils étaient adolescents, ils **jouaient** au volley-ball le jeudi.	*When they were teens, they would play volleyball on Thursdays.*

When *would* refers to a polite request, the **présent du conditionnel** is used. Note the following examples:

Voudrais-tu me **montrer** le chemin?	*Would you mind showing me the way?*
Est-ce que tu **voudrais** bien m'**aider** à résoudre ce problème?	*Could you help me solve that problem?*

When *would* refers to a specific action in the past, the **passé composé** of **vouloir** is used. Note the following examples:

Nous leur avons demandé de nous accorder un peu de temps; ils **n'ont pas voulu** le **faire**.	*We asked them to give us a little time; they would not do it.*
Je lui ai posé la question plusieurs fois; elle **n'a pas voulu répondre**.	*I asked her the question several times; she would not answer.*

Could, should, would? 271

When *would* refers to an idea of the future, a hypothesis, or a suggestion, the **présent du conditionnel** of the main verb is used. The **imparfait** is used in the **si** clause.

Je vous le **dirais** si je le **savais**. *I would tell you if I knew.*
Elle **serait** si heureuse s'il la **demandait** en mariage. *She would be so happy if he proposed to her.*

EXERCICE 19·3

Traduire en anglais les phrases suivantes.

1. S'il était moins paresseux, il aurait de meilleures notes à l'école.

2. Quand nous étions enfants, nos parents nous emmenaient en vacances au Maroc tous les ans.

3. Samuel a demandé un peu plus d'argent. Son patron n'a pas voulu le lui donner.

4. Si Emmanuelle était disponible, elle viendrait.

5. Quand elle était étudiante à Paris, elle allait au cinéma tous les dimanches.

6. Si Sylvie avait plus d'argent, elle s'achèterait de nouvelles chaussures.

7. S'ils avaient le choix, ils ne déménageraient pas.

8. Voudrais-tu me dire ce qui s'est passé à cette réunion?

9. Catherine voulait faire demi-tour, mais son mari n'a pas voulu le faire.

10. Pourriez-vous m'expliquer comment cela marche?

EXERCICE 19·4

*Traduire en français les phrases suivantes en utilisant **tu** et l'inversion si nécessaire.*

1. Could you read this document?

2. We should buy tickets for the concert.

3. Valérie could help you!

4. At that time, she could not go out very often.

5. Could you send me a copy of that letter?

6. I asked her to help me; she would not do it.

7. Pascal would play the violin if he had more time.

8. Marie could not tell him the truth.

9. When we were kids, we would play for hours on the beach.

10. Don't you think you should change your haircut?

EXERCICE 19·5

Could, would *ou* should? *Traduire les phrases suivantes.*

1. Pourrais-tu ouvrir la porte?

2. À cette heure, il devrait être à la maison.

3. Ils n'ont pas pu avoir de billets.

4. Voudriez-vous bien participer à ce projet?

_____

5. Je suis venu le chercher; il n'a pas voulu venir avec moi.

_____

6. Si tu étais moins égoïste, tu aurais plus d'amis.

_____

7. Voudrais-tu bien me montrer comment ça fonctionne?

_____

8. Il n'a pas pu partir à temps.

_____

9. Lorsque nous étions enfants, nous allions à la mer tous les étés.

_____

10. Il devrait réfléchir avant de parler.

_____

EXERCICE 19·6

Faire correspondre les deux colonnes.

_____ 1. Marie serait ravie   a. venir manger à la maison ce soir.

_____ 2. Vous devriez   b. elle circulait en vélo.

_____ 3. Quand elle habitait à la campagne,   c. si Marc l'invitait à dîner.

_____ 4. Je serais moins inquiet   d. me prévenir que tes parents venaient aussi.

_____ 5. Tu aurais dû   e. si tu me téléphonais en arrivant.

The present subjunctive and the past subjunctive

The present subjunctive

The subjunctive is a mood, not a tense. The mood of a verb determines how one views an event. You have already studied verb tenses in the indicative mood (**le présent**, **l'imparfait**, and **le futur**), stating objective facts, and in the conditional mood, relating to possibilities. In Chapter 23 we will study the imperative mood that gives commands. The subjunctive is another mood that refers to someone's opinion or deals with hypothetical actions.

For most verbs, the present of the subjunctive is formed by adding the subjunctive endings (**-e**, **-es**, **-e**, **-ions**, **-iez**, **-ent**) to the stem. The stem for **je**, **tu**, **il/elle**, **ils/elles** is found by dropping the **-ent** ending from the third-person plural present indicative form (**ils/elles**). Note that the sound of the verb will be the same for all these persons.

Let's look at the verb **penser** (*to think*). The third-person plural: **ils/elles pensent**. The stem: **pens-**

je pens**e**	*I speak*
tu pens**es**	*you speak*
il/elle pens**e**	*he/she speaks*
ils/elles pens**ent**	*they speak*

The stem for the **nous** and **vous** subjunctive forms is found by dropping the **-ons** from the first-person plural of the present indicative. For **nous** and **vous**, the present subjunctive is identical to the forms of the **imparfait**. The first-person plural: **nous pensons**. The stem: **pens-**

nous pens**ions**	*we speak*
vous pens**iez**	*you speak*

Let's conjugate the verb **dire** (*to say*) in the present subjunctive:

je **dise**	*I say*	nous **disions**	*we say*
tu **dises**	*you say*	vous **disiez**	*you say*
il/elle **dise**	*he/she says*	ils/elles **disent**	*they say*

And **mettre** (*to put*):

je **mette**	*I put*	nous **mettions**	*we put*
tu **mettes**	*you put*	vous **mettiez**	*you put*
il/elle **mette**	*he/she puts*	ils/elles **mettent**	*they put*

Some verbs have irregular forms in the present subjunctive. **Être** (*to be*) and **avoir** (*to have*) have both irregular stems and endings.

être

je **sois**	*I am*	nous **soyons**	*we are*
tu **sois**	*you are*	vous **soyez**	*you are*
il/elle **soit**	*he/she is*	ils/elles **soient**	*they are*

avoir

j'**aie**	*I have*	nous **ayons**	*we have*
tu **aies**	*you have*	vous **ayez**	*you have*
il/elle **ait**	*he/she has*	ils/elles **aient**	*they have*

The following three verbs have an irregular subjunctive stem but regular endings.

pouvoir *can, to be able to*

je **puisse**	*I can*	nous **puissions**	*we can*
tu **puisses**	*you can*	vous **puissiez**	*you can*
il/elle **puisse**	*he/she can*	ils/elles **puissent**	*they can*

savoir *to know*

je **sache**	*I know*	nous **sachions**	*we know*
tu **saches**	*you know*	vous **sachiez**	*you know*
il/elle **sache**	*he/she knows*	ils/elles **sachent**	*they know*

faire *to do, to make*

je **fasse**	*I do*	nous **fassions**	*we do*
tu **fasses**	*you do*	vous **fassiez**	*you do*
il/elle **fasse**	*he/she does*	ils/elles **fassent**	*they do*

Aller (*to go*) and **vouloir** (*to want*) have an irregular stem in the **je**, **tu**, **il/elle**, **ils/elles** forms and are partially irregular in the **nous** and **vous** forms.

aller *to go*

j'**aille**	*I go*	nous **allions**	*we go*
tu **ailles**	*you go*	vous **alliez**	*you go*
il/elle **aille**	*he/she goes*	ils/elles **aillent**	*they go*

vouloir *to want*

je **veuille**	*I want*	nous **voulions**	*we want*
tu **veuilles**	*you want*	vous **vouliez**	*you want*
il/elle **veuille**	*he/she wants*	ils/elles **veuillent**	*they want*

VOCABULAIRE

un ordinateur	*a computer*	**l'informatique** (*f.*)	*computer science*
une souris	*a mouse*	**un(e) internaute**	*a Internet surfer*
une touche	*a key (on keyboard)*	**une banque de données**	*a data bank*
un clavier	*a keyboard*	**une base de données**	*a database*
un écran	*a screen*	**une disquette**	*a floppy disk*
cliquer	*to click*	**une page d'accueil**	*a home page*
imprimer	*to print*	**la Toile**	*the Web*
une imprimante	*a printer*	**un disque dur**	*a hard drive*

276 PRACTICE MAKES PERFECT Complete French All-in-One

un logiciel	a software program	se connecter	to log on
numérique	digital	surfer sur Internet	to surf the Net
numériser	to digitize	télécharger	to download
sauvegarder	to save	un site Web	a website

Uses of the subjunctive

There are three main concepts that require the use of the subjunctive: wish, emotion, and doubt.

The subjunctive is used after verbs expressing the notion of *wish* and *desire*. It is used when the subject of the main clause is different from the subject of the dependent clause. Compare:

> **Je veux acheter** cet ordinateur. *I want to buy this computer.*
> **Je veux que tu achètes** cet ordinateur. *I want you to buy this computer.*

Compare:

> **Vous désirez suivre** un cours d'informatique. *You want to take a computer science class.*
> **Vous désirez que nous suivions** un cours d'informatique. *You want us to take a computer science course.*
> **Elle souhaite que tu ailles** en France. *She wishes you would go to France.*
> **J'exige que vous arriviez** à l'heure. *I demand that you arrive on time.*
> **Il demande que nous soyons** plus efficaces. *He is asking us to be more efficient.*

The subjunctive is used after expressions of *emotion*.

> **Je regrette qu'il ne puisse pas être** ici. *I am sorry he can't be here.*
> **Nous sommes ravis que tu prennes** tes vacances ici. *We are delighted you are vacationing here.*
> **Ils sont déçus que le cours soit annulé.** *They are disappointed that the class is canceled.*
> **Je suis content que tu viennes** dimanche. *I am happy you are coming on Sunday.*

The subjunctive is also used after expressions of *doubt*.

> **Je ne suis pas convaincu qu'il ait** raison. *I am not convinced he is right.*
> **Je doute qu'il comprenne** vos questions. *I doubt he understands your questions.*
> **Elle ne croit pas que vous trouviez** leur projet intéressant. *She does not think you find their project interesting.*
> **Je ne pense pas qu'il sache** ce qu'il fait. *I doubt he knows what he is doing.*

The verbs **penser** (*to think*) and **croire** (*to believe*) in the affirmative are followed by the indicative mood. However, in the negative and interrogative, the subjunctive can be used to underline the uncertainty of the event.

> **Je ne crois pas que Daniel est** coupable. *I don't think Daniel is guilty.*
> **Je ne crois pas que Daniel soit** coupable. *I don't think Daniel is guilty.*

The first sentence above means "I am actually sure Daniel is innocent." In the second example, there is some doubt about his guilt (or innocence). The difference will be detected in context and with the intonation of the voice or through gestures.

The present subjunctive and the past subjunctive   277

EXERCICE 20·1

Mettre les verbes au subjonctif.

1. Elle préfère que tout le monde (être) _____ là avant de commencer.
2. Je doute que vous (comprendre) _____ l'importance de cet événement.
3. Sa mère aimerait mieux qu'elle (ne pas sortir) _____ ce soir.
4. A-t-il fini le projet? Non. Mais je tiens à ce qu'il le (finir) _____ aujourd'hui.
5. Je doute qu'ils (gérer) _____ cette affaire correctement.
6. J'ai peur que ces logiciels (ne pas être) _____ compatibles.
7. Ils souhaitent que cette aventure (avoir) _____ une fin heureuse.
8. Il craint que ce projet (être) _____ un échec.
9. Elle est contente qu'il (pouvoir) _____ acheter la maison de ses rêves.
10. Le juge ne croit pas qu'il (dire) _____ la vérité.

The subjunctive is also used after certain impersonal expressions, in the same way that some verbs are followed by the indicative and others by the subjunctive. In most cases, the impersonal expressions followed by the subjunctive express will, obligation, necessity, emotion, and doubt. Here are some impersonal expressions that are followed by the *indicative*:

il est certain	*it is certain*	**il est sûr**	*it is sure*
il est évident	*it is obvious*	**il est vrai**	*it is true*
il est probable	*it is probable*	**il me semble**	*it seems to me*

And here are some impersonal expressions that are followed by the *subjunctive*:

il faut	*one must*	**il est possible**	*it is possible*
il est essentiel	*it is essential*	**il est indispensable**	*it is essential*
il est juste	*it is fair*	**il se peut**	*it may be*
il est important	*it is important*	**il vaut mieux**	*it is better*
il est préférable	*it is preferable*	**il est souhaitable**	*it is desirable*
il est naturel	*it is natural*	**il est normal**	*it is normal*
il est rare	*it is rare*	**il est utile**	*it is useful*
il est étrange	*it is strange*	**il est bizarre**	*it is odd*
il est étonnant	*it is amazing*	**il est surprenant**	*it is surprising*
il est triste	*it is sad*	**il est dommage**	*it is a shame*
il est regrettable	*it is unfortunate*	**cela ne vaut pas la peine**	*it is not worth it*

Let's compare the use of the indicative and the subjunctive with some impersonal expressions:

Il est **certain** qu'il **viendra** ce soir. — *It is certain he'll come tonight.*
Il est **possible** qu'il **vienne** ce soir. — *It is possible he'll come tonight.*

Look at these example sentences with impersonal expressions.

Il faut que vous commenciez vos recherches dès que possible. — *You have to begin your research as soon as possible.*

Il est étonnant que vous demandiez un salaire si élevé.	*It is surprising that you're asking for such a high salary.*
Il est rare qu'ils finissent leurs rapports à temps.	*It is rare for them to finish their reports on time.*
Il est regrettable que ce logiciel coûte si cher.	*It is unfortunate this software is so expensive.*
Il se peut que cette imprimante soit incompatible.	*It is possible this printer is not compatible.*
Il est triste que vous démissionniez cette semaine.	*It is sad you are resigning this week.*
Il faut que vous refassiez la page d'accueil de votre site.	*You must redo the home page of your website.*
Il est étrange qu'il télécharge tous vos documents.	*It is strange that he downloads all your documents.*
Il est possible que leurs dossiers soient numériques.	*Their files may be digital.*

Mettre les propositions subordonnées au subjonctif.

1. Il faut que vous (aller) _____ voir ce film.
2. Il est essentiel que vous (arriver) _____ avant la fin de la semaine.
3. Il est impensable que nous (accepter) _____ ces conditions.
4. Il est possible que nous (voyager) _____ cet été.
5. Il est important qu'il (être) _____ à l'heure.
6. Il vaut mieux que nous (ne rien dire) _____ .
7. Il est regrettable que ses enfants (habiter) _____ si loin.
8. Il est dommage que vous (vendre) _____ votre maison de campagne.
9. Il est indispensable qu'elle (suivre) _____ un cours d'informatique.
10. Il est rare que nous (emporter) _____ du travail à la maison.

When you use conjunctions, you will also have to decide whether to use the indicative or the subjunctive in the following clause.

afin que	*so that, in order to*	**pour que**	*so that, in order to*
de peur que	*for fear that*	**de crainte que**	*for fear that*
avant que	*before*	**jusqu'à ce que**	*until*
bien que	*although*	**quoique**	*although*
sans que	*without*	**à moins que**	*unless*
pourvu que	*provided that*	**à condition que**	*on the condition that*
en attendant que	*waiting for*		

The present subjunctive and the past subjunctive

Nous partirons demain **à moins qu**'il y **ait** une grève.	*We'll leave tomorrow unless there is a strike.*
Il viendra avec nous **à condition que** son patron lui **donne** un jour de congé.	*He'll come with us on the condition that his boss gives him a day off.*
Tout sera fini **avant qu**'ils **arrivent**.	*Everything will be done before they arrive.*
Je sauvegarde toutes ses données **de peur qu**'il les **perde**.	*I save all his data for fear he loses (he'll lose) it.*
Ils ont pris la décision **sans qu**'elle le **sache**.	*They made the decision without her knowing it.*
Il est tolérant **pourvu qu**'on **respecte** ses idées.	*He is tolerant provided one respects his ideas.*
Quoiqu'il **fasse** froid, ils se promènent dans la forêt.	*Although it is cold, they take a walk in the forest.*

Refer to Chapter 17 for the list of conjunctions that are followed by the indicative mood.

EXERCICE 20·3

Mettre les verbes entre parenthèses au subjonctif.

1. Il ne commencera pas son discours avant que vous (donner) _____ le signal.

2. Elle est généreuse quoiqu'elle (ne pas être) _____ riche.

3. Je t'aiderai à condition que tu me (faire) _____ une faveur.

4. Nous les inviterons pour qu'ils (ne pas se sentir) _____ délaissés.

5. Elle déposera un brevet de peur qu'on lui (voler) _____ son idée.

6. J'achèterai leur appartement pour qu'ils (pouvoir) _____ s'installer à la campagne.

7. Il téléchargera le dossier bien qu'il (ne pas répondre) _____ exactement à ses besoins.

8. Elle a un blog pour que ses lecteurs (donner) _____ leurs réactions.

9. Nous donnerons nos opinions pourvu qu'elles (rester) _____ anonymes.

10. Elle achètera un appareil numérique pour que sa fille (pouvoir) _____ lui envoyer des photos au cours de son voyage.

Pourvu que

Pourvu que has the sense of *provided that*.

Il ne démissionnera pas **pourvu que** le directeur lui **donne** une augmentation de salaire.	*He won't resign provided the director gives him a raise.*

When used in a single clause, **pourvu que** takes a different meaning. It is a handy expression, also followed by the subjunctive, that expresses hopes and desires.

Pourvu qu'il y **ait** un cybercafé!	*Let's hope there is a cybercafé!*
Pourvu qu'ils **aient** l'adresse!	*Let's hope they have the address!*
Pourvu qu'il **réussisse**!	*Let's hope he succeeds!*
Pourvu que leur base de données **soit** à jour!	*Let's hope their database is up to date!*

The subjunctive is also used after a superlative or an adjective conveying a superlative idea, such as: **premier** (*first*), **dernier** (*last*), **seul** (*only*), **unique** (*unique*), etc.

C'est **le meilleur** ordinateur **que** je **connaisse**.	*It's the best computer I know.*
C'est **le seul** logiciel **qui puisse** vous être utile.	*It's the only software that can be of use to you.*
C'est **la pire** chose **qui puisse** lui arriver.	*It's the worst thing that could happen to him.*
C'est la personne **la plus** sympathique **qu'il connaisse**.	*He's/She's the friendliest person he knows.*

The relative pronouns **qui** and **que** can sometimes be followed by the subjunctive. If there is some doubt about the existence of someone or the possible realization of something, the subjunctive may be used after the relative pronoun.

Connaîtriez-vous **quelqu'un qui sache** parler le chinois couramment?	*Would you know someone who can speak Chinese fluently?*
Il cherche **quelqu'un qui puisse** créer un logiciel pour son entreprise.	*He is looking for someone who can create a piece of software for his company.*

EXERCICE
20·4

Indicatif ou subjonctif?

1. Il dit que leur page d'accueil (être) _____ attrayante.
2. Elle doute qu'il (faire) _____ chaud demain.
3. Ils sont heureux que leurs enfants (pouvoir) _____ aller en Europe cet été.
4. Je pense que Maud (avoir) _____ raison.
5. Je veux que tu (faire) _____ la présentation jeudi.
6. Tu ne crois pas qu'ils (avoir) _____ assez d'expérience.
7. Vous savez qu'ils (être) _____ toujours en retard.
8. Nous souhaitons que vous (obtenir) _____ ce poste.
9. Ils exigent que vous (parler) _____ une langue étrangère.
10. Vous savez que cet ordinateur (être) _____ obsolète.

EXERCICE 20·5

Mettre les propositions subordonnées suivantes au subjonctif.

1. Il est rare que nous (voyager) _____ dans cette région.

2. Il me semble que vous (se tromper) _____ souvent.

3. Il faut que nous (trouver) _____ un bon restaurant.

4. Il est naturel que je (connaître) _____ cette ville. C'est ma ville natale!

5. Il est essentiel que nous (acheter) _____ un nouvel ordinateur.

6. Il est dommage que ce logiciel (ne pas être) _____ plus performant.

7. Elle reste chez elle de peur qu'il y (avoir) _____ une tempête de neige.

8. Nous vous contacterons avant que vous (envoyer) _____ la rédaction du contrat.

9. Vérifiez les chiffres afin qu'on (pouvoir) _____ communiquer le rapport.

10. Bien que son livre (être) _____ bien écrit, il ne trouvera guère de lecteurs.

EXERCICE 20·6

*Traduire les phrases suivantes en utilisant **vous** si nécessaire.*

1. Let's hope he is right!

   _____

2. She is happy he can study French.

   _____

3. It is possible you can buy this software here.

   _____

4. Call us before we go to France!

   _____

5. It is strange he is late.

   _____

6. Let's hope he can come!

   _____

7. She wants you to buy this computer.

   _____

282 PRACTICE MAKES PERFECT   Complete French All-in-One

8. Although he is tired, he reads the newspaper.

9. Although he makes a few mistakes, his French is very good.

10. It is the most beautiful city I know.

The past subjunctive

The past subjunctive is used in the same way as the present subjunctive. In such sentences, the action of the dependent clause is *anterior* to the action of the main clause. To form the past subjunctive, use the present subjunctive of **avoir** or **être** + the past participle of the verb.

penser *to think*

j'**aie pensé**	*I have thought*	nous **ayons pensé**	*we have thought*
tu **aies pensé**	*you have thought*	vous **ayez pensé**	*you have thought*
il/elle **ait pensé**	*he/she has thought*	ils/elles **aient pensé**	*they have thought*

venir *to come*

je **sois venu(e)**	*I have come*	nous **soyons venu(e)s**	*we have come*
tu **sois venu(e)**	*you have come*	vous **soyez venu(e)(s)**	*you have come*
il/elle **soit venu(e)**	*he/she has come*	ils/elles **soient venu(e)s**	*they have come*

Je suis désolé **que tu n'aies pas pu travailler** avec nous.
I am sorry you were not able to work with us.

Nous sommes ravis **qu'elle ait gagné** la médaille d'or.
We are delighted she won the gold medal.

EXERCICE
20·7

Mettre les verbes entre parenthèses au passé du subjonctif.

1. Je doute que tu (lire) _____ tout le livre.
2. Nous sommes ravis que vous (pouvoir) _____ être parmi nous.
3. Il est possible que le logiciel (être) _____ défectueux.
4. Je suis surpris que vous (ne pas voir) _____ ce film.
5. Il a peur que Charles (manquer) _____ le train.
6. Il n'est pas certain qu'il (réussir) _____ à son examen.
7. Je crains qu'il (plagier) _____ mes idées.
8. Il a envoyé le courriel avant que je (pouvoir) _____ ajouter un mot.
9. Il est douteux qu'ils (lire) _____ tous les dossiers.
10. Je suis content que vous (dire) _____ la vérité.

The present subjunctive and the past subjunctive

EXERCICE 20·8

Changer du présent au passé du subjonctif.

1. Il est content que nous partions.

2. Nous sommes ravis que tu puisses venir avec nous.

3. Je ne crois pas qu'il aille à l'exposition.

4. Il doute qu'elle réussisse.

5. Elle a peur qu'il ait un accident de moto.

6. Ils sont contents que Laurent se marie.

7. Nous sommes désolés que votre sœur soit malade.

8. Il est douteux qu'ils aillent en Patagonie.

9. Il est regrettable que leurs enfants soient si peu reconnaissants.

10. Il est incroyable que vous ne sachiez pas la réponse.

EXERCICE 20·9

Faire correspondre les deux colonnes.

_____ 1. Je pense   a. que nous ayons raté le dernier métro.

_____ 2. Il est bizarre   b. que leur fille ait obtenu son diplôme.

_____ 3. Marie! J'ai bien peur   c. que Jean ait refusé une telle offre!

_____ 4. Il est essentiel pour l'entreprise   d. qu'il pleuvra demain.

_____ 5. Ils sont ravis   e. que vous assistiez à la conférence de presse.

284 PRACTICE MAKES PERFECT Complete French All-in-One

Prepositions

A preposition is a liaison word. Invariable, it never changes. No masculine, no feminine. You are already familiar with several French prepositions: **à** (*to, at*), **avec** (*with*), **avant** (*before*), **en** (*in*), and **pour** (*for*).

A preposition may introduce a noun.

Le chat est **sur** le fauteuil.	*The cat is on the armchair.*

The preposition **sur** introduces the noun **fauteuil**. Proper names may also be introduced by prepositions.

Je vais **à** Paris, **en** France.	*I am going to Paris, in France.*

A preposition may also introduce a verb. Some verbs, in fact, are married to prepositions. Let's consider examples with the prepositions **à** and **de**.

Chloé m'a aidé **à** déménager.	*Chloé helped me to move.*

A verb that follows **aider** (*to help*) is introduced by the preposition **à**.

J'ai oublié **de** leur téléphoner.	*I forgot to call them.*

The verb **oublier** (*to forget*) is followed by the preposition **de**.

Some verbs, however, are single—they aren't accompanied by a preposition. Others are less faithful—they may take different prepositions and change their meaning in doing so.

J'ai parlé **à** Joséphine **à** Paris.	*I talked to Joséphine in Paris.*
J'ai parlé **de** Joséphine **à** Paris.	*I talked about Joséphine in Paris.*

If you want to stay out of trouble and avoid confusion, you must learn these prepositions well!

Common prepositions

Remember that a preposition is a part of speech that establishes a connection between words or word groups.

Je me promène **avec** Julien.	*I am walking with Julien.*
Ils sont tous venus **sauf** Chloé.	*They all came except Chloé.*

The prepositions **à** and **de**, when combined with the definite article, take on different forms.

◆ **à + le = au**

Jean et Vincent sont allés **au** cinéma.   *Jean and Vincent went to the movies.*

◆ **à + la = à la**

Anne est **à la** maison.   *Anne is at home.*

◆ **à + les = aux**

Elle montre des photos **aux** enfants.   *She shows pictures to the children.*

◆ **de + le = du**

Je lui ai parlé **du** film.   *I talked to him about the film.*

◆ **de + la = de la**

Le cheval s'approche **de la** rivière.   *The horse is moving toward the river.*

◆ **de + les = des**

Il a peur **des** souris.   *He is afraid of mice.*

The preposition **de** plus a noun can express possession.

C'est la maison **du** maire.	*It's the mayor's house.*
J'ai trouvé le portefeuille **de la** cliente sous le comptoir.	*I found the client's wallet under the counter.*
La voiture **des** voisins est grise.	*The neighbors' car is gray.*

The following are the most common one-word prepositions. Compound prepositions are discussed later in this chapter.

à	*at, in*
après	*after*
avant	*before*
avec	*with*
chez	*at, with*
contre	*against*
dans	*in*
de	*of, from*
derrière	*behind*
dès	*from*
devant	*in front of*
durant	*during*
en	*in, out of*
entre	*between*
envers	*toward*
hormis	*apart from*
hors	*except, apart from*
malgré	*in spite of*
par	*by, through*
parmi	*among*
pendant	*during*
pour	*for*
sans	*without*
sauf	*except*

selon	*according to*
sous	*under*
suivant	*according to*
sur	*on*
vers	*toward*
vu	*considering, given*

Translate the following sentences into French.

1. According to him, Julie is in Madrid. _____
2. We went to the theater with them. _____
3. Mélanie is waiting for him in front of the bakery. _____
4. Your (**tu**) shoes are under the bed. _____
5. He is walking toward the park. _____
6. The chair is against the wall. _____
7. He arrived after me. _____
8. He went out in spite of the rain. _____
9. Send me the letter before Tuesday! (**vous**) _____
10. The cat sat between us. _____

Some prepositions can have more than one meaning. Let's start with the essential **chez**.

Nous avons passé le week-end **chez** Bertrand.	*We spent the weekend at Bertrand's.*
Le restaurant **Chez** Benoît est dans le vingtième.	*The restaurant Chez Benoît is in the twentieth arrondissement.*
Chez Sony, vous trouverez des produits haut de gamme.	*At Sony, you will find top-of-the-line products.*
Chez Balzac, les descriptions sont merveilleusement détaillées.	*With Balzac, the descriptions are detailed in a wonderful way.*
Chez cet enfant, tout est obsessionnel.	*With this child, everything is obsessive.*

The preposition *with* presents a number of translation problems. Let's look at a few examples—the easy ones first.

J'irai à Miami **avec** Etienne.	*I'll go to Miami with Etienne.*
Elle voyage toujours **avec** son chat.	*She always travels with her cat.*

To refer to an attribute or feature of a person or thing, *with* is translated by **à** + the definite article.

L'homme **aux** yeux verts est acteur.	*The man with green eyes is an actor.*
La jeune fille **au** blouson de cuir est sa nièce.	*The young woman with the leather jacket is his niece.*

Prepositions **287**

Le coffre **aux** poignées incrustées de pierres précieuses est à elle.	*The chest with handles inlaid with precious stones is hers.*

To describe how to do something, *with* is translated by **de**.

Je l'ai remercié **d'**un sourire.	*I thanked him with a smile.*
Il a quitté la salle **d'**un air triste.	*He left the room with a sad look.*
D'un geste, elle lui indiqua la porte.	*With a gesture, she showed him the door.*

The preposition *with* is left untranslated when describing a way of doing things or carrying oneself.

Il avance vers eux, les manches retroussées.	*He is walking toward them with his sleeves rolled up.*
Elle le regarde, les yeux écarquillés.	*She is looking at him with wide eyes.*

Some adjectives followed by *with* in English take **de** in French.

Il est satisfait **de** son sort.	*He is happy with his lot.*
Elle est contente **de** son nouvel emploi.	*She is happy with her new job.*

EXERCICE
21·2

Complete each sentence with the appropriate preposition.

1. J'achète une baguette _____ le boulanger.

2. Le sculpteur regarde le buste _____ un air satisfait.

3. Elle ira en vacances dans le Midi, toute seule, _____ Marc.

4. _____ Baudelaire, tout est poésie.

5. Claude a pris rendez-vous _____ le médecin.

6. L'homme _____ chapeau gris, est professeur d'histoire.

7. Hier soir, nous avons dîné _____ Maxime.

8. _____ Verdi, tout est harmonie.

9. Elle voyagera _____ son mari en Amazonie.

10. L'enfant _____ cheveux noirs s'appelle Lucas.

The preposition **sur** presents different problems. It is not always translated by *on* in English.

L'ordinateur est **sur** le bureau.	*The computer is on the desk.*
Son appartement donne **sur** le Panthéon.	*His apartment looks out on the Pantheon.*
La villa donne **sur** la mer.	*The villa faces the ocean.*
Il a quinze mille euros **sur** son compte.	*He has 15,000 euros in his account.*
Elle n'a pas d'argent **sur** elle.	*She doesn't have any money on/with her.*
La cuisine fait deux mètres **sur** trois.	*The kitchen measures two by three meters.*
Il travaille quatre jours **sur** sept.	*He works four days out of seven.*

288 PRACTICE MAKES PERFECT Complete French All-in-One

| Elle a une chance **sur** deux de réussir. | *She has one chance out of two to succeed.* |
| Ce supermarché est ouvert vingt-quatre heures **sur** vingt-quatre. | *This supermarket is open twenty-four hours a day.* |

As you can see, **sur** is not always translated by *on* in English. And as the following examples show, *on* is not always translated by **sur**.

Ils se promènent **dans** la rue.	*They are walking on the street.*
Ils vont au théâtre **le** jeudi.	*They go to the theater on Thursdays.*
Son bureau se trouve **au** quatrième étage.	*Her office is on the fourth floor.*
Elle habite **au** dernier étage.	*She lives on the top floor.*
Le Louvre est **à** votre gauche.	*The Louvre is on your left.*

When expressing time, **en** and **dans** have different uses. **Dans** is used for an action about to begin.

| Le train part **dans** trois minutes. | *The train is leaving in three minutes.* |
| Je reviens **dans** cinq minutes. | *I'll be back in five minutes.* |

En indicates the length of time an action has taken, takes, or will take.

Ahmadou a couru le marathon **en** moins de quatre heures.	*Ahmadou ran the marathon in less than four hours.*
Cet enfant peut lire un livre **en** quelques heures.	*This child can read a book within a few hours.*
Elle pourra accomplir cette tâche **en** deux heures.	*She will be able to accomplish this task in two hours.*

EXERCICE 21·3

Complete each sentence with the appropriate preposition.

1. Ma chambre d'hôtel donne _____ la Seine.
2. Cet ouvrier travaille cinq jours _____ sept.
3. Nous partons pour Bali _____ quelques jours.
4. Il suit un cours d'informatique _____ mercredi.
5. Rappelez-moi _____ cinq minutes!
6. Henri a trouvé un trousseau de clés _____ la rue.
7. Dépose mille euros _____ son compte avant lundi.
8. Mon frère n'a jamais un centime _____ lui.
9. D'ordinaire, il peut traduire un texte de ce genre _____ une semaine.
10. Élodie habite _____ troisième étage.

In referring to time, **à** is used for hours of the day and **en** is used for months, years, and seasons, except for spring.

Les participants sont arrivés **à** midi.	The participants arrived at noon.
La réunion commencera **à** quinze heures.	The meeting will start at 3 P.M.
Sartre est né **en** 1905.	Sartre was born in 1905.
La guerre d'Indochine a pris fin **en** 1954.	The Indochina war ended in 1954.
Il fait froid **en** hiver.	It's cold in winter.
Victor prend ses vacances **en** été.	Victor takes his vacation in summer.
Elle va toujours à Venise **au** printemps.	She always goes to Venice in spring.

To express means of transportation, different prepositions are used.

aller à bicyclette / à/en vélo	to go by bicycle
aller à cheval	to ride
aller à pied	to walk, go on foot
aller en autobus	to go by bus
aller en autocar	to go by bus (intercity)
aller en avion	to go by plane
aller en bateau	to go by boat
aller en métro	to go by subway
aller en péniche	to go by barge
aller en train	to go by train
aller en voiture	to drive, go by car

Quentin va au bureau **à** pied.	Quentin walks to work.
Valérie va au travail **à** bicyclette.	Valérie bikes to work.
Ils vont à la campagne **en** voiture.	They drive to the country.

Note the difference between **en** and **dans** in distinguishing between general and specific.

À Paris, je circule **en** métro.	In Paris, I travel by subway.
Hier j'ai vu Arnaud **dans** le métro.	Yesterday I saw Arnaud in the subway.
Elle aime voyager **en** avion.	She likes to fly.
Dans l'avion, il y avait une équipe de basketteurs.	In the plane, there was a basketball team.
Vladimir vit **en** Russie.	Vladimir lives in Russia.
Dans la Russie des tsars, la vie était différente.	In czarist Russia, life was different.

EXERCICE
21·4

Complete each sentence with the appropriate preposition.

1. Elle rentre chez elle _____ pied.

2. Ils préfèrent aller à Amsterdam _____ printemps.

3. La Révolution française a eu lieu _____ 1789.

4. Elle est rentrée _____ minuit.

5. Ce sera plus rapide d'y aller _____ métro.

6. Il neige souvent _____ hiver.

7. Lucie ignore _____ quelle heure commence la réunion.

8. Louis XIV est mort _____ 1715.

9. À Amsterdam, on se balade partout _____ bicyclette.

10. Je ne veux pas y aller _____ voiture. Il y a trop de circulation.

The preposition **à** can denote nature, function, or purpose.

un gâteau **aux** noisettes	*a hazelnut pie*
une glace **à la** framboise	*a strawberry ice cream*
une machine **à** coudre	*a sewing machine*
une machine **à** écrire	*a typewriter*
une machine **à** laver	*a washing machine*
une machine **à** sous	*a slot machine*
un métier **à** tisser	*a loom*
un moulin **à** café	*a coffee mill*
un moulin **à** paroles	*a chatterbox*
un moulin **à** poivre	*a pepper mill*
un moulin **à** vent	*a windmill*
une mousse **au** chocolat	*a chocolate mousse*
une tasse **à** thé	*a tea cup*
un verre **à** eau	*a water glass*
un verre **à** vin	*a wine glass*
un verre **à** whisky	*a whisky glass*

Michel préfère la glace **à la** vanille.   *Michel prefers vanilla ice cream.*
Ses verres **à** vin sont ébréchés.   *His wine glasses are chipped.*

The preposition **de** can denote contents or composition.

une boîte **de** petits pois	*a can of peas*
un bol **de** soupe	*a bowl of soup*
une poignée **de** cerises	*a handful of cherries*
une tasse **de** thé	*a cup of tea*
un verre **d'**eau	*a glass of water*
un verre **de** vin	*a glass of wine*

Il n'avait qu'une boîte **de** haricots verts.   *He only had one can of string beans.*
Elle nous a offert une tasse **de** thé.   *She gave us a cup of tea.*

EXERCICE
21·5

Translate the following sentences into French. For questions, invert the subject and verb.

1. They'll leave for Ireland in a few days.

_____

2. With this little boy, everything is pathological.

_____

3. What do you (**vous**) do on Sundays?

_____

Prepositions   **291**

4. The woman with the straw hat is a famous actress.

5. He loves chocolate ice cream.

6. They opened a good bottle of wine for her birthday.

7. According to him, Carole is in Hawaii.

8. We saw many windmills in Holland.

9. Please give me a cup of tea. (**tu**)

10. Let's go to Aunt Sophie's this afternoon!

11. Simone de Beauvoir died in 1986.

12. Do you (**vous**) have a room facing the Seine?

13. I walk to work every day.

14. Their office is on the tenth floor.

15. She looked at him with an air of perplexity.

16. The castle faced the ocean.

17. Julie only works three days out of seven.

18. At what time does the meeting start?

19. The writer wrote this chapter in two weeks.

20. How much money do you (**tu**) have in your account in France?

Compound prepositions

Compound prepositions are prepositions made up of two or three words. Here's a list of the most common of these prepositions. There is no mystery about them—you just have to memorize them one by one.

à cause de	*because of*
à côté de	*beside, next to*
à défaut de	*for lack of*
à force de	*by dint of*
à l'égard de	*toward, with regard to*
à l'exception de	*except for*
à l'instar de	*following the example of*
à l'insu de	*without (somebody)'s knowing*
à la faveur de	*thanks to, owing to*
à la merci de	*at the mercy of*
à même	*straight from, next to*
à même de	*in a position to (do something)*
à partir de	*from*
à raison de	*at the rate of, on the basis of*
à travers	*across, through*
au bas de	*at the bottom of, at the foot of*
au bord de	*by, on the verge of, on the brink of*
au coin de	*at the corner of*
au lieu de	*instead of*
au milieu de	*in the middle of*
au moyen de	*by means of*
au nord de	*north of*
au prix de	*at the cost of*
au sud de	*south of*
au-dehors de	*outside*
au-delà de	*beyond*
au-dessous de	*under, below*
au-dessus de	*above, on top of*
auprès de	*next to, with*
autour de	*around*
aux alentours de	*in the vicinity of*
aux dépens de	*at the expense of*
aux environs de	*in the vicinity of*
d'après	*according to*
de façon à	*so as to*
de peur de	*for fear of*
en bas	*downstairs*
en bas de	*at the bottom of*
en comparaison de	*in comparison with*
en dépit de	*despite*
en face de	*in front of, opposite*
en guise de	*by way of*
en haut de	*at/to the top of*
en raison de	*because of, owing to*
en-dehors de	*outside, apart from*
face à	*against, faced with*
faute de	*for lack of, for want of*
grâce à	*thanks to*
le long de	*along*
loin de	*far from*

Prepositions **293**

lors de	*at the time of, during*
par rapport à	*in comparison with, in relation to, with regard to*
près de	*close to*
quant à	*as for, as to*
quitte à	*even if it means*
vis-à-vis de	*next to, against*

Elle était assise **à côté de** moi.	*She was sitting next to me.*
À force de chercher, on finira bien par trouver une solution.	*If we keep on looking, we'll end up finding a solution.*
À force de répéter ces poèmes, tu les sauras par cœur.	*By repeating these poems, you'll know them by heart.*
Marie a téléphoné à mon client **à mon insu**.	*Marie called my client without my knowing.*
Lors de son discours, le président a abordé les problèmes économiques.	*During his speech, the president discussed the economic problems.*
Quant à moi, je pense qu'il est fou.	*As far as I am concerned, I think he is crazy.*
Il n'ira pas à la réunion **quitte à** perdre son travail.	*He won't go to the meeting even if it means losing his job.*

EXERCICE 21·6

Translate the following sentences into French.

1. Armelle arrived in the middle of the night.

2. According to them, she works in Strasbourg.

3. They live far from Paris.

4. Following his mother's example, he became a singer.

5. I left the suitcases downstairs.

6. She became famous in spite of herself.

7. As for me, I have no plans for this summer.

8. For lack of money, he stayed home.

9. He is at our mercy.

10. They accepted for fear of disappointing them.

_____

11. Faced with such problems, he does not know how to react.

_____

12. Sign at the bottom of this page. (**vous**)

_____

13. Instead of wasting even more time, call her! (**tu**)

_____

14. He organized a trip to Argentina without his parents knowing.

_____

15. He learned this at his own expense.

_____

16. The rate of the dollar is lower in comparison with last year.

_____

17. I can see her through the window.

_____

18. This town has changed a lot through the centuries.

_____

19. Carmen likes to walk along the river.

_____

20. He gave me these flowers by way of thanks.

_____

_____

| EXERCICE |
| 21·7 |

Complete each sentence with the appropriate compound preposition.

1. Il est devenu architecte _____ son père.

2. Tu réussiras à tes examens _____ travailler.

3. Hughes est monté _____ la Tour Eiffel.

4. Mes voisins passent leurs vacances _____ la mer.

5. _____ les experts, la situation s'améliore peu à peu.

6. Il n'a pas acheté de voiture neuve _____ argent.

Prepositions 295

7. _____ toujours lui offrir des fleurs, offre-lui des chocolats!

8. Ton programme favori recommencera _____ la semaine prochaine.

9. Gérard a organisé une surprise-party _____ son copain Yves.

10. Impossible d'aller dans cette ville, c'est trop _____ chez nous.

Some compound prepositions with similar meanings have subtle nuances that distinguish them. **Grâce à** is positive, **à cause de** is negative, and **en raison de** is more neutral.

Christian a réussi à son examen **grâce à** toi.	*Christian passed his exam thanks to you.*
Xavier a perdu son travail **à cause de** toi.	*Xavier lost his job because of you.*
Le pique-nique a été annulé **en raison de** la pluie.	*The picnic was cancelled because of the rain.*

À même is an interesting preposition.

Ne bois pas **à même** la bouteille!	*Don't drink straight from the bottle!*
Elle porte toujours ses pulls **à même** la peau.	*She always wears her sweaters next to her skin.*
Le sans-abri dormait **à même** le sol.	*The homeless man was sleeping on the bare ground.*

À même de followed by a verb means *in a position to (do something).*

Je ne suis pas **à même de** vous aider.	*I am not in a position to help you.*
Il n'est pas **à même de** juger vos actes.	*He is not in a position to judge your actions.*

Fleur is often encountered as a noun, but it is also used in the compound preposition **à fleur de**.

Il a les nerfs **à fleur de** peau.	*He is a bundle of nerves.*
Elle a une sensibilité **à fleur de** peau.	*She's very touchy.*
L'écueil est **à fleur d'**eau.	*The reef is just above the water.*

EXERCICE
21·8

Complete each sentence with the appropriate compound preposition.

1. Ce jury n'est pas _____ juger le suspect.

2. Tout ce malheur est arrivé _____ sa stupidité.

3. Il est arrivé à l'heure _____ l'aide d'un mécanicien compétent.

4. Vous avez remercié le médecin. Vous vous sentez mieux _____ lui.

5. Le tarif est moins cher _____ jeune âge.

6. Les spectateurs étaient assis sur des coussins _____ la scène.

7. Seriez-vous _____ me donner quelques conseils?

8. Tout va mal _____ toi!

9. Les enfants n'iront pas à l'école _____ une éventuelle tempête de neige.

10. Il boit le jus d'orange _____ la bouteille.

296 PRACTICE MAKES PERFECT Complete French All-in-One

Prepositions with geographical names

To express *in* or *to* with a geographical name, the preposition varies in French. With cities, the preposition **à** is used.

> Nous sommes **à** Dakar. — *We are in Dakar.*
> Je vais **à** Paris en mars. — *I am going to Paris in March.*

Cities are usually not preceded by an article. Some exceptions are **La Nouvelle-Orléans**, **Le Havre**, **La Rochelle**, **Le Mans**, and **Le Caire**.

> Ils vivent **au** Caire depuis dix ans. — *They have been living in Cairo for 10 years.*
> Il va chaque année **à** La Rochelle. — *He goes every year to La Rochelle.*

With countries, states, and provinces, the preposition changes according to gender, number, and the initial sound of the word that follows.

en	feminine
en	masculine beginning with a vowel
au	masculine beginning with a consonant
aux	plural

> Elle voyagera **en** Allemagne puis **en** Italie. — *She'll travel to Germany, then to Italy.*
> Ils ont vécu **en** Iran et **en** Afghanistan. — *They lived in Iran and in Afghanistan.*
> J'ai travaillé **au** Japon et **au** Brésil. — *I worked in Japan and Brazil.*
> Irez-vous **aux** États-Unis cet été? — *Will you go to the United States this summer?*

Continents are feminine in French. Provinces and states ending in **-e** are also feminine, with a few exceptions, like **le Mexique** and **le Cambodge**.

> Elle travaille pour MSF (Médecins Sans Frontières) **en** Afrique. — *She is working for Doctors Without Borders in Africa.*
> Le président se rendra **au** Mexique la semaine prochaine. — *The president will go to Mexico next week.*

EXERCICE 21·9

Complete each sentence with a prepositional phrase, using the appropriate preposition plus the place name in parentheses.

1. Timothée ira _____ en décembre. (la Chine)
2. Léa vit _____ depuis quelques années. (le Mali)
3. Manon prend ses vacances _____. (le Maroc)
4. Patrice a acheté un terrain _____. (le Portugal)
5. Cléo prévoit un voyage _____. (les États-Unis)
6. Raphaël fait des études _____. (la Belgique)
7. Séverine chantera _____ samedi prochain. (Milan)
8. Aimé n'est jamais allé _____. (l'Argentine)
9. Julie rêve de faire un voyage _____. (la Patagonie)
10. Matéo part en mission _____. (le Vietnam)

11. Fatima envoie un paquet à des amis _____. (la Hongrie)

12. Émilie écrit à sa cousine _____. (le Kenya)

13. Anabelle est invitée _____ à un mariage. (Paris)

14. Lionel ne veut pas s'installer _____. (la Sibérie)

15. Zazie a contacté une agence _____. (le Caire)

16. Mélissa enverra ses enfants chez sa sœur _____. (Madrid)

17. Amaury a ouvert une agence _____. (l'Inde)

18. Alix a passé un mois _____. (la Turquie)

19. Olivia s'est arrêtée _____ avant de continuer vers le Vietnam. (le Laos)

20. Kim espère obtenir une bourse d'études _____. (le Canada)

EXERCICE 21·10

Create sentences from the elements below, following the example.

MODÈLE   Karen / Chicago / États-Unis

Je m'appelle Karen. J'habite à Chicago, aux États-Unis.

1. Christian / Amsterdam / Hollande

   _____

2. Paolo / Venise / Italie

   _____

3. Phong / Hanoi / Vietnam

   _____

4. Laure / Rouen / France

   _____

5. Christopher / Londres / Angleterre

   _____

6. Maria / Mexico / Mexique

   _____

7. Patrick / Bruxelles / Belgique

   _____

8. Ahmadou / Abidjan / Côte d'Ivoire

   _____

9. Akiko / Tokyo / Japon

10. Cheng / Shanghai / Chine

11. Vladimir / Moscou / Russie

12. Youssef / Marrakech / Maroc

13. Rachida / Alger / Algérie

14. Amin / Alexandrie / Égypte

15. Christina / Varsovie / Pologne

16. Karl / Berlin / Allemagne

17. Jean / Genève / Suisse

18. Hugo / Caracas / Venezuela

19. Pablo / Quito / Équateur

20. Karim / Istanbul / Turquie

With French provinces and departments, the preposition may vary. Before a feminine noun or a masculine noun beginning with a vowel, **en** is used.

la Bourgogne	**en** Bourgogne
la Bretagne	**en** Bretagne
la Charente	**en** Charente
la Provence	**en** Provence
la Touraine	**en** Touraine
l'Anjou	**en** Anjou

However, before a masculine noun beginning with a consonant, **dans le** is often used instead of **au**.

le Languedoc	**dans le** Languedoc
le Midi	**dans le** Midi
le Poitou	**dans le** Poitou

With names of American states, **en** is used before a feminine state name or a masculine state name beginning with a vowel. **Au** is used before a masculine state name beginning with a consonant.

la Californie	**en** Californie
la Caroline du Sud	**en** Caroline du Sud
la Floride	**en** Floride
l'Alabama	**en** Alabama
l'Arizona	**en** Arizona
l'Arkansas	**en** Arkansas
le Colorado	**au** Colorado
le Nevada	**au** Nevada
le Tennessee	**au** Tennessee

One often hears **dans le** or **dans l'État de** with many American states.

| le Maine | **dans le** Maine |
| le New Jersey | **dans le** New Jersey |

We sometimes need to differentiate between a city and state that share the same name.

Il est né **à** Washington.	*He was born in Washington.*
Elle voyage **dans l'État de** Washington.	*She is traveling in Washington State.*
Le président français se rendra **à** New York.	*The French president will go to New York City.*
Il prendra quelques jours de vacances **dans l'État de** New York.	*He'll take a few days of vacation in New York State.*

Although usage may vary, the preposition **à** (**aux** in the plural) is often used for islands.

| **à** Cuba |
| **à** Hawaii |
| **à** La Réunion |
| **à** Madagascar |
| **à** Tahiti |
| **aux** Maldives |
| **aux** Seychelles |

Some common exceptions follow.

| **en** Guadeloupe |
| **en** Haïti |
| **en** Martinique |

EXERCICE 21·11

Some people are planning a trip soon. Create sentences from the elements below, following the example.

MODÈLE   Maryse / Caroline du Nord et Virginie
         Maryse va en Caroline du Nord et en Virginie.

1. Mon ami Julien / Normandie et Bretagne

2. Nos voisins / Tahiti et Hawaii

3. Ma sœur et mon beau-frère / Montana et Wyoming

4. Corinne / Oregon et Alaska

5. Nous / Alsace et Auvergne

6. Mes amis / Aquitaine et Languedoc

7. Je / Haïti / Guadeloupe

8. Bernard / Lorraine et Champagne

9. Vous / Anjou et Vendée

10. Le camionneur / Californie et Arizona

EXERCICE 21·12

Complete the following sentences, matching the countries in the list with their famous citizens and using the appropriate preposition.

Afrique du Sud	Inde
Allemagne	Italie
Angleterre	Russie
États-Unis	Sénégal
France	Vietnam

1. J'ai rencontré Gustave Flaubert _____.
2. J'ai rencontré le Mahatma Gandhi _____.
3. J'ai rencontré Léopold Sédar Senghor _____.
4. J'ai rencontré Eleanor Roosevelt _____.
5. J'ai rencontré Fédor Dostoïevski _____.
6. J'ai rencontré Giuseppe Verdi _____.
7. J'ai rencontré Nelson Mandela _____.
8. J'ai rencontré Hô Chi Minh _____.
9. J'ai rencontré Goethe _____.
10. J'ai rencontré la reine Victoria _____.

Geographical origin is expressed by **de** for continents, feminine singular country names, provinces, regions, and states. For masculine and plural names, the definite article is kept.

Elle revient **d'**Australie.	*She is coming back from Australia.*
Il est originaire **de** Californie.	*He comes from California.*
Je reviens tout juste **du** Japon.	*I am just back from Japan.*
Il vient **des** Antilles.	*He comes from the West Indies.*

EXERCICE 21·13

Complete each sentence with a prepositional phrase, using the place name in parentheses.

1. Ces fruits exotiques viennent _____. (l'Inde)
2. Elle est originaire _____. (le Guatemala)
3. Ces vins délicieux sont importés _____. (le Chili)
4. Il est rentré _____ hier soir. (l'Espagne)
5. Cette lettre anonyme provient _____. (la Norvège)

6. La fondue est originaire _____. (la Suisse)

7. Il est natif _____. (le Colorado)

8. Les fromages en provenance _____ seront soumis à un contrôle strict. (la France)

9. Joseph vient _____. (les Antilles)

10. Rapporte-moi un cadeau _____. (le Togo)

EXERCICE 21·14

Complete each sentence with the appropriate country name from the list below, preceded by the appropriate preposition.

Cambodge	Grande-Bretagne
Chine	Grèce
Égypte	Inde
États-Unis	Italie
France	Pérou

1. Le Taj Mahal, c'est _____.

2. La Tour de l'Horloge Big Ben, c'est _____.

3. Le pont des Soupirs, c'est _____.

4. La Grande Muraille, c'est _____.

5. La Tour Eiffel, c'est _____.

6. Le Grand Canyon, c'est _____.

7. Le Machu Picchu, c'est _____.

8. Le Temple de Louxor, c'est _____.

9. L'Acropole, c'est _____.

10. Le Temple d'Angkor Vat, c'est _____.

EXERCICE 21·15

Translate the following sentences into French. For questions, invert the subject and verb.

1. Marc is the owner of a bookstore in Dublin.

_____

2. She went to Australia last summer.

_____

Prepositions **303**

3. I came back from Senegal last night.

4. Léo bought a house in Brazil.

5. Is he in Tahiti?

6. This singer has one house in Montana and another in Mexico.

7. Julie lost her earrings in Spain.

8. Karim's apartment is in Cairo.

9. This king has castles in Germany and Austria.

10. They opened a bakery in Vietnam.

11. Nabila goes to Provence twice a year.

12. Théo sent me a postcard from Ireland.

13. Her son found a job in California.

14. In India, food is delicious.

15. They import products from China.

16. She bought this necklace in Morocco.

17. Do you (vous) want to go to New York with me next week?

18. Ludovic wants to work in Toulouse.

19. Noémie teaches French in Poland.

_____

20. Let's go to Florida for the weekend!

_____

Infinitives with adjectival phrases

The infinitive is used as the object of an adjectival phrase.

1. The infinitive following an adjective is preceded by **de**:

◆ After the following common **être** + _adjective_ expressions (partial list)

être content(e) de	_to be satisfied to_
être déçu(e) de	_to be disappointed to_
être désolé(e) de	_to be sorry to_
être enchanté(e) de	_to be delighted to_
être fier (fière) de	_to be proud to_
être forcé(e) de	_to be forced to_
être heureux (heureuse) de	_to be happy to_
être libre de	_to be free to_
être obligé(e) de	_to be forced to, have to_
être (im)patient(e) de	_to be (im)patient, anxious to_
être ravi(e) de	_to be delighted to_
être reconnaissant(e) à qn de	_to be thankful to sb for . . . -ing_
être satisfait(e) de	_to be satisfied to_
être sûr(e) de	_to be sure of . . . -ing_
être surpris(e) de	_to be surprised to_
être triste de	_to be sad to_

Il est **content d'avoir gagné** le prix.	_He is happy to have won the prize._
Je suis **ravi/enchanté de** vous **connaître**.	_I am delighted to meet you._
Vous êtes **libre de dire** ce que vous pensez.	_You are free to say what you think._
Je vous suis **reconnaissant de** m'**avoir embauché**.	_I am grateful to you for having hired me._

◆ After the impersonal **il est** + _adjective_

il est bon **de**	_it is good to_
il est dangereux **de**	_it is dangerous to_
il est défendu **de** / il est interdit **de**	_it is forbidden to_
il est difficile (à qn) **de**	_it is difficult (for sb) to_
il est dur **de**	_it is hard to_
il est facile **de**	_it is easy to_
il est important **de**	_it is important to_
il est nécessaire **de**	_it is necessary to_
il est (im)possible **de**	_it is (im)possible to_
il est (in)utile **de**	_it is useful (useless) to_

Prepositions **305**

Il est interdit de **marcher** sur la pelouse. It's forbidden to walk on the grass.
*Il est difficile d'***apprendre** une langue étrangère. It's difficult to learn a foreign language.

Note: In informal French, **ce (c')** + **être** (+ *adjective* + **de**) frequently replaces the impersonal **il** + **être** (+ *adjective* + **de**).

C'est **interdit de fumer**. It's forbidden to smoke.
C'est **dur de plaire** à tout le monde. It's hard to please everyone.

EXERCICE 21·16

Comment dit-on en français?

1. We had to do it. _____
2. I am sorry to disturb you (*pol.*). _____
3. He is sad he forgot the appointment. _____
4. I am delighted to make your (*pol.*) acquaintance. _____
5. It is forbidden to park here. _____
6. It is useful to know a foreign language. _____
7. It is easy to learn French. _____
8. It is dangerous to drive without a seat belt. _____

2. The infinitive following an *adjective* is preceded by the preposition **à**

   ◆ when the subject (noun or pronoun) of the sentence or clause *precedes* the infinitive.

   Cette voiture est difficile **à réparer**. *This car is difficult to repair.*

   ◆ when **ce (c')** + **être** + *adjective* refers to a previously mentioned idea, i.e., is the speaker's reaction to what has already been said.

   C'est bon **à savoir**. *That's good to know.*
   C'est impossible **à dire**. *That's impossible to say.*

   ◆ when the infinitive follows one of these adjectives and past participles (partial list).

   être autorisé(e) à *to be authorized to*
   être déterminé(e) à *to be determined to*
   être habitué(e) à *to be used to . . . -ing*
   être lent(e) à *to be slow in . . . -ing*
   être long(ue) à *to take a long time to*
   être occupé(e) à *to be busy (doing)*
   être prêt(e) à *to be ready/prepared/willing to*

   Je **suis habitué à travailler** dur. *I am used to working hard.*
   C'est **long à faire**. *It takes a long time to do it.*
   Elle **est occupée à nettoyer** sa chambre. *She is busy cleaning her room.*

- after **(le) seul, (la) seule, (les) seuls, (les) seules**, and after **nombreux.**

    Vous êtes *le seul à* me **comprendre**.   *You are the only one who understands me.*

    Les gens sont *nombreux à* être inquiets.   *Numerous people are worried.*

- after an *ordinal number* (**le premier, la première, les premiers, les premières, le/la deuxième**, etc.) and after **le dernier, la dernière, les derniers, les dernières** with or without a noun.

    Nous sommes *les premiers à* **arriver** et *les derniers à* **partir**.   *We are the first to arrive and the last to leave.*

Note: Adjectives preceded by **trop** (*too*) or **assez** (*enough*) take **pour** before the following infinitive.

C'est *trop beau pour* **être** vrai.   *That's too good to be true.*
Tu es *assez grand pour* **comprendre** ça.   *You are old enough to understand this.*

EXERCICE 21·17

Comment dit-on en français?

1. We are ready to leave. _____
2. The taxi is slow in coming. _____
3. She is busy doing the laundry. _____
4. I am used to seeing him every day. _____
5. She was the only one who knew the answer. _____
6. You (*fam.*) are the first one (*fem.*) to contact me. _____
7. They (*fem.*) will not be the last ones to ask me that question. _____
8. He is too young to get married. _____

EXERCICE 21·18

Remplissez les tirets avec **à** *ou* **de/d'**, *selon le cas.*

1. Ils sont déçus _____ avoir perdu le match.
2. Je suis désolé _____ avoir été si long _____ te donner de mes nouvelles.
3. Je suis autorisé _____ visiter cet endroit.
4. Elle est fière _____ avoir obtenu la meilleure note.
5. Je suis impatient _____ te voir.

6. Ce serait trop long _____ expliquer.

7. Il est impossible _____ prédire l'avenir.

8. Quand est-ce qu'il va y avoir un tremblement de terre dans cette région? —C'est impossible _____ prédire.

9. Suivez mon conseil! —C'est plus facile _____ dire qu' _____ faire!

10. Elle est triste _____ le voir partir.

11. C'est triste _____ voir.

12. Les hôtels sont prêts _____ vous accueillir.

13. C'est difficile _____ croire.

14. Ce plat est lourd _____ digérer.

15. Il est facile _____ réparer cette voiture.

16. En 1980, Marguerite Yourcenar devient la première femme _____ être admise à l'Académie Française.

17. Je suis toujours le dernier _____ le savoir.

18. Ils étaient nombreux _____ manifester.

19. Il était obligé _____ démissionner.

20. La décision n'était pas facile _____ prendre.

21. Il est interdit _____ fumer dans les lieux publics.

22. La dernière personne _____ l'avoir vu, c'est sa secrétaire.

23. « Il est bon _____ parler et meilleur _____ se taire. » (La Fontaine)

24. Nos voisins étaient les seuls _____ avoir la climatisation (*air conditioning*).

25. On est heureux _____ être vivants.

The infinitive is used as the object of a noun. When used after a noun, the infinitive is most often preceded by the preposition **de**, especially after **il est** or **c'est**.

le besoin de *the need to*

J'éprouve le besoin **de me reposer**.   *I feel the need to rest.*

c'est dommage de *it's a pity to*

Ce serait dommage **de perdre** cet argent.   *It would be a pity to lose that money.*

ce n'est pas la peine de *there is no need to, there is no point in . . . -ing*

Ce n'est pas la peine **de parler** si fort.   *There is no need to speak so loud.*

il n'est pas question de *it's out of the question to*

Il n'est pas question **de céder**.   *It's out of the question to yield.*

il est (grand) temps de *it's (about) time to*

　　Il est temps *de* **partir**.　　　　　　　　　*It's time to leave.*

c'est un plaisir de *it's a pleasure to*

　　C'est un plaisir *de* vous **connaître**.　　　*It's a pleasure to meet you.*

c'est mon (ton, son...) tour de *it's my (your, his, her . . .) turn to*

　　C'est mon tour *de* **parler**.　　　　　　　*It's my turn to speak.*

The infinitive is used after **merci**. After the word **merci**, the infinitive is preceded by **de**.

Merci *de* **fumer** dehors.	*Thanks for smoking outside.*
Merci *d'***être** avec nous.	*Thanks for being with us.*
Merci *d'***avoir** appelé.	*Thanks for calling.*
Merci *de* m'**avoir** invité(e).	*Thanks for inviting me.*

Note: The *past infinitive* is used after **merci de** if the action (that someone is being thanked for) happened before the statement is made.

EXERCICE 21·19

Remplissez les tirets avec la préposition correcte.

1. Ce n'est pas le moment _____ parler.
2. C'est ton tour _____ jouer.
3. C'est un régal (*a delight*) _____ entendre ce pianiste.
4. C'est le seul moyen _____ trouver sa trace.
5. C'est l'heure _____ aller au lit.
6. La chance _____ trouver des survivants s'aménuise (*is diminishing*).
7. Ne manquez pas l'occasion _____ participer.
8. C'est une erreur _____ croire que le subjonctif ne s'utilise qu'à l'écrit.
9. Merci _____ avoir accepté notre invitation.
10. Ce n'est pas la peine _____ t'excuser.

EXERCICE 21·20

Sébastien parle de ses projets d'avenir. Traduisez en français ce qu'il dit.

Today, I feel like talking to you about my plans for the immediate future.
　　After graduating, I plan to rest a little. Before beginning to work, I want to have a good time. In order to be happy in life, one must try to fulfill one's dreams. Instead of searching for a job, I prefer to go abroad for a while. I hope to see many countries. I told my friends to come with me, but they thought that it was better to go to graduate school right away. That's a

shame! While they will be writing their boring term papers, I will spend my time reading good books, because I intend to learn something new every day. I will be able to listen to the radio without having to do my homework. I will no longer have to take required courses, and I will no longer be afraid to flunk a test. I will be free to do what (**ce que**) I want! Time will fly by (I will not see the time go by). My friends are going to be green with envy when they hear me describe my adventures. I am sure (that) I will always have good memories of this vacation.

I am going to let you go now. Before flying to Asia, I still have to pack my suitcases.

Good-bye!

Sébastien

VOCABULAIRE

to be green with envy	**pâlir d'envie**	to go to graduate school	**faire des études supérieures**
course	**le cours**	to graduate	**obtenir son diplôme**
to describe	**décrire**	to have good memories of	**garder un bon souvenir de**
to flunk a test	**rater un examen**	immediate	**immédiat(e)**
to fly (to a place)	**prendre l'avion pour**	a job	**un emploi**
for a while	**pendant un certain temps**	plans	**les projets (m.pl.)**
to fulfill	**réaliser**	required	**obligatoire**

310　PRACTICE MAKES PERFECT　Complete French All-in-One

VOCABULAIRE			
un aspirateur	*a vacuum cleaner*	une fourchette	*a fork*
une assiette	*a plate, a (soup) bowl*	un grille-pain	*a toaster*
		un lave-vaisselle	*a dishwasher*
un bol	*a bowl, wide cup (for morning coffee)*	une louche	*a ladle*
		une nappe	*a tablecloth*
		un ouvre-boîtes	*a can opener*
une cafetière	*a coffee pot*	un plateau	*a tray*
une casserole	*a pan, a pot*	une poêle	*a frying pan*
un congélateur	*a freezer*	un réfrigérateur	*a refrigerator*
un couteau	*a knife*	une serviette	*a napkin*
une cuillère	*a spoon*	une soucoupe	*a saucer*
une cuisinière	*a stove*	une tasse	*a cup*
un four	*an oven*	une théière	*a teapot*
un four à micro-ondes	*a microwave oven*	un tire-bouchon	*a corkscrew*
		un verre	*a glass*

Verbs that use different prepositions

In previous chapters we have seen how complicated verbs and their conjugations can be. Some verbs can be very capricious as they change preposition and meaning. Here are a few more examples, just for the fun of it!

It is important to remember that the same verb can be used with no preposition, simply followed by a direct object noun, or followed by different prepositions. The meaning of the verb changes. Such verbs have to be memorized with their meanings. For example:

finir *to finish, to end*

As-tu **fini** ton café?	*Have you finished your coffee?*
Elle **a fini** le tournage du film.	*She completed the shooting of the film.*
Elle **n'a pas fini d'**écrire son article.	*She hasn't finished writing her article.*
J'**ai fini de** manger.	*I am done eating.*
Il **a fini par** lui dire la vérité.	*He finally told her the truth.*
Elle **a fini par** accepter.	*She finally accepted.*

commencer *to begin, to start*

J'**ai commencé** un nouveau livre.	*I started a new book.*
Tu **as** bien **commencé** l'année?	*Did you start the year on the right foot?*
Il **commence à** pleuvoir.	*It's starting to rain.*
Tout à coup, il **a commencé à** pleurer.	*Suddenly, he started crying.*
Elle **a commencé par** se présenter.	*She started by introducing herself.*
On **va commencer par** des escargots.	*We'll start with snails.*

décider *to decide*

C'est **décidé**.	*It's (has been) decided.*
J'**ai décidé d'**aller au cinéma.	*I decided to go to the movies.*
Nous **avons décidé d'**aller au Japon.	*We decided to go to Japan.*
Ils **se sont** enfin **décidés à** se marier.	*They finally decided to get (got around to getting) married.*
Décide-toi!	*Make up your mind!*

Prepositions 311

demander to ask

Il lui **demande** une explication.	*He is asking her for an explanation.*
Demande-moi tout ce que tu veux.	*Ask me anything you want.*
Elle nous **a demandé de** ne rien dire.	*She asked us not to say anything.*
Je vous **demande d'**attendre.	*I am asking you to wait.*
Je **demande à** voir les preuves.	*I'm asking to see the evidence.*
Le patient **demande à** quitter l'hôpital.	*The patient is asking (permission) to leave the hospital.*

donner to give

Je te le **donnerai** demain.	*I'll give it to you tomorrow.*
Elle m'**a donné** sa réponse.	*She gave me her answer.*
L'hôtel **donne sur** la mer?	*The hotel faces the sea?*
Mon appartement **donne sur** la Place de la Bastille.	*My apartment looks out onto Place de la Bastille.*

jouer to play

Il faut **jouer le jeu**.	*You've got to play the game.*
Marie et Émile **jouent aux échecs**.	*Marie and Émile play chess.*
Marc **joue au poker** tous les jeudis.	*Marc plays poker every Thursday.*
Ils **jouent au chat et à la souris**.	*They are playing cat and mouse.*
Thierry **joue de la guitare**.	*Thierry plays the guitar.*
Pierre **joue de l'accordéon**.	*Pierre plays the accordion.*
Valérie aime **jouer des castagnettes**.	*Valérie likes to play castanets.*

parler to speak

Laisse-moi **parler à** ta sœur.	*Let me talk to your sister.*
Puis-je **lui parler**?	*May I talk to her/him?*
Il **a parlé de toi** à la radio.	*He talked about you on the radio.*
De quoi voulez-vous **parler** aujourd'hui?	*What do you want to talk about today?*

croire to believe

La police **le croit**.	*The police believe him.*
Je **crois sa version** de l'histoire.	*I believe his version of the story.*
Il ne **croit** pas **à la magie**.	*He doesn't believe in magic.*
Je **crois au progrès**.	*I believe in progress.*
Crois-tu **en Dieu**?	*Do you believe in God?*
Je **crois en toi**, mon fils.	*I have confidence in you, my son.*
Je **crois en l'humanité**.	*I have faith in mankind.*
Je **crois pouvoir** vous **dire** ce qui s'est réellement passé.	*I think I can tell you what really happened.*
Il **croit avoir garé** sa voiture dans cette rue.	*He thinks he parked his car in that street.*

tenir to hold

Je **tiens à** mes amis.	*I am attached to my friends.*
Je **tiens à voir** ce film.	*I am eager to see that movie.*
Tu **tiens de ton père**.	*You look like your father.*
Elle **tient de sa mère**.	*She takes after her mother.*

rêver to dream

La nuit dernière, j'**ai rêvé de lui**.	*Last night I dreamt about him.*
Patrice **rêve à une autre vie**.	*Patrice is dreaming of a different life.*
Ils **rêvent à un avenir meilleur**.	*They are hoping for better days (a better future).*

312 PRACTICE MAKES PERFECT   Complete French All-in-One

EXERCICE 21·21

Compléter avec la préposition appropriée.

1. Elle aime jouer _____ la clarinette.
2. Paul a décidé _____ partir tôt.
3. La chambre donne _____ une cour très calme.
4. Je crois _____ la vertu médicinale des plantes.
5. J'ai rêvé _____ toi.
6. Émilie tient _____ ses livres.
7. Hier, nous avons parlé _____ toi.
8. Est-ce qu'il croit _____ Dieu?
9. Nous nous sommes décidés _____ prendre de très longues vacances.
10. Elle m'a demandé _____ fermer la porte.

The verb manquer

Note how the preposition (or lack of preposition) changes the meaning of the verb **manquer** (*to miss*) in these examples:

J'**ai manqué le cours** la semaine dernière.	*I missed the class last week.*
Elle **a manqué le début** de la pièce.	*She missed the beginning of the play.*
Cette pièce **manque d'air**.	*This room lacks air.*
Tu **manques de générosité**.	*You lack generosity.*
Je **ne manque de rien**.	*I lack nothing.*
Frédérique **a manqué à sa promesse**.	*Frédérique failed to keep her word.*
Laura **a manqué à tous ses devoirs**.	*Laura neglected all of her duties.*
Tu **me manques**.	*I miss you (i.e., you are lacking to me)*
Paris **me manque**.	*I miss Paris.*

Traduire en anglais les phrases suivantes.

1. Paul me manque.

_____

2. Mon frère a manqué à sa parole.

_____

3. Cet écrivain manque de talent.

_____

4. J'ai manqué le début du cours.

5. Le patron a manqué à ses devoirs.

The infinitive mood ·22·

The **infinitif présent**

You will come across the **infinitif**, the infinitive mood, on many occasions. It is used more frequently in French than in English. The **infinitif** can be used as the subject of a verb. (Note that the present participle is used in English instead.)

Faire la cuisine est son passe-temps favori.	*Cooking is his favorite pastime.*
Suivre des cours de cuisine est amusant.	*Taking cooking classes is fun.*
Voyager par le train est rapide.	*Traveling by train is fast.*
Apprendre une langue étrangère est très utile.	*Learning a foreign language is very useful.*

The **infinitif** is also used for general instructions, prescriptions, public notices, and proverbs (where the imperative is often used in English).

Prendre une fois par jour.	*Take once a day.*
Ne pas se pencher par la fenêtre.	*Do not lean out of the window.*
Ne pas marcher sur la pelouse.	*Keep off the lawn.*
Lire le mode d'emploi avant utilisation.	*Read the instructions before using.*

Since a verb in the infinitive mood is not conjugated, the negation (**ne... pas**) does not surround the verb but rather precedes it, and is not separated.

Il a promis de **ne pas ajouter** trop d'ail.	*He promised not to add too much garlic.*
Je lui ai demandé de **ne pas faire frire** le poisson.	*I asked her not to fry the fish.*
Elle m'a dit de **ne pas mettre** d'huile.	*She told me not to put any oil in.*
Je lui ai conseillé de **ne pas mettre** le gâteau au four avant midi.	*I advised her not to put the cake in the oven before noon.*

VOCABULAIRE

ajouter	*to add*	**broyer**	*to grind, to crush*
assaisonner	*to season*	**caraméliser**	*to caramelize*
bouillir	*to boil*	**couper**	*to cut*
braiser	*to braise*	**cuire**	*to cook*

décortiquer	to shell, to husk	griller	to grill, to toast
écailler	to scale (fish)	hacher	to chop, to mince
écraser	to crush, to squash	macérer	to macerate, to soak
écumer	to skim (soup)	mariner	to marinate
émincer	to slice thinly	mettre au four	to put in the oven
épicer	to spice	mijoter	to simmer
éplucher	to peel (vegetables)	paner	to coat with bread crumbs
faire la cuisine	to cook	pétrir	to knead
faire revenir	to brown	piler	to crush
faire sauter	to sauté	pocher	to poach
farcir	to stuff	râper	to grate
flamber	to flambé	réduire	to reduce (by boiling)
frire	to fry	rôtir	to roast
garnir	to garnish	tremper	to soak
glacer	to glaze	verser	to pour
gratiner	to brown, to cook au gratin		

Although nowadays French household magazines tend to use the imperative mood in recipes and other instructions, the **infinitif présent** is often used in professional cookbooks and other instruction manuals.

Hacher le persil. *Chop the parsley.*
Farcir la dinde. *Stuff the turkey.*
Râper une demi-livre de fromage. *Grate half a pound of cheese.*
Pocher le poisson. *Poach the fish.*

EXERCICE 22·1

Traduire les phrases suivantes en utilisant l'infinitif présent.

1. Writing this book was a challenge.

2. Studying French is fun.

3. Working four days a week is ideal.

4. Finding a new job will be difficult.

5. Walking along the Seine is pleasant.

6. Waking up at five A.M. is too early.

316 PRACTICE MAKES PERFECT Complete French All-in-One

7. Cooking takes a lot of time.

_____

8. Take this medicine twice a day.

_____

9. Add some pepper.

_____

10. Do not put in any garlic.

_____

The infinitive is used after *verbs of perception* (where the present participle is used in English).

J'**ai vu** les moutons **traverser** la route.	*I saw the sheep crossing (cross) the road.*
Elle **a entendu** le coq **chanter**.	*She heard the rooster crowing (crow).*
On **entendait** le chef **fredonner** une chanson.	*We could hear the chef humming (hum) a song.*
Elle **a vu** la biche **sauter** par-dessus la clôture.	*She saw the doe jumping (jump) over the fence.*

The infinitive is used in the *interrogative infinitive*.

Que **répondre**?	*What can I (can we) answer?*
Comment le lui **expliquer**?	*How to explain it to him?*
Pourquoi **protester**?	*Why protest?*
Que **dire**?	*What is there to say?*
Quoi **faire**?	*What can we do?*

You learned **faire** in Chapter 13. This causative form with **faire** is used to express the idea of *having something done by someone* or of *causing something to happen.*

Il a **fait macérer** la viande vingt-quatre heures.	*He macerated the meat twenty-four hours.*
Elle **a fait rôtir** le poulet.	*She roasted the chicken.*
J'**ai fait griller** le pain.	*I toasted the bread.*
J'**ai fait tremper** les pruneaux.	*I soaked the prunes.*

The infinitive is used after expressions of *spending time*.

Elle **passe son temps à créer** de nouvelles recettes.	*She spends her time creating new recipes.*
Il **passe ses vacances à lire** des livres de cuisine.	*He spends his vacation reading cookbooks.*
Il **a gaspillé sa vie à ne rien faire**.	*He wasted his life doing nothing.*
Je **passe mon temps à chercher** de nouvelles épices.	*I spend my time looking for new spices.*

The infinitive is used after expressions of *position*. The preposition **à** precedes the infinitive. (Note the present participle equivalents in English.)

Il **est debout à éplucher** des carottes.	*He is standing peeling carrots.*
Elle **est assise à écosser** des petits pois.	*She is sitting shelling peas.*

The infinitive mood **317**

Il **est accroupi** dans le jardin **à cueillir** des fraises.
He is squatting in the garden picking strawberries.

Elle **est à genoux à arracher** les mauvaises herbes.
She is kneeling pulling out weeds.

EXERCICE 22·2

Réécrire les phrases suivantes en traduisant les expressions entre parenthèses.

1. Elle passe ses après-midi (*cooking*).

2. Ils passent leurs nuits (*dancing*).

3. Ils sont accoudés au comptoir (*talking*).

4. Elle est assise (*peeling vegetables*).

5. Il a gaspillé sa vie (*working for them*).

6. Tu as perdu ton temps (*looking for another job*).

7. Je suis allongée sur la plage (*reading*).

8. Elle est debout dans le jardin (*picking some flowers*).

9. Il passe son temps (*dreaming*).

10. Ils passent leurs journées (*shopping*).

EXERCICE 22·3

Translate the following sentences.

1. I saw Victorine eating a chocolate cake in her office.

   _____

2. His cousin Grégoire spends his time playing basketball.

   _____

3. My neighbor Carl spends his time watching television.

   _____

4. I heard him talking in the hallway.

   _____

5. Samuel spends his vacation visiting libraries in Paris.

   _____

6. In the summer, we spend our time traveling in Europe.

   _____

7. Carla saw him cutting wood in the garden.

   _____

8. Laurent spends his time learning foreign languages.

   _____

9. She heard them saying they would sell their house.

   _____

10. I was watching him sleeping.

   _____

EXERCICE 22·4

Match the two columns.

_____ 1. Tu es accroupi dans le jardin

_____ 2. Elle est étendue sur son lit

_____ 3. Ils sont accoudés au bar

_____ 4. Elle est assise, la tête dans les mains

_____ 5. Vous êtes debout sur une chaise

a. à réfléchir à son destin.

b. à boire une bière.

c. à arracher les mauvaises herbes.

d. à nettoyer les étagères de la bibliothèque.

e. à lire un roman d'amour.

The infinitive mood   **319**

EXERCICE 22·5

*Translate the following sentences, using the **tu** or **vous** form, as indicated.*

1. They are sitting in the grass watching the sunset.

2. The professor is standing reading a passage from *The Lover* by Marguerite Duras.

3. Xavier is lying on his bed reading the dictionary.

4. We are lying down on the sofa watching a new Italian film.

5. Yvon is squatting in the field picking some strawberries.

6. Édouard is leaning against the door of the refrigerator wondering what he is going to eat.

7. Lucien is leaning against the wall watching people dance.

8. You are standing on a chair cleaning the windows. (**vous**)

9. The novelist is sitting in front of her computer thinking about what she is going to write.

10. You are squatting in the kitchen trying to repair the door. (**tu**)

The **infinitif passé**

The **infinitif passé** (*past infinitive*) is used to mark anteriority. It is formed with the infinitive of **avoir** or **être** and the past participle of the main verb. (Note that, for verbs conjugated with **être**, the past participle of the **infinitif passé** agrees with the subject of the sentence.)

Les hôtes ont remercié le chef d'**avoir préparé** un si bon repas.
Nous nous sommes excusés d'**être partis** avant le dessert.

The guests thanked the chef for having prepared such a good meal.
We apologized for leaving before dessert.

320 PRACTICE MAKES PERFECT Complete French All-in-One

Il a regretté d'**avoir oublié** l'anniversaire de Clara. *He regretted having forgotten Clara's birthday.*

Comment pouvait-il **avoir brûlé** tout le dîner? *How could he have burnt the whole dinner?*

Mettre les verbes suivants à l'infinitif passé, au masculin singulier.

1. dormir _____
2. aller _____
3. manger _____
4. se promener _____
5. regarder _____
6. tomber _____
7. se lever _____
8. préparer _____
9. partir _____
10. allumer _____

One common occurrence of the **infinitif passé** is after the preposition **après** (*after*), while the **infinitif présent** follows **avant de** (*before*).

Gérard fait mariner la viande **avant d'éplucher** un oignon. *Gérard marinates the meat before peeling an onion.*

Gérard fait mariner la viande **après avoir épluché** un oignon. *Gérard marinates the meat after peeling an onion.*

Elle se lave les mains **avant de décortiquer** les crevettes. *She washes her hands before shelling the shrimp.*

Elle se lave les mains **après avoir décortiqué** les crevettes. *She washes her hands after shelling the shrimp.*

Je fais la cuisine **avant d'aller** au cinéma. *I cook before going to the movies.*

Je fais la cuisine **après être allé** au cinéma. *I cook after going to the movies.*

Elle lit le journal **avant de se lever**. *She reads the paper before getting up.*

Elle lit le journal **après s'être levée**. *She reads the paper after getting up.*

The infinitive mood

EXERCICE 22·7

*Changer **avant de** en **après** en utilisant l'infinitif passé.*

1. Elle prend des vacances avant de compléter son projet.

2. Il écrit la lettre avant de consulter son ami.

3. Je prépare un thé avant de cueillir des fruits.

4. Ils rendent visite à leurs amis avant d'aller au théâtre.

5. Il verse le vin avant de servir le dîner.

6. Elle se maquille avant de s'habiller.

7. Nous dînons avant de regarder le film à la télévision.

8. Ils se promènent avant de travailler.

9. Je réfléchis avant de téléphoner.

10. Nous allons chez Julien avant de choisir un cadeau.

Verbs with their prepositions

When a verb is followed by another verb in the infinitive (**j'aime danser**), the first thing to ask is whether or not it is followed by a preposition. There is no magic recipe, you need to learn them by heart as you go along. Some verbs are not followed by a preposition, others are followed by **à**, **de**, **sur**, etc., before an infinitive, and sometimes before a noun or pronoun.

Verbs not followed by a preposition

Let's start with verbs that are *not* followed by a preposition:

aimer	*to like, to love*
aller	*to go*

avouer	*to admit*
compter	*to intend, to plan*
désirer	*to desire, to wish*
détester	*to hate (to)*
devoir	*must, to have to*
écouter	*to listen to*
espérer	*to hope to*
faire	*to do*
falloir	*must, to be necessary to*
laisser	*to let, to allow*
oser	*to dare (to)*
paraître	*to appear, to seem*
penser	*to think*
pouvoir	*can, to be able to*
préférer	*to prefer*
prétendre	*to claim*
savoir	*to know (how to)*
sembler	*to seem to*
sentir	*to feel, to think*
souhaiter	*to wish to*
venir	*to come*
voir	*to see*
vouloir	*to want to*

Les Corbin **aiment manger** au restaurant.	*The Corbins love to eat out.*
Elle **voudrait devenir** traiteur.	*She would like to become a caterer.*
J'**avoue ne pas comprendre** son but.	*I admit I do not understand his goal.*
Il **sait faire** la sauce béchamel.	*He knows how to make béchamel sauce.*

In the above examples, the subject of the first verb is the same as the one for the second verb; that's why the infinitive form is used. When the subjects are different, a dependent clause introduced by **que** is required. Depending on the verb in the main clause, the dependent clause can be in the indicative or the subjunctive.

J'espère obtenir ce poste.	*I am hoping to get this position.*
J'espère **qu'elle obtiendra** ce poste.	*I am hoping she'll get this position.*
Tu veux apprendre ce métier.	*You want to learn this craft.*
Tu veux **qu'il apprenne** ce métier.	*You want him to learn this craft.*

In some cases, a French verb does not need a preposition even though its English equivalent requires one.

Elle **attend** le train.	*She is waiting **for** the train.*
Il **a abandonné** le projet.	*He gave **up** the project.*
Nous **écoutons** la conférence.	*We are listening **to** the lecture.*
Soudain, ils **sont entrés**.	*Suddenly they walked **in**.*

The infinitive mood **323**

EXERCICE 22·8

Mettre au présent les verbes entre parenthèses.

1. Il (détester) _____ attendre.

2. Ils (vouloir) _____ acheter un nouvel ordinateur.

3. Nous (devoir) _____ partir dans une heure.

4. Je (pouvoir) _____ vous aider.

5. Nous (désirer) _____ renouveler notre abonnement.

6. Tu (vouloir) _____ goûter ces plats.

7. Elle (sembler) _____ comprendre les conséquences.

8. Tu (penser) _____ pouvoir réussir?

9. Il (falloir) _____ faire mariner le poisson.

10. Vous (aller) _____ passer une bonne soirée.

Verbs followed by the preposition à

Many verbs are followed by the preposition **à** when they precede an infinitive. You have already encountered quite a few in previous chapters. These will also need to be memorized.

s'accoutumer à	*to get accustomed to*
aider à	*to help to*
s'amuser à	*to enjoy*
apprendre à	*to learn to, to show how to*
arriver à	*to manage to*
aspirer à	*to aspire to*
s'attendre à	*to expect to*
autoriser à	*to authorize to*
chercher à	*to try to, to attempt to*
commencer à	*to start to*
consentir à	*to agree to, to consent to*
continuer à	*to continue to, to keep on*
se décider à	*to make up one's mind to*
encourager à	*to encourage to*
se faire à	*to get used to*
faire attention à	*to pay attention to*
s'habituer à	*to get used to*
hésiter à	*to hesitate to*
inciter à	*to encourage to*
s'intéresser à	*to get interested in*
inviter à	*to invite to*
se mettre à	*to start to, to begin to*
parvenir à	*to manage to*
préparer à	*to get ready to*
renoncer à	*to give up*
se résigner à	*to resign oneself to*

réussir à	*to succeed in*
songer à	*to think about*
tenir à	*to insist on, to be eager to*
viser à	*to aim at*

Il **commence à travailler** à huit heures.	*He starts to work at eight o'clock.*
Ils **se préparent à partir**.	*They are getting ready to leave.*
Elle l'**a encouragé à s'inscrire**.	*She encouraged him to sign up.*
Tu **as réussi à obtenir** un prix.	*You managed to get an award.*

Verbs followed by the preposition **de**

Now that you have memorized some of the **à** verbs, let's look at some verbs followed by the preposition **de** when they precede an infinitive.

accepter de	*to accept, to agree to*
accuser de	*to accuse (of)*
s'arrêter de	*to stop*
avoir besoin de	*to need to*
avoir envie de	*to feel like, to want*
avoir l'intention de	*to intend to*
avoir peur de	*to be afraid of*
cesser de	*to stop, to cease*
choisir de	*to choose to*
conseiller de	*to advise (to)*
se contenter de	*to content oneself with*
convaincre de	*to convince (to)*
craindre de	*to fear (to)*
défendre de	*to forbid (to)*
demander de	*to ask (to)*
se dépêcher de	*to hurry to*
s'efforcer de	*to try hard to*
empêcher de	*to prevent (from)*
s'empêcher de	*to refrain from*
envisager de	*to contemplate*
essayer de	*to try to*
éviter de	*to avoid*
s'excuser de	*to apologize for*
faire semblant de	*to pretend to*
feindre de	*to feign to, to pretend to*
finir de	*to finish, to end up*
interdire de	*to forbid (to)*
menacer de	*to threaten to*
mériter de	*to deserve to*
offrir de	*to offer to*
oublier de	*to forget to*
permettre de	*to allow (to), to permit (to)*
persuader de	*to persuade (to), to convince (to)*
se plaindre de	*to complain of*
projeter de	*to plan to/on*
promettre de	*to promise to*
refuser de	*to refuse to*
regretter de	*to regret*
remercier de	*to thank (for)*
reprocher de	*to reproach for*

The infinitive mood **325**

soupçonner de	to suspect of
se souvenir de	to remember to
tâcher de	to try to

Il **a essayé de faire** un soufflé. *He tried to make a soufflé.*
Elle **a refusé de** nous **donner** sa recette. *She refused to give us her recipe.*
Ils **ont promis de l'envoyer** au Cordon Bleu. *They promised to send him to the Cordon Bleu cooking school.*
J'**ai fini de lire** le roman. *I finished reading the novel.*

À ou de? Mettre la préposition.

1. J'ai appris _____ faire une mousse au chocolat.
2. Ils ont choisi _____ s'installer dans une région gastronomique.
3. Il s'habitue _____ vivre dans une grande ville.
4. Elle nous reproche _____ ne jamais lui rendre visite.
5. Tu as renoncé _____ faire ce voyage.
6. Elle se souvient _____ la cuisine de sa grand-mère.
7. Il tient _____ sa voiture.
8. Tu lui as conseillé _____ suivre des cours de cuisine.
9. Ils se plaignent _____ tout.
10. Son grand-père a promis _____ faire des gâteaux.

*Traduire les phrases suivantes en utilisant la forme **vous** si nécessaire.*

1. They want to travel to France.

2. He spent hours peeling potatoes.

3. Cooking is her favorite pastime.

4. Do not forget to add some salt!

5. He is afraid of burning the meat.

6. They feel like eating a chocolate soufflé.

7. He stopped smoking.

8. They refused to go out.

9. She is learning how to cook.

10. Try to understand the situation!

The imperative mood

The imperative mood (**l'impératif**) is used to give orders, make suggestions, or give advice.

Formation of the imperative

To make the three forms of the imperative, take the **tu**, **nous**, and **vous** forms of the present tense. For the **-er** verbs, drop the **-s** of the present tense **tu** form.

parler *to speak*	
Parle!	*Speak!*
Parlons!	*Let's speak!*
Parlez!	*Speak!*

choisir *to choose*	
Choisis!	*Choose!*
Choisissons!	*Let's choose!*
Choisissez!	*Choose!*

répondre *to answer*	
Réponds!	*Answer!*
Répondons!	*Let's answer!*
Répondez!	*Answer!*

boire *to drink*	
Bois!	*Drink!*
Buvons!	*Let's drink!*
Buvez!	*Drink!*

Prends un café avant de partir!	*Have a coffee before you leave!*
Signez votre nom ici!	*Sign your name here!*
Allons leur rendre visite!	*Let's go visit them!*
Épelez votre nom, s'il vous plaît.	*Please spell your name.*
Faites un effort!	*Make an effort!*
Téléphone à Jérôme immédiatement!	*Call Jérôme immediately!*

In the negative form, the negation is placed around the verb. Note that object pronouns immediately precede the verb (following **ne** [**n'**]) in the negative imperative.

N'oubliez pas son anniversaire!	*Don't forget her birthday!*
Ne l'appelle pas dimanche!	*Don't call him on Sunday!*

N'y allons pas avant midi. Let's not go there before noon.
Ne parle pas si fort! Don't talk so loud!
Ne prends pas ma voiture! Don't take my car!
Ne signez pas ce document avant de l'avoir lu. Do not sign this document before reading it.

Mettre à l'impératif les phrases suivantes.

1. Prendre le train de neuf heures. (tu)

2. Regarder le film à la télé ce soir. (vous)

3. Dîner sur la terrasse. (nous)

4. Acheter le journal. (tu)

5. Boire à sa santé. (nous)

6. Expliquer les conditions. (vous)

7. Ne pas courir si vite. (tu)

8. Épeler ton nom. (tu)

9. Prêter votre dictionnaire à Marie. (vous)

10. Ne pas inviter Denis. (tu)

VOCABULAIRE

un nom	a name	**Comment épelez-vous votre nom?**	How do you spell your name?
un prénom	a first name		
un surnom	a nickname	**s'appeler**	to call oneself, to be named
épeler	to spell		

Comment vous appelez-vous?	*What is your name?*	un permis de conduire	*a driver's license*
Je m'appelle...	*My name is...*	un certificat de vaccination	*a vaccination certificate*
l'état civil (*m.*)	*civil status*	célibataire	*single*
la date de naissance	*birth date*	marié(e)	*married*
le lieu de naissance	*place of birth*	séparé(e)	*separated*
Où êtes-vous né(e)?	*Where were you born?*	divorcé(e)	*divorced*
Je suis né(e) à...	*I was born in...*	veuf, veuve	*widow, widower*
une naissance	*a birth*	une parenté	*a kinship*
un extrait de naissance	*a birth certificate*	un lien de parenté	*a family tie*
un mariage	*a marriage, a wedding*	un arbre généalogique	*a family tree*
un décès	*a death*	un(e) ancêtre	*an ancestor*
une adresse	*an address*	signer	*to sign*
une carte d'identité	*an identity card*	cocher	*to check off*
un passeport	*a passport*		

Irregular imperative forms

Some imperatives are irregular. Let's take a look at **être**, **avoir**, and **savoir**.

être *to be*	
sois	*be*
soyons	*let's be*
soyez	*be*

avoir *to have*	
aie	*have*
ayons	*let's have*
ayez	*have*

savoir *to know*	
sache	*know*
sachons	*let's know*
sachez	*know*

The irregular verb **vouloir** (*to want*) is used only in the **vous** imperative form.

Veuillez accepter mes excuses!	*Please accept my excuses!*
Sois sage!	*Be good!*
Aie plus de patience!	*Have more patience!*
Sachez que je suis avec vous!	*Be aware (Know that) I am with you!*
Ne soyez pas si rigide!	*Don't be so rigid!*
Veuillez signer le contrat.	*Please sign the contract.*

The position of object pronouns with the imperative

In the *affirmative imperative* the object pronoun follows the verb and is joined to it by a hyphen (**me** becomes **moi**).

Attendez-**moi**!	*Wait for me!*
Regarde-**nous**!	*Look at us!*

330 PRACTICE MAKES PERFECT Complete French All-in-One

Aidez-**les**!	*Help them!*
Demande-**lui**!	*Ask him!*
Allons-**y**!	*Let's go!*
Allez-**y**!	*Go ahead!*
Excusez-**moi**!	*Excuse me!*
Tenez-**moi** au courant!	*Keep me posted!*
Prévenez-**moi**!	*Inform me!*
Faites-**moi** confiance!	*Trust me!*
Bois-**en**!	*Drink some!*
Laissez-**moi** tranquille!	*Leave me alone!*

Note: If the familiar command is followed by the pronouns **y** or **en**, all -**er** ending verbs and those -**ir** ending verbs that are conjugated like -**er** verbs in the present tense (**ouvrir, souffrir,** and **offrir**) *retain* the -**s** in the second-person singular for phonetic reasons. Don't forget to make the liaison sound [z] between the -**s** and **y** or **en**.

Va**s**-**y**!	*Go ahead!*
Mange**s**-**en**!	*Eat some!*
Reste**s**-**y**!	*Stay there!*
Ouvre**s**-**en**!	*Open some!*
Profite**s**-**en**!	*Make the most of it!*

EXERCICE 23·2

Comment dit-on en français?

1. Listen to me (*fam.*)! _____
2. Trust me (*fam.*)! _____
3. Follow me (*pol.*)! _____
4. Let's hope so (**le**)! _____
5. Ask her (*pol.*)! _____
6. Go ahead (*fam.*)! _____
7. Help me (*fam.*)! _____
8. Phone them (*pol.*)! _____
9. Pass me (*fam.*) the salt! _____
10. Buy some (*fam.*)! _____
11. Do it (*pol.*)! _____
12. Keep me posted (*fam.*)! _____
13. Excuse me (*fam.*)! _____
14. Wait for me (*fam.*)! _____
15. Look at her (*fam.*)! _____
16. Try it (*pol.*)! _____

If there are two object pronouns with the imperative form, the direct object pronoun precedes the indirect object pronoun, but **y** and **en** always come last. The pronouns are joined to each other and to the verb by a hyphen. Note that before **en**, **moi** becomes **m'**.

Dis-**le-moi**!	*Tell me!*
Donnez-**m'en**!	*Give me some!*
Donnez-**les-leur**!	*Give them to them!*
Passez-**le-moi**!	*Let me talk to him! (on the phone)*
Dites-**le-lui**!	*Say it to him!*
Emmène-**les-y**!	*Take them there!*

Comment dit-on en français?

1. Give (*fam.*) it (*masc.*) to them! _____
2. Put (*pol.*) them there! _____
3. Give (*pol.*) him some! _____
4. Bring (*pol.*) it (*masc.*) to me! _____
5. Show (*pol.*) it (*fem.*) to them! _____
6. Lend (*fam.*) me some! _____

In the *negative imperative*, the object pronoun or pronouns precede the verb. There is no hyphen.

Ne **le** regarde pas!	*Don't look at him!*
N'**y** pensez plus!	*Don't think of it any more!*

Comment dit-on en français?

1. Don't leave (*fam.*) (**quitter**) me! _____
2. Don't believe (*pol.*) her! _____
3. Don't disturb (*pol.*) us! _____
4. Don't answer (*fam.*) him! _____
5. Don't make (*pol.*) me laugh! _____
6. Don't listen (*fam.*) to them! _____
7. Don't lie (*fam.*) to me! _____

If there are two object pronouns in the negative imperative, they have the same order as in a normal declarative sentence.

me (m')	before	le (l')	before	lui	before	y	before	en
te (t')		la (l')		leur				
se (s')		les						
nous								
vous								

Ne **me le** dites pas! — *Don't tell (it to) me!*
Ne **m'en** parlez pas! — *Don't talk to me about it!*
Ne **vous y** mariez pas! — *Don't get married there!*

EXERCICE 23·5

Dites en français.

1. Don't (*fam.*) show them to him! _____
2. Don't (*pol.*) sell it (*fem.*) to them! _____
3. Let's not offer it (*masc.*) to her! _____
4. Don't (*fam.*) give me any! _____
5. Let's not send it (*fem.*) to her! _____

The imperative of pronominal verbs

When putting pronominal verbs in the imperative, watch for the pronoun and its position. The pronoun *follows* the verb form in the affirmative imperative; **me (m')** and **te (t')** become **moi** and **toi**. However, the pronoun *precedes* the verb in the negative imperative. For a review of pronominal verbs, see Chapter 14.

Tu te lèves. — *You get up.*
Lève-toi! — *Get up!*
Ne te lève pas! — *Do not get up!*

Nous nous promenons. — *We take a walk.*
Promenons-nous! — *Let's take a walk!*
Ne nous promenons pas! — *Let's not take a walk!*

Vous vous reposez. — *You are resting.*
Reposez-vous! — *Take a rest!*
Ne vous reposez pas! — *Do not rest!*

EXERCICE 23·6

Mettre à l'impératif les phrases suivantes.

1. Se laver les mains. (tu)

2. Se balader dans la forêt. (vous)

3. S'écrire plus souvent. (nous)

4. Ne pas se coucher trop tard. (tu)

5. Se réveiller à cinq heures. (vous)

6. S'habiller vite. (tu)

7. Ne pas se tromper de route. (vous)

8. Se retrouver devant la Brasserie Lipp. (nous)

9. Se dépêcher. (tu)

10. Se rencontrer un jour à Paris. (nous)

EXERCICE 23·7

Traduire les phrases suivantes en utilisant l'impératif.

1. Don't forget your passport! (**tu**)

2. Let's rest on the bench! (**nous**)

3. Bring your identification card! (**vous**)

4. Tell us his first name! (**tu**)

5. Take this medicine! (**tu**)

6. Don't be late! (**vous**)

7. Let's go to Italy! (**nous**)

8. Close the door! (**tu**)

9. Wait for me! (**vous**)

10. Write your address on the envelope! (**vous**)

The present participle and gerund

The present participle

You have used the **participe passé** (*past participle*) many times with the compound tenses. Another participle is the **participe présent** (*present participle*). It is formed by dropping the **-ons** ending from the present tense **nous** form and adding **-ant**.

chanter *to sing*			
nous chantons	*we sing*	**chantant**	*singing*
partir *to leave*			
nous partons	*we leave*	**partant**	*leaving*
choisir *to choose*			
nous choisissons	*we choose*	**choisissant**	*choosing*
boire *to drink*			
nous buvons	*we drink*	**buvant**	*drinking*
voir *to see*			
nous voyons	*we see*	**voyant**	*seeing*
répondre *to answer*			
nous répondons	*we answer*	**répondant**	*answering*

Some spelling changes occur with some **-cer** and **-ger** verbs:

commencer *to start*			
nous commençons	*we start*	**commençant**	*starting*
influencer *to influence*			
nous influençons	*we influence*	**influençant**	*influencing*
manger *to eat*			
nous mangeons	*we eat*	**mangeant**	*eating*
nager *to swim*			
nous nageons	*we swim*	**nageant**	*swimming*

Pronominal verbs follow the same pattern. Do not forget the pronoun corresponding to the subject. Let's look at the present participle of **se promener** (*to take a walk*):

me promenant	*walking*	**nous** promenant	*walking*
te promenant	*walking*	**vous** promenant	*walking*
se promenant	*walking*	**se** promenant	*walking*

Three verbs have an irregular present participle:

être	*to be*	**étant**	*being*
avoir	*to have*	**ayant**	*having*
savoir	*to know*	**sachant**	*knowing*

VOCABULAIRE

jouer	*to play*	**la boxe**	*boxing*
un joueur, une joueuse	*a player*	**le cyclisme**	*biking, cycling*
un(e) adversaire	*an opponent*	**le football**	*soccer*
une équipe	*a team*	**le football américain**	*football*
gagner	*to win*	**le golf**	*golf*
remporter une victoire	*to win*	**le jogging**	*jogging*
battre	*to beat*	**la lutte**	*wrestling*
un vainqueur	*a winner*	**la natation**	*swimming*
un(e) gagnant(e)	*a winner*	**le patinage**	*ice skating*
un(e) perdant(e)	*a loser*	**la plongée**	*diving*
un match	*a game*	**le ski**	*skiing*
manquer	*to miss*	**la descente**	*downhill skiing*
courir	*to run*	**le ski de fond**	*cross-country skiing*
sauter	*to jump*	**le ski nautique**	*waterskiing*
lancer	*to throw*	**le tennis**	*tennis*
s'entraîner	*to train*	**la voile**	*sailing*
un entraîneur	*a trainer*	**un stade**	*a stadium*
le base-ball	*baseball*	**une raquette**	*a racket*
le basket-ball	*basketball*	**un ballon**	*a ball*

Some **participes présents** can be used as nouns. When used as a noun, the present participle changes according to gender and number. For example:

un gagnant	*a winner (masculine)*	**une gagnante**	*a winner (feminine)*
un perdant	*a loser (masculine)*	**une perdante**	*a loser (feminine)*

Many **participes présents** can be used as adjectives. When used as an adjective, the **participe présent** agrees with the noun it modifies. For example:

des matchs épuisants	*exhausting games*
un commentateur fascinant	*a fascinating commentator*
un sport exigeant	*a demanding sport*
une pièce amusante	*an amusing play*

The **participe présent** can also be used as a verb. Note that when used as a verb, the present participle is invariable.

La police l'a aperçu **entrant** dans un laboratoire médical.	*The police saw him entering (as he was entering) a medical lab.*
Étant blessé au genou, il n'a pas pu jouer.	*Since he has a knee injury, he was not able to play.*
Ne **sachant** pas comment nous excuser, nous lui avons offert des fleurs.	*Not knowing how to apologize, we gave her some flowers.*

The present participle and gerund **337**

Traversant la rue, elle a perdu son chapeau.	*Crossing (As she crossed) the street, she lost her hat.*

When an action precedes another one, **avoir** and **être** in the **participe présent** can be combined with a **participe passé**. Note that the past participle agrees with the subject of the sentence if the verb is conjugated with **être**.

ayant vu	*having seen*
ayant compris	*having understood*
ayant joué	*having played*
ayant traversé	*having crossed*
étant allé(e)(s)	*having gone*
étant parti(e)(s)	*having left*
nous étant promené(e)s	*having walked*
nous étant retrouvé(e)s	*having met*

Ayant accepté la défaite, les joueurs **sont rentrés** chez eux.	*Having accepted the defeat, the players went home.*
Étant partis très tôt, nous **sommes arrivés** les premiers.	*Having left very early, we were the first to arrive.*
Nous étant promenés toute la journée, nous **étions** fatigués.	*Having walked all day, we were tired.*
M'étant couchée à l'aube, j'**ai fait** la grasse matinée.	*Having gone to bed at dawn, I slept late.*
N'ayant pas dormi de la nuit, il **était** de mauvaise humeur.	*Not having slept all night, he was in a bad mood.*

EXERCICE 24·1

Mettre au participe présent les verbes suivants.

1. finir _____

2. savoir _____

3. donner _____

4. protéger _____

5. faire _____

6. avoir _____

7. avancer _____

8. être _____

9. prononcer _____

10. vendre _____

The gerund

When the present participle is introduced by **en**, it is referred to as the **gérondif** (*gerund*). It is formed with **en** + the present participle. It describes the relationship between two actions. It can express simultaneity, manner, condition, or causality.

Il s'est foulé la cheville **en jouant** au foot.	*He sprained his ankle while playing football.*
Elle écoute de la musique **en conduisant**.	*She listens to music while driving.*
M. Vincent a gagné beaucoup d'argent **en achetant** ces toiles.	*Mr. Vincent made a lot of money buying (when he bought) these paintings.*
En renvoyant ce joueur, vous feriez une grosse erreur.	*If you fired this player, you would make a big mistake.*

When **tout** precedes the gerund, it underscores a tension, a contradiction between two actions. For example:

Tout en étant un bon joueur, il ne marquait jamais de but.	*While being (Even though he was) a good player, he never scored a goal.*
Tout en faisant semblant d'écouter le professeur, il jouait avec son iPod.	*While pretending to listen to the teacher, he was playing with his iPod.*
Tout en pleurant, il riait.	*While crying, he was laughing.*
Tout en prétendant le contraire, elle voulait être élue.	*While claiming otherwise, she wanted to be elected.*

EXERCICE 24·2

Mettre au gérondif les verbes suivants.

1. C'est en (faire) _____ de l'exercice que vous serez en forme.
2. Elle chante en (prendre) _____ une douche.
3. Il s'est tordu la cheville en (jouer) _____ au volley.
4. Ils ont bronzé en (faire) _____ du ski de fond.
5. Il l'a invitée à dîner en (savoir) _____ que cela lui ferait plaisir.
6. En (aller) _____ en Inde, il a fait escale en Allemagne.
7. Tout en (se plaindre) _____, elle avait l'air satisfaite.
8. Ils ont découvert la basilique de Lisieux en (visiter) _____ la Normandie.
9. J'ai rencontré un ami en (arriver) _____ à Paris.
10. Il a tout perdu en (parier) _____ tous les jours au casino.

EXERCICE 24·3

Traduire les phrases suivantes.

1. He lost his keys while walking in the park.

The present participle and gerund 339

2. Not having seen the film, I can't make any comment.

_____

3. They saw Paul while crossing the street.

_____

4. Knowing the truth, she could not stay silent.

_____

5. He made money selling paintings.

_____

6. It was a fascinating game.

_____

7. Having finished the book, he left.

_____

8. They listen to music while working.

_____

9. I knit while watching television.

_____

10. He fell while jumping over the wall.

_____

EXERCICE
24·4

Traduisez en français les mots entre parenthèses en utilisant le gérondif.

1. On s'instruit (*by traveling*) _____ .

2. J'ai eu la voiture moins chère (*by bargaining*) _____ .

3. Renvoyez dès aujourd'hui ce bulletin (*by using*) _____ l'enveloppe ci-jointe.

4. Roméo s'est tué (*by drinking*) _____ une potion contenant un poison.

5. Il a trouvé sa montre (*when he tidied up*) _____ ses affaires.

6. Ne le dites pas (*while laughing*) _____ .

7. Il est parti (*while crying*) _____ .

8. Je vous quitte pour ce jour, (*[while] hoping*) _____ avoir bien vite de vos nouvelles.

9. (*[By] thanking you*) _____ à l'avance, je vous prie d'agréer, cher Monsieur, l'expression de mes sentiments les meilleurs.

340 PRACTICE MAKES PERFECT Complete French All-in-One

10. Ils sont sortis de l'appartement (*by slamming* [**claquer**] *the door*). _____ .

11. Ce qui m'a frappé (*while listening to this song*) _____ c'est la belle voix de la chanteuse.

12. (*Upon entering the house*) _____ , j'ai remarqué qu'on avait été cambriolés.

13. (*On receiving the award*) _____ elle a pleuré de joie.

14. Si nous parlions (*while having lunch*) _____?

15. Conduire (*while telephoning*) _____ est interdit en France.

EXERCICE
24·5

Traduisez en français en utilisant le gérondif.

1. Switch off the light as you (*pol.*) go out. _____

2. One must not speak while eating. _____

3. It is by visiting France that one learns best (**le mieux**) how to speak French. _____

4. You (*pol.*) succeeded by making an effort. _____

5. I earn my living by working. _____

6. He fell when he went down the stairs. _____

7. He broke his leg while skiing. _____

8. She found this job by reading the want ads (**les petites annonces**). _____

9. I lost weight (**maigrir**) by exercising (**faire du sport**) every day. _____

10. Nowadays, one often telephones while walking and one eats one's meals while watching television. _____

EXERCICE
24·6

Faites une seule phrase en employant en + *participe présent. Suivez le modèle.*

Exemple: Anne faisait la vaisselle. Elle a cassé une assiette.

En faisant la vaisselle, Anne a cassé une assiette.

1. Brice allait au théâtre. Il a rencontré un ami. _____

The present participle and gerund **341**

2. Mireille lisait le journal. Elle a découvert un article intéressant. _____

3. On regarde le journal télévisé. On se tient au courant de l'actualité. _____

4. Nous travaillons dur. Nous réussirons. _____

5. Je fais du yoga. Je me détends. _____

6. Les joueurs s'entraînent tous les jours. Ils ont gagné le match. _____

7. J'ai couru très vite. J'ai attrapé le bus. _____

8. Vous prenez la deuxième rue à droite. Vous arriverez à la gare. _____

The simple past, the passive voice, and indirect speech

The **passé simple** (simple past)

The **passé simple** (*simple past, historical past*) is a verb tense used mainly in written French, for literary and historical material. It may also be heard during a formal speech. It is the equivalent of the **passé composé**, used to recount a specific action in the past. When relating events, quality newspapers use the **passé simple** for refinement. Scandal sheets will often use it to convey a sense of drama. When reading French literature of all periods, you will need to recognize the **passé simple** to get a full appreciation of the text.

Formation of the **passé simple**

The **passé simple** of regular -**er** verbs is formed by adding the endings -**ai**, -**as**, -**a**, -**âmes**, -**âtes**, -**èrent** to the infinitive stem.

répéter to repeat			
je répét**ai**	*I repeated*	nous répét**âmes**	*we repeated*
tu répét**as**	*you repeated*	vous répét**âtes**	*you repeated*
il/elle répét**a**	*he/she repeated*	ils/elles répét**èrent**	*they repeated*

Verbs like **commencer** and **manger** have a spelling change. When the **passé simple** ending starts with -**a**, use the cedilla (**ç**) for verbs ending in -**cer** and add an extra -**e**- for verbs ending in -**ger**.

Elle prononça un discours.	*She made a speech.*
Je remplaçai le comédien malade.	*I replaced the sick actor.*
Il partagea sa fortune.	*He shared his fortune.*
Nous déménageâmes de nombreuses fois.	*We moved many times.*

The **passé simple** of regular -**ir** and -**re** verbs like **partir** (*to leave*) and **répondre** (*to answer*) is formed by adding the endings -**is**, -**is**, **it**, -**îmes**, -**îtes**, -**irent** to the infinitive stem.

partir to leave			
je part**is**	*I left*	nous part**îmes**	*we left*
tu part**is**	*you left*	vous part**îtes**	*you left*
il/elle part**it**	*he/she left*	ils/elles part**irent**	*they left*

répondre to answer			
je répond**is**	*I answered*	nous répond**îmes**	*we answered*
tu répond**is**	*you answered*	vous répond**îtes**	*you answered*
il/elle répond**it**	*he/she answered*	ils/elles répond**irent**	*they answered*

Avoir (*to have*) and **être** (*to be*) are irregular in the **passé simple**.

avoir *to have*			
j'**eus**	*I had*	nous **eûmes**	*we had*
tu **eus**	*you had*	vous **eûtes**	*you had*
il/elle **eut**	*he/she had*	ils/elles **eurent**	*they had*

être *to be*			
je **fus**	*I was*	nous **fûmes**	*we were*
tu **fus**	*you were*	vous **fûtes**	*you were*
il/elle **fut**	*he/she was*	ils/elles **furent**	*they were*

On **frappa** à la porte et il **se leva**. *Someone knocked on the door and he got up.*
Il **fut** surpris par notre réaction. *He was surprised by our reaction.*
Ils **répondirent** immédiatement à notre lettre. *They answered our letter immediately.*
Elles **partirent** aussitôt après le discours. *They left right after the speech.*

VOCABULAIRE

l'art (*m.*)	*art*	**une statue**	*a statue*
un musée	*a museum*	**une nature morte**	*a still life*
une collection	*a collection*	**un chef-d'œuvre**	*a masterpiece*
collectionner	*to collect*	**une photographie**	*a photograph*
un collectionneur,	*a collector*	**un vernissage**	*an opening (art show)*
une collectionneuse		**peindre**	*to paint*
une galerie	*a gallery*	**dessiner**	*to draw*
une visite guidée	*a guided tour*	**sculpter**	*to sculpt*
un conservateur,	*a curator*	**un peintre**	*a painter*
une conservatrice		**un(e) paysagiste**	*a landscape painter*
une exposition	*an exhibition*	**un(e) portraitiste**	*a portrait painter*
les beaux-arts (*m.pl.*)	*fine arts*	**une palette**	*a palette*
une toile	*a canvas, a painting*	**un pinceau**	*a paintbrush*
une peinture	*a painting*	**un chevalet**	*an easel*
un tableau	*a painting*	**un dessinateur,**	*a designer, a sketcher*
une aquarelle	*a watercolor (painting)*	**une dessinatrice**	
une gravure	*an etching*	**un sculpteur**	*a sculptor*
un dessin	*a drawing*	**un(e) photographe**	*a photographer*
une sculpture	*a sculpture*	**un atelier**	*a studio, a workshop*

The **passé simple** of irregular verbs

Other verbs have an irregular **passé simple**. For some verbs the stem of the **passé simple** is based on the past participle, but this is not a fixed rule.

Here are some of the irregular verbs in the **passé simple** that will let you start right in reading French newspapers or novels. It is especially useful to learn the third-person singular and plural forms.

boire (*to drink*)	il/elle **but**	*he/she drank*	ils/elles **burent**	*they drank*
conduire (*to drive*)	il/elle **conduisit**	*he/she drove*	ils/elles **conduisirent**	*they drove*
connaître (*to know*)	il/elle **connut**	*he/she knew*	ils/elles **connurent**	*they knew*
convaincre (*to convince*)	il/elle **convainquit**	*he/she convinced*	ils/elles **convainquirent**	*they convinced*
courir (*to run*)	il/elle **courut**	*he/she ran*	ils/elles **coururent**	*they ran*

couvrir (*to cover*)	il/elle **couvrit**	*he/she covered*	ils/elles **couvrirent**	*they covered*
craindre (*to fear*)	il/elle **craignit**	*he/she feared*	ils/elles **craignirent**	*they feared*
croire (*to believe*)	il/elle **crut**	*he/she believed*	ils/elles **crurent**	*they believed*
devoir (*to have to*)	il/elle **dut**	*he/she had to*	ils/elles **durent**	*they had to*
écrire (*to write*)	il/elle **écrivit**	*he/she wrote*	ils/elles **écrivirent**	*they wrote*
éteindre (*to turn off [the light]*)	il/elle **éteignit**	*he/she turned off*	ils/elles **éteignirent**	*they turned off*
faire (*to do*)	il/elle **fit**	*he/she did*	ils/elles **firent**	*they did*
falloir (*to have to*)	il **fallut**	*one had to, it was necessary to*		
introduire (*to introduce*)	il/elle **introduisit**	*he/she introduced*	ils/elles **introduisirent**	*they introduced*
lire (*to read*)	il/elle **lut**	*he/she read*	ils/elles **lurent**	*they read*
mettre (*to put*)	il/elle **mit**	*he/she put*	ils/elles **mirent**	*they put*
mourir (*to die*)	il/elle **mourut**	*he/she died*	ils/elles **moururent**	*they died*
naître (*to be born*)	il/elle **naquit**	*he/she was born*	ils/elles **naquirent**	*they were born*
obtenir (*to obtain*)	il/elle **obtint**	*he/she obtained*	ils/elles **obtinrent**	*they obtained*
offrir (*to offer*)	il/elle **offrit**	*he/she offered*	ils/elles **offrirent**	*they offered*
peindre (*to paint*)	il/elle **peignit**	*he/she painted*	ils/elles **peignirent**	*they painted*
plaire (*to please*)	il/elle **plut**	*he/she pleased*	ils/elles **plurent**	*they pleased*
pleuvoir (*to rain*)	il **plut**	*it rained*		
pouvoir (*can*)	il/elle **put**	*he/she could*	ils/elles **purent**	*they could*
prendre (*to take*)	il/elle **prit**	*he/she took*	ils/elles **prirent**	*they took*
recevoir (*to receive*)	il/elle **reçut**	*he/she received*	ils/elles **reçurent**	*they received*
rire (*to laugh*)	il/elle **rit**	*he/she laughed*	ils/elles **rirent**	*they laughed*
savoir (*to know*)	il/elle **sut**	*he/she knew*	ils/elles **surent**	*they knew*
sourire (*to smile*)	il/elle **sourit**	*he/she smiled*	ils/elles **sourirent**	*they smiled*
tenir (*to hold*)	il/elle **tint**	*he/she held*	ils/elles **tinrent**	*they held*
valoir (*to be worth*)	il/elle **valut**	*it was worth*	ils/elles **valurent**	*they were worth*
venir (*to come*)	il/elle **vint**	*he/she came*	ils/elles **vinrent**	*they came*
vivre (*to live*)	il/elle **vécut**	*he/she lived*	ils/elles **vécurent**	*they lived*
vouloir (*to want*)	il/elle **voulut**	*he/she wanted*	ils/elles **voulurent**	*they wanted*

EXERCICE 25·1

Mettre l'infinitif des verbes suivants.

1. Ils furent de grands collectionneurs. _____
2. J'eus un profond respect pour cet artiste. _____
3. Elles peignirent des natures mortes. _____
4. Nous fîmes un tour de son atelier. _____
5. Il vint nous rejoindre au vernissage. _____
6. Tu lus toutes ses œuvres. _____
7. Vous voulûtes lui faire un compliment. _____
8. Elle sut tout de suite que c'était un chef-d'œuvre. _____
9. Il plut à tout le monde. _____
10. J'éteignis la lumière. _____

EXERCICE 25·2

Mettre au passé simple les verbes entre parenthèses.

1. *Le Rouge et le Noir* (être) _____ publié en 1830.

2. En France, les femmes (obtenir) _____ le droit de vote en 1944.

3. Jacques Cartier (explorer) _____ la région de Montréal en 1535.

4. Charles de Gaulle (mourir) _____ en 1970.

5. Édouard Manet (peindre) _____ *Le déjeuner sur l'herbe* en 1863.

6. La terre (trembler) _____ au Japon en 1923.

7. Catherine de Médicis (introduire) _____ l'usage de la fourchette en France.

8. Le voyage inaugural du TGV (avoir lieu) _____ en 1981.

9. Johnny Hallyday (faire) _____ son premier concert à l'Olympia en 1961.

10. La Côte-d'Ivoire (devenir) _____ indépendante en 1960.

EXERCICE 25·3

Traduire les phrases suivantes en utilisant le passé simple.

1. He lived ten years in Amsterdam.

   _____

2. She introduced this new method.

   _____

3. They read all his books.

   _____

4. He died in Italy.

   _____

5. He was surprised.

   _____

6. I wanted to thank him.

   _____

7. She was born in Rouen.

   _____

8. They bought a new easel.

   _____

346 PRACTICE MAKES PERFECT Complete French All-in-One

9. She became a portrait painter.

_____

10. He smiled and left.

_____

EXERCICE 25·4

*Put the verbs in parentheses into the **passé simple**.*

1. Blanche _____ (être) ravie du bouquet de roses.

2. Il _____ (pleuvoir) pendant toute la semaine.

3. Ils _____ (vivre) à Chamonix pendant dix ans.

4. Je _____ (croire) connaître Ethan.

5. Delphine _____ (devenir) vétérinaire.

6. Elles _____ (manger) avec leurs amis.

7. Je _____ (guérir) rapidement.

8. Tu _____ (naître) au Brésil.

9. Gabriel _____ (admirer) le travail du sculpteur.

10. Joseph _____ (croire) voir un requin.

The passive voice

A sentence can either be in the active or the passive voice. In the active voice, the subject performs the action, while in the **voix passive** (*passive voice*), the subject is acted upon. That is, in the passive voice, the subject and the object exchange roles. Be aware that the passive voice is much more common in English than in French. In French, one tends to use the active voice.

Compare the active and the passive voices.

The active voice:	
Les croisés **envahissent** le pays.	*The crusaders are invading the country.*
La souris **mange** le fromage.	*The mouse eats the cheese.*

The passive voice:	
Le pays **est envahi** par les croisés.	*The country is being invaded by the crusaders.*
Le fromage **est mangé** par la souris.	*The cheese is being eaten by the mouse.*

The simple past, the passive voice, and indirect speech **347**

Formation of the passive voice

The passive voice is formed with **être** in the tense required + the past participle of the main verb.

il **est** construit	it is (being) built
il **a été** construit	it has been built
il **était** construit	it was built
il **fut** construit	it was built
il **sera** construit	it will be built
il **serait** construit	it would be built

VOCABULAIRE

la police	police	**prendre la fuite,**	to flee
le policier	police officer	**s'enfuir**	
arriver sur les lieux du crime	to arrive at the crime scene	**poursuivre**	to chase, to pursue
une fusillade	a shoot-out, a gun battle	**attraper**	to catch
		arrêter	to arrest
passer les menottes à quelqu'un	to handcuff someone	**un attentat**	a terrorist attack
		un détournement d'avion	a hijacking
voler	to steal		
un vol	a theft	**un témoin**	a witness
cambrioler	to burglarize	**un témoignage**	a testimony, a piece of evidence
un cambriolage	a burglary		
un vol à l'étalage	(a case of) shoplifting	**témoigner**	to testify
une agression	a mugging, an assault	**prévenir la police**	to call the police
le harcèlement	harassment	**les empreintes digitales** (f. pl.)	fingerprints
le blanchiment d'argent	money laundering		
le chantage	blackmail	**l'ADN** (m.)	DNA
l'escroquerie (f.)	swindle, fraud	**l'accusé(e)**	the accused
un escroc	a crook	**être condamné(e) à**	to be sentenced to
un meurtre	a murder	**une amende**	a fine
un assassin	a murderer	**une peine**	a sentence
un meurtrier, une meurtrière	a murderer		

EXERCICE 25·5

Mettre les phrases suivantes à la voix passive. Attention aux temps de verbe!

1. Le policier a attrapé le voleur.

2. Le roi a signé le traité.

3. Le médecin prescrit un nouveau traitement.

4. Le cambrioleur a volé le tableau.

5. Le chien a mordu l'homme au chapeau gris.

6. L'ennemi a pris l'otage.

7. L'enfant a déchiré le canapé.

8. Le marchand d'art vendra un célèbre tableau.

9. Les envahisseurs prennent la forteresse.

10. Le professeur félicite les étudiants.

EXERCICE
25·6

Mettre les phrases suivantes à la voix active. Attention aux temps des verbes!

1. Le gâteau a été fait par le chef.

2. L'objet a été conçu par l'artisan.

3. Le château a été érigé par le roi.

4. Le document sera signé par l'ambassadeur.

5. Le tableau a été vendu par le propriétaire.

6. Le fauteuil est griffé par le chat.

7. L'amende a été payée par le malfaiteur.

8. Le vase a été volé par l'antiquaire.

_____

9. Le livre sera écrit par un journaliste.

_____

10. Les élèves sont punis par le professeur.

_____

The agent with **par** and with **de** in the passive voice

In most cases, the agent is introduced by **par**.

Ce rapport **a été fait par** un consultant américain.	_This report was written by an American consultant._
Cette bague **a été retrouvée par** la police.	_This ring was found by the police._
Ce manoir **a été construit par** une famille fortunée.	_This mansion was built by a wealthy family._
Ces éditoriaux **seront écrits par** notre rédacteur en chef.	_These editorials will be written by our editor in chief._

However, the preposition **de** is commonly used after verbs expressing emotion or opinion.

Ce professeur **est apprécié de** ses étudiants.	_This teacher is appreciated by his students._
Ce gérant **est estimé de** ses employés.	_This manager is respected by his employees._

That is, when the **voix passive** is followed by the preposition **de** (rather than **par**), the agent plays a less active role.

Le voleur **est suivi de** ses complices.	_The thief is followed by his accomplices._
Le voleur **est suivi par** la police.	_The thief is followed by the police._
Le château **est entouré de** douves.	_The castle is surrounded by a moat._
Le château **est entouré par** les envahisseurs.	_The castle is surrounded by the invaders._

Uses of the passive voice

The **voix passive** is used to emphasize the subject.

Une écharpe blanche **a été retrouvée** sur les lieux du crime.	_A white scarf was found on the crime scene._
Le témoignage de M. Baulieu **a été entendu** ce matin.	_Mr. Baulieu's testimony was heard this morning._

The **voix passive** is also used to avoid specifying the agent of the action.

Aucune décision ne **sera prise** avant l'arrivée du nouveau directeur.	_No decision will be made before the new director's arrival._
Son incompétence **a été** très **remarquée**.	_His incompetence was clearly noticed._
Aucun rapport n'**a été envoyé**.	_No report was sent._

Avoiding the passive voice in French

The **voix passive** can be replaced by the active voice in French with the following reflexive verbs: **se laisser, se faire, se voir, s'entendre dire**. Note the passive voice forms in the English translations.

Elle **s'est fait faire** une robe pour son mariage.	*She had a dress made for her wedding.*
Il **s'est vu contraint** d'accepter.	*He found himself forced to accept.*
Ils **se sont laissés influencer** très facilement.	*They let themselves be influenced very easily.*

In Chapter 14, you studied one type of pronominal verb called the passive pronominal. This construction is another example of the **voix passive**.

Ça ne **se dit** pas.	*That isn't said.*
Comment ça **se traduit**?	*How is it translated?*
Ça **se voit**.	*It shows.*
Le vin blanc **se boit** frais.	*White wine is to be drunk chilled.*

French often prefers to use the third-person singular form **on** rather than the passive voice construction.

Ici, **on parle anglais**.	*English is spoken here.*
On vous demande au téléphone.	*You are wanted on the phone.*

EXERCICE 25·7

Traduire les phrases suivantes en utilisant la voix passive.

1. The castle is being built by the queen.

2. The painting was stolen by an art dealer.

3. A pink hat was found in the park yesterday.

4. This verb is followed by the indicative (mood).

5. The house is surrounded by the police.

6. A new remedy will be invented before 2050.

7. This vaccine was invented in 1885.

8. The decision was made on Monday.

9. The letter was read by a witness.

10. The house is surrounded by trees.

EXERCICE 25·8

Comment dit-on en français?

1. The vaccine (**Le vaccin**) against rabies (**la rage**) was invented by Louis Pasteur. _____

2. The movie star is followed by the photographers. _____

3. One thief out of three is never caught by the police. _____

4. Fifty people were hired by the airline company. (*to hire* = **embaucher**) _____

5. They (*masc.*) were forced to work. _____

6. In France, the death penalty (**la peine de mort**) was abolished in 1981. _____

7. Some day, a cure (**un remède**) for AIDS (**le sida**) will be discovered. _____

8. The visit has been postponed several times. _____

9. Thanksgiving is celebrated on the fourth Thursday in November. _____

10. The class (**Le cours**) has just been canceled. (*to cancel* = **annuler**) _____

11. Fortunately, nobody was injured in the accident. (*to injure* = **blesser**) _____

12. The ATM (**Le distributeur de billets**) was damaged. _____

13. You (*pol.*) are fired. (*to fire* = **renvoyer**) _____

14. That (**Cela**) has never been done. _____

15. She hopes to be invited. _____

EXERCICE 25·9

Écrivez des phrases à la forme active et à la forme passive avec les éléments donnés. Utilisez le passé composé.

EXEMPLE   Le roman *Madame Bovary* / écrire / Flaubert.

a. *Flaubert a écrit le roman* Madame Bovary.

b. *Le roman* Madame Bovary *a été écrit par Flaubert.*

1. La tour Eiffel / construire / en 1889 / Gustave Eiffel.

    a. _____

    b. _____

2. Les rayons X / découvrir / le physicien allemand Wilhelm Röntgen.

    a. _____

    b. _____

3. « La Marseillaise »* / composer / Rouget de Lisle.

    a. _____

    b. _____

4. Le tableau « Impression, soleil levant » / peindre / Monet.

    a. _____

    b. _____

5. Le poème « Le Lac » / écrire / Lamartine.

    a. _____

    b. _____

---

*"La Marseillaise" is the name of the French national anthem.

The simple past, the passive voice, and indirect speech   **353**

EXERCICE 25·10

Est-ce vrai ou faux?

_____ 1. Le château de Versailles a été construit par le Roi Soleil.

_____ 2. La première ligne du métro parisien a été ouverte en 1900.

_____ 3. La pénicilline a été découverte par Alexander Fleming.

_____ 4. La pièce « Hamlet » a été écrite par Molière.

_____ 5. Les présidents américains sont élus par un collège électoral.

_____ 6. Le président français est élu au suffrage universel direct.

_____ 7. La Bastille a été démolie par les révolutionnaires en 1900.

_____ 8. L'écriture pour les aveugles a été inventée par Louis Braille.

_____ 9. Le roi Louis XVI et sa femme Marie-Antoinette ont été guillotinés.

_____ 10. La Statue de la liberté a été sculptée par un Français.

EXERCICE 25·11

Traduisez en français le texte suivant.

During the last riots, many cars were set on fire and numerous display windows were broken by the rioters. Several stores were looted and merchandise worth several thousand euros was stolen. When the riot police arrived, one person was seriously injured by a Molotov cocktail. The victim (**La victime**) was taken to the hospital where he (**elle**) was operated on immediately. According to the doctors, he is in critical condition. A few people (**personnes** *[f.]*) were taken into custody. They (**Elles**) were sentenced to five months in jail. The juvenile delinquent who had thrown the Molotov cocktail ran away and has not yet been found by the police. As soon as the culprit is caught, he will be arrested and punished. The precise number of victims will be known in the coming days.

VOCABULAIRE

as soon as	**aussitôt que**	to operate	**opérer**
to be in critical condition	**être dans un état critique**	to punish	**sanctionner**
		riot police	**les CRS** *(m.pl.)*
to break	**briser**	rioter	**l'émeutier** *(m.)*
to catch	**attraper**	riots	**les émeutes** *(f.pl.)*
the culprit	**le/la coupable**	to run away	**s'enfuir**
display window	**la vitrine**	to sentence	**condamner**
during	**lors de**	seriously	**grièvement**
in the coming days	**dans les jours qui viennent**	to set on fire	**incendier**
		to take (to the hospital)	**transporter (à l'hôpital)**
juvenile delinquent	**le/la jeune délinquant(e)**	to take into custody	**interpeller**
to loot	**piller**		
merchandise	**les marchandises** *(m.pl.)*	to throw	**lancer**
		worth	**d'une valeur de**
a Molotov cocktail	**un cocktail Molotov**		

Indirect speech

Indirect speech is used, both in English and in French, to relate conversational exchanges or information in the third person.

Direct speech versus indirect speech

In direct speech (**le discours direct**), one says something or asks a question directly.

Quentin demande:	Quentin asks:
« Où allez-vous? »	"Where are you going?"
Pierre dit:	Pierre says:
« Le président est à Milan. »	"The president is in Milan."

In indirect speech (**le discours indirect**), the words of one or more people are reported or a question is asked indirectly. There are no quotation marks.

| Quentin demande **où vous allez**. | Quentin is asking where you are going. |
| Pierre dit **que le président est à Milan**. | Pierre is saying that the president is in Milan. |

Verbs in the main clause of indirect speech are followed by **que** (**où**, **si**, etc.); the verb in the dependent clause is usually in the indicative. Here are some typical main clause verbs:

affirmer	to say, to claim
annoncer	to announce
assurer	to ensure, to maintain
avouer	to confess
confier	to confide
constater	to note, to notice
crier	to shout
déclarer	to state
dire	to say
expliquer	to explain
observer	to notice, to observe
prétendre	to claim
promettre	to promise

The simple past, the passive voice, and indirect speech

remarquer	*to notice, to observe*
répondre	*to answer*
révéler	*to reveal*
s'apercevoir	*to realize*
savoir	*to know*
se rendre compte	*to realize*

Balancing tenses: **la concordance des temps**

If the verb in the main clause is in the present tense, the verb in the dependent clause remains in the same tense as it is in the direct speech.

Paul dit: « Ce n'**est** pas important. »	*Paul says: "It's not important."*
Paul dit que ce n'**est** pas important.	*Paul says it is not important.*
Je lui avoue: « Je **ne suis jamais allé** en Argentine. »	*I admit to him: "I have never been to Argentina."*
Je lui avoue que je **ne suis jamais allé** en Argentine.	*I admit to him that I have never been to Argentina.*
Il répond: « J'**avais** toujours faim quand j'étais jeune. »	*He answers: "I was always hungry when I was young."*
Il répond qu'il **avait** toujours faim quand il était jeune.	*He answers that he was always hungry when he was young.*

VOCABULAIRE

la politique	*politics*	**le droit de vote**	*right to vote*
le pouvoir	*power*	**l'électeur, l'électrice**	*voter*
le gouvernement	*government*	**le scrutin**	*ballot*
gouverner	*to govern*	**le bulletin de vote**	*(paper) ballot*
le/la politique	*politician*	**le suffrage universel**	*universal suffrage*
la gauche	*the left*	**la réforme**	*reform*
la droite	*the right*	**gagner les élections**	*to win the elections*
le centre	*the center*	**perdre les élections**	*to lose the elections*
le parti	*(political) party*	**le sondage**	*poll*
la coalition	*coalition*	**la démocratie**	*democracy*
l'élection (f.)	*election*	**la monarchie**	*monarchy*
la voix	*vote*	**le multipartisme**	*multiparty system*
le premier tour	*first round*	**la parité**	*equality between men and women*
le deuxième tour	*second round*		
élire	*to elect*	**l'abstention** (f.)	*abstention*
être élu(e)	*to be elected*	**boycotter**	*to boycott*
voter	*to vote*		

356 PRACTICE MAKES PERFECT Complete French All-in-One

EXERCICE 25·12

*Mettre les phrases suivantes au discours indirect en commençant la phrase par **Il veut savoir si**.*

1. Le programme du parti est bien défini.

2. Nous allons boycotter les prochaines élections.

3. Tu vas voter dimanche.

4. Le ministre de l'Éducation a proposé des réformes.

5. Elle acceptera notre proposition.

6. Le parti a choisi son candidat.

7. Les femmes peuvent voter dans ce pays.

8. Vous viendrez samedi soir.

9. Elle a fini ses recherches.

10. La parité sera jamais réalisée.

EXERCICE 25·13

Relier les deux membres de phrase.

1. Elle sera absente mardi. (Elle annonce que)

2. Paul s'est trompé. (Ils avouent que)

3. Ses produits sont les meilleurs. (La marchande dit)

4. Elles avaient tort. (Tu sais bien que)

_____

5. Le candidat a peu de chance de gagner. (On se rend compte que)

_____

6. Le musée est ouvert. (Ils ne savent pas si)

_____

7. Tu n'avais rien entendu. (Tu réponds que)

_____

8. Il n'est jamais allé en France. (Elle nous apprend que)

_____

9. Ils avaient dilapidé leur fortune. (Il nous déclare que)

_____

10. Le peintre habite. (Il ignore où)

_____

Learning **la concordance des temps**, that is, agreement of tenses, is one of the most difficult tasks of a French learner. When switching from direct to indirect speech, some changes of tense occur when the main clause verb is in the **passé composé**. Here are the three main scenarios:

Present recounted in the imparfait

If the direct speech is in the present tense, the dependent clause verb is changed into the **imparfait**.

Elle **est** en Inde.	*She is in India.*
J'**ai entendu dire** qu'elle **était** en Inde.	*I heard she was in India.*
Tu **travailles** pour France 2.	*You are working for France 2.*
J'**ai entendu dire** que tu **travaillais** pour France 2.	*I heard you were working for France 2.*
Il **pleut** à Londres.	*It is raining in London.*
J'**ai entendu dire** qu'il **pleuvait** à Londres.	*I heard it was raining in London.*
Ce candidat **a** une chance de gagner.	*This candidate has a chance of winning.*
On m'**a dit** que ce candidat **avait** une chance de gagner.	*I heard this candidate has (had) a chance of winning.*

Passé composé recounted in the plus-que-parfait

If the direct speech is in the **passé composé**, the verb in the dependent clause is changed into the **plus-que-parfait**.

Ils **ont élu** le candidat de gauche.	*They elected the candidate from the left.*
On m'**a dit** qu'ils **avaient élu** le candidat de gauche.	*I heard they had elected the candidate from the left.*

358 PRACTICE MAKES PERFECT Complete French All-in-One

Elle **a expliqué** son programme.	*She explained her program.*
On m'**a dit** qu'elle **avait expliqué** son programme.	*I heard she (had) explained her program.*
Il **a démissionné**.	*He resigned.*
On nous **a dit** qu'il **avait démissionné**.	*We heard he had resigned.*
Vous **avez voté** pour moi.	*You voted for me.*
J'**ai entendu dire** que vous **aviez voté** pour moi.	*I heard you had voted for me.*

Future recounted in the present conditional

If the direct speech is in the future, the dependent clause verb is changed into the **conditionnel** in the indirect speech.

Vous **vous présenterez** aux élections.	*You'll run for election.*
J'**ai entendu dire** que vous **vous présenteriez** aux élections.	*I heard you would run for election.*
Tu **iras** en France.	*You'll go to France.*
J'**ai entendu dire** que tu **irais** en France.	*I heard you would go to France.*
Ils **achèteront** une maison.	*They'll buy a house.*
J'**ai entendu dire** qu'ils **achèteraient** une maison.	*I heard they would buy a house.*
Ils **se retrouveront** à Lyon.	*They'll meet in Lyon.*
J'**ai entendu dire** qu'ils **se retrouveraient** à Lyon.	*I heard they would meet in Lyon.*

EXERCICE
25·14

*Commencer les phrases par **J'ai entendu dire que**. Attention à la concordance des temps.*

1. Tu as accepté leur offre la semaine dernière.

   _____

2. Elle a vendu sa voiture hier.

   _____

3. Tu travailleras à Chicago l'an prochain.

   _____

4. Elle ira en Asie demain.

   _____

5. Ils se sont mariés le mois dernier.

   _____

6. Il fait froid à Moscou aujourd'hui.

   _____

7. Ils s'installeront au Canada l'an prochain.

8. Il a quitté son poste vendredi dernier.

9. Elle est la candidate favorite en ce moment.

10. Tu as pris beaucoup de photos hier soir.

EXERCICE
25·15

*Traduire les phrases suivantes en utilisant **vous** si nécessaire.*

1. They know you are living in Paris.

2. I have heard you are living in Paris.

3. I heard you lived in Paris in 1995.

4. I heard you'll go to Paris next year.

5. He says his cat is adorable.

6. I heard you had a cat.

7. I heard you had a cat when you lived on the Victor Hugo Boulevard.

8. I heard your sister will give you her cat.

9. I was told you voted for me.

10. We realize she has a chance to win.

360 PRACTICE MAKES PERFECT Complete French All-in-One

Pronouns

Subject pronouns

There are many types of pronouns in French. Let's start with the *subject pronouns* you have already used when conjugating verbs.

je	*I*
tu	*you* (singular familiar)
il	*he, it* (masculine)
elle	*she, it* (feminine)
on	*one, we, they, people*
nous	*we*
vous	*you* (singular formal and all plurals)
ils	*they* (masculine, or mixed masculine and feminine)
elles	*they* (feminine)

The third-person pronouns apply to people, animals, or things.

Bertrand est chirurgien.	*Bertrand is a surgeon.*
Il est chirurgien.	*He is a surgeon.*
Les trois sœurs jouent dans le salon.	*The three sisters are playing in the living room.*
Elles jouent dans le salon.	*They are playing in the living room.*
Le chat est assis sur la chaise.	*The cat is sitting on the chair.*
Il est assis sur la chaise.	*It is sitting on the chair.*
La ville est très polluée.	*The city is very polluted.*
Elle est très polluée.	*It is very polluted.*

Remember that there are two ways of saying *you* in French. Use **tu** and its verb forms to talk to friends, family members, children, and animals. Use **vous** when you are addressing a stranger or someone you don't know well, or to maintain a certain degree of distance or respect. Note, however, that the contemporary trend is toward familiarity, especially among peers. It all depends on the setting and the crowd. However, it's always a good idea to let the native French speaker initiate your first exchange with **tu**.

The pronoun **on** has several meanings. It may mean *one*, *we*, or *they* depending on how it is used. **On** can replace an indefinite person.

On voudrait tout réussir.	*One would like to succeed in everything.*
On ne peut pas penser à tout.	*One cannot think of everything.*

361

On means *people* in general. It often refers to habits and customs of a culture.

En France, **on boit** du vin.	*In France, one drinks wine.*
Au Japon, **on boit** du saké.	*In Japan, one drinks sake.*

In informal conversation, **on** takes on the meaning of **nous**.

On va au cinéma cet après-midi?	*Shall we go to the movies this afternoon?*
Julien et moi, **on passe** toujours nos vacances en Corse.	*Julien and I, we always spend our vacation in Corsica.*

Another informal use of **on** replaces the pronoun **tu**.

Ah, **on s'amuse** ici!	*So, we are having fun here!*
Alors, **on se promène** au lieu de faire ses devoirs!	*So, we are taking a walk instead of doing our homework!*

On can also replace a passive voice in English.

Ici, **on parle** anglais.	*English is spoken here.*
On n'a pas encore trouvé de solution.	*A solution has not yet been found.*

VOCABULAIRE

un acteur, une actrice	*an actor, an actress*	**un(e) informaticien(ne)**	*a computer specialist*
un(e) architecte	*an architect*	**un ingénieur**	*an engineer*
un(e) artiste	*an artist*	**un(e) journaliste**	*a journalist*
un(e) avocat(e)	*a lawyer*	**un mannequin**	*a model*
un coiffeur, une coiffeuse	*a hairdresser, a barber*	**un médecin**	*a doctor, a physician*
un(e) commerçant(e)	*a store owner*	**un metteur en scène**	*a film/theater director*
un(e) comptable	*an accountant*	**un(e) musicien(ne)**	*a musician*
un cuisinier, une cuisinière	*a cook*	**un ouvrier, une ouvrière**	*a (factory) worker*
un(e) dentiste	*a dentist*	**un(e) pharmacien(ne)**	*a pharmacist*
un directeur, une directrice	*a manager*	**un(e) photographe**	*a photographer*
un écrivain	*a writer*	**un(e) pilote**	*a pilot*
		un plombier	*a plumber*
		un pompier	*a firefighter*
un homme, une femme d'affaires	*a businessman, -woman*	**un professeur**	*a teacher, a professor*
un(e) fleuriste	*a florist*	**un rédacteur, une rédactrice**	*an editor*
un infirmier, une infirmière	*a (hospital) nurse*	**une sage-femme**	*a midwife*
		un serveur, une serveuse	*a waiter, a waitress*

Direct object pronouns

Another type of pronoun is the *direct object pronoun* (**le pronom objet direct**). In English there are seven direct object pronouns: *me, you, him, her, it, us, them.* Note that in French there are two forms of the direct object pronoun *you*: the informal **te** and the formal or plural **vous**. English distinguishes between a direct object pronoun that replaces a person (*him* or *her*) or a thing (*it*); in French **le, la, les** can replace both people and things. **Les** refers to both masculine and feminine. **Me, te, le,** and **la** become **m', t',** and **l'** before vowels and mute **h**.

362 PRACTICE MAKES PERFECT Complete French All-in-One

SINGULAR		PLURAL	
me (m')	*me*	**nous**	*us*
te (t')	*you* (familiar)	**vous**	*you* (plural or formal)
le (l')	*him* or *it* (masculine)	**les**	*them* (masc. and fem.)
la (l')	*her* or *it* (feminine)		

Pronouns allow speakers to avoid being repetitious, to make communication more efficient, and to link ideas across sentences. An object is called *direct* if it immediately follows the verb without a preposition. The direct object pronoun replaces the direct object noun. In French, the direct object pronoun agrees in gender and number with the noun it replaces. Note that the French direct object pronoun precedes the verb. In a sentence with auxiliary or compound verbs, the direct object pronoun precedes the verb to which it directly refers. The direct object pronoun can replace a noun with a definite article (**le**, **la**, **les**), with a possessive adjective (**mon**, **ton**, **son**, etc.), or with a demonstrative adjective (**ce**, **cet**, **cette**, **ces**).

L'artiste **chante la chanson**.	*The artist sings the song.*
L'artiste **la chante**.	*The artist sings it.*
Quentin **appelle son ami**.	*Quentin calls his friend.*
Quentin **l'appelle**.	*Quentin calls him.*
Il **prend la décision**.	*He makes the decision.*
Il **la prend**.	*He makes it.*
L'infirmier **soigne ses patients**.	*The nurse takes care of his patients.*
L'infirmier **les soigne**.	*The nurse takes care of them.*
Il **m'appelle**.	*He is calling me.*
Nous **vous remercions**.	*We thank you.*
Elle **t'invite**.	*She invites you.*
Ils **nous accueillent**.	*They greet us.*

In a negative sentence, the direct object pronoun also comes immediately before the conjugated verb.

Nous n'acceptons **pas l'offre**.	*We do not accept the offer.*
Nous **ne l'acceptons pas**.	*We do not accept it.*
Ils **ne** comprennent **pas la question**.	*They do not understand the question.*
Ils **ne la** comprennent **pas**.	*They do not understand it.*
Elle **ne** suit **pas les directives**.	*She does not follow the directions.*
Elle **ne les** suit **pas**.	*She does not follow them.*

In the interrogative form, when using the inversion, the direct object pronoun comes immediately before the verb.

Connaissez-vous **ce dentiste**?	*Do you know this dentist?*
Le connaissez-vous?	*Do you know him?*
Approuvez-vous **sa décision**?	*Do you approve of his decision?*
L'approuvez-vous?	*Do you approve of it?*
Aimez-vous **les chansons de Brel**?	*Do you like Brel's songs?*
Les aimez-vous?	*Do you like them?*
Emmenez-vous **les enfants** au cirque?	*Are you taking the children to the circus?*
Les emmenez-vous au cirque?	*Are you taking them to the circus?*

When an infinitive has a direct object, the direct object pronoun immediately precedes the infinitive.

Pouvez-vous contacter **le journaliste**?	*Can you contact the journalist?*
Pouvez-vous **le** contacter?	*Can you contact him?*
Il doit finir **son article**.	*He must finish his article.*

Pronouns **363**

Il doit **le** finir.	*He must finish it.*
Je vais lire tous **les documents**.	*I am going to read all the documents.*
Je vais tous **les** lire.	*I am going to read all of them.*
Nous venons de voir **son nouveau film**.	*We just saw his new film.*
Nous venons de **le** voir.	*We have just seen it.*

In the **passé composé** and other compound tenses, the direct object pronoun is placed before the auxiliary verb. The past participle agrees in number and gender when the direct object precedes the verb.

Le journaliste a pris **les photos**.	*The journalist took the pictures.*
Le journaliste **les** a pris**es**.	*The journalist took them.*
Le comptable avait trié tous **ces papiers**.	*The accountant had sorted all these papers.*
Le comptable **les** avait tous triés.	*The accountant had sorted them all out.*
Le pompier a éteint **les flammes**.	*The fireman extinguished the flames.*
Le pompier **les** a éteint**es**.	*The fireman extinguished them.*
Le guitariste a joué **ses morceaux favoris**.	*The guitarist played his favorite pieces.*
Le guitariste **les** a joués.	*The guitarist played them.*

In the affirmative imperative, the direct object pronoun follows the verb. **Me (m')** and **te (t')** change to **moi** and **toi**. Remember to link the verb to the pronoun with a hyphen. In the negative imperative, the direct object pronoun remains before the verb.

Appelez **Jacques**!	*Call Jacques!*
Appelez-**le**!	*Call him!*
Rendez **les clés** à Antoine!	*Give the keys back to Antoine!*
Rendez-**les** à Antoine!	*Give them back to Antoine!*
Achetez **ces fleurs**!	*Buy these flowers!*
Achetez-**les**!	*Buy them!*
N'éteins pas **la lumière**!	*Do not turn off the light!*
Ne **l'**éteins **pas**!	*Do not turn it off!*
N'appelle pas **Caroline** si tard!	*Do not call Caroline so late!*
Ne **l'**appelle **pas** si tard!	*Do not call her so late!*
Invitez-**moi** à la soirée, s'il vous plaît.	*Please invite me to the party.*

EXERCICE 26·1

Remplacer les mots en caractères gras par un pronom objet direct.

1. Elle achète **les fleurs bleues**. _____
2. Il consulte **le médecin**. _____
3. Nous soutenons **votre projet**. _____
4. Ils construisent **la maison de leurs rêves**. _____
5. J'ouvre **la porte**. _____
6. Elle conduit **la voiture de son père**. _____
7. Il accepte **les résultats**. _____
8. Nous comprenons **leur décision**. _____
9. Tu visites **le château de Fontainebleau**. _____
10. Elle étudie **sa leçon**. _____

EXERCICE 26·2

*Traduire les phrases suivantes en utilisant **vous** et l'inversion si nécessaire.*

1. He thanks me. _____
2. The writer sends them. _____
3. They invite us. _____
4. We accept it. _____
5. She called them. _____
6. Bring them! _____
7. I am going to buy it. _____
8. Do not sell it! _____
9. We must see it. _____
10. Do you know her? _____

Indirect object pronouns

Now that you have mastered the **pronom objet direct**, let's take a look at the **pronom objet indirect** (*indirect object pronoun*).

In English there are five indirect object pronouns *me, you, him, her, us*. As always, French distinguishes between an informal *you* (**te**) and a formal or plural *you* (**vous**). The French indirect object pronoun does not, however, distinguish gender; **lui** and **leur** replace both masculine and feminine nouns. In French, the indirect object pronoun replaces only animate indirect objects (people, animals). Inanimate ideas and things are replaced with the indirect object pronouns **y** and **en**, which will be discussed later in this chapter. Let's look at the indirect object pronouns:

SINGULAR		PLURAL	
me (m')	*me*	**nous**	*us*
te (t')	*you* (familiar)	**vous**	*you* (formal or plural)
lui	*him, her*	**leur**	*them* (masc. and fem.)

The object is called *indirect* when the verb is controlled by a preposition (**parler à, répondre à, écrire à**, etc.). The indirect object pronoun is placed before the conjugated verb and before **avoir** in the compound tenses. Although the past participle agrees in gender and number with the *preceding* direct object, the past participle *never* agrees with an indirect object pronoun. The indirect object pronouns **me** and **te** become **m'** and **t'** before vowels and mute **h**. Make sure to distinguish between **leur**, the indirect object pronoun, and **leur(s)**, the possessive adjective.

Tu parles **au journaliste**.	*You are talking to the journalist.*
Tu **lui** parles.	*You are talking to him.*
Tu réponds **à Andrée**.	*You answer Andrée.*
Tu **lui** réponds.	*You answer her.*
Vous écrivez **à l'agent**.	*You write to the agent.*
Vous **lui** écrivez.	*You write to him.*
Vous expliquez la situation **aux clients**.	*You explain the situation to the customers.*
Vous **leur** expliquez la situation.	*You explain the situation to them.*

Pronouns

Elle **nous** enverra une confirmation.	*She'll send us a confirmation.*
Je **vous** donnerai un jour de congé.	*I'll give you a day off.*
Il **me** rendra le livre demain.	*He'll return the book to me tomorrow.*
Ils **t'**apporteront des fleurs.	*They'll bring you some flowers.*

In the interrogative or negative, the indirect object pronoun is placed immediately before the verb.

Lui as-tu parlé de ce livre?	*Did you talk to him about this book?*
M'avez-vous envoyé un courriel?	*Did you send me an e-mail?*
Vous fournit-il de bons produits?	*Does he provide you with good products?*
Leur avez-vous envoyé les révisions?	*Did you send them the revisions?*
Elle **ne nous** envoie **jamais** rien.	*She never sends us anything.*
Tu **ne m'**apportes **que** des mauvaises nouvelles.	*You only bring me bad news.*
Vous **ne lui** avez **pas** dit la vérité.	*You did not tell him the truth.*
Ils **te** prêteront leur voiture.	*They'll lend you their car.*

Indirect object pronouns in the imperative

In the affirmative imperative, the indirect object pronoun follows the verb. **Me (m')** and **te (t')** become **moi** and **toi**. Remember to link the verb to the following pronoun with a hyphen. In the negative imperative, the indirect object pronoun remains before the verb.

Téléphone-**moi** demain matin!	*Call me tomorrow morning!*
Prêtez-**lui** votre dictionnaire!	*Lend him your dictionary!*
Apportez-**nous** de nouveaux accessoires!	*Bring us new props!*
Envoyez-**leur** le script!	*Send them the script!*
Ne lui donnez **rien**!	*Don't give him anything!*
Ne nous téléphonez **pas** si tard!	*Don't call us so late!*

EXERCICE 26·3

Remplacer les mots en caractères gras par un pronom objet indirect.

1. La grand-mère a raconté une histoire **aux petits-enfants**.

2. Nous avons fait un cadeau **à Marie**.

3. Je ferai parvenir le dossier **à Jean** dès que possible.

4. Nous enverrons des fleurs **à notre collègue**.

5. Ce théâtre appartient **à un ancien comédien**.

6. Est-ce que tu as écrit **au rédacteur en chef**?

7. Téléphonez **à Louise** aussitôt que possible!

8. Ne mentionnez rien **à Odile**!

9. Il annoncera sa décision **à ses employés** demain.

10. Il donnera le scénario **aux acteurs** en fin de journée.

EXERCICE 26·4

*Traduire les phrases suivantes en utilisant **tu** et l'inversion si nécessaire.*

1. Bring me a book!

2. Do not call them after eight P.M.!

3. Send us your new play!

4. I will write him a letter.

5. She'll give me an answer on Monday.

6. He did not return the books to me.

7. This pen belongs to her.

8. He does not talk to us.

9. They told us a good story.

10. They'll lend you their house for the weekend.

Pronouns **367**

The pronoun y

Y is an indirect object pronoun that precedes the verb. It usually replaces an inanimate object (thing or idea). The object replaced by **y** is considered indirect because it is preceded by a preposition, usually the preposition **à**, but sometimes **sur**.

Elle répond **à l'annonce**.	She answers the ad.
Elle **y** répond.	She answers it.
Ils s'habituent **à cette ville**.	They are getting used to this city.
Ils s'**y** habituent.	They are getting used to it.
Nous pensons **à la situation**.	We are thinking about the situation.
Nous **y** pensons.	We are thinking about it.
Tu t'intéresses **à cette pièce**?	Are you interested in this play?
Tu t'**y** intéresses?	Are you interested in it?

In the **passé composé** and other compound tenses the indirect object pronoun **y** is placed before the auxiliary verb. Note that the past participle *does not* agree in gender or number with the indirect object **y**.

Ils ont réfléchi **à cette question**.	They thought about this issue.
Ils **y** ont réfléchi.	They thought about it.
Nous avons répondu **à vos questions**.	We answered your questions.
Nous **y** avons répondu.	We answered them.
Il a renoncé **à sa carrière**.	He gave up his career.
Il **y** a renoncé.	He gave it up.
Je n'ai pas goûté **à cette sauce**.	I did not taste this sauce.
Je n'**y** ai pas goûté.	I did not taste it.

EXERCICE
26·5

Remplacer les éléments en caractères gras par y.

1. Elle s'habitue **à tout**.

2. Tu devrais prêter attention **à ce qu'il dit**.

3. Nous nous intéressons **à son œuvre**.

4. Je m'abonne **à ce magazine**.

5. Elle tient **à ses bijoux**.

6. Nous ne croyons pas **à cette nouvelle théorie scientifique**.

7. Il ne pense jamais **aux conséquences de ses actes**.

8. Ils n'obéissent pas **à la loi**.

9. Elle réfléchira **au rôle que vous lui proposez**.

10. Pourquoi n'avez-vous jamais répondu **à notre demande**?

The pronoun en

En is an indirect object pronoun that precedes the verb. It usually replaces an inanimate object (thing or idea) preceded by **de**. The pronoun **en** immediately precedes the verb, except in the affirmative imperative where it follows the verb.

Nous nous occuperons **de tous les détails**.	We'll take care of all the details.
Nous nous **en** occuperons.	We'll take care of them.
Elle ne se souvient pas **de cette histoire**.	She does not remember this story.
Elle ne s'**en** souvient pas.	She does not remember it.
Avez-vous peur **de sa réaction**?	Are you afraid of his reaction?
En avez-vous peur?	Are you afraid of it?

In the **passé composé** and other compound tenses the indirect object pronoun **en** is placed before the auxiliary verb. Note that the past participle *does not* agree in gender and number with the indirect object **en**.

Il a parlé **de sa nouvelle idée** à Théo.	He talked about his new idea to Théo.
Il **en** a parlé à Théo.	He talked about it to Théo.
Elle s'est chargée **de cette affaire difficile**.	She took care of this difficult business.
Elle s'**en** est chargée.	She took care of it.
Je me suis approché **des remparts**.	I came closer to the ramparts.
Je m'**en** suis approché.	I came closer to them.
Tu t'es débarrassé **de toutes ces choses inutiles**.	You got rid of all these useless things.
Tu t'**en** es débarrassé.	You got rid of them.

EXERCICE
26·6

*Remplacer les éléments en caractères gras par le pronom **en**.*

1. J'ai parlé **de tous nos problèmes**.

2. Ils ont envie **d'aller en France en mai**.

3. Nous avons besoin **d'un logiciel plus performant**.

4. Il s'est approché **du château** très lentement.

5. Je me chargerai **de tout ce qui facilitera son séjour à Aix**.

6. Tu te sers **de ce dictionnaire**?

7. Il a peur **des changements**.

8. Je ne me souviens pas **de sa conférence**.

9. Elle s'est occupée **des réservations**.

10. Il ne pourra jamais se débarrasser **de ses livres de l'école primaire**.

EXERCICE 26·7

Faire correspondre les deux colonnes.

_____ 1. Il a peur   a. d'un ordinateur portable

_____ 2. Elle s'intéresse   b. à un magazine hebdomadaire

_____ 3. Je me sers   c. du nom de l'hôtel

_____ 4. Ils ne se souviennent pas   d. à ce nouveau candidat

_____ 5. Tu t'abonnes   e. des insectes

The order of object pronouns

When a direct and indirect pronoun appear in the same sentence, the indirect object pronoun comes first, unless the direct and indirect pronouns are in the third person, in which case the direct object pronoun comes first.

INDIRECT OBJECT	DIRECT OBJECT
me (m')	
te (t')	+ le, la, l', les
nous	
vous	

Elle **te** donne **le rôle**.	*She gives you the part.*
Elle **te le** donne.	*She gives it to you.*
Nous **vous** envoyons **le contrat**.	*We are sending you the contract.*
Nous **vous** l'envoyons.	*We are sending it to you.*
Vous **nous** montrez **les costumes**.	*You show us the costumes.*
Vous **nous les** montrez.	*You show them to us.*
Il **m'**offre **la bague de sa mère**.	*He gives me his mother's ring.*
Il **me** l'offre.	*He gives it to me.*

If the direct and indirect pronouns in the third person are combined, the direct object pronoun comes first.

DIRECT OBJECT	INDIRECT OBJECT
le (l') la (l') } les	+ **lui, leur**

J'envoie **la lettre au rédacteur**.	*I send the letter to the editor.*
Je **la lui** envoie.	*I send it to him.*
Elle tend **le document au médecin**.	*She hands the document to the doctor.*
Elle **le lui** tend.	*She hands it to him.*
Nous offrons **ce livre aux participants**.	*We give this book to the participants.*
Nous **le leur** offrons.	*We give it to them.*
Nous montrons **la route aux touristes**.	*We show the road to the tourists.*
Nous **la leur** montrons.	*We show it to them.*

In the **passé composé** and other compound tenses, the direct object pronoun is placed before the auxiliary verb. The past participle agrees in number and gender with the direct object when the direct object precedes the verb.

Il a écrit **ces articles**.	*He wrote these articles.*
Il **les** a écrit**s**.	*He wrote them.*
Elle a fait **ces tartes délicieuses**.	*She made these delicious pies.*
Elle **les** a fait**es**.	*She made them.*
J'ai envoyé **les lettres**.	*I sent the letters.*
Je **les** ai envoyé**es**.	*I sent them.*
Tu as mis **ta nouvelle chemise**.	*You put on your new shirt.*
Tu **l'**as mis**e**.	*You put it on.*

When **en** is combined with an indirect object pronoun, it is always in second position. The past participle *does not* agree in number and gender with **en** (nor does it agree with any other indirect object pronoun).

Elle **lui** a offert **des fleurs**.	*She gave her some flowers.*
Elle **lui en** a offert.	*She gave her some.*
Il **leur** a donné **des explications**.	*He gave them some explanations.*
Il **leur en** a donné.	*He gave them some.*
Nous **lui** avons prêté **de la farine**.	*We lent him some flour.*
Nous **lui en** avons prêté.	*We lent him some.*
Tu **nous** enverras **des photos**.	*You'll send us some pictures.*
Tu **nous en** enverras.	*You'll send us some.*

Pronouns **371**

EXERCICE 26·8

Remplacer les éléments en caractères gras par les pronoms appropriés.

1. Ne parlez pas **de ce détail à Zoé**!

2. Elle a emprunté **de l'argent à sa sœur**.

3. Je ferai parvenir **ce document à votre avocat.**

4. Patrick a raconté **ses aventures** (*f.pl.*) **à son frère**.

5. Le musicien a envoyé **sa nouvelle composition à son agent**.

6. L'ouvrier a donné **la lettre au patron**.

7. J'ai demandé **la photo au photographe**.

8. Il vendra **sa maison à son cousin**.

9. Le médecin **a prescrit ce médicament au malade**.

10. Je recommande **cet hôtel à tous mes amis**.

EXERCICE 26·9

*Traduire les phrases suivantes en utilisant **tu** si nécessaire.*

1. I am thinking about it.

2. He is not interested in it.

3. She took care of it.

372 PRACTICE MAKES PERFECT Complete French All-in-One

4. I sent it (*f.*) to you.

_____

5. We gave it (*m.*) to them.

_____

6. I use it every day.

_____

7. He spoke about it.

_____

8. I need it.

_____

9. She borrowed some from me.

_____

10. They gave us some.

_____

Disjunctive pronouns

There are many ways to use *disjunctive pronouns*, also known as stressed or tonic pronouns.

moi	*me*	**nous**	*us*
toi	*you*	**vous**	*you*
lui	*him*	**eux**	*them*
elle	*her*	**elles**	*them* (feminine)

The disjunctive pronouns can be used to add extra *emphasis* to a thought.

Lui, c'est un grand musicien!	*He is a great musician!*
Moi, je déteste les lentilles!	*I hate lentils!*
Lui, il est toujours contre tout!	*He is always against everything!*
Elle, c'est vraiment ma meilleure amie!	*She is really my best friend!*

Disjunctive pronouns are used after **c'est** or **ce sont** in order to stress identification. In this case, they are used where English would use intonation.

C'est moi qui ai trouvé la solution.	*I found the solution.*
C'est lui qui a raison.	*He is right.*
C'est toi qui dois aller les chercher.	*You have to go pick them up.*
Ce ne sont pas eux qui pourront le faire!	*They won't be able to do it!*

You'll find disjunctive pronouns in conjunction with another subject.

Bruno et moi, nous allons à Tokyo.	*Bruno and I are going to Tokyo.*
Lui et sa mère, ils sont toujours d'accord sur tout.	*He and his mother always agree on everything.*
Toi et ta collègue, vous avez gâché la soirée!	*You and your colleague spoiled the party!*

Pronouns **373**

Elle et Michel, ce sont les meilleurs voisins.	*She and Michel are the best neighbors.*

Disjunctive pronouns are also used as one-word questions or answers when there isn't a verb present.

Qui était absent hier? —**Moi!**	*Who was absent yesterday? —I was.*
Qui ne veut pas travailler le dimanche? —**Nous!**	*Who does not want to work on Sundays? —We don't!*
Elle aime le chocolat. **Moi aussi.**	*She likes chocolate. So do I.*
Elle n'aime pas le bruit. **Moi non plus.**	*She does not like noise. Neither do I.*

The disjunctive pronouns can also be used to solicit an opinion or ask for a contrasting piece of information.

Lui, il est pharmacien. **Et elle**, qu'est-ce qu'elle fait?	*He is a pharmacist. And what does she do?*
Moi, je pense que cette décision est absurde. **Et toi**, quelle est ton opinion?	*I think this decision is absurd. And what is your opinion?*
Eux, ils ne dépensent jamais un centime! **Et lui**, est-ce qu'il est moins radin?	*They never spend a cent! Is he less cheap?*
Elle, elle a toujours de la chance. **Et lui**, a-t-il la même veine?	*She is always lucky. Does he have the same luck?*

You'll see disjunctive pronouns used after a preposition.

Qu'est-ce qu'il a **contre eux**?	*What does he have against them?*
Cet employé travaille **pour nous**.	*This employee works for us.*
Vous allez **chez eux** ce soir?	*Are you going to their place tonight?*
Il n'achète rien **sans elle**.	*He never buys anything without her.*

Disjunctive pronouns are also used with **être** to indicate possession.

À qui est cette écharpe? —C'est **à moi**!	*Whose scarf is it? —It's mine!*
À qui sont ces gants? —Ce sont **à lui**!	*Whose gloves are these? —They are mine!*
C'est **à toi**? —Non, ce n'est pas à moi!	*Is it yours? —No, it's not mine!*

You can use disjunctive pronouns to make comparisons.

Caroline est **plus** intelligente **que lui**.	*Caroline is brighter than he is.*
Il court **plus** vite **que toi**.	*He runs faster than you do.*
Ils sont **aussi** riches **qu'elle**.	*They are as rich as she is.*
Elle n'est pas **aussi** douée **que vous**.	*She is not as gifted as you are.*

You can use disjunctive pronouns with -**même** (-*self*) to reinforce the pronoun.

Elle rédige tous ses discours **elle-même**.	*She writes all her speeches herself.*
Écrivez-le **vous-même**!	*Write it yourself!*
C'est **lui-même** qui l'a dit.	*He said it himself.*
On est **soi-même** conscient de ses propres erreurs.	*One is aware of one's own mistakes.*

Disjunctive pronouns are used with certain verbs when the indirect object is a *person*. Compare:

Je parle **de ce film**.	*I am talking about this film.*
J'**en** parle.	*I am talking about it.*

374 PRACTICE MAKES PERFECT Complete French All-in-One

and

Je parle **de ce metteur en scène**.	*I am talking about this film director.*
Je parle **de lui**.	*I am talking about him.*
Je pense **à ce livre**.	*I am thinking about this book.*
J'**y** pense.	*I am thinking about it.*

and

Je pense **à cette photographe**.	*I am thinking about this photographer.*
Je pense **à elle**.	*I am thinking about her.*
Tu as besoin **de cet avocat**.	*You need this lawyer.*
Tu as besoin **de lui**.	*You need him.*
Nous parlons **de nos enfants**.	*We are talking about our children.*
Nous parlons **d'eux**.	*We are talking about them.*
Fais attention **à cet homme**!	*Watch out for this man!*
Fais attention **à lui**!	*Watch out for him!*
Il a peur **de son professeur de chimie**.	*He is afraid of his chemistry teacher.*
Il a peur **de lui**.	*He is afraid of him.*
Nous tenons **à nos amis**.	*We are attached to our friends.*
Nous tenons **à eux**.	*We are attached to them.*
Elle songe **à son fils**.	*She is thinking about her son.*
Elle songe **à lui**.	*She is thinking about him.*

If a reflexive verb is followed by an animate indirect object (person, animal), the disjunctive pronoun is used and placed after the verb.

Nous nous intéressons **à cette candidate**.	*We are interested in this candidate.*
Nous nous intéressons **à elle**.	*We are interested in her.*
Elle s'est débarrassée **de cet employé incompétent**.	*She got rid of this incompetent employee.*
Elle s'est débarrassée **de lui**.	*She got rid of him.*
Il ne veut pas s'occuper **de vos enfants**.	*He does not want to take care of your children.*
Il ne veut pas s'occuper **d'eux**.	*He does not want to take care of them.*
Nous nous méfions **de ce consultant**.	*We do not trust this consultant.*
Nous nous méfions **de lui**.	*We do not trust him.*

EXERCICE 26·10

Mettre en relief le pronom sujet avec un pronom disjoint en utilisant l'expression **C'est... qui**.

1. **Il** a gagné le prix.

2. **Je** prendrai la décision.

3. **Vous** écrirez le discours.

4. **Nous** préparons le dîner.

5. **Tu** as fait cette erreur.

6. **Elle** lui fait toujours de beaux cadeaux.

7. **Je** vous ai invité.

8. **Ils** sont responsables de cette situation désastreuse.

9. **Elles** s'occuperont de tous les détails.

10. **Il** fait les courses.

EXERCICE 26·11

*Traduire les phrases suivantes en utilisant un pronom disjoint et la forme **tu** si nécessaire.*

1. He will go to France with me.

2. I hate coffee!

3. She works for us.

4. Whose book is this?

5. Do it yourself!

6. I can't make this decision without you.

7. He is taller than you are.

8. I am thinking about her.

9. They are afraid of him.

10. She said it herself.

EXERCICE 26·12

*Formuler une question-réponse en reliant les phrases et en utilisant **aussi** ou **non plus**.*

1. Il n'aime pas le froid. Je n'aime pas le froid.

2. Nous allons en France. Ils vont en France.

3. Je prends des vacances. Elle prend des vacances.

4. Nous commandons un dessert. Elles commandent un dessert.

5. Il lit beaucoup. Nous lisons beaucoup.

Possessive pronouns

Possessive pronouns replace nouns used with possessive adjectives. They agree in gender and number with the noun they replace, not with the possessor.

MASCULINE SINGULAR		FEMININE SINGULAR	
le mien	*mine*	**la mienne**	*mine*
le tien	*yours*	**la tienne**	*yours*
le sien	*his/hers*	**la sienne**	*his/hers*
le nôtre	*ours*	**la nôtre**	*ours*
le vôtre	*yours*	**la vôtre**	*yours*
le leur	*theirs*	**la leur**	*theirs*

MASCULINE PLURAL		FEMININE PLURAL	
les miens	*mine*	**les miennes**	*mine*
les tiens	*yours*	**les tiennes**	*yours*
les siens	*his/hers*	**les siennes**	*his/hers*
les nôtres	*ours*	**les nôtres**	*ours*
les vôtres	*yours*	**les vôtres**	*yours*
les leurs	*theirs*	**les leurs**	*theirs*

Pronouns   377

J'apporte mes notes et tu apportes **les tiennes**.	I bring my notes and you bring yours.
Tu fais tes devoirs et elle fait **les siens**.	You do your homework and she does hers.
Nous aimons votre chien et vous aimez **le nôtre**.	We like your dog and you like ours.
Les leurs sont de grande valeur.	Theirs are quite valuable.
Vous prenez vos billets et nous prenons **les nôtres**.	You take your tickets and we take ours.

When the possessive pronoun is preceded by **à** or **de**, the article is contracted as shown below.

Il a téléphoné à son avocat et elle a téléphoné **au sien**.	He called his lawyer and she called hers.
Elle a besoin de mon aide et tu as besoin **de la sienne**.	She needs your help and you need hers.

Expressing possession with être + à

Remember that the most common way of expressing possession is by using **être** + **à** + the disjunctive pronoun.

Cette valise **est à moi**.	This suitcase is mine.
Ce blouson en cuir **est à lui**.	This leather jacket is his.
Ces vélos **sont à eux**.	These bikes are theirs.
Ces journaux **sont à elles**.	These newspapers are theirs.

When one wants to stress the ownership or identify different items of a similar nature, the possessive pronoun is used.

C'est **le sien**? —Non, c'est **le mien**!	Is it his? —No, it's mine!
C'est ton avis et c'est aussi **le sien**.	It's your opinion and it's also his.

Contrary to English, sometimes a possessive adjective rather than a possessive pronoun is required in French.

C'est **un de vos associés**?	Is he a business partner of yours?
C'est **un de mes collègues**.	He is a colleague of mine.

Possessive pronouns are also used in idiomatic expressions.

À la tienne!	Cheers! (informal singular)
À la vôtre!	Cheers! (formal or plural)
Après des mois de cauchemar, elle est de nouveau **parmi les siens**.	After some nightmarish months, she is back with her family again.
Leur benjamin a encore **fait des siennes**!	Their youngest son has been acting up again!
Il faut **y mettre du tien**!	You have to make an effort!
Si elle n'**y met** pas **du sien**, elle ne réussira jamais.	If she does not make an effort, she'll never succeed.

EXERCICE
26·13

Traduire les pronoms possessifs entre parenthèses.

1. Mes documents sont en anglais. (*His*) _____ sont en français.

2. Ses parents viennent d'Écosse. (*Mine*) _____ viennent d'Irlande.

3. Il n'a pas trouvé son acte de naissance. Voici (*mine*) _____ .

4. Nous avons choisi notre itinéraire. Avez-vous choisi (*yours*) _____?

5. Elle a fini son roman. As-tu fini (*yours*) _____?

6. Ses idées sont étranges. Et (*theirs*) _____ aussi.

7. Je suis vos conseils et je vous demande de suivre (*ours*) _____.

8. Mon blouson est en cuir marron et (*hers*) _____ est en cuir noir.

9. Ton plat est trop épicé et (*mine*) _____ est trop salé.

10. Mon neveu est trop âgé et (*his*) _____ est trop jeune pour ce spectacle.

EXERCICE
26·14

*Traduire les phrases suivantes en utilisant **vous** si nécessaire.*

1. My family is larger than yours.

   _____

2. Our situation is more difficult than his.

   _____

3. Her brothers are younger than she is.

   _____

4. Their city is cleaner than ours.

   _____

5. My exercise is more advanced than theirs.

   _____

6. Your dog is more handsome than his.

   _____

7. Our neighbors are nicer than yours.

   _____

8. Your winters are colder than ours.

   _____

9. Their products are more expensive than yours.

   _____

10. Your children are more active than mine.

   _____

Pronouns **379**

Possessive pronouns with **aussi** and **non plus**

The possessive pronoun is also often used with **aussi** and **non plus** to confirm an affirmative or negative statement.

Son appartement coûtait cher.
   —Le mien aussi.
Nos meubles sont très modernes.
   —Les miens aussi.
Vos réponses ne sont pas correctes.
   —Les siennes non plus.
Son appartement n'est pas bruyant.
   —Le tien non plus.

His apartment was expensive.
   —So was mine.
Our furniture is very modern.
   —So is mine.
Your answers are not right.
   —His either. (Nor are his.)
His apartment is not noisy.
   —Yours either. (Nor is yours.)

Demonstrative pronouns

Earlier, you studied the demonstrative adjectives **ce, cet, cette, ces** (*this, that, these, those*) used to point out things and people.

ce restaurant	*this restaurant*	**cette galerie**	*this gallery*
ces chaises	*these chairs*	**ces bagues**	*these rings*

A demonstrative pronoun replaces a demonstrative adjective + a noun. It agrees in gender and number with the noun it replaces. It can refer to people or things. In a sentence, it can be the subject or object of the verb and be followed by **que, qui, de,** or another prepositional phrase.

Singular

celui	*the one* (masculine)	**celle**	*the one* (feminine)

Plural

ceux	*the ones* (masc.; masc. and fem.)	**celles**	*the ones* (feminine)

Cette dame est **celle qui habitait**
   autrefois à côté.
Il a adopté la méthode de Gérard.
   —Non, c'est celle de Francine.
À qui est ce téléphone?
   —C'est celui de Juliette?

That woman is the one who used to live
   next door.
He adopted Gérard's method.
   —No, it's Francine's.
Whose phone is it?
   —Is it Juliette's?

Compound demonstrative pronouns

Compound demonstrative pronouns are used to compare elements of the same nature or to indicate a choice between two objects or two people. The particles **-ci** and **-là** are added to demonstrative pronouns to indicate *this one, that one,* etc.

Singular

celui-ci	*this one* (masculine)	**celui-là**	*that one* (masculine)
celle-ci	*this one* (feminine)	**celle-là**	*that one* (feminine)

Plural

ceux-ci	*these* (*ones*) (masc.; masc. and fem.)	**ceux-là**	*those* (*ones*) (masc.; masc. and fem.)
celles-ci	*these* (*ones*) (fem.)	**celles-là**	*those* (*ones*) (feminine)

Celui-ci est en argent. **Celui-là** est en or.	*This one is silver. That one is gold.*
Celle-ci coûte cher. **Celle-là** est bon marché.	*This one is expensive. That one is cheap.*
Ceux-ci sont vrais. **Ceux-là** sont faux.	*These are real. Those are fake.*
Celles-ci sont belles. **Celles-là** sont laides.	*These are beautiful. Those are ugly.*

Note that **celui-ci** (**celle-ci**) and **celui-là** (**celle-là**) may carry a condescending or derogatory meaning when used to talk about a person who is not present. Therefore, be careful if you decide to use it to refer to a person.

Tu connais son frère?	*Do you know his brother?*
—Ah, **celui-là**! Il est odieux!	*—Ah, that one! He is obnoxious!*
Tu as posé la question à ta voisine?	*Did you ask your neighbor?*
—Ah, **celle-là**, je ne lui adresse jamais la parole!	*—Ah! That one! I don't talk to her!*

The demonstrative pronoun ce

The demonstrative pronoun **ce** (**c'**) is invariable and is often the subject of the verb **être**. It refers to an idea previously introduced. The adjective following **ce** (**c'**) is always in the masculine even if it refers to a feminine antecedent. See the example sentences below:

Les erreurs qu'elle a faites! **C'est idiot!**	*The mistakes she made! It's so stupid!*
Cette ville en hiver! **C'est si beau!**	*This city in the winter! It's so beautiful!*

Ceci, cela, and ça

The indefinite demonstrative pronouns **ceci** (*this*), **cela** (*that*), and **ça** (*this/that,* familiar) refer to indefinite things or ideas. **Ceci** may initiate a statement and also announce a following sentence. **Cela** may reflect on something already mentioned.

Mangez **ceci**!	*Eat this!*
Enlevez **cela**!	*Remove that!*
Ceci n'est pas une pipe.	*This is not a pipe.*
Ça, c'est de l'art!	*That's (really) art!*
Ça ne fait rien.	*It does not matter.*
Ça m'est égal.	*I don't mind.*

EXERCICE 26·15

*Traduire les phrases suivantes en utilisant **tu** et l'inversion si nécessaire.*

1. What dress are you going to wear? —The one (that) I bought in Paris.

2. What do you think of his new novel? —It's awful!

3. What are these rings made of? —This one is gold and that one is silver.

Pronouns

4. What do you think of my new house? —It's beautiful!

5. What dishes can we prepare? —We can prepare the ones you prefer.

6. Are these films available? —This one is available but that one is not.

7. Are they subtitled? —This one is subtitled in French and that one is in German.

8. Their children like games but not the ones that are difficult.

9. Look at these two books. Do you think my mother would like this one or that one?

10. Here are two bracelets. This one is Indian. That one is Egyptian.

EXERCICE 26·16

Remplacer l'adjectif démonstratif par le pronom démonstratif.

1. Cette robe est rose. Cette robe est blanche.

2. Ces écrivains sont inconnus. Ces écrivains sont célèbres.

3. Cet oncle est jeune. Cet oncle est plus âgé.

4. Ce rendez-vous est trop tôt. Ce rendez-vous est trop tard.

5. Ce roman est un best-seller. Ce roman est épuisé.

6. Cet ordinateur est vieux. Cet ordinateur est le dernier modèle.

7. Cette peinture est trop claire. Cette peinture est trop foncée.

8. Ces articles sont bien écrits. Ces articles sont mal écrits.

9. Cette valise est légère. Cette valise est lourde.

10. Ces arguments sont bons. Ces arguments sont nuls.

EXERCICE 26·17

*Traduire les phrases suivantes en utilisant des expressions idiomatiques contenant un pronom possessif et la forme **tu** si nécessaire.*

1. After ten difficult years, she went back to her family.

2. My friend René is not at ease among his peers.

3. His young dog has been acting up again!

4. Their granddaughter has been acting up again in school!

5. Cheers! It's your birthday.

6. You are going to lose everything if you don't make an effort!

7. If he does not contribute his share, the presentation will be a disaster!

Relative pronouns

It is essential to know how to connect several elements in the same sentence. One way to link ideas back to persons and things already mentioned is by using **pronoms relatifs** (*relative pronouns*). Relative pronouns link two sentences, making one dependent on the other. The dependent phrase is also called the subordinate clause; it contains a verb, but usually cannot stand alone. Choosing the correct relative pronoun depends on its function in the sentence (subject, direct object, or object of a preposition).

Qui

Let's start with the relative pronoun **qui** used as a subject. **Qui** may refer to people or things and may mean *who, whom, which, what,* or *that.*

J'écoute la personne **qui parle**.	*I am listening to the person who is speaking.*
Il aime les histoires **qui finissent** bien.	*He likes stories that end well.*
Elle remercie la cousine **qui l'a invitée**.	*She thanks the cousin who invited her.*
Nous félicitons l'artiste **qui a pris** cette photo.	*We congratulate the artist who took this picture.*

Note that the **-i** of **qui** is *never* dropped in front of a vowel sound (see above: **qui a pris**). **Qui** as a *subject* precedes the verb in the dependent clause.

When **qui** is the *subject* of the dependent clause, the verb following **qui** agrees with the noun or pronoun that **qui** replaces.

C'est **moi qui lui ai vendu** cette lampe.	*I am the one who sold him this lamp.*
C'est **toi qui es** responsable.	*You are the one who is responsible.*
C'est **vous qui avez restauré** cette chaise?	*Did you restore (Was it you who restored) this chair?*
C'est **vous qui êtes** le propriétaire?	*Are you the owner?*

VOCABULAIRE

un(e) antiquaire	*an antiques dealer*	**une vente aux enchères**	*an auction*
		faire une offre	*to bid*
un marché aux puces	*a flea market*	**baisser le prix**	*to lower the price*

marchander	*to bargain*	une lampe	*a lamp*
un meuble	*a piece of furniture*	une lampe de chevet	*a bedside lamp*
les meubles (*m.pl.*)	*furniture*	un miroir	*a mirror*
une chaise	*a chair*	une coiffeuse	*a dressing table*
un tabouret	*a stool*	un vase	*a vase*
une table	*a table*	un secrétaire	*a writing desk*
une table basse	*a coffee table*	une commode	*a chest of drawers*
un fauteuil	*an armchair*	un coffre	*a chest*
un canapé	*a sofa*	une bibliothèque	*a bookcase, a library*
un buffet	*a sideboard*	une étagère	*a shelf*
un lit	*a bed*	un tapis	*a rug*
un placard	*a closet, a cupboard*	une horloge	*a clock*
une penderie	*a wardrobe, a closet*	un rideau	*a curtain*
une armoire	*a wardrobe, a cupboard*	cher, chère	*expensive*
une armoire à pharmacie	*a medicine cabinet*	bon marché	*cheap, inexpensive*

EXERCICE

27·1

Conjuguer les verbes entre parenthèses au présent.

1. C'est moi qui (être) _____ en charge de l'exposition.

2. C'est lui qui (suivre) _____ l'affaire.

3. C'est nous qui (avoir) _____ les documents d'authenticité.

4. Ce sont eux qui (pouvoir) _____ prendre cette décision.

5. C'est elle qui (savoir) _____ la vérité.

6. C'est moi qui (avoir) _____ l'armoire de grand-mère.

7. C'est vous qui (devoir) _____ nous aider à choisir.

8. C'est lui qui (faire) _____ la restauration.

9. C'est toi qui (écrire) _____ l'article?

10. C'est eux qui (vouloir) _____ acheter ce buffet.

Que

When the dependent clause introduced by a relative pronoun already has a subject noun or pronoun, the relative pronoun **que** (*whom, which, that*) is used. Like **qui**, the relative pronoun **que** refers to both people and things.

Elle n'aime pas le cadre **que vous lui montrez**.	*She does not like the frame you are showing her.*
Voici le lustre **que Daniel a acheté**.	*Here's the chandelier Daniel bought.*

Relative pronouns **385**

J'ai contacté l'ébéniste **que tu as recommandé**.	*I contacted the cabinetmaker you recommended.*
Rends-moi le livre **que je t'ai prêté**.	*Give me back the book I lent you.*

In the following sentences, note that the **-e** of **que** is dropped before a vowel (**qu'**).

Les articles **qu'il vend** sont chers.	*The items he sells are expensive.*
Les statues **qu'il a chez lui** viennent d'Afrique.	*The statues that he has at home come from Africa.*
L'article **qu'elle écrit** sera publié en mai.	*The article she is writing will be published in May.*
Les objets **qu'ils fabriquent** sont de grande valeur.	*The objects they make are of great value.*

In the compound tenses, if the direct object is placed before the verb, the past participle agrees in gender and number with that direct object. This includes sentences where **que** (**qu'**) refers back to a direct object noun. See the following examples:

C'est **la table en marbre que** nous avons trouvé**e** au marché aux puces.	*Here's the marble table we found at the flea market.*
La pièce qu'il a écrit**e** n'a jamais été jouée.	*The play he wrote was never performed.*
Montrez-moi **la photo que** vous avez prise.	*Show me the picture you took.*
Les chaises qu'ils ont restaurées sont comme neuves.	*The chairs they restored look new.*

Note the following sentences where **qui** is the *object* of the verb in the dependent clause. In this case, a subject noun or pronoun comes between **qui** and the verb form. Remember that the **-i** of **qui** is never dropped.

Je ne sais pas **qui il est**.	*I don't know who he is.*
Le président n'a pas dit **qui il nommerait** à ce poste.	*The president did not say who(m) he would appoint to this position.*
Nous ignorons **qui elle renverra**.	*We don't know who(m) she'll fire.*
Le policier a révélé **qui il avait attrapé**.	*The police officer revealed who(m) he had caught.*

EXERCICE
27·2

Qui ou que?

1. Le magasin _____ se trouve place d'Italie a beaucoup de choix.

2. L'antiquaire _____ elle a conseillé est fermé le dimanche.

3. Tu veux me vendre le coffre _____ est dans le salon?

4. Les manteaux sont dans le placard _____ est à gauche de la porte.

5. Le livre _____ je lis en ce moment est passionnant.

6. Les clients _____ sont dans le magasin sont indécis.

7. Il choisit toujours des gravures _____ je déteste.

8. Achète quelque chose _____ fera plaisir aux enfants.

9. Le dessert _____ tu as acheté est délicieux.

10. Il n'est pas satisfait du tableau _____ il peint.

EXERCICE 27·3

Faire correspondre les deux colonnes.

_____ 1. Les chemises   a. qu'elle a lu

_____ 2. Les documents   b. qu'ils ont racontée

_____ 3. Le livre   c. qu'elle a lavées

_____ 4. L'histoire   d. que tu as prises

_____ 5. Les photos   e. qu'il a consultés

The relative clause is often inserted into the main clause. Note again that **qui** and **que** can refer to either people or things.

La commode **qui est dans la vitrine**, a appartenu à Talleyrand.	*The chest of drawers that is in the window belonged to Talleyrand.*
L'homme **que vous voyez au fond de l'atelier** est un des meilleurs artisans du pays.	*The man you see in the back of the shop is one of the best craftsmen in the country.*

Lequel

When verbs are followed by prepositions, the relative pronouns **qui** (*whom*), **quoi** (*what*), **lequel, laquelle, lesquels, lesquelles** (*that, which, whom*) are used. The preposition precedes these pronouns. **Qui** refers only to people; **quoi** is an indefinite thing or object; and **lequel, laquelle, lesquels, lesquelles** refer to specific things. (**Lequel, laquelle, lesquels, lesquelles** may also be used for people; but this use is less common.)

C'est l'antiquaire **à qui** je pensais. (*Less common:* C'est l'antiquaire auquel je pensais.)	*He's the antiques dealer I was thinking about.*
C'est le tableau **auquel** je pensais.	*It is the painting (that) I was thinking about.*
Tu sais **à quoi** il pense?	*Do you know what he is thinking about?*
C'est **le client pour lequel** je travaille.	*It's the client for whom I am working.*
C'est **la société pour laquelle** je travaille.	*It's the company for which I am working.*
Voici **le collègue avec qui** j'écris le rapport.	*Here is the colleague with whom I am writing the report.*
Les outils avec lesquels il travaille appartenaient à son père.	*The tools with which he is working belonged to his father.*
Je vous présente **la personne sans qui** je n'aurai pas pu réussir.	*Let me introduce you to the person without whom I would not have been able to succeed.*

Relative pronouns

| Merci pour **ces documents sans lesquels** je n'aurais pas pu authentifier ces œuvres. | *Thank you for these documents without which I would not have been able to authenticate these works.* |

Note that **qui** cannot be used with the preposition **parmi** (*among*).

| **Plusieurs peintres, parmi lesquels** celui-ci, étaient nés en Angleterre. | *Several painters, among whom this one, were born in England.* |

EXERCICE 27·4

Compléter avec un pronom relatif en utilisant la préposition entre parenthèses.

1. La femme, _____ je restaure ces meubles, est australienne. (pour)
2. La route _____ nous devons passer, est dangereuse. (par)
3. Le tissu _____ il recouvre le canapé, est de la soie sauvage. (avec)
4. L'époque _____ ils s'intéressent, est le dix-neuvième siècle. (à)
5. Les livres _____ je fais mes recherches, sont à Sylvie. (avec)
6. Le fauteuil _____ il est assis, appartenait à sa tante. (dans)
7. Le poste _____ elle aspire, sera vacant d'ici la fin de l'année. (à)
8. Les amis, _____ nous avons déjeuné dimanche, ont une belle collection de gravures. (chez)
9. Il pense à ses vacances? À ses projets? Je ne sais pas _____ il pense. (à)
10. Merci à Julie _____ ce projet n'aurait jamais vu le jour. (sans)

Où

The relative pronoun **où**, referring to a place, often replaces **dans lequel**, **sur lequel**, **par lequel**, etc. **Où** is more common in modern language.

C'est **le magasin dans lequel** je fais mes courses.	*It's the store where I do my shopping.*
C'est **le magasin où** je fais mes courses.	*It's the store where I do my shopping.*
La région dans laquelle ils habitent est très calme.	*The area where they live is very quiet.*
La région où ils habitent est très calme.	*The area where they live is very quiet.*

The relative pronoun **où** is also used when the antecedent expresses time.

| Tu te souviens de **l'année où** il est arrivé dans la région? | *Do you remember the year (when) he arrived in the region?* |
| **Le jour où** il a été élu, tout le monde était content. | *The day (when) he was elected, everyone was happy.* |

L'instant **où** nous sommes partis, il a commencé à pleuvoir.	The moment (when) we left, it started to rain.
Le dix-neuvième siècle fut **un siècle où** il y eut de nombreuses inventions.	The nineteenth century was a century (when) there were many inventions.

Dont

The relative pronoun **dont** acts as an object of the main clause and can refer to both people and things. It is used to refer to objects of verbs or verbal expressions that include the preposition **de**. (You may wish to review the verbs and their prepositions in Chapter 21.)

Il **a besoin de** ces documents.	He needs these documents.
Voici les documents **dont il a besoin**.	Here are the documents he needs.
Elle **se sert d'**un pinceau.	She uses a paintbrush.
Montrez-moi le pinceau **dont elle se sert**.	Show me the paintbrush she uses.
Tu **as parlé d'**un souffleur de verre.	You talked about a glassblower.
Où habite le souffleur de verre **dont tu nous as parlé**?	Where does the glassblower you told us about live?
Elle **est fière de** son fils.	She is proud of her son.
Denis est le fils **dont elle est fière**.	Denis is the son she is proud of.

In modern French, **dont** usually replaces **duquel**, **de laquelle**, **desquels**, and **desquelles**.

Le marchand **dont** (**duquel**) **je me souviens** est à Saint-Ouen.	The merchant I remember is in Saint-Ouen.
Les forgerons, **dont** (**desquels**) **je parle** dans mon roman, vivent dans ce quartier.	The blacksmiths I talk about in my book live in this neighborhood.

Dont is also used to express possession (*whose, of whom, of which*). After this construction, the word order is subject + verb + object.

Un artisan, **dont j'ai aussi rencontré le père**, m'a encouragé à devenir verrier.	A craftsman, whose father I also met, encouraged me to become a glassworker.
Ils ont des voisins **dont les amis sont bergers**.	They have neighbors whose friends are shepherds.

EXERCICE 27·5

*Compléter avec **qui**, **que** ou **dont**.*

1. L'artisan _____ tu parles est à la retraite.

2. Le film _____ nous regardons est sous-titré.

3. Le dictionnaire _____ ils se servent est bilingue.

4. Le cadre _____ vous plaît n'est pas à vendre.

5. Les pinceaux _____ elle a besoin sont dans l'autre atelier.

6. Le livre d'art _____ est sur la table appartient à un client.

7. Le seul incident _____ je me souviens c'est celui-ci.

8. Le coussin _____ tu regardes est en soie.

9. La maison _____ ils veulent acheter est en Camargue.

10. Les ouvriers _____ il est content recevront une augmentation de salaire.

EXERCICE 27·6

*Traduire les phrases suivantes en utilisant **vous** si nécessaire.*

1. I can remember the year he opened his shop.

2. The chandelier he bought is for the living room.

3. The tool with which she is working is very old.

4. Are you the owner?

5. The armchair you are sitting on belonged to my grandfather.

6. The city where they live is quite beautiful.

7. I know the person he is talking about.

8. It's the only detail I remember.

9. The documents you need are at Valérie's.

10. I don't know what he is thinking about.

Ce que, ce qui, ce dont, ce à quoi

When there is no specific word or antecedent for the relative pronoun to refer to, the antecedent **ce** is combined with the pronoun. **Ce qui**, **ce que**, **ce dont**, and **ce à quoi**, all meaning *what*, refer to ideas, not to persons, and do not have gender or number. Choosing the correct indefinite relative pronoun again depends on the pronoun's function in the sentence (subject, direct object, or object of a preposition). Here again, it will be useful to review the verbs and their prepositions in Chapter 21.

Ce qui is used as the subject of the dependent clause.

J'aime **ce qui est fabriqué** dans cet atelier.	*I like what is made (what they make) in this workshop.*
Il ne sait pas **ce qui a provoqué** leur réaction.	*He does not know what triggered their reaction.*
Qui sait **ce qui est arrivé**?	*Who knows what happened?*
J'aimerais savoir **ce qui lui plairait**.	*I'd like to know what she would like.*

Ce que is used as the direct object of the dependent clause.

Savez-vous **ce qu'il fait** ces jours-ci?	*Do you know what he is doing these days?*
Tu comprends **ce que ce journaliste écrit** (**ce qu'écrit ce journaliste**)?	*Do you understand what this journalist writes?*
Ils ont fait **ce qu'il ne fallait pas faire**.	*They did what shouldn't have been done.*
Elle écrit **ce qu'elle vit**.	*She writes what she lives.*

Ce dont is used when verbs take the preposition **de**.

Elle ne comprend pas **ce dont il a peur**. (avoir peur de)	*She does not understand what he's afraid of.*
Fais-moi voir **ce dont tu te sers**. (se servir de)	*Show me what you use.*
La police veut savoir **ce dont elle se souvient**. (se souvenir de)	*The police want to know what she remembers.*
Je m'intéresse à **ce dont vous avez parlé** ce matin. (parler de)	*I am interested in what you talked about this morning.*

Ce à quoi is used with verbs that take the preposition **à**.

J'ignore **ce à quoi il s'abonne**. (s'abonner à)	*I don't know what he subscribes to.*
C'est exactement **ce à quoi je m'attendais** de sa part. (s'attendre à)	*It's exactly what I expected from him.*
Ils ne savent pas **ce à quoi tu t'opposes**. (s'opposer à)	*They don't know what you are opposed to.*
Je voudrais savoir **ce à quoi elle aspire**. (aspirer à)	*I'd like to know what she is aspiring to.*

The indefinite relative pronouns **ce qui**, **ce que**, **ce à quoi**, and **ce dont** are frequently placed at the beginning of a sentence to stress a point. This construction compensates for the English intonation that is much more marked. When a verb requires a preposition, it is repeated in the second clause.

Ce qui est amusant, c'est les marchés aux puces.	*Flea markets are fun!*
Ce qu'elle adore, c'est acheter des vieilles chaises.	*She loves buying old chairs!*
Ce dont il a envie, c'est **de** cet automate.	*What he'd like is this automaton!*
Ce à quoi il s'intéresse, c'est **à** l'aromathérapie.	*He is interested in aromatherapy!*

Relative pronouns **391**

EXERCICE 27·7

*Compléter par **ce qui, ce que, ce à quoi** ou **ce dont**.*

1. _____ ils s'intéressent, c'est à l'opéra.

2. _____ elle se souvient, c'est de son enfance en Indochine.

3. _____ ils aiment, c'est l'art déco.

4. _____ tu as envie est beaucoup trop cher.

5. _____ j'ai besoin, c'est de votre aide.

6. _____ est arrivé hier risque d'avoir des conséquences graves.

7. _____ je ne comprends pas, c'est son indifférence.

8. _____ est fascinant, c'est sa collection.

9. _____ il parle n'a aucun intérêt.

10. _____ je décris dans mon roman, c'est le paysage savoyard.

EXERCICE 27·8

*Traduire les phrases suivantes en commençant par **ce qui, ce que, ce à quoi** ou **ce dont**.*

1. What he wants is more free time.

   _____

2. What the glassblower uses is in the other workshop.

   _____

3. What I can't remember is this incident in Camargue.

   _____

4. What I expected was different.

   _____

5. What he needs is this book.

   _____

6. What they are talking about is interesting.

   _____

7. What he does is difficult.

   _____

8. What she is interested in is this art collection.

   _____

392 PRACTICE MAKES PERFECT Complete French All-in-One

9. What they love is chocolate.

10. What happened last night is very sad.

The relative pronouns **qui** and **que** can sometimes be followed by the subjunctive. If there is a doubt about the existence of someone or the possible realization of anything, the subjunctive may be used after the relative pronoun.

Il cherche un artisan **qui puisse restaurer** ce fauteuil Louis XV.
Connaîtriez-vous un antiquaire **qui vende des pièces rares**?

He is looking for an artisan who might be able to restore this Louis XV armchair.
Would you know of an antiques dealer who sells rare coins?

When the antecedent of the relative pronoun **qui** or **que** is a superlative such as **le plus** (*the most*), **le moins** (*the least*), **le seul** (*the only*), **l'unique** (*the unique*), **le premier** (*the first*), **le dernier** (*the last*), etc., the subjunctive may be used.

Paolo est **le meilleur artisan qui vende** des objets à Burano.
C'est **le seul marché aux puces que je connaisse** dans cette ville.

Paolo is the best artisan who sells pieces in Burano.
It's the only flea market I know in this city.

EXERCICE 27·9

Compléter avec le pronom relatif qui convient.

1. Pourquoi la bibliothèque, _____ est dans le coin à gauche, est-elle si chère?
2. L'artiste _____ tu parles vit actuellement à Paris.
3. La chaise sur _____ elle est assise a besoin d'être repeinte.
4. _____ j'ai envie, c'est de faire le tour du monde.
5. Le chinois est une langue étrangère _____ est très utile de nos jours.
6. Je ne comprends pas _____ vous demandez.
7. C'est un lustre _____ vient d'Espagne.
8. Les objets _____ il s'intéresse sont du dix-huitième siècle.
9. L'ottoman _____ je veux faire recouvrir appartenait à un des mes ancêtres.
10. _____ est fait, est fait.

Adjectives

Agreement of adjectives

To describe things and people, we use qualificative adjectives. In French, adjectives agree in gender and number with the noun they modify. The feminine form of an adjective is very often created by adding an -**e** to the masculine form.

Frank est **allemand**.	*Frank is German.*
Heidi est **allemande**.	*Heidi is German.*
Le jardin est **grand**.	*The garden is big.*
La fille de Vincent est **grande**.	*Vincent's daughter is tall.*

Note that the final consonant **d** of **allemand** and **grand** is silent, while the **d** of **alleman*d*e** and **gran*d*e** is pronounced.

If an adjective ends with an -**e** in the masculine form, the feminine form remains the same.

Cet homme est **coupable**.	*This man is guilty.*
Cette femme est **coupable**.	*This woman is guilty.*
Cet éléphant est **énorme**.	*This elephant is huge.*
Cette baleine est **énorme**.	*This whale is huge.*

Note several irregular feminine forms of adjectives:

Il est **vietnamien**.	*He is Vietnamese.*
Elle est **vietnamienne**.	*She is Vietnamese.*
Marco est **italien**.	*Marco is Italian.*
Stefania est **italienne**.	*Stefania is Italian.*
Charles est **généreux**.	*Charles is generous.*
Caroline est **généreuse**.	*Caroline is generous.*
Ce produit est **dangereux**.	*This product is dangerous.*
Cette route est **dangereuse**.	*This road is dangerous.*
Ce jeu est **interactif**.	*This game is interactive.*
Cette activité est **interactive**.	*This activity is interactive.*
Cet employé est très **passif**.	*This employee is very passive.*
Cette femme est très **passive**.	*This woman is very passive.*
C'est un **faux** témoignage.	*It's perjury.*
C'est une **fausse** alerte.	*It's a false alarm.*

Many adjectives are simply irregular. See the boldfaced adjectives in the following list. Note the special forms of these adjectives when they precede a masculine singular noun that starts with a vowel:

Ce jeu est **fou**.	*This game is crazy.*
Tu as vu le film *Docteur **fol** amour*?	*Have you seen the film* Dr. Strangelove?

394

Cette idée est **folle**.	*This idea is crazy.*
Ce château est **vieux**.	*This castle is old.*
Ce **vieil édifice** appartenait à un prince.	*This old building belonged to a prince.*
Cette maison est **vieille**.	*This house is old.*
Son **nouveau** patron est suédois.	*His new boss is Swedish.*
Son **nouvel emploi** est ennuyeux.	*Her new job is boring.*
Ma **nouvelle** voiture est grise.	*My new car is gray.*
Ce village est très **beau**.	*This village is very beautiful.*
Ce **bel homme** est son cousin.	*This handsome man is her cousin.*
Quelle **belle** histoire!	*What a beautiful story!*
Le pelage de ce chien est **roux**.	*This dog's coat is red.*
Est-elle **rousse?**	*Is she a redhead?*

VOCABULAIRE

beige	*beige*	**orange**	*orange*
blanc, blanche	*white*	**rose**	*pink*
bleu(e)	*blue*	**rouge**	*red*
bleu ciel	*sky blue*	**vert(e)**	*green*
bleu clair	*light blue*	**vert olive**	*olive green*
bleu foncé	*dark blue*	**violet(te)**	*purple*
bleu marine	*navy blue*	**à carreaux**	*checked*
bordeaux	*burgundy*	**à rayures**	*striped*
gris(e)	*gray*	**à fleurs**	*flowered*
jaune	*yellow*	**à pois**	*polka-dotted*
marron	*brown*	**à volants**	*flounced*
noir(e)	*black*	**à plis**	*pleated*
ocre	*ochre*		

The placement of adjectives

As you continue studying French, you'll become familiar with the irregular feminine forms of certain adjectives. What is often more difficult is knowing where to place adjectives. In French, most qualificative adjectives follow the noun.

Carole aime les **plats italiens**.	*Carole loves Italian dishes.*
Danielle préfère la **cuisine chinoise**.	*Danielle prefers Chinese cooking.*
Il porte des **chaussures noires**.	*He is wearing black shoes.*
C'est un **remède efficace**.	*This is an effective remedy.*

Some adjectives precede the noun. You just need to memorize them.

C'est un **long trajet**.	*It's a long commute.*
C'est une **longue distance**.	*It's a long distance.*
C'est un **beau compliment**.	*It's a beautiful compliment.*
J'adore cette **belle chanson**.	*I love this beautiful song.*
Son **nouveau livre** est un polar.	*His new book is a detective novel.*
Sa **nouvelle armoire** est magnifique.	*His new armoire is magnificent.*
C'est un **bon prix**.	*It's a good price.*
C'est une **bonne affaire**.	*It's a good deal.*
C'est un **mauvais signe**.	*It's a bad sign.*
C'est une **mauvaise critique**.	*It's a bad review.*
Je déteste mon **vieux canapé**.	*I hate my old couch.*

Adjectives **395**

Cette **vieille maison** est à vendre.	*This old house is for sale.*
Ce **jeune chef** est vraiment doué.	*This young chef is really talented.*
Cette **jeune femme** est écrivain.	*This young woman is a writer.*

Beware: Some adjectives have different meanings, depending on whether they precede or follow the noun.

son ancien mari	*her former husband*	**une statue ancienne**	*an antique statue*
ma chère Carole	*my dear Carole*	**un cadeau cher**	*an expensive gift*
Notre pauvre chien!	*Our poor dog!*	**des pays pauvres**	*poor countries*
sa propre idée	*his own idea*	**une nappe propre**	*a clean tablecloth*
une sale affaire	*a nasty business*	**une fenêtre sale**	*a dirty window*
un grand homme	*an important man*	**une femme grande**	*a tall woman*
le dernier métro	*the last subway train*	**l'an dernier**	*last year*

Adjectives of color

Adjectives describing colors usually agree in gender and number with the noun they modify.

Elle a les **yeux verts**.	*She has green eyes.*
Il a acheté des **chemises blanches**.	*He bought some white shirts.*
Les **fleurs** sur la table sont **rouges**.	*The flowers on the table are red.*
En hiver, cette **pièce** est **froide**.	*In the winter, this room is cold.*
Ses trois **chats** sont **noirs**.	*His three cats are black.*
Tes **lunettes** sont **nouvelles**?	*Are your glasses new?*

Adjectives of color that are also nouns of fruit or plants generally remain in the masculine singular form.

Ces **chaussures orange** sont moches.	*These orange shoes are ugly.*
Mon frère a les **yeux marron**.	*My brother has brown (chestnut-colored) eyes.*
Ces **échantillons safran** sont parfaits!	*These saffron-colored samples are perfect!*

Another exception: **les adjectifs composés**. When two adjectives are combined to provide more specificity, both adjectives generally remain in the masculine singular form.

Cette peinture **vert clair** ne me plaît pas.	*I don't like this light-green paint.*
Sa veste **gris foncé** lui va très bien.	*Her dark gray jacket suits her well.*
Ces robes **rose bonbon** sont trop voyantes.	*These candy pink dresses are too flashy.*
Achète ces coussins **bleu azur**!	*Buy these azur blue cushions!*
Sa fille a les cheveux **châtain clair**.	*Her daughter has light-brown hair.*

EXERCICE 28·1

Traduire les adjectifs entre parenthèses.

1. Ta grand-mère est (*French*)? —Non, elle est (*Italian*).

_____

2. Ces fenêtres sont (*clean*)? —Non, ces fenêtres sont (*dirty*).

_____

3. Sa femme est (blond)? —Non, elle est (redhead).

4. Il porte ses chaussures (black)? —Non, il porte des chaussures (navy blue).

5. C'est une situation (serious)? —Oui, c'est une situation très (serious).

6. C'est une histoire (tragic)? —Non, c'est une histoire (funny).

7. C'est un (long) voyage? —Non, c'est assez (short).

8. Votre projet est (ambitious). —Non, c'est la directrice qui est (ambitious).

9. Ses idées sont (good)? —Oui, ses idées sont (better) que les nôtres.

10. Ton travail est (boring)? —Non, mon travail est très (interesting).

EXERCICE 28·2

Choisir l'adjectif logique.

1. Les antiquités sont _____ méchantes/vieilles/courtes.
2. Mon chat est _____ adorable/bavard/immense.
3. Le musée du Louvre est _____ brave/dernier/fascinant.
4. Le professeur d'italien est _____ silencieux/intéressant/final.
5. Sa nouvelle histoire est _____ première/folle/violette.

EXERCICE 28·3

Mettre les adjectifs au féminin en remplaçant Patrick par Sonia.

1. Patrick est français. Sonia est _____.
2. Patrick est charmant. Sonia est _____.
3. Patrick est amoureux. Sonia est _____.

4. Patrick est beau. Sonia est _____ .

5. Patrick est agressif. Sonia est _____ .

6. Patrick est actif. Sonia est _____ .

7. Patrick est fou. Sonia est _____ .

8. Patrick est généreux. Sonia est _____ .

9. Patrick est roux. Sonia est _____ .

10. Patrick est doué. Sonia est _____ .

Comparatives and superlatives
Comparison of adjectives and adverbs

In French, comparisons of adjectives and adverbs can take three forms, **plus... que** (*more . . . than*), **moins... que** (*less . . . than*), **aussi... que** (*as . . . as*). For example:

Ce modèle est **plus** récent **que** le mien.	*This model is more recent than mine.*
New York est **plus** grand **que** San Francisco.	*New York is bigger than San Francisco.*
Marc est **moins** riche que **Paul**.	*Mark is less rich than Paul.*
Luc est **aussi** célèbre **que** Bertrand.	*Luc is as famous as Bertrand.*

Comparison of nouns

To compare quantities, use the following expressions. Note the use of **de (d')** with expressions of quantity:

Elle a **plus de** temps **que** Valérie.	*She has more time than Valérie.*
Il a **moins de** chance **que** toi.	*He is less lucky than you are.*
Elle a **autant de** jouets **que** toi.	*She has as many toys as you do.*

Irregular comparatives

Some comparatives have irregular forms.

Ce livre est **bon**.	*This book is good.*
Ce livre-ci est **meilleur que** ce livre-là.	*This book is better than that book.*
Il se porte **bien**.	*He's feeling well.*
Il se porte **mieux qu'**avant.	*He is feeling better than before.*
La situation économique est **mauvaise**.	*The economic situation is bad.*
La situation économique est **pire qu'**avant.	*The economic situation is worse than before.*
Cela n'a pas **le moindre** intérêt.	*That does not have the slightest interest.*

Superlatives

To express the ideas of *the most, the least, the best, the worst,* etc., one uses the *superlative*. To form the superlative in French, simply precede the comparative form by the definite article. Note that before naming a group or entity, the superlative is followed by **de** + the definite article.

C'est **le plus grand** spectacle **du monde**.
C'est **la plus belle** histoire que j'aie jamais lue.
C'est l'endroit **le moins ennuyeux de toute la ville**.

It's the greatest show on earth.
It's the most beautiful story I ever read.
It's the least boring place in the whole city.

The irregular adjectives you learned with the comparatives are also used in the superlative.

Ce roman est **bon**.
C'est son **meilleur** roman.
C'est un **mauvais** cauchemar.
C'est son **pire** cauchemar.

This novel is good.
It's his best novel.
It's a bad nightmare.
It's his worst nightmare.

EXERCICE 28·4

Traduire les éléments entre parenthèses.

1. Je suis (*more optimistic*) que lui.

2. Cécile est (*as efficient*) que Carole.

3. Ce vin-ci est (*better*) que ce vin-là.

4. Sa sœur est (*as intelligent*) qu'elle.

5. Votre chambre est (*less expensive*) que la mienne.

6. Arnaud a (*as much*) argent que vous?

7. Ce prix est (*the best*)!

8. Marie a (*fewer*) paires de chaussures que toi.

9. Elle est (*more organized*) que lui.

10. Cet appartement est (*the most beautiful*) de l'immeuble.

EXERCICE 28·5

Formuler une phrase avec les éléments ci-dessous.

1. Charlotte/Lucie/grande/+

2. Charles/Xavier/drôle/=

3. Véronique/Sébastien/optimiste/−

4. Lucien/sa sœur/intelligent/+

5. Élodie/Thérèse/bronzée/=

EXERCICE 28·6

Traduire les phrases suivantes.

1. It's a good idea.

2. They bought an old house in Normandy.

3. This young man is ambitious.

4. This white shirt is mine.

5. Her aunt loves old French songs.

6. I do not have your new address.

7. England is smaller than France.

8. She does not like this yellow jacket.

9. She is as ambitious as he is.

10. This story is boring.

EXERCICE 28·7

Faire correspondre les deux colonnes.

_____ 1. Il travaillait ici dans le passé.   a. Elles sont toutes sales.

_____ 2. Ils n'ont pas d'argent.   b. Elle mesure 1,80 m.

_____ 3. Il n'a pas de chemise à porter.   c. Son pauvre genou!

_____ 4. C'est une femme grande.   d. Ils sont pauvres.

_____ 5. Elle est tombée.   e. C'est l'ancien directeur.

Demonstrative adjectives

Sometimes you need to be very specific when identifying things. To do so, you use demonstrative adjectives (*this, that, these, those*). In French, demonstratives, like all adjectives, agree in gender and number with the noun they modify.

Masculine singular

ce livre	*this book*
cet auteur	*this author*
cet homme	*this man*

Note that the demonstrative adjective **ce** adds a **-t** before a masculine singular noun that starts with a vowel or a mute **h** (**cet appartement, cet arbre**).

Feminine singular

cette lampe	*this lamp*
cette télévision	*this television*
cette histoire	*this story*

Masculine and feminine plural

ces cahiers (*m.pl.*)	*these notebooks*
ces arbres (*m.pl.*)	*these trees*
ces chemises (*f.pl.*)	*these shirts*
ces homards (*m.pl.*)	*these lobsters*

To make a distinction between two elements, **-ci** and **-là** are added to the noun following the demonstrative adjective.

Préférez-vous **cette** chemise-**ci** ou **cette** chemise-**là**?	*Do you prefer this shirt or that shirt?*

Adjectives **401**

Combien coûtent **ce** livre-**ci** et **ce** livre-**là**?	*How much do this book and that book cost?*		
Préférez-vous **ces** lunettes-**ci** ou **ces** lunettes-**là**?	*Do you prefer these glasses or those glasses?*		
Vous recommandez **cet** hôtel-**ci** ou **cet** hôtel-**là**?	*Do you recommend this hotel or that hotel?*		

VOCABULAIRE

une famille	*a family*	**un oncle**	*an uncle*
un(e) adulte	*an adult*	**une tante**	*an aunt*
un mari	*a husband*	**un(e) cousin(e)**	*a cousin*
une femme	*a wife, a woman*	**un beau-père**	*a father-in-law, a stepfather*
un père	*a father*		
une mère	*a mother*	**une belle-mère**	*a mother-in-law a stepmother*
un fils	*a son*		
une fille	*a daughter, a girl*	**un beau-frère**	*a brother-in-law*
un enfant	*a child*	**une belle-sœur**	*a sister-in-law*
un bébé	*a baby*	**un neveu**	*a nephew*
un frère	*a brother*	**une nièce**	*a niece*
une sœur	*a sister*	**un grand-père**	*a grandfather*
ainé(e)	*older, eldest*	**une grand-mère**	*a grandmother*
cadet(te)	*younger, youngest*	**un petit-fils**	*a grandson*
un(e) benjamin(e)	*a youngest son, daughter*	**une petite-fille**	*a granddaughter*
		les petits-enfants (m.pl.)	*grandchildren*
un(e) parent(e)	*a relative*		

EXERCICE 28·8

*Compléter avec **ce**, **cet**, **cette** ou **ces**.*

1. Ma sœur n'aime pas (*this*) _____ robe rouge.

2. Mon petit frère préfère (*this*) _____ dessin animé.

3. Nos parents arrivent (*this*) _____ semaine.

4. Tu vas voir ton cousin (*this*) _____ soir.

5. J'achète (*these*) _____ cadeaux pour mes enfants.

6. (*This*) _____ maison est trop petite pour notre famille.

7. Son neveu trouve (*this*) _____ jeu difficile.

8. Ma cousine fait toujours (*these*) _____ plats pour sa belle-mère.

9. (*This*) _____ famille habite ici depuis longtemps et les enfants aiment (*this*) _____ quartier.

10. (*This*) _____ bébé est adorable.

402   PRACTICE MAKES PERFECT   Complete French All-in-One

EXERCICE 28·9

Faire la distinction entre les deux éléments en ajoutant -ci et -là aux noms qui suivent les adjectifs démonstratifs.

1. Ma mère achète les biscuits dans (*this*) _____ pâtisserie et les gâteaux dans (*that*) _____ pâtisserie.
2. Leur enfant joue avec (*this*) _____ jouet mais il ne joue pas avec (*that*) _____ jouet.
3. Mes parents habitent loin d'ici. (*This*) _____ cousin habite à San Francisco, (*that*) _____ cousin est à New York.
4. (*This*) _____ maison appartient à Tante Marthe, (*that*) _____ maison appartient à son fils.
5. (*This*) _____ neveu et (*that*) _____ neveu sont nés le même jour.
6. Mon mari aime (*this*) _____ belle-sœur, mais il n'aime pas (*that*) _____ belle-sœur.
7. Son frère a écrit (*this*) _____ roman, mais il n'a pas écrit (*that*) _____ roman.
8. Leurs enfants aiment (*this*) _____ jeu mais ils n'aiment pas (*that*) _____ jeu.
9. (*This*) _____ poupée et (*that*) _____ poupée sont des cadeaux de Tante Agathe.
10. Notre tante a envoyé (*this*) _____ carte à son fils et (*that*) _____ carte à sa mère, notre grand-mère.

Possessive adjectives

Possessive adjectives modify nouns and are used to express relationship and ownership. They agree in gender and number with the noun they modify.

Masculine singular

mon ordinateur	*my computer*	**notre ordinateur**	*our computer*
ton ordinateur	*your computer*	**votre ordinateur**	*your computer*
son ordinateur	*his/her computer*	**leur ordinateur**	*their computer*

Feminine singular

ma vie	*my life*	**notre vie**	*our life*
ta vie	*your life*	**votre vie**	*your life*
sa vie	*his/her life*	**leur vie**	*their life*

Masculine and feminine plural

mes cousin(e)s	my cousins	nos cousin(e)s	our cousins
tes cousin(e)s	your cousins	vos cousin(e)s	your cousins
ses cousin(e)s	his/her cousins	leurs cousin(e)s	their cousins

Note that the masculine singular form of the possessive adjective (**mon, ton, son**) is used before *singular feminine* nouns beginning with a vowel or a mute **h**.

Mon amie Suzanne travaille à Rennes.	*My friend Suzanne works in Rennes.*
Ton amitié est importante.	*Your friendship is important.*
Son honnêteté est suspecte.	*His honesty is suspect.*

Son, sa, ses can mean either *his* or *hers*, since they modify the noun (not the owner). The context will usually prevent any ambiguity about the identity of the owner. If there is ambiguity, the sentence needs to be rephrased for clarity.

son roman	*his/her novel*
sa pièce	*his/her play*
ses contes de fée	*his/her fairy tales*

Another way of expressing possession is to use **à** + a noun or a disjunctive pronoun.

C'est **à qui**?	*Whose is it?*
C'est **à Pierre**?	*Is it Pierre's?*
Non, ce n'est pas **à Pierre**.	*No, it's not Pierre's.*
C'est **à moi**.	*It's mine.*

EXERCICE 28·10

*Compléter avec l'adjectif possessif approprié en utilisant **vous** si nécessaire.*

1. Aimez-vous (*his*) _____ nouvelle pièce?

2. Non, mais j'aime (*his*) _____ nouveau conte de fée.

3. Que penses-tu de (*her*) _____ dernier roman?

4. (*Her*) _____ dernière pièce est plus intéressante.

5. As-tu besoin de (*our*) _____ voiture?

6. Oui, j'ai besoin de (*your*) _____ voiture.

7. (*Your*) _____ sœur est actrice?

8. Non, (*my*) _____ sœur est architecte.

9. Quel âge a (*their*) _____ fille?

10. (*Their*) _____ filles sont jumelles. Elles ont quatre ans.

EXERCICE 28·11

Faire correspondre les deux colonnes.

_____ 1. frère   a. ma

_____ 2. amies   b. mon

_____ 3. oncle   c. ma

_____ 4. maison   d. mon

_____ 5. belle-sœur e. mes

Adverbs

Adverbs and expressions of time

The following expressions are useful when talking about time:

aujourd'hui	today
demain	tomorrow
hier	yesterday
après-demain	the day after tomorrow
avant-hier	the day before yesterday
dans trois jours	in three days (from today)
dans une quinzaine	in two weeks
dans un mois	in a month
dans un an	in a year
la semaine prochaine	next week
la semaine dernière	last week

Il ira en France **dans un an**. — *He'll go to France in a year.*
Je t'appellerai **après-demain**. — *I'll call you the day after tomorrow.*

The adverbs listed above are ordinarily used when you are speaking directly to people, in what is known as direct style or direct speech. If you are discussing past and future events, or telling a story, you are more likely to use an indirect style, the **discours indirect** (*indirect speech*), which you studied in Chapter 25. Here are a few time expressions typically used in indirect speech:

la veille	the day before
le jour même	the very day
le lendemain	the day after
l'avant-veille	two days before
le surlendemain	two days later
la semaine suivante	the following week
la dernière semaine	the last week (of a sequence)

Elle est arrivée **la veille** de mon anniversaire. — *She arrived the day before my birthday.*
Nous sommes partis **le lendemain**. — *We left the day after.*

406

Here are some additional adverbs or expressions of time:

chaque jour	*every day*	**tous les jours**	*every day*
maintenant	*now*	**en ce moment**	*at this present time*
actuellement	*presently*	**à l'heure actuelle**	*at this very moment*
d'habitude	*usually*	**d'ordinaire**	*ordinarily*
toujours	*always, still*	**souvent**	*often*
ne... jamais	*never*	**longtemps**	*for a long time*
autrefois	*formerly*	**rarement**	*seldom*
tôt	*early*	**tard**	*late*
parfois	*sometimes*	**quelquefois**	*sometimes*
de temps en temps	*from time to time*	**de temps à autre**	*from time to time*

Il assiste **rarement** aux réunions.   *He rarely attends meetings.*
Que fait-elle **actuellement**?   *What is she presently doing?*

Compléter les phrases avec l'adverbe approprié.

1. Virginie arrive (*tomorrow*) _____? —Oui, elle arrive (*tomorrow evening*) _____.

2. Vous êtes libres (*next week*) _____? —Non, nous ne sommes pas libres (*next week*) _____.

3. Où vas-tu (*today*) _____? —Je vais à Nantes (*today*) _____.

4. Vous mangez des fruits (*every day*) _____? —Non, je mange des fruits (*every other day*) _____.

5. Tu rentres (*late*) _____ ce soir? —Non, je rentre vers sept heures.

6. Est-ce qu'ils arrivent (*often*) _____ en avance? —Non, ils arrivent (*rarely*) _____ en avance.

7. Est-ce qu'elles vont (*sometimes*) _____ à la plage? —Non, elles ne vont (*never*) _____ à la plage.

8. Vous avez beaucoup de travail (*right now*) _____? —Non, (*right now*) _____, c'est très calme.

9. Ton anniversaire est (*next week*) _____? —Non, mon anniversaire est (*the day after tomorrow*) _____.

10. Il est parti (*yesterday*) _____? —Non, il est parti (*the day before yesterday*) _____.

EXERCICE 29·2

*Traduire les phrases suivantes en utilisant **tu** et la forme **est-ce que** si nécessaire.*

1. Today is the first day of winter.

   _____

2. She often travels.

   _____

3. I am never on time. I am always late.

   _____

4. He arrives the day after tomorrow.

   _____

5. Her appointment is in two weeks.

   _____

6. We are working tomorrow, but we are not working the day after tomorrow.

   _____

7. They sold their house last week.

   _____

8. Are you going to the opera tonight?

   _____

9. You are early. I am not ready.

   _____

10. The bakery will be closed next week.

    _____

VOCABULAIRE

une agence de voyages	*a travel agency*	un épicier, une épicière	*a grocer*
un(e) antiquaire	*an antiques dealer*	un(e) fleuriste	*a florist*
une banque	*a bank*	un horloger	*a watchmaker*
une bijouterie	*a jewelry store*	un kiosque à journaux	*a newsstand*
un boucher, une bouchère	*a butcher*	un magasin	*a store*
un boulanger, une boulangère	*a baker*	un magasin d'appareils photo	*a camera store*
un bureau de tabac	*a tobacco shop*	un magasin de chaussures	*a shoe shop*
un coiffeur, une coiffeuse	*a hairdresser*	un magasin de disques	*a record store*
une confiserie	*a candy store*	un magasin de jouets	*a toy store*
un cordonnier	*a shoemaker*		

408   PRACTICE MAKES PERFECT   Complete French All-in-One

un(e) marchand(e) au détail	a retailer	une papeterie	a stationery store
un(e) marchand(e) de gros	a wholesaler	une pharmacie	a pharmacy
un(e) marchand(e) de journaux	a newspaper dealer	un(e) pharmacien(ne)	a pharmacist
un(e) marchand(e) de légumes	a produce dealer	un pâtissier, une pâtissière	a pastry cook
un(e) marchand(e) de poisson	a fishmonger		
un(e) marchand(e) de tableaux	an art dealer	une poissonnerie	a fish market
un(e) marchand(e) de vin	a wine merchant	une quincaillerie	a hardware store
un(e) libraire	a bookseller	un salon de coiffure	a hairdressing salon
une librairie	a bookstore	un supermarché	a supermarket
un(e) opticien(ne)	an optician	un pressing, une teinturerie	a dry cleaner

Expressing duration

Remember: If you are asking a question about the duration of an action that began in the past and still continues in the present, you have several options: **depuis**, **il y a... que**, or **cela (ça) fait... que**, used along with the duration. Note that French uses a present tense verb whereas English uses the past.

Let's review **depuis**. To ask a question about the duration of an action, use **Depuis quand?** (*Since when?*) or **Depuis combien de temps?** (*How long?*)

Depuis quand (Depuis combien de temps) Julie est-elle pharmacienne?	*Since when has Julie been a pharmacist?*
—Julie est pharmacienne **depuis dix ans**.	—*Julie has been a pharmacist for ten years.*
J'achète mes livres chez ce libraire **depuis des années**.	*I have been buying my books at this bookseller's for years.*

EXERCICE 29·3

Traduire les éléments entre parenthèses.

1. (*Since when*) _____ habites-tu à New York? —J'habite à New York depuis 1998.

2. (*How long*) _____ est-ce que ce boulanger est installé ici? —Depuis cinq ans.

3. (*Since when*) _____ est-elle malade? —Elle est malade depuis jeudi.

4. (*How long*) _____ est-il fleuriste? —Depuis six mois.

5. (*Since when*) _____ cette bijouterie est-elle ouverte? —Elle est ouverte depuis le premier septembre.

6. (*How long*) _____ est-ce que vous attendez? —Nous attendons (*for*) _____ quinze minutes.

7. (*Since when*) _____ voyages-tu en France régulièrement? —Depuis plusieurs années.

Adverbs

8. (*Since when*) _____ êtes-vous amis? —Nous sommes amis depuis notre enfance.

9. (*How long*) _____ le marchand de journaux a-t-il pris sa retraite? Depuis trois mois.

10. Cette laverie se trouve ici (*for*) _____ plusieurs années.

There is an important exception to the construction with **depuis**: In negative sentences, the **passé composé** is used instead of the present. For example:

Il n'a pas revu sa sœur depuis dix ans.	*He has not seen his sister for ten years.*
Nous ne sommes pas allées à Madrid **depuis** dix ans.	*We have not been to Madrid for ten years.*

EXERCICE 29·4

Répondre aux questions à l'aide des éléments entre parenthèses.

1. Depuis combien de temps travailles-tu pour cette agence de voyages? (5 ans)

   _____

2. Depuis combien de temps cherches-tu un nouvel appartement? (le mois de janvier)

   _____

3. Depuis quand allez-vous chez cet opticien? (des années)

   _____

4. Cela fait longtemps que vous êtes mariés? (14 ans)

   _____

5. Cela fait combien de temps que nous nous connaissons? (9 ans)

   _____

6. Cela fait longtemps que tu m'attends sous la pluie? (45 minutes)

   _____

7. Vous prenez cette ligne de métro depuis combien de temps? (5 ans)

   _____

8. Cela fait longtemps que le coiffeur est situé par ici? (6 mois)

   _____

9. Depuis quand est-ce que tu ne fumes plus? (la semaine dernière)

   _____

10. Depuis combien de temps est-il en vacances? (3 semaines)

   _____

EXERCICE 29·5

*Changer **depuis** ou **cela fait... que** en **il y a... que**.*

1. J'attends depuis une demi-heure.

2. Cela fait quatre mois que Valérie a sa voiture.

3. Cela fait dix jours que nous essayons de joindre le banquier.

4. Il est en voyage d'affaires depuis deux jours.

5. Sophie étudie le chinois depuis un an.

6. Elle veut adopter un enfant depuis cinq ans.

7. Cela fait des semaines que nous cherchons un appartement.

8. Cela fait trois mois que j'attends votre réponse.

9. Ses idées sont dénuées d'intérêt depuis longtemps.

10. Le chien de nos voisins est perdu depuis une semaine.

Using adverbs with the **passé composé**

In the **passé composé**, shorter adverbs of quantity, quality, and frequency are placed between **avoir** or **être** and the past participle. See the following example sentences:

Elle étudie **beaucoup**.	*She studies a lot.*
Elle a **beaucoup** étudié.	*She studied a lot.*
Ils dépensent **trop**.	*They spend too much.*
Ils ont **trop** dépensé.	*They spent too much.*
Nous travaillons **assez**.	*We work enough.*
Nous avons **assez** travaillé.	*We worked enough.*
Il écrit **très bien** la musique.	*He writes music very well.*
Il a **très bien** écrit la musique.	*He wrote music very well.*
Tu t'exprimes **mal**.	*You express yourself badly.*
Tu t'es **mal** exprimé(e).	*You expressed yourself badly.*

Adverbs **411**

Je voyage **souvent** en Italie.	*I often travel in Italy.*
J'ai **souvent** voyagé en Italie.	*I often traveled in Italy.*
Vous mentez **rarement**.	*You rarely lie.*
Vous avez **rarement** menti.	*You have rarely lied.*

To express time with the **passé composé**, **pendant** (*for, during*) is commonly used (although it can actually be omitted). However, **pour** (*for*) is *never* used to talk about duration in the past.

Il a habité **pendant cinq ans** à Londres.	*He lived for five years in London.*
Il a habité **cinq ans** à Londres.	*He lived five years in London.*
Nous avons voyagé **pendant un mois** en Italie.	*We traveled for a month in Italy.*
Nous avons voyagé **un mois** en Italie.	*We traveled one month in Italy.*

EXERCICE 29·6

Mettre les phrases suivantes au passé composé.

1. Ils voyagent souvent en Asie.

2. On mange bien chez eux.

3. Elle dépense beaucoup.

4. Il lit rarement des romans policiers.

5. Nous ne travaillons pas assez.

6. Je parle trop.

7. Elle écrit très peu.

8. Tu vas souvent au théâtre.

9. Il s'exprime toujours très mal.

10. Nous aimons bien la maison.

Interrogative forms; question words

When you want to formulate questions, interrogative words come in handy. Here are some important ones:

pourquoi	*why*
où	*where*
quand	*when*
comment	*how*
combien	*how much*
que	*what*
qui	*who, whom*
dans quelle mesure	*to what extent*

EXERCICE 29·7

Traduire les mots entre parenthèses.

1. (How many) _____ livres lisez-vous? —Je lis deux livres.
2. (How) _____ allons-nous à la plage? —Nous allons à la plage en voiture.
3. (Who) _____ loue la maison bleue? —Suzanne loue la maison bleue.
4. (What) _____ pensez-vous de ce roman? —C'est un mauvais roman.
5. (How much) _____ coûte l'appartement de Stéphane? —L'appartement de Stéphane coûte cher.
6. (Where) _____ travaille votre mari? —Il travaille à Berlin.
7. (When) _____ vont-ils au théâtre? —Ils vont au théâtre samedi soir.
8. (Why) _____ étudiez-vous le français? —J'étudie le français pour mon travail.
9. (When) _____ arrive-t-il? —Il arrive la semaine prochaine.
10. (Who) _____ chante? —C'est Laurent qui chante.

Adverbs and expressions of location

Here are some words that are helpful when talking about location:

ici	*here*	**là**	*there*
là-bas	*over there*	**ailleurs**	*elsewhere*
ça et là	*here and there*	**à cet endroit**	*in this place*
là-haut	*up there*	**partout**	*everywhere*
près	*near, close*	**loin**	*far*
à côté	*next to, beside*	**auprès**	*next to, close to*
dehors	*outside*	**dedans**	*inside*
devant	*in front of*	**derrière**	*behind*
dessus	*on top*	**dessous**	*under*

Ici, tout est possible.	*Here, everything is possible.*
Les femmes **d'ici** sont très belles.	*Local women are very beautiful.*
Fitzgerald est mort **ici** même.	*Fitzgerald died in this very place.*
Je le vois **là**, sur l'étagère.	*I see it over there, on the shelf.*
Mets ton sac **dessous**.	*Put your bag underneath.*
C'est écrit **dessus**.	*It's written on it.*
Nous désirons voyager **ailleurs**.	*We want to travel elsewhere.*
Tu es juste **devant**.	*You are right in front of it.*
Vous êtes juste **derrière**.	*You are right behind it.*
C'est beaucoup trop **loin**.	*It is much too far.*
Je vois des erreurs **çà et là**.	*I see mistakes here and there.*

EXERCICE 29·8

*Traduire les phrases suivantes en utilisant **vous** et l'inversion si nécessaire.*

1. He planted flowers everywhere.

2. Do you want to live here?

3. My car is parked just behind yours.

4. We'll go somewhere else.

5. He is outside.

6. I live near the river.

7. You live too far.

8. I see strange things here and there.

9. He is in front of you.

10. Come sit next to me.

Written French: Making transitions and written correspondence

Transitional words or phrases serve to link parts of a sentence or to connect one sentence to another as well as one paragraph to another. They help build organized paragraphs that can be read smoothly, and help to ultimately construct extended pieces of writing such as letters.

Linking thoughts within a sentence

Smooth transitions from one thought to another within a sentence are clearly important to communicate effectively. This can be achieved by the use of adverbs and conjunctions.

Using coordinating and subordinating conjunctions

Using conjunctions will help sentences flow in a logical manner, making your message clear to the reader. These conjunctions may serve in a variety of ways such as adding an idea, e.g., **et** (*and*); explaining an idea, e.g., **car** (*for*); or opposing an idea, e.g., **bien que** (*although*). You may review Chapter 9 for coordinating conjunctions and subordinating conjunctions.

Coordinating conjunctions

Coordinating conjunctions such as **et** (*and*), **car** (*for*), **ou** (*or*), **mais** (*but*), **donc** (*so*), and **ni...ni** (*neither . . . nor*) are commonly used to link two or more verbs, nouns, adverbs, adjectives, or clauses.

Elle a fait la lessive **et** la vaisselle.	*She did the laundry **and** the dishes.*
Il est allé manger **car** il avait faim.	*He went to eat **for** he was hungry.*
Elle veut aller au cinéma **ou** au restaurant.	*She wants to go to the movies **or** to the restaurant.*
Il avait fini **donc** il est parti.	*He had finished, **so** he left.*
Il ne veut **ni** nager **ni** marcher.	*He does not want to swim **nor** walk.*
Elle est fatiguée **mais** elle veut finir son travail.	*She is tired but wants to finish her work.*

Subordinating conjunctions

Subordinating conjunctions link two clauses. Some conjunctions govern the subjunctive mood. The following are some commonly used subordinating conjunctions:

alors que	*while*	pendant que	*while*
bien que	*although*	pourvu que	*provided that*
parce que	*because*	tandis que	*while*

Il est parti tôt **parce qu'**il était pressé. — *He left early **because** he was in a hurry.*
Elle dansait **alors que/tandis que** je chantais. — *She was dancing **while** I was singing.*

In the following sentences, note that the conjunctions **bien que** and **pourvu que** are followed by a verb in the subjunctive mood:

Elle a planté des fleurs **bien qu'**elle n'y connaisse pas grand-chose. — *She planted flowers **although** she does not know anything about gardening.*
Je te pardonne **pourvu que** tu ne le fasses plus. — *I forgive you **provided** you do not do this again.*

EXERCICE 30·1

Complete each sentence with one of the following coordinating conjunctions.

ni / et / donc / mais / car / ou

1. Comme sport, je fais de la marche _____ de la natation.
2. Je n'aime ni courir _____ escalader les montagnes.
3. Pour nager, je vais à la piscine _____ à la plage.
4. J'adore la mer _____ quelquefois les vagues sont trop hautes pour nager.
5. Je vais quand même souvent à la plage _____ je peux toujours y faire de la marche.
6. Je fais beaucoup d'exercice physique, _____ je suis en assez bonne forme.

EXERCICE 30·2

Complete each sentence with one of the following subordinating conjunctions.

alors que / tandis que / parce que / pourvu que / bien que / pendant que

1. Comme sport, Mimi monte et descend l'escalier une ou deux fois par jour _____ moi, je vais au gym, au parc et à la plage.
2. Mimi croit qu'elle est en forme _____ elle ne soit pas malade.
3. Je ne suis pas contente _____ je sais que Mimi ne fait pas assez d'exercice.

4. _____ je sois plus âgée et plus raisonnable, Mimi ne m'écoute pas.

5. La plupart du temps Mimi écoute des CD, couchée sur son lit, _____ moi, j'écoute mon iPod tout en marchant.

6. Je m'inquiète pour Mimi _____ c'est ma petite sœur.

Using adverbs and adverbial conjunctions

Just like coordinating and subordinating conjunctions, adverbs and adverbial conjunctions can be classified in categories such as adding, contrasting, illustrating, and sequencing ideas.

Addition

It is sometimes good style to use an adverb or adverbial clause such as the following to illustrate or provide an additional detail in a sentence:

ainsi que	*as well as*	également	*also/too*
aussi	*also/too*	encore	*still*
d'ailleurs	*besides*		

L'eau était trop froide pour y nager; il y avait **aussi** de grandes vagues.	*The water was too cold to swim in it; **also** there were big waves.*
J'ai apporté les boissons; j'ai **également** fait un dessert.	*I brought the drinks; I **also** made a dessert.*
Il a nettoyé l'évier mais il y avait **encore** des débris de verre.	*He cleaned the sink, but **still** there was some broken glass in it.*

Note: Unlike the adverb *also*, which is often used at the head of a sentence or clause in English, **aussi**, **également**, and **encore** should never appear at the head of a French sentence but rather after the verb.

subject + verb + aussi/encore

Il + avait + encore...
He still had . . .

Elle enseigne le violon **ainsi que** le piano.	*She teaches the violin **as well as** the piano.*
Il a rendu le livre; **d'ailleurs** il ne l'avait pas lu.	*He returned the book; **besides** he had not read it.*

Note: It is not unusual to use a coordinating conjunction such as **et** or **mais** as well as an adverb to make a transition from one thought to another. Remember that a great majority of adverbs follow the verb in a French sentence. Consider the following examples:

Il a pris la retraite **mais** il travaille **encore** un peu.	*He retired **but** he **still** works a little.*
Il répond au téléphone **mais** il commande **aussi** les fournitures.	*He answers the phone **but** he **also** orders office supplies.*

Contrast

In some instances, adverbs or adverbial phrases such as the following help transition from one idea to another by establishing a contrast:

au lieu de cela	*instead of that*	pourtant	*yet*
cependant	*however*	malgré tout	*in spite of everything/ all the same*
sinon	*otherwise*		

Written French: Making transitions and written correspondence **417**

Tu devais surveiller les enfants; **au lieu de cela**, tu dormais.	*You were supposed to watch the children; **instead of that**, you were sleeping.*
Prends ton petit déjeuner; **sinon** tu auras faim.	*Have your breakfast; **otherwise** you will be hungry.*

Emphasis

In other instances, adverbs or adverbial phrases such as the following help transition from one idea to another by adding emphasis to what has already been stated:

bien sûr que	*of course*	en fait	*in fact*
certainement	*certainly*	naturellement	*naturally*
en effet	*indeed*	sûrement	*surely*

Quand on m'a demandé de venir, **bien sûr que** je suis venue.	*When they asked me to come, **of course** I came.*
Je croyais que c'était l'adresse correcte; **en fait**, elle était fausse.	*I thought that it was the correct address; **in fact** it was wrong.*
Quand on l'a insulté, **naturellement** il s'est révolté.	*When they insulted him, **naturally** he rebelled.*

Illustration

Adverbs or adverbial phrases such as the following help transition from one idea to another by giving an example or an illustration:

autrement dit	*in other words*	par exemple	*for example/for instance*
en particulier	*specifically*	surtout	*especially*

J'adore les pierres précieuses, **par exemple** les rubis.	*I adore precious stones, **for example** rubies.*
Il dessine beaucoup d'animaux, **en particulier** les chats.	*He draws many animals, **specifically** cats.*
J'aime bien le Colorado **surtout** en été.	*I like Colorado **especially** in the summer.*

Time sequence

Often, adverbs or adverbial phrases such as the following help transition from one idea to another by establishing a time sequence:

actuellement	*presently*	enfin	*finally*
alors	*then/so*	ensuite	*then*
après	*afterward*	finalement	*finally*
autrefois	*formerly*	maintenant	*now*
avant	*before*	par la suite	*afterward*
bientôt	*soon*	puis	*then*
d'abord	*first (of all)*		

Il est inscrit à l'Université de Paris 8 **mais actuellement** il est en vacances.	*He is enrolled at the University of Paris 8, **but currently** he is on vacation.*
Avant il ne faisait pas de gym **mais maintenant** il en fait tous les jours.	***Before** he did not do any exercise, **but now** he does some every day.*
Il a pris une douche, **puis** il s'est habillé **et enfin**, il a pu partir.	*He took a shower, **then** he got dressed, **and finally** he was able to leave.*

EXERCICE 30·3

Complete each sentence with an appropriate transition word or phrase from the list provided.

tandis que / mais / car / et / bien que / ou / puisque / donc / ainsi que

1. J'ai toujours rêvé d'aller à Monaco _____ je n'en ai jamais eu l'occasion.

2. _____ nous serons sur la Côte d'Azur cet été, je veux vraiment y aller.

3. Je veux jouir de la vue de la mer _____ nous passerons par de petits ports de pêche.

4. À Monaco, nous pourrons voir la relève de la garde _____ le célèbre casino.

5. Il paraît qu'il y a de nombreux cafés et restaurants; _____ nous déjeunerons là-bas.

6. Il faudra aussi acheter un souvenir _____ nous n'aimions pas trop dépenser pour ce genre de choses.

EXERCICE 30·4

Choose the appropriate transitional word or phrase to complete each sentence in the following paragraph.

pourtant / et / ainsi que / mais actuellement / bientôt / en effet / bien que

Le jeune Sarkozy se distinguait déjà au lycée par son talent de négociateur (1) _____ son charme. Il savait énoncer clairement ses arguments (2) _____ affirmer ses points de vue. (3) _____ il n'était pas arrogant, simplement sûr de lui. Il n'avait que vingt ans quand il s'est affilié à la campagne électorale de Jacques Chirac. (4) _____ les deux hommes avaient des convictions communes, (5) _____ Sarkozy ait changé de direction par la suite. (6) _____ Sarkozy a réussi à faire une belle carrière politique. Élu président de la République française, il est devenu leader d'une importante nation européenne et a su (7) _____ s'affirmer sur la scène internationale. (8) _____ le président Sarkozy a fait face à un nombre de problèmes, mais «Qui vivra verra!»

EXERCICE 30·5

Reconstitute each sentence of this paragraph by placing the sentence fragments in the correct order and adding punctuation. Pay particular attention to transitional words such as **sinon** *or* **aussi** *that provide important clues.*

1. encore beaucoup à apprendre / mais il me reste / j'ai beaucoup appris

_____

2. ainsi que de la grammaire / j'étudie du vocabulaire / il faut que

_____

Written French: Making transitions and written correspondence **419**

3. aussi / la culture française / comprendre mieux / je voudrais

_____

4. c'est frustrant / être patient / sinon / il faut / quand on apprend une langue

_____

5. faire des progrès en écriture / en particulier / je vais continuer / bien sûr avec un peu de diligence /dans

_____

6. quelques phrases / je sais écrire / actuellement

_____

7. un paragraphe entier / je pourrai écrire / mais bientôt

_____

Linking sentences and paragraphs

Smooth, orderly, and logical transitions from one sentence to the next, and from one paragraph to another, are key to creating clear meaning and flow in any document. This can be achieved by using prepositional and adverbial phrases, impersonal expressions, verbs, and conjunctions. These structures are organized here according to their meaning rather than their grammatical definition.

Expressing personal viewpoints

You may begin a sentence with a phrase such as **Selon moi** or with a verb phrase such as **Je crois** to make it clear that you are giving your own point of view. Here are some examples followed by a paragraph in which you will notice how transitional words allow the smooth development of ideas:

Selon moi	*In my opinion*
À mon avis	*In my opinion*
D'après moi	*In my opinion*
Je crois que	*I believe that*
Je ne crois pas que	*I do not believe that*
Je pense que	*I think that*
Je ne pense pas que	*I do not think that*
Je suis convaincu(e) que	*I am convinced that*

Je ne pense pas que ce problème soit grave. **Selon moi**, ce voyage est bien organisé. **Je crois que** nous reviendrons. **D'après moi**, on devrait remercier le guide. **Je suis convaincue qu'**il est honnête.

I do not think that *this problem is serious.* ***In my opinion****, this trip is well organized.* ***I believe that*** *we will come back.* ***In my opinion****, we should thank the guide.* ***I am convinced that*** *he is honest.*

Expressing certainty or uncertainty

You may begin a sentence with one of many impersonal expressions that help convey varying degrees of certainty or uncertainty. Remember that expressions that convey uncertainty must be followed by a verb in the subjunctive mood. (See Chapter 20.) The following expressions are frequently used in French. Note the use of transitional words in the short paragraph following these expressions:

FOLLOWED BY INDICATIVE MOOD		FOLLOWED BY SUBJUNCTIVE MOOD	
Il est certain que	*It is certain that*	Il n'est pas certain que	*It is not certain that*
Il est évident que	*It is evident that*	Il est possible que	*It is possible that*
Il est probable que	*It is probable that*	Il est peu probable que	*It is improbable that*
Il va de soi que	*It is self-evident that*	Il est contestable que	*It is questionable/ debatable that*

Ce n'est pas clair. **Il est contestable qu'il** ait gagné. Quelle surprise! **Il est certain qu'**on ne peut pas tout prévoir. Mais quel mensonge! **Il est évident que** la vérité est rare. Il est si têtu. **Il n'est pas certain qu'**on puisse raisonner avec lui. Il n'écoute pas. **Il est peu probable qu'**il fasse ce qu'on lui demande.

*It is not clear. **It is questionable that** he won. What a surprise! **It is certain that** we cannot predict everything. But what a lie! **It is evident that** truth is rare. He is so stubborn. **It is not certain that** we can reason with him. He does not listen. **He is not likely to** do what they ask.*

Illustrating a point

You may begin a sentence with one of the following terms when you are ready to give evidence for the point you are making. Note the use of transitional words in the short paragraph following these expressions:

Notamment	*Notably/In particular*
Par exemple	*For example*
On peut préciser que	*Let us point out that/One should point out that*
On peut souligner que	*Let us stress that*

Il avait des raisons très claires pour commettre le délit. **On peut préciser qu'**il y avait beaucoup réfléchi. Mais il a fait plusieurs erreurs. **Par exemple**, le mois dernier, il a oublié de payer une facture. Et il avait un dossier: il avait été emprisonné plusieurs fois, **notamment** l'an dernier.

*He had very clear reasons to commit the felony. **One should point out that** he had thought about it a lot. But he made several mistakes. **For example**, last month he forgot to pay a bill. And he had a record: he had been incarcerated several times, **in particular** last year.*

Giving a reason

Except for **comme**, which must begin a sentence in order to mean *as/since*, you may use the following terms *to begin* or *develop* a sentence when you want to explain why. Note the use of transitional words in the short paragraph following these expressions:

À cause de	*Because of*
Comme	*As/Since*
Étant donné que, vu que	*Given that*
Parce que	*Because*
Puisque	*Since*

Written French: Making transitions and written correspondence **421**

À **cause de** l'examen ce matin, Mireille était pressée. **Étant donné qu'**elle était en retard, elle a décidé de prendre la voiture de sa sœur. **Comme** elle en avait besoin tout de suite, elle l'a prise sans demander. Ce n'était pas sympa **parce que** la sœur de Mireille a eu très peur quand elle n'a pas vu sa voiture.

*Because of the exam this morning, Mireille was in a hurry. **Given that** she was late, she decided to take her sister's car. **Since** she needed it immediately, she took it without asking. It was not nice, **because** Mireille's sister got very scared when she did not see her car.*

Stating a consequence

You may use the following terms when you want to show consequences. Note the use of transitional words in the short paragraph following these expressions:

Ainsi	*Thus*
C'est pour cette raison que	*It is for this reason that*
C'est pourquoi	*That is why*
Donc	*So/Thus*
Par conséquent	*Consequently*
Voilà pourquoi	*That is why*

L'économie n'est pas très bonne. **Ainsi** Jacques a perdu son travail. **Voilà pourquoi** il en cherche un autre. **C'est aussi pour cette raison qu'**il regarde les petites annonces chaque jour. Il a rendez-vous chez un employeur demain. **Donc** il faut qu'il prépare son CV.

*The economy is not very good. **Thus** Jacques lost his job. **That's why** he is looking for another. **It is also for this reason** that he looks at ads every day. He has an appointment with an employer tomorrow. **So** he has to prepare his résumé.*

Stating a contrast

There are many expressions that help compare and contrast. Here are a few common ones. Note the use of transitional words in the short paragraph following these expressions:

Au contraire	*On the contrary*	Mais	*But*
Cependant	*However*	Malgré	*Despite*
D'une part	*On one hand*	Même si	*Even though/Even if*
D'autre part, par contre	*On the other hand*	Pourtant	*Yet*
En dépit de	*In spite of*		

Le jeune homme était vendeur dans un grand magasin. **Malgré** le fait qu'il gagnait bien sa vie, il désirait faire des études de kinésithérapeute. Il était très bon en anatomie **même s'**il n'avait pas poursuivi ses études. **D'autre part**, comment allait-il payer ses factures? **Même si** ses études allaient durer quelques années, il serait patient.

*The young man was a salesman in a department store. **Despite** the fact that he earned a good living, he wanted to become a physical therapist. He was good in anatomy **even if** he had not pursued his studies. **On the other hand**, how was he to pay his bills? **Even if** his studies were going to last a few years, he would be patient.*

Establishing a sequence

To show a sequence of events in a sentence or paragraph, you may use any of the previously seen adverbs or adverbial conjunctions, which are used to begin and develop sentences, as well as the following expressions, which may be useful when developing an argument. Note the use of transitional words in the short paragraph following these expressions:

422 PRACTICE MAKES PERFECT Complete French All-in-One

En premier lieu	In the first place
Premièrement	First/Firstly
En deuxième lieu	In the second place
Deuxièmement	Secondly
En troisième lieu	In the third place
Troisièmement	Thirdly
En dernier lieu	Lastly

Non, je ne suis pas allé en Corse. **En premier lieu**, je ne connaissais personne là-bas. **En deuxième lieu**, je n'avais plus que deux jours de vacances et **en troisième lieu**, on m'a invité à rester à Èze.	No, I did not go to Corsica. **In the first place**, I did not know anybody there. **In the second place**, I only had two days vacation left, and i**n the third place**, I was invited to stay in Eze.

Concluding

You may use one of the following terms when you finish an argument, an illustration, or an explanation. In the paragraph following these expressions, note how transitional terms make the entire paragraph easy to read and understand:

En conclusion	To conclude
En résumé	To summarize
En somme	In short
Somme toute	All in all

Je n'étais pas du tout satisfait du service à votre hôtel. **Premièrement**, le personnel n'était pas attentif: **par exemple**, on a oublié de me réveiller le premier matin. **Deuxièmement**, ma chambre n'a pas été nettoyée pendant deux jours. **Troisièmement,** on m'a facturé pour un film que je n'ai pas vu. **En conclusion**, le service était lamentable.	I was not at all satisfied with the service at your hotel. **First**, the personnel were not attentive: **for example**, they forgot to wake me up on the first morning. **Secondly**, my room was not cleaned for two days. **Thirdly**, I was charged for a movie I did not see. **To conclude**, the service was deplorable.

EXERCICE 30·6

Circle the appropriate transition from the choices in parentheses to complete each sentence.

Je suis désolée de ne pas pouvoir accepter votre invitation. (1) (Probablement, Malheureusement) mon mari et moi serons en plein déménagement. Mon mari vient d'apprendre qu'il va travailler pour une dans une succursale de sa banque dans une ville voisine et (2) (c'est pourquoi, parce que) nous devons emballer tous nos effets aussitôt que possible. (3) (Tandis que, Cependant) je dois vous dire que nous apprécions beaucoup votre amitié et (4) (pourtant, même si) nous habitons à une certaine distance, nous voulons continuer de vous voir. (5) (Puisque, Certainement) nos enfants ont le même âge et s'entendent bien, il est important que nous fassions des efforts pour nous voir souvent. (6) (Ainsi que, Donc) le fait que nous ne soyons plus voisins ne devrait pas nous empêcher de rester amis.

Written French: Making transitions and written correspondence **423**

EXERCICE 30·7

Translate the phrases in parentheses to complete each sentence.

1. _____ qu'il fasse mauvais temps aujourd'hui. (*It is not at all sure*)

2. _____ que nous aurons de la pluie. (*It is probable*)

3. _____ que nos amis viennent. (*It is not certain*)

4. _____ que la meilleure équipe gagne ce match. (*It is not evident*)

5. _____ que tous les gens soient honnêtes. (*It is debatable*)

EXERCICE 30·8

Circle the most appropriate choice to complete each sentence.

1. (Par conséquent, À mon avis), beaucoup de gens ne font pas confiance aux promesses des politiciens.

2. (Je doute, Je crois) que beaucoup d'entre eux ont été déçus ces dernières années.

3. (D'après moi, Je suis convaincue) que les choses peuvent changer.

4. Nous aurons bientôt une nouvelle vague de politiciens, (je crois, je ne pense pas).

5. Il suffit que nous votions raisonnablement, (je pense, j'espère).

6. (Malgré, Selon moi), tout est possible!

7. (C'est pourquoi, En dépit) je vais voter dans ces élections.

8. (Au contraire, Ainsi) je ferai mon devoir de citoyen.

EXERCICE 30·9

*Outline the five steps you take to prepare and write an essay for class, using expressions such as **en premier lieu** with the following ideas.*

1. _____
(réfléchir et organiser les idées)

2. _____
(réviser et finir le plan)

424 PRACTICE MAKES PERFECT Complete French All-in-One

3. _____
(commencer à écrire et développer l'essai)

4. _____
(relire et faire des corrections à l'essai)

5. _____
(rendre l'essai au prof et quitter la salle de classe)

EXERCICE 30·10

*Reconstitute each sentence of this paragraph by placing the sentence fragments in the correct order and adding punctuation. Let the transitional word clues such as **C'est pourquoi** guide you.*

1. est toujours complexe / selon moi / la politique

2. qu'il est difficile / de dire toute la vérité / je suis convaincu / pour un politique / et rien que la vérité

3. à admettre / la vérité est quelquefois difficile / il est certain que

4. que les gens / il va de soi / notamment / n'aiment pas entendre la vérité / quand elle est désagréable

5. peu de politiques ont le courage / de toujours dire la vérité / étant donné que / il faut observer leurs actions de très près

6. c'est pourquoi / et les interviews / je suis les débats

EXERCICE 30·11

*Translate the following paragraph using the **imparfait** and **passé composé** tenses. Remember that the words **aussi** and **également** cannot head a sentence in French.*

Formerly I was very shy. I used to worry (s'inquiéter) a lot when I had to talk, in particular before a group of people. Also, I always blushed (rougir) in front of people. But soon I learned to calm down (se calmer). Now I can even make presentations (faire des interventions) in front of an audience. Naturally this did not happen (se passer) in one day.

Written correspondence

French and English formats of letter writing are quite similar in the way letters are addressed but often differ in the way they are closed. In both languages there is a formal style used for legal matters, business, and trade, and there is a familiar style used with friends and relatives.

Addressing an envelope

When writing a person's address on an envelope, the order of lines is the same in English and in French but the order in which information is given on those lines varies slightly.

The number of the house or building should be separated from the name of the street by a comma. However, that rule is frequently disregarded.

> 19, rue du Roethig *or* 19 rue Roethig
> 40, boulevard des Alouettes *or* 40 boulevard des Alouettes

Beware that in French-speaking countries, a street (**rue**) may be called **allée** (*alley*), **chemin** (*path*), **quai** (*riverside*), **promenade** (*promenade*) or other such creative names. These substitutes for **rue** are sometimes capitalized because they have become an inherent part of the location.

> 136, Allée des Aubépines *or* 136 Allée des Aubépines
> 22, Promenade des Anglais *or* 22 Promenade des Anglais

The zip code (**le code postal**) consists of five digits and appears before the name of the town or city in a French address. In France the first two digits of the zip code identify the county (**le département**) in which the person resides.

> **13**004 Marseille **69**002 Lyon
> France France

In France's overseas departments and territories, the first three digits identify the town or city.

> **971**00 Basse-Terre
> Guadeloupe

When writing to Québec, Canada, remember that the first language of the province is French; try to follow the rule of the comma after the street number. Also be sure to indicate **Québec** in parentheses after the town/city *and then* the zip code.

> 99, avenue Jacques Cartier
> Montréal (Québec) H1X 1X1

In addition, a person's title is usually omitted in English, but not in French. Titles may be abbreviated on an envelope as follows. But do not use abbreviations in the body of the letter itself.

Docteur/Dr	*Doctor/Dr.*
Maître/Me	*Esquire/Esq.*
Madame/Mme	*Madam/Mrs.*
Mesdames/Mmes	
Mademoiselle/Mlle	*Miss/Miss*
Mesdemoiselles/Mlles	
Monsieur/M.	*Mister/Mr.*
Messieurs/MM.	
Professeur/Pr	*Professor/Prof.*

Compare the following formats:

ENGLISH	FRENCH	FRENCH
Paul Smith	Monsieur Jules Lemand	M. Jules Lemand
215 Riverside Road	19, rue du Roethig	19, rue Roethig
Colorado Springs, CO 80918	67 000 Strasbourg	67 000 Strasbourg

When writing to a person who lives with a relative or rents a room in another person's home, add a line after the person's name to whom you are writing. This will be followed by the name and address of the home's owner.

Mlle Michelle Verban
Chez Mme Aubin
12, rue du Maréchal Foch
5660 Liège
Belgique

When writing to a company rather than a specific person, write the company's name on the first line, then the specific department and/or the name of the person (if applicable) on the second line, the street address on the third line, the zip code followed by the city on the fourth line, and the country on the fifth line. See the following example:

Société Générale
Section Assurances (*Insurance Department*)/Mlle Butin
29, boulevard Haussmann
75009 Paris
France

EXERCICE
30·12

Using the information provided, write each address as if on an envelope.

1. avenue Leclerc / 12 / Monique Meru / Lille / Madame / 59000 / France

_____
_____
_____
_____

2. 75009 / MM. / Royen et Sanson / Société Productrice d'Electricité / Paris / boulevard Haussmann / 10

_____

_____

_____

_____

3. Fort de France / Martinique / 5 / rue de la Liberté / Hôtel Le Lafayette / 97200

_____

_____

_____

_____

Writing a letter

In both informal and formal French letters, there usually does not appear any address at the top: A business letter is written on letterhead that provides the sender's information, and a personal letter is often written on personalized stationery that also provides the sender's information.

Place and date

Regardless of whether or not letterhead is used, the sender's location (usually a city) appears at the top right of a letter and is separated from the date by a comma as follows:

Avignon, le 11 mars 2014

Salutations

In French and in English, the main difference between informal and formal salutations is the use of a title used in formal letters.

Informal salutations

In an informal letter to a friend or relative, use the word **cher** (*dear*) in the form that is appropriate (masculine, feminine, plural) before the person's name. You may also add the corresponding possessive article **mon**, **ma**, **mes** (*my*) before the adjective **cher**.

Cher François	***Dear*** *François*
Mon cher François	***My dear*** *François*
Chère Michelle	***Dear*** *Michelle*
Ma chère Michelle	***My dear*** *Michelle*
Chers François et Michelle	***Dear*** *François and Michelle*
Chers amis	***Dear*** *friends* (males or mixed group)
Chères amies	***Dear*** *friends* (females)
Mes chères amies	***My dear*** friends (female group)

428 PRACTICE MAKES PERFECT Complete French All-in-One

Formal salutations

In a formal letter, you may use a salutation with or without a name. If you know the person to whom you are writing, use the appropriate form of the word **cher**. If you do not know the person, use only the title.

Writing to a known person:

Chère madame,	*Dear Madam,*
Chère madame Flaubert,	*Dear Mrs. Flaubert,*

Writing to an unknown person:

À qui de droit,	*To whom it may concern,*
Monsieur,	*Sir,*
Messieurs,	*Dear Sirs,*

With individuals who bear a professional title, use **monsieur** or **madame** followed by the professional title. Remember that according to the dictionary of the French Academy, some professions such as **écrivain** (*writer*) and **juge** (*judge*) do not have a feminine form. However, in Québec and parts of Switzerland, it has become standard practice to use a feminine form for these professions: e.g. **la professeure** (*female teacher*) and **l'écrivaine** (*female writer*).

Monsieur le Directeur/Madame la Directrice,	*Dear Director,*
Monsieur le Professeur/Madame le Professeur,	*Dear Professor,*

Closings

There are numerous closing formulas for both informal and formal letters. Many of them differ greatly from closings you would use in English.

Informal closings

In English and in French the closing of a letter will depend on the degree of intimacy one shares with the intended reader. Sometimes the closing is an entire sentence (which ends with a period); sometimes it is just a phrase or a word (which usually ends with a comma or an exclamation mark). As these expressions cannot be translated literally, note that many include the notion of friendship (**amitié**), and others reflect the fact that the French *kiss* (**baisers/bises**) rather than *hug*.

Je vous envoie mes amitiés./Amitiés.	*Regards,*
Je vous envoie mon très amical souvenir.	*Best regards,*
Je vous envoie mes pensées bien amicales.	*Best wishes,*
Amicalement,/Cordialement,	*Yours sincerely,*
Chaleureusement,	*Warm regards,*
Bien à toi/Ton ami(e) dévoué(e),	*Yours truly,*
Je t'embrasse.	*Love,/With love,*
Bons baisers!	*Lots of love,*
Bises!	*Hugs and kisses!*
Grosses bises!	*Lots of hugs and kisses!*

Formal closings

Formal French closing formulas tend to be long and flowery. They cannot be translated literally into English, because in English a formal closing is quite simply the word *Sincerely*. Here are a few examples of some frequently used French formulas. Note that the title embedded in the closing (sir, madam, miss) must refer to the title used in the opening salutation.

Je vous prie d'agréer, Madame/Monsieur/Mademoiselle, l'expression de mes sentiments distingués.

Veuillez agréer, Madame/Monsieur/Mademoiselle, mes cordiales salutations.

Je vous prie d'accepter, Madame/Monsieur/Mademoiselle, mes sincères salutations.

The final closing of a letter will be your signature. Sometimes it will be followed by a postscript (P.S.), which will yield some additional information that was not included in the letter.

EXERCICE 30·13

Using the information provided, write three lines that give the date, the salutation, and the closing of each letter.

1. Paris / July 4, 2008 / Doctor Mason (your physician)

2. Metz / May 23, 2009 / Jeanine Rosier (your girlfriend)

EXERCICE 30·14

Using the information in the following paragraph, compose a note that Tina is writing to a French friend named Marie-Josée who is presently in Cannes with her aunt. Include proper opening and closing expressions.

Depuis que Marie-Josée est partie à Cannes, Tina s'ennuie beaucoup. Elle n'a personne pour l'accompagner au cinéma. Marie-Josée manque terriblement à Tina. Elle ne peut pas attendre qu'elle revienne de France. Mais elle espère que Marie-Josée s'amuse quand même en France. Elle demande si ça lui plaît là-bas et lui dit de donner le bonjour à sa tante.

EXERCICE 30·15

Write a note to a woman who is renting an apartment in Nice. Tell her you saw her ad online, and you very much like the description of the apartment and the monthly rental fee. Add that you hope the apartment is still for rent and that you would like to see it when you are in Nice on June 15. Ask if that is convenient and say that you are waiting for a reply. Use proper opening and closing expressions.

EXERCICE 30·16

*Write a letter to Mr. Fauchon, the manager of a hotel on the Left Bank (**Rive Gauche**) in Paris where you have stayed before. Tell him you and your spouse have stayed at his hotel on several occasions and would like to reserve a room for two weeks in July. You would like your usual room with a view of the Eiffel Tower. You also want breakfast included in the room rate. Ask if you could have a discounted rate since you are a regular customer. Thank him courteously. Use proper opening and closing expressions.*

Written French: Making transitions and written correspondence 431

E-mails

Using e-mails for formal and informal communication has become a way of life all over the world. In French, e-mail is most commonly called by its English name, **le email**, but it is also called **le courriel** (especially in Canada) or **le courrier électronique** (*electronic mail*). The format of e-mails is the same in French as it is in English.

EXERCICE
30·17

Follow the directions for each exercise.

1. Write an e-mail to Mme Sorot, a friend of the family who hosted you in France and just forwarded your mail to you. Tell her you just received the package containing the mail she had the kindness to send you. Add that you will always remember the days you spent as her guest. Thank her for having sent your mail to you and close appropriately.

2. Write an e-mail to your friend Jonathan. Tell him to please send you his new phone number in France. Tell him that if he is available this afternoon, you would like to talk to him. Tell him to answer quickly.

Text messaging

Text messaging is called **le SMS** in French. The essential idea of text messaging is to express one-self with the least number of characters, making use of pure reliance on sounds, abbreviations, and acronyms to convey a message. Beware that it is customary not to use accents in text messages. Consider the following examples of French abbreviations and acronyms used in text messaging:

A2m1	À demain.	*See you tomorrow.*	FDS	le week-end	*weekend*
ALP	À la prochaine.	*See you soon.*	G	j'ai	*I have*
auj	aujourd'hui	*today*	Je t'M	Je t'aime.	*I love you.*
BAL	boîte aux lettres	*mailbox*	KDO	cadeau	*gift*
BCP	beaucoup	*a lot*	Koi29	Quoi de neuf?	*What's new?*
Bjr	Bonjour.	*Hello.*	Mr6	Merci.	*Thanks.*
C	c'est	*it is*	Pkoi	Pourquoi?	*Why?*
CPG	C'est pas grave.	*It does not matter.*	rdv	rendez-vous	*date/appointment*
DSL	Désolé(e).	*Sorry.*	STP	S'il te plaît.	*Please.*
DQP	Dès que possible.	*As soon as possible.*			

Common abbreviations used in informal communication

Along with the previously mentioned shortcuts in written communication, there are many other words in French that are commonly abbreviated in written *and* spoken communication. Here are a few examples:

un apart	un appartement	*an apartment*
cet aprem	cet après-midi	*this afternoon*
le ciné	le cinéma	*the movie theater*
un/une coloc	un/une colocataire	*a cotenant*
dac	d'accord	*OK*
la fac	la faculté	*the school (university or college)*
le foot	le football	*soccer*
le frigo	le réfrigérateur	*the fridge*
impec	impeccable	*terrific*
le petit dej	le petit déjeuner	*breakfast*
une promo	une promotion	*a promotion*
un/une proprio	un/une propriétaire	*an owner*
un resto	un restaurant	*a restaurant*

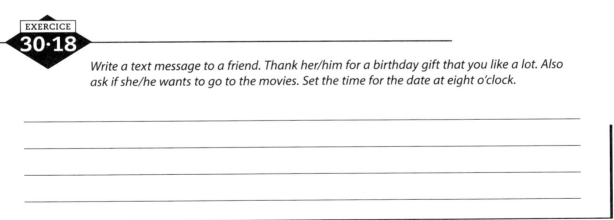

EXERCICE 30·18

Write a text message to a friend. Thank her/him for a birthday gift that you like a lot. Also ask if she/he wants to go to the movies. Set the time for the date at eight o'clock.

Verb transfers and confusing verbs

Verb transfers

The concept of *language transfer*, borrowed from the psychology of learning, refers to a technique, conscious or unconscious, that falls back on acquired knowledge to construct a phrase in the target language.

This transfer can be either positive or negative. Here's an example of positive transfer: An English speaker is deciphering a French text. No vocabulary problems, except for the word **idée**, which the reader, after some hesitation, recognizes as *idea*. Since English and French share an enormous number of cognates and even some identical words with similar meanings, positive transfers can greatly facilitate language acquisition within a language family.

Faux amis

Unfortunately, transfers can also go awry, pointing the learner in the wrong direction. How does a negative transfer work? The engine that powers negative transfers, so to speak, is our belief in a mythical parallelism of form and content across language boundaries. If the word **illusion** means pretty much the same thing in English, why shouldn't all shared words be equally accommodating? Well, they are not, because each language relies on a unique alchemy of form and meaning, which explains why the friendly looking word **location** does not mean *location* in English. Linguists have named these problematic pairings *false friends*, or **faux amis**, because they offer nothing but false hope and confusion.

The purpose of this chapter is to debunk the myth that false friends are an unavoidable fact of life. Nothing could be further from the truth. Systematic study, enriched by relevant exercises and pertinent examples, enables you to grasp underlying patterns. For example, take the phrase, "I have made my decision." You probably recognize that this phrase would transfer poorly into French, where a decision is *taken*, not *made*. You may analyze the different mental processes underlying the challenge of decision making in both languages. For example, while the English speaker takes full ownership of the process, in French, it seems that making the right decision is perceived as a question of choosing between several possibilities—in other words, picking or taking the right one.

What makes this chapter unique is its emphasis on verbs, which usually play second fiddle in **faux amis** discussions—usually the emphasis is on nouns. Unlike nouns, verbs express movement, processes, developments, in other words: *change*. Under these circumstances, it is safe to say that verb transfers present an extraordinary challenge for the learner.

Readers may find themselves uncomfortable with the following left-to-right English-to-French format—a departure from our usual format so far in this book. But I've chosen this layout for this chapter because of the immense power—conscious and unconscious—of English syntactic and idiomatic patterns. These patterns are the main cause of negative transfers.

Here are some examples of the negative transfer:

| "I returned the book," said Anne to the librarian. | « J'ai retourné le livre », a dit Anne au bibliothécaire. |

Since Anne returned the book, but didn't turn it over with its cover facing the desk, the correct translation is:

« J'ai rendu le livre », dit Anne au bibliothécaire.

Michael really needs to get into the habit of finishing his homework. Tempting as it may be to start translating this sentence as **XMichael doit prendre l'habit de finir ses devoirs**, it would comically undermine the meaning of the original sentence, for in French, **prendre l'habit** means to *take the habit*, that is, *join a religious order*.

Naturally, I am not recommending translation from English into French as a method of learning! However, in certain situations, especially for the native English speaker who doesn't think in French, it is necessary to shed light on the initial stages of forming a French phrase, for they encompass unconscious or barely conscious thought processes that are informed by the speaker's tacit knowledge of rules pertaining to his or her own language. This, of course, does not call into question the fundamental principle that for a bilingual person, learning, so to speak, moves in both directions. Nevertheless, in this particular context, using English as a starting point will, as we shall see, yield many valuable insights.

To have

The temptation to overuse this verb, in both languages, should not surprise us: owing to its remarkable versatility and universality, this verb may, covering a wide semantic field, fit into a variety of phrases and expressions. However, count to ten when you feel the urge to "cut and paste" the English semantic field of *have* into a French phrase that *you feel* will work with **avoir**. Remember that highly idiomatic phrases are particularly dangerous. For example: *Thanks for having me* should not be translated as **XMerci de m'avoir eu(e)**, for that means *Thanks for playing a trick on me*. The proper sentence is **Merci de m'avoir invité(e)**.

As a rule, French is often more precise than English:

| Pierre has many friends among artists. | *Pierre compte beaucoup d'amis parmi les artistes.* |

Here are some other examples:

May I have another look?	*Je peux jeter un autre coup d'œil?*
We had a goat cheese sandwich in the park.	*Nous avons mangé un sandwich au fromage de chèvre dans le parc.*
They had breakfast in the garden.	*Ils ont pris le petit déjeuner dans le jardin.*
Ambroise had another serving of egg and bacon quiche.	*Ambroise a repris de la quiche lorraine.*
I had lunch with my best friend yesterday.	*J'ai déjeuné avec mon meilleur ami hier.*
We have dinner at 8 o'clock.	*Nous dînons à 20 heures.*
My grandfather always had a cognac after dinner.	*Mon grand-père buvait toujours un cognac après le dîner.*
Adèle had sex with Jonas last weekend.	*Adèle a couché avec Jonas le week-end dernier.*
Did you have a nice evening with your friends?	*Tu as passé une bonne soirée avec tes amis?*
This summer, they had a lot of visitors in their country house.	*Cet été, ils ont reçu beaucoup de monde dans leur maison de campagne.*

Verb transfers and confusing verbs **435**

Elizabeth had a good time with her friends in Spain.	*Elizabeth a passé de bons moments avec ses amis en Espagne.*
Have fun!	*Amuse-toi!/Amusez-vous bien!*
Jacques had a hard time last year.	*Jacques a traversé une période difficile l'année dernière.*
I am sure you'll have a very nice vacation in Scotland.	*Je suis sûr que vous passerez de bonnes vacances en Écosse.*
Can I have my books back?	*Tu peux me rendre mes livres?*
Noémie had a pink cap on.	*Noémie portait une casquette rose.*
You'd better go now before it starts raining.	*Il vaut mieux que vous partiez avant qu'il pleuve.*
Violaine had her hair cut.	*Violaine s'est fait couper les cheveux.*
The music teacher soon had them all singing in tune.	*Le professeur de musique a réussi très vite à les faire chanter juste.*
"Yvon, you have not done your homework!" "Yes, I have!"	*—Yvon, tu n'as pas fait tes devoirs!—Mais si!*
"You have lied to your sister!" "No, I haven't!"	*—Tu as menti à ta sœur!—Mais non!*
I've had it!	*J'en ai marre!*

To be

Like **avoir** (*to have*), *to be* (**être**) is a verb of great power, since it determines if someone or something is or isn't. One could say that French is less accepting of *to be,* often insisting on a more specific verb in many phrases in which, to an inexperienced learner of French, **être** would seem quite acceptable. For example:

How are you?	*Comment allez-vous?*

Remember, French verbs are more context-sensitive than their English counterpart:

I am well.	*Je vais bien.*
How much is it?	*Combien ça coûte?*
Here's your passport.	*Voici ton passeport.*
Here are your tennis rackets.	*Voici vos raquettes de tennis.*
My sister is afraid of the dark.	*Ma sœur a peur du noir.*
Mathéo is ashamed of his behaviour.	*Mathéo a honte de sa conduite.*
We were very cold last winter.	*Nous avons eu très froid l'hiver dernier.*
I am hot. I think I have a fever.	*J'ai très chaud. Je crois que j'ai de la fièvre.*
My cat Félix must be hungry. He doesn't stop meowing.	*Mon chat Félix doit avoir faim. Il n'arrête pas de miauler.*
You are lucky at card games.	*Tu as de la chance au jeu.*
Julia is forty-three years old.	*Julia a quarante-trois ans.*
How old are you?	*Quel âge as-tu?*
Frédéric, are you sure you're right?	*Frédéric, êtes-vous sûr d'avoir raison?*
They were very thirsty because of the heat.	*Ils avaient très soif à cause de la chaleur.*
Renaud is always wrong.	*Renaud a toujours tort.*
The weather was nice all week long.	*Il a fait beau toute la semaine.*
Ten and two are twelve.	*Dix et deux font douze.*
Émilie is nice, isn't she?	*Émilie est gentille, non/n'est-ce pas?*
"Your brother is going to sue you." "Oh, is he?"	*—Ton frère va te faire un procès.—Ah, vraiment?*
There must be a reason.	*Il doit y avoir une raison.*
It is always windy in Brittany.	*Il y a toujours du vent en Bretagne.*
It's 100 degrees in the shade.	*Il fait 38 degrés à l'ombre.*

EXERCICE 31·1

*Translate the following sentences using the **est-ce que** form where needed and **tu** or **vous**, as indicated.*

1. We'll have dinner late tonight.

2. Jeanne, can I have my pen back? (**tu**)

3. You'd better buy another cake. There will be a lot of guests at the party. (**vous**)

4. I am so cold! There must be another blanket in the armoire.

5. Here's the book you wanted. (**tu**)

6. Your brother is eight? And he is not afraid to speak in public? (**tu**)

7. The weather is nice in Normandy this week. Have a nice vacation! (**vous**)

8. How much is it? Only twenty euros.

9. Henri is lucky. He got a new job near his apartment.

10. The musician had a blue baseball cap on.

To get

A jack-of-all-trades with no true French equivalent, this verb should be handled very gingerly. Do not translate the phrase *I got it!* as **XJe l'ai reçu**, unless you're talking about a package, because the correct translation is **J'ai compris!** Here are some examples:

I got a promotion.	*J'ai eu une promotion.*
You got so many birthday cards!	*Tu as reçu tant de cartes d'anniversaire!*
Timothée got his diploma with distinction.	*Timothée a obtenu son diplôme avec distinction.*
Sabrina got a new job.	*Sabrina a obtenu/décroché un nouvel emploi.*
It's difficult to get a parking space downtown.	*Il est difficile de trouver une place de parking dans le centre-ville.*
Where does your carpenter get his wood?	*Où est-ce que votre menuisier achète son bois?*

Verb transfers and confusing verbs

Could you get my packages at the post office?	Pourrais-tu aller chercher mes colis à la poste?
She got a well-deserved reputation.	Elle a acquis une réputation bien méritée.
I am sorry. I did not get your first name.	Je suis désolé(e). Je n'ai pas entendu/compris votre prénom.
Got it?	T'as compris?/T'as pigé?
The first runner has gotten ahead of his competitors.	Le premier coureur a pris de l'avance sur ses concurrents.
My cat and my dog get along very well.	Mon chat et mon chien s'entendent très bien.
Claire would like to get away from it all and go to Tierra del Fuego.	Claire voudrait tout quitter et partir pour la Terre de Feu.
You should get back home.	Tu devrais rentrer chez toi.
Lily got her credit card back.	Lily a récupéré sa carte de crédit.
Get down from this tree! You are going to fall.	Descends de cet arbre! Tu vas tomber.
Her dismissal got her down.	Son licenciement l'a déprimée.
You will get off the train at the end of the line.	Tu descendras du train au terminus.
The police got the burglar today. He was having lunch with a friend.	La police a attrapé le cambrioleur aujourd'hui. Il déjeunait avec un ami.
Naïm got over a rather serious stomach flu.	Naïm s'est remis d'une gastro-entérite assez grave.
I phoned many times but I could not get through to the manager.	J'ai appelé de nombreuses fois, mais je n'ai pas pu avoir le patron.
We should get together to discuss the details of the contract.	Nous devrions nous réunir pour discuter des détails du contrat.
Get up, it's already ten o'clock!	Lève-toi, il est déjà dix heures!
Let's get going!	Allons-y!
Yann was not able to get the car going this morning, so he was late.	Yann n'a pas réussi à faire démarrer sa voiture ce matin, alors il est arrivé en retard.
Don't hesitate to get help from others!	N'hésite pas à te faire aider par les autres!
My kitchen gets a lot of sun.	Ma cuisine est très ensoleillée.
Armelle got the flu when she was on vacation.	Armelle a attrapé la grippe pendant ses vacances.
I must get my essay to the professor.	Je dois remettre mon essai au professeur.
Jean got into the habit of typing his novels on his new iPad.	Jean a pris l'habitude de taper ses romans sur son nouvel iPad.

EXERCICE 31·2

*Translate the following sentences using the **est-ce que** form where needed and **tu** or **vous**, as indicated.*

1. Bertrand never got over Paul's death.

   _____

2. Tomorrow we must get up at seven to have breakfast with the marketing director.

   _____

3. Sonia borrowed a lot of money from you. Did you get it back? (**tu**)

   _____

4. There is so much noise here. I did not get your last name.

_____

5. Can you get this novel quickly? I really need it for my French course. (**vous**)

_____

6. Get off the subway at the Louvre station! (**tu**)

_____

7. How did you get the flu in July on the Riviera? (**tu**)

_____

8. We'll meet once a month to talk about the new project.

_____

9. Luc's parents don't want him to get back home after 10 P.M.

_____

10. Where does the baker get his flour? His bread is so good.

_____

To take

While this verb often corresponds to the French **prendre**, you need to watch out for a plethora of connotations, metaphorical and literal, without French parallels. Because *to take* is more versatile than **prendre**, it is imperative to avoid literal translations. For example:

> Bus number 12 will take you to the airport.

should not be translated as:

> **X** *Le bus 12 vous prendra vers l'aéroport.*

for that is not a French sentence. The correct sentence is:

> *Le bus 12 vous conduira à l'aéroport.*

Similarly, we may *take a trip*, but being allergic to the idea of **X***prendre* **un voyage**, a French person will say: **Je vais faire un voyage**. Here are some other examples:

I took his hand.	*J'ai pris sa main.*
Marie-Lys took her daughter by the hand.	*Marie-Lys a pris sa fille par la main.*
Martin took the baby into his arms.	*Martin a pris le bébé dans ses bras.*
Can you take the vase on the shelf and put it in the garden?	*Peux-tu prendre le vase sur l'étagère et le mettre dans le jardin?*
Don't forget to take your passport.	*N'oublie pas d'emporter ton passeport.*
Is this seat taken?	*Cette place est occupée?*
The detective took his name and address.	*Le détective a relevé son nom et son adresse.*
The soldiers took the town in a few hours.	*Les soldats se sont emparés de/ont saisi la ville en quelques heures.*

Verb transfers and confusing verbs **439**

This novelist takes her ideas from real life.	Cette romancière tire ses idées de la réalité.
I take it you have already made your decision.	Je suppose que tu as déjà pris ta décision.
I took me three hours to get to Caen.	Cela m'a pris/J'ai mis/Il m'a fallu trois heures pour arriver à Caen.
Gabrielle has a foul temper; she takes after her grandmother.	Gabrielle a un sale caractère; elle tient de sa grand-mère.
Raoul took apart each of their arguments.	Raoul a démoli chacun de leurs arguments.
Selma took back her DVDs.	Selma a repris ses DVD.
We slowly took down the pictures.	Nous avons lentement décroché les tableaux.
Her plane took off for Rio de Janeiro.	Son avion s'est envolé pour Rio de Janeiro.
I took off my clothes before jumping in the swimming pool.	J'ai enlevé mes vêtements avant de sauter dans la piscine.
They took us to the opera.	Ils nous ont emmenés à l'opéra.
Basil did not take the news very well.	Basil a été très affecté par les nouvelles.
I can't take it anymore.	Je n'en peux plus.
Take it or leave it!	C'est à prendre ou à laisser!

EXERCICE 31·3

*Translate the following sentences using inversion as needed and **tu** or **vous**, as indicated.*

1. Where are you taking us tonight? (**tu**)

2. It will take me two hours to finish this translation. (*three possible answers*)

3. The Grand Palais will take down the Manet exhibition on March 15.

4. Take the first street on the right! (**vous**)

5. I am sure Carole will take at least three suitcases.

6. This seat is not taken. Sit down, please. (**vous**)

7. Take off your shoes before entering the temple! (**vous**)

8. Take this bracelet, and put it in your bag! It's a gift. (**tu**)

9. The children like to watch the planes take off at the Orly airport.

_____

10. Joséphine is so nice. She takes after her mother.

_____

To put

Loosely corresponding to the French verb **mettre**, this handy English verb, because it covers enormous semantic ground, often misleads the unsuspecting learner of French, who may be oblivious to this verb's monumental idiomatic productivity. For example:

How shall we put our demands to the boss?

You may have guessed that a French person would never say:

X_Comment allons-nous mettre nos demandes au chef?_

The correct sentence is:

Comment allons-nous présenter nos demandes au chef?

Alexandre put the fan on the table.	_Alexandre a mis le ventilateur sur la table._
Olivia always puts on lipstick to go out.	_Olivia met toujours du rouge à lèvres pour sortir._
We put an advertisement in the paper to rent out our apartment.	_Nous avons passé une annonce dans le journal pour louer notre appartement._
They put us on the train.	_Ils nous ont accompagnés au train._
I wouldn't put Offenbach on a list of best composers.	_Je ne classerais pas Offenbach parmi les plus grands compositeurs._
How should I put it?	_Comment dirais-je?_
As Victor Hugo puts it: "To love beauty is to see light."	_Comme le dit Victor Hugo « Aimer la beauté, c'est vouloir la lumière »._
You put forward pros and cons. We'll see . . .	_Tu as présenté le pour et le contre. On verra . . ._
Raphaël put a lot of money into this paper factory.	_Raphaël a investi beaucoup d'argent dans cette usine à papier._
We've put a lot of time into this project.	_Nous avons consacré beaucoup de temps à ce projet._
Cassandre puts great effort into explaining Latin to her students.	_Cassandre se démène pour faire comprendre le latin à ses élèves._
I put aside some money to go to Polynesia.	_J'ai mis de l'argent de côté pour partir en Polynésie._
Put away your toys in the box.	_Range tes jouets dans la boîte._
After his psychic breakdown, Ivan was put in a mental hospital.	_Après sa crise de démence, on a enfermé Ivan dans un hôpital psychiatrique._
Put the antique doll back in its place!	_Remets la poupée antique à sa place!_
Benjamin put his hat down and sat in an armchair.	_Benjamin a posé son chapeau et s'est assis dans un fauteuil._
My aunt Margaud puts down everybody except her darling son.	_Ma tante Margaud critique tout le monde sauf son fils chéri._
Aurélie put down two thousand euros on a house by the sea.	_Aurélie a versé une caution de deux mille euros pour une maison au bord de la mer._
The boss put you down as an intern.	_Le patron a mis que tu étais stagiaire._

Verb transfers and confusing verbs   **441**

They have put in a request for a scholarship.	*Ils ont fait une demande de bourse.*
The filth everywhere put us off.	*La saleté partout nous a dégoûtés.*
I put money on Tornade at the time of the Prix de Diane race in Chantilly.	*J'ai parié sur Tornade au Prix de Diane à Chantilly.*
After everything his brother put him through, he still talks to him.	*Après tout ce que son frère lui a fait subir, il lui parle toujours.*
Mélanie's boss puts her through hell.	*Le patron de Mélanie lui mène la vie dure.*
I'm not going to put up with this behavior! Enough!	*Je ne vais pas tolérer ce comportement! Ça suffit!*

EXERCICE 31·4

*Translate the following sentences using the **est-ce que** form as needed and **tu** or **vous**, as indicated.*

1. Put your red dress on! We're going out tonight. (**tu**)

2. Will you put an ad in the paper to sell your house? (**vous**)

3. Quentin put his computer down on the desk; then he had lunch.

4. My colleague put aside several personal letters to read after work.

5. Juliette put all the vegetables into the refrigerator in perfect order.

6. Mrs. Deville put all her money into her daughter's new shop.

7. Put everything back in its place before they come back! (**tu**)

8. Jonathan put in a request for financial aid.

9. You need to put down a fifty-euro deposit to rent this bicycle. (**vous**) (**verser**)

10. I put you down as a part-time worker. (**vous**) (**mis que vous**)

To hold

Just like the verbs previously discussed, *to hold* may be related to a particular French verb, which in this case is **tenir**. However, as we already know, the semantic fields of the two verbs may only occasionally overlap, which leaves large areas of uncertainty. It is very easy to step out onto thin ice. For example:

> Jack has never held a job for more than a week.

Which verb should be used in French? **Tenir**?

> X*Jack n'a jamais tenu un emploi plus d'une semaine.*

Although a French person would probably understand the preceding phrase, being merely understood is not enough! The correct sentence is:

> *Jack n'ai jamais gardé/conservé un emploi plus d'une semaine.*

Let's look at some other examples:

Can you hold my umbrella?	*Tu peux tenir mon parapluie?*
Noah and Agathe were holding hands.	*Noah et Agathe se tenaient par la main.*
The older brother was holding his youngest brother's hand.	*Le frère aîné tenait son plus jeune frère par la main.*
The wooden stake holds the rosebush in place.	*Le tuteur en bois maintient le rosier en place.*
Audrey's hair was held in place with clips.	*Les cheveux d'Audrey étaient attachés avec des barrettes.*
Everybody holds an opinion about global warming.	*Tout le monde a une opinion sur le réchauffement climatique.*
The nice weather seems to be holding.	*Le beau temps semble se maintenir.*
The press conference will be held in the Japanese garden.	*La conférence de presse aura lieu dans le jardin japonais.*
Antonia and Ingrid are holding a party to celebrate the success of their new company.	*Antonia et Ingrid ont prévu une fête pour célébrer le succès de leur nouvelle entreprise.*
Your car will hold all our suitcases?	*Ta voiture est assez grande pour contenir toutes nos valises?*
Could you hold this money until I return from China?	*Pourrais-tu garder cet argent jusqu'à ce que je revienne de Chine?*
The police held them for the whole night because they were drunk.	*La police les a gardés toute la nuit car ils étaient ivres.*
The police held back the crowd.	*La police a contenu la foule.*
The press held back the number of killings.	*La presse n'a pas divulgué le nombre de meurtres.*
Louis managed with difficulty to hold back his dogs.	*Louis a réussi à retenir ses chiens avec difficulté.*
Hold the line!	*Ne quittez pas!*
Well, well! This is really strange.	*Tiens, tiens! C'est vraiment bizarre.*

Verb transfers and confusing verbs **443**

EXERCICE 31·5

*Translate the following sentences using the **tu** or **vous** form, as indicated.*

1. We hope the warm weather will hold during the weekend.

2. A policeman is accused of having held back the name of an accomplice.

3. The wedding will be held in a nineteenth-century castle.

4. There are several ways to hold a pencil.

5. Pierre, how can you hold such opinions? You should be more objective! (**vous**)

6. Well, well! Léa and Xavier at the beach!

7. Hold the ladder a minute! (**tu**)

8. My school is holding a party to celebrate its fiftieth anniversary.

9. I am going to try and find Mrs. Bernardin. Hold the line! (**vous**)

10. Olivier will hold these documents until I come back.

To go

While *to go* and **aller** both express the idea of literal (and metaphorical) motion, their numerous semantic and idiomatic differences remain a challenge for every learner. For example, instead of using **aller**, a French person will consider the context and then pick another word. Imagine yourself as a boss telling an employee that you don't need him or her at this time:

> You may go.

Would a French employee understand the literal translation?

> X*Vous pouvez vous en aller.*

The correct sentence would be:

> *Vous pouvez disposer.*

Here are some other examples:

How's it going?
Ça va?/Comment ça va?

We are going to the Galeries Lafayette.
Nous allons aux Galeries Lafayette.

Has Stéphane already gone?
Stéphane est déjà parti?

My father always goes too fast on the highway.
Mon père roule toujours trop vite sur l'autoroute.

You are pregnant. You can go next.
Vous êtes enceinte. Vous pouvez passer devant.

Add nutmeg, stirring as you go.
Ajoutez de la noix de muscade en remuant au fur et à mesure.

The children went down the hill full speed.
Les enfants ont descendu la colline à toute vitesse.

Justine went up all the stairs to the top of the Eiffel Tower.
Justine a monté tous les escaliers jusqu'au sommet de la Tour Eiffel.

Ismaël went on a journey to Turkey.
Ismaël a fait un voyage en Turquie.

The ambassador went to a rice field in Vietnam.
L'ambassadeur s'est rendu dans une rizière au Vietnam.

My iPhone is gone!
Mon iPhone a disparu!

200 workers are supposed to be let go at Moulinex.
200 ouvriers sont censés être licenciés chez Moulinex.

After two days in Saint-Tropez, all my money was gone!
Après deux jours à Saint-Tropez, j'avais dépensé tout mon argent!

The way things are going, the firm is going to have to file for bankruptcy.
Si ça continue comme ça, l'entreprise va devoir déposer son bilan.

The ceremony at the Académie française went very well.
La cérémonie à l'Académie française s'est très bien passée.

The Sahara desert goes from Mauritania to Sudan.
Le désert du Sahara s'étend de la Mauritanie au Soudan.

$100 does not go very far.
On ne va pas très loin avec 80 euros.

What's wrong with Carla? Has she gone mad?
Qu'est-ce qui ne va pas chez Carla? Elle est folle?/Elle est devenue folle?

The light went red.
Le feu est passé au rouge.

Marc went through a red light.
Marc a brûlé un feu rouge.

There goes another crystal glass!
Encore un verre en cristal de cassé!

My great-uncle's mind is going.
Mon grand-oncle n'a plus toute sa tête.

The opera singer was supposed to sing *La Traviata* but his voice was gone.
Le chanteur était censé chanter La Traviata *mais il n'avait plus de voix.*

The story goes that a princess of Denmark is going to marry a tightrope walker.
Le bruit court qu'une princesse du Danemark va épouser un funambule.

Anything goes.
Tout est permis.

That goes without saying.
Cela va sans dire.

Irina doesn't know how the words of the song go.
Irina ne connaît pas les paroles de cette chanson.

Kiyo is not bad, as far as fashion designers go.
Kiyo n'est pas mauvais comme styliste.

There are three weeks to go before the swimming competition.
Il reste trois semaines avant la compétition de natation.

He had gone only three miles when a tire burst.
Il n'avait fait que cinq kilomètres quand un pneu a éclaté.

We were going across the street when suddenly I saw Lyne on the sidewalk.
Nous traversions la rue quand, soudain, j'ai vu Lyne sur le trottoir.

Madeleine has gone away on vacation without her cell phone.
Madeleine est partie en vacances sans son portable.

We went back to Nepal the third time.
Nous sommes retournés au Népal pour la troisième fois.

This story goes back to the 19th century.
Cette histoire remonte au XIXe siècle.

You've got to go by the book!
Vous devez appliquer strictement le règlement!

Verb transfers and confusing verbs **445**

EXERCICE 31·6

Translate the following sentences.

1. Her family goes back to Louis XVIII.

2. How did Pierre's birthday party go?

3. I was going across the Boulevard des Capucines when I saw Christian Lacroix!

4. There goes another plate!

5. Louise went through a red light last night.

6. Let's go to Nohant tomorrow. I want to visit George Sand's house.

7. Nora wants to go back to Brazil next year. It will be the fourth time.

8. The prime minister of Great Britain will go to Dakar at the end of the month.

9. The story goes that the prince lied to his family.

10. I can't teach today. My voice has gone.

To keep

Keep in mind that the French equivalents of *to keep* that you might think of, such as **garder**, work only in the right context. Unfortunately, what seems to be the right context in English may often strike a French person as odd, if not incomprehensible. For example, even the simplest English phrase may pose a challenge:

> Pierre kept his promise.

In English, it seems, a promise is like a keepsake, something to be treasured; one is faithful to a promise. However, this idea does not work in French:

> X*Pierre a gardé sa promesse.*

The correct sentence is:

Pierre a tenu sa promesse.

Here are a few other examples:

May I keep the cork of this Mouton Cadet 1947?	*Puis-je garder le bouchon de ce Mouton Cadet 1947?*
You must keep the cake in a cold place.	*Il faut conserver le gâteau au frais.*
These peaches do not keep long.	*Ces pêches ne se conservent pas longtemps.*
How long could you keep this Venetian mirror for me?	*Combien de temps pouvez-vous mettre de côté ce miroir vénitien?*
Where do you keep your medicine?	*Où ranges-tu tes médicaments?*
After the accident, Joanne was kept in the hospital for two days.	*Après l'accident, Joanne a dû passer deux jours à l'hôpital.*
This chiropractor has the bad habit of keeping his patients waiting.	*Ce chiropracteur a la sale habitude de faire attendre ses patients.*
I tried to say something, but Leïla kept talking.	*J'ai essayé de dire quelque chose, mais Leïla a continué à parler.*
My secretary keeps forgetting to take down some important messages.	*Mon secrétaire oublie tout le temps de noter des messages importants.*
Her lawyer kept saying I was a bad driver.	*Son avocat ne cessait de dire que j'étais un mauvais conducteur.*
I was holding the ladder to keep Michel from falling.	*Je tenais l'échelle pour empêcher Michel de tomber.*
Keep quiet!	*Tais-toi!*
Keep your stomach in!	*Rentre le ventre!*
Keep out.	*Défense d'entrer.*

EXERCICE 31·7

Translate the following sentences using inversion as needed and **tu** *or* **vous**, *as indicated.*

1. I am sure the clinic will keep Étienne at least a week.

2. Where do you keep your tea cups? (**tu**) (**ranger**)

3. We are in a theater. Keep quiet! (**vous**)

4. This bread won't keep more than three days.

5. Don't keep me waiting! (**tu**)

6. Patrick keeps complaining about everything.

7. Keep the change! (**vous**)

_____

8. You cannot keep him from seeing his ex-mother-in-law. (**tu**)

_____

9. Anne promised to keep the secret.

_____

10. He keeps forgetting to buy olive oil.

_____

Faire

In the previous sections, we illustrated the numerous discrepancies between English and French verbs by providing examples of incorrect usage caused by the learner's good-natured belief that verbs like to play nice! Well, as you know by now, they play, but as far as their mannerisms are concerned, the word _nice_ does not come to mind.

Until now, the English examples on the left side of the page have given you a selection of verbs known for their uncanny ability to attract false friends. So moving from left to right, you were to seek a safe route between Scylla and Charybdis, hoping to land on a friendly French verb.

Let's see what happens when we ask the two mythological monsters to take a break and play a game of Scrabble. On the left, you will still find English sentences with a variety of verbs, which, as you will discover on the right side, all become **faire** in French. The purpose of this particular exercise is not only to demonstrate the productivity of a frequently used French verb, but also to familiarize you with an important part of French idiomatic vocabulary and to enable you to investigate these key verbs on your own.

Can you bake a cake?	_Tu peux faire un gâteau?_
What about going for a walk?	_Si on faisait une promenade?_
I am going to play hooky.	_Moi, je vais faire l'école buissonnière._
The doctor will probably give you a shot.	_Le médecin vous fera sans doute une piqûre._
I have several checks to write.	_Je dois faire plusieurs chèques._
What about a cruise?	_Et si on faisait une croisière?_
Our bedroom is twenty feet wide.	_Notre chambre fait six mètres de large._
I went around all the libraries, but I could not find the book I needed.	_J'ai fait toutes les bibliothèques mais je n'ai pas pu trouver le livre dont j'avais besoin._
I am only repeating what Christine said.	_Je ne fais que répéter ce que Christine a dit._
It has been five years since we last went to Amsterdam.	_Cela fait cinq ans que nous ne sommes pas allés à Amsterdam._
She is a self-made woman.	_Elle s'est faite toute seule._
It does not matter.	_Cela ne fait rien._
Don't worry!	_Ne t'en fais pas!/Ne vous en faites pas!_

EXERCICE 31·8

*Translate the following sentences using inversion as needed and **tu** or **vous**, as indicated.*

1. She is writing a check.

   _____

2. The nurse gave me a shot.

   _____

3. It has been three months since I visited my grandfather.

   _____

4. Let's go for a walk!

   _____

5. Can you cook? (**vous**)

   _____

6. I am only telling you what I heard. (**tu**)

   _____

7. His living room must be twenty feet wide.

   _____

8. I am not worried.

   _____

9. It has been a year since she called her sister.

   _____

10. Lucie would like to go on a cruise.

   _____

EXERCICE 31·9

Select the theme corresponding to each sentence.

activité artistique	communication	cuisine	dessert	études
maison	problème	sortie	sport	voyage

1. Est-ce que Damien fait du théâtre? _____

2. Cela fait six mois que nous ne sommes pas allés au cinéma. _____

3. Ils ont fait plusieurs pâtisseries pour trouver un gâteau original. _____

Verb transfers and confusing verbs   **449**

4. Je ferai une salade pour le déjeuner. _____

5. Vous avez fait toute la Sicile pendant vos vacances. _____

6. La terrasse fait dix mètres carrés. _____

7. Alexandre fait une école d'ingénieur. _____

8. —J'ai oublié ton dictionnaire.—Cela ne fait rien. _____

9. Arrête de crier, je ne fais que te transmettre le message d'Astrid! _____

10. Si on faisait une randonnée dans les calanques de Cassis. _____

Confusing verbs

As you have noticed so far, the French language is full of surprises. The previous section introduced you to **faux amis** (*false friends*), especially as they occur in verbs. Now the confusion continues—we look at verbs that often confuse English learners of French.

Prêter/emprunter

There is some confusion in English when speakers use the verb *to loan*, without making a clear distinction between the verbs *to lend* and *to borrow*. There is no such confusion in French.

Prêter

Ils **prêtent** à 8%.	*They give loans at 8%.*
Pourrais-tu me **prêter** ta voiture samedi?	*Could you lend me your car on Sunday?*
Vous devrez **prêter** serment.	*You'll have to take an oath.*
Tu **devrais prêter un peu plus attention** à ce qu'ils disent.	*You should pay more attention to what they have to say.*
Isabelle Huppert **a prêté** son nom à une organisation de bienfaisance.	*Isabelle Huppert lent her name to a charity.*

Emprunter

Les Tanguy **ont emprunté** 50 000 euros à la banque.	*The Tanguys borrowed 50,000 euros from the bank.*
Pourquoi **n'empruntes-tu pas** ce nouveau roman à la bibliothèque?	*Why don't you borrow this new novel from the library?*
Ces métaphores **sont empruntées** à la musique baroque.	*These metaphors are derived from baroque music.*
Les randonneurs **ont emprunté** un sentier escarpé pour arriver au col du Ventoux.	*The hikers used a steep path to get to the Ventoux mountain pass.*
N'empruntez pas ce passage souterrain!	*Do not use this underpass!*

Poser/demander/interroger/mettre ou remettre en question

These verbs are used in specific ways and are often confused. Most important, remember to **poser une question**.

Poser

Le propriétaire leur **a posé** des questions.	*The owner asked them some questions.*
Vous devriez lui **poser la question**.	*You should ask him about it.*

450 PRACTICE MAKES PERFECT Complete French All-in-One

Demander

Il a **demandé** l'autorisation de créer une association.	He **asked for** permission to create an association.
Elle **a demandé** une réponse d'ici jeudi.	She **asked for** an answer by Thursday.

Interroger

La police **a interrogé** le suspect pendant trois heures.	The police **questioned** the suspect for three hours.
Vendredi, vous **serez interrogés par écrit** sur la géographie de la France.	On Friday, you'**ll be given a written test** on the geography of France.

Mettre en question/remettre (se remettre) en question

These two verbs are interchangeable most of the time. It all depends on the context:

Le directeur du marketing **a mis en question** la compétence de ce candidat.	The marketing director **questioned** this candidate's competence.
Un scientifique de renom **met en question** cette nouvelle théorie.	One well-known scientist **questions** this theory.
Ce projet artistique **est** sans cesse **remis en question**.	This artistic project **is** continually **being called into question**.
Selon Sartre, il est important de **se remettre en question** de temps en temps.	According to Sartre, it is important **to do some soul-searching** now and then.

Commander/ordonner

Commander

Mesdames, **avez**-vous déjà **commandé**?	Ladies, **have** you already **ordered**?
J'**ai commandé** trois livres et un DVD sur Amazon.fr.	I **ordered** three books and one DVD on Amazon.fr.

Ordonner

Il leur **a ordonné** de se taire.	He **ordered** them to be quiet.
Le général **va ordonner** que ce soit fait sur-le-champ.	The general **will order** that it be done immediately.

EXERCICE
31·10

*Translate the following sentences, using **tu** or **vous**, as indicated.*

1. Ask for an appointment for Friday morning. (**tu**)

   _____

2. Paul wants to borrow my car on Sunday afternoon.

   _____

3. Céline ordered a chocolate mousse.

   _____

4. Alexandre continually questions his choice of career.

_____

5. Can you lend me the notes you took at the conference? (**vous**)

_____

6. The mayor of Strasbourg has ordered the closing of a discotheque.

_____

7. This expression is probably derived from the German language.

_____

8. I would like to ask you a delicate question. (**vous**)

_____

9. Inès borrowed a dress from her best friend, Noami.

_____

10. The detective questioned Jean and his brother.

_____

Apporter/emporter/rapporter/amener/emmener

These verbs indicate someone bringing or taking things somewhere. It is important to use these verbs only with *things*, not human beings. **Apporter** and **amener** start with an **a-**, so the thing or the person comes to the speaker. **Emporter** and **emmener** start with an **e-**, actually an **ex** in Latin, so it goes out, away from the speaker. This is one trick to remember. Some exceptions can be found in literary discourse and abstract statements. However, this is the basic rule you need to refer to in everyday conversation. And be careful, even French people tend to make this mistake. You have to prove them wrong!

Apporter

Apporte-moi une tasse de thé!	**Bring** me a cup of tea!
Le président **a apporté** bien des changements.	The president **brought** many changes.

Emporter

Ma tante Jeanne **emporte** au moins trois valises en vacances.	My aunt Jeanne **takes** at least three suitcases on vacation.
Dans ce petit restaurant, il y a des plats chauds **à emporter**.	At this restaurant, there are hot dishes **to take out**.

Rapporter

Quand voulez-vous que je **rapporte** votre couscoussier?	When do you want me to **bring back** your couscous maker?
Érica **rapportera** une baguette en rentrant.	Érica **will bring** a baguette when she gets back.

452 PRACTICE MAKES PERFECT Complete French All-in-One

Amener/emmener

Amène les enfants chez moi vers dix heures!	***Bring*** the children home around 10 o'clock.
Qu'est-ce qui vous **amène** ici?	What ***brings*** you here?
J'**emmène** Alice à la piscine en matin.	I'll take Alice to the swimming pool this morning.

Here are some exceptions when **amener** means *to be the cause, to provoke*.

La sécheresse **a amené** la famine.	*The drought **brought about** famine.*
Cela pourrait l'**amener** à démissionner.	*This could **bring** him to resign.*

Aménager/emménager/déménager

Aménager

Aménager is an important verb to know how to handle. You'll read it in the press every day.

L'État **va aménager** de nouveaux espaces dans le bois de Vincennes.	*The government **is going to develop** some new areas in the bois de Vincennes.*
Le patron **a décidé d'aménager** les horaires de travail.	*The boss **has decided to adjust** the working hours.*

But you can also use **aménager** at home:

Florence **va aménager** cette chambre en bureau.	*Florence **is going to convert** this bedroom into a study.*
Dans ce catalogue figurent des cuisines **aménagées en design contemporain**.	*This catalog features **fully equipped and modernly designed** kitchens.*

Emménager

Emménager starts with an **e-**, which indicates that you are going from point A to point B.

Les Gautier **viennent d'emménager** dans un nouvel appartement.	*The Gautiers **just moved into** a new apartment.*
Théo **a fini par emménager** avec sa compagne.	*Théo **finally moved in** with his partner.*

Déménager

Here comes the problem! **Déménager** simply indicates the idea of moving out of somewhere, not of moving in, like **emménager**. This is a typical mistake. Be aware of it. Remember Théo and Véronique!

Véronique **doit déménager** avant le 31 mars.	*Véronique **must move out** before March 31st.*
L'entreprise **va déménager** ses bureaux sur l'île de la Jatte.	*The company **will move** its offices on the Île de la Jatte.*

Rencontrer/rejoindre/retrouver/se joindre à

Here are some other tough ones. Here again, the English language is the culprit because the verb *to meet* is so elastic. Look carefully at the examples and familiarize yourself with the nuances.

Verb transfers and confusing verbs **453**

Rencontrer

As a rule, **rencontrer** is used when you meet someone for the first time or by chance:

| Nella et Fabrice **se sont rencontrés** dans un cours de français. | Nella and Fabrice **met** in a French class. |
| J'**ai rencontré** Félicie ce matin au marché aux puces. | I **ran into** Félicie this morning at the flea market. |

However, in formal situations, **rencontrer** does not necessarily refer to a first encounter. It emphasizes the importance of the meeting, but it does not mean that the persons involved had never met before.

| Le Premier ministre français **a rencontré** son homologue britannique lors du Sommet européen. | The French prime minister **had a meeting with** his British counterpart during the European Summit. |

Rejoindre

Rejoindre means that one person or more will meet another or several persons in a specific place. **Retrouver** is a synonym.

Rejoindre

| On **se rejoint** à la gare à midi. | Let's **meet** at the station at noon. |
| Je n'ai pas fini mon article. Je vous **rejoins** tous les deux au Café de la Paix dans une heure. | I have not finished my article. I'll **meet** you both at the Café de la Paix in an hour. |

Retrouver

| Je **te retrouve** devant le cinéma à 19 heures. | I'll **meet you** outside the movie theater at 7 P.M. |
| On **se retrouve** à quinze heures? | **Should** we **meet** at 3 P.M.? |

Se joindre à

When one or more persons join a group already formed, an association, or a club, **se joindre à** is the proper verb.

| Voudriez-vous **vous joindre à** nous dimanche pour le pique-nique annuel? | Would you like **to join** us on Sunday for the annual picnic? |
| N'hésitez pas à vous **joindre** à notre discussion! On a besoin de votre avis. | Do not hesitate **to join** in the discussion. We need your opinion. |

EXERCICE 31·11

*Translate the following sentences, using the **est-ce que** form as needed and the **tu** or **vous** form, as indicated.*

1. We'll have a party at the pool tonight. Would you like to join us? (**tu**)

   _____

2. The prime ministers of France and Great Britain will meet in Berlin in May.

   _____

3. Lise, you want to take these two huge suitcases for just two days? Are you crazy? (**tu**)

_____

4. Ask Pierre to be at La Perle, rue Vieille du Temple. I'll meet you around 8 P.M. (**vous**)

_____

5. Bring Léonie a nice bouquet of flowers! (**vous**)

_____

6. Rémi is moving out on Saturday. Can you come and help us? (**tu**)

_____

7. I took my niece to l'Opéra Bastille. She loves _Carmen_.

_____

8. You are moving in with Simon! Congratulations! (**tu**)

_____

9. Don't bring your brother-in-law on Sunday! I don't like him at all. (**tu**)

_____

10. Laura's school knows how to adjust the children's schedule to give them more time for arts and sports.

_____

EXERCICE
31·12

Complete each sentence with the appropriate verb, using the **tu** or **vous** form, as indicated.

1. _____ un parapluie! Je pense qu'il va pleuvoir. (**tu**)

2. Je _____ Jérémie pour la première fois, boulevard Montparnasse. Je l'adore!

3. Lila et Loïs _____ en février et se sont mariés en décembre de la même année.

4. _____-moi au bout du monde! (**tu**)

5. Les voleurs se sont introduits dans la maison et ils _____ tous nos bijoux.

6. _____-moi un sari en soie sauvage de Madras!

7. Pars avant moi! Nous _____ tous à la Brasserie Mollard vers 21 heures.

8. Cela me ferait tant plaisir si vous pouviez _____ nous. Toute la famille sera là.

9. J'adore cet appartement. Je refuse de _____ une autre fois. Ça suffit!

10. Le propriétaire du château _____ l'ancienne écurie en quatre chambres d'hôtes. C'est vraiment magnifique!

Verb transfers and confusing verbs **455**

Arrêter/s'arrêter

A common mistake is the omission of the reflexive pronoun in front of the verb. The verb **arrêter** does exist, but it has a different meaning. Here are some examples.

Arrêter

La police **a arrêté** un dealer de drogue, rue de Verneuil.	*The police **arrested** a drug dealer on the rue de Verneuil.*
Arrêtez la voiture ici!	***Stop** the car here!*

S'arrêter

Je me **suis arrêtée** devant les vitrines de Sonia Rykiel.	*I **stopped** in front of Sonia Rykiel's windows.*
Ce train **ne s'arrête pas** à Orléans.	*This train **does not stop** in Orleans.*

Pousser/faire pousser

More subtleties! Yes, *to grow* is so easy in English. But in French, you must analyze the meaning before making the decision.

Pousser

Katiana **pousse** le landau de son bébé.	*Katiana **pushes** her baby's pram.*
Mes tomates **poussent bien** cette année.	*My tomatoes **are doing nicely** this year.*

Faire pousser

Ils **font pousser** du seigle dans le Massif Central.	*They **grow** rye in the Massif Central.*
Comment **faire pousser** un avocatier à la maison?	*How **to grow** an avocado tree at home?*

Visiter/rendre visite/faire visiter

As a rule, **visiter** is used when refering to places.

Visiter

Roland et moi **avons visité** l'abbaye de Cluny près de Macon.	*Roland and I **visited** the Cluny Abbey near Macon.*
Nous **avons visité** trois maisons à vendre.	*We **viewed** three houses for sale.*

Rendre visite

When you visit someone socially, use **rendre visite à**:

Nous **allons rendre visite** à mes beaux-parents ce week-end.	*We'll **visit** my in-laws this weekend.*
Éolia **voudrait rendre visite** à ses amis en Italie.	*Éolia **would like to visit** her friends in Italy.*

However, if your teeth hurt, you neither **visiter** nor **rendre visite** to the dentist. You simply go to the dentist's:

Tu **devrais aller chez** un dentiste.	*You **should visit (go to, see)** a dentist.*

Visiter can be used when referring to people in a hospital or jail setting. This usage is **discutable**. Although it is correct, today people may just say **aller voir**.

456 PRACTICE MAKES PERFECT Complete French All-in-One

Le Dr Clément **visitera** le patient
à l'hôpital demain matin.
L'avocat **visitera** sa cliente à la prison
de la Roquette.

Dr. Clément **will visit** the patient at the
hospital tomorrow morning.
The lawyer **will visit** his client in the la Roquette
prison.

Faire visiter

Un chercheur du CNRS **m'a fait visiter**
son laboratoire.
Tu **me fais visiter** ton appartement?

A CNRS researcher **showed me around**
his laboratory.
Can you **show me around** your apartment?

EXERCICE 31·13

Translate the following sentences, using the **est-ce que** form as needed and the **tu** or **vous** form, as indicated.

1. Mélanie will visit her friend Léa in Rouen this summer.

2. Push this chair against the wall! (**tu**)

3. Stop asking questions! (**tu**)

4. Inspector Clouseau is so happy today. He arrested Sir Charles Lytton.

5. You must visit the Futuroscope in Poitiers. (**vous**)

6. My uncle grows corn in his garden.

7. Léa's parents showed me around their house.

8. They stopped in a beautiful village in Corrèze.

9. Our cauliflowers refused to grow this year.

10. You need to ask for authorization to visit someone in this prison. (**tu**)

Vouloir/en vouloir à

Vouloir

The general meaning of **vouloir** is *to want, to wish*. It is followed by either a direct object or a verb in the infinitive. When the partitive article and an object are replaced, **en** is used.

Nous **voulons** une réforme.	*We **want** a reform.*
Ils **veulent vendre** leur maison.	*They **want to sell** their house.*
Je **voudrais** bien que tu me donnes des roses de ton jardin.	*I really **would like** you to give me some roses from your garden.*
Tu **en veux** combien?	*How many do you **want**?*
J'**en voudrais** quatre.	*I'**d like** four.*
Je peux t'en donner autant que tu **veux**.	*I can give you as many as you **wish**.*

En vouloir à

En vouloir means "to have a grudge against someone." The **en** here is part of the verb. So be careful when you see or hear a **en** with **vouloir**. It can lead to total misunderstanding.

Pourquoi tu lui **en veux**?	*Why do you **have a grudge against** him?*
Benoît **en veut à** son frère d'avoir fait échouer leurs projets.	*Benoît **holds it against** his brother that he made their projects fail.*
Ne m'**en veux** pas. Je ne l'ai pas fait exprès.	*Don't **hold it against** me. I did not do it on purpose.*
Tu ne m'**en veux** pas?	*No hard feelings?*

Envier/avoir envie de/avoir une envie de

They may look similar, but their meaning is quite different.

Envier

Je t'**envie**.	*I **envy** you.*
Denis vous **envie** de pouvoir faire ce voyage.	*Denis **envies** you for being able to take this trip.*

Avoir envie de

Nicolas **a envie de** s'installer à Menton.	*Nicolas **would like to** move to Menton.*
Qu'est-ce que vous **avez envie de** faire?	*What do you **feel like** doing?*
Loïc **avait** très **envie de** rire pendant la conférence.	*Loïc really **felt like** laughing during the conference.*
J'**ai envie de** toi.	*I **want** you.*

Avoir une envie de

Hélène, qui est enceinte, **a une envie** de chocolat.	*Hélène, who is pregnant, **has a craving** for chocolate.*
Gabriel **a des envies** subites de cornichons.	*Gabriel **has** sudden **cravings** for pickles.*

Attendre/s'attendre à

Attendre

Attendre can be followed by a direct object (notice there is no preposition before the object), an infinitive, or a dependent clause.

458 PRACTICE MAKES PERFECT Complete French All-in-One

J'**attends** une livraison.	I **am waiting** for a delivery.
Nous **attendons** d'en savoir plus.	We **are waiting** to know more about it.
Ils **attendent** que vous preniez une décision.	They **are waiting** for you to make a decision.
J'**attends** votre réponse avec impatience.	I'**m looking forward to** your answer.
En attendant, je te souhaite bonne chance.	**Meanwhile**, I wish you good luck.

S'attendre à

When **attendre** is used in the pronominal form, it means *to expect*. It is followed by the preposition **à** and the subjunctive in a dependent clause.

Attendez-vous **à** des grèves!	You **should expect** some strikes.
Tu **t'attends** vraiment **à** ce qu'il dise la vérité?	Do you really **expect** him to tell the truth?
Paul **ne s'attendait pas à** gagner une médaille d'or.	Paul **did not expect** to win a gold medal.
Je **ne m'y attendais pas**.	I **did not expect** it.

EXERCICE 31·14

Translate the following sentences, using inversion where needed and the **tu** or **vous** form, as indicated.

1. They don't expect me to know how to play the piano.

2. Don't hold it against him! He is tired and he forgot the appointment. (**tu**)

3. I don't feel like going out tonight.

4. "I want to give you some oranges. How many do you want?" "I want three." (**tu**)

5. I did not expect his reaction. I was so surprised.

6. I envy you. You are so lucky! (**vous**)

7. I'll wait for you in front of the statue of George Sand in the Luxembourg Garden. (**tu**)

8. Marion does not talk to her brother. She holds a grudge against him. I don't know why.

9. Charlotte has cravings for strawberries.

10. I expect his victory in May.

Manquer/manquer de/manquer à/il manque

The verb **manquer** (*to miss*) is a teacher's favorite when examination time comes. There are many rules to remember. Try and memorize some examples in context.

Manquer

First is **manquer** with a direct object, no preposition:

J'**ai manqué** le train à cause d'un accident dans le métro.	I **missed** the train because of an accident in the subway.
Bastien **a manqué** le cours d'informatique.	Bastien **missed** the computer science course.
Vous **avez manqué** Tara de cinq minutes.	You **missed** Tara by five minutes.
Le film était horrible. Vous **n'avez** rien **manqué**.	The film was horrible. You **did not miss** anything.
Marion **a manqué** une marche et elle est tombée.	Marion **missed** a step and she fell.

Manquer de

When the preposition **de** follows **manquer**, it means that something is lacking, insufficient, and sometimes weak.

Ce soufflé **manque de** goût. Tu as oublié d'ajouter de la noix de muscade?	This soufflé **lacks** flavor. Did you forget to add some nutmeg?
Odile **manque d'**imagination.	Odile **lacks** imagination.
Notre entreprise **manque de** main-d'œuvre.	Our company **has a shortage of** labor.
On **manque d'**air ici. Ouvrez les fenêtres!	There **is no** air in here! Open the windows!
Cette Adèle! Elle **ne manque pas d'audace!**	That Adèle! She **has got some nerve!**
Ne vous en faites pas! Ces enfants **ne manquent de rien**.	Don't worry! These children **have everything they need**.

Manquer à

When **manquer** is followed by the preposition **à**, the spectrum of meanings is quite impressive:

Tu me **manques**.	I **miss** you.

If you want to stay out of trouble, do not confuse:

Tu me **manques**.	I **miss** you.

with:

Je te **manque**?	You **miss** me?

Here are more examples:

Nous te **manquons**?	*Do you **miss** us?*
Leur ancien quartier leur **manque**.	*They **miss** their old neighborhood.*
Manuel te **manque** vraiment?	*Do you really **miss** Manuel?*
Manuel me **manque** terriblement.	*I **miss** Manuel terribly.*
Elle vous **manque**.	*You **miss** her.*
Vous me **manquez** tant.	*I **miss** you so much.*
Venise me **manque**.	*I **miss** Venice.*
Ses blagues nous **manquent**.	*We **miss** his jokes.*

To fail can be sometimes be translated with **manquer à**.

Valentin a **manqué à** ses devoirs.	*Valentin **failed** to do his duty.*
Vanessa a **manqué à** ses promesses.	*Vanessa **failed** to keep her word.*

Il manque

Il manque is an impersonal expression that takes on a lot of meanings.

Il manque deux pieds à la table.	*There are two legs **missing** from the table.*
Il leur manque 300 euros pour acheter cette chaise.	*They are **short** of 300 euros to buy this chair.*
Il ne manquait plus que ça!	*That's all we needed!*

EXERCICE
31·15

*Translate the following sentences, using the **est-ce que** form as needed and the **tu** or **vous** form, as indicated.*

1. Our organization is five thousand euros short of having a chance to win.

2. Édouard won't be here tonight. He missed his plane.

3. Andréa does not lack talent, but she is too shy.

4. I miss my grandmother Victorine.

5. Some pages are missing in this novel. That is strange . . .

6. I am so sad. I missed Amélien by three minutes.

7. Do you miss us? (**tu**)

8. If you fail to do your duty, Clara will leave you. (**tu**)

Verb transfers and confusing verbs

9. I miss our trips in Brittany.

10. There are buttons missing on this cardigan.

Savoir/connaître

You are aware of the verb **savoir** (*to know*), as the phrase *savoir faire* (*know-how*) is commonly used in English. However, you cannot learn **savoir** without becoming acquainted with the verb **connaître**, so that you can distinguish one from the other. **Connaître** means to know, to be acquainted with, and to be familiar with. In a figurative way, it means to enjoy, to live, and to experience. **Savoir** can be followed by a direct object or a dependent clause. It can also be translated in many ways.

Maryse **sait jouer** de la flûte.	*Maryse **can play** the flute.*
Eva **sait négocier** avec ses clients.	*Eva **knows how to negotiate** with her clients.*
Savez-vous où Éric habite?	*Do you **know** where Éric lives?*
Je **ne savais pas** qu'il était célibataire.	*I **did not know** he was single.*
Ça se **saurait** si c'était vrai.	*People **would know** about it if it were true.*
Elle **sait parler** aux ados.	*She **is good at talking** to teenagers.*
Savez-vous la nouvelle?	***Have** you **heard** the news?*
Claire **sait écouter**.	*Claire **is a good listener**.*
Savoir, c'est pouvoir.	***Knowledge** is power.*
Nous **savons bien** que le comptable est impliqué dans le complot.	*We **are well aware** that the accountant is involved in the plot.*

In many cases, *how* is used with *to know*. It is not used in French unless the speaker knows how something should be done and what needs to be emphasized.

Common usage:

Mon frère **sait changer** un pneu.	*My brother **knows how to change** a tire.*

Emphasis:

Je ne **sais vraiment pas comment** vous exprimer ma gratitude.	*I **really don't know how** to express my gratitude.*
Il **ne sait vraiment pas comment** expliquer ce qui s'est passé.	*He **really does not know how** to explain what happened.*

Connaître is always followed by a direct object. But it is never followed by a dependent clause. Remember, if you need a dependent clause with a conjunction after *to know*, don't think twice—**savoir** is the only answer.

Ils **connaissent** tous les musées de Lyon.	*They **know** all the museums in Lyon.*
Ma sœur **connaît** le rédacteur en chef du Monde.	*My sister **knows** the editor-in-chief of Le Monde.*
Elle l'**a connu** à la fac.	*She **met** him at the university.*
Sa bonté **ne connaît pas** de bornes.	*His/her kindness **knows no** limits.*
Bon nombre d'artistes **ont connu** la pauvreté.	*Many artists **have experienced** poverty.*

462 PRACTICE MAKES PERFECT Complete French All-in-One

Il **a connu** la faim pendant son enfance.	He **experienced** hunger during his youth.
La Grèce **connaît** une grave crise économique.	Greece **is going through** a serious economic crisis.
Ils **ne connaissent pas** encore les coutumes de cette tribu.	They **are not** yet **familiar with** the customs of this tribe.

Savoir and **connaître** can be used together with an interesting nuance:

| **Savez**-vous cette chanson? | Do you **know** this song? (i.e., by heart) |
| **Connaissez**-vous cette chanson? | Do you **know** this song? (i.e., Are you familiar with it?) |

Savoir and pouvoir

Savoir is often used in French in contrast with **pouvoir**, depending on the meaning:

Tu **sais** nager?	**Can** you swim?
Il ne **sait** pas lire.	He **can't** read.
Je **sais** nager mais je ne peux pas nager aujourd'hui car je suis enrhumé.	I **can** swim, but I am not able to today because I have a cold.
Il **sait** lire mais il ne peut pas lire maintenant car il a oublié ses lunettes.	He **can** read, but he cannot read right now because he forgot his glasses.

EXERCICE
31·16

*Translate the following sentences, using inversion as needed and the **tu** or **vous** form, as indicated.*

1. Do you know at what time they'll arrive? (**vous**)

2. Camille experienced hunger when she was young.

3. Can you drive? (**vous**)

4. I know she is always late.

5. The Langlois know how to organize a party.

6. I am sure Jonas knows the truth.

7. When will you know if we can visit them in Normandy? (**vous**)

Verb transfers and confusing verbs   **463**

8. Véronique is going through a serious personal crisis.

_____

9. These children cannot even read. Please do something! (**vous**)

_____

10. Have you heard the news? (**tu**)

_____

EXERCICE
31·17

Match the two columns.

_____ 1. Claire a envie de	a. sa tante.
_____ 2. Tu ne peux pas t'imaginer à quel point	b. du piano.
_____ 3. Vanessa emprunte trop d'argent à	c. un miracle.
_____ 4. Ne vous attendez pas à	d. faire le tour du monde.
_____ 5. Louise ne sait pas vraiment jouer	e. tu me manques.

Whatever, whenever, wherever: French oddities and fun with prepositions ·32·

The present subjunctive is used with the indefinite expressions that are the French equivalents of *whatever, whenever, wherever,* and *whoever*.

When the English *whatever* is followed by subject + verb, use the neuter **quoi que** + present subjunctive.

Quoi que tu fasses, je t'aimerai toujours.	*Whatever you do, I will always love you.*
Quoi qu'elle dise, je ne changerai pas d'avis.	*Whatever she says, I will not change my mind.*

When the English *whatever* is followed by a noun, use **quel que** (**quelle que, quels que, quelles que**) + the subjunctive of **être** + noun. **Quel que** agrees in gender and number with the noun that follows it.

Quel que soit votre conseil, je prendrai rendez-vous avec le patron.	*Whatever your advice, I will make an appointment with the boss.*
Quelle que soit leur décision, elle démissionnera.	*Whatever their decision, she will resign.*

Look at the following examples that express *wherever* (**où que**) in French:

Où que tu sois, appelle-moi.	*Wherever you are, call me.*
Où qu'elle aille, il ira aussi.	*Wherever she goes, he will go, too.*

The subjunctive is also used following the expression of *whoever* (**qui que**). For example:

Qui que tu sois, tu peux lui parler.	*Whoever you are, you can talk to him.*
Qui que vous soyez, ouvrez votre cœur.	*Whoever you are, open up your heart.*

EXERCICE 32·1

*Traduire les phrases entre parenthèses en utilisant **tu** si nécessaire.*

1. (*Whatever you say*), je reste sur ma position.

_____

2. (*Whatever her decision*), la mienne est prise.

_____

3. (*Whoever you are*), je ne t'autorise pas à me parler sur ce ton.

_____

4. (*Wherever you go*), j'irai avec toi.

_____

5. (*Whoever she is*), elle n'est pas autorisée à venir!

_____

6. (*Whatever you think*), je m'en moque.

_____

7. (*Wherever they live*), je les retrouverai.

_____

8. (*Whatever their suggestion*), je trouve mon idée très bonne.

_____

9. (*Whoever you are*), aide-moi.

_____

10. (*Whatever your mother may think*), c'est ta décision.

_____

Avoir beau and quitte à

The expression **avoir beau** + infinitive can usually be translated by *although* or *however*.

Il a beau être aisé, il n'est pas heureux.	*Although he has a lot of money, he is not happy.*
Il a beau dormir, il est toujours fatigué.	*However much he sleeps, he is always tired.*
Il avait beau habiter au bord de la mer, il n'a jamais appris à nager.	*Although he lived by the sea, he never learned how to swim.*
Elle aura beau essayer, ce sera inutile.	*However much she tries, it will be useless.*

The expression **quitte à** + infinitive can usually be translated by *even if it means*.

Je vais lui dire ce que je pense, **quitte à me fâcher** avec elle.	*Even if it means arguing with her, I am going to tell her what I think.*

466 PRACTICE MAKES PERFECT Complete French All-in-One

Quitte à payer plus, je préfère voyager en première classe.	*Even if it means paying more, I prefer traveling first class.*
Je n'accepterai pas leur offre, **quitte à être renvoyé**.	*I won't accept their offer even if it means being fired.*
Quitte à s'ennuyer, ils préfèrent rester chez eux.	*They prefer to stay home even if it means being bored.*

EXERCICE 32·2

*Traduire les phrases suivantes en utilisant **tu** si nécessaire.*

1. Even if it means not sleeping, I am going with you to that party.

2. He will resign even if it means having financial problems.

3. However intelligent he is, he is very lonely.

4. Although they are friends, they cannot talk politics together.

5. I'll take two years off even if it means losing my position.

6. However hard they tried, they failed.

7. However magnificent this teapot is, it is not worth 200 euros.

8. Although you are swearing to tell the truth, I still have doubts.

9. Even if it means bothering you, I need to ask you a few questions.

10. He will not leave the room even if it means bothering everyone.

Verbs and prepositions

When a verb is followed by another verb in the infinitive, the first thing to ask yourself is whether or not there is a preposition between them. In sentences based on the pattern of **j'aime lire** (*I like to read*), this is a question of life and death: many French sentences, which follow the same pattern, insist on inserting a preposition between the two verbs, so the preposition precedes the infinitive. All this comes naturally to the French, who don't even wonder why it's necessary to say, **Je songe à prendre ma retraite** (*I'm thinking of retiring*).

Things are simpler in English because the only preposition we need to worry about is *to*, which functions as an infinitive marker. For example, if a verb is standing alone, we have no idea of its form, because modern English does not have an infinitive ending. For all practical purposes, it's just a word. On the other hand, *to read* and *to write* are infinitives. In French, when we write the word **parler**, we know it's an infinitive, because we recognize the infinitive ending -**er**.

So how do we learn when to drop the preposition and how to choose among **de**, **à**, **sur**, and so on? While we wait for some genius to discover a magic formula, we can take advantage of a mnemonic technique, which has helped us learn the correct gender of a noun. When you learned the word *moon*, you memorized it as **la lune**, not just **lune**. So when you form a mental image of a particular infinitive that isn't followed by a preposition, you can visualize it followed by a "zero"—for example, **vouloir 0**. You will then know that **Je veux lire** is correct!

When you run into verbs that must be followed by a preposition, look for patterns, and memorize them, according to preposition, always forming a unit consisting of a verb and its preposition. Imagine you're learning the verb **apprendre**. If you memorize it as **apprendre à**, you will always use the correct preposition.

Verbs not followed by a preposition

Let's start with verbs that are *not* followed by a preposition:

aimer	*to like, to love*
aller	*to go*
avouer	*to admit*
compter	*to intend, to plan*
désirer	*to desire, to wish*
détester	*to hate (to)*
devoir	*must, to have to*
écouter	*to listen to*
espérer	*to hope to*
faire	*to do*
falloir	*must, to be necessary to*
laisser	*to let, to allow*
oser	*to dare (to)*
paraître	*to appear, to seem*
penser	*to think*
pouvoir	*can, to be able to*
préférer	*to prefer*
prétendre	*to claim*
savoir	*to know (how to)*
sembler	*to seem to*
sentir	*to feel, to think*
souhaiter	*to wish to*
venir	*to come*
voir	*to see*
vouloir	*to want to*

Nous **allons skier** tous les hivers.	*We **go skiing** every winter.*
Ludivine **souhaite partir** en Argentine.	*Ludivine **wishes to travel** to Argentina.*
Je **n'ose pas demander** à Benoît de m'aider.	*I **don't dare ask** Benoît to help me.*

468 PRACTICE MAKES PERFECT Complete French All-in-One

Préfères-tu aller chez Ludovic sans nous?	*Do you prefer going to Ludovic's without us?*
Il faut démolir ce vieux bâtiment, sinon il va s'effondrer.	*This old building **must be demolished**, otherwise it is going to collapse.*
Viens voir!	***Come take a look!***

Note the single subject in the preceding examples: these sentences exemplify the subject–indicative verb–infinitive verb pattern. In fact, the infinitive comes in handy when we need to avoid repeating the same subject. For example, one may say in improper French: **XJe pense que je suis en mesure de le faire** (*I think I can do it*). But saying **Je pense être en mesure de le faire** not only is more elegant but also is correct French.

Let's see what happens when there are two subjects. Remember, we are still discussing sentences based on the subject–indicative verb–infinitive verb pattern. With one subject, we can get away with a simple sentence. When there are two subjects, we need to create a complex sentence and introduce the dependent clause with **que**. The verb in the main clause will determine the mood (indicative or subjunctive) of the verb in the dependent clause.

Ils préfèrent oublier cette sale histoire.	*They prefer to forget this nasty story.*
Ils préfèrent **qu'elle oublie** cette sale histoire.	*They prefer her to forget this nasty story.*
Tu détestes être en retard.	*You hate being late.*
Tu détestes **que je sois** en retard.	*You hate me being late.*

Remember that there are many zero-preposition verbs in French whose English equivalents require a preposition, and vice versa.

Colombe cherche un livre d'Ananda Devi.	*Colombe is looking **for** a book by Ananda Devi.*
Regarde l'arc-en-ciel!	*Look **at** the rainbow!*
Maxence n'a pas répondu **aux** critiques.	*Maxence didn't answer the critics.*
J'ai permis **aux** enfants de regarder un film de kung-fu.	*I let the children watch a kung fu movie.*

EXERCICE
32·3

Choose the right verb in the following list to complete each sentence.

aimez	désirent	a détesté	devons	laisse
pensent	pourrais	sembles	viendra	voudrais

1. Candice _____ toujours _____ faire le ménage.

2. Tu _____ angoissé par la présence du directeur.

3. Je _____ devenir chorégraphe.

4. Vous _____ enseigner le dessin aux enfants.

5. Est-ce qu'Émilie _____ au rendez-vous qu'elle m'a fixé ?

6. Faustin et Aimée _____ ardemment avoir un enfant.

7. _____-la prendre ses décisions elle-même !

8. _____-tu me prêter ton enregisteur numérique ?

9. Nous _____ écrire un livre sur le subjonctif en français.

10. Elles _____ que le juge est corrompu.

Verbs followed by the preposition à

Sometimes, although rarely, even native French speakers have to refresh their memory when it comes to **à** verbs and **de** verbs. Clearly, we are dealing with a fundamental dichotomy. As mentioned previously, a verb and its appropriate preposition should be memorized as a unit.

aider à	to help to
s'amuser à	to enjoy
apprendre à	to learn to, to show how to
arriver à	to manage to
aspirer à	to aspire to
s'attendre à	to expect to
autoriser à	to authorize to
avoir à	to have to
chercher à	to try to, to attempt to
commencer à	to start to
consentir à	to agree to, to consent to
continuer à	to continue to, to keep on
se décider à	to make up one's mind to
encourager à	to encourage to
se faire à	to get used to
faire attention à	to pay attention to
s'habituer à	to get used to
hésiter à	to hesitate to
inciter à	to encourage to
s'intéresser à	to get interested in
inviter à	to invite to
se joindre à	to join
se mettre à	to start to, to begin to
parvenir à	to manage to
préparer à (se)	to get ready to
renoncer à	to give up
se résigner à	to resign oneself to
réussir à	to succeed in
songer à	to think about
tenir à	to want, to insist on, to be eager to
viser à	to aim at

Maria apprend **à** monter à cheval.	Maria is learning how to ride a horse.
Nous les avons invités **à** prendre un verre.	We invited them to have a drink.
Le président du conseil d'administration tient **à** vous voir cet après-midi.	The chairman of the board wants to see you this afternoon.
Nous ne sommes pas parvenus **à** le convaincre **d'**inviter Laura **à** se joindre à nous.	We did not manage to convince him to invite Laura to join us.

EXERCICE 32·4

Match the two columns.

_____ 1. Ils pensent   a. au progrès de la science.

_____ 2. Je pense   b. en son fils aîné.

_____ 3. Cet universitaire croit   c. à leurs prochaines vacances.

_____ 4. Elle croit   d. il y a trop de risques.

_____ 5. Nous pensons que   e. les inviter à devenir membres de notre club.

Verbs followed by the preposition de

While you're memorizing these verbs, try not to use this particular preposition as a crutch. French teachers have noticed that students sometimes imagine that **de** is a generic preposition that will do when they draw a blank. For example, the sentence **XJ'aime de lire** is many a French teacher's nightmare. It is important, therefore, to remember that the **à/de** divide must never be ignored.

accepter de	*to accept, to agree to*
accuser de	*to accuse (of)*
s'arrêter de	*to stop*
avoir besoin de	*to need to*
avoir envie de	*to feel like, to want*
avoir l'intention de	*to intend to*
avoir peur de	*to be afraid of*
cesser de	*to stop, to cease*
choisir de	*to choose to*
conseiller de	*to advise (to)*
se contenter de	*to content oneself with*
convaincre de	*to convince (to)*
craindre de	*to fear (to)*
défendre de	*to forbid (to)*
demander de	*to ask (to)*
se dépêcher de	*to hurry to*
s'efforcer de	*to try hard to*
empêcher de	*to prevent (from)*
s'empêcher de	*to refrain from*
envisager de	*to contemplate*
essayer de	*to try to*
éviter de	*to avoid*
s'excuser de	*to apologize for*
faire semblant de	*to pretend to*
feindre de	*to feign to, to pretend to*
finir de	*to finish, to end up*
interdire de	*to forbid (to)*
menacer de	*to threaten to*
mériter de	*to deserve to*
offrir de	*to offer to*
oublier de	*to forget to*

Whatever, whenever, wherever: French oddities and fun with prepositions   **471**

parler à	*to speak to*
parler de	*to speak about*
permettre de	*to allow (to), to permit (to)*
persuader de	*to persuade (to), to convince (to)*
se plaindre de	*to complain of*
projeter de	*to plan to/on*
promettre de	*to promise to*
refuser de	*to refuse to*
regretter de	*to regret*
remercier de	*to thank (for)*
reprocher de	*to reproach for*
soupçonner de	*to suspect of*
se souvenir de	*to remember to*
tâcher de	*to try to*

Vincent a accepté **de** participer **à** l'événement.	*Vincent has accepted to attend the event.*
J'ai conseillé **à** Élise **d'**aller voir un avocat.	*I advised Élise to see a lawyer.*
Florent se plaint toujours **d'**avoir trop de travail.	*Florent always complains about having too much work.*
Stéphanie a refusé **de** lui révéler le secret.	*Stéphanie refused to reveal the secret to him/her.*

Did you know that prepositions can be glamorous? In World War II, Dutch resistance fighters had no problem catching German spies, because there are certain place names that foreigners, even fluent Dutch speakers, regularly mispronounce. A spy trying to pass as a native French speaker better watch his or her prepositions, for an incorrect preposition can derail not only an otherwise elegant speech in French, but perhaps a career as well. For example, let us imagine a meeting of European business executives, taking place in July, during which an independent contractor, ostensibly from France, describes himself as more efficient than any of his competitors. No doubt in his mind that he should be awarded the lucrative contract for a project that is to be launched in October. Listen to the conclusion of his pitch: **Je peux le faire dans quatre semaines**. Before he could finish his sentence, he was asked to leave. What went wrong? Well, a Francophone member of the group immediately noticed that the "French" entrepreneur used the wrong preposition. He obviously wanted to say, *It would take me four weeks to finish the job*, but what he actually said was *I can finish that job in four weeks*, which made no sense, because the job was supposed to start in October. Had he learned the correct preposition, he would have said: **Je peux le faire en quatre semaines**, or *It would take me four weeks to finish the job*, and that would not have aroused any suspicion.

Having fun with prepositions

On the other end of the knowledge spectrum, here's a witty letter, written by a student of mine, who not only knows her grammar, but also composes her missive as a charming bouquet of colorful prepositions, homonyms, and *faux amis*.

Les prépositions caméléonesques et capricieuses

Ma chère petite-fille Chloé,

Je t'applaudis! Je suis ravie **d'**apprendre que tu as l'intention **de** faire une maîtrise de Lettres à New York University. Lorsque tu commenceras **à** apprendre la langue de Voltaire, tu tomberas amoureuse **de** la belle littérature française. Mais il faut faire attention: on dit que la grammaire,

472 FRACTICE MAKES PERFECT Complete French All-in-One

c'est *une chanson douce*—je paraphrase le titre d'un livre célèbre d'Érik Orsenna. Moi, je dis qu'elle est parsemée **de** mystères, hérissée **de** pièges et épicée **de** magie!

Par exemple, quelques prépositions sont des sorcières, de vrais caméléons, qui ont le pouvoir de métamorphoser le sens d'un verbe. Voici quelques exemples:

de/par: Je fêterai mon prochain anniversaire **dans** la vallée de Napa, entourée **de** ma tribu californienne. Madame Obama y fêtera son prochain anniversaire, comme moi, entourée **de** sa tribu et aussi **par** le Secret Service—la sauvegarde contre un éventuel danger.

de/à/par: Elle tient sa petite-fille **par** la main; la petite tient **d'**elle le bleu de ses yeux, le blond platine de ses cheveux; bouquinovore et francophile, elle tient **à** sa collection de livres français, de Gustave Flaubert **à** Amélie Nothomb.

Il y a un mec que je connais qui est vraiment agaçant, **ennuyeux** et **ennuyant**. Il n'a pas le droit **de** tutoyer LÉO, mon chaton chéri; il n'a pas droit **à** cette forme d'adresse—(c'est différent si *droit* est suivi **d'**un nom ou **d'**un verbe). Une princesse ne peut jamais échapper **à** sa cage dorée; Charles Manson ne pourra jamais s'échapper **de** prison (figuratif ou littéral).

dans/en (général/spécifique; temps): D'habitude, les vedettes volent **en** jet privé; moi, je suis **dans** l'avion à destination **de** Paris, j'étudie *French Demystified* par Annie Heminway; je dois maîtriser les pièges et les défis de la langue française **avant** l'atterrissage. **En** deux heures, j'ai lu le « Chapitre 14: All About Prepositions ». **Dans** quatre heures, je serai **à** Paris, les prépositions peaufinées!

Il y a des prépositions capricieuses qui flirtent avec les verbes, sans formule:

de/en: Jeanne Gonzalès éclata **en** sanglots quand elle vit le portrait de Berthe Morisot par Édouard Manet; elle écumait **de** rage et elle fondit **en** larmes. Sa rivale éclata-t-elle **de** rire, ou riait-elle **aux** éclats ou **jusqu'**aux larmes lorsqu'elle décortiqua ce portrait?

de/au: La mère d'Édouard Manet adore jouer **du** piano; pianoter; elle s'évade **de** la vie quotidienne; elle n'a aucune envie **de** jouer **au** golf, un passe-temps inutile, à son avis.

Les verbes s'amusent aussi bien que les prépositions; sans règle:

Gervaise, la blanchisseuse de Zola, s'occupe **de** tout: elle **fait** la vaisselle, elle **fait** la lessive et elle **lave** le linge au lavoir. À noter, c'est le **blanchissage**, ce n'est pas le **blanchiment** d'argent.

Je **jette** un coup d'œil à la garde-robe de notre cher écrivain, Alain Mabanckou, et je lui **fais** un clin d'œil.

Et les verbes qui trafiquent avec leurs prépositions:

Avoir les pieds **sur** terre: si jamais un tremblement **de** terre vous frappe, vous tombez **à** terre; on n'a pas envie **de** vous mettre **en** terre; on se flanque **par** terre; on veut rentrer **sous** terre (de honte); ne pas toucher terre.

Le sens d'un verbe peut changer selon la présentation d'un pronom réfléchi:

Eva Gonzalès, élève de Manet, peintre célèbre, **éclipse** sa sœur cadette Jeanne; tout à coup, juste après la mort du maître, elle **s'éclipse** et décède.

On se **met à** nu, comme Ananda Devi; on **est nu** comme un ver, comme Amélie Nothomb à Burning Man.

On ne peut pas négliger la position des adjectifs; avant ou après le nom—figuratif ou littéral.

Charles de Gaulle était de grande taille. C'était un homme **grand**—il mesurait 1,93 mètre. En période de crise, il a vraiment été un **grand** homme. Il restera dans les annales de l'Histoire.

Et les accents, le circonflexe, par exemple?

Elle revient de son séjour à l'Île de Ré **hâlée**; les marins ont **hâlé** une grosse baleine à bord.

Et les homonymes, féminin ou masculin? Et les homonymes euphoriques?

En face de **son poêle à** bois, mon fils cadet Guillaume trouve un **poil** de son chat Aphrodite dans **la poêle à galettes**, ce n'est pas marrant.

J'en ai marre: je me cache **sous un voile** et je mets **les voiles** (f.)

En **vers**, elle écrit la vie d'un **ver vert** qui se trouve dans un **verre** de rosé à Ver-sur-Mer.

Chez moi, à la campagne, le terrain est couvert **de pins**, le panier est rempli **de pain**.

Whatever, whenever, wherever: French oddities and fun with prepositions **473**

Érik Orsenna me dit que la **mer** est sa **mère** pas son **maire**.
Ça suffit! J'espère que mes conseils n'ont pas gâché ton appétit pour les études du français!
Bon courage, ma petite-fille chérie!
Je t'embrasse très fort, Lili
Lisa Ehrenkranz

See Translations *in the back of this book for English version of letter.*

EXERCICE 32·5

Complete with a preposition if necessary.

1. Nous vous remercions vivement _____ être venus si nombreux.

2. L'ambassadeur voudrait _____ éviter _____ provoquer une crise diplomatique.

3. J'ai besoin _____ acheter un nouveau climatiseur. Tu peux m'aider _____ en choisir un?

4. Pourquoi hésites-tu _____ le contacter?

5. Mon beau-père a l'intention _____ investir dans l'or.

6. Je doute qu'il accepte _____ signer un contrat de mariage.

7. Le directeur tient _____ vous parler immédiatement!

8. Je te promets, je vais essayer _____ apprendre tous ces verbes par cœur.

9. Philippe est très timide. Il n'ose pas _____ contredire ses collègues de bureau.

10. Je n'ai pas pu m'empêcher _____ rire quand il a fait son discours.

11. L'éditeur de Claire s'attend _____ recevoir des critiques favorables à la parution de son livre.

12. N'oublie pas _____ prendre de l'essence. Le réservoir est presque vide.

13. Le syndicat menace _____ faire grève si les conditions ne s'améliorent pas.

14. Le nouveau ministre de l'Éducation voudrait _____ « mieux payer » les professeurs.

15. Est-ce que tu te souviens _____ l'année la naissance de Julien?

16. Quand commencerez-vous _____ travailler chez Guerlain?

17. Dépêche-toi _____ finir tes devoirs. Je voudrais _____ sortir prendre l'air.

18. Il faut _____ comparer les deux propositions.

19. Édouard ne peut pas s'habituer _____ son nouvel emploi.

20. Fabien m'a encouragé _____ suivre des cours en ligne.

EXERCICE 32·6

*Translate the following sentences, using the **tu** or **vous** form, as indicated.*

1. José and Julie invited us to spend our vacation with them.

   _____

2. We are going to buy a new computer.

   _____

3. Joël hates to cook.

   _____

4. Sophie cannot get used to getting up at 6 A.M. every morning.

   _____

5. They managed to meet the president of Air France.

   _____

6. I suspect him of pretending to be sick this weekend.

   _____

7. Nicolas is afraid he will lose the elections.

   _____

8. They promised to visit us at the end of the month.

   _____

9. You have to learn how to play the guitar. (**tu**)

   _____

10. I hope you like your new apartment.

    _____

EXERCICE 32·7

Restore the missing prepositions in front of nouns or verbs, when necessary.
(See Translations *in the back of this book for the English.)*

Port-au-Prince
Je suis né **à** Port-au-Prince **en** Haïti, j'ai grandi et passé mon enfance **à** Petit-Goâve. **À** Port-au-Prince, j'ai travaillé comme journaliste, puis j'ai dû quitté mon pays, exilé, pour venir **à** Montréal où j'ai travaillé **à** l'usine, **dans** différentes usines avant **d'**écrire mon premier roman.

Montréal à écrire
C'est au Carré Saint-Louis que j'ai commencé _____ écrire. Pour moi, Montréal, c'est la machine _____ écrire. C'est la modernité. Je n'ai jamais cru que je pourrais

Whatever, whenever, wherever: French oddities and fun with prepositions **475** écrire _____ la main _____ Montréal. Montréal, c'est aussi la distance. Je suis _____ cette petite chambre et j'écris _____ Petit-Goâve, Port-au-Prince tout en sachant que les gens qui vont me lire, pour la plupart, ne connaissent pas ces villes. Ça me donne une certaine liberté. Je n'ai pas _____ fictionaliser ces villes. Elles sont déjà fictions pour mes lecteurs.

Ville en images
Quand j'ai fait un film _____ Montréal, j'ai voulu que ce soit _____ hiver. Un hiver aussi fort que l'été du tournage de *Comment faire l'amour.* Parce que je trouvais que c'était comme si je regardais Montréal cette fois-ci pour lui-même, pour elle-même. Et _____ Montréal, il y a un hiver. Je ne peux pas _____ passer ma vie _____ croire que Montréal est une ville du Sud. Montréal, c'est aussi une ville nordique. J'ai voulu m'approcher _____ cet hiver-là et essayer _____ l'apprivoiser, essayer _____ sentir cela parce que je crois que c'est l'image fondamentale de Montréal et du Québec. D'ailleurs Gilles Vigneault, le grand poète québécois, a dit: « D'un glaçon, j'ai fait l'hiver. Mon pays, ce n'est pas un pays, c'est l'hiver ». Je ne peux pas continuer _____ ne pas voir qu'il y a un hiver dans ce pays, et j'ai voulu qu'il soit le plus fort. Et dans « Comment conquérir l'Amérique _____ une nuit », il me semblait que je devais _____ faire quelque chose qui réconcilie les deux villes et Montréal et Port-au-Prince, deux villes qui m'habitent. J'ai pensé qu'il faudrait qu'un film montre un peu les passages successifs entre les deux villes comme s'il n'y avait même pas d'espace. Je parle _____ l'espace tendre _____ Montréal et Port-au-Prince. Donc c'était un plaisir que je voulais me faire, de faire ce film. J'ai pas été surpris _____ la ville. Je voulais que l'image me fasse voir la ville sous un autre angle, d'une autre manière, et ça je l'ai voulu. Oui, tout à fait. Et je l'ai eu. J'ai voulu aussi qu'il y ait des choses que l'être humain ne peut pas _____ voir. C'est trop minuscule, on y passe . . . On voit la ville tellement avec nos émotions quand on y passe et que je me suis dit que peut-être je, en regardant _____ le film, je regarderai _____ les choses que je n'ai pas vues parce que je les avais tellement absorbées rapidement en émotion et non en images.

Un petit tour de ville et puis s'ennuie
Je ne regarde pas _____ les villes précisément. Une grande majorité de mes chroniques à l'étranger se passent _____ une salle de bain ou _____ une chambre d'hôtel. Mon rêve, c'est de ne jamais être un touriste. Le touriste pour moi, c'est celui qui regarde, qui cherche à savoir. Moi, je ne cherche pas _____ savoir. Je cherche à sentir. Il me faut un but. Je marche, je vais _____ un copain dans une ville que je viens à peine _____ connaître. C'est le trajet qui m'intéresse et le désir _____ être chez le copain. C'est beaucoup plus les intérieurs qui me plaisent, être _____ un bar, être _____ une librairie, être _____ un ami, être un peu partout. Le trajet, quand je vais dans une ville généralement—comme j'y vais comme conférencier et pour mes livres—je suis reçu par quelqu'un et qui me fait toujours faire un petit tour de la ville. C'est la partie la moins agréable pour moi parce que je n'aime pas qu'on me raconte une ville et son histoire. Et je n'aime pas qu'on me montre surtout les monuments ou les endroits importants. Ce qui m'intéresse, c'est juste _____ marcher et _____ voir le peu possible qui arrive _____ attirer ma rétine. Et finalement—incubation, _____ finir—sentir la ville. Je veux que la ville s'amène _____ moi. Je ne veux pas la découvrir. Je veux qu'elle me découvre.

Extrait d'un entretien de Dany Laferrière réalisé par Annie Heminway à Montréal en février 2009, pour blog *La ville est ailleurs*, aubepine.blog.lemonde.fr de Frédéric Antoine Brosson et Annie Heminway.

A final thought

Allow me to reinforce the mantra of this chapter—watch your prepositions!—by imagining a rather catastrophic misunderstanding that highlights the perils of ignorance. A cautionary tale for the prepositionally challenged.

Louise: Lucas, je t'**en** veux terriblement d'avoir offert un si joli cadeau à Lola.
Lucas: Eh bien, comme tu me veux malgré cette gaffe, *tout est pour le mieux dans le meilleur des mondes possibles.*

French in conversation: Meeting people

Now that you have a solid foundation in French grammar and vocabulary, it's time to start communicating in French. The following four chapters feature sample dialogues and key structures to get you started.

Dialogue 1

Chloé meets a young American at a party. She has never met him face to face, but she seems to know him . . .

CHRIS: **Bonjour**, je m'appelle Chris. **Ça va?**	*Hello, my name is Chris. How's it going?*
CHLOÉ: Oui, très bien, merci. **Moi, je** suis Chloé. Tu es le copain américain de Didier, n'est-ce pas?	*Yes, very well, thanks. I'm Chloé. You're Didier's American friend, right?*
CHRIS: Oui, **c'est ça**. Comment le sais-tu?	*Yes, that's it. How do you know (it)?*
CHLOÉ: Parce que j'aide souvent Didier avec l'anglais.	*Because I often help Didier with English.*
CHRIS: **Je vois.** Alors quand il m'envoie des emails, c'est **toi** qui écris?	*I see. So when he sends me e-mails, are you the one who writes?*
CHLOÉ: Disons que **lui, il** écrit, et **moi, je** traduis et je corrige.	*Let's say that he writes, and I translate and correct.*
CHRIS: Tu es très bonne en anglais. **Je pige** toujours très bien.	*You're very good in English. I always understand very well.*
CHLOÉ: Et moi, je vois que tu parles bien français, **même** l'argot.	*And I see that you speak French well, even slang.*
CHRIS: **Merci pour** le compliment.	*Thanks for the compliment.*
CHLOÉ: **Pas de quoi.**	*Don't mention it.*

Testez votre compréhension. *Check your comprehension. Write* T *for true or* F *for false.*

1. _____ Chris connaît déjà Chloé.

2. _____ Chris est français.

3. _____ Chloé est américaine.

4. _____ Chris est l'ami de Didier.

5. _____ Chloé traduit des emails en français.

Review the following explanations of some interesting phrases found in the previous dialogue. Make them your own.

Bonjour

To say *hello*, the words **bonjour** (literally, *good day*), **bonsoir** (literally, *good evening*), or **salut** (*hi*) may be used. **Bonjour** is usually used until around six P.M., whereas **bonsoir** is used after six P.M. On the other hand, **salut** can be used any time of day.

—**Salut**, Paul. Ça va bien?   —***Hi**, Paul. Is everything going well?*
—Très bien, merci.   —*Very well / Great, thanks.*

—**Bonjour**, Pierre. Comment ça va?   —***Hello**, Pierre. How are you?*
—Bien, merci.   —*Fine, thank you.*

Ça va bien?

This question has several variations. **Ça va?** may be interpreted as *How are you?*, *How's it going?*, or *Is everything OK?* Therefore, there is flexibility in the response.

—Bonsoir, Sophie. **Ça va?**   —*Hello, Sophie. **Is everything OK?***
—Oui, **ça va**.   —*Yes, **everything is OK.***

—Bonsoir, Sophie. **Ça va?**   —*Hello, Sophie. **How are you?***
—(**Ça va**) pas mal.   —*(**I'm**) not bad.*

The question **Ça va bien?** is more specific and requires a *yes* or *no* answer.

—**Ça va bien**, Sophie?   —***Are you fine / Is it going well**, Sophie?*
—Oui, très bien, merci.   —*Yes, quite fine, thank you.*

—**Ça va bien**, Sophie?   —***Are you fine / Is it going well**, Sophie?*
—Non, pas trop bien.   —*No, (I'm) not (doing) very well.*

Moi, je/toi, tu/lui, il/elle, elle

In English, voice inflexion and tone are used to emphasize the subject; in French, emphasis is conveyed by adding a stress pronoun before the subject pronoun.

moi, je	*I*		**nous, nous**	*we*
toi, tu	*you* (familiar)		**vous, vous**	*you* (formal)
elle, elle	*she*		**elles, elles**	*they* (f.)
lui, il	*he*		**eux, ils**	*they* (m.)

Didier, **lui**, **il** écrit.   *Didier, **he** writes.*
Moi, **je** corrige ses méls.   *I correct his e-mails.*

C'est ça

Use this phrase to confirm what someone says to you.

—Il va nous rejoindre?   —*Is he going to join us?*
—**C'est ça**. À dix-sept heures.   —*Yes, **he is (that's it)**. At five P.M.*

French in conversation: Meeting people   **479**

Je vois

Use this phrase to confirm that you understood what was conveyed to you.

—Je ne peux pas sortir. Je suis malade.   —*I can't go out. I'm sick.*
—**Je vois.** Repose-toi bien!   —***I see.*** *Rest well!*

Je pige

This phrase is slang fo r **Je comprends** (*I understand*).

—Il faut vouvoyer les gens qu'on ne   —*You have to use* vous *with people you don't know.*
    connaît pas. Tu **piges**?   ***Do you understand? (Are you getting it?)***
—Ah oui! **J'ai pigé.**   —*Oh yes!* ***I understand (I get it).***

Merci pour...

Use this phrase to thank someone for something specific.

Merci pour ce beau cadeau.   ***Thanks for*** *this beautiful gift.*

Pas de quoi / il n'y a pas de quoi

Use either of these phrases as a reply for a *thank you*. Know that **pas de quoi** is an abbreviated version of **il n'y a pas de quoi** and is therefore more informal than the longer phrase.

—Merci pour cette carte.   —*Thanks for this card.*
—**Il n'y a pas de quoi. / Pas de quoi.**   —***Don't mention it.***

Même

Use this word to intensify and give emphasis to what you just said.

Je sais parler français, **même** l'argot.   *I know how to speak French,* ***even*** *slang.*

EXERCICE 33·2

Entre amis! *Between friends! Complete the sentence with the appropriate word or phrase from the list provided. Capitalize when necessary.*

bien	ça	je pige
même	pas	sais
salut	suis	toi

1. JOËL: _____, Karina. _____ va?

2. KARINA: _____ mal. Et _____, Joël?

3. JOËL: Très _____, merci. Tu _____, je _____ toujours content, moi.

4. KARINA: Moi aussi, je suis toujours contente, _____ aujourd'hui.

5. JOËL: _____, Karina. Tu as un examen aujourd'hui.

480   PRACTICE MAKES PERFECT   Complete French All-in-One

EXERCICE 33·3

Insistons sur la différence! *Let's emphasize the difference! Complete each sentence with a stress pronoun:* **moi**, **toi**, **elle**, **lui**, **nous**, **vous**, **elles**, *or* **eux**.

1. Vous, _____ parlez bien français.
2. Elle, _____ s'appelle aussi Karina.
3. _____, tu es François, n'est-ce pas?
4. Non, _____, je m'appelle Nicolas.
5. Ah! Alors, _____, il s'appelle François.

Dialogue 2

Now Chloé walks over to greet Didier, who is talking to Marie-Josée.

DIDIER: Dis, Chloé, je voudrais te présenter **mon pote**, Chris.

CHLOÉ: Trop tard, mon cher! Je le connais déjà.

DIDIER: Ah bon? **Comment ça?**

CHLOÉ: On s'est rencontrés tout à l'heure, et il sait maintenant que je lis ses emails et que j'écris les tiens.

DIDIER: Quelle copine tu es! Tu ne sais jamais rien garder pour toi. **Comment ça se fait?**

CHLOÉ: Pourquoi garder des secrets, Didier? On est tous copains. Bonsoir. **À un de ces jours!**

DIDIER: **Salut**, Chloé! **À bientôt!**

MARIE-JOSÉE: Au revoir, Chloé. **À un de ces jours.**

Say, Chloé, I would like you to meet my pal, Chris.

Too late, my dear! I already know him.

Really? How is that?

We met a little while ago, and now he knows that I read his e-mails and that I write yours.

What a friend you are! You never know how to keep anything to yourself. How come?

Why keep secrets, Didier? We're all friends. Good night. See you around!

Bye, Chloé! See you soon!

Good-bye, Chloé. See you around.

EXERCICE 33·4

Testez votre compréhension. *Check your comprehension. Write T for true or F for false.*

1. _____ Chris est un bon ami de Didier.
2. _____ Chloé aide Didier avec ses emails à Chris.
3. _____ Marie-Josée aime écrire les emails de Chris à Didier.
4. _____ Didier n'aime pas Chloé.
5. _____ Didier est aimable avec Chloé.

French in conversation: Meeting people

Review the following conversational and grammatical concepts that help structure and perfect your communicative skills.

Mon pote

This phrase is very colloquial and is used for only a *male friend*, to replace **mon ami** or **mon copain**.

Je peux tout te dire, **mon pote**.   *I can tell you everything, **my friend**.*

Comment ça se fait? / comment se fait-il?

This question is used to show surprise and elicit more information.

Tu connais ce jeune homme? **Comment ça se fait?**   *You know this young man? **How is that?***

Elle parle parfaitement le français. **Comment ça se fait?**   *She speaks French perfectly. **How can that be?***

Salut

This familiar term is used to say *Hi* but can also be used to say *Bye*.

Salut, mon pote. Ça va?   ***Hi**, buddy. How are you?*

Salut, Jean-Jacques. À demain.   ***Bye**, Jean-Jacques. See you tomorrow.*

À un de ces jours / à bientôt / à demain

Here, the preposition **à** helps express *see you*; **un de ces jours** literally means *one of these days*. This structure can be used with specific days of the week or moments in time.

Au revoir et **à dimanche**.   *Good-bye; **see you Sunday**.*

Au revoir et **à demain**.   *Good-bye; **see you tomorrow**.*

Salut, Dominique. **À un de ces jours!**   *Bye, Dominique. **See you later!***

Je file maintenant. **À bientôt**, tout le monde.   *I'm taking off now. **See you soon**, everybody.*

Mon/ma/mes

The masculine singular possessive adjective is **mon** (*my*); this form is also used in front of feminine singular nouns starting with a vowel sound. The feminine form of **mon** is **ma** (used before feminine singular nouns starting with a consonant), and the plural is **mes**.

mon ami / **mon** copain	*my friend* (male)	**mon** amie / **ma** copine	*my friend* (female)
mes amis / **mes** copains (*m. pl.*)	*my friends* (male)	**mes** amies / **mes** copines (*f. pl.*)	*my friends* (female)

Je voudrais voir **mon** amie Marie-Josée.   *I would like to see **my** friend Marie-Josée.*

Ton/ta/tes and son/sa/ses

Similarly, the possessive adjective for the familiar *your* has three forms: **ton, ta, tes**; and the possessive adjective for *his* or *her* has three forms: **son, sa, ses**. **Ton** and **son** also precede a feminine singular noun that starts with a vowel sound.

Tu as **ton** argent?	*Do you have **your** money?*
Elle a **son** ticket?	*Does she have **her** ticket?*
Sarah, c'est **ton** amie?	*Is Sarah **your** friend?*

Connaître and savoir

Connaître and **savoir** both mean *to know*. However, **connaître** is generally used to express *being familiar* with a place or person, whereas **savoir** is used to express *knowing a fact* or *knowing how to do something*.

Je **connais** ton copain. Il **sait** parler anglais.	*I **know** your friend. He **knows how** to speak English.*
—Chris **connaît** bien Paris?	*—Does Chris **know** Paris well?*
—Je ne **sais** pas.	*—I don't **know**.*

The verb **connaître** has an irregular conjugation in the present tense: **je/tu connais, il/elle/on connaît, nous connaissons, vous connaissez, ils/elles connaissent**.

Tu **connais** mon copain Bill?	*Do you **know** my friend Bill?*

The verb **savoir** has an irregular conjugation in the present tense: **je/tu sais, il/elle/on sait, nous savons, vous savez, ils/elles savent**.

Ses parents **savent** toujours où elle est.	*Her parents always **know** where she is.*

EXERCICE 33·5

Quelle est la réponse? *What is the answer? Write the letter of the appropriate response on the line provided.*

1. _____ Tu connais bien Paris?

2. _____ Tu sais bien parler anglais?

3. _____ Ça va?

4. _____ Il est là, Chris?

5. _____ Marie-Josée est avec Chris?

6. _____ Je voudrais rentrer à la maison.

7. _____ C'est vous deux, Al et Bob?

8. _____ Je voudrais te présenter Sophie.

a. Bonjour. Je m'appelle Kathy.

b. Bon, au revoir.

c. Oui, c'est nous deux.

d. Oui, c'est ma ville.

e. Oui, le voilà!

f. Oui, je suis américain.

g. Non, je suis fatigué.

h. Non, elle est avec moi.

French in conversation: Meeting people **483**

Dialogue 3

Didier takes his friend Chris home to meet his parents. Only his father is at home.

DIDIER: Bonsoir, papa. **Je te présente** mon ami Chris.	Hello, Dad. I'd like you to meet my friend Chris.
CHRIS: Bonsoir, monsieur Dupoint.	Hello, Mr. Dupoint.
M. DUPOINT: **Enchanté de faire votre connaissance**, jeune homme!	Delighted to make your acquaintance, young man!
DIDIER: Tu sais, papa, c'est mon correspondant des États-Unis.	You know, Dad, he's my pen pal from the United States.
M. DUPOINT: Oui, oui, bien sûr! Mais vous ne restez pas **chez nous**?	Yes, yes, of course! But aren't you staying with us?
CHRIS: J'ai une tante et un oncle qui habitent en ville. Je reste **chez eux**.	I have an aunt and an uncle who live in town. I'm staying with them.
M. DUPOINT: Ah! D'accord. Je comprends.	Ah! OK, I understand.
CHRIS: Il est quelle heure? **Chez ma tante**, nous dînons à dix-neuf heures.	What time is it? At my aunt's, we eat dinner at seven P.M.
M. DUPOINT: Vous ne pouvez pas dîner avec nous?	Can't you have dinner with us?
CHRIS: Pas aujourd'hui. Mais **peut-être une autre fois**.	Not today. But perhaps another time.
M. DUPOINT: Considérez-vous invité pour samedi. D'accord?	Consider yourself invited for Saturday. OK?
CHRIS: Merci, monsieur. Je veux bien! Au revoir, monsieur.	Thank you, sir. Gladly! Good-bye, sir.
M. DUPOINT: À samedi. Au revoir.	See you on Saturday. Good-bye.
DIDIER: Salut, Chris. Dis, tu prends le métro ou le bus?	Bye, Chris. Say, are you taking the subway or the bus?
CHRIS: Le métro.	The subway.
DIDIER: Tu sais où est la station la plus proche?	Do you know where the nearest station is?
CHRIS: **Ne t'inquiète pas. Je sais me débrouiller.**	Don't worry. I can manage.
DIDIER: Bon, je t'appelle demain.	Good. I'll call you tomorrow.

EXERCICE 33·6

Testez votre compréhension. *Check your comprehension. Write T for true or F for false.*

1. _____ Didier présente Chris à son père.
2. _____ Le père de Didier est très aimable avec Chris.
3. _____ Chris peut dîner aujourd'hui avec la famille de Didier.
4. _____ Chris peut dîner un autre jour avec Didier.
5. _____ Chris habite chez sa tante.

Review the following conversational and grammatical concepts that help structure and perfect your communicative skills.

Je te présente

Use this expression to introduce someone to a friend or relative. Use the same expression, substituting **vous** for **te**, to introduce someone in a formal setting.

Sonia, **je te présente** Damien.
Madame Chartier, **je vous présente** le nouvel employé.

*Sonia, **I'd like you to meet** Damien.*
*Mrs. Chartier, **I would like you to meet** the new employee.*

Enchanté(e) de faire votre connaissance

This rather formal expression is used when meeting someone. The expression is often abbreviated to **Enchanté**(e).

—Mademoiselle, je suis **enchanté de faire votre connaissance**.
—**Enchantée**, monsieur.

—***Delighted to make your acquaintance**, miss.*
—***Delighted**, sir.*

Chez...

Use this preposition followed by the name or identity of a person to express *at* or *to that person's place/house/home*.

Il habite **chez sa tante**.
Nous allons **chez Rémy**.

*He lives **at his aunt's**.*
*We are going **to Remy's house**.*

The preposition **chez** is followed by a stress pronoun (**moi/toi/lui/elle/nous/vous/eux/elles**) when you want to replace the person's name.

Je suis **chez moi**.
Nous allons **chez eux**.

*I'm **at home (at my house)**.*
*We're going **to their house**.*

Peut-être une autre fois

Use this expression to tell someone that you would like to take a rain check on an offer.

Je ne peux pas rester aujourd'hui, mais **peut-être une autre fois**.

*I can't stay today, but **perhaps another time**.*

Ne t'inquiète pas

Use this phrase to tell a friend that there is no need for concern or worry.

Je sais comment rentrer chez moi. **Ne t'inquiète pas.**

*I know how to get home. **Don't worry.***

Je sais me débrouiller

Use this phrase to say that you do not need help; you can manage.

Il y a beaucoup de lignes de métro, mais **je sais** déjà **me débrouiller**.

*There are lots of subway lines, but **I** already **know how to manage**.*

French in conversation: Meeting people   **485**

Je suis débutant en français, mais **je sais me débrouiller** au restaurant pour commander.

*I'm a beginner in French, but **I can figure out** how to order at the restaurant.*

Prendre and comprendre

The verbs **prendre** and **comprendre** follow the same irregular pattern in the present tense: **je/tu (com)prends, il/elle/on (com)prend, nous (com)prenons, vous (com)prenez, ils/elles (com)prennent**.

Moi, je **prends** le bus. Et toi?
Tu le **comprends**?

*I **take** the bus. How about you?*
*Do you **understand** him?*

Pouvoir and vouloir

Conjugations for the verbs **pouvoir** and **vouloir** follow similar irregular patterns in the present tense: **je/tu peux/veux, il/elle/on peut/veut, nous pouvons/voulons, vous pouvez/voulez, ils/elles peuvent/veulent**. They are both often followed by an infinitive.

Je **veux** absolument apprendre le français.
Nous **pouvons** étudier ensemble.

*I definitely **want** to learn French.*
*We **can** study together.*

Vouloir

When the verb **vouloir** is followed by the adverb **bien**, with or without an infinitive, it expresses willingness.

Je **veux bien**.

*I **would be happy to**. / **Gladly**.*

EXERCICE 33·7

Une invitation à dîner. *A dinner invitation. Complete the blanks in the following dialogue according to the English guidelines in parentheses.*

1. —Tu peux dîner avec nous?
   —Oui, _____. (*I can*)

2. —Tu prends le bus?
   —Non, je préfère _____ le métro. (*to take*)

3. —Tes parents peuvent venir aussi?
   —Non, pas cette fois, mais _____. (*perhaps another time*)

4. —Tu peux arriver à dix-huit heures?
   —Oui, je pense que _____ arriver vers dix-huit heures. (*I can*)

5. —Ta famille habite à Paris?
   —Non, seulement ma tante _____ à Paris. (*lives*)

6. Et toi, comment _____ que tu habites à Paris? (*how is it*)

EXERCICE 33·8

Visite chez les Dupoint. *Visiting the Dupoints. Reconstitute the following dialogue by filling in the blanks with the appropriate words from the list. Capitalize when necessary.*

là	très	bonjour
pote	voilà	enchanté
l'ami	madame	monsieur
je m'appelle	va	

1. CHRIS: _____ Madame Dupoint. _____ de faire votre connaissance.

2. MME DUPOINT: Bonjour, _____. Vous êtes _____ de Didier.

3. CHRIS: Oui, _____. _____ Chris.

4. MME DUPOINT: Didier, ton ami est _____. Ah! Le _____!

5. DIDIER: Salut, mon _____. Ça _____?

6. CHRIS: _____ bien, merci.

Dialogue 4

Today is Saturday. Chris comes to Didier's house to have dinner with him and his parents. He is surprised when he walks into a room filled with people.

CHRIS: Salut, Didier. **C'est bien** samedi aujourd'hui? Ce n'est pas dimanche, **n'est-ce pas**?

Hi, Didier. Isn't it Saturday today? It's not Sunday, right?

DIDIER: Oui, mais **le samedi**, on dîne généralement en famille. Je vais te présenter.

Yes, but on Saturdays, we generally eat dinner with the family. I'm going to introduce you.

CHRIS: **Bonjour, monsieur** Dupoint.

Hello, Mr. Dupoint.

M. DUPOINT: Bonjour, Chris!

Hello, Chris!

DIDIER: Maman, je te présente Chris.

Mom, let me present Chris.

MME DUPOINT: Bonjour, Chris. Je vous **fais la bise**.

Hello, Chris. Here's a kiss for you.

CHRIS: **Bonjour, madame**.

Hello, madam.

DIDIER: Je te présente ma sœur Hélène et son mari.

This is my sister Hélène and her husband.

CHRIS: Bonsoir, madame. Bonsoir, monsieur. **Comment allez-vous?**

Hello, madam. Hello, sir. How are you?

HÉLÈNE: Bien, merci. Et vous?

Fine, thank you. How about you?

CHLOÈ: Moi, je suis Chloé, la cousine de Didier.

I'm Chloé, Didier's cousin.

CHRIS: **Ça alors!** Tu es vraiment sa cousine?

How about that! Are you really his cousin?

CHLOÈ: Eh bien, oui! Et voilà Marie-Josée. Tu sais, c'est la copine de Didier.

Well, yes! And here's Marie-Josée. You know, she's Didier's girlfriend.

French in conversation: Meeting people **487**

EXERCICE 33·9

Testez votre compréhension. *Check your comprehension. Write* T *for true or* F *for false.*

1. _____ Chris va chez Didier dimanche.

2. _____ Chris fait la connaissance de la mère de Didier.

3. _____ La maman de Didier est affectueuse avec Chris.

4. _____ Chris connaît déjà la sœur de Didier.

5. _____ Chloé est la cousine de Didier.

C'est bien...

Use this expression to confirm that you are right about an assumption you made.

C'est bien l'adresse correcte?	***Isn't it (this)** the correct address?*
C'est bien lundi aujourd'hui?	***Isn't it** Monday today?*

N'est-ce pas?

This is another expression to confirm that you are right about an assumption you made.

On va au concert vendredi, **n'est-ce pas**?	*We are going to the concert on Friday, **aren't we**?*
Ta copine s'appelle Chloé, **n'est-ce pas**?	*Your girlfriend's name is Chloé, **isn't it**?*

Le samedi

Use a day of the week with the definite article **le** in front of it to indicate that you mean *regularly* on that day.

Je ne vais pas en cours **le samedi**.	*I don't go to school **on Saturdays**.*
Nous sortons dîner **le dimanche**.	*We go out to dinner **on Sundays**.*

Bonjour, monsieur / bonjour, madame

Use the title **monsieur**, **madame**, or **mademoiselle** with or without the last name of the person whenever you address someone in a formal setting. Don't forget to use the titles in the evening, when say **bonsoir**.

—**Bonjour, monsieur** Ramu.	*—**Hello, Mr.** Ramu.*
—**Bonsoir, madame**.	*—**Good evening, madam**.*

Faire la bise

Faire la bise reflects a cultural habit. It is customary in France to give two or more kisses on the cheek when greeting friends or relatives.

Je ne te fais pas la bise parce que j'ai un rhume.	***I'm not kissing you**, because I have a cold.*
Jean, **fais la bise** à ta tante!	*Jean, **kiss** your aunt!*

488 PRACTICE MAKES PERFECT Complete French All-in-One

Ça alors!

Use this expression to express surprise.

Tu es déjà là? **Ça alors!** *You're already there? **How about that!***

Comment allez-vous?

Use this phrase to ask a person whom you address formally (someone older, a store clerk, employee, server, etc.) how he or she is. This expression is followed by the person's title (**monsieur, madame,** or **mademoiselle**).

Comment allez-vous, monsieur? *How are you, sir?*

Days of the week

When introducing a day of the week, do not try to translate the English preposition that precedes the day (*on Mondays*). Say simply **le lundi**, or, in the case of a single event, just **lundi**.

le lundi *on Mondays (every Monday)*
Mercredi, je vais voir Guy. *I'm going to see Guy (on) Wednesday.*

Relationships and possessions

To express relationships and possession, use the appropriate structure and include the preposition **de** (*of*) as in the following examples:

la famille **de** Didier *Didier's family*
la copine **de** Didier *Didier's girlfriend*
la maison **de** Didier *Didier's house*

Votre and vos

There are two words for formal *your*: **votre** (used before all singular nouns) and **vos** (used before all plural nouns).

J'admire **votre** mère. *I admire **your** mother.*
J'admire **vos** parents. *I admire **your** parents.*

C'est / ce sont

Use **C'est / ce sont** before noun phrases.

C'est Didier. **C'est** mon meilleur ami. ***This is** Didier. **He's** my best friend.*

Faire

Remember that the verb **faire** (*to do/make*) is irregular in the present tense: **je/tu fais, il/elle/on fait, nous faisons, vous faites, ils/elles font. Faire** is used in numerous idiomatic expressions where the English equivalent is not always *to do* or *to make*.

Tu fais du vélo? *Are you riding a bike?*
Les voisins **font** du bruit. *The neighbors **are making** noise.*

French in conversation: Meeting people **489**

EXERCICE 33·10

La famille de Didier. *Didier's family. Write the appropriate possessive adjective* **son, sa,** *or* **ses** *in the blank spaces.*

Dans la famille de Didier, il y a (1) _____ mère, Mme Dupoint; il y a (2) _____ père, M. Dupoint; il y a (3) _____ sœur Hélène; il y a (4) _____ beau-frère; il y a aussi (5) _____ cousins et (6) _____ cousines.

Qui est-ce? *Who is this? Translate the sentences in parentheses into French.*

7. M. Dupoint? _____. (*He is Didier's father.*)

8. _____. (*He is delighted to make Chris's acquaintance.*)

9. Mme Dupoint? _____. (*She is his mother.*)

10. _____. (*She is affectionate.*)

11. Hélène? _____. (*She is his sister.*)

12. _____. (*She is married.*)

EXERCICE 33·11

La rencontre d'Hélène et de Chris. *Hélène's and Chris's meeting. In this dialogue, Chris meets Didier's sister Hélène for the first time. Write the dialogue between these two people using the English guidelines provided.*

1. Hélène greets Chris in a formal manner by saying hello and asking him how he is.

    HÉLÈNE: _____

2. Chris says he is fine and then expresses how delighted he is to make her acquaintance.

    CHRIS: _____

3. Hélène asks Chris if he is indeed Didier's English friend.

    HÉLÈNE: _____

4. Chris tells her that is not exactly the case. Then he explains that he is his American friend.

    CHRIS: _____

5. Hélène apologizes. Then she adds that she does know that he is American.

    HÉLÈNE: _____

6. Chris states that today being Saturday, they both have a little free time.

    CHRIS: _____

7. Hélène says that it's nice. Then she adds that on Saturdays, the family always eats together and that everyone wanted to meet him.

    HÉLÈNE: _____

490   PRACTICE MAKES PERFECT   Complete French All-in-One

French in conversation: Making conversation and making plans

Dialogue 1

Chris approaches a young woman he meets at his friend's house and finds out she was interested in meeting him because he is American.

CHRIS: Bonjour, mademoiselle. Je m'appelle Chris.

ANNE: Je m'appelle Anne et je suis la cousine de Didier.

CHRIS: Et moi, je suis son copain. J'habite aux États-Unis et **je suis ici en visite**.

ANNE: Ah oui, **j'ai entendu parler de vous. J'avais justement envie de** vous rencontrer.

CHRIS: Ah bon. Je ne savais pas que j'étais célèbre!

ANNE: Célèbre? Je ne sais pas! Mais j'étais aux États-Unis il y a deux ans et j'ai des copains américains, moi aussi.

CHRIS: **Je plaisantais**, bien sûr! Où est-ce que vous étiez aux USA?

ANNE: J'étais en Californie et au Colorado.

CHRIS: Ah bon, à l'Ouest! Moi, j'habite au Nevada, à Las Vegas!

ANNE: Las Vegas, pour moi, c'est les casinos au milieu du désert.

CHRIS: **Je comprends qu'on pense cela**, mais il y a aussi des gens tout à fait ordinaires là-bas.

ANNE: **C'est vrai qu'**on peut imaginer Paris comme la ville de la Tour Eiffel, de l'Arc de Triomphe, des Champs-Élysées et du Louvre.

CHRIS: **Exactement. Et pourtant** c'est tellement plus que cela, n'est-ce pas?

Hello, miss. My name is Chris.

My name is Anne, and I'm Didier's cousin.

I'm his friend. I live in the United States, and I am here visiting.

Oh yes, I've heard about you. It just so happens I wanted to meet you.

Well. I didn't know I was famous!

Famous? I don't know about that! But I was in the United States two years ago, and I too have American friends.

I was joking, of course! Where were you in the U.S.?

I was in California and in Colorado.

Oh, in the West! I live in Nevada, in Las Vegas!

For me, Las Vegas is casinos in the desert.

I understand that people think that, but there are also very ordinary people there.

It's true that we could imagine Paris as the city of the Eiffel Tower, the Arch of Triumph, the Champs-Élysées, and the Louvre.

Exactly. And yet, it's so much more than that, isn't it?

EXERCICE 34·1

Testez votre compréhension. *Check your comprehension. Write* T *(true) or* F *(false).*

1. _____ Didier a deux cousines, Chloé et Anne.

2. _____ Anne connaît les États-Unis.

3. _____ Chris habite en Californie.

4. _____ Anne était sur la côte Ouest des États-Unis.

5. _____ Anne pense que Chris est célèbre.

En visite

This phrase helps you say you are visiting without specifying whom or what you are visiting.

Nous sommes ici **en visite.**   *We are here **visiting**.*

J'ai entendu parler de vous

This expression can be used when you meet someone you've heard about prior to your meeting.

Enchanté de faire votre connaissance.   *Delighted to make your acquaintance.*
J'ai souvent **entendu parler de vous.**   *I've often **heard about you**.*

J'avais justement envie de (d')...

This expression can be used when you meet a person you've heard of prior to your meeting. In this case, you are saying that you expected and looked forward to your meeting.

Ah! Voilà ta copine. **J'avais justement**   *Ah! Here's your girlfriend. **It just so**
envie de la rencontrer.   ***happened I wanted** to meet her.*

Je plaisantais

This nice ice-breaker is for people who like to use humor in their conversation.

Je parle dix langues!... Bon, pas vraiment.   *I speak ten languages! . . . Well, not really.*
Je plaisantais.   ***I was joking**.*

Je comprends qu'on pense...

This expression can be used to confirm or deny a preconceived notion.

J'ai un petit accent en français.   *I have a little accent in French. **I understand**
Je comprends qu'on pense que je   **(that) people think** I am a foreigner.*
suis étranger.

C'est vrai que (qu')...

These expressions are transitions or replies that confirm a previous statement.

Je parle assez bien le français. **C'est vrai**   *I speak French pretty well. **It's true**
que je passe beaucoup de temps en   **that** I spend a lot of time in
France.   France.*

Exactement

This short phrase is used to confirm an interlocutor's statement.

—Vous êtes américain, monsieur? —Are you American, sir?
—Oui, **exactement**. —Yes, **that's right**.

Et pourtant...

This short phrase can be used to deny or temper a preconceived notion or statement.

Elle parle très bien l'anglais, **et pourtant** elle ne l'étudie que depuis deux ans. She speaks English very well, **and yet** she's studied it for only two years.

En and au/aux

When mentioning where you live, use the preposition **en** followed by the name of a feminine country, state, or province, or use **au/aux** followed by the name of a masculine country, state, or province.

J'habite **en** France / **en** Normandie / **au** Colorado / **aux** États-Unis. I live **in** France / Normandy / Colorado / the United States.

EXERCICE 34·2

On est intéressé! *We're interested! By completing the sentences of the following dialogue with words or expressions from the list provided, you will reconstruct a meeting between Chris and Anne.*

au Colorado	J'ai entendu parler	exactement
grandes villes	moi	vous
c'est vrai	aux États-Unis	plaît
j'avais envie	des copains	m'appelle
Qu'est-ce qui		

1. ANNE: C'est _____, Chris, le copain de Didier?
2. CHRIS: Oui, c'est bien _____. Et qui êtes-vous?
3. ANNE: Je _____ Anne et je suis la cousine de Didier.
4.–5. CHRIS: Ah oui. _____ de vous. Vous avez voyagé _____.
6. ANNE: Oui, _____ que tout le monde le sait.
7. CHRIS: Et où _____?
8.–9. ANNE: En Californie et _____. La Californie me _____ beaucoup.
10. CHRIS: Ah oui? _____ vous plaît surtout là-bas?
11. ANNE: J'adore ses _____.
12. CHRIS: Vous avez _____ américains?
13. ANNE: Mais oui! C'est pourquoi _____ de vous parler.

Dialogue 2

As Chris and Anne continue their conversation, Chris finds out about Anne's American experience.

CHRIS: Dites, Anne, **cela vous dérangerait si on se tutoyait**?	Say, Anne, would it bother you if we used the familiar?
ANNE: Mais non, pas du tout.	Of course not, not at all.
CHRIS: Alors, **dis-moi, qu'est-ce qui te plaît** aux États-Unis?	So, tell me, what do you like in the United States?
ANNE: Beaucoup de choses. Les grandes villes de Californie et la personnalité ouverte de ses habitants, par exemple.	Lots of things. The big California cities and the open personality of the people, for example.
CHRIS: J'ai de la famille à San Francisco. Je connais et **j'aime bien** la ville.	I have family in San Francisco. I know and like the city well.
ANNE: Au Colorado, j'adore les paysages et la nature.	In Colorado, I love the scenery and nature.
CHRIS: Tu as fait de l'escalade et des randonnées au Colorado, je suppose.	You went climbing and hiking in Colorado, I suppose.
ANNE: On s'est promenés en montagne, bien sûr, mais l'escalade, c'est pour les professionnels.	We went walking in the mountains, of course, but climbing is for pros.
CHRIS: Tu n'aimes pas le sport?	Don't you like sports?
ANNE: Oh! Tu sais, pour moi, la marche **me suffit** et elle **fait partie** de ma routine quotidienne.	Oh you know, for me, walking is enough and it's part of my daily life.
CHRIS: C'est vrai que je marche beaucoup depuis que je suis à Paris.	It's true that I walk a lot since I've been in Paris.
ANNE: Tu vois. Tu t'adaptes à la vie parisienne.	You see, you are adapting to Parisian life.
CHRIS: **Il le faut!** Ça ne me dérange pas du tout.	It's necessary! I don't mind at all.

EXERCICE 34·3

Testez votre compréhension. *Check your comprehension. Write T (true) or F (false).*

1. _____ Chris peut tutoyer Anne.
2. _____ Anne n'aime pas les États-Unis.
3. _____ Anne aime faire des promenades.
4. _____ Anne est très sportive.
5. _____ Chris marche beaucoup à Paris.

Cela te/vous dérangerait?

This expression allows you to ask for a favor in a very courteous manner because you acknowledge that you might be imposing on someone.

Cela vous dérangerait, madame, si je parlais anglais?	***Would it bother you**, madam, if I spoke English?*

Dis / dis-moi

This expression is best used in familiar settings. Note that you are using the command form of the verb **dire** as a direct approach to someone.

Dis, Joël, tu peux venir me chercher?	***Hey/Say**, Joël, can you pick me up?*
Dis-moi, elle te plaît, cette voiture?	***Say**, do you like that car?*

Qu'est-ce qui te plaît?

This familiar question is frequently used instead of **Qu'est-ce que tu aimes?** Note that the literal translation of the question is *What is pleasing to you / pleases you?*

—**Qu'est-ce qui te plaît** ici, Suzanne?	—***What do you like** here, Suzanne?*
—J'aime bien les montagnes.	—*I like the mountains.*

Asking this question in a formal manner requires substituting the pronoun **vous** for **te**.

Qu'est-ce qui vous plaît, mademoiselle?	***What do you like**, miss?*

J'aime bien

Since the verb **aimer** means both *to like* and *to love*, use the adverb **bien** to specify or emphasize that you mean *to like*.

J'aime bien les comédies.	***I like** comedies.*
J'aime bien cette actrice.	***I like** this actress.*

Cela/ça me suffit

This versatile expression is used to express that you have had enough of something. The word **ça** is simply an abbreviated form of **cela**.

—Tu veux encore du café?	—*Do you want more coffee?*
—Non merci. **Ça me suffit**.	—*No, thanks. **That's enough.***
Ah non! Plus de télé ce soir. **Ça suffit**.	*Oh, no! No more TV tonight. **Enough.***

Faire partie de (d')...

Use this idiomatic **faire** expression to express being a part of or belonging to something.

Ma sœur **fait partie d'**une sororité à l'université.	*My sister **belongs to** a sorority at the university.*
Cette ceinture **fait partie d'**un ensemble que j'ai depuis longtemps.	*This belt **is part of** an outfit I've had for a long time.*

French in conversation: Making conversation and making plans

Il le faut

Use this impersonal phrase to express that something is a *must*.

—Tu réponds toujours? —*Do you always answer?*
—Bien sûr. **Il le faut**. —*Of course, **I must / It's necessary**.*

—Vous travaillez le week-end? —*You work on weekends?*
—**Il le faut**. —***We have to**.*

Et puis...

This phrase is used to add a detail. It is used as a somewhat emphatic *and* or *in addition*.

J'ai faim, **et puis** je voudrais goûter ces hors-d'œuvre. *I'm hungry, **and** I would like to taste these appetizers.*

Je veux bien

Use the verb **vouloir** with the adverb **bien** when you mean *I want to* as in *I don't mind* or *I'm willing*.

—Tu veux aller au restaurant? —*Do you want to go to the restaurant?*
—Oui, **je veux bien**. —*Yes, **I don't mind**.*

EXERCICE 34·4

Quelle est la réponse appropriée dans le dialogue suivant? *What is the appropriate reply in the following dialogue? Write the letter of the response on the line provided.*

1. _____ Je connais très bien les États-Unis.
2. _____ Je connais, par exemple, la Californie.
3. _____ J'adore les grandes villes.
4. _____ Dis, tu aimes bien Paris?
5. _____ Tu marches beaucoup.
6. _____ Tu fais du sport?
7. _____ On va au parc?
8. _____ Cela te dérangerait si on marchait?

a. Oh non! La marche me suffit.
b. Ah! Je vois! Tu as voyagé aux États-Unis.
c. Pas du tout. Un peu d'exercice, c'est bon!
d. Oui, j'adore la ville et ses habitants.
e. Je veux bien. Allons-y!
f. Ah bon! Tu connais San Francisco?
g. Oui, comme les Parisiens. Il le faut.
h. Moi aussi.

Dialogue 3

Now Anne is interested enough to want to know more about Chris and what he is doing this summer in Paris.

ANNE: Alors, **combien de temps** tu vas rester en France? *So, how long are you going to stay in France?*

CHRIS: Je suis là pour l'été. Mais, avec ma tante qui habite à Paris, nous allons voyager.

I'm here for the summer. But, with my aunt who lives in Paris, we're going to travel.

ANNE: **Comment se fait-il que** tu aies une tante à Paris?

How is it that you have an aunt in Paris?

CHRIS: Elle est tout simplement mariée à un Français.

She is simply married to a Frenchman.

ANNE: Ah! Je vois. **Depuis quand** elle est mariée? **Et ça fait longtemps qu'**elle habite à Paris?

Oh, I see. How long has she been married? And has she lived in Paris long?

CHRIS: **Depuis** à peu près dix ans, je crois.

For about ten years, I think.

ANNE: Et où est-ce que vous comptez aller alors?

And where do you intend to go then?

CHRIS: En Normandie et en Touraine.

To Normandy and Touraine.

ANNE: Vous n'allez pas en Provence comme la moitié de la population française?

Won't you go to Provence like half the French population?

CHRIS: Eh bien non. Ma tante dit qu'il y a **trop de monde** sur La Côte méditerranéenne en été.

Well no. My aunt says that there are too many people on the Mediterranean coast during the summer.

ANNE: Elle a raison! Et pourtant elle est belle, la Côte d'Azur!

She's right! However, the Riviera is beautiful!

Testez votre compréhension. *Check your comprehension. Write T (true) or F (false).*

1. _____ Chris va passer l'été en France.
2. _____ La tante américaine de Chris est mariée à un Français.
3. _____ La tante de Chris habite en Normandie.
4. _____ Chris et sa tante vont voyager en Provence.
5. _____ Anne aime la Côte d'Azur.

Combien de temps... ?

Use this expression when you want to ask for how long an event took place, is taking place, or will take place.

Combien de temps dure le film? *How long does the movie last?*
Combien de semaines passeras-tu là-bas? *How many weeks will you spend over there?*

Comment se fait-il que (qu')... ?

This expression shows your puzzlement or surprise that something is true or may be happening. Note that the verb in the dependent clause is in the *subjunctive* mood.

Comment se fait-il qu'il neige en été? / *How can it snow in the summer?*
Comment se fait-il que vous étudiiez encore à cette heure? / *Why are you still studying at this hour?*

Depuis quand / ça fait combien de temps que (qu')... ?

Use one of these expressions to ask for how long something has been going on. Be sure to use the present tense to indicate that the action is still going on.

Depuis quand est-ce qu'il a cette voiture? / *How long has he had this car?*
Ça fait combien de temps qu'elle attend? / *How long has she been waiting?*

Trop de monde

Use this expression to talk about *too many people*.

Il y a **trop de monde** dans ce café. Allons ailleurs! / *There are **too many people** in this café. Let's go somewhere else!*

EXERCICE 34·6

Une rencontre. *A meeting. Reconstitute the following dialogue. The first sentence is identified as **a**. Write **b**, **c**, **d**, **e**, or **f** for each of the remaining sentences, putting them in the appropriate chronological order.*

1. __a__ Bonjour, je m'appelle John. Enchanté de faire votre connaissance.
2. _____ Mais oui, c'est mon copain aussi.
3. _____ Vous le connaissez depuis longtemps?
4. _____ Bonjour. Je m'appelle Hélène. Vous êtes l'étudiant américain?
5. _____ Oh oui. Depuis à peu près dix ans.
6. _____ Oui, je passe l'été chez Jean-Luc. Vous le connaissez?

Une conversation. *A conversation. Complete this exercise as you did the one above.*

7. __a__ J'avais justement envie de faire votre connaissance, Hélène.
8. _____ Vous savez que j'ai voyagé aux États-Unis, c'est ça?
9. _____ C'est vrai. Je connais bien la Californie.
10. _____ Ah bon. Pourquoi?
11. _____ Parfaitement.
12. _____ Parce que j'ai entendu parler de vous.

Dialogue 4

Now Chris is curious about how Anne plans to spend her summer and is surprised to find out that she loves to stay home.

CHRIS: Et toi, Anne, **qu'est-ce que tu fais**, cet été?	And you, Anne, what are you doing this summer?
ANNE: Moi, **je profite de** Paris pendant que tout le monde quitte la ville.	I enjoy Paris while everybody leaves the city.
CHRIS: Super bonne idée! Tu as la ville pour toi toute seule.	What a great idea! You have the city to yourself.
ANNE: J'ai les berges de la Seine où je peux me reposer.	I have the banks of the Seine where I can rest.
CHRIS: Pas mal! Mais tu ne peux pas te baigner!	Not bad! But you can't swim!
ANNE: Non, mais j'adore lire, couchée dans l'herbe ou sur le sable.	No, but I love to read lying in the grass or on the sand.
CHRIS: Du sable à Paris?	Sand in Paris?
ANNE: Mais oui, le long de la Seine. **Et puis**, tu sais, **je suis des cours** aussi.	Of course, along the Seine. And, you know, I also take classes.
CHRIS: Ah oui? De quoi?	Really? In what?
ANNE: Je suis un cours de littérature anglaise en ce moment. C'est fascinant.	I'm taking an English literature class at the moment. It's fascinating.
CHRIS: **Tiens**, tu sais **donc** bien parler l'anglais?	What do you know, so you know English well?
ANNE: Pas trop mal, mais je sais **mieux** lire que parler.	Not too badly, but I read better than I speak.

Testez votre compréhension. *Check your comprehension. Write T (true) or F (false).*

1. _____ Anne va voyager cet été.

2. _____ Anne aime se promener le long de la Seine.

3. _____ Anne nage dans la Seine.

4. _____ Anne va à l'université pendant l'été.

5. _____ Anne va suivre des cours de français.

Qu'est-ce que tu fais?

Use this phrase to ask what someone is doing or will do soon.

Qu'est-ce que tu fais en ce moment?	*What are you doing at the moment?*
Qu'est-ce que tu fais demain?	*What will you do tomorrow?*

Profiter de (d')

Use this verb and structure to express that you are enjoying and taking full advantage of an opportunity.

Je n'ai pas de cours aujourd'hui. **Je profite de** ma journée de congé.	*I don't have class today. **I'm enjoying** my day off.*
Il habite au bord de la mer. Alors **il en profite** pour se détendre souvent sur la plage.	*He lives near the sea. So **he takes advantage of it** by relaxing often on the beach.*

Mais oui!

Use this emphatic phrase to express a most definite *yes* as in *of course*.

—Tu viens ce soir?	*—Are you coming tonight?*
—Mais oui!	*—Of course!*

Et puis...

This expression, which, in its literal sense, means *and then*, can be used to mean *on top of that*.

Je vais finir cet exercice **et puis** je vais dormir.	*I'm going to finish this exercise **and then** go to sleep.*
Je ne peux pas sortir. Je suis fatigué. **Et puis** j'ai encore du travail.	*I can't go out. I'm tired. **On top of that** I still have some work.*

Tiens!

This interjection has a variety of uses and meanings. It usually conveys surprise.

Ils vont en France? **Tiens**, je ne savais pas.	*They're going to France? **Well**, I didn't know.*
Où sont les clés? **Tiens**, les voilà!	*Where are the keys? **Look**, there they are!*

Donc...

This adverb also has a variety of uses and meanings. It often accompanies an urgent command, in which case it has no translation. It can also be used to indicate a *cause* (*so/therefore*).

Viens **donc**!	*Come on! / Let's go!*
Ils sont à la retraite. **Donc** ils voyagent beaucoup.	*They are retired. **So they travel a lot.***
Tu es **donc** déjà professeur?	*So you're already a teacher?*

Suivre un cours

This idiomatic phrase includes the irregular verb **suivre** (literally meaning *to follow*); it is used to indicate that you are *taking a class*.

Nous **suivons un cours d'anglais**.	*We're **taking an English class**.*

Mieux

This adverb modifies the meaning of the action verb to say it's being done *better* than before or than in other circumstances.

J'étudie **mieux** tout seul.	*I study **better** alone.*
Vous jouez **mieux** aujourd'hui.	*You're playing **better** today.*

With a verb that indicates a state (rather than an action), such as **être** (*to be*), the superlative adverb **le mieux** means *the best*.

Tout est pour **le mieux**.	*All is for **the best**.*

Meilleur(e)(s) and mieux

Remember to distinguish the adjective (**le/la/les**) **meilleur(e)(s)** (*better; best*) from the adverb (**le**) **mieux** (*better; the best*). **Aimer mieux** is a synonym for **préférer**.

C'est **le meilleur** film de cette année.	*It is **the best** movie this year.*
J'**aime mieux** rester à la maison.	*I **prefer** staying home / I **like** staying home **better**.*

Reflexive verbs

Many regular -**er** verbs such as **se baigner** and **se promener** are also reflexive. So remember to add the appropriate reflexive pronoun before the conjugated verb.

se baigner (*present tense*) (*to bathe / to swim*)

je me baigne	nous nous baignons
tu te baignes	vous vous baignez
il/elle/on se baigne	ils/elles se baignent

se promener (*present tense*) (*to go for a walk*)

je me promène	nous nous promenons
tu te promènes	vous vous promenez
il/elle/on se promène	ils/elles se promènent

Nous **nous baignons** dans ce lac en été.	*We **swim/bathe** in this lake during the summer.*
Tout le monde **se promène** aujourd'hui.	*Everybody **is going for a walk** today.*

Suivre

The conjugation of the irregular verb **suivre** (*to follow; to take* [*a class*]) in the present tense is as follows: **je/tu suis, il/elle/on suit, nous suivons, vous suivez, ils/elles suivent**.

Vas-y! Je te **suis** dans une minute.	*Go ahead! I'll **follow** you in a minute.*
Ma sœur **suit** un cours d'anthropologie.	*My sister **is taking** a class in anthropology.*
Ils **suivent** bien nos instructions.	*They **follow** our instructions well.*

EXERCICE 34·8

Quelle coïncidence! *What a coincidence! Write the letter of the most appropriate reply to each line of dialogue in the space provided.*

1. __*a*__ Qu'est-ce que tu fais pendant l'été?

2. _____ Oui, mais tu voyages par exemple?

3. _____ Pourquoi? Tu as de la famille là-bas?

4. _____ Ah. Je comprends. Tu y vas toute seule?

5. _____ Tu sais, moi aussi, je vais en Normandie!

6. _____ Oui, tu vois, j'ai un oncle qui habite là-bas.

7. _____ Il habite à Caen. Tu connais?

8. _____ Ce n'est pas trop mal comme ville.

a. Je profite des vacances.

b. Tiens! Quelle coïncidence!

c. Ah oui, je connais très bien.

d. Pas trop mal? Moi, j'adore cette petite ville.

e. Bien sûr! Je vais toujours en Normandie.

f. Exactement. Mes parents ne quittent pas Paris.

g. Justement oui: mes grands-parents.

h. Où en Normandie habite-t-il?

EXERCICE 34·9

J'aime me détendre. *I like to relax. Complete each sentence with an appropriate term or expression from the list provided.*

suis	quitter	lire
me suffit	profite	tout seul
Et puis	me baigner	me bronzer
me promener		

En été, je _____ (1) de mes vacances. Je ne _____ (2) généralement pas de

cours à l'université. J'adore _____ (3) le long des berges de la Seine. Les Parisiens

aiment _____ (4) la ville en été; moi, non. C'est vrai, je ne peux pas _____ (5),

mais je peux _____ (6) et _____ (7) un bon livre, couché dans l'herbe ou sur

le sable. Cela _____ (8). _____ (9) j'adore la tranquillité et le calme; cela ne

me dérange pas d'être _____ (10).

Dialogue 5

Since Chris is going to be in Paris for a few more weeks, he wonders if Anne could show him around town.

CHRIS: Tu sais, Anne, Didier va bientôt partir en Italie avec sa famille.	*You know, Anne, Didier is soon going to leave for Italy with his family.*
ANNE: C'est parce qu'ils ont une maison de campagne en Toscane où ils vont chaque été.	*It's because they have a house in Tuscany where they go every summer.*
CHRIS: **Dommage** pour moi! Je perds mon copain.	*Too bad for me! I'm losing my friend.*
ANNE: Si tu veux, je peux te montrer mes endroits favoris à Paris.	*If you want, I can show you my favorite places in Paris.*
CHRIS: C'est gentil, Anne! Mais tu vas être occupée avec tes études, non?	*That's nice, Anne! But you're going to be busy with your studies, aren't you?*
ANNE: **Mais non, pas tout le temps, voyons**!	*Of course not, not all the time, come on!*
CHRIS: Tu vas m'emmener me promener le long de la Seine?	*Are you going to take me for a walk along the Seine?*
ANNE: Ah non! Ça, je le fais toute seule. Mais on peut sortir le soir.	*Certainly not! That I do alone. But we can go out in the evenings.*
CHRIS: Ah! **Ça m'intéresse!** Où par exemple?	*Oh! I'm interested! Where for example?*
ANNE: Il y a mille choses à faire. Tu aimes la musique, la danse, le théâtre, la bonne bouffe?	*There are a thousand things to do. Do you like music, dance, theater, good food?*
CHRIS: J'adore le théâtre.	*I love the theater.*
ANNE: Eh bien, moi aussi. **Alors**, on va décider ensemble **ce qui est le plus** intéressant à voir.	*Well, me too. So we'll decide together what is the most interesting to see.*
CHRIS: D'accord! Je suis prêt!	*OK, I'm ready!*

EXERCICE 34·10

Testez votre compréhension. *Check your comprehension. Write* T *(true) or* F *(false).*

1. _____ La famille de Didier a une maison en Italie.
2. _____ Didier va partir en vacances cet été.
3. _____ Anne ne veut pas sortir avec Chris.
4. _____ Chris et Anne vont faire des promenades le long de la Seine.
5. _____ Chris et Anne adorent le théâtre.

Dommage!

Use this adverb to show empathy or express disappointment.

Élaine est malade. **Dommage!** *Élaine is sick. **Too bad!***
Il pleut. **Dommage** pour le pique-nique. *It's raining. **Too bad** for the picnic!*

Mais non, voyons!

The expression **mais non** is an emphatic *no* or *of course not*. The verb **voyons** (literally, *let's see*), added to the phrase, makes a reply more forceful and somewhat indignant.

—Tu as encore eu un accident de voiture? —*Have you had another car accident?*
—**Mais non, voyons!** —***Of course not!** (implying "How can you think that?")*

Ça m'intéresse!

Use this structure to express that you are interested in something (rather than trying to make a literal translation of *I'm interested*).

La politique? **Ça m'intéresse** beaucoup. *Politics? **It interests me** a lot.*

(Pas) tout le temps

This is one of several expressions that include the noun **le temps** with the meaning of *time*.

J'aime lire, mais **pas tout le temps**. *I like to read but **not all the time**.*
Lui, il regarde **tout le temps** la télé. *He watches TV **all the time**.*

Alors...

Use this transitional adverb, at the beginning or end of a sentence, to predict an effect or draw a conclusion.

Tu aimes les films d'aventures. **Alors,** trouvons-en un! *You like adventure movies. **So** let's find one!*

Ce qui est le plus...

Use this phrase to talk about something that's the most boring, interesting, expensive, etc., in a given circumstance.

Ce qui est le plus ennuyeux ici, c'est qu'il faut toujours attendre. ***What is most** annoying here is that you always have to wait.*

The near future tense

The near future tense (*to be going to*) uses a conjugated form of the verb **aller** followed by an infinitive:

Je **vais partir**. *I'm **going to leave**.*

Remember that the verb **aller** has an irregular conjugation in the present tense: **je vais, tu vas, il/elle/on va, nous allons, vous allez, ils/elles vont.**

Ils **vont voyager**.	*They **are going to travel**.*
Mes copains **vont organiser** une fête.	*My friends **are going to organize** a party.*
Nous **allons nous amuser**.	*We're **going to have fun**.*

EXERCICE 34·11

Un petit incident! *A little incident!* Complete each line of dialogue with an appropriate term or expression from the list provided. Capitalize as necessary.

c'est gentil	c'est parce que	si tu veux
alors	d'accord	mais non, voyons!
dommage	ce qui est intéressant	il y a mille choses à faire
prêt		

1. DENISE: Tu es _____, chéri? Voilà le taxi!
2. JEAN-LOUIS: Oui, oui, _____. J'arrive. Mais ce n'est pas un taxi, c'est un autobus, c'est un car de tourisme!
3. DENISE: _____! Tu exagères toujours!
4. JEAN-LOUIS: _____, c'est que tu adores quand j'exagère, n'est-ce pas?
5. DENISE: C'est vrai. _____ tu es drôle!
6. JEAN-LOUIS: Merci pour le compliment. _____.
7. DENISE: _____ on y va?
8. JEAN-LOUIS: Oui, _____, allons-y!
9. DENISE: Oui, je veux. _____ ce soir. Mais... où est le taxi?
10. JEAN-LOUIS: _____ pour nous! Le taxi est parti avec d'autres clients.

Dialogue 6

Anne and Chris are planning to see a modern play at Anne's university and then go out to a café for a bite to eat.

ANNE: Allô, Chris. Ici, Anne. J'ai deux billets pour une pièce à l'université samedi soir. Ça t'intéresse?

CHRIS: Bien sûr, Anne! C'est sympa de ne pas m'avoir oublié. Mais **dis-moi** un peu **de quoi il s'agit**.

ANNE: Écoute, tout ce que je peux dire, c'est que mon professeur d'anglais a vu la pièce et l'a trouvée **géniale**.

Hello, Chris. This is Anne. I have two tickets for a play at the university Saturday night. Are you interested?

Of course, Anne! It's nice that you didn't forget me. But tell me something about it.

Listen, all I can say is that my English professor saw it and found it amazing.

CHRIS:	Tu ne sais pas **quel en est le sujet**?	*You don't know what it's about?*
ANNE:	C'est une adaptation de *La Tempête* de Shakespeare, mais dans un contexte moderne.	*It's an adaptation of Shakespeare's* The Tempest, *but in a modern context.*
CHRIS:	Bon, d'accord. **On verra bien!**	*OK, good. We'll see!*
ANNE:	**Tu veux venir me chercher chez moi ou me rejoindre** au théâtre?	*Do you want to pick me up at home or meet me at the theater?*
CHRIS:	Donne-moi ton adresse et l'heure où je dois être chez toi et **j'y serai**.	*Give me your address and the time I have to be at your house and I'll be there.*
ANNE:	Ça va! Tiens, je vais t'envoyer tout ça à ton adresse email, d'accord?	*Fine! Hey, I'm going to send all that to your e-mail address, OK?*
CHRIS:	Ça va. Parfait.	*Fine. (It's) perfect.*
ANNE:	Si tu veux, après la pièce, on peut aller dans un café avec quelques amis.	*If you like, after the play, we can go to a café with a few friends.*
CHRIS:	**Volontiers.** Je te suivrai où que tu ailles, Anne!	*Gladly. I'll follow you wherever you go, Anne!*

Testez votre compréhension. *Check your comprehension. Write* T *(true) or* F *(false).*

1. _____ Anne invite Chris au cinéma.
2. _____ Le prof d'Anne recommande une pièce à ses étudiants.
3. _____ Chris veut venir chercher Anne chez elle.
4. _____ Anne va envoyer l'adresse du théâtre à Chris.
5. _____ Anne et Chris vont aller au café samedi soir.

Dis-moi / dites-moi de quoi il s'agit

This expression may be used to ask what something is about, such as a movie, a play, a book, or a lecture.

Je veux bien aller voir cette pièce, mais **dis-moi de quoi il s'agit**.	*I don't mind going to see this play, but **tell me what it's about**.*

Génial!

This adjective may be used in multiple contexts to express admiration or excitement.

Quel beau tableau! Il est **génial**!	*What a beautiful painting! It's **brilliant**!*
Tu as acheté les tickets de concert? **Génial!**	*You bought the concert tickets? **Great!/Fabulous!***

Quel en est le sujet?

This question asks what the subject or topic of an article or a book is. The pronoun **en** (*of it / in it*) replaces the article or book being discussed.

Tu as lu ce livre. **Quel en est le sujet?**	*You read this book. **What is its topic?***

On verra bien

Use this expression to show skepticism or restrained optimism.

Je ne sais pas si on pourra apprécier le spectacle de si loin. **On verra bien.**	*I don't know if we'll be able to appreciate the show from so far away. **We'll see.***

Tu veux venir me chercher? Ou tu veux me rejoindre?

Ask this question to find out if your friend will pick you up or if he or she prefers to meet you at the venue.

Je ne sais pas où c'est. **Tu veux me venir chercher?**	*I don't know where it is. **Do you want to pick me up?***
Je suis devant le cinéma. **Tu veux me rejoindre?**	*I'm in front of the movie theater. **Do you want to meet me?***

J'y serai

This phrase assures your friend you'll get to your agreed-upon rendezvous on time. Change the subject and the form of the verb to adapt the expression as necessary.

Le cinéma Rex? D'accord. **J'y serai!**	*The Rex cinema? OK, **I'll be there!***
Rendez-vous devant le restaurant? D'accord, **nous y serons**.	*Let's me outside the restaurant? OK, **we'll be there**.*

Volontiers

Use this adverb to agree with or accede to a request.

—Tu peux me rejoindre au théâtre?	*—Can you join me at the theater?*
—**Volontiers.**	*—**Sure.***

N'importe où

Use **n'importe** followed by an interrogative adverb (**quand/où/comment**) to indicate *any time/ any place* or *by any means*.

Tu peux téléphoner **n'importe quand**.	*You can phone **any time**.*
J'irai **n'importe où** avec toi.	*I'll go **any place/anywhere** with you.*

Commands

The command forms of verbs are the conjugated **tu/nous/vous** forms of the verb *without* the subject pronouns that normally precede them in statements.

Dis-le!	***Say it!** (familiar)*
Disons-le!	***Let's say it!***
Dites-le!	***Say it!** (formal or plural)*

French in conversation: Making conversation and making plans

For regular **-er** verbs and the verb **aller**, remember to drop the **-s** ending of the conjugated **tu** form of the verb (**vas**) to create the familiar command.

Écoute!	*Listen!*
Va!	*Go!*

EXERCICE 34·13

Tu vas me rejoindre? *Are you going to meet me? Write the letter of the most appropriate reply on the line provided. The first one has been done for you.*

1. __a__ J'ai des billets pour un récital de danse.
2. _____ C'est à dix-neuf heures. Tu peux y aller?
3. _____ C'est de la danse expérimentale.
4. _____ Oui, je sais. Tu veux me rejoindre au théâtre?
5. _____ D'accord. Tu arrives à quelle heure?
6. _____ L'heure où il y a le plus de circulation.

a. Génial, c'est à quelle heure?
b. Non, je vais te chercher chez toi.
c. Je sais, mais on verra bien.
d. Je serai chez toi à dix-sept heures.
e. Volontiers! Ça m'intéresse!
f. Écoute, tu sais que j'adore n'importe quelle danse.

EXERCICE 34·14

Allons au cinéma! *Let's go to the movies! In the following dialogue, write Marc's replies to his friend Juliette according to the English guidelines in parentheses.*

1. JULIETTE: Allô, Marc. Ici Juliette. J'ai les billets de cinéma. Tu veux venir me chercher ou me rejoindre?

   MARC: _____
   (*I am going to pick you up.*)

2. JULIETTE: À quelle heure?

   MARC: _____
   (*Any time.*)

3. JULIETTE: D'accord. Je serai prête. On peut prendre le taxi.

   MARC: _____
   (*Gladly*)

4. JULIETTE: Ça va être génial.

   MARC: _____
   (*It is about Facebook. I'm interested.*)

508 PRACTICE MAKES PERFECT Complete French All-in-One

5. JULIETTE: Ah oui. Bien sûr! Et moi aussi!

   MARC: _____

   (*The topic is good, but the movie? We'll see.*)

6. JULIETTE: Tout ce que je peux dire, c'est que c'est un film à voir.

   MARC: _____

   (*Listen, I'll be at your house at six.*)

EXERCICE
34·15

Karen et François deviennent amis. *Karen and François become friends. In this dialogue, Karen tells François she is taking an art history class on Wednesdays with Professor Pouce. Write the dialogue between these two people using the English guidelines provided.*

1. Karen tells François that she's taking an art history class on Wednesdays with Professor Pouce.

   KAREN: _____

2. François is surprised because he is also taking an art history class with Professor Pouce, but on Mondays.

   FRANÇOIS: _____

3. Karen tells François that her course is only an introduction and asks about his course.

   KAREN: _____

4. François replies that his course is a second year course and that he loves it.

   FRANÇOIS: _____

5. Karen asks François if he goes regularly to museums then.

   KAREN: _____

6. François says that, of course, he spends all his free time in museums and art galleries. Then he asks if she wants to join him tomorrow for a modern art exhibit.

   FRANÇOIS: _____

7. Karen says that she would be glad to and asks at what time.

   KAREN: _____

8. François says they can go any time after seven P.M.

   FRANÇOIS: _____

French in conversation: Making conversation and making plans   **509**

French in conversation: Discussing current events

Dialogue 1

Didier and his family can't get back from Italy by train because of a railroad workers' strike.

ANNE: Allô, Chris. Ici Anne. Ça va bien?

Hello, Chris. This is Anne. Is everything OK?

CHRIS: Oui, très bien, Anne. Et toi? **Quoi de neuf?**

Yes, fine, Anne. How about you? What's new?

ANNE: Moi, **j'ai des nouvelles de** Didier. Je viens de lui parler.

I heard from Didier. I just spoke to him.

CHRIS: Il devrait **être de retour** bientôt, non?

He should be back soon, shouldn't he?

ANNE: **Tu n'es pas au courant?** Les employés de la SNCF **sont en grève**.

Don't you know? The workers of the French National Railroad Company (the SNCF) are on strike.

CHRIS: **Ça veut dire** pas de trains pour quelques jours!

That means no trains for a few days!

ANNE: Exact! **C'est déjà assez embêtant. Mais en plus**, les conducteurs d'autobus veulent se joindre à la grève.

Correct! That's already pretty annoying. But in addition, the bus drivers want to join the strike.

CHRIS: Ah oui, par solidarité, sans doute. **À mon avis**, c'est admirable.

Of course, out of solidarity, no doubt. In my opinion, it's admirable.

ANNE: **C'est toujours comme ça** en France. **Quelle poisse!**

It's always like that in France. What a pain!

CHRIS: Je sais. Ma tante m'en a souvent parlé.

I know. My aunt often talked to me about it.

ANNE: **Tu trouves ça bien que** les travailleurs emploient tant de force de persuasion contre leur employeur?

Do you think that's good that workers use so much persuasive force against their employers?

CHRIS: **Ça dépend.** C'est bien pour les travailleurs, **c'est sûr et certain**!

That depends. It's good for workers, that much is certain!

ANNE: Pas si bien pour les voyageurs et les touristes. **Ça arrive** toujours **en pleine saison**, ces grèves!

Not so good for travelers and tourists. It always happens in the high season, those strikes!

CHRIS: Alors **on dirait que** Didier et sa famille vont être coincés en Italie.

So it looks like Didier and his family will be stuck in Italy.

ANNE: Pour l'instant. On verra si la SNCF et le syndicat de travailleurs pourront **se mettre d'accord** bientôt.

For the moment. We'll see if the SNCF and the workers' union can come to an agreement soon.

EXERCICE 35·1

Testez votre compréhension. *Check your comprehension. Write* T *(true) or* F *(false).*

1. _____ Anne voudrait des nouvelles de Didier.

2. _____ Anne sait où est Didier.

3. _____ Anne pense que les grèves sont embêtantes.

4. _____ Chris trouve que les grèves sont bonnes pour les travailleurs.

5. _____ Chris pense que Didier est de retour à la maison.

Quoi de neuf?

Use this familiar expression with friends to start a conversation.

Salut, Marie-Josée. **Quoi de neuf?**   *Hi, Marie-Josée. **What's up?***

Avoir des nouvelles de (d')...

Use this expression to inquire or give updates about what is happening with friends.

Tu **as des nouvelles d'**Arnaud?   *Do you **have any news from** Arnaud?*
Aujourd'hui j'**ai eu des nouvelles de** Lucie.   *Today I **got news from** Lucie.*

Non?

Always placed at the end of a statement, this word is a synonym for the expression **n'est-ce pas?** (*isn't it so?*).

Tu comprends, **non**?   *You understand, **don't you?***
Elle est là, **non**?   *She's there, **isn't she?***

Être idioms

There are many expressions using the verb **être**; some do not translate literally from French into English.

Arnaud **est** finalement **de retour**.   *Arnaud **is** finally **back**.*
Nous **ne sommes pas au courant** de ce qui se passe.   *We **are not abreast** of what's happening. (We **are not in the loop**.)*
Les travailleurs **sont en grève**.   *The workers **are on strike**.*

Zut!

Use this short interjection to express dissatisfaction or annoyance colloquially.

Je vais arriver en retard à mon rendez-vous. **Zut!**   *I'm going to arrive late for my appointment. **Darn!***

French in conversation: Discussing current events   **511**

Ça veut dire…

Use this phrase to paraphrase, clarify, or summarize statements.

Ils ne téléphonent pas. **Ça veut dire** qu'ils sont fâchés.	*They aren't calling. **That means** that they're angry.*

C'est embêtant!

This colloquial expression expresses annoyance.

Le café est fermé. **C'est embêtant!**	*The café is closed. **That's annoying!***

Assez

Use this adverb before an adjective to convey the meaning of *rather, pretty,* or *quite.*

Tu es **assez grand** pour ton âge.	*You're **rather tall** for your age.*
C'est **assez gênant**.	*This is **pretty embarrassing**.*

Et en plus…

Use this transitional phrase to add details to statements.

J'ai faim et soif, **et en plus** je suis fatiguée.	*I am hungry and thirsty, **and on top of that** I'm tired.*

À mon avis…

Use this phrase to indicate that you are about to express your personal opinion.

À mon avis, nous ne pourrons pas avoir de billets.	***In my opinion,** we will not be able to get tickets.*

C'est toujours comme ça

Use this transitional phrase to trivialize or generalize occurrences.

Il y a trois pharmacies en plein centre. **C'est toujours comme ça.**	*There are three pharmacies in the city center. **It's always like that.***

Quelle poisse!

This slang expression, which shows extreme exasperation, should only be used in very colloquial settings.

Il faut attendre trois heures l'arrivée du train? **Quelle poisse!**	*We have to wait three hours for the arrival of the train? **Just my luck!***

Tu trouves ça bien que (qu')… ?

Start a question with this expression to ask someone's opinion about something. The verb after **que (qu')** will be in the subjunctive mood.

Tu trouves ça bien que le pourboire soit inclus?	***Do you think it's right that** the tip be included?*

512   PRACTICE MAKES PERFECT   Complete French All-in-One

Ça dépend de (d')...

Use this transitional phrase to interject nuances, details, or examples.

Tu penses que nos amis vont arriver à l'heure? **Ça dépend de** la circulation.

You think our friends are going to arrive on time? ***It depends on*** *the traffic.*

C'est sûr et certain!

Use this expression to agree vehemently with a statement.

Je t'assure qu'il va neiger. **C'est sûr et certain.**

I assure you it's going to snow. ***It is absolutely certain.***

Ça arrive

Use this transitional phrase to trivialize or generalize occurrences.

Il y a des accidents de voiture sur l'autoroute? Oui, **ça arrive.**

There are traffic accidents on the highway? Yes, ***it happens.***

En pleine saison

This expression is generally used in the context of tourism.

Les prix des chambres sont plus élevés **en pleine saison.**

The prices of rooms are higher ***in high season.***

On dirait que (qu')...

Use this phrase to express an opinion or a point of view.

On dirait que beaucoup de célébrités ont des problèmes de drogue.

It would seem that *many celebrities have drug problems.*

Se mettre d'accord

Use this **mettre** idiom to refer to a negotiation that leads to an agreement. Note that the verb **mettre** is an irregular verb in the present tense; it normally means *to put* or *to put on*.

Peut-on **se mettre d'accord** sur le fait qu'il vaut mieux lire les journaux que de regarder le journal télévisé?

Can we ***agree*** *that it is better to read the newspapers than watch the televised news?*

Pas de (d') + *nom*

Pas de (**d'**) + *noun* is an invariable expression used before a noun, regardless of the noun's gender or number. Note that the noun is expressed without an article.

Il n'y a **pas de trains**?
Pas de nouvelles aujourd'hui?

There are ***no trains?***
No news *today?*

En

The pronoun **en** replaces **de** (**d'**) + *noun* or *verb*. The translation of the pronoun **en** varies according to what it replaces and can sometimes be omitted in the English sentence.

French in conversation: Discussing current events **513**

—Tu es de retour **d'Italie**?	—*You're back **from Italy**?*
—Oui, j'**en** viens.	—*Yes, I'm just coming **from there**.*

—Tu as envie **de manger**?	—*You feel like **eating**?*
—Oui, j'**en** ai envie.	—*Yes, I feel like **it**.*

The **futur simple**

The **futur simple** tense consists of the infinitive (minus the **-e** ending for infinitives ending in **-e**) used as a stem and the following endings: **je (j') -ai, tu -as, il/elle/on -a, nous -ons, vous -ez, ils/ elles -ont.**

J'**arriverai** bientôt.	*I **will arrive** soon.*
Nous **répondrons** demain.	*We **will answer** tomorrow.*

The **futur simple** tense of some common verbs have irregular stems. They should be memorized.

être	→	**ser-**
pouvoir	→	**pourr-**
voir	→	**verr-**
vouloir	→	**voudr-**

Ce **sera** super.	*That/It **will be** great.*
On **pourra** rentrer.	*We**'ll be able** to go back home.*
On **verra**!	*We**'ll see**.*
Tu **voudras** rester.	*You**'ll want** to stay.*

EXERCICE 35·2

Tu es au courant? *Do you know what's happening? Complete the following lines of dialogue with words or expressions from the list provided.*

poisse	Pas de	comme ça
Ici	Quoi de neuf	Ça arrive
Zut	ce sera super	non
On dirait	grève	en pleine saison

1. MARC: Allô, Sabine. _____ Marc.

2. SABINE: Bonjour, Marc. _____?

3. MARC: Les conducteurs de bus font _____.

4. SABINE: Quelle _____! Heureusement qu'il y a le métro.

5. MARC: Désolé! _____ métro non plus!

6. SABINE: _____! C'est vraiment embêtant!

7. MARC: C'est toujours _____ pendant les vacances.

8. SABINE: _____ que tu n'es pas surpris!

9. MARC: _____ assez souvent, non?

10. SABINE: Tu as raison, mais vraiment, _____, ce n'est pas bien!

11. Marc: C'est une bonne excuse pour ne pas aller au cours, _____?

12. Sabine: Pour nous, bien sûr, _____.

EXERCICE 35·3

Tu plaisantes? *Are you kidding? Write Sonia's replies to Luc's statements or questions as indicated.*

1. Luc: Tu es au courant? Tous les travailleurs des transports publics font la grève.

Sonia: _____

(*Darn! What a pain!*)

2. Luc: Tu as des cours aujourd'hui?

Sonia: _____

(*Yes, I do have some.*)

3. Luc: Mais non, Sonia! Pas de cours aujourd'hui!

Sonia: _____

(*Are you kidding?*)

4. Luc: Non! Crois-moi! C'est sûr et certain! Tu n'as pas de nouvelles de tes profs ou de ta faculté?

Sonia: _____

(*No news at all!*)

5. Luc: Regarde la télé! Tu verras!

Sonia: _____

(*I see. It looks like you're right!*)

6. Luc: Tu devrais être contente. Une journée de vacances!

Sonia: _____

(*That depends! Not so good when you like your class.*)

7. Luc: Tu es assez bonne élève. Tu pourras te débrouiller (*manage*).

Sonia: _____

(*We'll see.*)

8. Luc: Et en plus, il fait si beau aujourd'hui. Tu voudras sans doute te promener avec moi.

Sonia: _____

(*You think they're great, those strikes, don't you?*)

French in conversation: Discussing current events **515**

Dialogue 2

Chris and Anne talk about the weather forecast and particularly about the upcoming heat wave.

ANNE: **Dis donc**, Chris. On annonce qu'il va y avoir une vague de chaleur la semaine prochaine.	*Say, Chris. They announce that there's going to be a heat wave next week.*
CHRIS: Zut! Il fait déjà assez chaud.	*Darn! It is pretty hot already.*
ANNE: Tu sais, ici **c'est grave**. Les maisons et les bureaux n'ont généralement pas l'air a climatisation.	*You know, here it is serious. Houses and offices generally don't have air conditioning.*
CHRIS: **Pas drôle, ça!**	*That's no fun!*
ANNE: Tout le monde transpire dans les bus et dans le métro. **Tu verras.**	*Everybody sweats in the buses and in the subway. You'll see.*
CHRIS: **Plus personne** aux terrasses des cafés! Ce sera parfait pour toi qui aimes être seule.	*Nobody left on the terraces of the cafés! That will be perfect for you who likes to be alone.*
ANNE: **Tu m'énerves**, tu sais. J'espère que tu souffriras bien.	*You are getting on my nerves, you know. I hope you'll suffer.*
CHRIS: Désolée, Anne. Je serai en Normandie où je profiterai de la brise atlantique.	*Sorry, Anne. I'll be in Normandy where I'll enjoy the Atlantic breeze.*
ANNE: **Veinard!** Moi, il faudra que je supporte la canicule avec ses températures extrêmes. On prévoit quarante-deux degrés Celsius.	*Lucky you! I will have to bear the heat wave with its extreme temperatures. They predict forty-two degrees Celsius.*
CHRIS: Quelle horreur! **Franchement** j'espère que les météorologues se trompent. Ça arrive!	*How awful! Frankly I hope that the meteorologists are wrong. It happens!*
ANNE: Je voudrais bien mais **ça m'étonnerait**.	*I'd like that, but I'd be surprised.*

Jugez votre compréhension. *Check your comprehension. Write* T *(true) or* F *(false).*

1. _____ La météo annonce du temps chaud.
2. _____ Anne dit que tout le monde a l'air conditionné.
3. _____ Chris va souffrir de la chaleur à Paris.
4. _____ La Normandie est sur la mer Méditerranée.
5. _____ Anne dit que les météorologues se trompent toujours.

Dis donc

Use this expression to begin a discussion, but only in familiar situations.

Dis donc, Rémy, tu as des nouvelles de Stéphane?	*Hey, Rémy, do you have any news of Stéphane?*

C'est grave

Use this expression to indicate that something is serious. The opposite would be **Ce n'est pas grave** (*It's not serious / It's no big deal*).

Il est malade et **c'est grave**.	*He is sick and **it's serious**.*
Elle a oublié de téléphoner mais **ce n'est pas grave**.	*She forgot to call but **it's no big deal**.*

C'est pas drôle, ça!

Use this slightly sarcastic phrase to convey annoyance.

Quoi? L'hôtel est fermé? **C'est pas drôle, ça!**	*What? The hotel is closed? **That's not funny!***

Plus personne

Use this double negative structure to declare that *there is nobody left*.

Nous sommes en retard. Il n'y a **plus personne** ici!	*We're late. Everyone left! (**No one** here anymore!)*

Tu m'énerves!

Use this expression only with close friends and relatives to express irritation.

Arrête de parler si fort! **Tu m'énerves.**	*Stop talking so loud! **You're getting on my nerves.***

Veinard(e)!

Use this adjective in familiar settings to exclaim that a person is really lucky.

Veinard, tu as encore gagné.	***Lucky you**, you won again.*

Franchement!

Use this adverb as an exclamation to show disapproval or dismay.

Tu n'as pas encore fini? **Franchement!**	*You haven't finished yet? **Why, really!***

Ça m'étonnerait!

Use this exclamation to show skepticism and doubt.

Tu dis que le restaurant sera fermé en pleine saison? **Ça m'étonnerait!**	*You say that the restaurant will be closed in high season? **I'd be surprised!***

Faire idioms

Most expressions describing the weather are **faire** idioms beginning with **Il fait** (*It is*), including the question **Quel temps fait-il?** (*What's the weather like?*):

Il fait beau	*It's nice*	**... chaud**	*hot*
... du soleil	*sunny*	**... mauvais**	*bad*
... frais	*cool*	**... nuageux** (colloq.)	*cloudy*
... froid	*cold*		

French in conversation: Discussing current events   **517**

Notable exceptions are:

il grêle	*it hails / it's hailing*	**il pleut**	*it rains / it's raining*
il neige	*it snows / it's snowing*		

EXERCICE 35·5

Croire ou ne pas croire la météo? *To believe or not believe the weather report? Write the letter of the most appropriate completion on the line provided.*

1. _____ MARIETTE: Dis donc, Jacques, la météo annonce...
2. _____ JACQUES: ... il faut prendre les skis et partir tout de suite.
3. _____ MARIETTE: ... que les routes seront dangereuses?
4. _____ JACQUES: ... Nous serons seuls sur la route!
5. _____ MARIETTE: C'est pas drôle, ça!... tu sais.
6. _____ JACQUES: ... quand on perd le sens de l'humour, Mariette.
7. _____ MARIETTE: Écoute! Moi, je ne voudrais pas...
8. _____ JACQUES: ... Ils n'ont pas toujours raison!

a. Tu ne crois pas
b. Tant mieux! Quelle chance!
c. qu'il neige dans les Alpes depuis ce matin.
d. À mon avis,
e. me trouver coincée dans une tempête de neige.
f. Ça m'étonnerait, Mariette.
g. Tu m'énerves,
h. C'est grave

EXERCICE 35·6

Coincé en montagne. *Stuck in the mountains. Complete the following dialogue by choosing the most appropriate word or phrase from the list provided. Capitalize as necessary.*

zut	veinard	on dirait que
plaisanter	franchement	raison
neige	être de retour	

1. MARIETTE: Tu vois, Jacques, les routes sont couvertes de _____.
2. JACQUES: _____! Comment est-ce qu'on va rentrer?
3. MARIETTE: Tiens! _____ tu as perdu ton sens de l'humour, Jacques.
4. JACQUES: Je dois _____ au travail demain.
5. MARIETTE: _____! Tu vas avoir un jour de congé.

6. JACQUES: Arrête de _____, Mariette!

7. MARIETTE: Ça alors! C'était ton idée de venir. _____, tu m'énerves.

8. JACQUES: Tu as _____! Je m'excuse.

Dialogue 3

This time, Anne and Chris talk about an article Anne came across in the newspaper about the future of French transportation.

ANNE: Il y a un article super dans le journal sur l'avenir des transports en France.

There is a great article in the newspaper about the future of transportation in France.

CHRIS: Ça m'intéresse beaucoup! La production des voitures électriques augmente de plus en plus aux États-Unis. **Où en est-on** en France?

I'm very interested! The production of electric cars is increasing more and more in the United States. Where do they stand in France?

ANNE: On en fait. Mais un problème majeur, c'est de pouvoir recharger son véhicule rapidement et n'importe où. **On parle de** créer un réseau national de sites de recharge.

We make them. But a major problem is to be able to recharge your vehicle rapidly and from anywhere. They're talking about creating a national network of recharging sites.

CHRIS: **Ce n'est pas évident, ça!**

That's not easy!

ANNE: **Une autre idée qui circule**, c'est des batteries interchangeables.

Another idea going around is interchangeable batteries.

CHRIS: Ça existe déjà, **il me semble**.

That exists already, I think.

ANNE: **Je me demande** si on ne **fantasme** pas **à force de** vouloir rompre la dépendance pétrolière.

I wonder if it's not wishful thinking because we want to be free from oil dependency.

CHRIS: Admets que tous les pays ont été **des accros** du pétrole pendant trop longtemps. Il est temps de **faire marche arrière.**

Admit that we have all been dependent on oil for too long. It's time to go backward.

ANNE: Ou plutôt **marche avant.**

Or rather forward.

CHRIS: J'ai entendu dire que certaines villes françaises ont déjà des bus hybrides. C'est vrai?

I heard that some French cities already have hybrid buses. Is it true?

ANNE: **Bien sûr que** c'est vrai. Nous sommes très **écolo** en France. Si ça t'intéresse **tant que ça**, tu devrais aller à l'exposition qui aura lieu **à l'occasion de** la Fête des transports la semaine prochaine.

Of course it's true. We are very ecologically minded in France. If you're that interested, you should go to the exhibition taking place along with the Transportation Fair next week.

CHRIS: La fête des transports! **Décidément, vous autres Français,** vous avez des fêtes pour tout. **C'est tordant!**

The transportation festival! Honestly, you French have festivals for everything. It's hilarious!

French in conversation: Discussing current events **519**

EXERCICE 35·7

Testez votre compréhension. *Check your comprehension. Write* T *(true) or* F *(false).*

1. _____ La France ne fabrique pas de voitures électriques.

2. _____ Chris pense que les batteries interchangeables existent.

3. _____ Chris pense qu'il faut limiter l'utilisation du pétrole.

4. _____ Anne déclare que les Français veulent protéger l'environnement

5. _____ Anne conseille à Chris d'aller à une exposition pour s'informer sur les transports.

Où en est-on?

Ask this question to find out how a project is coming along.

Le gâteau n'est pas encore prêt? **Où en es-tu?**	*The cake isn't ready yet?* **How far along are you?**

On parle de (d')...

Use this expression to report something you heard.

Il y a eu un accident. **On parle de** trois blessés.	*There has been an accident.* **They're talking about** *three injured people.*
Le temps est horrible en montagne. **On parle d'**avalanches.	*The weather is horrible in the mountains.* **They're talking about** *avalanches.*

Ce n'est pas évident, ça! / c'est pas évident, ça!

Use this phrase to convey that something is hard to conceive of. **C'est pas évident** is an abbreviated and more familiar form of **Ce n'est pas évident**. Note that the negative adverb **ne (n')** is often omitted in familiar language.

Tu dois finir ce travail ce soir? **C'est pas évident!**	*You have to finish this work tonight?* **That's not / won't be easy!**

Une autre idée qui circule...

This phrase is used to talk about unconfirmed news.

Une autre idée qui circule est qu'on a commandé des bus hybrides.	**Another idea that's around** *is that they've ordered hybrid buses.*

Il me semble que (qu')...

Use this phrase to express an opinion that you share.

Il me semble que nos amis sont en retard.	**It seems to me that** *your friends are late.*
Il me semble que les Français ont beaucoup de fêtes.	**It looks like** *the French have many celebrations.*

520 PRACTICE MAKES PERFECT Complete French All-in-One

Je me demande...

Use this reflexive verb when you are wondering about something.

Je me demande quand les batteries interchangeables seront disponibles.

I wonder when interchangeable batteries will be available.

On fantasme sur...

Use this verb when you want to convey the notion of *dreaming about something*, desirable but perhaps hard to obtain or outside the scope of reality.

Je suis très optimiste. **Je fantasme sur** un avenir de paix.

*I am very optimistic. **I dream about** a peaceful future.*

À force de (d')...

Use this prepositional phrase to link ideas of cause and effect. This phrase introduces the cause.

Elle a réussi à me persuader **à force de** me donner des exemples.
À **force de** persévérance, j'ai atteint mon but.

*She managed to persuade me **by** giving me examples.*
***By** persevering, I reached my goal.*

Un(e) accro

This noun is derived from the adjective **accroché(e)** (*attached to / hooked on to*). It is often used to describe people who are dependent and addicted.

C'est **un accro** du tabac!

*He is **addicted** to tobacco!*

Faire marche avant / marche arrière

Use this phrase to express *forward* or *backward* motion, literally or figuratively.

Faisons marche avant et parlons de l'avenir!
Tu es trop près de la rue. **Fais marche arrière!**

***Let's move forward** and talk about the future!*
*You are too close to the street. **Back up!***

Bien sûr que (qu')...

Use this phrase to confirm something vehemently.

Bien sûr que je sais parler français!

***Of course** I know how to speak French!*

Écolo

This abbreviated form of the adjective **écologique** is used to describe people who believe in promoting habits and processes that are good for the planet.

Il faut être **écolo** et recycler autant que possible.

*We must be **ecologically minded** and recycle as much as possible.*

Tant que ça

Use this phrase to add emphasis to what a person does or feels.

French in conversation: Discussing current events **521**

| Si tu veux protéger l'écologie **tant que ça**, tu dois adhérer à une organisation «verte»! | *If you want to protect ecology **so much**, you have to join a "green" organization!* |
| Une personne qui travaille **tant que ça** doit gagner beaucoup. | *A person who works **that much** must earn a lot.* |

À l'occasion de (d')...

Use this phrase to introduce any special occasion or moment.

| **À l'occasion de** la sortie de son nouveau livre, elle a en dédicacé plusieurs. | ***When** her new book came out, she autographed several.* |
| **À l'occasion de** ton anniversaire, nous dînerons ensemble. | ***For** your birthday, we'll have dinner together.* |

Décidément

Use this adverb as an exclamation to show a variety of emotions you want to emphasize.

| Tu travailles encore? **Décidément!** | *Are you still working? **Honestly!*** |
| Quelle corruption dans ce gouvernement! **Décidément!** | *What corruption in this government! **Honestly!*** |

Vous autres...

Use this all-encompassing phrase to address several people.

| Vous ne faites jamais d'objections, **vous autres**? | *Don't **you (all)** ever object?* |
| Vous avez bien de la chance, **vous autres**! | *You are quite lucky, **you all**!* |

C'est tordant!

Use this exclamation to show how amused you are!

| Tu es rouge comme une tomate! **C'est tordant!** | *You're red as a tomato! **It's hilarious!*** |

EXERCICE
35·8

Les voitures du futur. *Cars of the future. Write the letter of the most appropriate completion on the line provided.*

1. _____ MARIETTE: On devrait acheter...

2. _____ JACQUES: Et pourquoi pas une voiture... ?

3. _____ MARIETTE: Il paraît qu'il faut souvent recharger...

4. _____ JACQUES: Oui, mais je pense que bientôt elles seront...

5. _____ MARIETTE: Ce serait bien, ça! Il faut être... !

6. _____ JACQUES: Je suis d'accord. Je ne veux pas...

a. les batteries.

b. interchangeables.

c. une voiture hybride.

d. écolo de nos jours.

e. être un accro du pétrole.

f. électrique

522   PRACTICE MAKES PERFECT   Complete French All-in-One

EXERCICE 35·9

Les transports de demain. *Tomorrow's transportation. Complete the following dialogue by choosing the most appropriate word or phrase from the list provided. Capitalize as necessary.*

je me demande	évident	batteries
où en est-on	écologiques	qui circule
on parle	il paraît	tant que ça
décidément		

1. MARIETTE: Dis, Jacques, _____ avec le projet de bus hybrides?

2. JACQUES: _____ qu'il y en a déjà pas mal en France.

3. MARIETTE: _____ si notre ville va en avoir aussi.

4. JACQUES: C'est une idée _____! Espérons-le!

5. MARIETTE: Dans notre proche avenir, je vois des voitures et des bus

   à _____!

6. JACQUES: Bien sûr qu'on aura des transports en commun _____! J'en suis sûr.

7. MARIETTE: _____! Nous sommes très optimistes!

8. JACQUES: Écoute, _____ même de sites de recharge partout dans le pays.

9. MARIETTE: Alors, ça, c'est pas _____. Mais il le faut évidemment!

10. JACQUES: Si nous voulons protéger l'environnement _____, c'est une bonne idée!

EXERCICE 35·10

Les dernières nouvelles. *The latest news. In this dialogue, Jacques and Mariette are watching a YouTube video on Jacques's iPod about the wedding of two celebrities. Write the dialogue using the English guidelines provided.*

Jacques tells Mariette to watch the short video he just found online. He tells her that she will love it.

1. JACQUES: _____. _____!

Mariette asks what it is about.

2. MARIETTE: _____?

Jacques tells her it is the wedding of two celebrities (*you may use any real or imaginary names*).

3. JACQUES: _____.

French in conversation: Discussing current events **523**

Mariette comments that the bride is magnificent in white and that the groom is as handsome as a god.

4. MARIETTE: _____.

Jacques wonders how much such a wedding costs.

5. Jacques: _____.

Mariette says it costs more than he can imagine or afford.

6. MARIETTE: _____.

French in conversation: Asking for help

Dialogue 1

This morning, Chris met Anne at the Louvre. After visiting the museum and stopping at the gift shop, they went to a bistro.

CHRIS: Décidément, Anne, on ne **se lasse** jamais du Louvre. La Joconde **me manquera** quand je rentrerai aux États-Unis!

No doubt about it, Anne, you never get tired of the Louvre. I'll miss the Mona Lisa when I go back to the United States!

ANNE: Il faudra revenir quand tu le pourras. En tout cas, tu as acheté quelques souvenirs.

You'll just have to come back when you can. In any case, you bought a few souvenirs.

CHRIS: Oui, j'ai acheté des reproductions de tableaux du Louvre qui me plaisent beaucoup.

Yes, I bought reproductions of the Louvre paintings that I like a lot.

ANNE: C'est pour décorer ta chambre à l'université quand tu rentreras?

Is it / Are they to decorate your room at the university when you get back?

CHRIS: Certaines, oui. D'autres seront sans aucun doute des cadeaux.

Some, yes, others will no doubt be gifts.

LE SERVEUR: Bonjour, mademoiselle, monsieur. Que puis-je vous servir?

Hello, miss, sir. What would you like?

ANNE: Pour moi, une eau minérale et une salade niçoise. **J'ai une faim de loup**.

For me, a mineral water and a salade niçoise. I'm starving.

CHRIS: Tu as faim et tu ne veux qu'une salade? Prends encore quelque chose!

You're hungry and you only want a salad? Have something else!

ANNE: **Tu sais ce que c'est**, une salade niçoise, Chris? Avec des légumes, des œufs, du thon et tout ça. C'est **rassasiant comme tout**.

Do you know what a salade niçoise is, Chris? With vegetables, eggs, tuna, and all that. It's really filling.

CHRIS: Ah! **Je t'ai encore eue**, ma petite! Bon, pour moi, un steak au poivre avec des frites, s'il vous plaît.

Ah! Got you again, sweetie! All right, for me, a pepper steak with fries, please.

LE SERVEUR: Parfaitement. Et comme boissson, monsieur?

Certainly. And to drink, sir?

CHRIS: Un coca, s'il vous plaît.

A coke, please.

LE SERVEUR: Bien, **je reviens tout de suite**.

Fine, I'll be right back.

ANNE: **Petit blagueur!** Tu me manqueras dès que tu seras parti.

Little joker! I'll miss you as soon as you leave.

EXERCICE 36·1

Testez votre compréhension. *Check your comprehension. Write* T *(true) or* F *(false).*

1. _____ Chris a acheté des affiches à la boutique du Louvre.

2. _____ Ce sont des cadeaux pour Chris et Anne.

3. _____ Anne n'a pas très faim.

4. _____ Chris aime beaucoup plaisanter.

5. _____ Le serveur n'est pas patient avec ses clients.

Se lasser de (d')...

This reflexive verb is used to express that *you are tired of* or *bored with* something.

Les enfants **se lassent** très vite **de** leurs noveaux jouets.	*Children **get tired** quickly of their new toys.*

... me manquera / ... me manqueront

Use this expression to say that *you will miss something or someone*. Remember that what or whom you will miss is always the *subject* of the verb in a sentence with the verb **manquer**.

La cuisine française **me manquera**.	*I will miss French cooking.*
Mes amis **me manqueront**.	*I will miss my friends.*

Sans doute

This adverbial expression is used to express a distinct probability.

Il a **sans doute** acheté quelque chose de cher.	*He **probably** bought something expensive.*

Avoir une faim de loup

This idiomatic **avoir** expression is used to stress how hungry you are, that is, *hungry as a wolf*.

Quand je fais du sport toute la journée, **j'ai** toujours **une faim de loup**.	*When I exercise all day, **I am** always **hungry as a wolf**.*

Rassasiant(e)/rassasié(e)

Use the first adjective to talk about *how filling a dish is* and the second to say *how filled up you are*.

Le bœuf bourguignon est un plat **rassasiant**.	*Beef bourguignon is a **filling** dish.*
Je ne peux plus manger. Je suis **rassasié(e)**.	*I can't eat any more. I'm **full** / I've **had enough**.*

526 PRACTICE MAKES PERFECT Complete French All-in-One

Comme tout

Use this phrase to stress (*really*) what someone or something is like.

Il est gentil **comme tout**.	*He is **really** nice.*
Ce plat est délicieux **comme tout**.	*This dish is **really** delicious.*

Je t'ai eu(e)

This familiar expression should only be used with friends after you have tricked them.

Tu as cru mon histoire. **Je t'ai eu**, John!	*You believed my story. **I got you**, John!*
Je t'ai bien eue, Mireille! Poisson d'avril!	***I got you**, Mireille! April Fool's!*

Je reviens tout de suite

This expression is frequently used to say that you will be back promptly.

Je **reviens tout de suite** avec votre addition, monsieur.	***I'll be right back** with your check, sir.*

Petit blagueur / petite blagueuse

This familiar expression can be used to chide friends and family members.

Tu m'as joué un bon tour, **petite blagueuse**.	*You played a good trick on me, **little joker**.*

EXERCICE 36·2

Au rayon de maquillage. *In the cosmetics department. Complete each line of the following dialogue with an appropriate word or phrase from the choices given.*

lasses	faim	le rayon
blagues	quelque chose	t'ai eue
comme tout	reviens	

1. SUZE: Je vais aux toilettes, Sandrine. Je _____ tout de suite.

2. SANDRINE: D'accord. Je serai ici dans _____ du maquillage.

3. SUZE: Encore, Sandrine. Tu fais toujours ça. Tu ne te _____ pas d'acheter du rouge à lèvres et du rimmel?

4. SANDRINE: Jamais. C'est amusant _____.

5. SUZE: Me voilà, Sandrine. Dis, on va manger quelque chose? J'ai une

   _____ de loup.

6. SANDRINE: Je veux bien mais je veux acheter _____ de plus.

7. SUZE: Tu _____, Sandrine. Je veux vraiment manger quelque chose.

8. SANDRINE: Je _____, ma petite. Allons-y!

EXERCICE 36·3

Que faire d'abord? *What should we do first? Write the letter of the most appropriate completion for each line of dialogue.*

1. NICOLAS: _____ Appelle-moi...   a. des balles de tennis aujourd'hui.
2. MARC: _____ Où est-ce que...   b. on ira au rayon des sports.
3. NICOLAS: _____ Je vais au rayon des sports...   c. quand tu seras prêt, Marc.
4. MARC: _____ Tu ne veux pas m'aider...   d. pour acheter des balles de tennis.
5. NICOLAS: _____ Avec plaisir, mais il me faut...   e. à choisir un pull?
6. MARC: _____ Dès que nous aurons trouvé mon pull...   f. tu vas?

Dialogue 2

Anne is taking Chris to a big department store. He is looking for a gift for his mom.

CHRIS: C'est gentil **de ta part**, Anne, de m'accompagner. J'ai besoin de toi pour trouver le cadeau parfait pour ma mère.

It's nice of you, Anne, to accompany me. I need you to find the perfect gift for my mother.

ANNE: Tu n'as rien trouvé dans la boutique du Louvre? Ça m'étonne. J'y ai vu de très beaux foulards et sacs à main.

You haven't found anything in the Louvre boutique? That's surprising. I saw some very beautiful scarves and purses.

CHRIS: Eh bien, tu vois, je ne les ai pas remarqués.

Well, you see, I didn't notice them.

ANNE: Bon. Où veux-tu commencer?

All right. Where do you want to start?

CHRIS: Eh bien, les foulards, c'est une bonne idée. Ça ne pèse pas lourd dans la valise.

Well, scarves, that's a good idea. That doesn't weigh much in the suitcase.

ANNE: Nous sommes au **bon** étage alors. Madame, s'il vous plaît, les foulards, **c'est où?**

We're on the right floor then. Madam, please, the scarves, where are they?

LA VENDEUSE: **Suivez-moi.** Le rayon est au bout de ce couloir. C'est pour vous, mademoiselle?

Follow me. The department is at the end of this hallway. Is it for you, miss?

CHRIS: **En fait**, c'est pour ma mère.

Actually, it's for my mother.

LA VENDEUSE: Vous connaissez ses goûts en couleurs?

Do you know her taste in colors?

CHRIS: **Euh!** Je pense que je saurai quand je verrai.

Ehm! I think I'll know when I see.

ANNE: Si par hasard, **ça ne lui va pas** ou si ça ne lui plaît pas, Chris, tu pourras toujours me l'envoyer.

If, by chance, it doesn't suit her or if she doesn't like it, Chris, you can send it back to me.

528 PRACTICE MAKES PERFECT Complete French All-in-One

EXERCICE 36·4

Testez votre compréhension. *Check your comprehension. Write* T *(true) or* F *(false).*

1. _____ Chris a vu de beaux foulards au Louvre.

2. _____ Anne veut bien accompagner Chris aux Galeries Lafayette.

3. _____ Anne et Chris sont au bon étage pour trouver les foulards.

4. _____ La vendeuse n'est pas serviable.

5. _____ Chris sait quelles couleurs sa mère aime bien.

De ma/ta part

Use one of these phrases to indicate the originator of an act or a communication.

Dis-lui bonjour **de ma part**.	*Say hello to him/her **from me**.*
C'est gentil **de ta part** de m'inviter.	*It is nice **of you** to invite me.*

Bon(ne)/mauvais(e)

Use the adjective **bon(ne)** before a noun to indicate that it is the *right* one and the adjective **mauvais(e)** to indicate the *wrong* one.

C'est la **bonne** direction.	*This is the **right** direction.*
Il a donné la **mauvaise** réponse.	*He gave the **wrong** answer.*

C'est où?

Use this informal question whenever you are looking for something.

La pharmacie, **c'est où**?	***Where's** the pharmacy?*
Les articles de toilette, **c'est où**?	***Where are** the toiletries?*

Suivez-moi

This expression is used by someone who offers to lead you to a location.

Vous cherchez l'ascenseur? **Suivez-moi.**	*You're looking for the elevator? **Follow me.***

En fait

Use this short transitional phrase to express the English word *actually*.

Je cherchais un cadeau pour ma mère, mais **en fait** je n'ai rien trouvé.	*I was looking for a gift for my mother, but **actually** I didn't find anything.*
Tu crois que je suis français? Non, **en fait**, je suis américain.	*You think I'm French? No, **actually**, I'm American.*

Euh

Expect to hear this interjection frequently in the speech of native French speakers. It shows hesitation.

French in conversation: Asking for help **529**

—Où est le rayon des appareils ménagers?	—*Where is the home appliance department?*
—Euh...	—*Ehm / Let's see . . .*

Ça lui va

This phrase is used to say that something fits a person or looks good on the person.

Marie-Laure porte un béret. **Ça lui va bien!** Tu ne trouves pas?	*Marie-Laure is wearing a beret.* ***It looks good on her!*** *Don't you think?*
François ne devrait pas acheter ce pull. **Ça ne lui va pas.** Il est bien trop grand pour lui.	*François should not buy this sweater.* ***It doesn't fit him.*** *It's much too big for him.*

EXERCICE 36·5

Luc et Marc se mettent d'accord. *Luc and Marc are in agreement. Complete the following dialogue according to the English guidelines in parentheses.*

1. LUC: _____ de vouloir faire du shopping tout seul. (*It's not very nice*)

2. MARC: Euh! _____. C'est pour ça. (*But I'm in a hurry*)

3. LUC: Qu'est-ce qu' _____, Marc? (*do you need*)

4. MARC: _____. (*I need new sweaters and new shirts*)

5. LUC: Moi, _____ de gel après-rasoir et de l'eau de Cologne. (*I need*)

6. MARC: Bon, je viens et _____ tes articles de toilette, on ira faire mes achats. (*as soon as we have*)

7. LUC: Voilà, mon pote. Ça, _____. (*it's nice of you*)

8. MARC: _____? (*Where is it?*)

9. LUC: Pardon, monsieur, le rayon des articles de toilette, _____? (*is it on this floor*)

10. LE VENDEUR: Oui, _____, monsieur. (*Follow me*)

Dialogue 3

After Anne left, Chris walked around the **quartier** (*neighborhood*) and is now looking for a subway station to go back home. He first stops a woman and then a man to get directions.

CHRIS: Pardon, madame, **pouvez-vous m'indiquer** la station de métro la plus proche?	*Pardon me, madam, can you show me the nearest subway station?*
UNE DAME: Désolée, je suis pressée!	*Sorry! I'm in a hurry!*
CHRIS: Pardon, monsieur, **excusez-moi de vous déranger**. Je cherche une station de métro.	*Excuse me for the interruption, sir. I'm looking for a subway station.*

Un monsieur: Où allez-vous, monsieur?	*Where are you going, sir?*
Chris: **Il me faut** la ligne Orange direction Défense.	*I need the Orange line going to the Défense.*
Un monsieur: Bon, alors, je vous conseille d'aller tout droit jusqu'à la Madeleine. Vous trouverez une station devant l'église.	*All right, then I advise you to go straight ahead up to the Madeleine (church). You'll find a station in front of the church.*
Chris: Merci, monsieur. **Vous êtes très aimable.**	*Thank you, sir. You're very kind.*

Chris is now in front of the church of the Madeleine, and since he is in a hurry, he asks a policeman where the station is exactly.

Chris: **Monsieur l'agent**, s'il vous plaît, **pouvez-vous me dire** où est la station de métro?	*Officer, can you please tell me where the subway station is?*
L'agent: **Avec plaisir**, jeune homme. Traversez la place! La station est au coin de ces deux rues.	*My pleasure, young man. Go across the square! The station is at the corner of those two streets.*
Chris: Merci beaucoup, **monsieur l'agent**.	*Thank you very much, officer.*

EXERCICE 36·6

Testez votre compréhension. *Check your comprehension. Write* T *(true) or* F *(false).*

1. _____ Une dame aide Chris à trouver sa station.
2. _____ Un monsieur trop pressé ne peut pas aider Chris.
3. _____ Chris sait quelle ligne de métro il veut prendre.
4. _____ Chris prend la mauvaise route pour aller à la Madeleine.
5. _____ Chris demande de l'aide à un agent de police.

Pouvez-vous m'indiquer... ? / Pouvez-vous me dire... ?

Use one of these expressions when you are asking a passerby for directions.

Pouvez-vous m'indiquer où se trouve la rue Jean-Jaurès?	*Can you tell me where Jean-Jaurès Street is?*

Excusez-moi de vous déranger

Use this expression as a lead-in when you have to ask a passerby for directions. This shows that you acknowledge that you may be imposing upon someone and that his or her help will be appreciated.

Excusez-moi de vous déranger, mais pouvez-vous me dire où sont les toilettes?	***I apologize for interrupting you***, *but can you tell me where the restroom is?*

Il me faut

This idiomatic impersonal expression followed by a noun, is used to express that you need something. Remember to use the appropriate object pronoun (**me** [**m'**], **te** [**t'**], etc.) before the verb to indicate who needs something.

| **Il me faut** un taxi. | **I need** a taxi. |
| **Il te faut** quelque chose? | **Do you need** something? |

Vous êtes très aimable

Use this sentence in addition to **merci** to thank people emphatically for any help they give you.

Oui, c'est exactement ce que je cherche. Merci, **vous êtes très aimable**.
*Yes, it is exactly what I'm looking for. Thank you, **you're very kind**.*

Monsieur l'agent

Use this title when addressing a police officer.

Pardon, **monsieur l'agent**. Je cherche un bureau de police.
*Excuse me, **officer**. I'm looking for a police station.*

Avec (grand) plaisir

This phrase is used to confirm that a service is being rendered or an invitation is accepted with (great) pleasure.

Je suis invité chez toi? D'accord, je viendrai **avec plaisir**.
*I am invited to your house? OK, I'll come **with pleasure**. / I'll **gladly** come.*

EXERCICE 36·7

Corinne est un peu perdue. *Corinne is a little lost. Complete each line of dialogue with an appropriate word from the list.*

plaisir   droite   mauvaise
déranger   mademoiselle monsieur

1. CORINNE: Bonjour, _____ l'agent. Pouvez-vous me dire où se trouve la rue Victor Hugo?

2. L'AGENT: Avec _____, mademoiselle. Allez tout droit et vous la trouverez à deux rues d'ici.

3. CORINNE: Excusez-moi encore de vous _____, mais ce sera à droite ou à gauche?

4. L'AGENT: Ce sera à _____, mademoiselle, après la station de métro.

5. CORINNE: Alors, en fait, j'allais dans la _____ direction.

6. L'AGENT: Euh! Oui, _____. Je pense que oui.

Dialogue 4

Chris goes to a **syndicat d'initiative** (*tourist office*) to inquire about the latest ecological tourist trend in Paris: bicycle tours around the city.

L'EMPLOYÉE: Bonjour, monsieur. **Puis-je vous aider?**	*Hello, sir. May I help you?*
CHRIS: Oui, bonjour, madame. Je voudrais des renseignements sur **les tours** de Paris à bicyclette.	*Yes, hello, madam. I would like some information regarding bicycle tours of Paris.*
L'EMPLOYÉE: Certainement, monsieur. Nous avons plusieurs options. Voulez-vous regarder ces brochures et me dire ce qui vous intéresse?	*Certainly, sir. Do you want to look at these brochures and tell me what interests you?*
CHRIS: Je les ai déjà regardées et je peux vous dire que **je préférerais la balade à vélo** dans Paris accompagnée d'**un guide-interprète** expérimenté.	*I've already looked at them, and I can tell you that I'd like the bike tour of Paris with an experienced guide-interpreter.*
L'EMPLOYÉE: Très bien, monsieur. Vous paraissez informé. Vous voulez partir du Pont-Neuf ou plutôt de la place de la Concorde?	*Very well, sir. You seem informed. Do you want to leave from the Pont-Neuf or rather from the Place de la Concorde?*
CHRIS: Je préfère la place de la Concorde si c'est le même prix.	*I prefer the Place de la Concorde if it's the same price.*
L'EMPLOYÉE: C'est le même prix **d'où que vous partiez**. Et le **forfait comprend** la visite guidée des quartiers et des monuments cités dans la brochure.	*It's the same price no matter where you leave from. And the set price includes the guided tour of the neighborhoods and the monuments mentioned in the brochure.*
CHRIS: **C'est bien ce qu'il me semblait.** Bon, ça va. Je vais réserver une bicyclette pour le tour de mardi matin, s'il vous plaît.	*That's what I thought. Good, that's fine. I'm going to reserve a bicycle for Tuesday morning's tour, please.*

Testez votre compréhension. *Check your comprehension. Write* T *(true) or* F *(false).*

1. _____ Chris est bien informé sur les tours de Paris à bicyclette.
2. _____ Chris veut commencer son tour au Pont-Neuf.
3. _____ Le tour qui part du Pont-Neuf est plus cher.
4. _____ Le tour est limité à un seul quartier.
5. _____ Le tour est guidé.

Dialogue 5

Chris wants to buy a few books before returning home. He was advised to go to the Fnac (a French chain that has a huge inventory of books, music, and videos).

CHRIS: **Excusez-moi**, mademoiselle, je cherche **le rayon** des romans francophones du vingtième et vingt-et-unième siècles.

Excuse me, miss, I'm looking for the section for twentieth- and twenty-first-century Francophone novels.

LA VENDEUSE: Vous avez les romans français modernes là-bas **à gauche**, monsieur. Les prix Goncourt des dernières années sont ici, sur ces étagères-là.

You have modern French novels over there to the left, sir. The Goncourt prize winners of the past few years are here, on these shelves.

CHRIS: Est-ce qu'il y a une section pour les romans africains? Et pour les romans canadiens?

Is there a section for African novels? And how about Canadian novels?

LA VENDEUSE: Oui, ils sont **en haut au deuxième étage à droite** contre le mur. Vous voyez le panneau?

Yes, they're upstairs on the third floor against the wall. Do you see the sign?

CHRIS: Oui, je le vois. **Je vous remercie**, mademoiselle.

Yes, I see it. Thank you, miss.

LA VENDEUSE: S'il y a des titres ou des auteurs particuliers que vous voulez, je peux faire une recherche rapide et vous dire ce que nous avons et où ils sont.

If there are specific titles or authors you want, I can make a quick search and tell you what we have and where they are.

CHRIS: Non, je préfère flâner dans le magasin et voir de moi-même. Mais **merci bien**.

No, I prefer roaming the store to see for myself. But thank you.

LA VENDEUSE: **Je vous en prie**, monsieur. Quand vous serez prêt, vous trouverez les caisses **en bas** au **rez-de-chaussée**.

You're welcome, sir. When you're ready, you'll find the cashiers downstairs on the ground floor.

EXERCICE 36·9

Testez votre compréhension. *Check your comprehension. Write* T *(true) or* F *(false).*

1. _____ Chris préfère les vieux romans.
2. _____ Chris aime seulement les romans français.
3. _____ La vendeuse de la Fnac est polie et serviable.
4. _____ Chris veut trouver ses livres lui-même.
5. _____ Les livres de la Fnac sont gratuits.

Excusez-moi

This expression may be used not only to excuse oneself, but also to catch someone's attention.

Excusez-moi de vous déranger, madame.	*I'm sorry to bother you, madam.*
Excusez-moi, monsieur, je cherche un dictionnaire.	*Excuse me, sir. I'm looking for a dictionary.*

Le rayon

This word may be used in supermarkets, department stores, and bookstores to designate a specialized department.

Où est **le rayon** des livres de cuisine?	*Where is the cookbook **department**?*

À gauche / à droite

These phrases are useful in many contexts to give directions.

Le rayon de la musique pop est là-bas **à droite**.	*The pop music department is over there **on the right**.*
Les meilleurs livres de l'année sont exposés à l'entrée du magasin, là-bas **à gauche**.	*The best books of the year are displayed at the entrance of the store, over there **on the left**.*

En haut / en bas

These phrases also serve to give directions.

Les guides touristiques sont **en haut** ou **en bas**?	*Are the tourist guides **upstairs** or **downstairs**?*

Le deuxième étage / le rez-de-chaussée

Note that a store or other building in France has a **rez-de-chaussée**, which is the street- or ground-level floor (usually called *first floor* in the United States), a **premier étage** which is a *second floor* in the United States, and so on.

Nous sommes au **premier étage**.	*We're on the **second floor**.*
Il faut monter au **deuxième étage**.	*You have to go up to the **third floor**.*

Je vous remercie / merci bien

Use either of these expressions to thank a salesperson. Remember to use a title whenever you address someone in a business setting.

Je **vous remercie**, mademoiselle.	*Thank you, miss.*
Ah oui, je vois. **Merci bien**, mademoiselle.	*Oh yes, I see. **Thank you**, miss.*

Je vous en prie

This expression is a bit more formal than the customary **de rien** or **il n'y a pas de quoi** (for *you're welcome*) and should always be accompanied by the appropriate title of the person you are addressing.

—Merci bien.	*—Thank you.*
—**Je vous en prie**, monsieur.	*—**You're welcome**, sir.*

French in conversation: Asking for help

> **EXERCICE**
> **36·10**

Denise fait des achats. *Denise is shopping. Write the following dialogue in French.*

1. DENISE: _____

   (*Excuse me, madam, I'm looking for the ladies' clothing department.*)

2. LA VENDEUSE: _____

   (*That department is downstairs, miss.*)

3. DENISE: _____

   (*Are we on the second floor?*)

4. LA VENDEUSE: _____

   (*Yes, miss.*)

5. DENISE: _____

   (*I thank you, madam.*)

6. LA VENDEUSE: _____

   (*You're welcome, miss.*)

A taste of French literature

·37·

A sampling of the subjunctive in French literature and theater

There is no reason to be subjunctophobic. **Au contraire**, I hope that you have become a true subjunctophile! You now have a sense of the nuances and subtleties of this mood in French. You know the rules. No more mystery. **Le subjonctif** is no longer a dusty and esoteric aspect of grammar. You will use it every day, you will hear it every day and you will read it in French newspapers, magazines, essays, novels, and poetry.

That's why I want to share with you quotations from journalism and excerpts from some of my favorite French authors. Read them; use your dictionary or an online dictionary such as WordReference.com. Look for further excerpts of these works on http://books.google.fr. And perhaps you'll want to read the whole book, essay, poem, or play. When you encounter **le subjonctif** in context—whether your tastes run to science, art, music, or literature—you will savor the words, master the forms, and retain them. Pure pleasure. So now start reading aloud:

Que les Haïtiens ne **soient** pas **écoutés**, c'est une évidence.

—Lionel Trouillot, *Le Monde*, 9 janvier 2011

§

Moi, je suis fatigué là, vraiment. Épuisé. Je n'ai pas beaucoup couru, mais nerveusement, ça a sûrement été l'un des matches les plus difficiles qu'on **ait eu** à jouer. Il a vraiment fallu aller puiser profond à la fin pour s'en sortir. […] Vous devez vous rendre compte que l'équipe vit bien, qu'il y a une espèce de plaisir, de joie, de sérénité. Tout ça se passe bien, les journées s'enchaînent avec facilité, il n'y a pas besoin de recadrer **quoi que ce soit**.

—Claude Onesta, "Joueur de handball",
Le Monde Blogs, 31 janvier 2011

§

Oui, Michel, il faut que je **sache** comment tu m'aimes sinon qu'est-ce que moi je vais penser? [...]
Ils [les oiseaux] voyagent beaucoup et chantent pour qu'il **fasse** toujours beau sur Terre.

—Alain Mabanckou, *Demain j'aurai vingt ans*,
@ Éditions Gallimard (2010)

§

Que tout **soit allé** si vite et se trouve désormais accompli. **Qu'il** y **ait eu** toute cette accumulation d'instants avant d'attendre la fin. Autour de lui, il cherchait quelqu'un qu'il **puisse** prendre à témoin de son étonnement. Et il n'y avait personne, bien sûr.

—Philippe Forest, *Le Siècle des nuages*,
@ Éditions Gallimard (2010)

§

J'ai toujours pensé
que c'était le livre qui franchissait
les siècles pour parvenir à nous.
Jusqu'à ce que je **comprenne**
en voyant cet homme
que c'est le lecteur qui fait le déplacement.

—Dany Laferrière, *L'énigme du retour*,
Grasset (2009)

§

Une petite localité au centre du pays. Je m'y suis rendu. Seul. Il m'a fallu du temps pour repérer quelqu'un qui me **fasse confiance** et qui **se souvienne de** cette nuit.

—Gary Victor, *Treize nouvelles vaudou*,
Mémoire d'encrier (2007)

§

Ils poussent les pions avec un enthousiasme sans pareil. Peut-être pour échapper à la fatalité? Peut-être pour oublier hier? La mémoire du pays est celle de l'oubli. Un autre pays est déjà en train de naître **sans qu**'on **s'en aperçoive**.

—Rodney Saint-Éloi, *Haïti Kenbe la!*,
Michel Lafon (2010)

§

Il rêvait d'un borsalino. Je ne crois pas qu'il en **ait eu** un vrai... peut-être une copie.

—Éric Fottorino, *Question à mon père*,
@ Éditions Gallimard (2010)

§

Le 30 décembre 1957

Le train entra en gare de Guang-Ning. Mugissements de la sirène. Grincements des freins. Quelques secousses brutales.

Avant même **que** le train ne **s'arrêtât** complètement, les voyageurs se pressaient devant les portières avec cette fièvre qui marque la fin d'un long voyage.

—Wei-Wei, *La couleur du bonheur*,
L'Aube (1996)

§

Il voulait juste que nous **nous gavions** de mangues, que nous **mordions** dans ces fruits en faisant gicler leur jus […].

—Kim Thuy, *Rú*, Éditions Liana Levi (2009)

§

Je ne suis pas sûre que ce **soit** le lieu pour en parler. Cela manque de discrétion! Et nos affaires de famille en imposent. Nos affaires mais aussi les tiennes, Louise… Berthon.

—Aliette Armel, *Pondichéry, à l'aurore*,
Le Passage (2010)

§

Je suis resté dans la voiture comme ça. Et alors tout à coup j'ai été heureux que la voiture **soit** bloquée dans la neige, que je ne **puisse** plus bouger, plus du tout.

—Laurent Mauvignier, *Des hommes*,
Éditions de Minuit (2009)

§

Bien qu'elle **sût** que c'était inutile s'il se trouvait en cet instant dans une salle de cinéma, elle composa le numéro de portable de Jakob.

—Marie NDiaye, *Trois femmes puissantes*,
@ Éditions Gallimard (2009)

§

—Combien de temps avez-vous?
—Il faut que je **réunisse** le maximum de renseignements avant demain soir.

—Jean-Christophe Rufin, *Katiba*,
Flammarion (2010)

§

Je n'ai pas souhaité d'autre enfant. Je voulais que mon garçon **ait** toutes les chances, concentrer toutes mes forces sur lui—comme faisaient les autres mères dont les fils arrivaient.

—Gilles Leroy, *Zola Jackson*,
Mercure de France (2010)

§

« Que veux-tu que j'y **fasse**? » répondit-elle sans lever les yeux. «Je suis pas responsable de ce genre de choses.» [...] **Quoi qu'**il en **soit,** personne ne les avait vus sortir ensemble, ce soir-là, cette fameuse Barbara et lui. [...] Cela avait-il à voir avec **le fait que** Richard **se trouvât** à la tête du département de littérature et que Marc **fût** sous ses ordres?

—Philippe Djian, *Incidences,*
@ Éditions Gallimard (2010)

§

J'avais envie de le dire à Hélène mais je craignais que cet enthousiasme **soit** déplacé. [...] Debout à côté de Patrice qui félicitait son beau-frère, j'ai eu peur qu'il **dise** que j'étais là. [...] Il se peut que leur dossier **ait été déclaré** irrecevable et qu'ils **contestent** cette décision.

—Emmanuel Carrère, *D'autres vies que la mienne*, P.O.L
(2009)

§

Je tourne une page de l'album; maman tient dans ses bras un bébé qui n'est pas moi; je porte une jupe plissée, un béret, j'ai deux ans et demi, et ma sœur vient de naître. J'en fus, paraît-il, jalouse, mais pendant peu de temps. **Aussi loin que** je **m'en souvienne,** j'étais fière d'être l'aînée; la première.

—Simone de Beauvoir,
Mémoires d'une jeune fille rangée,
@ Éditions Gallimard (1958)

§

C'est le seul âge où j'**aie connu** l'angoisse de la page blanche, mais il a duré des années d'enfance, c'est-à-dire des siècles.

—Amélie Nothomb, *Une forme de vie*,
Albin Michel (2010)

§

27 février
Au demeurant, Amélie n'éleva plus la moindre protestation. Il semblait qu'elle **eût réfléchi** pendant la nuit et **pris** son parti de cette charge nouvelle; même elle y semblait prendre quelque plaisir et je la vis sourire après qu'elle eut achevé d'apprêter Gertrude.

—André Gide, *La symphonie pastorale*,
@ Éditions Gallimard (1919)

§

Tchen tenterait-il de lever la moustiquaire? Frapperait-il au travers? [...] Bêtement: car il savait qu'il le tuerait. Pris ou non, exécuté ou non, peu importait. Rien n'existait que ce pied, cet homme qu'il devait frapper **sans qu**'il **se défendît**, —car, s'il se défendait, il appellerait.

—André Malraux, *La condition humaine*,
@ Éditions Gallimard (1933)

§

Quoi qu'il en **fût**, Gwynplaine était admirablement réussi.

Gwynplaine était un don fait par la providence à la tristesse des hommes. Par quelle providence? Y a-t-il une providence Démon comme il y a une providence Dieu? Nous posons la question sans la résoudre.

Gwynplaine était un saltimbanque. Il se faisait voir en public. Pas d'effet comparable au sien. Il guérissait les hypocondries rien qu'en se montrant.

—Victor Hugo, *L'Homme qui rit* (1869)

§

[...] pour le bonheur qui dure je doute qu'il y **soit** connu. À peine est-il dans nos plus vives jouissances un instant où le cœur **puisse** véritablement nous dire: *Je voudrais que cet instant durât toujours*; et comment peut-on appeler bonheur un état fugitif qui nous laisse encore le cœur inquiet et vide, qui nous fait regretter quelque chose avant, ou désirer encore quelque chose après?

—Jean-Jacques Rousseau,
Les rêveries du promeneur solitaire,
Publication posthume (1782)

§

Il **avait beau** porter de bonnes chaussures de marche, des Galibier, ses chaussettes étaient trempées [...]

—Philippe Djian, *Incidences,*
@ Éditions Gallimard (2010)

§

Elle **a eu beau** interroger ses tantes, ses oncles, toi, tous ceux qui l'ont connue, elle n'a eu aucune réponse.

—Ananda Devi, *Le sari vert*,
@ Éditions Gallimard (2009)

§

[...] j'**ai beau** aller trois fois par semaine chez le psychanalyste, je vois de moins en moins de raison **pour que** ça **change**.

—Emmanuel Carrère, *Un roman russe*, P.O.L (2007)

§

J'**avais beau** le maintenir tout au fond depuis des années, j'**avais beau** l'étouffer, le forcer à se tapir, il remontait.

—Olivier Adam, *Le cœur régulier*,
Éditions de l'Olivier (2010)

§

[...] Georges Diderot **avait beau** être une légende, il avait vieilli... [...]

—Maylis de Kerangal, *Naissance d'un pont*, Verticales (2010)

§

Mais elle **avait beau** faire, aucun des mots qu'elle a prononcés n'est venu se loger dans mon cerveau. [...] et l'acteur élastique **a eu beau** déployer toute l'étendue de son génie comique, personne n'a ri.

—Olivier Adam, *À l'abri de rien*,
Éditions de l'Olivier (2007)

§

Je voulais que les villes **fussent** splendides, aérées, arrosées d'eaux claires, peuplées d'êtres humains dont le corps ne **fût** détérioré ni par les marques de la misère ou de la servitude, ni par l'enflure d'une richesse grossière; que les écoliers **récitassent** d'une voix juste des leçons point ineptes; que les femmes au foyer **eussent** dans leurs mouvements une espèce de dignité maternelle, de repos puissant; que les gymnases **fussent** fréquentés par des jeunes hommes point ignorants des jeux ni des arts; que les vergers **portassent** les plus beaux fruits et les champs les plus riches moissons.

—Marguerite Yourcenar, *Mémoires d'Hadrien*,
@ Éditions Gallimard (1951)

§

Mais aussitôt après je pris garde que, pendant que je voulais aussi penser que tout était faux, il fallait nécessairement que moi, qui le pensais, **fusse** quelque chose: et remarquant que cette vérité, je pense, donc je suis, était si ferme et si assurée que toutes les plus extravagantes suppositions des sceptiques n'étaient pas capables de l'ébranler, je jugeai que je pouvais la recevoir sans scrupule pour le premier principe de la philosophie que je cherchais.

—René Descartes, *Discours de la méthode*:
Les passions de l'âme,
Booking International (1649)

§

Encore une fois, nous voulions une philosophie qui **se soumît** au contrôle de la science et qui **pût** aussi la faire avancer.

—Henri Bergson, *La pensée et le mouvant*,
Presses Universitaires de France (1903)

§

And to end on a humorous note:

La célèbre tirade du nez dans *Cyrano de Bergerac*
Acte I, scène 4

Le Vicomte: Vous... vous avez un nez... heu... un nez... très grand.

Cyrano (*gravement*): Très.

Le Vicomte (*riant*): Ha!

Cyrano (*imperturbable*): C'est tout?

Le Vicomte: Mais...

Cyrano: Ah! non! c'est un peu court, jeune homme!
On pouvait dire... Oh ! Dieu!... bien des choses en somme...
En variant le ton, —par exemple, tenez:

Agressif: «Moi, monsieur, si j'avais un tel nez,
Il faudrait sur-le-champ que je me l'**amputasse**!»

Amical: «Mais il doit tremper dans votre tasse!
Pour boire, faites-vous fabriquer un hanap!»

Descriptif: «C'est un roc !... c'est un pic!... c'est un cap!
Que dis-je, c'est un cap?... C'est une péninsule!»

—Edmond Rostand. Pièce écrite entre 1896 et 1897; elle est
jouée pour la première fois en 1897.

Je vous conseille de louer le film de Jean-Paul Rappeneau, *Cyrano de Bergerac* (1990) où Gérard Depardieu incarne Cyrano avec brio. Vous trouverez aussi cette tirade sur YouTube.

§

A sampling of past tenses and translation obstacles in French literature

The purpose of the following excerpts, some exemplifying the quintessential, breathtaking virtuosity of French writing, is to move you profoundly, perhaps even spark a desire to look for the works quoted, and let you embark on a pilgrimage throughout the infinitely rich world of French literature. What sets French writers apart is their extraordinary ability to attain a unique balance of intellectual depth and technical virtuosity. Furthermore, they are never intimidated by metaphysical challenges.

A case in point is the mysterious being of time, which writers literally conjure up, particularly in prose, knowing that the many modalities of time add contrapuntal richness, texture, and depth to any narrative. While the past, for example, may be as incomprehensible as time itself, language—and particularly the French language—provides some keys, grammatical tenses, which enable us to differentiate, rationally and at a visceral level, between the various ways a person or an event can exist in the past.

Moving beyond any rational or grammatical rules, French writers, emulating the interplay of melody and harmony in music, use tenses to express perceptible and imperceptible nuances within a defined temporal framework. For example, there are times when the spirit of the narrative requires the **passé simple**, to indicate a clearly perceived, singular past event, but the narrative can inexplicably veer into the **imparfait**, without any obvious justification. In other words, although these two tenses describe two distinct modalities of the past, there are times when they intersect, leaving it to the writer's intuition to decide when a simple fact belongs to the simple past, and when it is better described by the somewhat ambivalent **imparfait**.

It is not a coincidence that time figures so prominently in French literature and philosophy, for the French spirit has a privileged rapport with time. Unlike their counterparts in other Western traditions, who have approached time as an intellectual problem, French writers have understood that only lived experience can unlock the portal of time. Brilliant exponents of this conception of time include Marcel Proust, Henri Bergson, and Vladimir Jankélévitch, who wrote that not only is time our essence, but we human beings are its incarnation. Therefore, by reading and experiencing these literary fragments, by incorporating them into your own lived experience, you will not only improve your knowledge of the language but also experience the tremendous power of literature to illuminate crucial realms of life that in the cold light of everyday banality appear hopelessly distant and inaccessible. Thinking about the mystery of time may not reward you with scientific insights, but it will change your life.

Read aloud these excerpts over and over. Write them in a small notebook, and try and memorize some of them to enjoy the delicious taste of tenses.

À 95 ans, il tire encore

À Marseille, un nonagénaire **soupçonnait** son voisin septuagénaire qui lui **rendait** quelques services dans son pavillon de lui **avoir dérobé** de l'argent dissimulé sous un matelas. L'explication **se termina** devant le canon d'un fusil: le vieux **tira** sur le plus jeune et lui **plomba** le bras et une main. Le vieux fusil de 95 ans **a été retrouvé** dans une maison de retraite de la banlieue marseillaise et **placé** en garde à vue.

—Libération, 5 mai 2003

§

Pendant un quart d'heure, l'Enquêteur **resta** immobile, bien droit, sa valise posée à côté de lui tandis que les gouttes de pluie et les flocons de neige **continuaient** de mourir sur son crâne et son imperméable. Il ne **bougea** pas. Pas du tout. Et durant ce moment, il ne **pensa** à rien.

Aucune voiture n'**était passée**, aucun piéton. On l'**avait oublié**. Ce n'**était** pas la première fois.

—Philippe Claudel, *L'Enquête*, Stock (2010)

§

Elle **est morte** bien avant ma naissance, quelques années après le mariage de mes parents.

Je ne **connaissais** d'elle qu'une photographie couleur sépia signée Cattan, le meilleur artiste de l'époque. Posée sur le dessus du piano où je **faisais** mes gammes, la femme qu'elle **représentait** portait une robe ornée d'un large col de dentelle, ce qui lui **donnait** l'air d'une écolière.

—Maryse Condé, *Victoire, les saveurs et les mots*, Mercure de France (2006)

§

J'**avais décidé** de rentrer à pied impasse de l'Astrolabe. Je n'**avais** pas **dîné**. J'**avalai** une crêpe brûlante dans une guitoune en plein air à l'angle du boulevard Raspail. Il **devait** être onze heures du soir. Les Parisiens **étaient** encore nombreux dans les rues. Tous n'**avaient** pas **remisé** leurs manteaux mais ils **marchaient** sans hâte et bien droits, libérés du poids de l'hiver. Les femmes **portaien**t des robes de demi-saison. Une fois ou deux, je **reconnus** Jardins de Bagatelle.

—Eric Fottorino, *Baisers de cinéma*, @ Éditions Gallimard (2007)

§

Le samedi 29 janvier, le cortège nuptial **quitta** à six heures du soir le manoir des Siloé. Il **avait** trois cents mètres environ à parcourir jusqu'à l'église. Une double haie l'**attendait** depuis la fin de l'après-midi. Une clameur mêlée d'applaudissements **accueillit** Hadriana au bras de son père.

— Vive la mariée! Bravo Nana!

De toutes parts **fusaient** des fleurs, des confettis, des serpentines, des cris d'admiration (oh la sacrée jolie fille!). Sur le côté est de la place, elle **avançait**, élancée, romantique, sensuellement fluide dans ses voiles blancs.

—René Depestre, *Hadriana dans tous mes rêves*, @ Éditions Gallimard (1988)

§

Elle **se dirigeait** vers un centre commercial qui **venait** d'être ouvert dans un quartier chic. Elle **s'enfonçait** dans un univers de voitures de luxe, de magasins branchés, de blocs d'appartements cossus. Elle **détonnait** de plus en plus dans cet environnement, mais cela ne la **troublait** pas. Elle **avait** du soleil dans les yeux. À l'entrée du centre commercial, un garde de sécurité **l'avait arrêtée**. En s'approchant, Subha **avait entendu** le garde lui demander si elle **avait** une carte de crédit.

—Ananda Devi, *Indian Tango*,
@ Éditions Gallimard (2007)

§

C'était l'été sans doute. Les vacances **étaient** déjà **commencées**. Il **avait couché** son vélo dans l'herbe toute brûlée par la chaleur du soleil. Peut-être **attendait**-il allongé sur le sol ou bien se **tenait**-il assis sur le ponton, les jambes se balançant au-dessus du courant très lent. À perte de vue, le grand ciel bleu du beau temps **recouvrait** le monde. Il **regardait** descendre vers lui le signe en forme de croix de la carlingue et des ailes. Lorsque l'avion **heurtait** l'eau, le choc le **ralentissait** net.

—Philippe Forest, *Le siècle des nuages*,
@ Éditions Gallimard (2010)

§

Ce jour-là, parce que je **me sentais** un brin fiévreux, je **suis rentré** plus tôt que d'ordinaire. Il ne **devait** pas être dix-sept heures quand le tram **m'a déposé** dans ma rue, un sac de provisions à chaque bras. Il est rare que je me trouve si tôt chez moi pendant la semaine, aussi **ai**-je **eu** l'impression d'y entrer par effraction.

—Éric Faye, *Nagasaki,* Stock (2010)

§

L'aviateur **avait** des bras immenses, des bras enveloppants, deux ailes chaudes où je tremblais. L'aviateur n'**avait** que moi à aimer—**disait**-il. Il **prétendait** aussi que j'**étais** la seule, la seule à l'aimer.

Seule? Sans blague...

—Gilles Leroy, *Alabama Song,*
Mercure de France (2007)

§

Pendant quatre jours et quatre nuits, il **avait** violemment plu. La terre **avait tremblé** au nord de Yuorma le jour où la tornade **prit** fin. Personne n'**avait quitté** sa maison pendant la tornade, ce qui **rendit** la catastrophe du séisme plus meurtrière: la radio nationale **annonça** trois cents morts, deux mille blessés et d'innombrables sans-abri.

—Sony Labou Tansi, *La vie et demie*, Le Seuil (1979)

§

La première séance de cinéma au monde **eut** lieu au mois de décembre 1895 à Paris, boulevard des Capucines, dans le salon indien du Grand Café. Un an seulement plus tard, le cinéma **arriva** en Égypte. La première projection **eut** lieu en novembre 1896 à Alexandrie, dans la salle possédée par un Italien qui **s'appelait** Dillo Astrologo. Ce **fut** un événement extraordinaire dans la vie des Égyptiens et des résidants en Égypte et le journaux de l'époque **étaient** pleins de commentaires enthousiastes sur la nouvelle invention.

—Alaa el Aswany, *J'aurais voulu être égyptien*,
Actes Sud (2009)

§

Quand je **fréquentais** l'école primaire, je **plongeais** avec enthousiasme ma plume dans l'encrier du pupitre. Je **prenais** le temps de contempler la goutte de liquide noir ou bleu. Je la **regardais** comme le Créateur **a** probablement **regardé** le néant au moment où il **se disposait** à en faire un univers. J'**étais** un peu comme lui. J'**allais** donner vie, grâce au bout de ma plume, à un chat, à une peuplade, à un adjectif ou à une périphrase.

—Gilles Lapouge, *L'encre du voyageur*,
Albin Michel (2007)

§

L'homme **se dirigea** vers le rideau noir et le **tira** d'un seul coup. Entourée d'un cadre en bois noir, une photographie y **était** accrochée: une femme jeune, jolie, en robe brodée traditionnelle, **tenait** par la main une fillette d'au plus trois ans. L'une et l'autre **souriaient** vaguement à l'objectif. L'image en noir et blanc **était** tellement agrandie que les contours des visages en **devenaient** flous, comme tracés par un crayon de fusain argentique.

—Anouar Benmalek, *Le rapt*, Fayard (2009)

§

Cosmétique, l'homme **se lissa** les cheveux avec le plat de la main. Il **fallait** qu'il **fût** présentable afin de rencontrer sa victime dans les règles de l'art.

Les nerfs de Jérôme Angust **étaient** déjà à vif quand la voix de l'hôtesse **annonça** que l'avion, en raison de problèmes techniques, **serait retardé** pour une durée indéterminée.

« Il ne **manquait** plus que ça », **pensa**-t-il.

Il **détestait** les aéroports et la perspective de rester dans cette salle d'attente pendant un laps de temps pas même précisé l'**exaspérait**. Il **sortit** un livre de son sac et **s'y plongea** rageusement.

—Amélie Nothomb, *Cosmétique de l'ennemi*,
Albin Michel (2001)

§

L'enfant va voir vers le bar, elle n'entre pas bien sûr, elle va sur l'autre pont. Là il n'y a personne. Les voyageurs sont à bâbord pour guetter l'arrivée du vent de la haute mer.

De ce côté-là du navire il y a seulement un très jeune homme. Il est seul. Il **est accoudé** au bastingage. Elle passe derrière lui. Il ne se retourne pas sur elle. Il ne l'**a** sans doute pas **vue**. C'est curieux qu'à ce point il ne l'**ait** pas **vue**.

Elle non plus n'**a** pas **pu** voir son visage, mais elle se souvient de ce manque à voir de son visage comme d'un manque à voir du voyage. Oui, c'est bien ça, il **portait** une sorte de blazer. Bleu. À rayures blanches. Un pantalon du même bleu il **portait** aussi, mais uni.

—Marguerite Duras, *L'Amant de la Chine du Nord,*
@ Éditions Gallimard (1991)

§

Ce jour-là, je **suis rentré** plus tôt. Tu m'**attendais** sur le trottoir. Tu **faisais** les cent pas devant la porte de l'immeuble. Quand tu m'**as vu** arriver, tu **as souri** de tout ton corps. Je t'**ai demandé** ce qu'il se passait, ce que tu faisais dehors. Tu **n'as** rien **répondu**. Tu m'**as serré** dans tes bras et j'**ai senti** que tu **pleurais**. Je n'oublierai jamais cette étreinte baignée de pleurs et de sourires. Tu m'**as murmuré** à l'oreille que ça y **était**, que la maison d'édition **venait** d'appeler, qu'ils **avaient lu** mes poèmes et **voulaient** les publier.

—Laurent Gaudé, *Dans la nuit Mozambique,*
Babel (2007)

§

Je **naquis** donc en mars 1705, le premier des fils de Suzanne Rousseau. Quelques jours après cet heureux événement Isaac Rousseau, mon père, **s'enfuit** sans mot dire. Il **quitta** ma mère, Genève et l'Europe dans un seul et même mouvement. Il ne **manquait** pas de courage, puisque, pour bien marquer son éloignement, il **s'en fut** jusque dans les faubourgs de Constantinople.

—Stéphane Audeguy, *Fils unique,*
@ Éditions Gallimard (2006)

§

L'inspecteur Azémar **ouvrit** la portière pour prendre à nouveau place sur le siège avant. Il **indiqua** la nouvelle adresse où il **comptait** se rendre. Le chauffeur **démarra** sans dire un mot. Ils **se retrouvèrent** bien vite dans la chaleur suffocante des embouteillages. Le cerveau de l'inspecteur **fonctionnait** tant bien que mal.

—Gary Victor, *Saison de porcs,*
Mémoire d'encrier (2009)

§

— Tu as **oublié**?

— J'ignore ce qui m'**est arrivé**, aujourd'hui. Jamais je n'**ai connu** cette impression-là auparavant, pas même lorsque nous **avons perdu** notre maison. J'**étais** comme dans les vapes et j'**errais** comme ça, à l'aveuglette, incapable de reconnaître les rues que j'**arpentais** de long en large sans parvenir à les traverser. Vraiment bizarre. J'**étais** dans une sorte de brouillard, je n'**arrivais** ni à me souvenir de mon chemin ni à savoir où je **voulais** aller.

—Yasmina Khadra, *Les hirondelles de Kaboul,* Julliard
(2002)

§

Ma chance **fut** de me trouver, un matin, place du Réghistan. Une caravane **passait**, une caravane courte; elle ne **comptait** que six ou sept chameaux de Bactriane, à la fourrure épaisse, aux sabots épais. Le vieux chamelier s'était arrêté, non loin de moi, devant l'échoppe d'un potier, retenant contre sa poitrine un agneau nouveau-né; il **proposait** un échange, l'artisan **discutait**; sans éloigner ses mains de la jarre ni du tour, il **indiquait** du menton une pile de terrines vernissées.

—Amin Maalouf, *Samarcande*, Lattès (1988)

§

Moi, je **suis resté** gringalet malgré les plats de semoule et de fécule que certains compatriotes **avaient jugé** utile de me recommander dès mon arrivée en France dans l'espoir que ce corps étique **prendrait** quelques kilos et **cesserait** de ternir l'image que le pays **se faisait** des Parisiens, les vrais: des hommes joufflues, à la peau claire et à l'allure élégante.

—Alain Mabanckou, *Bleu blanc rouge*,
Présence Africaine (1998)

§

Un jour, **j'avais** sept ans, mon grand-père n'y **tint** plus: il me **prit** par la main, annonçant qu'il m'**emmenait** en promenade. Mais, à peine **avions**-nous **tourné** le coin de la rue, il me **poussa** chez le coiffeur en me disant: « Nous allons faire une surprise à ta mère ». J'**adorais** les surprises. Il y en **avait** tout le temps chez nous. [...]. Bref les coups de théâtre **faisaient** mon petit ordinaire et je **regardai** avec bienveillance mes boucles rouler le long de la serviette blanche qui me **serrait** le cou et tomber sur le plancher, inexplicablement ternies; je **revins** glorieux et tondu.

Il y **eut** des cris mais pas d'embrassements et ma mère **s'enferma** dans sa chambre pour pleurer: on **avait troqué** sa fillette contre un garçonnet.

—Jean-Paul Sartre, *Les mots*,
@ Éditions Gallimard (1964)

§

Comme il **faisait** une chaleur de trente-trois degrés, le boulevard Bourdon **se trouvait** absolument désert. Plus bas le canal Saint-Martin, fermé par les deux écluses **étalait** en ligne droite son eau couleur d'encre. Il y **avait** au milieu, un bateau plein de bois, et sur la berge deux rangs de barriques. Au-delà du canal, entre les maisons que séparent des chantiers le grand ciel pur **se découpait** en plaques d'outremer, et sous la réverbération du soleil, les façades blanches, les toits d'ardoises, les quais de granit **éblouissaient**. Une rumeur confuse **montait** du loin dans l'atmosphère tiède; et tout **semblait** engourdi par le désœuvrement du dimanche et la tristesse des jours d'été. Deux hommes **parurent**. L'un **venait** de la Bastille, l'autre du Jardin des Plantes. Le plus grand, vêtu de toile, **marchait** le chapeau en arrière, le gilet déboutonné et sa cravate à la main. Le plus petit, dont le corps **disparaissait** dans une redingote marron, **baissait** la tête sous une casquette à visière pointue. Quand ils **furent arrivés** au milieu du boulevard, ils **s'assirent** à la même minute, sur le même banc. Pour s'essuyer le front, ils **retirèrent** leurs coiffures, que chacun **posa** près de soi; et le petit homme **aperçut** écrit dans le chapeau de son voisin: Bouvard; pendant que celui-ci **distinguait** aisément dans la casquette du particulier en redingote le mot: Pécuchet.

—Gustave Flaubert, *Bouvard et Pécuchet* (1881)

§

Port-au-Prince, c'est une autre odeur. C'est l'odeur de la gasoline, de ses milliers de voitures qui chaque jour encombrent la ville. Et quand le soir, les voitures **se retiraient**, Port-au-Prince autrefois **avait** l'odeur d'ilang-ilang et de jasmin. C'est aussi l'odeur du parfum très bon marché qu'on **appelait** Florida et que les jeunes filles des quartiers populaires **portaient**. Cette odeur-là aussi m'habite. Et j'aime beaucoup parce que c'est les bouteilles de parfum qu'on **mettait** aussi dans les petits oratoires pour le voudou. C'est très parfumé. Le voudou, c'est une religion très parfumée.

—Dany Laferrière, entretien réalisé par
Annie Heminway (2009)

§

As you will see in the following excerpt, the **passé composé** punctuates a narrative that takes the reader into a cold, stark, and indifferent world. A sequence of events is presented, and there seems to be no room for any feelings.

In *L'Étranger* by Camus, the **passé composé** is the basic tense of the novel to underline the loneliness of the characters and the scene. The words exchanged are banal, automatic, and empty. In an absurd world, the character Meursault lives the moment without a real notion of past and future. Later, the **imparfait** will be used to describe Meursault's perceptions.

J'**ai pris** l'autobus à deux heures. Il **faisait** très chaud. J'**ai mangé** au restaurant, chez Céleste, comme d'habitude. Ils **avaient** tous beaucoup de peine pour moi et Céleste m'a dit: « On n'a qu'une mère. » Quand je **suis parti**, ils m'**ont accompagné** à la porte. J'**étais** un peu étourdi parce qu'il **a fallu** que je monte chez Emmanuel pour lui emprunter une cravate noire et un brassard. Il **a perdu** son oncle, il y a quelques mois.

J'**ai couru** pour ne pas manquer le départ. Cette hâte, cette course, c'est à cause de tout cela sans doute, ajouté aux cahots, à l'odeur d'essence, à la réverbération de la route et du ciel, que je **me suis assoupi**. J'**ai dormi** pendant presque tout le trajet. Et quand je me **suis réveillé**, j'**étais tassé** contre un militaire qui m'**a souri** et qui **a demandé** si je **venais** de loin. J'**ai dit** « oui » pour n'avoir plus à parler. L'asile est à deux kilomètres du village. J'**ai fait** le chemin à pied. J'**ai voulu** voir maman tout de suite. Mais le concierge m'**a dit** qu'il **fallait** que je rencontre le directeur. Comme il **était occupé**, j'**ai attendu** un peu. Pendant tout ce temps, le concierge **a parlé** et ensuite, j'**ai vu** le directeur: il m'**a reçu** dans son bureau. C'**était** un petit vieux, avec la Légion d'honneur. Il m'**a regardé** de ses yeux clairs. Puis il m'**a serré** la main qu'il **a gardée** si longtemps que je ne **savais** trop comment la retirer. Il **a consulté** un dossier et m'**a dit**: « Mme Meursault **est entrée** ici il y a trois ans. Vous **étiez** son seul soutien. » J'**ai cru** qu'il me **reprochait** quelque chose et j'**ai commencé** à lui expliquer. Mais il m'**a interrompu**: « Vous n'avez pas à vous justifier, mon cher enfant. J'**ai lu** le dossier de votre mère. [...] »

550 PRACTICE MAKES PERFECT Complete French All-in-One

As far as translation is concerned, Camus has been a challenge for translators all over the world. Stuart Gilbert translated the novel in 1946, four years after the publication. Gilbert's translation had a very formal tone not in synch with Camus, influenced by Hemingway, Dos Passos, who had admitted using an American method for the first part of his book. Other translations were published; then in 1988, Matthew Ward, a thirty-seven-year-old New Yorker, a graduate of Stanford University, and a brilliant translator and poet, decided to undertake the translation of the book he had admired for years. Forty-two years after Gilbert, twenty-six years after the independence of Algeria, Matthew Ward had another perception of the world, and he knew he had to Americanize *L'Étranger* to be truthful to Camus.

Here's an example: At one point, the main character, Mersault, observes: **Il *était* avec son chien.** Gilbert, in a conventional manner added an adverbial phrase, stressing the British relationship between man and animal: *As usual, he **had** his dog with him.* Ward, in a straightforward manner said: *He **was** with his dog,* conveying the way a person would be with a friend and presenting a clear picture of the world through Meursault's eyes. Here the tenses remain the same but the verb has changed. Students and faculty should take *L'Étranger* and compare both translations. It is a feast for the language lovers.

§

What could be further from the precise, austere, almost clinical prose of *L'Étranger* than the richly textured, multifaceted, almost synaesthetic nature of Gustave Flaubert's writing?

Marcel Proust was fascinated by the way Gustave Flaubert used the tenses and was convinced he was the precursor of the **Nouveau Roman**, a new exploration of the novel in the mid-1950s. In the **Nouvelle Revue Française** of January 1920, Proust said:

... dans *L'Éducation sentimentale*, la révolution est accomplie; ce qui jusqu'à Flaubert était action devient impression. Les choses ont autant de vie que les hommes, car c'est le raisonnement qui après coup assigne à tout phénomène visuel des causes extérieures, mais dans l'impression première que nous recevons cette cause n'est pas impliquée.

For Proust, Flaubert's sentences are exceptional because of their rhythmic value and the bold usage of tenses. Note the mélange of tenses in this passage:

Il **voyagea**.

Il **connut** la mélancolie des paquebots, les froids réveils sous la tente, l'étourdissement des paysages et des ruines, l'amertume des sympathies interrompues.

Il **revint**.

Il **fréquenta** le monde, et il **eut** d'autres amours, encore. Mais le souvenir continuel du premier les lui **rendait** insipides; et puis la véhémence du désir, la fleur même de la sensation **était perdue**. Ses ambitions d'esprit **avaient** également **diminué**. Des années **passèrent;** et il **supportait** le désœuvrement de son intelligence et l'inertie de son cœur.

—Flaubert, *L'Éducation sentimentale* (1869)

Sometimes, Flaubert mixes his **éternels imparfaits** (that are supposed to transmit not only the words of his characters but also their lives) and other past tenses with the present. The sudden **découvre** casts a light on the sea, **on a réalité plus durable**. You can imagine the challenge it has been for the numerous translators of this work.

A taste of French literature **551**

C'**était** une maison basse, à un seul étage, avec un jardin rempli de buis énormes et une double avenue de châtaigniers montant jusqu'au haut de la colline, d'où l'on découvre la mer.

— « Je vais m'asseoir là, sur un banc, que j'**ai appelé**: le banc Frédéric. »

Puis elle **se mit** à regarder les meubles, les bibelots, les cadres, avidement, pour les emporter dans sa mémoire. Le portrait de la Maréchale **était** à demi **caché** par un rideau. Mais les ors et les blancs, qui **se détachaient** au milieu des ténèbres, l'**attirèrent**.

In *L'affaire Lemoine*, Proust will publish an interesting pastiche of Flaubert, juggling all kinds of tenses and the direct and indirect speech.

And to close with one of the most beautiful pieces of literature, rich in past tenses, the feverish scene with Emma Bovary in the ballroom:

Charles **vint** l'embrasser sur l'épaule.

— Laisse-moi! dit-elle, tu me chiffonnes.

On **entendit** une ritournelle de violon et les sons d'un cor. Elle **descendit** l'escalier, se retenant de courir. Les quadrilles **étaient** commencés. Il **arrivait** du monde. On **se poussait**. Elle **se plaça** près de la porte, sur une banquette.

Quand la contredanse **fut finie**, le parquet **resta** libre pour les groupes d'hommes causant debout et les domestiques en livrée qui **apportaient** de grands plateaux. Sur la ligne des femmes assises, les éventails peints **s'agitaient**, les bouquets **cachaient** à demi le sourire des visages, et les flacons à bouchon d'or **tournaient** dans des mains entrouvertes dont les gants blancs **marquaient** la forme des ongles et **serraient** la chair au poignet. Les garnitures de dentelles, les broches de diamants, les bracelets à médaillon **frissonnaient** aux corsages, **scintillaient** aux poitrines, **bruissaient** sur les bras nus. Les chevelures, bien collées sur les fronts et tordues à la nuque, **avaient**, en couronnes, en grappes ou en rameaux, des myosotis, du jasmin, des fleurs de grenadier, des épis ou des bleuets. Pacifiques à leurs places, des mères à figure renfrognée **portaient** des turbans rouges.

Le cœur d'Emma lui **battit** un peu lorsque, son cavalier la tenant par le bout des doigts, elle **vint** se mettre en ligne et **attendit** le coup d'archet pour partir. Mais bientôt l'émotion **disparut;** et, se balançant au rythme de l'orchestre, elle **glissait** en avant, avec des mouvements légers du cou. Un sourire lui **montait** aux lèvres à certaines délicatesses du violon, qui **jouait** seul, quelquefois, quand les autres instruments **se taisaient;** on **entendait** le bruit clair des louis d'or qui **se versaient** à côté, sur le tapis des tables; puis tout **reprenait** à la fois, le cornet à pistons **lançait** un éclat sonore, les pieds **retombaient** en mesure, les jupes **se bouffaient** et **frôlaient,** les mains **se donnaient, se quittaient**; les mêmes yeux, s'abaissant devant vous, **revenaient** se fixer sur les vôtres.

—Flaubert, *Madame Bovary* (1857)

Bonne chance à toutes et à tous!

Appendix A
French pronunciation

Beginning students of French usually have no difficulty writing the words they have learned, but find it hard to pronounce them. In French, numerous letters are silent and some represent sounds that do not exist in English. Depending on its environment within the word, one letter may have several different pronunciations, and one sound may have several different spellings. Although French uses the same alphabet as English, the rules of English pronunciation do not apply. The sounds that the letters of the alphabet produce in French are frequently quite different from those they produce in English.

To indicate how a letter or combination of letters is pronounced, the symbols of the International Phonetic Alphabet are often used, i.e., the letters are transcribed phonetically. Phonetic transcriptions are always placed in square brackets. The word **temps** for example is transcribed [tã], the word **homme** [ɔm]. Note that silent letters (**m, p, s** in the first example, **h** and **e** in the second example) do not appear in phonetic transcriptions.

There are thirty-six phonetic symbols that represent the thirty-six sounds of the French language. If you learn these extremely useful symbols, and if you know which sounds they describe, you will be able to understand the transcriptions given in this book, and look up the pronunciation of French words in many dictionaries.

Consonants

Most of the symbols representing the consonants and half-consonants (or semi-vowels) are derived from the Latin alphabet that we use to write French and English.

SYMBOL	FRENCH WORDS THAT CONTAIN THIS SOUND	ENGLISH WORDS THAT CONTAIN A SIMILAR SOUND
[b]	barbe	boy
[d]	madame	day
[f]	fenêtre	fox
[g]	garçon	garage
[k]	cœur (Contrary to English, the sound [k] is *never* aspirated, i.e., *never* articulated with air.)	ski
[l]	livre (Contrary to English, [l] is always pronounced with the tongue pressing against the upper front teeth.)	late

(continued)

553

SYMBOL	FRENCH WORDS THAT CONTAIN THIS SOUND	ENGLISH WORDS THAT CONTAIN A SIMILAR SOUND
[m]	monsieur	man
[n]	banane	banana
[p]	plage (Contrary to English, the sound [p] is never aspirated.)	spouse
[ʀ]	rouge (Contrary to English the sound [ʀ] is produced between the back of the tongue and the upper part of the back of the mouth.)	no equivalent in English
[s]	merci	sun
[t]	table (Contrary to English, the sound [t] is never aspirated.)	stop
[v]	voilà	van
[j]	bien	yes
[w]	oui	west
[z]	chaise	zebra

The following phonetic symbols are *not* taken from the Latin alphabet:

SYMBOL	FRENCH WORDS THAT CONTAIN THIS SOUND	ENGLISH WORDS THAT CONTAIN A SIMILAR SOUND
[ʃ]	chocolat	shoe
[ʒ]	jeu	pleasure
[ɲ]	montagne	onion
[ŋ]	smoking	smoking
[ɥ]	nuit	no equivalent in English

Vowels

Note that French vowel sounds are much tenser than the English ones.

SYMBOL	FRENCH WORDS THAT CONTAIN THIS SOUND	ENGLISH WORDS THAT CONTAIN A SIMILAR SOUND
[a]	papa	car
[e]	été (To produce the [e] sound, extend your lips as if you were smiling; no equivalent in English.)	
[ɛ]	très (To produce the [ɛ] sound, open the jaw.)	bad
[i]	midi	fit
[o]	stylo	no equivalent in English
[ɔ]	porte	not
[ø]	deux (To produce the [ø] sound, project your lips forward to form a circle.)	no equivalent in English
[œ]	beurre	fur
[u]	vous	shoe
[y]	sur (To produce the [y] sound, place the tip of the tongue behind the lower front teeth and project your lips forward as far as possible as if to whistle.)	no equivalent in English

[ə]   je (The sound [ə] is similar to the
[ø] sound, but weaker. The lips are
projected less far forward; no
equivalent in English.)

Nasal vowels

Note that these vowels are transcribed with a tilde [~] above them and that the sounds they represent resonate in the nose.

SYMBOL	FRENCH WORDS THAT CONTAIN THIS SOUND	ENGLISH WORDS THAT CONTAIN A SIMILAR SOUND
[ã]	comm**ent**	no equivalent in English
[ɛ̃]	v**in**	no equivalent in English
[ɔ̃]	b**on**	no equivalent in English
[œ̃]	l**un**di	no equivalent in English

Abbreviations

The following abbreviations are used in this book:

adj.	adjective
e.g.	for example
fam.	familiar (you [*fam.*] = **tu**)
f. or fem.	feminine
f.pl.	feminine plural
i.e.	that is, that is to say
inf.	infinitive
lit.	literally (indicating a literal translation of a French expression or sentence)
m. or masc.	masculine
m.pl.	masculine plural
p.	page
pl. or plur.	plural
pol.	polite (you [*pol.*] = **vous**)
qch	**quelque chose** (*something*)
qn	**quelqu'un** (*someone*)
sing.	singular
sb	somebody
sth	something

Appendix A: French pronunciation   **555**

Appendix B
Grammatical terminology for verbs

Infinitive

The *infinitive* is the basic, unconjugated form of the verb. In English, all infinitives are preceded by *to*. In French, infinitives end in -**er, -ir,** or -**re** (**donn***er* [*to give*], **chois***ir* [*to choose*], **vend***re* [*to sell*]).

Subject

The *subject* of a sentence is the person or thing that performs the action. The subject determines the form of the verb: *I go. You sing. David asks. We dance. The students work.* The subject can be a noun (*David, the students*) or a pronoun (*I, you, he*, etc.).

Conjugation

When one lists the six existing verb forms in a particular tense by adapting the verb to each of the subject pronouns, one *conjugates* the verb. Contrary to English, most French verb forms change from one person to another during the conjugation.

Compare the following two present tense conjugations:

French: **je parle, tu parles, il/elle/on parle, nous parlons, vous parlez, ils/elles parlent.** (Only two forms are alike.)

English: *I speak, you speak, he/she/one speaks, we speak, you speak, they speak.* (All forms are the same except one.)

Stem

The *stem* is what is left of the verb after dropping the infinitive ending -**er, -ir,** or -**re**. Thus, the stem of **parler** is **parl-**, the stem of **réussir** is **réuss-,** and the stem of **attendre** is **attend-**.

Verb ending

A verb *ending* is what is added to the stem during the conjugation. Regular -**er** verbs, for example, have the endings -**e, -es, -e, -ons, -ez, -ent** in the present indicative. The verb ending indicates the subject, tense, and mood, i.e., it shows who or what performs the action, when this action occurs, and how it is perceived.

Tense

The *tense* of a verb indicates when the action takes place, in the present, past, or future. The verb can be in a *simple tense,* which consists of one word only (such as the present tense), or in a *compound tense,* which consists of two words: the auxiliary and the past participle (such as the **passé composé**).

Mood

Grammatical *mood* means "manner." It shows how the speaker perceives what he or she is saying. There are four personal and two impersonal moods in French.

The indicative, subjunctive, imperative, and conditional are *personal* moods. The infinitive and the participle (present and past) are *impersonal* moods. Impersonal moods do not show who performs the action.

Elision

A vowel is *elided* when it is dropped and replaced by an apostrophe (**je danse**, but **j'adore**).

Subject pronouns

The following set of *subject pronouns* are used when conjugating a verb in French:

	SINGULAR		PLURAL	
first person	**je**	*I*	**nous**	*we*
second person	**tu**	*you*	**vous**	*you*
third person	**il**	*he, it*	**ils**	*they*
	elle	*she, it*	**elles**	*they*
	on	*one*		

The French subject pronouns differ from their English counterparts in the following way:

- ◆ There are two ways to say *you,* depending on whom one addresses (see Note).
- ◆ There are two ways to say *they,* due to gender (see Note).
- ◆ There is no specific word for *it.* French refers instead to a masculine thing with **il** (*he*) and to a feminine thing with **elle** (*she*).

Note: The **e** in **je** is elided (i.e., dropped), and **je** becomes **j'** before a verb that starts with a vowel or mute **h**: **j'aime, j'habite.**

The pronouns **il** and **elle** can be used for persons, animals, and things.

The pronoun **il** expresses

- ◆ *he* (replacing a masculine person)
- ◆ *it* (replacing a masculine thing—or an animal—and used as a subject in impersonal expressions)

The pronoun **elle** expresses

- ◆ *she* (replacing a feminine person)
- ◆ *it* (replacing a feminine thing or animal)

The indefinite pronoun **on** expresses *one, they, people.*

Comment dit-**on** « chair » en français?	*How does **one** say "chair" in French?*
On parle français en Belgique.	***People** (= They) speak French in Belgium.*

558 Appendix B: Grammatical terminology for verbs

Note that in informal French, **on** is frequently used instead of **nous**.

On s'aime.   *We love each other.*

There are two ways to express *you* in French.

1. The pronoun **tu** is familiar singular and is used to address one person whom one would call by his/her first name in France, i.e., a family member, a good friend or colleague, a fellow student, or a child. **Tu** is also used when praying to God and when talking to a pet.

2. The pronoun **vous** is both singular and plural formal and addresses one adult or a number of adults whom one doesn't know very well (strangers, service personnel, professional contacts, acquaintances, etc.). It is also the plural of **tu**, i.e., used when speaking to more than one family member, close friend, fellow student, or child.

In the exercises in this book, *fam.* (= familiar) indicates that **tu** should be used, *pol.* (= polite) indicates that **vous** should be used to translate *you*.

There are two ways to express *they* in French.

1. The pronoun **ils** replaces masculine beings or things, or masculine *and* feminine beings or things combined.

2. The pronoun **elles** replaces feminine beings or things only.

Verb categories

- ◆ **Regular verbs.** The conjugation of these verbs follows a fixed pattern. Once you learn this pattern, you can conjugate each verb within one group (**-er**, **-ir**, or **-re** verbs). With regular verbs, the stem of the infinitive remains intact during the conjugation, and all verbs within one group have the same endings.
- ◆ **Irregular verbs.** The conjugation of each of these verbs does not follow a fixed pattern and therefore must be memorized.
- ◆ **Auxiliaries.** These verbs (**avoir** and **être** in French) are also called *helping verbs* because they help to build a compound tense.
- ◆ **Transitive verbs.** These are verbs that can take an (direct or indirect) object. An object is a person who (or a thing that) receives the action of the subject. In the sentence **je visite le musée** (*I visit the museum*), **le musée** is the object. The verb **visiter** is *transitive*.

    In dictionaries, transitive verbs are often indicated by the abbreviation *v.tr.* (**verbe transitif**).
- ◆ **Intransitive verbs.** Intransitive verbs, such as **aller** (*to go*), **venir** (*to come*), and **rester** (*to stay*), cannot take an object. You cannot *go, come,* or *stay* "someone" or "something." In dictionaries, intransitive verbs are usually indicated by the abbreviation *v.i.* (**verbe intransitif**).
- ◆ **Reflexive verbs.** The infinitive of these verbs is preceded by the reflexive pronoun **se** (or **s'** before a vowel or mute **h**). The verbs **se coucher** (*to go to bed*) and **s'amuser** (*to have a good time*) are reflexive verbs.
- ◆ **Impersonal verbs.** These are verbs that are only used in the third-person singular (= **il**) form. Many impersonal verbs describe the weather: *Il pleut*. (*It is raining.*)

Appendix B: Grammatical terminology for verbs **559**

Appendix C
French verb tables

Regular verbs
Regular -er ending verbs
travailler (*to work*)

Present indicative	je travaille, tu travailles, il/elle/on travaille, nous travaillons, vous travaillez, ils/elles travaillent
Imperative	travaille, travaillons, travaillez
Passé composé	j'ai travaillé, tu as travaillé, il/elle/on a travaillé, nous avons travaillé, vous avez travaillé, ils/elles ont travaillé
Imperfect	je travaillais, tu travaillais, il/elle/on travaillait, nous travaillions, vous travailliez, ils/elles travaillaient
Pluperfect	j'avais travaillé, tu avais travaillé, il/elle/on avait travaillé, nous avions travaillé, vous aviez travaillé, ils/elles avaient travaillé
Passé simple	je travaillai, tu travaillas, il/elle/on travailla, nous travaillâmes, vous travaillâtes, ils/elles travaillèrent
Future	je travaillerai, tu travailleras, il/elle/on travaillera, nous travaillerons, vous travaillerez, ils/elles travailleront
Futur antérieur	j'aurai travaillé, tu auras travaillé, il/elle/on aura travaillé, nous aurons travaillé, vous aurez travaillé, ils/elles auront travaillé
Present conditional	je travaillerais, tu travaillerais, il/elle/on travaillerait, nous travaillerions, vous travailleriez, ils/elles travailleraient
Past conditional	j'aurais travaillé, tu aurais travaillé, il/elle/on aurait travaillé, nous aurions travaillé, vous auriez travaillé, ils/elles auraient travaillé
Present subjunctive	que je travaille, que tu travailles, qu'il/elle/on travaille, que nous travaillions, que vous travailliez, qu'ils/elles travaillent
Past subjunctive	que j'aie travaillé, que tu aies travaillé, qu'il/elle/on ait travaillé, que nous ayons travaillé, que vous ayez travaillé, qu'ils/elles aient travaillé

Regular -*ir* ending verbs

finir (*to finish*)

Present indicative	je finis, tu finis, il/elle/on finit, nous finissons, vous finissez, ils/elles finissent
Imperative	finis, finissons, finissez
Passé composé	j'ai fini, tu as fini, il/elle/on a fini, nous avons fini, vous avez fini, ils/elles ont fini
Imperfect	je finissais, tu finissais, il/elle/on finissait, nous finissions, vous finissiez, ils/elles finissaient
Pluperfect	j'avais fini, tu avais fini, il/elle/on avait fini, nous avions fini, vous aviez fini, ils/elles avaient fini
Passé simple	je finis, tu finis, il/elle/on finit, nous finîmes, vous finîtes, ils/elles finirent
Future	je finirai, tu finiras, il/elle/on finira, nous finirons, vous finirez, ils/elles finiront
Futur antérieur	j'aurai fini, tu auras fini, il/elle/on aura fini, nous aurons fini, vous aurez fini, ils/elles auront fini
Present conditional	je finirais, tu finirais, il/elle/on finirait, nous finirions, vous finiriez, ils/elles finiraient
Past conditional	j'aurais fini, tu aurais fini, il/elle/on aurait fini, nous aurions fini, vous auriez fini, ils/elles auraient fini
Present subjunctive	que je finisse, que tu finisses, qu'il/elle/on finisse, que nous finissions, que vous finissiez, qu'ils/elles finissent
Past subjunctive	que j'aie fini, que tu aies fini, qu'il/elle/on ait fini, que nous ayons fini, que vous ayez fini, qu'ils/elles aient fini

Regular -*re* ending verbs

vendre (*to sell*)

Present indicative	je vends, tu vends, il/elle/on vend, nous vendons, vous vendez, ils/elles vendent
Imperative	vends, vendons, vendez
Passé composé	j'ai vendu, tu as vendu, il/elle/on a vendu, nous avons vendu, vous avez vendu, ils/elles ont vendu
Imperfect	je vendais, tu vendais, il/elle/on vendait, nous vendions, vous vendiez, ils/elles vendaient
Pluperfect	j'avais vendu, tu avais vendu, il/elle/on avait vendu, nous avions vendu, vous aviez vendu, ils/elles avaient vendu
Passé simple	je vendis, tu vendis, il/elle/on vendit, nous vendîmes, vous vendîtes, ils/elles vendirent
Future	je vendrai, tu vendras, il/elle/on vendra, nous vendrons, vous vendrez, ils/elles vendront
Futur antérieur	j'aurai vendu, tu auras vendu, il/elle/on aura vendu, nous aurons vendu, vous aurez vendu, ils/elles auront vendu
Present conditional	je vendrais, tu vendrais, il/elle/on vendrait, nous vendrions, vous vendriez, ils/elles vendraient
Past conditional	j'aurais vendu, tu aurais vendu, il/elle/on aurait vendu, nous aurions vendu, vous auriez vendu, ils/elles auraient vendu
Present subjunctive	que je vende, que tu vendes, qu'il/elle/on vende, que nous vendions, que vous vendiez, qu'ils/elles vendent
Past subjunctive	que j'aie vendu, que tu aies vendu, qu'il/elle/on ait vendu, que nous ayons vendu, que vous ayez vendu, qu'ils/elles aient vendu

Regular reflexive verbs

se coucher (*to go to bed*)

Present indicative	je me couche, tu te couches, il/elle/on se couche, nous nous couchons, vous vous couchez, ils/elles se couchent
Imperative	couche-toi, couchons-nous, couchez-vous
Passé composé	je me suis couché(e), tu t'es couché(e), il/elle/on s'est couché(e), nous nous sommes couché(e)s, vous vous êtes couché(e)(s), ils/elles se sont couché(e)s
Imperfect	je me couchais, tu te couchais, il/elle/on se couchait, nous nous couchions, vous vous couchiez, ils/elles se couchaient
Pluperfect	je m'étais couché(e), tu t'étais couché(e), il/elle/on s'était couché(e), nous nous étions couché(e)s, vous vous étiez couché(e)(s), ils/elles s'étaient couché(e)s
Passé simple	je me couchai, tu te couchas, il/elle/on se coucha, nous nous couchâmes, vous vous couchâtes, ils/elles se couchèrent
Future	je me coucherai, tu te coucheras, il/elle/on se couchera, nous nous coucherons, vous vous coucherez, ils/elles se coucheront
Futur antérieur	je me serai couché(e), tu te seras couché(e), il/elle/on se sera couché(e), nous nous serons couché(e)s, vous vous serez couché(e)(s), ils/elles se seront couché(e)s
Present conditional	je me coucherais, tu te coucherais, il/elle/on se coucherait, nous nous coucherions, vous vous coucheriez, ils/elles se coucheraient
Past conditional	je me serais couché(e), tu te serais couché(e), il/elle/on se serait couché(e), nous nous serions couché(e)s, vous vous seriez couché(e)(s) ils/elles se seraient couché(e)s
Present subjunctive	que je me couche, que tu te couches, qu'il/elle/on se couche, que nous nous couchions, que vous vous couchiez, qu'ils/elles se couchent
Past subjunctive	que je me sois couché(e), que tu te sois couché(e), qu'il/elle/on se soit couché(e), que nous nous soyons couché(e)s, que vous vous soyez couché(e)(s), qu'ils/elles se soient couché(e)s

Regular verbs with spelling changes

acheter (*to buy*)

Present indicative	j'achète, tu achètes, il/elle/on achète, nous achetons, vous achetez, ils/elles achètent
Imperative	achète, achetons, achetez
Passé composé	j'ai acheté, tu as acheté, il/elle/on a acheté, nous avons acheté, vous avez acheté, ils/elles ont acheté
Imperfect	j'achetais, tu achetais, il/elle/on achetait, nous achetions, vous achetiez, ils/elles achetaient
Pluperfect	j'avais acheté, tu avais acheté, il/elle/on avait acheté, nous avions acheté, vous aviez acheté, ils/elles avaient acheté
Passé simple	j'achetai, tu achetas, il/elle/on acheta, nous achetâmes, vous achetâtes, ils/elles achetèrent
Future	j'achèterai, tu achèteras, il/elle/on achètera, nous achèterons, vous achèterez, ils/elles achèteront
Futur antérieur	j'aurai acheté, tu auras acheté, il/elle/on aura acheté, nous aurons acheté, vous aurez acheté, ils/elles auront acheté
Present conditional	j'achèterais, tu achèterais, il/elle/on achèterait, nous achèterions, vous achèteriez, ils/elles achèteraient

Appendix C: French verb tables **563**

Past conditional	j'aurais acheté, tu aurais acheté, il/elle/on aurait acheté, nous aurions acheté, vous auriez acheté, ils/elles auraient acheté
Present subjunctive	que j'achète, que tu achètes, qu'il/elle/on achète, que nous achetions, que vous achetiez, qu'ils/elles achètent
Past subjunctive	que j'aie acheté, que tu aies acheté, qu'il/elle/on ait acheté, que nous ayons acheté, que vous ayez acheté, qu'ils/elles aient acheté

Verbs conjugated like **acheter**: **amener** (*to bring*), **emmener** (*to take*), **peser** (*to weigh*)

appeler (*to call*)

Present indicative	j'appelle, tu appelles, il/elle/on appelle, nous appelons, vous appelez, ils/elles appellent
Imperative	appelle, appelons, appelez
Passé composé	j'ai appelé, tu as appelé, il/elle/on a appelé, nous avons appelé, vous avez appelé, ils/elles ont appelé
Imperfect	j'appelais, tu appelais, il/elle/on appelait, nous appelions, vous appeliez, ils/elles appelaient
Pluperfect	j'avais appelé, tu avais appelé, il/elle/on avait appelé, nous avions appelé, vous aviez appelé, ils/elles avaient appelé
Passé simple	j'appelai, tu appelas, il/elle/on appela, nous appelâmes, vous appelâtes, ils/elles appelèrent
Future	j'appellerai, tu appelleras, il/elle/on appellera, nous appellerons, vous appellerez, ils/elles appelleront
Futur antérieur	j'aurai appelé, tu auras appelé, il/elle/on aura appelé, nous aurons appelé, vous aurez appelé, ils/elles auront appelé
Present conditional	j'appellerais, tu appellerais, il/elle/on appellerait, nous appellerions, vous appelleriez, ils/elles appelleraient
Past conditional	j'aurais appelé, tu aurais appelé, il/elle/on aurait appelé, nous aurions appelé, vous auriez appelé, ils/elles auraient appelé
Present subjunctive	que j'appelle, que tu appelles, qu'il/elle/on appelle, que nous appelions, que vous appeliez, qu'ils/elles appellent
Past subjunctive	que j'aie appelé, que tu aies appelé, qu'il/elle/on ait appelé, que nous ayons appelé, que vous ayez appelé, qu'ils/elles aient appelé

Verbs conjugated like **appeler:** **jeter** (*to throw*)

commencer (*to begin*)

Present indicative	je commence, tu commences, il/elle/on commence, nous commençons, vous commencez, ils/elles commencent
Imperative	commence, commençons, commencez
Passé composé	j'ai commencé, tu as commencé, il/elle/on a commencé, nous avons commencé, vous avez commencé, ils/elles ont commencé
Imperfect	je commençais, tu commençais, il/elle/on commençait, nous commencions, vous commenciez, ils/elles commençaient
Pluperfect	j'avais commencé, tu avais commencé, il/elle/on avait commencé, nous avions commencé, vous aviez commencé, ils/elles avaient commencé
Passé simple	je commençai, tu commenças, il/elle/on commença, nous commençâmes, vous commençâtes, ils/elles commencèrent
Future	je commencerai, tu commenceras, il/elle/on commencera, nous commencerons, vous commencerez, ils/elles commenceront
Futur antérieur	j'aurai commencé, tu auras commencé, il/elle/on aura commencé, nous aurons commencé, vous aurez commencé, ils/elles auront commencé

Present conditional	je commencerais, tu commencerais, il/elle/on commencerait, nous commencerions, vous commenceriez, ils/elles commenceraient
Past conditional	j'aurais commencé, tu aurais commencé, il/elle/on aurait commencé, nous aurions commencé, vous auriez commencé, ils/elles auraient commencé
Present subjunctive	que je commence, que tu commences, qu'il/elle/on commence, que nous commencions, que vous commenciez, qu'ils/elles commencent
Past subjunctive	que j'aie commencé, que tu aies commencé, qu'il/elle/on ait commencé, que nous ayons commencé, que vous ayez commencé, qu'ils/elles aient commencé

Verbs conjugated like **commencer: effacer** (*to erase*)**, forcer** (*to force*)**, placer** (*to place*)**, remplacer** (*to replace*)

essayer (*to try*)

Present indicative	j'essaie, tu essaies, il/elle/on essaie, nous essayons, vous essayez, ils/elles essaient
Imperative	essaie, essayons, essayez
Passé composé	j'ai essayé, tu as essayé, il/elle/on a essayé, nous avons essayé, vous avez essayé, ils/elles ont essayé
Imperfect	j'essayais, tu essayais, il/elle/on essayait, nous essayions, vous essayiez, ils/elles essayaient
Pluperfect	j'avais essayé, tu avais essayé, il/elle/on avait essayé, nous avions essayé, vous aviez essayé, ils/elles avaient essayé
Passé simple	j'essayai, tu essayas, il/elle/on essaya, nous essayâmes, vous essayâtes, ils/elles essayèrent
Future	j'essaierai, tu essaieras, il/elle/on essaiera, nous essaierons, vous essaierez, ils/elles essaieront
Futur antérieur	j'aurai essayé, tu auras essayé, il/elle/on aura essayé, nous aurons essayé, vous aurez essayé, ils/elles auront essayé
Present conditional	j'essaierais, tu essaierais, il/elle/on essaierait, nous essaierions, vous essaieriez, ils/elles essaieraient
Past conditional	j'aurais essayé, tu aurais essayé, il/elle/on aurait essayé, nous aurions essayé, vous auriez essayé, ils/elles auraient essayé
Present subjunctive	que j'essaie, que tu essaies, qu'il/elle/on essaie, que nous essayions, que vous essayiez, qu'ils/elles essaient
Past subjunctive	que j'aie essayé, que tu aies essayé, qu'il/elle/on ait essayé, que nous ayons essayé, que vous ayez essayé, qu'ils/elles aient essayé

Verbs conjugated like **essayer: balayer** (*to sweep*)**, payer** (*to pay*)

lever (*to lift*)

Present indicative	je lève, tu lèves, il/elle/on lève, nous levons, vous levez, ils/elles lèvent
Imperative	lève, levons, levez
Passé composé	j'ai levé, tu as levé, il/elle/on a levé, nous avons levé, vous avez levé, ils/elles ont levé
Imperfect	je levais, tu levais, il/elle/on levait, nous levions, vous leviez, ils/elles levaient
Pluperfect	j'avais levé, tu avais levé, il/elle/on avait levé, nous avions levé, vous aviez levé, ils/elles avaient levé
Passé simple	je levai, tu levas, il/elle/on leva, nous levâmes, vous levâtes, ils/elles levèrent
Future	je lèverai, tu lèveras, il/elle/on lèvera, nous lèverons, vous lèverez, ils/elles lèveront

Appendix C: French verb tables **565**

Futur antérieur	j'aurai levé, tu auras levé, il/elle/on aura levé, nous aurons levé, vous aurez levé, ils/elles auront levé
Present conditional	je lèverais, tu lèverais, il/elle/on lèverait, nous lèverions, vous lèveriez, ils/elles lèveraient
Past conditional	j'aurais levé, tu aurais levé, il/elle/on aurait levé, nous aurions levé, vous auriez levé, ils/elles auraient levé
Present subjunctive	que je lève, que tu lèves, qu'il/elle/on lève, que nous levions, que vous leviez, qu'ils/elles lèvent
Past subjunctive	que j'aie levé, que tu aies levé, qu'il/elle/on ait levé, que nous ayons levé, que vous ayez levé, qu'ils/elles aient levé

Verbs conjugated like **lever: élever** (*to raise*), **enlever** (*to take off, kidnap*)

manger (*to eat*)

Present indicative	je mange, tu manges, il/elle/on mange, nous mangeons, vous mangez, ils/elles mangent
Imperative	mange, mangeons, mangez
Passé composé	j'ai mangé, tu as mangé, il/elle/on a mangé, nous avons mangé, vous avez mangé, ils/elles ont mangé
Imperfect	je mangeais, tu mangeais, il/elle/on mangeait, nous mangions, vous mangiez, ils/elles mangeaient
Pluperfect	j'avais mangé, tu avais mangé, il/elle/on avait mangé, nous avions mangé, vous aviez mangé, ils/elles avaient mangé
Passé simple	je mangeai, tu mangeas, il/elle/on mangea, nous mangeâmes, vous mangeâtes, ils/elles mangèrent
Future	je mangerai, tu mangeras, il/elle/on mangera, nous mangerons, vous mangerez, ils/elles mangeront
Futur antérieur	j'aurai mangé, tu auras mangé, il/elle/on aura mangé, nous aurons mangé, vous aurez mangé, ils/elles auront mangé
Present conditional	je mangerais, tu mangerais, il/elle/on mangerait, nous mangerions, vous mangeriez, ils/elles mangeraient
Past conditional	j'aurais mangé, tu aurais mangé, il/elle/on aurait mangé, nous aurions mangé, vous auriez mangé, ils/elles auraient mangé
Present subjunctive	que je mange, que tu manges, qu'il/elle/on mange, que nous mangions, que vous mangiez, qu'ils/elles mangent
Past subjunctive	que j'aie mangé, que tu aies mangé, qu'il/elle/on ait mangé, que nous ayons mangé, que vous ayez mangé, qu'ils/elles aient mangé

Verbs conjugated like **manger: changer** (*to change*), **nager** (*to swim*), **partager** (*to share*), **ranger** (*to arrange, tidy up*), **voyager** (*to travel*)

préférer (*to prefer*)

Present indicative	je préfère, tu préfères, il/elle/on préfère, nous préférons, vous préférez, ils/elles préfèrent
Imperative	préfère, préférons, préférez
Passé composé	j'ai préféré, tu as préféré, il/elle/on a préféré, nous avons préféré, vous avez préféré, ils/elles ont préféré
Imperfect	je préférais, tu préférais, il/elle/on préférait, nous préférions, vous préfériez, ils/elles préféraient
Pluperfect	j'avais préféré, tu avais préféré, il/elle/on avait préféré, nous avions préféré, vous aviez préféré, ils/elles avaient préféré
Passé simple	je préférai, tu préféras, il/elle/on préféra, nous préférâmes, vous préférâtes, ils/elles préférèrent

Future	je préférerai, tu préféreras, il/elle/on préférera, nous préférerons, vous préférerez, ils/elles préféreront
Futur antérieur	j'aurai préféré, tu auras préféré, il/elle/on aura préféré, nous aurons préféré, vous aurez préféré, ils/elles auront préféré
Present conditional	je préférerais, tu préférerais, il/elle/on préférerait, nous préférerions, vous préféreriez, ils/elles préféreraient
Past conditional	j'aurais préféré, tu aurais préféré, il/elle/on aurait préféré, nous aurions préféré, vous auriez préféré, ils/elles auraient préféré
Present subjunctive	que je préfère, que tu préfères, qu'il/elle/on préfère, que nous préférions, que vous préfériez, qu'ils/elles préfèrent
Past subjunctive	que j'aie préféré, que tu aies préféré, qu'il/elle/on ait préféré, que nous ayons préféré, que vous ayez préféré, qu'ils/elles aient préféré

Verbs conjugated like **préférer: espérer** (*to hope*), **posséder** (*to possess, own*), **répéter** (*to repeat*)

Irregular verbs

aller (*to go*)

Present indicative	je vais, tu vas, il/elle/on va, nous allons, vous allez, ils/elles vont
Imperative	va, allons, allez
Passé composé	je suis allé(e), tu es allé(e), il/elle/on est allé(e), nous sommes allé(e)s, vous êtes allé(e)(s), ils/elles sont allé(e)s
Imperfect	j'allais, tu allais, il/elle/on allait, nous allions, vous alliez, ils/elles allaient
Pluperfect	j'étais allé(e), tu étais allé(e), il/elle/on était allé(e), nous étions allé(e)s, vous étiez allé(e)(s), ils/elles étaient allé(e)s
Passé simple	j'allai, tu allas, il/elle/on alla, nous allâmes, vous allâtes, ils/elles allèrent
Future	j'irai, tu iras, il/elle/on ira, nous irons, vous irez, ils/elles iront
Futur antérieur	je serai allé(e), tu seras allé(e), il/elle/on sera allé(e), nous serons allé(e)s, vous serez allé(e)(s), ils/elles seront allé(e)s
Present conditional	j'irais, tu irais, il/elle/on irait, nous irions, vous iriez, ils/elles iraient
Past conditional	je serais allé(e), tu serais allé(e), il/elle/on serait allé(e), nous serions allé(e)s, vous seriez allé(e)(s), ils/elles seraient allé(e)s
Present subjunctive	que j'aille, que tu ailles, qu'il/elle/on aille, que nous allions, que vous alliez, qu'ils/elles aillent
Past subjunctive	que je sois allé(e), que tu sois allé(e), qu'il/elle/on soit allé(e), que nous soyons allé(e)s, que vous soyez allé(e)(s), qu'ils/elles soient allé(e)s

s'asseoir (*to sit down*)

Present indicative	je m'assieds (m'assois), tu t'assieds (t'assois), il/elle/on s'assied (s'assoit), nous nous asseyons (nous assoyons), vous vous asseyez (vous assoyez), ils/elles s'asseyent (s'assoient)
Imperative	assieds-toi, asseyons-nous, asseyez-vous
Passé composé	je me suis assis(e), tu t'es assis(e), il/elle/on s'est assis(e), nous nous sommes assis(es), vous vous êtes assis(e)(es), ils/elles se sont assis(es)
Imperfect	je m'asseyais, tu t'asseyais, il/elle/on s'asseyait, nous nous asseyions, vous vous asseyiez, ils/elles s'asseyaient
Pluperfect	je m'étais assis(e), tu t'étais assis(e), il/elle/on s'était assis(e), nous nous étions assis(es), vous vous étiez assis(e)(es), ils/elles s'étaient assis(es)
Passé simple	je m'assis, tu t'assis, il/elle/on s'assit, nous nous assîmes, vous vous assîtes, ils/elles s'assirent

Appendix C: French verb tables **567**

Future	je m'assiérai, tu t'assiéras, il/elle/on s'assiéra, nous nous assiérons, vous vous assiérez, ils/elles s'assiéront
Futur antérieur	je me serai assis(e), tu te seras assis(e), il/elle/on se sera assis(e), nous nous serons assis(es), vous vous serez assis(e)(es), ils/elles se seront assis(es)
Present conditional	je m'assiérais, tu t'assiérais, il/elle/on s'assiérait, nous nous assiérions, vous vous assiériez, ils/elles s'assiéraient
Past conditional	je me serais assis(e), tu te serais assis(e), il/elle/on se serait assis(e), nous nous serions assis(es), vous vous seriez assis(e)(es), ils/elles se seraient assis(es)
Present subjunctive	que je m'asseye, que tu t'asseyes, qu'il/elle/on s'asseye, que nous nous asseyions, que vous vous asseyiez, qu'ils/elles s'asseyent
Past subjunctive	que je me sois assis(e), que tu te sois assis(e), qu'il/elle/on se soit assis(e), que nous nous soyons assis(es), que vous vous soyez assis(e)(es), qu'ils/elles se soient assis(es)

avoir (*to have*)

Present indicative	j'ai, tu as, il/elle/on a, nous avons, vous avez, ils/elles ont
Imperative	aie, ayons, ayez
Passé composé	j'ai eu, tu as eu, il/elle/on a eu, nous avons eu, vous avez eu, ils/elles ont eu
Imperfect	j'avais, tu avais, il/elle/on avait, nous avions, vous aviez, ils/elles avaient
Pluperfect	j'avais eu, tu avais eu, il/elle/on avait eu, nous avions eu, vous aviez eu, ils/elles avaient eu
Passé simple	j'eus, tu eus, il/elle/on eut, nous eûmes, vous eûtes, ils/elles eurent
Future	j'aurai, tu auras, il/elle/on aura, nous aurons, vous aurez, ils/elles auront
Futur antérieur	j'aurai eu, tu auras eu, il/elle/on aura eu, nous aurons eu, vous aurez eu, ils/elles auront eu
Present conditional	j'aurais, tu aurais, il/elle/on aurait, nous aurions, vous auriez, ils/elles auraient
Past conditional	j'aurais eu, tu aurais eu, il/elle/on aurait eu, nous aurions eu, vous auriez eu, ils/elles auraient eu
Present subjunctive	que j'aie, que tu aies, qu'il/elle/on ait, que nous ayons, que vous ayez, qu'ils/elles aient
Past subjunctive	que j'aie eu, que tu aies eu, qu'il/elle/on ait eu, que nous ayons eu, que vous ayez eu, qu'ils/elles aient eu

boire (*to drink*)

Present indicative	je bois, tu bois, il/elle/on boit, nous buvons, vous buvez, ils/elles boivent
Imperative	bois, buvons, buvez
Passé composé	j'ai bu, tu as bu, il/elle/on a bu, nous avons bu, vous avez bu, ils/elles ont bu
Imperfect	je buvais, tu buvais, il/elle/on buvait, nous buvions, vous buviez, ils/elles buvaient
Pluperfect	j'avais bu, tu avais bu, il/elle/on avait bu, nous avions bu, vous aviez bu, ils/elles avaient bu
Passé simple	je bus, tu bus, il/elle/on but, nous bûmes, vous bûtes, ils/elles burent
Future	je boirai, tu boiras, il/elle/on boira, nous boirons, vous boirez, ils/elles boiront
Futur antérieur	j'aurai bu, tu auras bu, il/elle/on aura bu, nous aurons bu, vous aurez bu, ils/elles auront bu

Present conditional	je boirais, tu boirais, il/elle/on boirait, nous boirions, vous boiriez, ils/elles boiraient
Past conditional	j'aurais bu, tu aurais bu, il/elle/on aurait bu, nous aurions bu, vous auriez bu, ils/elles auraient bu
Present subjunctive	que je boive, que tu boives, qu'il/elle/on boive, que nous buvions, que vous buviez, qu'ils/elles boivent
Past subjunctive	que j'aie bu, que tu aies bu, qu'il/elle/on ait bu, que nous ayons bu, que vous ayez bu, qu'ils/elles aient bu

conduire (*to drive*)

Present indicative	je conduis, tu conduis, il/elle/on conduit, nous conduisons, vous conduisez, ils/elles conduisent
Imperative	conduis, conduisons, conduisez
Passé composé	j'ai conduit, tu as conduit, il/elle/on a conduit, nous avons conduit, vous avez conduit, ils/elles ont conduit
Imperfect	je conduisais, tu conduisais, il/elle/on conduisait, nous conduisions, vous conduisiez, ils/elles conduisaient
Pluperfect	j'avais conduit, tu avais conduit, il/elle/on avait conduit, nous avions conduit, vous aviez conduit, ils/elles avaient conduit
Passé simple	je conduisis, tu conduisis, il/elle/on conduisit, nous conduisîmes, vous conduisîtes, ils/elles conduisirent
Future	je conduirai, tu conduiras, il/elle/on conduira, nous conduirons, vous conduirez, ils/elles conduiront
Futur antérieur	j'aurai conduit, tu auras conduit, il/elle/on aura conduit, nous aurons conduit, vous aurez conduit, ils/elles auront conduit
Present conditional	je conduirais, tu conduirais, il/elle/on conduirait, nous conduirions, vous conduiriez, ils/elles conduiraient
Past conditional	j'aurais conduit, tu aurais conduit, il/elle/on aurait conduit, nous aurions conduit, vous auriez conduit, ils/elles auraient conduit
Present subjunctive	que je conduise, que tu conduises, qu'il/elle/on conduise, que nous conduisions, que vous conduisiez, qu'ils/elles conduisent
Past subjunctive	que j'aie conduit, que tu aies conduit, qu'il/elle/on ait conduit, que nous ayons conduit, que vous ayez conduit, qu'ils/elles aient conduit

Verbs conjugated like **conduire: construire** (*to build, construct*), **traduire** (*to translate*)

connaître (*to know*)

Present indicative	je connais, tu connais, il/elle/on connaît, nous connaissons, vous connaissez, ils/elles connaissent
Imperative	connais, connaissons, connaissez
Passé composé	j'ai connu, tu as connu, il/elle/on a connu, nous avons connu, vous avez connu, ils/elles ont connu
Imperfect	je connaissais, tu connaissais, il/elle/on connaissait, nous connaissions, vous connaissiez, ils/elles connaissaient
Pluperfect	j'avais connu, tu avais connu, il/elle/on avait connu, nous avions connu, vous aviez connu, ils/elles avaient connu
Passé simple	je connus, tu connus, il/elle/on connut, nous connûmes, vous connûtes, ils/elles connurent
Future	je connaîtrai, tu connaîtras, il/elle/on connaîtra, nous connaîtrons, vous connaîtrez, ils/elles connaîtront
Futur antérieur	j'aurai connu, tu auras connu, il/elle/on aura connu, nous aurons connu, vous aurez connu, ils/elles auront connu
Present conditional	je connaîtrais, tu connaîtrais, il/elle/on connaîtrait, nous connaîtrions, vous connaîtriez, ils/elles connaîtraient

Appendix C: French verb tables **569**

	Past conditional	j'aurais connu, tu aurais connu, il/elle/on aurait connu, nous aurions connu, vous auriez connu, ils/elles auraient connu
	Present subjunctive	que je connaisse, que tu connaisses, qu'il/elle/on connaisse, que nous connaissions, que vous connaissiez, qu'ils/elles connaissent
	Past subjunctive	que j'aie connu, que tu aies connu, qu'il/elle/on ait connu, que nous ayons connu, que vous ayez connu, qu'ils/elles aient connu

courir (*to run*)

	Present indicative	je cours, tu cours, il/elle/on court, nous courons, vous courez, ils/elles courent
	Imperative	cours, courons, courez
	Passé composé	j'ai couru, tu as couru, il/elle/on a couru, nous avons couru, vous avez couru, ils/elles ont couru
	Imperfect	je courais, tu courais, il/elle/on courait, nous courions, vous couriez, ils/elles couraient
	Pluperfect	j'avais couru, tu avais couru, il/elle/on avait couru, nous avions couru, vous aviez couru, ils/elles avaient couru
	Passé simple	je courus, tu courus, il/elle/on courut, nous courûmes, vous courûtes, ils/elles coururent
	Future	je courrai, tu courras, il/elle/on courra, nous courrons, vous courrez, ils/elles courront
	Futur antérieur	j'aurai couru, tu auras couru, il/elle/on aura couru, nous aurons couru, vous aurez couru, ils/elles auront couru
	Present conditional	je courrais, tu courrais, il/elle/on courrait, nous courrions, vous courriez, ils/elles courraient
	Past conditional	j'aurais couru, tu aurais couru, il/elle/on aurait couru, nous aurions couru, vous auriez couru, ils/elles auraient couru
	Present subjunctive	que je coure, que tu coures, qu'il/elle/on coure, que nous courions, que vous couriez, qu'ils/elles courent
	Past subjunctive	que j'aie couru, que tu aies couru, qu'il/elle/on ait couru, que nous ayons couru, que vous ayez couru, qu'ils/elles aient couru

craindre (*to fear*)

	Present indicative	je crains, tu crains, il/elle/on craint, nous craignons, vous craignez, ils/elles craignent
	Imperative	crains, craignons, craignez
	Passé composé	j'ai craint, tu as craint, il/elle/on a craint, nous avons craint, vous avez craint, ils/elles ont craint
	Imperfect	je craignais, tu craignais, il/elle/on craignait, nous craignions, vous craigniez, ils/elles craignaient
	Pluperfect	j'avais craint, tu avais craint, il/elle/on avait craint, nous avions craint, vous aviez craint, ils/elles avaient craint
	Passé simple	je craignis, tu craignis, il/elle/on craignit, nous craignîmes, vous craignîtes, ils/elles craignirent
	Future	je craindrai, tu craindras, il/elle/on craindra, nous craindrons, vous craindrez, ils/elles craindront
	Futur antérieur	j'aurai craint, tu auras craint, il/elle/on aura craint, nous aurons craint, vous aurez craint, ils/elles auront craint
	Present conditional	je craindrais, tu craindrais, il/elle/on craindrait, nous craindrions, vous craindriez, ils/elles craindraient
	Past conditional	j'aurais craint, tu aurais craint, il/elle/on aurait craint, nous aurions craint, vous auriez craint, ils/elles auraient craint
	Present subjunctive	que je craigne, que tu craignes, qu'il/elle/on craigne, que nous craignions, que vous craigniez, qu'ils/elles craignent

Past subjunctive	que j'aie craint, que tu aies craint, qu'il/elle/on ait craint, que nous ayons craint, que vous ayez craint, qu'ils/elles aient craint

Verbs conjugated like **craindre: plaindre** (*to pity, feel sorry for sb*)

croire (*to believe*)

Present indicative	je crois, tu crois, il/elle/on croit, nous croyons, vous croyez, ils/elles croient
Imperative	crois, croyons, croyez
Passé composé	j'ai cru, tu as cru, il/elle/on a cru, nous avons cru, vous avez cru, ils/elles ont cru
Imperfect	je croyais, tu croyais, il/elle/on croyait, nous croyions, vous croyiez, ils/elles croyaient
Pluperfect	j'avais cru, tu avais cru, il/elle/on avait cru, nous avions cru, vous aviez cru, ils/elles avaient cru
Passé simple	je crus, tu crus, il/elle/on crut, nous crûmes, vous crûtes, ils/elles crurent
Future	je croirai, tu croiras, il/elle/on croira, nous croirons, vous croirez, ils/elles croiront
Futur antérieur	j'aurai cru, tu auras cru, il/elle/on aura cru, nous aurons cru, vous aurez cru, ils/elles auront cru
Present conditional	je croirais, tu croirais, il/elle/on croirait, nous croirions, vous croiriez, ils/elles croiraient
Past conditional	j'aurais cru, tu aurais cru, il/elle/on aurait cru, nous aurions cru, vous auriez cru, ils/elles auraient cru
Present subjunctive	que je croie, que tu croies, qu'il/elle/on croie, que nous croyions, que vous croyiez, qu'ils/elles croient
Past subjunctive	que j'aie cru, que tu aies cru, qu'il/elle/on ait cru, que nous ayons cru, que vous ayez cru, qu'ils/elles aient cru

devoir (*to have to, must*)

Present indicative	je dois, tu dois, il/elle/on doit, nous devons, vous devez, ils/elles doivent
Imperative	dois, devons, devez
Passé composé	j'ai dû, tu as dû, il/elle/on a dû, nous avons dû, vous avez dû, ils/elles ont dû
Imperfect	je devais, tu devais, il/elle/on devait, nous devions, vous deviez, ils/elles devaient
Pluperfect	j'avais dû, tu avais dû, il/elle/on avait dû, nous avions dû, vous aviez dû, ils/elles avaient dû
Passé simple	je dus, tu dus, il/elle/on dut, nous dûmes, vous dûtes, ils/elles durent
Future	je devrai, tu devras, il/elle/on devra, nous devrons, vous devrez, ils/elles devront
Futur antérieur	j'aurai dû, tu auras dû, il/elle/on aura dû, nous aurons dû, vous aurez dû, ils/elles auront dû
Present conditional	je devrais, tu devrais, il/elle/on devrait, nous devrions, vous devriez, ils/elles devraient
Past conditional	j'aurais dû, tu aurais dû, il/elle/on aurait dû, nous aurions dû, vous auriez dû, ils/elles auraient dû
Present subjunctive	que je doive, que tu doives, qu'il/elle/on doive, que nous devions, que vous deviez, qu'ils/elles doivent
Past subjunctive	que j'aie dû, que tu aies dû, qu'il/elle/on ait dû, que nous ayons dû, que vous ayez dû, qu'ils/elles aient dû

Appendix C: French verb tables **571**

dire (*to say, tell*)

Present indicative	je dis, tu dis, il/elle/on dit, nous disons, vous dites, ils/elles disent
Imperative	dis, disons, dites
Passé composé	j'ai dit, tu as dit, il/elle/on a dit, nous avons dit, vous avez dit, ils/elles ont dit
Imperfect	je disais, tu disais, il/elle/on disait, nous disions, vous disiez, ils/elles disaient
Pluperfect	j'avais dit, tu avais dit, il/elle/on avait dit, nous avions dit, vous aviez dit, ils/elles avaient dit
Passé simple	je dis, tu dis, il/elle/on dit, nous dîmes, vous dîtes, ils/elles dirent
Future	je dirai, tu diras, il/elle/on dira, nous dirons, vous direz, ils/elles diront
Futur antérieur	j'aurai dit, tu auras dit, il/elle/on aura dit, nous aurons dit, vous aurez dit, ils/elles auront dit
Present conditional	je dirais, tu dirais, il/elle/on dirait, nous dirions, vous diriez, ils/elles diraient
Past conditional	j'aurais dit, tu aurais dit, il/elle/on aurait dit, nous aurions dit, vous auriez dit, ils/elles auraient dit
Present subjunctive	que je dise, que tu dises, qu'il/elle/on dise, que nous disions, que vous disiez, qu'ils/elles disent
Past subjunctive	que j'aie dit, que tu aies dit, qu'il/elle/on ait dit, que nous ayons dit, que vous ayez dit, qu'ils/elles aient dit

dormir (*to sleep*)

Present indicative	je dors, tu dors, il/elle/on dort, nous dormons, vous dormez, ils/elles dorment
Imperative	dors, dormons, dormez
Passé composé	j'ai dormi, tu as dormi, il/elle/on a dormi, nous avons dormi, vous avez dormi, ils/elles ont dormi
Imperfect	je dormais, tu dormais, il/elle/on dormait, nous dormions, vous dormiez, ils/elles dormaient
Pluperfect	j'avais dormi, tu avais dormi, il/elle/on avait dormi, nous avions dormi, vous aviez dormi, ils/elles avaient dormi
Passé simple	je dormis, tu dormis, il/elle/on dormit, nous dormîmes, vous dormîtes, ils/elles dormirent
Future	je dormirai, tu dormiras, il/elle/on dormira, nous dormirons, vous dormirez, ils/elles dormiront
Futur antérieur	j'aurai dormi, tu auras dormi, il/elle/on aura dormi, nous aurons dormi, vous aurez dormi, ils/elles auront dormi
Present conditional	je dormirais, tu dormirais, il/elle/on dormirait, nous dormirions, vous dormiriez, ils/elles dormiraient
Past conditional	j'aurais dormi, tu aurais dormi, il/elle/on aurait dormi, nous aurions dormi, vous auriez dormi, ils/elles auraient dormi
Present subjunctive	que je dorme, que tu dormes, qu'il/elle/on dorme, que nous dormions, que vous dormiez, qu'ils/elles dorment
Past subjunctive	que j'aie dormi, que tu aies dormi, qu'il/elle/on ait dormi, que nous ayons dormi, que vous ayez dormi, qu'ils/elles aient dormi

écrire (*to write*)

Present indicative	j'écris, tu écris, il/elle/on écrit, nous écrivons, vous écrivez, ils/elles écrivent
Imperative	écris, écrivons, écrivez
Passé composé	j'ai écrit, tu as écrit, il/elle/on a écrit, nous avons écrit, vous avez écrit, ils/elles ont écrit

Imperfect	j'écrivais, tu écrivais, il/elle/on écrivait, nous écrivions, vous écriviez, ils/elles écrivaient
Pluperfect	j'avais écrit, tu avais écrit, il/elle/on avait écrit, nous avions écrit, vous aviez écrit, ils/elles avaient écrit
Passé simple	j'écrivis, tu écrivis, il/elle/on écrivit, nous écrivîmes, vous écrivîtes, ils/elles écrivirent
Future	j'écrirai, tu écriras, il/elle/on écrira, nous écrirons, vous écrirez, ils/elles écriront
Futur antérieur	j'aurai écrit, tu auras écrit, il/elle/on aura écrit, nous aurons écrit, vous aurez écrit, ils/elles auront écrit
Present conditional	j'écrirais, tu écrirais, il/elle/on écrirait, nous écririons, vous écririez, ils/elles écriraient
Past conditional	j'aurais écrit, tu aurais écrit, il/elle/on aurait écrit, nous aurions écrit, vous auriez écrit, ils/elles auraient écrit
Present subjunctive	que j'écrive, que tu écrives, qu'il/elle/on écrive, que nous écrivions, que vous écriviez, qu'ils/elles écrivent
Past subjunctive	que j'aie écrit, que tu aies écrit, qu'il/elle/on ait écrit, que nous ayons écrit, que vous ayez écrit, qu'ils/elles aient écrit

Verbs conjugated like **écrire: décrire** (*to describe*)

être (*to be*)

Present indicative	je suis, tu es, il/elle/on est, nous sommes, vous êtes, ils/elles sont
Imperative	sois, soyons, soyez
Passé composé	j'ai été, tu as été, il/elle/on a été, nous avons été, vous avez été, ils/elles ont été
Imperfect	j'étais, tu étais, il/elle/on était, nous étions, vous étiez, ils/elles étaient
Pluperfect	j'avais été, tu avais été, il/elle/on avait été, nous avions été, vous aviez été, ils/elles avaient été
Passé simple	je fus, tu fus, il/elle/on fut, nous fûmes, vous fûtes, ils/elles furent
Future	je serai, tu seras, il/elle/on sera, nous serons, vous serez, ils/elles seront
Futur antérieur	j'aurai été, tu auras été, il/elle/on aura été, nous aurons été, vous aurez été, ils/elles auront été
Present conditional	je serais, tu serais, il/elle/on serait, nous serions, vous seriez, ils/elles seraient
Past conditional	j'aurais été, tu aurais été, il/elle/on aurait été, nous aurions été, vous auriez été, ils/elles auraient été
Present subjunctive	que je sois, que tu sois, qu'il/elle/on soit, que nous soyons, que vous soyez, qu'ils/elles soient
Past subjunctive	que j'aie été, que tu aies été, qu'il/elle/on ait été, que nous ayons été, que vous ayez été, qu'ils/elles aient été

faire (*to do, make*)

Present indicative	je fais, tu fais, il/elle/on fait, nous faisons, vous faites, ils/elles font
Imperative	fais, faisons, faites
Passé composé	j'ai fait, tu as fait, il/elle/on a fait, nous avons fait, vous avez fait, ils/elles ont fait
Imperfect	je faisais, tu faisais, il/elle/on faisait, nous faisions, vous faisiez, ils/elles faisaient
Pluperfect	j'avais fait, tu avais fait, il/elle/on avait fait, nous avions fait, vous aviez fait, ils/elles avaient fait
Passé simple	je fis, tu fis, il/elle/on fit, nous fîmes, vous fîtes, ils/elles firent
Future	je ferai, tu feras, il/elle/on fera, nous ferons, vous ferez, ils/elles feront

Futur antérieur	j'aurai fait, tu auras fait, il/elle/on aura fait, nous aurons fait, vous aurez fait, ils/elles auront fait
Present conditional	je ferais, tu ferais, il/elle/on ferait, nous ferions, vous feriez, ils/elles feraient
Past conditional	j'aurais fait, tu aurais fait, il/elle/on aurait fait, nous aurions fait, vous auriez fait, ils/elles auraient fait
Present subjunctive	que je fasse, que tu fasses, qu'il/elle/on fasse, que nous fassions, que vous fassiez, qu'ils/elles fassent
Past subjunctive	que j'aie fait, que tu aies fait, qu'il/elle/on ait fait, que nous ayons fait, que vous ayez fait, qu'ils/elles aient fait

falloir (*to be necessary*)

Present indicative	il faut
Passé composé	il a fallu
Imperfect	il fallait
Pluperfect	il avait fallu
Passé simple	il fallut
Future	il faudra
Futur antérieur	il aura fallu
Present conditional	il faudrait
Past conditional	il aurait fallu
Present subjunctive	qu'il faille
Past subjunctive	qu'il ait fallu

lire (*to read*)

Present indicative	je lis, tu lis, il/elle/on lit, nous lisons, vous lisez, ils/elles lisent
Imperative	lis, lisons, lisez
Passé composé	j'ai lu, tu as lu, il/elle/on a lu, nous avons lu, vous avez lu, ils/elles ont lu
Imperfect	je lisais, tu lisais, il/elle/on lisait, nous lisions, vous lisiez, ils/elles lisaient
Pluperfect	j'avais lu, tu avais lu, il/elle/on avait lu, nous avions lu, vous aviez lu, ils/elles avaient lu
Passé simple	je lus, tu lus, il/elle/on lut, nous lûmes, vous lûtes, ils/elles lurent
Future	je lirai, lu liras, il/elle/on lira, nous lirons, vos lirez, ils/elles liront
Futur antérieur	j'aurai lu, tu auras lu, il/elle/on aura lu, nous aurons lu, vous aurez lu, ils/elles auront lu
Present conditional	je lirais, tu lirais, il/elle/on lirait, nous lirions, vous liriez, ils/elles liraient
Past conditional	j'aurais lu, tu aurais lu, il/elle/on aurait lu, nous aurions lu, vous auriez lu, ils/elles auraient lu
Present subjunctive	que je lise, que tu lises, qu'il/elle/on lise, que nous lisions, que vous lisiez, qu'ils/elles lisent
Past subjunctive	que j'aie lu, que tu aies lu, qu'il/elle/on ait lu, que nous ayons lu, que vous ayez lu, qu'ils/elles aient lu

Verbs conjugated like **lire: élire** (*to elect*)

mentir (*to lie, tell a lie*)

Present indicative	je mens, tu mens, il/elle/on ment, nous mentons, vous mentez, ils/elles mentent
Imperative	mens, mentons, mentez
Passé composé	j'ai menti, tu as menti, il/elle/on a menti, nous avons menti, vous avez menti, ils/elles ont menti

Imperfect	je mentais, tu mentais, il/elle/on mentait, nous mentions, vous mentiez, ils/elles mentaient
Pluperfect	j'avais menti, tu avais menti, il/elle/on avait menti, nous avions menti, vous aviez menti, ils/elles avaient menti
Passé simple	je mentis, tu mentis, il/elle/on mentit, nous mentîmes, vous mentîtes, ils/elles mentirent
Future	je mentirai, tu mentiras, il/elle/on mentira, nous mentirons, vous mentirez, ils/elles mentiront
Futur antérieur	j'aurai menti, tu auras menti, il/elle/on aura menti, nous aurons menti, vous aurez menti, ils/elles auront menti
Present conditional	je mentirais, tu mentirais, il/elle/on mentirait, nous mentirions, vous mentiriez, ils/elles mentiraient
Past conditional	j'aurais menti, tu aurais menti, il/elle/on aurait menti, nous aurions menti, vous auriez menti, ils/elles auraient menti
Present subjunctive	que je mente, que tu mentes, qu'il/elle/on mente, que nous mentions, que vous mentiez, qu'ils/elles mentent
Past subjunctive	que j'aie menti, que tu aies menti, qu'il/elle/on ait menti, que nous ayons menti, que vous ayez menti, qu'ils/elles aient menti

mettre (*to put, to put on*)

Present indicative	je mets, tu mets, il/elle/on met, nous mettons, vous mettez, ils/elles mettent
Imperative	mets, mettons, mettez
Passé composé	j'ai mis, tu as mis, il/elle/on a mis, nous avons mis, vous avez mis, ils/elles ont mis
Imperfect	je mettais, tu mettais, il/elle/on mettait, nous mettions, vous mettiez, ils/elles mettaient
Pluperfect	j'avais mis, tu avais mis, il/elle/on avait mis, nous avions mis, vous aviez mis, ils/elles avaient mis
Passé simple	je mis, tu mis, il/elle/on mit, nous mîmes, vous mîtes, ils/elles mirent
Future	je mettrai, tu mettras, il/elle/on mettra, nous mettrons, vous mettrez, ils/elles mettront
Futur antérieur	j'aurai mis, tu auras mis, il/elle/on aura mis, nous aurons mis, vous aurez mis, ils/elles auront mis
Present conditional	je mettrais, tu mettrais, il/elle/on mettrait, nous mettrions, vous mettriez, ils/elles mettraient
Past conditional	j'aurais mis, tu aurais mis, il/elle/on aurait mis, nous aurions mis, vous auriez mis, ils/elles auraient mis
Present subjunctive	que je mette, que tu mettes, qu'il/elle/on mette, que nous mettions, que vous mettiez, qu'ils/elles mettent
Past subjunctive	que j'aie mis, que tu aies mis, qu'il/elle/on ait mis, que nous ayons mis, que vous ayez mis, qu'ils/elles aient mis

Verbs conjugated like **mettre: admettre** (*to admit*), **commettre** (*to commit*), **permettre** (*to allow*), **promettre** (*to promise*), **remettre** (*to put back*)

mourir (*to die*)

Present indicative	je meurs, tu meurs, il/elle/on meurt, nous mourons, vous mourez, ils/elles meurent
Imperative	meurs, mourons, mourez
Passé composé	je suis mort(e), tu es mort(e), il/elle/on est mort(e), nous sommes mort(e)s, vous êtes mort(e)(s), ils/elles sont mort(e)s
Imperfect	je mourais, tu mourais, il/elle/on mourait, nous mourions, vous mouriez, ils/elles mouraient

Appendix C: French verb tables **575**

Pluperfect	j'étais mort(e), tu étais mort(e), il/elle/on était mort(e), nous étions mort(e)s, vous étiez mort(e)(s), ils/elles étaient mort(e)s
Passé simple	je mourus, tu mourus, il/elle/on mourut, nous mourûmes, vous mourûtes, ils/elles moururent
Future	je mourrai, tu mourras, il/elle/on mourra, nous mourrons, vous mourrez, ils/elles mourront
Futur antérieur	je serai mort(e), tu seras mort(e), il/elle/on sera mort(e), nous serons mort(e)s, vous serez mort(e)(s), ils/elles seront mort(e)s
Present conditional	je mourrais, tu mourrais, il/elle/on mourrait, nous mourrions, vous mourriez, ils/elles mourraient
Past conditional	je serais mort(e), tu serais mort(e), il/elle/on serait mort(e), nous serions mort(e)s, vous seriez mort(e)(s), ils/elles seraient mort(e)s
Present subjunctive	que je meure, que tu meures, qu'il/elle/on meure, que nous mourions, que vous mouriez, qu'ils/elles meurent
Past subjunctive	que je sois mort(e), que tu sois mort(e), qu'il/elle/on soit mort(e), que nous soyons mort(e)s, que vous soyez mort(e)(s), qu'ils/elles soient mort(e)s

naître (*to be born*)

Present indicative	je nais, tu nais, il/elle/on naît, nous naissons, vous naissez, ils/elles naissent
Imperative	nais, naissons, naissez
Passé composé	je suis né(e), tu es né(e), il/elle/on est né(e), nous sommes né(e)s, vous êtes né(e)(s), ils/elles sont né(e)s
Imperfect	je naissais, tu naissais, il/elle/on naissait, nous naissions, vous naissiez, ils/elles naissaient
Pluperfect	j'étais né(e), tu étais né(e), il/elle/on était né(e), nous étions né(e)s, vous étiez né(e)(s), ils/elles étaient né(e)s
Passé simple	je naquis, tu naquis, il/elle/on naquit, nous naquîmes, vous naquîtes, ils/elles naquirent
Future	je naîtrai, tu naîtras, il/elle/on naîtra, nous naîtrons, vous naîtrez, ils/elles naîtront
Futur antérieur	je serai né(e), tu seras né(e), il/elle/on sera né(e), nous serons né(e)s, vous serez né(e)(s), ils/elles seront né(e)s
Present conditional	je naîtrais, tu naîtrais, il/elle/on naîtrait, nous naîtrions, vous naîtriez, ils/elles naîtraient
Past conditional	je serais né(e), tu serais né(e), il/elle/on serait né(e), nous serions né(e)s, vous seriez né(e)(s), ils/elles seraient né(e)s
Present subjunctive	que je naisse, que tu naisses, qu'il/elle/on naisse, que nous naissions, que vous naissiez, qu'ils/elles naissent
Past subjunctive	que je sois né(e), que tu sois né(e), qu'il/elle/on soit né(e), que nous soyons né(e)s, que vous soyez né(e)(s), qu'ils/elles soient né(e)s

ouvrir (*to open*)

Present indicative	j'ouvre, tu ouvres, il/elle/on ouvre, nous ouvrons, vous ouvrez, ils/elles ouvrent
Imperative	ouvre, ouvrons, ouvrez
Passé composé	j'ai ouvert, tu as ouvert, il/elle/on a ouvert, nous avons ouvert, vous avez ouvert, ils/elles ont ouvert
Imperfect	j'ouvrais, tu ouvrais, il/elle/on ouvrait, nous ouvrions, vous ouvriez, ils/elles ouvraient
Pluperfect	j'avais ouvert, tu avais ouvert, il/elle/on avait ouvert, nous avions ouvert, vous aviez ouvert, ils/elles avaient ouvert

Passé simple	j'ouvris, tu ouvris, il/elle/on ouvrit, nous ouvrîmes, vous ouvrîtes, ils/elles ouvrirent
Future	j'ouvrirai, tu ouvriras, il/elle/on ouvrira, nous ouvrirons, vous ouvrirez, ils/elles ouvriront
Futur antérieur	j'aurai ouvert, tu auras ouvert, il/elle/on aura ouvert, nous aurons ouvert, vous aurez ouvert, ils/elles auront ouvert
Present conditional	j'ouvrirais, tu ouvrirais, il/elle/on ouvrirait, nous ouvririons, vous ouvririez, ils/elles ouvriraient
Past conditional	j'aurais ouvert, tu aurais ouvert, il/elle/on aurait ouvert, nous aurions ouvert, vous auriez ouvert, ils/elles auraient ouvert
Present subjunctive	que j'ouvre, que tu ouvres, qu'il/elle/on ouvre, que nous ouvrions, que vous ouvriez, qu'ils/elles ouvrent
Past subjunctive	que j'aie ouvert, que tu aies ouvert, qu'il/elle/on ait ouvert, que nous ayons ouvert, que vous ayez ouvert, qu'ils/elles aient ouvert

Verbs conjugated like **ouvrir: couvrir** (*to cover*), **découvrir** (*to discover*), **offrir** (*to offer*), **souffrir** (*to suffer*)

partir (*to leave*)

Present indicative	je pars, tu pars, il/elle/on part, nous partons, vous partez, ils/elles partent
Imperative	pars, partons, partez
Passé composé	je suis parti(e), tu es parti(e), il/elle/on est parti(e), nous sommes parti(e)s, vous êtes parti(e)(s), ils/elles sont parti(e)s
Imperfect	je partais, tu partais, il/elle/on partait, nous partions, vous partiez, ils/elles partaient
Pluperfect	j'étais parti(e), tu étais parti(e), il/elle/on était parti(e), nous étions parti(e)s, vous étiez parti(e)(s), ils/elles étaient parti(e)s
Passé simple	je partis, tu partis, il/elle/on partit, nous partîmes, vous partîtes, ils/elles partirent
Future	je partirai, tu partiras, il/elle/on partira, nous partirons, vous partirez, ils/elles partiront
Futur antérieur	je serai parti(e), tu seras parti(e), il/elle/on sera parti(e), nous serons parti(e)s, vous serez parti(e)(s), ils/elles seront parti(e)s
Present conditional	je partirais, tu partirais, il/elle/on partirait, nous partirions, vous partiriez, ils/elles partiraient
Past conditional	je serais parti(e), tu serais parti(e), il/elle/on serait parti(e), nous serions parti(e)s, vous seriez parti(e)(s), ils/elles seraient parti(e)s
Present subjunctive	que je parte, que tu partes, qu'il/elle/on parte, que nous partions, que vous partiez, qu'ils/elles partent
Past subjunctive	que je sois parti(e), que tu sois parti(e), qu'il/elle/on soit parti(e), que nous soyons parti(e)s, que vous soyez parti(e)(s), qu'ils/elles soient parti(e)s

Verbs conjugated like **partir: sortir** (*to go out*)

peindre (*to paint*)

Present indicative	je peins, tu peins, il/elle/on peint, nous peignons, vous peignez, ils/elles peignent
Imperative	peins, peignons, peignez
Passé composé	j'ai peint, tu as peint, il/elle/on a peint, nous avons peint, vous avez peint, ils/elles ont peint
Imperfect	je peignais, tu peignais, il/elle/on peignait, nous peignions, vous peigniez, ils/elles peignaient

Appendix C: French verb tables **577**

Pluperfect	j'avais peint, tu avais peint, il/elle/on avait peint, nous avions peint, vous aviez peint, ils/elles avaient peint
Passé simple	je peignis, tu peignis, il/elle/on peignit, nous peignîmes, vous peignîtes, ils/elles peignirent
Future	je peindrai, tu peindras, il/elle/on peindra, nous peindrons, vous peindrez, ils/elles peindront
Futur antérieur	j'aurai peint, tu auras peint, il/elle/on aura peint, nous aurons peint, vous aurez peint, ils/elles auront peint
Present conditional	je peindrais, tu peindrais, il/elle/on peindrait, nous peindrions, vous peindriez, ils/elles peindraient
Past conditional	j'aurais peint, tu aurais peint, il/elle/on aurait peint, nous aurions peint, vous auriez peint, ils/elles auraient peint
Present subjunctive	que je peigne, que tu peignes, qu'il/elle/on peigne, que nous peignions, que vous peigniez, qu'ils/elles peignent
Past subjunctive	que j'aie peint, que tu aies peint, qu'il/elle/on ait peint, que nous ayons peint, que vous ayez peint, qu'ils/elles aient peint

Verbs conjugated like **peindre: atteindre** (*to reach, attain*), **éteindre** (*to switch off*)

plaire (*to please*)

Present indicative	je plais, tu plais, il/elle/on plaît, nous plaisons, vous plaisez, ils/elles plaisent
Imperative	plais, plaisons, plaisez
Passé composé	j'ai plu, tu as plu, il/elle/on a plu, nous avons plu, vous avez plu, ils/elles ont plu
Imperfect	je plaisais, tu plaisais, il/elle/on plaisait, nous plaisions, vous plaisiez, ils/elles plaisaient
Pluperfect	j'avais plu, tu avais plu, il/elle/on avait plu, nous avions plu, vous aviez plu, ils/elles avaient plu
Passé simple	je plus, tu plus, il/elle/on plut, nous plûmes, vous plûtes, ils/elles plurent
Future	je plairai, tu plairas, il/elle/on plaira, nous plairons, vous plairez, ils/elles plairont
Futur antérieur	j'aurai plu, tu auras plu, il/elle/on aura plu, nous aurons plu, vous aurez plu, ils/elles auront plu
Present conditional	je plairais, tu plairais, il/elle/on plairait, nous plairions, vous plairiez, ils/elles plairaient
Past conditional	j'aurais plu, tu aurais plu, il/elle/on aurait plu, nous aurions plu, vous auriez plu, ils/elles auraient plu
Present subjunctive	que je plaise, que tu plaises, qu'il/elle/on plaise, que nous plaisions, que vous plaisiez, qu'ils/elles plaisent
Past subjunctive	que j'aie plu, que tu aies plu, qu'il/elle/on ait plu, que nous ayons plu, que vous ayez plu, qu'ils/elles aient plu

pleuvoir (*to rain*)

Present indicative	il pleut
Passé composé	il a plu
Imperfect	il pleuvait
Pluperfect	il avait plu
Passé simple	il plut
Future	il pleuvra
Futur antérieur	il aura plu

578 Appendix C: French verb tables

Present conditional	il pleuvrait
Past conditional	il aurait plu
Present subjunctive	qu'il pleuve
Past subjunctive	qu'il ait plu

pouvoir (*can, to be able to*)

Present indicative	je peux *or* je puis, tu peux, il/elle/on peut, nous pouvons, vous pouvez, ils/elles peuvent
Passé composé	j'ai pu, tu as pu, il/elle/on a pu, nous avons pu, vous avez pu, ils/elles ont pu
Imperfect	je pouvais, tu pouvais, il/elle/on pouvait, nous pouvions, vous pouviez, ils/elles pouvaient
Pluperfect	j'avais pu, tu avais pu, il/elle/on avait pu, nous avions pu, vous aviez pu, ils/elles avaient pu
Passé simple	je pus, tu pus, il/elle/on put, nous pûmes, vous pûtes, ils/elles purent
Future	je pourrai, tu pourras, il/elle/on pourra, nous pourrons, vous pourrez, ils/elles pourront
Futur antérieur	j'aurai pu, tu auras pu, il/elle/on aura pu, nous aurons pu, vous aurez pu, ils/elles auront pu
Present conditional	je pourrais, tu pourrais, il/elle/on pourrait, nous pourrions, vous pourriez, ils/elles pourraient
Past conditional	j'aurais pu, tu aurais pu, il/elle/on aurait pu, nous aurions pu, vous auriez pu, ils/elles auraient pu
Present subjunctive	que je puisse, que tu puisses, qu'il/elle/on puisse, que nous puissions, que vous puissiez, qu'ils/elles puissent
Past subjunctive	que j'aie pu, que tu aies pu, qu'il/elle/on ait pu, que nous ayons pu, que vous ayez pu, qu'ils/elles aient pu

prendre (*to take*)

Present indicative	je prends, tu prends, il/elle/on prend, nous prenons, vous prenez, ils/elles prennent
Imperative	prends, prenons, prenez
Passé composé	j'ai pris, tu as pris, il/elle/on a pris, nous avons pris, vous avez pris, ils/elles ont pris
Imperfect	je prenais, tu prenais, il/elle/on prenait, nous prenions, vous preniez, ils/elles prenaient
Pluperfect	j'avais pris, tu avais pris, il/elle/on avait pris, nous avions pris, vous aviez pris, ils/elles avaient pris
Passé simple	je pris, tu pris, il/elle/on prit, nous prîmes, vous prîtes, il/elles prirent
Future	je prendrai, tu prendras, il/elle/on prendra, nous prendrons, vous prendrez, ils/elles prendront
Futur antérieur	j'aurai pris, tu auras pris, il/elle/on aura pris, nous aurons pris, vous aurez pris, ils/elles auront pris
Present conditional	je prendrais, tu prendrais, il/elle/on prendrait, nous prendrions, vous prendriez, ils/elles prendraient
Past conditional	j'aurais pris, tu aurais pris, il/elle/on aurait pris, nous aurions pris, vous auriez pris, ils/elles auraient pris
Present subjunctive	que je prenne, que tu prennes, qu'il/elle/on prenne, que nous prenions, que vous preniez, qu'ils/elles prennent
Past subjunctive	que j'aie pris, que tu aies pris, qu'il/elle/on ait pris, que nous ayons pris, que vous ayez pris, qu'ils/elles aient pris

Appendix C: French verb tables **579**

Verbs conjugated like **prendre: apprendre** (*to learn*), **comprendre** (*to understand*), **surprendre** (*to surprise*)

recevoir (*to receive*)

Present indicative	je reçois, tu reçois, il/elle/on reçoit, nous recevons, vous recevez, ils/elles reçoivent
Imperative	reçois, recevons, recevez
Passé composé	j'ai reçu, tu as reçu, il/elle/on a reçu, nous avons reçu, vous avez reçu, ils/elles ont reçu
Imperfect	je recevais, tu recevais, il/elle/on recevait, nous recevions, vous receviez, ils/elles recevaient
Pluperfect	j'avais reçu, tu avais reçu, il/elle/on avait reçu, nous avions reçu, vous aviez reçu, ils/elles avaient reçu
Passé simple	je reçus, tu reçus, il/elle/on reçut, nous reçûmes, vous reçûtes, ils/elles reçurent
Future	je recevrai, tu recevras, il/elle/on recevra, nous recevrons, vous recevrez, ils/elles recevront
Futur antérieur	j'aurai reçu, tu auras reçu, il/elle/on aura reçu, nous aurons reçu, vous aurez reçu, ils/elles auront reçu
Present conditional	je recevrais, tu recevrais, il/elle/on recevrait, nous recevrions, vous recevriez, ils/elles recevraient
Past conditional	j'aurais reçu, tu aurais reçu, il/elle/on aurait reçu, nous aurions reçu, vous auriez reçu, ils/elles auraient reçu
Present subjunctive	que je reçoive, que tu reçoives, qu'il/elle/on reçoive, que nous recevions, que vous receviez, qu'ils/elles reçoivent
Past subjunctive	que j'aie reçu, que tu aies reçu, qu'il/elle/on ait reçu, que nous ayons reçu, que vous ayez reçu, qu'ils/elles aient reçu

Verbs conjugated like **recevoir: apercevoir** (*to perceive*), **décevoir** (*to disappoint*)

rire (*to laugh*)

Present indicative	je ris, tu ris, il/elle/on rit, nous rions, vous riez, ils/elles rient
Imperative	ris, rions, riez
Passé composé	j'ai ri, tu as ri, il/elle/on a ri, nous avons ri, vous avez ri, ils/elles ont ri
Imperfect	je riais, tu riais, il/elle/on riait, nous riions, vous riiez, ils/elles riaient
Pluperfect	j'avais ri, tu avais ri, il/elle/on avait ri, nous avions ri, vous aviez ri, ils/elles avaient ri
Passé simple	je ris, tu ris, il/elle/on rit, nous rîmes, vous rîtes, ils/elles rirent
Future	je rirai, tu riras, il/elle/on rira, nous rirons, vous rirez, ils/elles riront
Futur antérieur	j'aurai ri, tu auras ri, il/elle/on aura ri, nous aurons ri, vous aurez ri, ils/elles auront ri
Present conditional	je rirais, tu rirais, il/elle/on rirait, nous ririons, vous ririez, ils/elles riraient
Past conditional	j'aurais ri, tu aurais ri, il/elle/on aurait ri, nous aurions ri, vous auriez ri, ils/elles auraient ri
Present subjunctive	que je rie, que tu ries, qu'il/elle/on rie, que nous riions, que vous riiez, qu'ils/elles rient
Past subjunctive	que j'aie ri, que tu aies ri, qu'il/elle/on ait ri, que nous ayons ri, que vous ayez ri, qu'ils/elles aient ri

Verbs conjugated like **rire: sourire** (*to smile*)

savoir (*to know*)

Present indicative	je sais, tu sais, il/elle/on sait, nous savons, vous savez, ils/elles savent
Imperative	sache, sachons, sachez
Passé composé	j'ai su, tu as su, il/elle/on a su, nous avons su, vous avez su, ils/elles ont su
Imperfect	je savais, tu savais, il/elle/on savait, nous savions, vous saviez, ils/elles savaient
Pluperfect	j'avais su, tu avais su, il/elle/on avait su, nous avions su, vous aviez su, ils/elles avaient su
Passé simple	je sus, tu sus, il/elle/on sut, nous sûmes, vous sûtes, ils/elles surent
Future	je saurai, tu sauras, il/elle/on saura, nous saurons, vous saurez, ils/elles sauront
Futur antérieur	j'aurai su, tu auras su, il/elle/on aura su, nous aurons su, vous aurez su, ils/elles auront su
Present conditional	je saurais, tu saurais, il/elle/on saurait, nous saurions, vous sauriez, ils/elles sauraient
Past conditional	j'aurais su, tu aurais su, il/elle/on aurait su, nous aurions su, vous auriez su, ils/elles auraient su
Present subjunctive	que je sache, que tu saches, qu'il/elle/on sache, que nous sachions, que vous sachiez, qu'ils/elles sachent
Past subjunctive	que j'aie su, que tu aies su, qu'il/elle/on ait su, que nous ayons su, que vous ayez su, qu'ils/elles aient su

sentir (*to feel, to smell*)

Present indicative	je sens, tu sens, il/elle/on sent, nous sentons, vous sentez, ils/elles sentent
Imperative	sens, sentons, sentez
Passé composé	j'ai senti, tu as senti, il/elle/on a senti, nous avons senti, vous avez senti, ils/elles ont senti
Imperfect	je sentais, tu sentais, il/elle/on sentait, nous sentions, vous sentiez, ils/elles sentaient
Pluperfect	j'avais senti, tu avais senti, il/elle/on avait senti, nous avions senti, vous aviez senti, ils/elles avaient senti
Passé simple	je sentis, tu sentis, il/elle/on sentit, nous sentîmes, vous sentîtes, ils/elles sentirent
Future	je sentirai, tu sentiras, il/elle/on sentira, nous sentirons, vous sentirez, ils/elles sentiront
Futur antérieur	j'aurai senti, tu auras senti, il/elle/on aura senti, nous aurons senti, vous aurez senti, ils/elles auront senti
Present conditional	je sentirais, tu sentirais, il/elle/on sentirait, nous sentirions, vous sentiriez, ils/elles sentiraient
Past conditional	j'aurais senti, tu aurais senti, il/elle/on aurait senti, nous aurions senti, vous auriez senti, ils/elles auraient senti
Present subjunctive	que je sente, que tu sentes, qu'il/elle/on sente, que nous sentions, que vous sentiez, qu'ils/elles sentent
Past subjunctive	que j'aie senti, que tu aies senti, qu'il/elle/on ait senti, que nous ayons senti, que vous ayez senti, qu'ils/elles aient senti

servir (*to serve*)

Present indicative	je sers, tu sers, il/elle/on sert, nous servons, vous servez, ils/elles servent
Imperative	sers, servons, servez

Appendix C: French verb tables **581**

Passé composé	j'ai servi, tu as servi, il/elle/on a servi, nous avons servi, vous avez servi, ils/elles ont servi
Imperfect	je servais, tu servais, il/elle/on servait, nous servions, vous serviez, ils/elles servaient
Pluperfect	j'avais servi, tu avais servi, il/elle/on avait servi, nous avions servi, vous aviez servi, ils/elles avaient servi
Passé simple	je servis, tu servis, il/elle/on servit, nous servîmes, vous servîtes, ils/elles servirent
Future	je servirai, tu serviras, il/elle/on servira, nous servirons, vous servirez, ils/elles serviront
Futur antérieur	j'aurai servi, tu auras servi, il/elle/on aura servi, nous aurons servi, vous aurez servi, ils/elles auront servi
Present conditional	je servirais, tu servirais, il/elle/on servirait, nous servirions, vous serviriez, ils/elles serviraient
Past conditional	j'aurais servi, tu aurais servi, il/elle/on aurait servi, nous aurions servi, vous auriez servi, ils/elles auraient servi
Present subjunctive	que je serve, que tu serves, qu'il/elle/on serve, que nous servions, que vous serviez, qu'ils/elles servent
Past subjunctive	que j'aie servi, que tu aies servi, qu'il/elle/on ait servi, que nous ayons servi, que vous ayez servi, qu'ils/elles aient servi

suivre (*to follow, to take [a class]*)

Present indicative	je suis, tu suis, il/elle/on suit, nous suivons, vous suivez, ils/elles suivent
Imperative	suis, suivons, suivez
Passé composé	j'ai suivi, tu as suivi, il/elle/on a suivi, nous avons suivi, vous avez suivi, ils/elles ont suivi
Imperfect	je suivais, tu suivais, il/elle/on suivait, nous suivions, vous suiviez, ils/elles suivaient
Pluperfect	j'avais suivi, tu avais suivi, il/elle/on avait suivi, nous avions suivi, vous aviez suivi, ils/elles avaient suivi
Passé simple	je suivis, tu suivis, il/elle/on suivit, nous suivîmes, vous suivîtes, ils/elles suivirent
Future	je suivrai, tu suivras, il/elle/on suivra, nous suivrons, vous suivrez, ils/elles suivront
Futur antérieur	j'aurai suivi, tu auras suivi, il/elle/on aura suivi, nous aurons suivi, vous aurez suivi, ils/elles auront suivi
Present conditional	je suivrais, tu suivrais, il/elle/on suivrait, nous suivrions, vous suivriez, ils/elles suivraient
Past conditional	j'aurais suivi, tu aurais suivi, il/elle/on aurait suivi, nous aurions suivi, vous auriez suivi, ils/elles auraient suivi
Present subjunctive	que je suive, que tu suives, qu'il/elle/on suive, que nous suivions, que vous suiviez, qu'ils/elles suivent
Past subjunctive	que j'aie suivi, que tu aies suivi, qu'il/elle/on ait suivi, que nous ayons suivi, que vous ayez suivi, qu'ils/elles aient suivi

tenir (*to hold*)

Present indicative	je tiens, tu tiens, il/elle/on tient, nous tenons, vous tenez, ils/elles tiennent
Imperative	tiens, tenons, tenez
Passé composé	j'ai tenu, tu as tenu, il/elle/on a tenu, nous avons tenu, vous avez tenu, ils/elles ont tenu
Imperfect	je tenais, tu tenais, il/elle/on tenait, nous tenions, vous teniez, ils/elles tenaient

Pluperfect	j'avais tenu, tu avais tenu, il/elle/on avait tenu, nous avions tenu, vous aviez tenu, ils/elles avaient tenu
Passé simple	je tins, tu tins, il/elle/on tint, nous tînmes, vous tîntes, ils/elles tinrent
Future	je tiendrai, tu tiendras, il/elle/on tiendra, nous tiendrons, vous tiendrez, ils/elles tiendront
Futur antérieur	j'aurai tenu, tu auras tenu, il/elle/on aura tenu, nous aurons tenu, vous aurez tenu, ils/elles auront tenu
Present conditional	je tiendrais, tu tiendrais, il/elle/on tiendrait, nous tiendrions, vous tiendriez, ils/elles tiendraient
Past conditional	j'aurais tenu, tu aurais tenu, il/elle/on aurait tenu, nous aurions tenu, vous auriez tenu, ils/elles auraient tenu
Present subjunctive	que je tienne, que tu tiennes, qu'il/elle/on tienne, que nous tenions, que vous teniez, qu'ils/elles tiennent
Past subjunctive	que j'aie tenu, que tu aies tenu, qu'il/elle/on ait tenu, que nous ayons tenu, que vous ayez tenu, qu'ils/elles aient tenu

valoir (*to be worth*)

Present indicative	je vaux, tu vaux, il/elle/on vaut, nous valons, vous valez, ils/elles valent
Imperative	vaux, valons, valez
Passé composé	j'ai valu, tu as valu, il/elle/on a valu, nous avons valu, vous avez valu, ils/elles ont valu
Imperfect	je valais, tu valais, il/elle/on valait, nous valions, vous valiez, ils/elles valaient
Pluperfect	j'avais valu, tu avais valu, il/elle/on avait valu, nous avions valu, vous aviez valu, ils/elles avaient valu
Passé simple	je valus, tu valus, il/elle/on valut, nous valûmes, vous valûtes, ils/elles valurent
Future	je vaudrai, tu vaudras, il/elle/on vaudra, nous vaudrons, vous vaudrez, ils/elles vaudront
Futur antérieur	j'aurai valu, tu auras valu, il/elle/on aura valu, nous aurons valu, vous aurez valu, ils/elles auront valu
Present conditional	je vaudrais, tu vaudrais, il/elle/on vaudrait, nous vaudrions, vous vaudriez, ils/elles vaudraient
Past conditional	j'aurais valu, tu aurais valu, il/elle/on aurait valu, nous aurions valu, vous auriez valu, ils/elles auraient valu
Present subjunctive	que je vaille, que tu vailles, qu'il/elle/on vaille, que nous valions, que vous valiez, qu'ils/elles vaillent
Past subjunctive	que j'aie valu, que tu aies valu, qu'il/elle/on ait valu, que nous ayons valu, que vous ayez valu, qu'ils/elles aient valu

venir (*to come*)

Present indicative	je viens, tu viens, il/elle/on vient, nous venons, vous venez, ils/elles viennent
Imperative	viens, venons, venez
Passé composé	je suis venu(e), tu es venu(e), il/elle/on est venu(e), nous sommes venu(e)s, vous êtes venu(e)(s), ils/elles sont venu(e)s
Imperfect	je venais, tu venais, il/elle/on venait, nous venions, vous veniez, ils/elles venaient
Pluperfect	j'étais venu(e), tu étais venu(e), il/elle/on était venu(e), nous étions venu(e)s, vous étiez venu(e)(s), ils/elles étaient venu(e)s
Passé simple	je vins, tu vins, il/elle/on vint, nous vînmes, vous vîntes, ils/elles vinrent
Future	je viendrai, tu viendras, il/elle/on viendra, nous viendrons, vous viendrez, ils/elles viendront

Appendix C: French verb tables **583**

Futur antérieur	je serai venu(e), tu seras venu(e), il/elle/on sera venu(e), nous serons venu(e)s, vous serez venu(e)(s), ils/elles seront venu(e)s
Present conditional	je viendrais, tu viendrais, il/elle/on viendrait, nous viendrions, vous viendriez, ils/elles viendraient
Past conditional	je serais venu(e), tu serais venu(e), il/elle/on serait venu(e), nous serions venu(e)s, vous seriez venu(e)(s), ils/elles seraient venu(e)s
Present subjunctive	que je vienne, que tu viennes, qu'il/elle/on vienne, que nous venions, que vous veniez, qu'ils/elles viennent
Past subjunctive	que je sois venu(e), que tu sois venu(e), qu'il/elle/on soit venu(e), que nous soyons venu(e)s, que vous soyez venu(e)(s), qu'ils/elles soient venu(e)s

Verbs conjugated like **venir: devenir** (*to become*), **revenir** (*to come back*)

vivre (*to live*)

Present indicative	je vis, tu vis, il/elle/on vit, nous vivons, vous vivez, ils/elles vivent
Imperative	vis, vivons, vivez
Passé composé	j'ai vécu, tu as vécu, il/elle/on a vécu, nous avons vécu, vous avez vécu, ils/elles ont vécu
Imperfect	je vivais, tu vivais, il/elle/on vivait, nous vivions, vous viviez, ils/elles vivaient
Pluperfect	j'avais vécu, tu avais vécu, il/elle/on avait vécu, nous avions vécu, vous aviez vécu, ils/elles avaient vécu
Passé simple	je vécus, tu vécus, il/elle/on vécut, nous vécûmes, vous vécûtes, ils/elles vécurent
Future	je vivrai, tu vivras, il/elle/on vivra, nous vivrons, vous vivrez, ils/elles vivront
Futur antérieur	j'aurai vécu, tu auras vécu, il/elle/on aura vécu, nous aurons vécu, vous aurez vécu, ils/elles auront vécu
Present conditional	je vivrais, tu vivrais, il/elle/on vivrait, nous vivrions, vous vivriez, ils/elles vivraient
Past conditional	j'aurais vécu, tu aurais vécu, il/elle/on aurait vécu, nous aurions vécu, vous auriez vécu, ils/elles auraient vécu
Present subjunctive	que je vive, que tu vives, qu'il/elle/on vive, que nous vivions, que vous viviez, qu'ils/elles vivent
Past subjunctive	que j'aie vécu, que tu aies vécu, qu'il/elle/on ait vécu, que nous ayons vécu, que vous ayez vécu, qu'ils/elles aient vécu

Verbs conjugated like **vivre: survivre** (*to survive*)

voir (*to see*)

Present indicative	je vois, tu vois, il/elle/on voit, nous voyons, vous voyez, ils/elles voient
Imperative	vois, voyons, voyez
Passé composé	j'ai vu, tu as vu, il/elle/on a vu, nous avons vu, vous avez vu, ils/elles ont vu
Imperfect	je voyais, tu voyais, il/elle/on voyait, nous voyions, vous voyiez, ils/elles voyaient
Pluperfect	j'avais vu, tu avais vu, il/elle/on avait vu, nous avions vu, vous aviez vu, ils/elles avaient vu
Passé simple	je vis, tu vis, il/elle/on vit, nous vîmes, vous vîtes, ils/elles virent
Future	je verrai, tu verras, il/elle/on verra, nous verrons, vous verrez, ils/elles verront
Futur antérieur	j'aurai vu, tu auras vu, il/elle/on aura vu, nous aurons vu, vous aurez vu, ils/elles auront vu

Present conditional	je verrais, tu verrais, il/elle/on verrait, nous verrions, vous verriez, ils/elles verraient
Past conditional	j'aurais vu, tu aurais vu, il/elle/on aurait vu, nous aurions vu, vous auriez vu, ils/elles auraient vu
Present subjunctive	que je voie, que tu voies, qu'il/elle/on voie, que nous voyions, que vous voyiez, qu'ils/elles voient
Past subjunctive	que j'aie vu, que tu aies vu, qu'il/elle/on ait vu, que nous ayons vu, que vous ayez vu, qu'ils/elles aient vu

Verbs conjugated like **voir: revoir** (*to see again*)

vouloir (*to want*)

Present indicative	je veux, tu veux, il/elle/on veut, nous voulons, vous voulez, ils/elles veulent
Imperative	veuille, veuillons, veuillez
Passé composé	j'ai voulu, tu as voulu, il/elle/on a voulu, nous avons voulu, vous avez voulu, ils/elles ont voulu
Imperfect	je voulais, tu voulais, il/elle/on voulait, nous voulions, vous vouliez, ils/elles voulaient
Pluperfect	j'avais voulu, tu avais voulu, il/elle/on avait voulu, nous avions voulu, vous aviez voulu, ils/elles avaient voulu
Passé simple	je voulus, tu voulus, il/elle/on voulut, nous voulûmes, vous voulûtes, ils/elles voulurent
Future	je voudrai, tu voudras, il/elle/on voudra, nous voudrons, vous voudrez, ils/elles voudront
Futur antérieur	j'aurai voulu, tu auras voulu, il/elle/on aura voulu, nous aurons voulu, vous aurez voulu, ils/elles auront voulu
Present conditional	je voudrais, tu voudrais, il/elle/on voudrait, nous voudrions, vous voudriez, ils/elles voudraient
Past conditional	j'aurais voulu, tu aurais voulu, il/elle/on aurait voulu, nous aurions voulu, vous auriez voulu, ils/elles auraient voulu
Present subjunctive	que je veuille, que tu veuilles, qu'il/elle/on veuille, que nous voulions, que vous vouliez, qu'ils/elles veuillent
Past subjunctive	que j'aie voulu, que tu aies voulu, qu'il/elle/on ait voulu, que nous ayons voulu, que vous ayez voulu, qu'ils/elles aient voulu

Appendix C: French verb tables **585**

Appendix D
French-English / English-French glossary

An asterisk follows expressions of informal or colloquial French. Regular adjectives are listed in their masculine singular form.

French-English glossary

A

abdiquer to abdicate
accident *(m.)* accident
   accident de voiture car accident
achat *(m.)* purchase
acheter to buy
achever to finish
acteur *(m.)* actor
actrice *(f.)* actress
actuellement presently
addition *(f.)* bill (in a restaurant), check
admettre to admit
admirer to admire
adolescent *(m.),* **adolescente** *(f.)* teenager
adresse *(f.)* address
adulte *(m./f.)* adult
aéroport *(m.)* airport
affaires *(f.pl.)* personal effects, business
Afrique *(f.)* Africa
âge *(m.)* age
agent immobilier *(m.)* real-estate agent
agir to act
agrafeuse *(f.)* stapler
agréable pleasant
aider to help
aimer to like, love
   aimer mieux to prefer
alcool *(m.)* alcohol
Allemagne *(f.)* Germany
allemand *(m.)* German
aller to go
   aller chercher qch to get sth
   aller chercher qn to pick up sb
allumer to switch on
ambassade *(f.)* embassy
(s')améliorer to improve
amener to bring (a person)

Amérique *(f.)* America
ami *(m.),* **amie** *(f.)* friend
amoureux, amoureuse (de) in love (with)
amuser to amuse
   s'amuser to have a good time, have fun
an *(m.)* year
analphabète *(m./f.)* illiterate person
anglais *(m.)* English
Angleterre *(f.)* England
animal *(m.) (plur.:* **animaux***)* animal
   animal domestique pet
anniversaire *(m.)* birthday
annuler to cancel
anorak *(m.)* anorak
août August
apéritif *(m.)* before-dinner drink
appareil photo *(m.)* camera
appartement *(m.)* apartment
appartenir à to belong to
appeler to call
apporter to bring
apprenant *(m.),* **apprenant(e)** *(f.)* learner
apprendre to learn
après after
après-demain the day after tomorrow
après-midi *(m.)* afternoon
arbre *(m.)* tree
arc-en-ciel *(m.)* rainbow
argent *(m.)* money, silver
armée *(f.)* army
(s')arrêter to stop, arrest
arriver to arrive, happen
ascenseur *(m.)* elevator
Asie *(f.)* Asia
aspirateur *(m.)* vacuum cleaner
s'asseoir to sit down
assiette *(f.)* plate

587

assister à to attend
attendre to wait (for)
atterrir to land
attraper to catch
aujourd'hui today
aussitôt que as soon as
autobus *(m.)* bus
automne *(m.)* fall
autoroute *(f.)* freeway
autre other
autrefois formerly, in the past
Autriche *(f.)* Austria
avant (que) before
avec with
avenir *(m.)* future
avertissement *(m.)* warning
aveugle blind
avion *(m.)* airplane
avis *(m.)* opinion
   à mon/ton avis in my/your opinion
avocat *(m.),* **avocate** *(f.)* lawyer
avoir to have
   avoir besoin de to need
   avoir chaud to be hot (people)
   avoir envie de to feel like, want to
   avoir faim to be hungry
   avoir froid to be cold (people)
   avoir lieu to take place
   avoir mal (à) to have a pain (in)
   avoir mal au cœur to feel nauseated
   avoir peur to be afraid
   avoir raison to be right (people)
   avoir soif to be thirsty
   avoir tort to be wrong (people)
avril April

B

balayer to sweep
balle *(f.)* ball, bullet
banc *(m.)* bench
bande dessinée *(f.)* comic strip
bande sonore *(f.)* soundtrack
banque *(f.)* bank
barre *(f.)* bar *(candy)*
   barre de céréales granola bar
bataille *(f.)* battle
bateau *(m.)* ship
bâtir to build
   bâtir des châteaux en Espagne to build castles in the
     air
battre to beat
bavarder to chat
beau, bel, belle beautiful, handsome
beaucoup (de) a lot (of), many, much
bébé *(m.)* baby
Belgique *(f.)* Belgium
belle-mère *(f.)* mother-in-law

beurre *(m.)* butter
   beurre de cacahuètes peanut butter
bibliothèque *(f.)* library
biche *(f.)* doe
bicyclette *(f.)* bicycle
bien well
bien que although
bientôt soon
   à bientôt see you soon
bienvenue welcome
bière *(f.)* beer
billet *(m.)* ticket
bisou* *(m.)* kiss
blanc, blanche white
blessé *(adj.)* wounded, injured
blessé *(m.) (noun)* injured (person)
blesser to wound, injure
bleu blue
blouson *(m.)* jacket, windbreaker
boire to drink
bois *(m.)* wood
boisson *(f.)* drink, beverage
boîte *(f.)* box
bon, bonne good
bonbons *(m. pl.)* candy
bottes *(f.pl.)* boots
boucherie *(f.)* butcher shop
bougie *(f.)* candle
boulanger *(m.),* **boulangère** *(f.)* baker
boulangerie *(f.)* bakery
boum* *(f.)* party *(teenagers')*
bourse *(f.)* scholarship
bouteille *(f.)* bottle
boutique *(f.)* shop
bouton *(m.)* button
braqueur* *(m.)* robber
bras *(m.)* arm
Brésil *(m.)* Brazil
brosser to brush
   se brosser les dents to brush one's teeth
brouillard *(m.)* fog
bruit *(m.)* noise
brûler to burn
   brûler un feu rouge to run a red light
bûche *(f.)* **de Noël** Yule log *(traditional French Christmas*
   pastry in the shape of a log richly decorated with frosting)
bureau *(m.)* office, desk

C

ça (cela) that
   ça m'est égal it's all the same to me
cabine téléphonique *(f.)* phone booth
cadeau *(m.)* gift
café *(m.)* coffee, café
cahier *(m.)* notebook
calculatrice *(f.)* calculator
camarade *(m./f.)* **de chambre** roommate

cambrioler to burglarize
cambrioleur *(m.)*, **cambrioleuse** *(f.)* burglar
canapé *(m.)* sofa, couch
canard *(m.)* duck
    il fait un froid de canard* it is freezing cold
caniche *(m.)* poodle
car because
carotte *(f.)* carrot
carrefour *(m.)* intersection
carte *(f.)* menu, map
    carte de crédit credit card
    carte postale postcard
cauchemar *(m.)* nightmare
cave *(f.)* cellar
ce, cet, cette this, that
céder to yield
ceinture *(f.)* belt
    ceinture de sécurité safety belt, seat belt
cela (ça) that
célèbre famous
céleri *(m.)* celery
célibataire single
centre commercial *(m.)* shopping center, mall
c'est-à-dire that is to say
chair *(f.)* **de poule** goose bumps
chaise *(f.)* chair
chambre *(f.)* room, bedroom
chance *(f.)* luck
    bonne chance! good luck!
chanceux, chanceuse lucky
changer to change
    changer d'avis to change one's mind
chanson *(f.)* song
chanter to sing
chanteur *(m.)*, **chanteuse** *(f.)* singer
chapeau *(m.)* hat
chaque each, every
chasseur *(m.)* hunter
chat *(m.)*, **chatte** *(f.)* cat
château *(m.)* castle
chaud hot, warm
chaussettes *(f.pl.)* socks
chaussures *(f.pl.)* shoes
chemise *(f.)* shirt
cher, chère expensive, dear
chercher to look for
cheval *(m.)* *(plur.:* **chevaux***)* horse
cheveux *(m.pl.)* hair
chez at (to, in) the home of
chien *(m.)*, **chienne** *(f.)* dog
Chine *(f.)* China
chinois *(m.)* Chinese
chocolat *(m.)* chocolate
choisir to choose
choix *(m.)* choice
chômage *(m.)* unemployment
chose *(f.)* thing

chute *(f.)* fall, descent
ciel *(m.)* sky
cinéma *(m.)* movie theater, movies
circulation *(f.)* traffic
cirque *(m.)* circus
ciseaux *(m.pl.)* scissors
classe *(f.)* class
    en classe in, to class
clé *(f.)* key
client *(m.)*, **cliente** *(f.)* customer
climatisation *(f.)* air conditioning
clôture *(f.)* fence
coiffeur *(m.)*, **coiffeuse** *(f.)* hairdresser
colis *(m.)* package
colline *(f.)* hill
colocataire *(m./f.)* housemate
combien (de) how much, how many
comédie musicale *(f.)* musical
comique *(m./f.)* comedian
commander to order
commencer to begin
comment how
commode *(f.)* chest of drawers
comprendre to understand
compter to count, plan (on, to)
concert *(m.)* concert
conducteur *(m.)*, **conductrice** *(f.)* driver
conduire to drive
conférence *(f.)* lecture
confiture *(f.)* jam
congé *(m.)* vacation, time off work, leave
congrès *(m.)* conference
connaître to know
conseil *(m.)* (piece of) advice
conseiller to advise
conte *(m.)* story
    conte de fées fairy tale
content happy
contravention *(f.)* traffic ticket
convaincre to convince
coordonnées *(f.pl.)* address and phone number
copain *(m.)* friend, boyfriend
copine *(f.)* friend, girlfriend
corne *(f.)* horn *(animal)*
costume *(m.)* suit *(men's)*
côte *(f.)* coast
    Côte d'Azur French Riviera
côté *(m.)* side
se coucher to go to bed
coudre to sew
couleur *(f.)* color
Coupe *(f.)* **du monde** World Cup
courage *(m.)* courage
couramment fluently
courir to run
courriel *(m.)* e-mail

Appendix D: French-English / English-French glossary **589**

courrier *(m.)* mail
   courrier électronique e-mail
cours *(m.)* course, class
course *(f.)* errand, race
cousin *(m.)*, **cousine** *(f.)* cousin
coût *(m.)* cost
   coût de la vie cost of living
couteau *(m.)* knife
coûter to cost
   coûter les yeux de la tête* to cost an arm and a leg
couverture *(f.)* blanket
couvrir to cover
craindre to fear
cravate *(f.)* tie
crever* to die
croire to believe
cuiller (cuillère) *(f.)* spoon
cuisine *(f.)* kitchen, cooking, food
cuisiner to cook
cuisse *(f.)* **de grenouille** frog leg
curriculum vitae *(m.)* résumé, CV

D

d'abord at first
d'accord okay, O.K.
   être d'accord (avec) to agree (with)
dame *(f.)* lady, woman
dangereux, dangereuse dangerous
dans in
danser to dance
d'après according to
de from, of
début *(m.)* beginning
décembre December
déçu disappointed
défaite *(f.)* defeat
défendre to forbid
dehors outside
déjà already
déjeuner *(m.)* lunch
déjeuner to have lunch
demain tomorrow
demander to ask
déménager to move (change residence)
dent *(f.)* tooth
se dépêcher to hurry
dépenser to spend (*money*)
déposer (qn) to drop (sb) off
déprimé depressed
depuis since, for
déranger to disturb, bother
dernier, dernière last
derrière behind
dès que as soon as
descendre to go down, get out of (a vehicle)
désolé sorry
dessert *(m.)* dessert

dessin animé *(m.)* cartoon
se détendre to relax
détester to hate, detest
dette *(f.)* debt
devant in front of
devenir to become
deviner to guess
devoir *(verb)* to have to, must, owe
devoirs *(m.pl.)* homework
diable *(m.)* devil
Dieu God
difficile hard, difficult
dimanche *(m.)* Sunday
dîner *(m.)* dinner
dîner *(verb)* to have, eat dinner
diplôme *(m.)* diploma, (university) degree
dire to say
diseuse *(f.)* **de bonne aventure** fortune teller
se disputer to argue
dissertation *(f.)* term paper
doigt *(m.)* finger
dommage *(m.)* pity, shame
   c'est dommage that's too bad
donner to give
dormir to sleep
dos *(m.)* back
douane *(f.)* customs
douche *(f.)* shower
douter to doubt
drapeau *(m.)* flag
droit right
tout droit straight ahead
droite: à droite on (to) the right
drôle funny
dur hard
durer to last

E

eau *(f.)* water
échecs *(m.pl.)* chess
échouer to fail
   échouer à un (l') examen to fail an (the) exam
école *(f.)* school
Écosse *(f.)* Scotland
écouter to listen (to)
écrire to write
écrivain *(m.)* writer
église *(f.)* church
Égypte *(f.)* Egypt
électricité *(f.)* electricity
élève *(m./f.)* student, pupil (*primary and secondary school*)
email *(m.)* e-mail
embouteillage *(m.)* traffic jam
embrasser to hug, kiss
emmener to take (sb somewhere)
empêchement *(m.)* unforeseen difficulty
emprunter to borrow

590   Appendix D: French-English / English-French glossary

enceinte pregnant
encore still, again
s'endormir to fall asleep
endroit *(m.)* place
enfance *(f.)* childhood
enfant *(m./f.)* child
enfin finally
ennuyeux, ennuyeuse boring
enseigner to teach
ensemble together
ensuite then
entendre to hear
s'entraîner to practice
entrer (dans) to enter
enveloppe *(f.)* envelope
envoyer to send
épeler to spell
épouser to marry
équipe *(f.)* team
erreur *(f.)* error
escalier *(m.)* stairs
escargot *(m.)* snail
Espagne *(f.)* Spain
espagnol *(m.)* Spanish
espérer to hope
essayer to try (on)
essence *(f.)* gasoline
et and
étage *(m.)* floor (of a building)
état *(m.)* state, condition
États-Unis *(m.pl.)* United States
été *(m.)* summer
éternuer to sneeze
étoile *(f.)* star
  étoile filante shooting star
étranger *(m.)*, **étrangère** *(f.)* stranger, foreigner
étranger, étrangère *(adj.)* foreign
  à l'étranger abroad
être to be
  être à to belong to
  être à l'aise to be comfortable
  être à l'heure to be on time
  être chanceux, chanceuse to be lucky
  être de bonne/mauvaise humeur to be in a good/bad mood
  être en retard to be late
  être en train de to be in the process of
  être sur le point de to be about to
études *(f.pl.)* studies
étudiant *(m.)*, **étudiante** *(f.)* student (*at university*)
étudier to study
Europe *(f.)* Europe
européen, européenne European
événement *(m.)* event
exagérer to exaggerate
examen *(m.)* exam, test
exiger (que) to demand (that)

exil *(m.)* exile
explication *(f.)* explanation

F

fâché angry
se fâcher to get angry
facile easy
facilement easily
façon *(f.)* manner, way
facteur *(m.)* mailman
facture *(f.)* the bill
faire to do, make
  faire attention to pay attention
  faire de son mieux to do one's best
  faire des courses to run errands
  faire des économies to save money
  faire du lèche-vitrines to do window-shopping
  faire la cuisine to cook
  faire la fête to party, celebrate
  faire la grasse matinée to sleep late
  faire (la) grève to be on strike
  faire la lessive to do the laundry
  faire la queue to stand in line
  faire la sieste to take a nap
  faire la vaisselle to do the dishes
  faire le ménage to do the housework
  faire un stage to do an internship
  faire ses valises to pack (one's suitcases)
  faire un voyage to go on a trip, take a trip
falloir to be necessary
fané wilted
fatigué tired
fauché* broke, without money
faute *(f.)* mistake, fault
fauteuil *(m.)* armchair
faux, fausse false, wrong
femme *(f.)* woman, wife
  femme de ménage cleaning woman
fenêtre *(f.)* window
fermé closed
fermer to close
fête *(f.)* holiday, party, celebration
  fête nationale national holiday
feu *(m.)* traffic light, fire
  feu d'artifice fireworks
  feu rouge red light
feuilleton *(m.)* soap opera, serial
février February
fiable reliable
fier, fière proud
fièvre *(f.)* fever
fille *(f.)* daughter, girl
film *(m.)* movie, film
fils *(m.)* son
fin *(f.)* end
finir to finish
fleur *(f.)* flower

Appendix D: French-English / English-French glossary   **591**

foie *(m.)* liver
  foie gras *goose liver pâté, foie gras*
fois *(f.)* time
  la prochaine fois *next time*
  une fois *one time, once*
fonctionner to work, function
fonder to found
football *(m.)* soccer
forêt *(f.)* forest
fort strong
four *(m.)* **à micro-ondes** microwave oven
fourchette *(f.)* fork
foyer *(m.)* home, fireplace, hearth
frais, fraîche fresh
fraise *(f.)* strawberry
franc, franche frank
français *(m.)* French
France *(f.)* France
frapper to strike, hit
  ce qui m'a frappé* *what struck me*
fréquemment frequently
frère *(m.)* brother
frigo* *(m.)* fridge
frites *(f.pl.)* French fries
froid *(adj.)* cold
fromage *(m.)* cheese
fruit *(m.)* (a piece of) fruit
  fruits de mer *seafood*
fuite *(f.)* leak, flight, escape
fumer to smoke
furieux, furieuse angry, furious
fusil *(m.)* gun, rifle

G

gagnant *(m.)*, **gagnante** *(f.)* winner
gagner to win, earn
  gagner à la loterie *to win the lottery*
  gagner sa vie *to make, earn a living*
gant *(m.)* glove
garage *(m.)* garage
garçon *(m.)* boy, waiter
garder to look after, keep
gare *(f.)* train station
gâteau *(m.)* cake
gâter to spoil
gauche left
  à gauche *on (to) the left*
gens *(m.pl.)* people
glace *(f.)* mirror, ice cream
gorge *(f.)* throat
grand big, tall
  grand magasin *(m.) department store*
grand-mère *(f.)* grandmother
grand-père *(m.)* grandfather
gratte-ciel *(m.)* skyscraper
gratuit free (of charge)
gravement (malade) seriously (ill)

grec *(m.)* *Greek*
Grèce *(f.)* Greece
grenier *(m.)* attic
grève *(f.)* strike
grille-pain *(m.)* toaster
grippe *(f.)* flu
gros, grosse big, fat
guérir to cure, get well
guerre *(f.)* war
gymnase *(m.)* gymnasium

H

habile skillful
s'habiller to get dressed
habiter to live, reside
habitude *(f.)* habit
  d'habitude *usually*
haut high
herbe *(f.)* grass
héritage *(m.)* inheritance
heure *(f.)* hour, time, o'clock
  à l'heure *on time*
  à quelle heure *(at) what time*
  quelle heure est-il? *what time is it?*
heureux, heureuse happy
hier yesterday
  hier soir *last night*
histoire *(f.)* story, history
hiver *(m.)* winter
homme *(m.)* man
hôpital *(m.)* hospital
horoscope *(m.)* horoscope
hors-d'œuvre *(m.)* appetizer
hôtel *(m.)* hotel
hôtesse *(f.)* **de l'air** *(female)* flight attendant

I

ici here
idée *(f.)* idea
il faut it is necessary
il vaut mieux it is better
il y a there is, there are, ago
île *(f.)* island
illettré illiterate
immeuble *(m.)* building, apartment building
imperméable *(m.)* raincoat
impôt *(m.)* tax
incendie *(m.)* fire
Inde *(f.)* India
infirmier *(m.)*, **infirmière** *(f.)* nurse
informatique *(f.)* computer science
inquiet, inquiète worried
s'inquiéter to worry
intentionnellement intentionally
interdire to forbid
interdit forbidden
internaute *(m./f.)* Web surfer

592 Appendix D: French-English / English-French glossary

Internet *(m.)* Internet
interrompre to interrupt
inutile useless
invité *(m.)*, **invitée** *(f.)* guest
inviter to invite
Irlande *(f.)* Ireland
Italie *(f.)* Italy
italien, italienne *(adj.)* Italian

J

jamais ever, never
    ne... jamais never
jambe *(f.)* leg
janvier January
Japon *(m.)* Japan
japonais *(m.)* Japanese
jardin *(m.)* garden, yard
jaune yellow
jean *(m.)* jeans
jeter to throw
    jeter par la fenêtre to throw out the window
jeu *(m.)* *(plur.:* **jeux***)* game
jeu vidéo video game
jeudi *(m.)* Thursday
jeune young
joie *(f.)* joy
joindre to reach, join
joli pretty
jouer to play
jouet *(m.)* toy
joueur *(m.)*, **joueuse** *(f.)* player
jour *(m.)* day
    un jour some day
journal *(m.)* *(plur.:* **journaux***)* newspaper
juillet July
juin June
jupe *(f.)* skirt
jus *(m.)* juice
jusqu'à until

K

kilo *(m.)* kilogram
kiosque *(m.)* newsstand

L

là there
lâche coward, cowardly
laisser to leave, let
lait *(m.)* milk
langue *(f.)* language
    langue maternelle mother tongue
lapin *(m.)* rabbit
lave-vaisselle *(m.)* dishwasher
laver to wash
légume *(m.)* vegetable
lendemain *(m.)* next day
lent slow

lentement slowly
lettre *(f.)* letter
leur *(pron.)* (to) them
leur, leurs *(adj.)* their
se lever to get up
librairie *(f.)* bookstore
libre free
lire to read
lit *(m.)* bed
littérature *(f.)* literature
livre *(m.)* book
logiciel *(m.)* software
loi *(f.)* law
loin (de) far (from)
long, longue long
longtemps a long time
lorsque when
louer to rent
loup *(m.)* wolf
lui (to) him, (to) her
lumière *(f.)* light
lundi *(m.)* Monday
lune *(f.)* moon
    lune de miel honeymoon
lunettes *(f.pl.)* (eye)glasses
lutter (contre) to fight (against), struggle
lycée *(m.)* high school

M

machine *(f.)* **à laver** washing machine
magasin *(m.)* store
    grand magasin department store
magnétoscope *(m.)* VCR
mai May
maigre skinny
maigrir to lose weight
mail (= mél) *(m.)* e-mail
maillot *(m.)* **de bain** bathing suit
main *(f.)* hand
maintenant now
mairie *(f.)* city hall
mais but
maison *(f.)* house
    à la maison home, at home
mal badly
malade *(adj.)* ill
malade *(m./f.)* sick person, patient
maladie *(f.)* disease, illness
malentendu *(m.)* misunderstanding
malgré in spite of
malheureusement unfortunately
manger to eat
    manger sur le pouce* to have a quick bite to eat
manifester to demonstrate
mannequin *(m.)* fashion model, store dummy
manquer (à) to miss
manteau *(m.)* coat

Appendix D: French-English / English-French glossary   **593**

marcher to walk, work (= function)
mardi *(m.)* Tuesday
mari *(m.)* husband
mariage *(m.)* marriage, wedding
marié *(adj.)* married
marié *(m.)* bridegroom
mariée *(f.)* bride
se marier (avec) to get married (to)
marron brown
mars March
match *(m.)* game
matin *(m.)* morning
mauvais bad
méchant mean, vicious
médecin *(m.)* doctor
meilleur better
même same, even
mendiant *(m.),* **mendiante** *(f.)* beggar
menu *(m.)* (fixed price) menu
mercredi *(m.)* Wednesday
mère *(f.)* mother
merveilleux, merveilleuse marvelous, wonderful
message *(m.)* message
météo *(f.)* weather forecast, weather
métier *(m.)* profession, trade
métro *(m.)* subway, metro
mettre to put
 se mettre à (+ *inf.*) to begin (doing)
meubles *(m.pl.)* furniture
Mexique *(m.)* Mexico
midi *(m.)* noon
mieux better
milieu *(m.)* middle
(des) milliers *(m.pl.)* thousands
mince slim, thin
minuit midnight
moins less, minus
mois *(m.)* month
mon, ma, mes *(adj.)* my
monde *(m.)* world
 tout le monde everybody
monnaie *(f.)* (small) change, currency
monsieur (M.) *(m.)* sir, gentleman (Mr.)
monstre *(m.)* monster
montagne *(f.)* mountain
monter to go up, get into (*a vehicle*)
montre *(f.)* watch
montrer to show
morceau *(m.)* piece
mordre to bite
mot *(m.)* word, (written) note
moto(cylette) *(f.)* motorcycle
mourir to die
mouton *(m.)* sheep
muguet *(m.)* lily-of-the-valley
mur *(m.)* wall

musée *(m.)* museum
musique *(f.)* music

N

nager to swim
nappe *(f.)* tablecloth
neige *(f.)* snow
neiger to snow
ne… jamais never
ne… pas not
ne… personne no one, nobody, not anyone
ne… que only
ne… rien nothing, not anything
Net *(m.)* Net (= Internet)
nettoyer to clean
neveu *(m.)* *(plur.:* **neveux***)* nephew
nièce *(f.)* niece
Noël *(m.)* Christmas
 père Noël *(m.)* *Santa Claus*
noir black
nom *(m.)* name
note *(f.)* grade (*in a course*)
nouveau, nouvel, nouvelle new
nouvelle *(f.)* (a piece of) news, short story
novembre November
nuage *(m.)* cloud
numéro *(m.)* **de téléphone** telephone number

O

obéir to obey
obtenir to get
occupé busy
octobre October
œil *(m.)* *(plur.:* **les yeux***)* eye
offrir to offer
oiseau *(m.)* bird
oncle *(m.)* uncle
ongle *(m.)* finger nail
opéra *(m.)* opera
or *(m.)* gold
orage *(m.)* thunderstorm
ordinateur *(m.)* computer
oser to dare
otage *(m.)* hostage
ou or
où where
oublier to forget
ouvert open
ouvrier *(m.),* **ouvrière** *(f.)* worker
ouvrir to open

P

pain *(m.)* bread
paix *(f.)* peace
pâle pale
pamplemousse *(m.)* grapefruit

panne: tomber en panne to break down (*car*)
pantalon (*m.*) (pair of) pants
papillon (*m.*) butterfly
Pâques (*f.pl.*) Easter
paquet (*m.*) package
parabole (*f.*) satellite dish
parapluie (*m.*) umbrella
parce que because
parents (*m.pl.*) parents, relatives
paresseux, paresseuse lazy
parler to speak
partager to share
partir to leave
partout everywhere
passager (*m.*), **passagère** (*f.*) passenger
passer to pass, spend (*time*), take (*a test*)
   se passer to happen
patiemment patiently
patience (*f.*) patience
patient (*adj.*) patient
patienter to wait
patiner to ice skate
pâtisserie (*f.*) pastry shop, pastry
patron (*m.*), **patronne** (*f.*) boss
pauvre poor
payer to pay (for)
   payer en espèces to pay cash
pays (*m.*) country
peau (*f.*) skin
pelouse (*f.*) lawn
pendant during, for
penser to think
perdre to lose
   perdre la tête to lose one's mind, one's temper
père (*m.*) father
   père Noël Santa Claus
permettre to allow
permis (*m.*) **de conduire** driver's license
personne (*f.*) person
peser to weigh
petit small, short
   petit ami (m.), petite amie (f.) boyfriend, girlfriend
   petit déjeuner (m.) breakfast
   petit pain (m.) roll (bread)
peur (*f.*) fear
peut-être perhaps, maybe
pharmacie (*f.*) pharmacy
piano (*m.*) piano
pièce (*f.*) play (*theater*), coin, room (of a house)
   pièce montée tiered wedding cake
piège (*m.*) trap
pied (*m.*) foot
   à pied on foot
piquer to sting, bite
pire worse, worst
piscine (*f.*) swimming pool

place (*f.*) seat, room (space), (public) square
plage (*f.*) beach
plaire à to please
plaisanter to joke
plaisanterie (*f.*) joke
plaisir (*m.*) pleasure
plancher (*m.*) floor (*of a room*)
plat (*m.*) dish, course
   plat principal main course
pleurer to cry
pleuvoir to rain
   pleuvoir à verse to rain hard, pour
   pleuvoir des cordes* to rain cats and dogs
pluie (*f.*) rain
plus more
   plus longtemps longer
   plus vite faster
plusieurs several
poème (*m.*) poem
poignée (*f.*) handle, doorknob
poisson (*m.*) fish
policier (*m.*) policeman
pomme (*f.*) apple
pompier (*m.*) firefighter
pont (*m.*) bridge
(téléphone) portable (*m.*) cell phone
porte (*f.*) door
portefeuille (*m.*) wallet
porte-monnaie (*m.*) coin purse
porter to wear, carry
   porter bonheur to bring good luck
portugais (*m.*) Portuguese
posséder to own
poste (*f.*) post office
poster to mail
poubelle (*f.*) garbage can
poupée (*f.*) doll
pour for, in order to
   pour que so that
pourboire (*m.*) tip (*waiter*)
pourquoi why
pouvoir (*m.*) power
pouvoir (*verb*) to be able to
prédire to predict
préférer to prefer
premier, première first
prendre to take
   prendre une décision to make a decision
presque almost
pressé in a hurry
prêter to loan, lend
prier to pray, beg
printemps (*m.*) spring
prison (*f.*) prison, jail
priver to deprive
prix (*m.*) price, prize, award

Appendix D: French-English / English-French glossary   **595**

prochain next
professeur *(m.)* teacher, professor
projet *(m.)* plan
se promener to take a walk
promesse *(f.)* promise
promettre to promise
prononcer to pronounce
proposer to suggest
propre clean, own
prudemment carefully
prudent careful
puis then
puissant powerful
pull-over (pull) *(m.)* sweater
PV (procès verbal) *(m.)* (traffic) ticket

Q

quand when
quartier *(m.)* neighborhood
que that, which; what?
quel, quelle which? what?
quelque chose something
quelque part somewhere
quelquefois sometimes
quelques some, a few
quelqu'un someone, somebody
qu'est-ce que what?
questionnaire *(m.)* questionnaire
queue *(f.)* line
qui who, whom; who? whom?
quitter to leave
quoi what?
quoique although

R

raconter to tell
radio *(f.)* radio
ragots* *(m.pl.)* gossip
rappeler to call back, remind
  se rappeler to remember
rarement rarely
ravi delighted
recevoir to receive
recherche *(f.)* search
  recherches (f.pl.) research
recommander to recommend
récompense *(f.)* reward
reçu *(m.)* receipt
rédaction *(f.)* composition, essay
réfrigérateur *(m.)* refrigerator
refuser to refuse
regarder to look at, watch
regretter to regret, be sorry
remède *(m.)* cure
remercier to thank
rencontrer to meet
rendez-vous *(m.)* (social) date, appointment

rendre to give back, hand in *(homework)*
rentrée *(f.)* beginning of the (new)
  school year
rentrer to go home, come home
repas *(m.)* meal
répéter to repeat
répondeur *(m.)* answering machine
répondre (à) to answer
réponse *(f.)* answer
se reposer to rest
représentation *(f.)* performance
respirer to breathe
rester to stay, remain
resto-U* (= **restaurant universitaire**) *(m.)* dining
  commons, university cafeteria
résultat *(m.)* result
retour *(m.)* return
retourner to return, go back
réunion *(f.)* meeting
réussir (à) to succeed, pass *(a test)*
rêve *(m.)* dream
réveil *(m.)* alarm clock
se réveiller to wake up
revenir to come back
réviser to review
revue *(f.)* magazine
rez-de-chaussée *(m.)* first floor, ground floor
rhume *(m.)* cold
rire to laugh
riz *(m.)* rice
robe *(f.)* dress
roi *(m.)* king
roman *(m.)* novel
rouge red
rougir to blush
roux, rousse red (-haired)
rue *(f.)* street
russe *(m.)* Russian
Russie *(f.)* Russia

S

sac *(m.)* bag, handbag
  sac à dos backpack
  sac à main handbag
  sac de couchage sleeping bag
sage well-behaved, wise
salaire *(m.)* salary
sale dirty
salle *(f.)* room; hall
  salle à manger dining room
  salle de bains bathroom
  salle de classe classroom
salon *(m.)* living room
saluer to greet
samedi *(m.)* Saturday
sans without
santé *(f.)* health

596 Appendix D: French-English / English-French glossary

sapeur-pompier *(m.)* firefighter
savoir to know
savon *(m.)* soap
selon according to
semaine *(f.)* week
sembler to seem
septembre September
serpent *(m.)* snake
serveur *(m.)*, **serveuse** *(f.)* waiter, waitress
service *(m.)* favor, service
serviette *(f.)* napkin, towel
seul alone
seulement only
short *(m.)* (pair of) shorts
si if, whether
siècle *(m.)* century
singe *(m.)* monkey
skier to ski
smoking *(m.)* tuxedo
sœur *(f.)* sister
soin *(m.)* care
soir *(m.)* evening
   ce soir tonight
soldat *(m.)* soldier
solde: en solde on sale
soleil *(m.)* sun
sonner to ring (*bell, telephone, alarm clock*)
sortie *(f.)* exit, outing
sortir to go out, exit
souffrir to suffer
souhaiter (que) to wish (that)
sourire to smile
souris *(f.)* mouse
sous under
sous-sol *(m.)* basement
se souvenir (de) to remember
souvent often
spectacle *(m.)* show
stage *(m.)* internship
   faire un stage to do an internship
stylo *(m.)* pen
suggérer to suggest
Suisse *(f.)* Switzerland
suisse *(adj.)* Swiss
suivre to follow, take (*a course*)
supermarché *(m.)* supermarket
sur on
sûr sure, safe
surpris surprised
survivre to survive

T

table *(f.)* table
tableau *(m.)* blackboard; painting
tant (de) so much, so many
tante *(f.)* aunt
tapis *(m.)* rug

tard late
   plus tard later
tarte *(f.)* pie, tart
tasse *(f.)* cup
taureau *(m.)* bull
tee-shirt *(m.)* tee-shirt
télé* *(f.)* TV
télécarte *(f.)* (prepaid) phone card
télécharger to download
télécommande *(f.)* remote control
téléphone *(m.)* telephone
   (téléphone) portable (m.) *cell phone*
téléphoner (à) to call, phone
téléviseur *(m.)* television set
télévision *(f.)* television
tempête *(f.)* storm
   tempête de neige snowstorm, blizzard
temps *(m.)* time, weather
   à temps in time
tenir to hold
   tenir à to insist on, be anxious to
terminaison *(f.)* ending
terminer to end
terre *(f.)* earth, land
tête *(f.)* head
TGV (train *[m.]* **à grande vitesse)** French high-speed
   train
thé *(m.)* tea
théâtre *(m.)* theater
ticket *(m.)* **de caisse** sales slip, receipt
timbre *(m.)* (postage) stamp
tirer to pull
tiroir *(m.)* drawer
toilettes *(f.pl.)* restroom
tomber to fall
   tomber à l'eau* to fall through **(plans)**
   tomber dans les pommes* to faint, pass out
   tomber en panne to break down **(car)**
   tomber malade to become, fall ill
tondre la pelouse to mow the lawn
tôt early
   plus tôt earlier
toujours always
tour *(f.)* tower
tour *(m.)* turn, walk, ride
tourner to turn
tout everything
   tout à coup suddenly
   tout le monde everybody
   tout le temps all the time
train *(m.)* train
tramway *(m.)* streetcar, light rail
travail *(m.)* work
travailler to work
travers: à travers across
traverser to cross
tremblement *(m.)* **de terre** earthquake

Appendix D: French-English / English-French glossary   **597**

très very
trésor *(m.)* treasure
triste sad
trop (de) too, too much, too many
trou *(m.)* hole
trouver to find
tuer to kill
Turquie *(f.)* Turkey

U

université *(f.)* university
usine *(f.)* factory
utile useful
utiliser to use

V

vacances *(f.pl.)* vacation
vaisselle *(f.)* dishes
valeur *(f.)* value
valise *(f.)* suitcase
  faire ses valises to pack one's
    suitcase(s)
valoir to be worth
  valoir mieux to be better
vedette *(f.)* star, movie star
veille (la) *(f.)* the night before
vélo* *(m.)* bike
vendeur *(m.)* salesperson, salesman
vendeuse *(f.)* saleslady, saleswoman
vendre to sell
vendredi *(m.)* Friday
venir to come
vent *(m.)* wind
vérité *(f.)* truth
verre *(m.)* glass

vers toward, at about (with clock time)
verser to pour
vert green
veste *(f.)* jacket
vêtements *(m.pl.)* clothes, clothing
viande *(f.)* meat
victoire *(f.)* victory
vie *(f.)* life
vieux, vieil, vieille old
ville *(f.)* city, town
  ville natale home town
vin *(m.)* wine
violet, violette purple
visiter to visit (*a place*)
vite fast, quickly
vitre *(f.)* (window) pane
vivre to live
vœu *(m.)* wish
voir to see
voisin *(m.),* **voisine** *(f.)* neighbor
voiture *(f.)* car
voix *(f.)* voice
volant *(m.)* steering wheel
voler to fly, steal
volontiers gladly
vouloir to want
voyage *(m.)* trip
voyager to travel
vrai true
vue *(f.)* view
  de vue by sight

Y

y there
yeux *(m.pl.)* eyes

English-French glossary

A

a lot (of) beaucoup
abolish abolir
about environ
abroad à l'étranger
accident accident *(m.)*
acquaintance connaissance *(f.)*
   make the acquaintance of faire la connaissance de
across à travers
act jouer, agir
actor acteur *(m.)*
actress actrice *(f.)*
address adresse *(f.)*
admit admettre
adult adulte *(m./f.)*
adventure aventure *(f.)*
advice (piece of) conseil *(m.)*
advise conseiller
advisor conseiller *(m.)*, conseillère *(f.)*
Africa Afrique *(f.)*
afraid: be afraid avoir peur, craindre
after après (que)
afternoon après-midi *(m.)*
age âge *(m.)*
ago il y a
agree (with) être d'accord (avec)
air conditioning climatisation *(f.)*
airline company compagnie aérienne
   (f.)
airplane avion *(m.)*
airport aéroport *(m.)*
aisle couloir *(m.)*
alarm (clock) réveil *(m.)*
alive en vie, vivant
allow permettre, laisser
almost presque
alone seul
already déjà
also aussi
although bien que, quoique
always toujours
America Amérique *(f.)*
and et
angry fâché; furieux, furieuse
   get angry se fâcher
animal animal *(m.)* *(plur.: animaux)*
answer *(noun)* réponse *(f.)*
answer *(verb)* répondre
answering machine répondeur *(m.)*
apartment appartement *(m.)*
apologize s'excuser
appetizer hors-d'œuvre *(m.)*

applaud applaudir
apple pomme *(f.)*
appointment rendez-vous *(m.)*
appreciate apprécier
April avril
argue se disputer
armchair fauteuil *(m.)*
arrest *(verb)* arrêter
arrive arriver
article article *(m.)*
Asia Asie *(f.)*
ask demander
   ask a question poser une question
assignment devoir *(m.)*
at à
   at first d'abord
   at least au moins
ATM (automated teller machine) distributeur
   (automatique) *(m.)* de billets
attend assister (à)
attention: pay attention faire attention
attentively attentivement
attic grenier *(m.)*
August août
aunt tante *(f.)*
Austria Autriche *(f.)*
autumn automne *(m.)*
avoid éviter
award *(noun)* prix *(m.)*

B

baby bébé *(m.)*
backpack sac *(m.)* à dos
bad mauvais
badly mal
bag sac *(m.)*
baker boulanger *(m.)*, boulangère *(f.)*
bakery boulangerie *(f.)*
balcony balcon *(m.)*
bank banque *(f.)*
bar bar *(m.)*
   (candy) bar barre (f.)
bargain *(noun)* bonne affaire *(f.)*
bargain *(verb)* marchander
basement sous-sol *(m.)*
basket panier *(m.)*
bathing suit maillot *(m.)* de bain
bathroom salle *(f.)* de bains
be être
   be able to ("can") pouvoir
   be afraid avoir peur
   be hungry avoir faim

(continued)

Appendix D: French-English / English-French glossary **599**

be être *(continued)*
    be interested in s'intéresser à
    be lucky avoir de la chance; être chanceux,
       chanceuse
    be mistaken se tromper
    be named s'appeler
    be quiet se taire
    be right avoir raison
    be situated se trouver
    be sleepy avoir sommeil
    be thirsty avoir soif
    be wrong (person) avoir tort
beach plage *(f.)*
bear *(noun)* ours *(m.)*
beat *(verb)* battre, frapper
beautiful beau, bel, belle
because parce que, car
    because of à cause de
become devenir
bed lit *(m.)*
bedroom chambre *(f.)* à coucher
beer bière *(f.)*
before avant (que)
begin commencer, se mettre à
behave se comporter, se conduire
Belgium Belgique *(f.)*
believe croire
belong to appartenir à , être à
belt ceinture *(f.)*
    seat belt, safety belt ceinture de sécurité
bench banc *(m.)*
better *(adj.)* meilleur
better *(adv.)* mieux
between entre
bicycle bicyclette *(f.)*, vélo* *(m.)*
big grand
bike vélo* *(m.)*
bill facture *(f.)*, *(in restaurant)* addition *(f.)*
bird oiseau *(m.)*
birthday anniversaire *(m.)*
bite *(verb)* mordre
black noir
blackboard tableau noir *(m.)*
blanket couverture *(f.)*
blue bleu
blush *(verb)* rougir
boat bateau *(m.)*, *(small)* barque *(f.)*
bomb *(noun)* bombe *(f.)*
book livre *(m.)*
bookstore librairie *(f.)*
boots bottes *(f.pl.)*
boring ennuyeux, ennuyeuse
borrow emprunter
boss patron *(m.)*, patronne *(f.)*
both (tous) les deux *(m.pl.)*, (toutes) les deux *(f.pl.)*
bother *(verb)* déranger
bottle bouteille *(f.)*

box boîte *(f.)*
boy garçon *(m.)*
boyfriend petit ami *(m.)*, copain *(m.)*
Brazil Brésil *(m.)*
bread pain *(m.)*
break *(verb)* casser
    break down (car) tomber en panne
breakfast petit déjeuner *(m.)*
bride mariée *(f.)*
bridegroom marié *(m.)*
bridge pont *(m.)*
bring apporter
broke *(no money)* fauché*
broken cassé
brother frère *(m.)*
brush *(verb)* (se) brosser
building bâtiment *(m.)*
burglar cambrioleur *(m.)*, cambrioleuse *(f.)*,
    braqueur* *(m.)*
bus autobus *(m.)*
busy occupé
but mais
butcher shop boucherie *(f.)*
butter beurre *(m.)*
    peanut butter beurre de cacahuètes
butterfly papillon *(m.)*
buy acheter

C

cake gâteau *(m.)*
calculator calculatrice *(f.)*
call *(verb)* appeler, téléphoner (à)
camera appareil photo *(m.)*
camping camping *(m.)*
    go camping faire du camping
can (be able to) pouvoir
cancel annuler, supprimer
candle bougie *(f.)*
candy bonbons *(m.pl.)*
car voiture *(f.)*
card carte *(f.)*
    credit card carte de crédit
    postcard carte postale
careful prudent
carefully prudemment
carry porter
cartoon dessin animé *(m.)*
cash register caisse *(f.)*
castle château *(m.)*
cat chat *(m.)*, chatte *(f.)*
catch attraper
cathedral cathédrale *(f.)*
cause *(verb)* causer
celebrate fêter, célébrer, faire la fête
cell phone (téléphone) portable *(m.)*
cellar cave *(f.)*
century siècle *(m.)*

600   Appendix D: French-English / English-French glossary

chair chaise *(f.)*
champagne champagne *(m.)*
change changer
    change one's mind *changer d'avis*
chat *(verb)* bavarder
cheese fromage *(m.)*
chicken poulet *(m.)*
child enfant *(m./f.)*
childhood enfance *(f.)*
Chinese chinois *(m.)*
chocolate chocolat *(m.)*
choice choix *(m.)*
choose choisir
Christmas Noël *(m.)*
church église *(f.)*
citizenship nationalité *(f.)*
city ville *(f.)*
class classe *(f.)*, cours *(m.)*
classroom salle *(f.)* de classe
clean *(verb)* nettoyer
clean *(adj.)* propre
clock *(big)* horloge *(f.)*, *(small)* pendule *(f.)*
close *(verb)* fermer
closed fermé
clothes, clothing vêtements *(m.pl.)*
cloud nuage *(m.)*
coach *(sports)* entraîneur *(m.)*
coat manteau *(m.)*
coffee café *(m.)*
cold froid *(m.)*
    be cold *(person)* *avoir froid*
    be cold *(weather)* *faire froid*
college université *(f.)*
color couleur *(f.)*
comb *(verb)* se peigner
come venir
comedy comédie *(f.)*
comic strip bande dessinée *(f.)*
complain (about) se plaindre (de)
composition *(writing)* rédaction *(f.)*
computer ordinateur *(m.)*
    computer science *informatique (f.)*
    laptop computer *ordinateur portable*
concert concert *(m.)*
consume consommer
continue continuer
cook *(noun)* cuisinier *(m.)*, cuisinière *(f.)*
cook *(verb)* cuisiner, faire la cuisine
cooking cuisine *(f.)*
correctly correctement
cost *(noun)* coût *(m.)*
cost *(verb)* coûter
country pays *(m.)*
cousin cousin *(m.)*, cousine *(f.)*
crazy fou, folle
credit card carte *(f.)* de credit
cross *(verb)* traverser

cruise *(noun)* croisière *(f.)*
    go on a cruise *faire une croisière*
cry *(verb)* pleurer
cup tasse *(f.)*
cure remède *(m.)*
customer client *(m.)*, cliente *(f.)*
cut *(verb)* couper

D

dad papa *(m.)*
damage *(verb)* endommager
dance *(verb)* danser
dangerous dangereux, dangereuse
dare *(verb)* oser
date *(noun)* date *(f.)*, *(social)* rendez-vous *(m.)*
daughter fille *(f.)*
day jour *(m.)*, journée *(f.)*
    every day *chaque jour*
    some day *un jour*
    the day before yesterday *avant-hier*
deadline date limite *(f.)*
dear cher, chère
death mort *(f.)*
debt dette *(f.)*
decade décennie *(f.)*
December décembre
deer *(female)* biche *(f.)*
delicious délicieux, délicieuse
delighted ravi
demand *(verb)* exiger (que)
demonstrate *(protest)* manifester
demonstration *(protest)* manifestation *(f.)*
dentist dentiste *(m./f.)*
department *(of a store)* rayon *(m.)*
    department store *grand magasin (m.)*
    shoe department *rayon des chaussures*
depressed déprimé
desk bureau *(m.)*
dessert dessert *(m.)*
destroy détruire
detest détester
devil diable *(m.)*
die mourir
difficult difficile
dining room salle *(f.)* à manger
dinner dîner *(m.)*
diploma diplôme *(m.)*
dirty sale
disappear disparaître
disappoint décevoir
disappointed déçu
dish plat *(m.)*
dishes vaisselle *(f.)*
dishwasher lave-vaisselle *(m.)*
disturb déranger
divorce *(noun)* divorce *(m.)*
divorce *(verb)* divorcer

Appendix D: French-English / English-French glossary   **601**

do faire
doctor médecin *(m.)*
doe biche *(f.)*
dog chien *(m.)*, chienne *(f.)*
doll poupée *(f.)*
door porte *(f.)*
doubt *(noun)* doute *(m.)*
doubt *(verb)* douter
dream *(noun)* rêve *(m.)*
dream *(verb)* rêver
dress *(noun)* robe *(f.)*
drink *(noun)* boisson *(f.)*
drink *(verb)* boire
drive conduire, rouler
driver conducteur *(m.)*, conductrice *(f.)*
    driver's license permis *(m.) de conduire*
drown se noyer
during pendant

E

each chaque
early tôt, de bonne heure
earn gagner
earring boucle *(f.)* d'oreille
earthquake tremblement *(m.)* de terre
easy facile
Easter Pâques *(f.pl.)*
eat manger
    eat dinner dîner
    eat lunch dejeuner
    eat out dîner au restaurant
effort effort *(m.)*
Egypt Égypte *(f.)*
elevator ascenseur *(m.)*
e-mail courrier électronique *(m.)*, e-mail *(m.)*, mail *(m.)*, courriel *(m.)*
employ employer
engineer ingénieur *(m.)*
England Angleterre *(f.)*
English anglais *(m.)*
enough assez (de)
enter entrer (dans)
envelope enveloppe *(f.)*
Europe Europe *(f.)*
    in/to Europe en Europe
European *(adj.)* européen, européenne
even même
evening soir *(m.)*, soirée *(f.)*
event événement *(m.)*
every chaque
everybody tout le monde
everyone tout le monde
everything tout
everywhere partout
exaggerate exagérer
exam examen *(m.)*

except sauf
exit *(noun)* sortie *(f.)*
expect s'attendre à
expensive cher, chère
experienced expérimenté
explode exploser
explosion explosion *(f.)*
eye œil *(m.) (plur.:* yeux)
eyeglasses lunettes *(f.pl.)*

F

face visage *(m.)*
factory usine *(f.)*
fail échouer
    fail an exam échouer à un examen, rater* un examen
fall *(verb)* tomber
    fall asleep s'endormir
fall *(noun) (season)* automne *(m.), (snow-, water-)* chute *(f.)*
false faux, fausse
family famille *(f.)*
famous célèbre
far (from) loin (de)
fashion model mannequin *(m.)*
fast rapide *(adj.)*, vite *(adv.)*
father père *(m.)*
father-in-law beau-père *(m.)*
favor service *(m.)*
favorite favori, favorite; préféré
fax *(noun)* fax *(m.)*
fear *(noun)* peur *(f.)*
fear *(verb)* craindre, avoir peur
February février
feel (se) sentir
fence *(noun)* clôture *(f.)*
fever fièvre *(f.)*
fill (up, out) remplir
finally enfin
find trouver
finger doigt *(m.)*
fingernail ongle *(m.)*
finish finir, terminer, achever
fire *(from a job)* licencier, renvoyer, virer*
firefighter pompier *(m.)*, sapeur-pompier *(m.)*
fireworks feu *(m.)* d'artifice
first premier, première
    at first d'abord
fish *(noun)* poisson *(m.)*
flag drapeau *(m.)*
flight vol *(m.)*
    flight attendant (female) hôtesse (f.) de l'air
floor *(of a building)* étage *(m.)*
    on the ground (first) floor au rez-de-chaussée
    on the second floor au premier étage
    on the third floor au deuxième étage
floor *(of a room)* plancher *(m.)*

602 Appendix D: French-English / English-French glossary

flower fleur *(f.)*
flu grippe *(f.)*
fluently couramment
fly *(verb)* voler
fog brouillard *(m.)*
foggy: be foggy out faire du brouillard
follow suivre
foot pied *(m.)*
   on foot à pied
for pour, depuis, pendant
forbid défendre, interdire
foreign *(adj.)* étranger, étrangère
forest forêt *(f.)*
forget oublier
forgive pardonner
fork fourchette *(f.)*
fortune fortune *(f.)*
France France *(f.)*
frank franc, franche
free libre
free *(of charge)* gratuit
freeway autoroute *(f.)*
French fries frites *(f.pl.)*
Friday vendredi *(m.)*
friend ami *(m.)*, amie *(f.)*, copain *(m.)*, copine *(f.)*
frog grenouille *(f.)*
from de
front: in front of devant
furniture meubles *(m.pl.)*
furthermore de plus
future avenir *(m.)*

G

game jeu *(m.)*, *(football, basketball)* match *(m.)*
garage garage *(m.)*
garden jardin *(m.)*
gasoline essence *(f.)*
gentleman monsieur *(m.)*
German allemand *(m.)*
Germany Allemagne *(f.)*
get obtenir, recevoir
   get along (with) s'entendre *(avec)*
   get angry se fâcher
   get bored s'ennuyer
   get dressed s'habiller
   get engaged se fiancer
   get lost se perdre
   get married se marier
   get undressed se déshabiller
   get up se lever
   get used to s'habituer à
gift cadeau *(m.)*
girl fille *(f.)*, jeune fille *(f.)*
girlfriend petite amie *(f.)*, copine *(f.)*
give donner
   give back rendre

glass verre *(m.)*
glasses *(eye)* lunettes *(f.pl.)*
glove gant *(m.)*
go aller
   go away s'en aller
   go down descendre
   go for a walk se promener
   go out sortir
   go swimming se baigner
   go to bed se coucher
   go up monter
God Dieu
gold or *(m.)*
good bon, bonne; *(well-behaved)* sage
good-bye au revoir
goose bumps chair *(f.)* de poule
grade *(in course)* note *(f.)*
graduate *(verb)* obtenir son diplôme, finir ses études
grandchildren petits-enfants *(m.pl.)*
grandfather grand-père *(m.)*
grandmother grand-mère *(f.)*
grass herbe *(f.)*
Greece Grèce *(f.)*
Greek *(adj.)* grec, grecque
green vert
greet saluer
gun pistolet *(m.)*, fusil *(m.)*
gym(nasium) gymnase *(m.)*

H

hair cheveux *(m.pl.)*
half moitié *(f.)*
hallway couloir *(m.)*
ham jambon *(m.)*
hand main *(f.)*
hand in *(homework)* rendre, remettre
handbag sac *(m.)* à main
handsome beau, bel
happen arriver, se passer
happy heureux, heureuse; content
hard dur, difficile
hat chapeau *(m.)*
hate *(verb)* détester
have avoir
   have a good time / have fun s'amuser
   have lunch déjeuner
   have to (do something) devoir
head tête *(f.)*
health santé *(f.)*
healthy en bonne santé
hear entendre
help *(verb)* aider
her *(adj.)* son, sa, ses
here ici
hesitate hésiter

Appendix D: French-English / English-French glossary **603**

hide *(verb)* (se) cacher
high school lycée *(m.)*
hijack détourner
his *(adj.)* son, sa, ses
hit *(crash into)* percuter, *(beat)* frapper, battre
hold tenir
home town ville natale *(f.)*
homework devoirs *(m.pl.)*
honeymoon lune *(f.)* de miel
hope *(verb)* espérer
horse cheval *(m.)* *(plur.: chevaux)*
hostage otage *(m.)*
hot chaud
hotel hôtel *(m.)*
hour heure *(f.)*
house maison *(f.)*
housemate colocataire *(m./f.)*
housework ménage *(m.)*
how comment
    how many combien
    how much combien
hug *(verb)* embrasser
hunger faim *(f.)*
hungry: be hungry avoir faim
hurricane ouragan *(m.)*
hurry se dépêcher
    be in a hurry être pressé
husband mari *(m.)*

I

ice cream glace *(f.)*
ice skate *(verb)* patiner
if si
ill malade
immediately immédiatement
important important
improve (s')améliorer
in dans
  + city *à*
  + feminine country *en*
  + masculine country *au*
    in a hurry pressé
    in love (with) amoureux, amoureuse (de)
injure blesser
inspector inspecteur *(m.)*, inspectrice *(f.)*
instead of au lieu de
interested: be . . . in être intéressé par
Internet Internet *(m.)*
introduce (oneself) (se) présenter
invent inventer
invite inviter
Ireland Irlande *(f.)*
island île *(f.)*
Italian italien *(m.)*
Italy Italie *(f.)*

J

jacket blouson *(m.)*, veste *(f.)*, anorak *(m.)*
jail prison *(f.)*
jam *(fruit)* confiture *(f.)*
January janvier
Japan Japon *(m.)*
Japanese japonais *(m.)*
jeans *(pair of)* jean *(m.)*
jewelry bijoux *(m.pl.)*
job travail *(m.)*, emploi *(m.)*
join rejoindre
joke *(noun)* plaisanterie *(f.)*
joke *(verb)* plaisanter
judge juge *(m.)*
juice jus *(m.)*
July juillet
June juin

K

keep garder, tenir *(promise)*
key clé *(f.)*
kidnap enlever
kill tuer
kilogram kilo *(m.)*
king roi *(m.)*
kiss *(verb)* (s')embrasser
kitchen cuisine *(f.)*
knife couteau *(m.)*
knock *(verb)* frapper
know savoir, *(person or place)* connaître

L

lady dame *(f.)*
lake lac *(m.)*
land *(verb)* atterrir
landscape paysage *(m.)*
language langue *(f.)*
laptop computer ordinateur portable *(m.)*
last *(adj.)* dernier, dernière
    last night hier soir
last *(verb)* durer
late tard
    be late être en retard
later plus tard
laugh *(verb)* rire
laundry lessive *(f.)*
lawn pelouse *(f.)*
lawyer avocat *(m.)*, avocate *(f.)*
lay off *(work)* licencier
lay the table mettre la table
lazy paresseux, paresseuse
learn apprendre
learner apprenant *(m.)*, apprenante *(f.)*
leave *(verb)* partir, quitter *(place or a person)*, laisser *(tip, message)*
lecture conférence *(f.)*

604 Appendix D: French-English / English-French glossary

left gauche *(f.)*
   on/to the left à gauche
   turn left tourner à gauche
leg jambe *(f.)*
lend prêter
less moins
let laisser, permettre
letter lettre *(f.)*
library bibliothèque *(f.)*
license: driver's license permis *(m.)* de conduire
lie *(verb)* mentir
lie *(noun)* mensonge *(m.)*
life vie *(f.)*
light *(noun)* lumière *(f.)*
like *(verb)* aimer
link *(noun)* lien *(m.)*
listen to écouter
little: a little (un) peu (de)
live *(verb)* habiter, vivre
living room salon *(m.)*, séjour *(m.)*
loan *(verb)* prêter
long time: a long time longtemps
look (at) regarder
   look for chercher
lose perdre
   lose patience perdre patience
   lose weight maigrir
lot: a lot beaucoup
love *(verb)* aimer
luck chance *(f.)*
   good luck bonne chance
luckily heureusement
lucky: be lucky avoir de la chance, être chanceux, chanceuse
lunch déjeuner *(m.)*
   have/eat lunch déjeuner

M

magazine magazine *(m.)*
mail courrier *(m.)*
mailman facteur *(m.)*
major in se spécialiser en
make faire
   make a decision prendre une décision
   make fun of se moquer de
   make oneself comfortable se mettre à l'aise
man homme *(m.)*
many beaucoup (de)
March mars
marriage mariage *(m.)*
married marié
marry se marier, épouser
mask masque *(m.)*
May mai
maybe peut-être
meal repas *(m.)*

mean *(adj.)* méchant
measure *(verb)* mesurer
meat viande *(f.)*
meet rencontrer
meeting réunion *(f.)*
memory souvenir *(m.)*
mention mentionner
menu carte *(f.)*
merchant commerçant *(m.)*, commerçante *(f.)*
message message *(m.)*
Mexico Mexique *(m.)*
middle milieu *(m.)*
midnight minuit
milk lait *(m.)*
minute minute *(f.)*
miracle miracle *(m.)*
mirror miroir *(m.)*
miss manquer
Miss Mlle (mademoiselle)
mistake faute *(f.)*
model: fashion model mannequin *(m.)*
mom maman *(f.)*
Monday lundi *(m.)*
money argent *(m.)*
month mois *(m.)*
moon lune *(f.)*
more plus (de)
morning matin *(m.)*
mother mère *(f.)*
mother-in-law belle-mère *(f.)*
motorcycle motocyclette *(f.)*, moto* *(f.)*
mountain montagne *(f.)*
mouse souris *(f.)*
move bouger, déménager *(change residence)*
movie film *(m.)*
   movie star vedette *(f.)* de cinéma
   movie theater cinéma *(m.)*
   movies cinéma *(m.)*
mow the lawn tondre la pelouse
Mr. M. (monsieur)
Mrs. Mme (madame)
much beaucoup (de)
museum musée *(m.)*
music musique *(f.)*
musical (comedy) comédie musicale *(f.)*
must *(have to)* devoir
my *(adj.)* mon, ma, mes

N

name *(noun)* nom *(m.)*
napkin serviette *(f.)*
near près (de)
necklace collier *(m.)*
need *(verb)* avoir besoin (de)
neighbor voisin *(m.)*, voisine *(f.)*
nephew neveu *(m.)* *(plur.: neveux)*

Appendix D: French-English / English-French glossary **605**

Net (= Internet) Net *(m.)*
never ne… jamais
new nouveau, nouvel, nouvelle
news informations *(f.pl.)*, nouvelle(s) *(f.)*
newspaper journal *(m.)* *(plur.: journaux)*
newsstand kiosque *(m.)*
next prochain
nice gentil, gentille
niece nièce *(f.)*
night nuit *(f.)*
  at night le soir
  last night hier soir
nightmare cauchemar *(m.)*
no longer, not any more ne… plus
no one ne… personne
nobody ne… personne
noise bruit *(m.)*
noon midi
north nord *(m.)*
not ne… pas
  not any more ne… plus
notebook cahier *(m.)*
nothing ne… rien
notice *(verb)* remarquer, s'apercevoir
novel *(noun)* roman *(m.)*
November novembre
now maintenant
nowadays de nos jours
nurse infirmier *(m.)*, infirmière *(f.)*

O

obey obéir (à)
object *(noun)* objet *(m.)*
October octobre
of de
offer *(verb)* offrir
office bureau *(m.)*
often souvent
old vieux, vieil, vieille
on sur
  on sale en solde
  on/to the left à gauche
  on/to the right à droite
once une fois
only seulement, ne… que
open *(verb)* ouvrir
open *(adj.)* ouvert
opinion avis *(m.)*
  in my (your, etc.) opinion à mon (ton, etc.)
    avis
or ou
other autre
our *(adj.)* notre, nos
outside dehors
owe devoir
own *(verb)* posséder, avoir
owner propriétaire *(m./f.)*

P

package paquet *(m.)*, colis *(m.)*
paint *(verb)* peindre
pants *(pair of)* pantalon *(m.)*
paper papier *(m.)*, *(term)* dissertation *(f.)*
parents parents *(m.pl.)*
park *(noun)* parc *(m.)*
park *(verb)* stationner, se garer
parliament parlement *(m.)*
party fête *(f.)*, boum* *(f.)*, soirée *(f.)*
pass an exam réussir à un examen
passenger passager *(m.)*, passagère *(f.)*
passport passeport *(m.)*
pastry pâtisserie *(f.)*
pastry shop pâtisserie *(f.)*
patience patience *(f.)*
  lose patience perdre patience
pay payer
peanut butter beurre *(m.)* de cacahuètes
pedagogy pédagogie *(f.)*
pen stylo *(m.)*
people gens *(m.pl.)*, *(with a number)* personnes
  (f.pl.)
per par
performance représentation *(f.)*
perhaps peut-être
person *(male or female)* personne *(f.)*
pet animal domestique *(m.)*
pharmacy pharmacie *(f.)*
piano piano *(m.)*
pick up sb aller/venir chercher qn
picture photo *(f.)*, image *(f.)*
pie tarte *(f.)*
piece morceau *(m.)*
place endroit *(m.)*, lieu *(m.)*
plan *(to do)* compter (+ *inf.*)
plate assiette *(f.)*
play *(noun)* pièce (de théâtre) *(f.)*
play *(verb)* jouer (à, de)
player joueur *(m.)*, joueuse *(f.)*
please *(interj.)* s'il vous plaît
please *(verb)* plaire à
pleasure plaisir *(m.)*
poem poème *(m.)*
police police *(f.)*
polite poli
political science sciences politiques *(f.pl.)*
politics politique *(f.)*
poor pauvre
Portuguese portugais *(m.)*
post office bureau *(m.)* de poste
postcard carte postale *(f.)*
postman facteur *(m.)*
postpone remettre, reporter, repousser
pour verser
prefer préférer
pregnant enceinte

606 Appendix D: French-English / English-French glossary

prepare préparer
pretend (to) faire semblant (de)
pretty joli
previews *(movies)* bande annonce *(f.)*
price prix *(m.)*
prince prince *(m.)*
principal *(school)* proviseur *(m.)*
printer *(equipment)* imprimante *(f.)*
prize prix *(m.)*
promise *(noun)* promesse *(f.)*
promise *(verb)* promettre
pronounce prononcer
proof preuve *(f.)*
protect protéger
proud fier, fière
provided that pourvu que
purple violet, violette
put mettre

Q

question *(noun)* question *(f.)*
questionnaire questionnaire *(m.)*
quick rapide
quickly vite, rapidement

R

rabbit lapin *(m.)*
radio radio *(f.)*
rain *(noun)* pluie *(f.)*
rain *(verb)* pleuvoir
raincoat imperméable *(m.)*
raise (a child) élever (un enfant)
rarely rarement
rather assez
read lire
reader lecteur *(m.)*, lectrice *(f.)*
realize *(notice)* se rendre compte (de)
really vraiment
receive recevoir
reception réception *(f.)*
recommend recommander
recreational vehicle (RV) camping-car *(m.)*
red rouge
refrigerator réfrigérateur *(m.)*, frigo* *(m.)*
region région *(f.)*
regret *(verb)* regretter
relax se détendre
remember se rappeler, se souvenir (de)
remote control télécommande *(f.)*
rent *(noun)* loyer *(m.)*
rent *(verb)* louer
repeat *(verb)* répéter
report *(noun)* rapport *(m.)*
resign démissionner
responsible responsable
rest *(verb)* se reposer
restaurant restaurant *(m.)*

restroom toilettes *(f.pl.)*
résumé curriculum vitae *(m.)*
return retourner, revenir, *(home)* rentrer
reward récompense *(f.)*
rice riz *(m.)*
rich riche
right droit *(m.)* droite *(f.)*
   on/to the right à droite
right away tout de suite
ring *(bell, telephone, alarm clock)* sonner
riot émeute *(f.)*
road route *(f.)*
roof toit *(m.)*
room chambre *(f.)*, pièce *(f.)*, salle *(f.)*
roommate camarade *(m./f.)* de chambre
row *(tier)* rang *(m.)*
rug tapis *(m.)*
run *(verb)* courir
Russia Russie *(f.)*
Russian russe *(m.)*

S

sad triste
safe *(adj.)* sûr
   feel safe se sentir en sécurité
safe *(noun)* coffre-fort *(m.)*
salad salade *(f.)*
salary salaire *(m.)*
salesman vendeur *(m.)*
saleswoman vendeuse *(f.)*
salt sel *(m.)*
same même
sandwich sandwich *(m.)*
Santa Claus père Noël *(m.)*
satisfy satisfaire
Saturday samedi *(m.)*
say dire
scallops coquilles Saint.-Jacques *(f.pl.)*
scholarship bourse *(f.)*
school école *(f.)*
   high school lycée *(m.)*
   middle school collège *(m.)*
seafood fruits *(m.pl.)* de mer
seat place *(f.)*
   aisle seat place *(f.)* côté couloir
   seat belt ceinture *(f.)* de sécurité
   window seat place *(f.)* côté fenêtre
secret secret *(m.)*
secretary secrétaire *(m./f.)*
see voir
seem sembler, paraître
selfish égoïste
sell vendre
semester semestre *(m.)*
send envoyer
sentence phrase *(f.)*
September septembre

Appendix D: French-English / English-French glossary   **607**

serial feuilleton *(m.)*
set the table mettre la table
several plusieurs
share *(verb)* partager
shave *(verb)* se raser
ship *(noun)* bateau *(m.)*, *(small)* barque *(f.)*
shirt chemise *(f.)*
shoes chaussures *(f.pl.)*
shop *(noun)* magasin *(m.)*, *(small)* boutique *(f.)*
shopping center centre commercial *(m.)*
short court *(hair)*, petit *(person)*
shorts *(pair of)* short *(m.)*
show *(noun)* spectacle *(m.)*
show *(verb)* montrer
shower *(noun)* douche *(f.)*
sick malade
since depuis, *(because)* puisque
sing chanter
singer chanteur *(m.)*, chanteuse *(f.)*
single *(unmarried)* célibataire
sister sœur *(f.)*
sit down s'asseoir
ski *(verb)* skier
skin peau *(f.)*
skirt jupe *(f.)*
sky ciel *(m.)*
skyscraper gratte-ciel *(m.)*
sleep *(noun)* sommeil *(m.)*
sleep *(verb)* dormir
slim mince
slow lent
slowly lentement
small petit
snail escargot *(m.)*
snow *(noun)* neige *(f.)*
snow *(verb)* neiger
so *(+ adj.)* si *(+ adj.)*
    so that pour que
soap opera feuilleton *(m.)*
society société *(f.)*
socks chaussettes *(f.pl.)*
software logiciel *(m.)*
soldier soldat *(m.)*
somebody quelqu'un
someone quelqu'un
something quelque chose
sometimes quelquefois
somewhere quelque part
son fils *(m.)*
song chanson *(f.)*
soon bientôt
sorry désolé
soup soupe *(f.)*
Spain Espagne *(f.)*
Spanish espagnol *(m.)*
speak parler

speaker conférencier *(m.)*, conférencière *(f.)*
speech discours *(m.)*
speed vitesse *(f.)*
spend *(money)* dépenser
spend *(time)* passer
spoil gâter
spoon cuiller (cuillère) *(f.)*
spring printemps *(m.)*
squirrel écureuil *(m.)*
stairs escalier *(m.)*
stamp *(postage)* timbre *(m.)*
stapler agrafeuse *(f.)*
star étoile *(f.)*
start commencer, se mettre à
stay *(noun)* séjour *(m.)*
stay *(verb)* rester
steal voler
stewardess hôtesse *(f.)* de l'air
still encore, toujours
stop (s')arrêter
store magasin *(m.)*
    department store grand magasin
story histoire *(f.)*, conte *(m.)*
straight ahead tout droit
stranger inconnu *(m.)*, inconnue *(f.)*, étranger *(m.)*,
    étrangère *(f.)*
strawberry fraise *(f.)*
street rue *(f.)*
strike *(noun)* grève *(f.)*
strike *(verb)* frapper, battre
strong fort
student élève *(m./f.)*, *(university)* étudiant *(m.)*,
    étudiante *(f.)*
studies études *(f.pl.)*
study *(verb)* étudier
subway métro *(m.)*
succeed réussir
successful: be successful réussir, avoir du succès
suddenly soudain, tout à coup
suffer souffrir
suggest proposer, suggérer
suit *(men's)* costume *(m.)*
    suit (women's) tailleur *(m.)*
    bathing suit maillot *(m.)* de bain
suitcase valise *(f.)*
summer été *(m.)*
sun soleil *(m.)*
Sunday dimanche *(m.)*
supermarket supermarché *(m.)*
supposed: be supposed to être censé, devoir
sure sûr
surf *(verb)* surfer
    surf the Net surfer sur Internet
surgeon chirurgien *(m.)*, chirurgienne *(f.)*
survive survivre (à)
survivor survivant *(m.)*, survivante *(f.)*

suspect *(verb)* se douter (de)
suspicious suspect
sweater pull(-over) *(m.)*
sweep balayer
swim nager
swimming pool piscine *(f.)*
swimsuit maillot *(m.)* de bain
switch off éteindre
Swiss *(adj.)* suisse
Switzerland Suisse *(f.)*

T

T-shirt tee-shirt *(m.)*
table table *(f.)*
   set the table mettre la table
tablecloth nappe *(f.)*
take prendre
   take (a class) suivre (un cours)
   *take (sb somewhere) emmener (qn quelque
     part)*
   take a nap faire la sieste
   take a test passer un examen
   take a trip faire un voyage
   take a walk faire une promenade
   take care of s'occuper de
   take place avoir lieu
talk *(verb)* parler
tall grand
tea thé *(m.)*
teach enseigner
teacher professeur *(m.)*
team équipe *(f.)*
teddy bear ours *(m.)* en peluche
teenager adolescent *(m.)*, adolescente *(f.)*
telephone *(noun)* téléphone *(m.)*
telephone *(verb)* téléphoner à
television télévision *(f.)*
tell raconter, dire
terrorist terroriste *(m./f.)*
thank remercier
the le, la, l', les
theater théâtre *(m.)*
their *(adj.)* leur, leurs
then puis, ensuite
there là, y
there is/are il y a
these *(adj.)* ces
thief voleur *(m.)*, voleuse *(f.)*
thing chose *(f.)*
think penser, trouver, croire
thirst soif *(f.)*
thirsty: be thirsty avoir soif
this *(adj.)* ce, cet, cette
throat gorge *(f.)*
throw jeter
Thursday jeudi *(m.)*

ticket contravention *(f.) (traffic)*, billet *(m.) (train, plane, etc.)*
tidy up ranger
tie *(noun)* cravate *(f.)*
time temps *(m.)*, heure *(f.)*, fois *(f.)*
   a long time longtemps
   all the time tout le temps
   from time to time de temps en temps
tip *(waiter)* pourboire *(m.)*
tired fatigué
toast *(noun)* pain grillé *(m.)*
today aujourd'hui
together ensemble
tomorrow demain
tonight ce soir
too trop, *(also)* aussi
   too many trop (de)
   too much trop (de)
tooth dent *(f.)*
towel serviette *(f.)*
tower tour *(f.)*
town ville *(f.)*
toy jouet *(m.)*
traffic circulation *(f.)*
   traffic jam embouteillage (m.)
   traffic light feu (m.) (de signalisation)
train train *(m.)*
   train station gare (f.)
translate traduire
trap piège *(m.)*
travel *(verb)* voyager
tray plateau *(m.)*
tree arbre *(m.)*
trip voyage *(m.)*
truck camion *(m.)*
true vrai
truth vérité *(f.)*
try, try on essayer
Tuesday mardi *(m.)*
Turkey Turquie *(f.)*
turn tourner
tuxedo smoking *(m.)*

U

umbrella parapluie *(m.)*
uncle oncle *(m.)*
under sous
understand comprendre
unfortunately malheureusement
United States États-Unis *(m.pl.)*
   in/to the United States aux États-Unis
university université *(f.)*
unless à moins que
until jusqu'à (ce que)
use *(verb)* se servir de, utiliser, employer
useful utile
usually d'habitude, en général

Appendix D: French-English / English-French glossary **609**

V

vacation vacances *(f.pl.)*
vegetable légume *(m.)*
very très
victim victime *(f.)*
video game jeu vidéo *(m.)*
visit *(noun)* visite *(f.)*
visit *(verb)* visiter *(places)*, rendre visite à *(people)*
voice voix *(f.)*

W

wait (for) attendre
waiter serveur *(m.)*, garçon *(m.)*
waitress serveuse *(f.)*
wake up se réveiller
walk marcher, aller à pied
wallet portefeuille *(m.)*
want (to) vouloir, avoir envie de
war guerre *(f.)*
warning avertissement *(m.)*
wash (se) laver
washing machine machine *(f.)* à laver
watch *(noun)* montre *(f.)*
watch *(verb)* regarder
water eau *(f.)*
wear porter
weather temps *(m.)*
wedding mariage *(m.)*
Wednesday mercredi *(m.)*
week semaine *(f.)*
weekend week-end *(m.)*
weigh peser
well bien
what que, qu'est-ce que, quel, quoi
  what is the weather like? quel temps fait-il?
  what time is it? quelle heure est-il?
when quand, lorsque
where où
whether si
which quel, quelle, quels, quelles
while pendant que
white blanc, blanche
who qui
why pourquoi

wife femme *(f.)*, épouse *(f.)*
win gagner
  win the lottery gagner à la loterie
wind vent *(m.)*
windbreaker blouson *(m.)*, anorak *(m.)*
window fenêtre *(f.)*
wine vin *(m.)*
winter hiver *(m.)*
wish *(noun)* souhait *(m.)*, vœu *(m.)*
  make a wish faire un vœu
wish (to) *(verb)* vouloir, avoir envie de
with avec
without sans
witness témoin *(m.)*
wolf loup *(m.)*
woman femme *(f.)*
wonder *(verb)* se demander
word mot *(m.)*
work *(noun)* travail *(m.)*
work *(verb)* travailler, *(function)* marcher,
  fonctionner
world monde *(m.)*
worried inquiet, inquiète
worry *(verb)* s'inquiéter
wound *(verb)* blesser
write écrire
writer écrivain *(m.)*
wrong faux, fausse
  be wrong (person) avoir tort

X

X-ray radio *(f.)*
  have an X-ray passer la radio

Y

yard jardin *(m.)*
year an *(m.)*, année *(f.)*
yellow jaune
yes oui
yesterday hier
yogurt yaourt *(m.)*
young jeune
your *(adj.)* ton, ta, tes, votre, vos

Answer key

1 Articles

1·1 1. des   2. du   3. des   4. de la   5. de l'   6. des   7. du   8. des   9. des   10. de la

1·2 1. annonçait   2. voyageons   3. reconnaissez   4. rangèrent   5. mangea   6. as été réveillé   7. reconnaîtrais   8. finançons   9. ai reçu   10. empêchèrent

1·3 La porte étroite

—Tiens! Ma porte n'était donc pas fermée? dit-elle.

—J'ai frappé; tu n'as pas répondu, Alissa, tu sais que je pars demain?

Elle ne répondit rien, mais posa sur la cheminée le collier qu'elle ne parvenait pas à agrafer. Le mot: fiançailles me paraissait trop nu, trop brutal, j'employai je ne sais quelle périphrase à la place. Dès qu'Alissa me comprit, il me parut qu'elle chancela, s'appuya contre la cheminée … mais j'étais moi-même si tremblant que craintivement j'évitais de regarder vers elle.

J'étais près d'elle et, sans lever les yeux, lui pris la main; elle ne se dégagea pas, mais, inclinant un peu son visage et soulevant un peu ma main, elle y posa ses lèvres et murmura, appuyée à demi contre moi:

—Non, Jérôme, non; ne nous fiançons pas, je t'en prie … […]

—Pourquoi?

—Mais c'est moi qui peux te demander: pourquoi? pourquoi changer?

Je n'osais lui parler de la conversation de la veille, mais sans doute elle sentit que j'y pensais, et, comme une réponse à ma pensée, dit en me regardant fixement:

—Tu te méprends, mon ami: je n'ai pas besoin de tant de bonheur. Ne sommes-nous pas heureux ainsi?

Elle s'efforçait en vain à sourire.

—Non, puisque je dois te quitter.

—Écoute, Jérôme, je ne puis te parler ce soir … Ne gâtons pas nos derniers instants… Non, non. Je t'aime autant que jamais; rassure-toi. Je t'écrirai; je t'expliquerai. Je te promets de t'écrire, dès demain… dès que tu seras parti. Va, maintenant!

1·4 1. La hiérarchie dans cette organisation est un jeu de hasard.   2. Le héros de ce nouveau film est un homme qui habite dans le hameau près de notre village.   3. La haine entre les deux frères est bien connue.   4. Nora est surprise par la hausse des prix du restaurant de l'hôtel.   5. Les hors-d'œuvre qu'ils ont servis étaient délicieux.   6. Est-ce que tu veux commander le homard sur le menu?   7. Le père de Carole s'est fracturé la hanche la semaine dernière.   8. Le hamac dans le jardin est un cadeau de Laurent.   9. L'hiver froid dans cette ville est le handicap principal pour nos grands-parents.   10. La honte de sa défaite est difficile à accepter.

1·5 1. Jean est belge.   2. Isabella est hongroise.   3. Les enfants de Bruno parlent français avec leurs amis et anglais avec leurs parents.   4. En Grèce, l'hiver est doux.   5. Lucie est née le 28 février.   6. Le festival de jazz a lieu du premier au quatre juillet.   7. La mer Méditerranée est moins salée que la mer Morte.   8. L'espagnol et le portugais sont les langues principales en Amérique latine.   9. Le pôle Sud est en Antarctique.   10. Quand tu fais du ski dans les Alpes, tu peux aller de France jusqu'en Slovénie.

2 Basic gender endings: **Masculin** and **féminin**

2·1   1. la tolérance   2. le pain   3. le compliment   4. le sapin   5. la présence   6. le courage   7. l'agneau (*masc.*)   8. l'orangeraie (*fem.*)   9. la chaîne   10. la plage   11. le ruisseau   12. l'architecture (*fem.*)   13. le classement   14. le symbolisme   15. l'égalité (*fem.*)   16. l'odeur (*fem.*)   17. la pudeur   18. le vignoble   19. la paille   20. le calepin

2·2   J'aime l'eau
J'aime l'eau dans ma baignoire
Et sur le carrelage de la cuisine quand maman le nettoie
J'aime l'eau sur la plage
J'aime les vaguelettes
Qui me chatouillent les doigts de pieds
Et s'en vont avec la marée
J'aime l'eau des flaques et des étangs
Des lacs et des barrages où elle se heurte en écumant
J'aime la pluie qui me mouille la langue
Et qui fait pousser les plantes dans le jardin
J'aime l'eau des fleuves
L'eau où pullulent les petits poissons
J'aime l'eau quand elle est bien chaude
Le matin dans mon lavabo
J'aime l'eau quand elle est gelée
Quand je peux patiner sur les mares glacées.

2·3   1. le meuble   2. le soja   3. la référence   4. le cocktail   5. le rail   6. la fin   7. l'attitude (*fem.*)   8. le lainage   9. le parlement   10. la centaine   11. la sculpture   12. le libéralisme   13. le signal   14. la délicatesse   15. l'horlogerie (*fem.*)   16. le citadin   17. le tact   18. l'orthographe (*fem.*)   19. le clavecin   20. la fraternité

2·4   1. l'acacia (*masc.*)   2. la chanson   3. le portefeuille   4. le domino   5. la signature   6. l'écaille (*fem.*)   7. le millefeuille   8. le cinéma   9. la tribu   10. le tracteur   11. l'établissement (*masc.*)   12. l'altitude (*fem.*)   13. le hamac   14. le ghetto   15. la confirmation   16. la noix   17. la main   18. l'inclinaison (*fem.*)   19. la soif   20. la faim

3 More French nouns and their gender

3·1   1. Il est directeur. Elle est directrice.
2. Il est chanteur. Elle est chanteuse.
3. Il est gardien. Elle est gardienne.
4. Il est commerçant. Elle est commerçante.
5. Il est pédiatre. Elle est pédiatre.
6. Il est consultant. Elle est consultante.
7. Il est traducteur. Elle est traductrice.
8. Il est agriculteur. Elle est agricultrice.
9. Il est technicien. Elle est technicienne.
10. Il est psychologue. Elle est psychologue.
11. Il est assistant technique. Elle est assistante technique.
12. Il est astrologue. Elle est astrologue.
13. Il est mécanicien. Elle est mécanicienne.
14. Il est boucher. Elle est bouchère.
15. Il est électricien. Elle est électricienne.
16. Il est archiduc. Elle est archiduchesse.
17. Il est dessinateur. Elle est dessinatrice.
18. Il est baron. Elle est baronne.

19. Il est infirmier. Elle est infirmière.
20. Il est viticulteur. Elle est viticultrice.

3·2
1. Son cousin est une célébrité dans le monde du spectacle.
2. Une altesse royale que nous n'avons pas vraiment reconnue, a fait halte dans notre village hier.
3. Ta tante est un ange!
4. Mathieu est une personne sur qui on peut compter.
5. Sandrine est un mannequin célèbre pour ses coiffures excentriques.
6. Monsieur Thibault est un génie en informatique.
7. Sa femme est un gourmet par excellence.
8. Ce chanteur, c'est une idole depuis des années.
9. Ce type, c'est une véritable crapule!
10. Julie est un témoin que le juge veut entendre.

3·3
1. L'impresario et sa star prenaient un verre sur la Croisette.
2. Mélanie voudrait inviter son oncle et sa tante pour son anniversaire.
3. La police n'a pas encore retrouvé son assassin.
4. Hervé est arrivé avec Anna, son successeur.
5. Alice, tu es son sauveur!
6. Son parrain lui a offert un joli bracelet.
7. Lui et son acolyte, ils ne font que des bêtises!
8. Yan est venu nous voir avec son beau-frère et sa belle-mère.
9. Ce pays ne peut pas se débarrasser de son tyran.
10. Quelle est sa vedette préférée?

3·4
1. La vache est agacée par la mouche qui tourne autour de sa tête.
2. En théorie, le lièvre court plus vite que la tortue.
3. Le perroquet de la tante de Xavier répète sans cesse les mêmes mots.
4. Je veux choisir le chameau qui me plaît pour faire un tour dans le désert.
5. La louve et l'ourse protègent farouchement leurs petits.
6. La cigale chante pendant que la fourmi travaille.
7. LÉO, le chat de Mademoiselle Gallatin est un magnifique Maine Coon.
8. L'oiseau qui se perche sur notre balcon est un rouge-gorge.
9. As-tu mangé le saumon que tu as attrapé?
10. La guêpe qui était sur la table a fini par la piquer.

3·5
1. la chamelle/le chameau   2. la chèvre/le bouc   3. la truie/le porc   4. la louve/le loup   5. l'oie/le jars   6. la chevrette/le chevreuil   7. la jument/le cheval   8. l'agnelle/l'agneau   9. la biche/le cerf   10. la brebis/le bélier

3·6
1. la Californie   2. la Seine-Saint-Denis   3. la Louisiane   4. la Bretagne   5. la Guadeloupe   6. le Caire   7. le Languedoc   8. la Dordogne   9. le Nebraska   10. le Vermont   11. le Maine   12. la Lorraine   13. le New Jersey   14. le Limousin   15. le Gard   16. le Poitou   17. le Missouri   18. la Provence   19. la Martinique   20. les Alpes-Maritimes

3·7
1. la France   2. le Danemark   3. la Grèce   4. le Mexique   5. la Belgique   6. le Japon   7. le Chili   8. le Guatemala   9. le Brésil   10. le Cambodge   11. l'Italie   12. le Portugal   13. la Chine   14. la Turquie   15. la Russie   16. la Bolivie   7. la Malaisie   18. la Nouvelle-Calédonie   19. le Costa Rica   20. les Philippines

3·8
1. Le Népal est un endroit idéal pour le trekking.
2. La Jordanie abrite l'ancienne cité de Pétra, patrimoine mondial de l'UNESCO.
3. En mars, Erwan visitera le Togo, le Bénin et la Sierra Leone.
4. La Nouvelle-Zélande attire Carla depuis longtemps.
5. La Guyane est un département ultramarin.
6. Le Burkina Faso organise un gigantesque festival de cinéma tous les deux ans.
7. Le Qatar a invité des architectes français pour construire des édifices.
8. Le Viêt-Nam a fortement influencé l'écriture de Marguerite Duras.
9. Les Pays-Bas sont de grands exportateurs de tulipes.
10. Le Québec est traversé par le Saint-Laurent.

3·9
1. le Rio Grande   2. la Somme   3. le Mékong   4. la Volga   5. la Loire   6. le Mississippi   7. le Têt   8. le Drâ   9. le Niger   10. la Rance   11. le Potomac   12. le Tumen   13. le Loir   14. la Seine   15. le Pô   16. la Drôme   17. le Nil   18. le Rhône   19. la Dordogne   20. la Vienne

Answer key   **613**

3·10 L'automne (*masc.*) prochain, j'irai à l'Île Maurice dans l'océan (*masc.*) Indien. L'Île Maurice est merveilleuse car c'est une île volcanique. Puis l'été (*masc.*) suivant, mon amie Anne et moi envisageons de faire une croisière en Norvège. Anne connaît la mer Noire et le golfe du Mexique. En raison du travail de ses parents, elle a beaucoup voyagé. Elle rêve de voir l'océan (*masc.*) Pacifique. Nous irons sans doute ensemble un de ces jours.

3·11
1. Dans le jardin de Victoire, il y a un lilas et un laurier rose.
2. La rose sur ton chapeau est fanée.
3. Nous étions à la campagne et il a cueilli un bouton d'or.
4. Quand il était jeune, Bernard est tombé sur un cactus.
5. Le chrysanthème est l'emblème national du Japon.
6. La mariée tenait une orchidée de la main gauche.
7. Le séquoia que j'ai pris en photo faisait huit mètres de diamètre.
8. L'automobiliste s'est écrasé contre un platane.
9. Sur chaque table du restaurant, il y avait une rose rouge dans un vase noir.
10. Le chêne dans le jardin de mon grand-père a près de 150 ans.

3·12
1. La pivoine rose signifie la sincérité. Vous pouvez compter sur moi.
2. Le tournesol signifie que vous êtes mon soleil; je ne vois que vous.
3. La pensée signifie que je ne veux pas que vous m'oubliiez.
4. Le mimosa signifie que je doute de votre amour.
5. La jacinthe signifie que je suis conscient de votre beauté.
6. Le bégonia signifie que mon amitié pour vous est sincère.
7. La véronique signifie fidélité, âme sœur.
8. Le bouton d'or signifie que vous vous moquez de moi.
9. Le narcisse signifie l'égoïsme.
10. La rue signifie que j'aime l'indépendance.

3·13 Lucie a mis au milieu un demi-kiwi, puis un abricot, une petite poire. Ensuite, en forme de bouquet, une mirabelle, un cassis, une cerise, une myrtille, une framboise, un cassis. À chaque coin, elle a placé un marron et une cacahouète. Pour finir, elle a mis une truffe au chocolat pour chaque invité tout autour du gâteau.

3·14
—Alex, qu'est-ce que tu prends? Un médoc et un beaufort?
—Non, aujourd'hui, je voudrais un rosé d'Anjou et un gorgonzola.
—Et toi, Yves?
—Une vodka et un vacherin.
—Une vodka? En quel honneur? Tu prends toujours un saumur!
—Oui mais demain, on part pour Moscou. Je veux m'habituer.
—D'accord, une vodka pour Yves et un chablis pour Raoul?
—Exact. Un chablis et un crottin de Chavignol.
—Tout le monde est servi?
—Non, Julien, tu m'as oublié. Un pernod et un chabichou.
—Désolé. Ça arrive tout de suite.

3·15 1. l'émeraude (*fem.*) 2. le diamant 3. la tourmaline 4. l'étain (*masc.*) 5. le potassium 6. le fer 7. le lithium 8. le marbre 9. la chaux 10. le charbon 11. la citrine 12. le quartz 13. la topaze 14. le bronze 15. le corail 16. le plomb 17. la bauxite 18. le sel 19. le jade 20. le rubis

3·16 Le père de mon copain Luc adore sa BMW alors que sa femme préfère sa Mini. Luc voudrait bien avoir son Pajero à lui tout seul mais ses parents ne sont pas d'accord. S'il passe le bac, il pourra rendre ses copains jaloux avec sa Smart ou sa Coccinelle.

3·17
1. Antoine apprend le japonais car il veut aussi apprendre le karaté.
2. Le marketing pour la vodka Van Gogh a bien réussi.
3. Le tweet a été envoyé par un gourou de l'ashram d'Aurobindo.
4. La pizza et la polenta qu'elle a préparées étaient délicieuses.
5. Je cherche un interprète qui parle très bien le chinois et le russe.
6. Le Carnaval de Venise a lieu en février.
7. Dans la datcha, cela sentait le bortsch et la vodka.
8. Akiko, aimez-vous le saké? Et le karaoké?
9. Le nouveau manga de Yoshihiro Togashi connaît un grand succès.
10. Ils ont chevauché dans la steppe de Mongolie.

614 Answer key

3·18	1. Le nouvel abat-jour que tu as acheté est trop grand.
	2. Le devant de la maison a besoin de réparations.
	3. Je ne peux pas trouver le casse-noisette. Où l'as-tu mis?
	4. Thierry lui a offert le presse-papier en cristal dont elle rêvait.
	5. Clara se demandait le pourquoi de toute chose.
	6. Ils envisagent de construire le plus haut gratte-ciel du monde.
	7. Quentin étudie la philosophie et le droit à la Sorbonne.
	8. À quelle heure ouvre la voiture-restaurant?
	9. Le sous-marin *Le Redoutable* a fait une escale à Hawaï.
	10. Le lave-vaisselle est en panne. Allons au restaurant!

3·19	1. Le livre qu'Éric a écrit est sur la mode en Italie.
	2. Il a marché dans la vase et ses chaussures sont sales.
	3. Le seul légume que mon fils accepte de manger, c'est le broccoli chinois.
	4. Elles m'ont suggéré le gîte dans le Lot où elles ont séjourné l'an passé.
	5. La crêpe a collé à la poêle. Elle est immangeable!
	6. Tu savais que Jean s'était laissé pousser la barbe?
	7. Voudrais-tu faire de la voile au large de l'Île de Ré?
	8. On doit lire le roman jusqu'à la page 150?
	9. Xavier a oublié le mémoire qu'il doit remettre à son professeur.
	10. La mousse pour le bain est parfumée à la lavande.

3·20	1. Je n'ai pas pu enlever la tache de vin sur ta chemise.
	2. Le maître-nageur a mis le drapeau rouge car la mer est très agitée.
	3. La diva a perdu la voix au beau milieu de l'aria.
	4. Vous aurez la peau lisse si vous utilisez cette crème hydratante.
	5. La police a trouvé le repaire des trafiquants de drogue.
	6. Attention! La sole jaune est tombée sur le sol.
	7. Je ne connais pas la tribu dont elle a parlé lors de sa conférence.
	8. Lucie a vu le plus vieux chêne de sa vie dans la forêt de Tronçais.
	9. Prépare un bon repas. Bertrand aime la bonne chère.
	10. Le verre dans lequel tu bois est en cristal de Baccarat.

4   Numbers

4·1 1. six   2. quatorze   3. vingt-trois   4. vingt-huit   5. trente-cinq   6. trente-neuf   7. quarante et un   8. quarante-six   9. quarante-neuf   10. cinquante-deux

4·2 1. He lost for the third time.   2. I live on the thirty-first floor.   3. She sold her second car.   4. It's his fifty-eighth birthday.   5. We skied for the first time.   6. It's the fourth time we have run into each other on the street.   7. He got forty-eighth place.   8. I love Beethoven's Ninth Symphony.   9. He lives at the corner of Twenty-third Street and Seventh Avenue.   10. Is it his second year?

4·3 1. 53   2. 59   3. 62   4. 70   5. 71   6. 78   7. 83   8. 87   9. 90   10. 93

4·4 1. cent un   2. cent quatorze   3. cent vingt-six   4. cent trente-neuf   5. cent quarante-cinq   6. cent cinquante-six   7. cent soixante   8. cent soixante dix-huit   9. cent quatre-vingt-un   10. cent quatre-vingt-dix-neuf

4·5 1. deux cent douze   2. trois cent quinze   3. quatre cent vingt   4. cinq cent trente et un   5. six cent vingt-trois   6. sept cent quatre-vingt-dix   7. huit cent quarante-huit   8. neuf cent quatre   9. six cent quarante-cinq   10. cent un

4·6 1. deux cent cinq   2. trois cent quatre-vingt-neuf   3. quatre cent cinquante-six   4. cinq cent quatre   5. six cent soixante-dix-huit   6. sept cent quarante-cinq   7. huit cents   8. huit cent quinze   9. neuf cent un   10. neuf cent quarante

4·7 1. mille cinq   2. deux mille quatre cent cinquante-six   3. trois mille vingt et un   4. quatre mille sept cent quatre-vingt-neuf   5. dix mille quatre cent cinquante   6. vingt-quatre mille huit   7. cent soixante-dix mille huit cent quatre-vingt-dix   8. un million deux cent trente mille   9. trente million trente mille   10. un milliard six cent millions

4·8 1. deux mille quinze   2. cent cinquante mille   3. mille neuf cent soixante-dix-huit   4. deux mille sept   5. un milliard   6. mille cinq cents   7. deux mille six / un million   8. mille huit cent quatre-vingt-cinq   9. cinq mille   10. six milliards

Answer key   **615**

5 Vocabulary: Thoughts, feelings, communicating, home, travel, science, leisure, and technology

5·1   1. B   2. E   3. C   4. F   5. G   6. H   7. D   8. A

5·2   1. d   2. g   3. j   4. a   5. b   6. h   7. i   8. e   9. c   10. f

5·3   *Answers may vary. Suggested answers are given.*   1. V   2. F   3. V   4. F   5. V   6. V   7. F   8. V   9. V   10. V

5·4   1. annonce   2. appelle   3. s'excuse   4. révise   5. explique   6. discute   7. comprend   8. publie   9. s'abonne   10. inculque

5·5   1. F   2. B   3. A   4. J   5. E   6. D   7. G   8. H   9. C   10. I

5·6   1. e   2. f   3. h   4. a   5. d   6. g   7. j   8. b   9. i   10. c

5·7   1. aider   2. soulager   3. prendre soin   4. s'occuper   5. offrir   6. divertir   7. plaisanter   8. jouer   9. imiter   10. consoler

5·8   1. f   2. j   3. g   4. i   5. h   6. a   7. c   8. e   9. b   10. d

5·9   1. loger   2. meubler   3. accrocher   4. ranger   5. clouer   6. peindre   7. aérer   8. nettoyer   9. s'installer   10. s'habituer

5·10   1. oui   2. non   3. oui   4. non   5. non   6. oui   7. non   8. non

5·11   1. F   2. F   3. V   4. V   5. F   6. V   7. V   8. F   9. V   10. V

5·12   1. D   2. H   3. F   4. A   5. E   6. C   7. G   8. B

5·13   1. s'intéresse   2. fait des expériences   3. recueille   4. observe   5. découvre   6. annonce   7. réussit   8. prouve   9. partage   10. dirige

5·14   1. F   2. V   3. V   4. F   5. V   6. F   7. F   8. V   9. V   10. F

5·15   1. mal   2. bien   3. bien   4. mal   5. mal   6. bien   7. mal   8. mal

5·16   1. afficher   2. transmettre   3. télécharger   4. communiquer   5. s'abonner   6. gérer   7. simuler   8. perfectionner   9. bloquer   10. initier

5·17   1. sites   2. abonnés   3. dictionnaires   4. fichiers   5. fossé   6. podcaster   7. données   8. utilisateurs   9. requête   10. téléconférences

5·18   1. V   2. F   3. F   4. V   5. F   6. V   7. F   8. V   9. V   10. F

5·19   1. j   2. d   3. g   4. i   5. h   6. a   7. b   8. f   9. e   10. c

5·20   1. B   2. E   3. D   4. A   5. F   6. C

5·21   1. F   2. V   3. V   4. F   5. F   6. V   7. F   8. F   9. V   10. V

5·22   1. l'icône   2. l'arobase   3. la poubelle   4. fournisseur   5. la chronologie   6. numérique   7. caractères   8. prénom   9. d'utilisateur   10. archives

5·23   1. applications   2. innovation   3. virtuel   4. chat   5. billets   6. lectures   7. photographie   8. touche

5·24   1. V   2. V   3. V   4. F   5. F   6. V   7. V   8. V

5·25   1. fichier   2. reporter   3. témoins   4. partages   5. bulletins   6. heures   7. reportages   8. en ligne

5·26   1. h   2. e   3. f   4. g   5. b   6. d   7. c   8. a

5·27   1. V   2. V   3. F   4. V   5. F   6. F   7. V   8. F   9. V   10. F

5·28   1. b   2. c   3. e   4. d   5. a

6 Building sentences

6·1   1. Mon frère est très jeune.   2. Il a dix-huit ans.   3. Il s'appelle Marc.   4. Je l'ai appelé hier./Je lui ai téléphoné hier.   5. Il n'était pas à la maison./Il n'était pas chez lui.   6. Il me répondra bientôt.

6·2   1. Lili et Mélanie; jouent   2. Leur maman; fait   3. Le papa; travaille   4. Les dessins animés; sont   5. Le poulet; rôtit   6. Les petites filles; se lavent

6·3   1. Le contrôleur demande les billets.
             S   V   O
      2. Les passagers ont composté leurs billets.
             S   V   O

3. Je lis mon livre.
   S V   O

4. J'admire les illustrations.
   S   V   O

5. Mon voisin regarde le journal.
     S   V   O

6. Il parle à sa femme.
   S V   O

6·4 1. N 2. N 3. P 4. P 5. N 6. P

6·5 1. l'anniversaire de Viviane 2. une fête 3. None 4. Viviane 5. le repas 6. la chaîne hi-fi

6·6 1. une voiture 2. les voitures confortables 3. un rêve 4. la performance de la voiture 5. des sièges de velours 6. son mari

6·7 1. un film aux étudiants/élèves 2. une note à ses étudiants/élèves 3. leur devoir 4. leur travail à leurs parents 5. un petit cadeau à leurs enfants

6·8 1. Jean habite la ville de Paris. 2. Lucie est la femme de Jean. 3. Les parents de Jean achètent une maison à Jean et à Lucie. 4. Lucie et Jean partent en lune de miel aujourd'hui. 5. Nous avons lu l'annonce de leur mariage dans le journal. 6. Ils vont passer une semaine à Tahiti.

6·9 1. Aujourd'hui mon ami/copain Jean et moi étudions le français. 2. Nous parlons déjà le français. 3. Nous finissons toujours notre travail. 4. Nous donnons notre travail au professeur/à l'enseignant. 5. Quelquefois j'aide mon ami/copain. 6. Il m'aide aussi.

6·10 1. Je n'achète jamais de vin ici. 2. L'employé n'est pas très aimable. 3. Je n'aime pas payer de prix élevés. 4. Le propriétaire ne dit jamais bonjour. 5. Nous ne perdons pas de temps ici.

6·11 1. plus 2. jamais 3. personne 4. rien 5. rien/personne

6·12 1. J'ai jeté mon ancien téléphone parce que je n'en voulais plus. 2. Mais je ne peux trouver mon nouveau cellulaire nulle part. 3. Ces jours-ci je ne me rappelle plus rien. 4. Bon. Je ne peux appeler personne d'autre ce soir. 5. Je n'oublierai plus jamais de le remettre dans mon sac.

7 Asking questions

7·1 1. Mon copain est en retard? 2. Tu as ma liste? 3. Le passager est patient? 4. Nous attendons? 5. Il y a un taxi au coin? 6. Il fait chaud ici?

7·2 1. Tu as compris les instructions? 2. À ton avis, elles étaient claires? 3. On va arriver à faire ce travail? 4. Tu es certain que ce ne sera pas trop difficile? 5. Tu veux commencer ce soir? 6. Tu ne crains pas d'échouer?

7·3 1. Oui./Pas encore./Pas ici. 2. Si./Pas encore./Pas ici. 3. Si./Pas encore./Pas ici. 4. Oui./Pas encore./Pas ici. 5. Oui./Pas encore. 6. Si./Pas encore.

7·4 1. pas 2. jamais 3. plus 4. personne 5. rien

7·5 1. Est-ce que le soleil brille aujourd'hui? 2. Est-ce qu'on va à la plage? 3. Est-ce que tu as envie de prendre le petit déjeuner sur la terrasse? 4. Est-ce qu'on ira nager dans la mer après le petit déjeuner? 5. Est-ce que tu es encore un peu endormi? 6. Est-ce que tu as besoin d'une bonne douche?

7·6 1. Marie écoute-t-elle bien les conseils de sa maman? 2. Est-elle attentive? 3. Les frères jumeaux travaillent-ils ensemble? 4. Sont-ils inséparables? 5. Ne vois-tu pas le bus? 6. Faut-il se dépêcher?

7·7 1. Aimez-vous cette robe, mademoiselle? 2. Puis-je recommander une paire de chaussures, mademoiselle? 3. Avez-vous besoin d'un foulard, mademoiselle? 4. Etes-vous prête à payer, mademoiselle? 5. Avez-vous une carte de crédit, mademoiselle? 6. Aimeriez-vous/Voudriez-vous un sac, mademoiselle?

7·8 *Suggested answers:* 1. Pardonnez-moi/Pardon, mademoiselle, aimez-vous cette robe? 2. Pardonnez-moi/Pardon, mademoiselle, puis-je recommander une paire de chaussures? 3. Pardonnez-moi/Pardon, mademoiselle, avez-vous besoin d'un foulard? 4. Excusez-moi de vous déranger mademoiselle, êtes-vous prête à payer ? 5. Pardonnez-moi/Pardon, mademoiselle, avez-vous une carte de crédit? 6. Pardonnez-moi/Pardon, mademoiselle, aimeriez-vous/voudriez-vous un sac?

7·9 1. Préfères-tu un citron pressé, un coca ou une bière? 2. Arrivez-vous cet après-midi ou demain? 3. Désirent-ils aller à la plage ou nager dans la piscine? 4. Achetons-nous le parasol, la chaise-

Answer key **617**

longue ou une serviette? 5. Veulent-elles voir un film ou dîner au restaurant? 6. Dormez-vous dans le lit ou sur le canapé?

7·10 1. d 2. e 3. a 4. b 5. c

7·11 1. Tu aimes ce livre, pas vrai? 2. Tu sais qui l'a écrit, n'est-ce pas? 3. Cet auteur est bon, tu ne penses pas? 4. C'est un maître du suspense, non? 5. Tu as lu son livre précédent, pas vrai?

7·12 1. Qui est-ce que 2. Qui est-ce que 3. Qui est-ce qui 4. Qui est-ce qui 5. Qui est-ce qui

7·13 1. Whom did you meet last night? —An old friend. 2. Whom did you invite? —The family. 3. Whom is Raymond going to congratulate? —His new employee. 4. Whom are you looking for? —The saleslady. 5. Whom do your parents prefer? —Me, of course. 6. Whom does Suzanne kiss? —Her boyfriend.

7·14 1. appelez-vous 2. invitez-vous 3. avez-vous vu 4. préférez-vous 5. allez-vous chercher 6. allez-vous renvoyer

7·15 1. c 2. e 3. a 4. b 5. d

7·16 1. aimez-vous recevoir comme cadeaux 2. vous offrent vos parents 3. dites-vous quand on vous donne un cadeau 4. faites-vous pour vous amuser 5. n'aimez-vous pas faire le jour de votre annniversaire

7·17 1. Que 2. Qu' 3. Qu'est-ce que 4. Qu'est-ce que 5. Qu'est-ce qui 6. Que

7·18 1. Tu vas où maintenant?/Où tu vas maintenant? 2. Tu vas au travail comment?/Comment tu vas au travail? 3. Tu rentres quand aujourd'hui?/Quand rentres-tu aujourd'hui? 4. Pourquoi tu ne manges pas? 5. Tu veux combien de café?/Combien de cafés tu veux-tu? 6. Ça va comment?/Comment ça va?

7·19 1. Où est-ce que tu vas maintenant? 2. Comment est-ce que tu vas au travail? 3. Quand est-ce que tu rentres aujourd'hui? 4. Pourquoi est-ce que tu ne manges pas? 5. Comment est-ce que tu veux de cafés? 6. Comment est-ce que ça va?

7·20 1. Quelle heure est-il? 2. Quelle est sa date de naissance? 3. Quel est son numéro de téléphone? 4. Quel temps fait-il aujourd'hui? 5. Quelles sont ses couleurs favorites? 6. Quel choix est-ce que j'ai?

7·21 1. Comment 2. Où 3. Quelle 4. Que 5. Où/Comment 6. Où/Comment 7. Où/Qui/Comment 8. Où/Comment 9. Où/Comment 10. Qui

7·22 1. Où 2. Qu' 3. Qu'est-ce qu' 4. Qu'est-ce qui 5. où 6. Qu'

7·23 1. D'où es-tu? 2. Où vas-tu? 3. Depuis quand étudies-tu le français? 4. Quand vas-tu finir cet exercice? 5. Jusqu'à quand vas-tu attendre? 6. À qui écris-tu la plupart de tes e-mails?

7·24 1. avez-vous/est-ce que vous avez 2. Quelle est 3. habitez-vous/est-ce que vous habitez 4. Quel est 5. ne venez-vous pas/est-ce que vous ne venez pas 6. avez-vous/est-ce que vous avez

7·25 1. Où voudriez-vous aller? 2. Combien pouvez-vous dépenser? 3. Qui voyage avec vous? 4. Quelle ligne aérienne préférez-vous? 5. Pourquoi voulez-vous voyager en première classe?

7·26 1. qui 2. où 3. Quand/Où/Comment 4. Quel 5. Quand/Où 6. Quand/Comment

7·27 1. Quel âge 2. Que 3. Où 4. Qui 5. Que/Pour qui/Où 6. Où 7. Comment 8. Qu'est-ce qu' 9. Qu'est-ce qu' 10. Qu'est-ce qui

7·28 1. Laquelle 2. Lequel 3. Lesquels 4. Combien de 5. Combien de 6. Laquelle/Lesquelles

8 Exclamations and commands

8·1 1. la lune est belle 2. Nous aimons 3. il fait chaud dehors 4. la limonade est froide 5. Lucie est si fatiguée! 6. Bon! Maintenant nous sommes prêtes!

8·2 1. Je suis si mignon(ne)! 2. Je danse si bien! 3. J'ai tant d'amis! 4. Mon patron m'aime beaucoup! 5. Je suis très riche! 6. Tout le monde m'admire!

8·3 1. One finds so many pleasures in life! 2. It offers so many surprises! 3. What innocence we see in children! 4. We are so attached to life! 5. How happy we are! 6. How lucky we are!

8·4 1. Que ce monsieur conduit vite! 2. Combien d'accidents il y a sur les routes! 3. Comme les chauffards sont dangereux! 4. Que d'obstacles il y a sur la route! 5. Combien de fous brûlent les feux rouges!

8·5 1. f 2. e 3. b 4. d 5. a 6. f

618 Answer key

8·6	*Suggested answers:* 1. Zut! 2. Au secours!/À l'aide! 3. Super!/Hourra! 4. Attention! 5. Zut! 6. Tant mieux!
8·7	1. Chut! Il y a trop de bruit! 2. Ciel! La conférence commence à midi! 3. Hé!/Eh!/Hep! Nous sommes arrivés! 4. Hélas! Je n'ai pas le temps! 5. Tu veux gagner? Espérons! 6. Oh là là! Cette montre est belle!
8·8	1. Regarde un bon film! 2. Viens à onze heures! 3. Prends un café! 4. Va chez Paul! 5. Finis cet exercice! 6. Descends au premier étage!
8·9	1. pars 2. ne fais pas 3. prends 4. ne téléphone pas 5. rentre
8·10	1. 1 2. 1 3. + 4. + 5. + 6. 1
8·11	1. Écoute ta maman! 2. Choisis ton film! 3. Descends! 4. Finis tes devoirs! 5. Ne regarde pas ta sœur! 6. Va à ta chambre!
8·12	1. Ne criez pas! 2. Fermez la télé! 3. Sortez dans le jardin! 4. Ne salissez pas le divan! 5. Donnez-moi cette serviette! 6. Restez dans votre chambre!
8·13	1. Mangeons au restaurant! 2. Invitons Jeanine! 3. Vérifions les horaires des films! 4. Allons-y! 5. Prenons un taxi!

9 Independent clauses and subordinate clauses

9·1	1. Jean va arriver ce soir. 2. Nous préparons un bon repas. 3. Tout le monde est content. 4. Il était longtemps absent. 5. Il va dormir dans sa chambre.
9·2	1. Brigitte ne dort pas bien. 2. Ginette n'aime plus les gâteaux. 3. Nous ne voulons rien boire. 4. Vous ne pouvez pas lire tout le roman. 5. Elles n'ont rien à dire. 6. Vous n'avez pas encore vingt ans.
9·3	1. Est-ce que le ciel est bleu? 2. Est-ce que les oiseaux chantent? 3. Est-ce que le chien court derrière moi? 4. Est-ce que je vais au parc? 5. Est-ce que tu viens avec moi?
9·4	1. Décore ta chambre! 2. Peins les murs! 3. Organise le placard! 4. Change les rideaux! 5. Accroche des tableaux! 6. Déplace le lit!
9·5	1. A 2. N 3. N 4. A 5. IMP 6. A
9·6	1. d 2. e 3. f 4. a 5. b 6. c
9·7	1. Toute la journée Mimi était chez ses grands-parents et elle jouait avec leur chien Médor. 2. Je voulais déjeuner avec elle mais elle avait rendez-vous chez le dentiste. 3. Elle a dû aller à son rendez-vous mais elle n'aime pas aller chez le dentiste. 4. Mimi n'a pas mangé de toute la journée ni le soir. 5. Aujourd'hui elle doit se sentir mieux sinon elle doit retourner chez le dentiste. 6. Mimi est très gentille mais elle est aussi très indécise.
9·8	1. Mes parents restent à la maison le samedi et le dimanche. 2. Papa ne mange pas de viande de bœuf ni de poulet. 3. Maman prépare la salade et la vinaigrette. 4. Nous allons manger vers six heures ou sept heures. 5. Avant le dîner, nous buvons un verre de vin ou un apéritif. 6. Après le dîner, nous faisons du thé ou du café.
9·9	1. J'ai envie d'écrire un roman donc je vais au bureau. 2. J'écris le premier chapitre mais je ne l'aime pas. 3. Je dois récrire le premier chapitre sinon la fin sera impossible. 4. Je peux changer le début ou la fin du chapitre. 5. Je n'ai pas d'idées donc je vais me promener. 6. J'entre dans un café et je commande un expresso.
9·10	1. Tu écris bien et tu parles encore mieux. 2. Le pauvre n'entend ni ne parle. 3. Tu es en retard donc dépêche-toi! 4. Tu arrives et/mais tu repars. 5. Ce manteau est cher mais j'ai assez d'argent pour l'acheter. 6. Le magasin ne ferme ni à six heures ni à sept heures.
9·11	1. Zoé se lève, s'habille et se maquille. 2. Elle prend son sac, sort et ferme la porte à clef. 3. Elle prend le vélo, le bus ou le métro. 4. Elle ne boit ni thé ni café, mais elle boit un verre de jus. 5. Il fait de l'orage et il pleut fort, donc elle se dépêche.
9·12	1. Quelquefois/Parfois j'aime rester à la maison/chez moi et lire un bon livre. 2. Il y a des jours où je ne veux ni sortir ni parler à personne. 3. Je réponds au téléphone mais seulement si c'est la famille. 4. Je peux voir le nom de mon correspondant, donc je sais qui appelle/téléphone. 5. Je n'ai ni scrupules ni regrets.
9·13	1. pendant que; quand 2. que 3. afin que; pour que 4. où 5. de manière que; de sorte que; en sorte que; si bien que; de façon que 6. Quand bien même; Même si 7. avant que 8. trop… pour que 9. Plus… moins 10. Bien que… car

Answer key   **619**

10 The present tense of -er verbs

10·1 1. travaille 2. acceptons 3. cherchent 4. apportes 5. bavardez 6. commande 7. habitent 8. déjeune 9. dessinez 10. visitons

10·2 1. Nous refusons l'invitation. 2. Elle annule le voyage. 3. Il parle français. 4. Vous apportez des fleurs. 5. Je coupe le pain. 6. Ils (Elles) déjeunent avec Julie. 7. Il emprunte dix euros. 8. Je commande un dessert. 9. Tu étudies le russe. 10. Ils (Elles) cherchent un bon restaurant.

10·3 1. commençons 2. avancez 3. déplace 4. devançons 5. annonçons 6. effaces 7. remplaçons 8. exercent 9. finançons 10. menace

10·4 1. mélangez 2. range 3. exigeons 4. déménagent 5. héberge 6. corrigez 7. mangeons 8. nages 9. encourageons 10. change

10·5 1. renouvelle 2. emmène 3. achetez 4. ensorcelle 5. espère 6. exagérez 7. s'appelle 8. étincellent 9. répète 10. célébrons

10·6 1. achète 2. travaillent 3. empruntez 4. aimes 5. renonçons 6. J'habite 7. préfère 8. s'appelle 9. bavardons 10. rappelle

10·7 1. i 2. e 3. h 4. a 5. b 6. j 7. c 8. d 9. f 10. g

10·8 1. Nous sommes en train de chanter une chanson. 2. Elle est en train de dessiner un mouton. 3. Je suis en train de travailler dans la cuisine. 4. Tu es en train d'effacer le tableau. 5. Vous êtes en train d'étudier l'histoire européenne. 6. Nous sommes en train de bavarder dans le jardin. 7. Il est en train de corriger les copies. 8. Tu es en train de laver la chemise. 9. Je suis en train de ranger mes affaires. 10. Elle est en train de manger une omelette aux champignons.

10·9 1. Elle chante dans cette chorale depuis trois ans. 2. Je partage cet appartement depuis six mois. 3. Il nage dans cette piscine depuis un mois. 4. J'habite à Montpellier depuis 2004. 5. Il possède cette propriété depuis dix ans. 6. Je regarde cette émission depuis des années. 7. Il travaille dans cette entreprise depuis 2002. 8. Je porte des lunettes depuis dix ans. 9. Il est président depuis 2005. 10. Ce magasin est fermé depuis deux mois.

10·10 1. J'étudie le français. 2. J'épelle mon nom. 3. Ils (Elles) déménagent demain. 4. Elle aime voyager en bateau. 5. Depuis combien de temps étudiez-vous le français? 6. Tu répètes la phrase. 7. Nous finançons le projet. 8. Elle annule la réunion. 9. Depuis combien de temps habitez-vous dans cette maison? 10. Je pèse les légumes.

11 The present tense of -ir and -re verbs

11·1 1. cueillons 2. finissent 3. remplis 4. investissons 5. mentent 6. ouvres 7. réfléchissez 8. sens 9. offrent 10. meurt

11·2 1. h 2. j 3. a 4. e 5. i 6. b 7. d 8. f 9. g 10. c

11·3 1. Nous partons à dix heures. 2. Elle ouvre la porte. 3. Vous cueillez des fleurs dans le jardin de Florence. 4. La voiture ralentit. 5. Nous sortons ce soir. 6. Elle saisit l'occasion. 7. Elle rougit facilement. 8. Ils (Elles) courent vite. 9. Elle résout le mystère. 10. Ils (Elles) dorment dans la chambre de Sonia.

11·4 1. répondons 2. répand 3. rendez 4. vendent 5. descends 6. attends 7. tend 8. perd 9. prétend 10. étendent

11·5 1. h 2. e 3. g 4. i 5. a 6. c 7. b 8. j 9. d 10. f

11·6 1. prenons 2. entreprend 3. apprends 4. comprenez 5. apprennent 6. surprend 7. prenez 8. comprenons 9. prends 10. comprend

11·7 1. Il apprend le chinois. 2. Elle prend le métro tous les jours. 3. Il perd souvent ses clés. 4. J'entends Pierre dans la rue. 5. Il prétend être le frère du roi. 6. Vous répondez rapidement. 7. Elle vend des fleurs. 8. Nous descendons les Champs-Élysées. 9. Je descends. 10. Nous attendons une réponse.

11·8 1. Remplissent-ils les formulaires? 2. Réfléchit-il au problème? 3. Aimez-vous aller au théâtre? 4. Préfère-t-elle voyager en Italie? 5. Écoutes-tu le discours du président? 6. Influencent-ils le public? 7. Annule-t-elle son voyage au Brésil? 8. Travailles-tu le jeudi? 9. Apportez-vous un nouveau livre? 10. Agrandit-elle les photos?

11·9   1. Est-ce qu'ils parlent de la nouvelle transaction?   2. Est-ce qu'elle apprend le portugais?   3. Est-ce que vous commandez une bouteille de vin blanc?   4. Est-ce que tu demandes une augmentation de salaire?   5. Est-ce qu'ils financent un grand projet?   6. Est-ce que vous choisissez une autre direction?   7. Est-ce qu'ils finissent tard?   8. Est-ce qu'il prétend être pauvre?   9. Est-ce qu'ils défendent cette théorie?   10. Est-ce que vous descendez par l'escalier?

11·10   1. Il n'encourage pas ses employés.   2. Ils ne visitent pas le musée.   3. Tu ne gagnes pas à la loterie.   4. Elle n'enlève pas son chapeau.   5. Vous n'exprimez pas vos opinions.   6. Tu ne pèses pas les fruits.   7. Il ne danse pas la valse.   8. Vous ne corrigez pas les copies des étudiants.   9. Nous n'étudions pas l'arabe.   10. Il ne maigrit pas en vacances.

11·11   1. J'apprends le japonais.   2. Il ne parle pas italien.   3. Elle ne mange ni viande ni fromage.   4. Ils (Elles) n'écoutent jamais personne.   5. Vous travaillez tard.   6. Ils (Elles) n'aiment ni le thé ni le café.   7. Comprenez-vous la question?   8. Nous cueillons des fleurs dans le jardin.   9. Il n'enlève jamais son chapeau.   10. Elle ne ment jamais.

12   Être, avoir, and other irregular verbs

12·1   1. est   2. sommes   3. sont   4. es   5. sont   6. êtes   7. C'est   8. ne sont pas   9. est   10. suis

12·2   1. Oui, ils sont en retard.   2. Oui, le climat est sec.   3. Oui, je suis libre ce soir.   4. Oui, il est heureux.   5. Oui, elle est sympathique.   6. Oui, ce restaurant français est cher.   7. Oui, je suis fatigué.   8. Oui, vous êtes à la bonne adresse.   9. Oui, ce film est amusant.   10. Oui, le musée est ouvert.

12·3   1. avons   2. n'as pas   3. J'ai   4. avez   5. a   6. ont   7. as   8. n'avons pas   9. n'avez pas   10. J'ai

12·4   1. g   2. j   3. a   4. i   5. b   6. h   7. c   8. e   9. d   10. f

12·5   1. Je suis fatigué(e).   2. Il a très faim.   3. Ils (Elles) ont toujours raison.   4. Sont-ils français? (Sont-elles françaises?)   5. Avez-vous peur de sa réaction?   6. Il a honte.   7. Ils (Elles) ont un chien.   8. Elle a un nouveau chapeau.   9. C'est très cher.   10. Fermez la fenêtre. Nous avons froid.

12·6   1. savez   2. sais   3. ne sait pas   4. savons   5. sais   6. sais   7. ne sait pas   8. Savez   9. sais   10. savez

12·7   1. connaissent   2. connaissons   3. connaît   4. connais   5. connaît   6. connaissez   7. connaissez   8. connais   9. connaît   10. Connaissez

12·8   1. sais   2. sait   3. sais   4. connaissons   5. sais   6. connaissent   7. connaît   8. connaissez   9. sait   10. connaissons

12·9   1. voulons   2. ne peux pas   3. veux   4. pouvons   5. veux   6. pouvez   7. peut   8. veulent   9. voulez   10. peuvent

12·10   1. J'aperçois   2. prévoit   3. pleut   4. voyons   5. déçois   6. promeut   7. vaut   8. faut   9. émeut   10. recevez

12·11   1. Est-ce que tu sais nager?   2. Est-ce qu'il sait faire la cuisine?   3. Je ne sais pas où il est.   4. Est-ce qu'elle peut remplir ce formulaire?   5. Elle connaît Caroline.   6. Est-ce que tu sais cette chanson française par cœur?   7. Il pleut en France.   8. Tu dois arriver à midi.   9. Il prévoit une grande amélioration.   10. Je vois le château.

12·12   1. doit   2. dois   3. devez   4. doit   5. ne doivent pas   6. dois   7. doit   8. doivent   9. dois   10. dois

12·13   1. Vous devez faire la cuisine ce soir.   2. Elle ne doit pas travailler aujourd'hui.   3. À quelle heure est-ce qu'il doit arriver?   4. Combien est-ce que je vous dois?   5. Pourquoi est-ce qu'il doit vendre sa voiture?   6. Elle doit une excuse à Carole.   7. Est-ce que nous devons connaître ces verbes?   8. Il doit deux mille dollars à la banque.   9. Vous devriez appeler Vincent.   10. Vous ne devriez pas inviter Pierre.

12·14   1. e   2. a   3. d   4. c   5. b

12·15   1. craint   2. feint   3. plaignent   4. ceint   5. feignez   6. craignons   7. peignez   8. craignent   9. teint   10. se plaint

12·16   1. Elle peint la cuisine.   2. Il y a un chien dans la voiture.   3. Ils (Elles) plaignent le pauvre enfant.   4. Dans ce livre, il s'agit du président français.   5. De quoi est-ce qu'il s'agit?   6. Il craint le pire.   7. Il y a des livres sur la table.   8. Est-ce qu'il y a un ordinateur?   9. Est-ce que tu peins les fleurs?   10. Il s'agit de passion.

Answer key   **621**

13 The immediate future, the immediate past, and the causative form

13·1 1. allons 2. vont 3. vais 4. va 5. allez 6. va 7. va 8. vais 9. va 10. allez

13·2 1. Nous allons acheter une nouvelle machine à laver. 2. Il va prendre des vacances cet automne. 3. Vous allez investir au Japon. 4. Elle va avoir vingt ans. 5. Cette agence va promouvoir cette marchandise. 6. Il va être président. 7. Nous allons choisir un cadeau. 8. Tu vas dîner au restaurant. 9. Ils vont déménager en janvier. 10. Elle va travailler au centre-ville.

13·3 1. vient 2. viennent 3. viens 4. vient 5. revenez 6. prévient 7. venons 8. devient 9. revenez 10. viens

13·4 1. Je viens de téléphoner à Bernard. 2. Il vient d'annuler son vol. 3. Elle vient de remplacer tous ses meubles. 4. La police vient de révéler le secret. 5. Vous venez de commencer à travailler. 6. Elle vient de manquer le train. 7. Tu viens d'avoir trente ans. 8. Il vient d'achever ses études. 9. Nous venons de parler à la directrice. 10. Ils viennent de voir un bon film.

13·5 1. Vas-tu au cinéma dimanche? 2. Ils (Elles) vont bientôt déménager. 3. Comment vas-tu? 4. Ils (Elles) vont investir au Portugal. 5. Elle vient de commencer un nouveau travail. 6. Ce chapeau te va bien. 7. Ils viennent d'annuler mon vol. 8. Il va à la bibliothèque le samedi. 9. Elle vient d'appeler François. 10. Elle va finir le livre cet après-midi.

13·6 1. c 2. d 3. e 4. a 5. b

13·7 1. fait 2. font 3. fais 4. fait 5. faisons 6. fait 7. fait 8. font 9. faites 10. fait

13·8 1. Je fais lire le dossier. 2. Vous faites laver la voiture. 3. Il fait réparer la télévision. 4. Elle fait investir sa fortune. 5. Je fais envoyer le paquet. 6. Il fait annuler le voyage. 7. Tu fais remplacer l'employé malade. 8. Il fait visiter l'entreprise. 9. Je fais corriger les copies des étudiants. 10. Je fais chanter la chanson.

13·9 1. Ils (Elles) font envoyer la lettre à Paris. 2. Je fais la queue depuis dix minutes. 3. Ils (Elles) tiennent à leurs amis. 4. Il tient à chanter cette chanson. 5. Elle tient un vase. 6. Il tient de son père. 7. Il pleut. 8. Est-ce que vous savez faire la cuisine? 9. Elle fait laver sa voiture. 10. Il fait froid.

13·10 1. Je ferai réparer mon ordinateur. 2. Emmanuel fera remplacer toutes les lampes dans la bibliothèque. 3. J'ai fait visiter les nouveaux bureaux de l'agence. 4. Shah Jahan a fait construire le Taj Mahal en mémoire de sa femme. 5. Fais envoyer le paquet en express! 6. Victoria fera faire une robe pour le mariage de sa cousine. 7. Faites rédiger une demande de bourse de recherche! 8. Il fera livrer les fleurs à Madame de Guermantes avant midi. 9. Vous ferez corriger les fautes d'orthographe dans votre essai. 10. Raphaël a fait laver sa voiture avant de partir en vacances.

14 Pronominal verbs

14·1 1. m'habille 2. nous levons 3. se coupe 4. te couches 5. se lavent 6. te peignes 7. vous baladez 8. se reposent 9. nous amusons 10. se détend

14·2 1. se marient 2. vous embrassez 3. nous écrivons 4. se retrouvent 5. se voient 6. nous téléphonons 7. vous quittez 8. nous disputons 9. se détestent 10. nous rencontrons

14·3 1. s'aperçoit 2. se dépêchent 3. t'attends 4. se passe 5. vous servez 6. me rends compte 7. te demandes 8. se dépêche 9. te trompes 10. s'envole

14·4 1. me promener 2. te lever 3. nous rendre compte 4. se souvenir 5. se marier 6. vous demander 7. nous écrire 8. m'habiller 9. vous voir 10. nous plaindre

14·5 1. e 2. a 3. d 4. c 5. b

14·6 1. Lève-toi! 2. Elle s'habille pour la soirée. 3. Elle se coupe les cheveux. 4. Nous nous promenons dans le parc. 5. Ils (Elles) se reposent car leurs jambes sont fatiguées. 6. Il se rase. 7. Ils viennent de se marier. 8. Ils (Elles) s'écrivent. 9. Il est fatigué. Il s'assoit sur un banc. 10. Ils s'aiment.

15 The passé composé

15·1 1. a invité 2. avons refusé 3. as travaillé 4. a compris 5. a apporté 6. J'ai voyagé 7. avez loué 8. a sous-titré 9. avez téléphoné 10. as assisté

622 Answer key

15·2	1. ont investi 2. a applaudi 3. ont réfléchi 4. a ralenti 5. ont attendu 6. avons réussi 7. a perdu 8. as grandi 9. a senti 10. a vendu
15·3	1. Ils (Elles) ont vendu la maison en France. 2. J'ai attendu dix minutes. 3. Il a fini le roman. 4. Elle a perdu son dictionnaire. 5. J'ai appelé Marc. 6. Ils (Elles) ont servi un dîner élégant. 7. Il a acheté une voiture. 8. J'ai choisi un très bon fromage. 9. Nous avons regardé le film. 10. Ils (Elles) ont applaudi le comédien.
15·4	1. J'ai pris 2. n'avons pas pu 3. ont suivi 4. a peint 5. a plu 6. avez reçu 7. avons lu 8. J'ai fait 9. a mis 10. a ouvert
15·5	1. e 2. d 3. a 4. b 5. c
15·6	1. est-il monté 2. sommes rentré(e)s 3. est tombée 4. sont descendus 5. sont revenues 6. est-il parti 7. est allée 8. est allé 9. est mort 10. est resté
15·7	1. Elle a lu le journal. 2. Nous sommes allé(e)s à Paris. 3. Ils sont partis (Elles sont parties) hier soir. 4. Il a dû partir à cinq heures. 5. Ils (Elles) ont habité en Italie. 6. Zola est mort en 1902. 7. J'ai écrit une longue lettre. 8. Elle a peint le mur en blanc. 9. Elle est restée à la maison. 10. Il a pris des vacances.
15·8	1. se sont promenés 2. s'est douté 3. se sont maquillées 4. se sont écrit 5. nous sommes arrêté(e)s 6. se sont occupés 7. se sont baladées 8. se sont rencontrés 9. t'es coupé 10. nous sommes demandé
15·9	1. e 2. a 3. d 4. b 5. c
15·10	1. Ils (Elles) ont passé un mois en Chine. 2. Elle s'est évanouie. 3. Ils se sont embrassés. 4. Ils se sont amusés (Elles se sont amusées) à la soirée. 5. Elle a descendu les valises. 6. Il s'est brossé les dents. 7. Il s'est réveillé fatigué. 8. Ils (Elles) se sont écrit régulièrement. 9. Anna s'est arrêtée dix minutes. 10. Il a retourné l'omelette.

16   The **imparfait** and the **plus-que-parfait**

16·1	1. voyageait 2. faisais 3. étions 4. buvaient 5. J'étais 6. aimions 7. partageaient 8. prenait 9. encourageait 10. alliez
16·2	1. croyait 2. J'étais 3. pensait 4. espéraient 5. avait 6. savais 7. étions 8. paraissiez 9. était 10. faisait
16·3	1. suivions 2. faisais 3. était 4. faisions 5. habitaient 6. buvions 7. assistaient 8. faisait 9. vous voyiez 10. travaillait
16·4	1. faisait 2. dormais 3. bavardions 4. se reposaient 5. parliez 6. étudiait 7. dansaient 8. réfléchissait 9. travaillait 10. J'attendais
16·5	1. Je jouais au tennis tous les jeudis. 2. Tu étudiais quand le téléphone a sonné. 3. Nous dormions quand tout à coup nous avons entendu un bruit fort. 4. Le restaurant était bondé. 5. Il faisait froid à la montagne. 6. Ils (Elles) avaient l'air fatigué. 7. La pièce était fascinante. 8. Elle travaillait aux Galeries Lafayette. 9. Nous attendions l'autobus quand il a commencé à pleuvoir. 10. Elle savait qu'ils (elles) avaient tort.
16·6	1. allait 2. déjeunait 3. apportait 4. attendait 5. commandait 6. faisait 7. ouvrait 8. investissait 9. réfléchissait 10. choisissait
16·7	1. Je suis allé(e) chez le dentiste hier. 2. Quand il était adolescent, il jouait au football. 3. À cette époque-là, ils tenaient une brasserie place d'Italie. 4. Ils ont randonné dans les Alpes le week-end passé. 5. Nous dînions dans ce restaurant tous les samedis. 6. Si on prenait un café? 7. Tu avais l'air fatigué. 8. Chaque jour, il écrivait une lettre à son amie. 9. Je regardais un film quand elle est arrivée. 10. La campagne était si belle.
16·8	1. J'avais dîné 2. avait expliqué 3. aviez investi 4. étaient arrivées 5. avais décidé 6. avions roulé 7. avait échoué 8. étais allé(e) 9. J'avais obtenu 10. avait bu
16·9	1. avait pris 2. nous étions réveillé(e)s 3. t'étais demandé(e) 4. s'était habillée 5. s'étaient mariés 6. s'étaient couchées 7. s'était souvenu 8. nous étions promené(e)s 9. s'était reposée 10. s'étaient écrites
16·10	1. était tombée 2. avait eu 3. n'avais pas expliqué 4. avait prescrit 5. avait oublié 6. était parti 7. avait invité 8. avait rencontré 9. avait souffert 10. avait reçu

Answer key   **623**

16·11   1. d   2. c   3. e   4. b   5. a

16·12   1. Si seulement vous n'aviez pas été en retard!   2. Si seulement tu avais étudié le français plus jeune!   3. Si seulement nous avions su la vérité!   4. Si seulement elle était restée plus longtemps!   5. Si seulement il avait rendu visite à sa cousine Flore!   6. Si seulement j'avais pris une meilleure décision!   7. Si seulement elle avait expliqué la situation plus clairement!   8. Si seulement vous aviez pu venir à la réception!   9. Si seulement tu avais compris les problèmes!   10. Si seulement il avait conseillé autre chose!

16·13   1. Il a pris le médicament que le médecin avait prescrit.   2. Elle savait qu'ils (elles) avaient fait une erreur.   3. Il était malade car il avait mangé trop de dessert.   4. Je me suis demandé pourquoi elle était restée trois mois à Vienne.   5. Je pensais qu'ils (elles) avaient compris le problème.   6. Si seulement il n'avait pas été en retard!   7. Elle était fatiguée parce qu'elle n'avait dormi que cinq heures.   8. Il avait faim parce qu'il n'avait pas mangé depuis sept heures du matin.   9. Nous pensions qu'il avait vu ce film.   10. Il pensait qu'elle avait lu le livre.

17   The simple future and the past future

17·1   1. suivrez   2. dînerons   3. entendras   4. cherchera   5. n'oublieront jamais   6. travaillerai   7. rendrons visite   8. finira   9. remplacera   10. partiras

17·2   1. sera   2. fera   3. sauras   4. aurons   5. ira   6. préférera   7. verrons   8. faudra   9. pourra   10. pleuvra

17·3   1. Vous irez à l'opéra quand vos amis seront à Lyon.   2. Nous prendrons une décision dès que la presse annoncera les résultats.   3. L'exposition aura lieu en janvier quand tous les tableaux seront réunis.   4. Le professeur emmènera les élèves au musée dès qu'il pourra.   5. Il devra nous appeler dès qu'il sera en contact avec M. Clément.   6. Tant qu'il y aura des hommes, il y aura des guerres.   7. Elle enseignera le français quand elle habitera au Vietnam.   8. Nous jouerons au bridge quand nous rendrons visite à nos amis.   9. Elle se reposera quand elle aura de longues vacances.   10. Dès qu'il obtiendra l'accord, il partira.

17·4   1. L'avion décollera à onze heures.   2. Tu apprendras à conduire.   3. Je peindrai le salon.   4. Ils sortiront avec des amis.   5. Vous recevrez une invitation.   6. Nous débarquerons à midi.   7. Elle écrira une lettre au président.   8. Tu mettras ton chapeau gris.   9. Ils iront en Bolivie.   10. Il vivra jusqu'à cent ans.

17·5   1. c   2. e   3. a   4. b   5. d

17·6   1. aura appris   2. aura fini   3. aurons visité   4. auront trouvé   5. aura découvert   6. J'aurai répondu   7. se sera reposée   8. auront complété   9. sera mort   10. J'aurai vu

17·7   1. Nous jouerons au tennis.   2. Vous aurez besoin d'acheter une nouvelle voiture.   3. Je suivrai un cours d'histoire.   4. Nous visiterons Venise quand nous serons en Italie.   5. Ils (Elles) iront à Dakar.   6. Nous marcherons le long de la plage.   7. Il étudiera le français quand il sera à Bordeaux.   8. Ils (Elles) verront l'exposition Picasso quand ils (elles) seront à Paris.   9. Elle voyagera en Asie quand elle obtiendra son diplôme.   10. Il deviendra médecin.

17·8   1. n'ira pas   2. fera   3. ne pourra pas   4. gèlera   5. nous promènerons   6. enverrai   7. ferai   8. ira   9. découvriras   10. contacterai

18   The present conditional and the past conditional

18·1   1. irions   2. voyagerait   3. dirions   4. j'aurais   5. mangeraient   6. prendrait   7. serais   8. demanderiez   9. j'écrirais   10. saurais

18·2   1. Iriez-vous   2. Pourrions-nous   3. Pourriez-vous   4. M'achèteriez-vous   5. Signerait-il   6. Pourriez-vous   7. Pourrait-elle   8. Iriez-vous   9. Pourrions-nous   10. Accompagneraient-ils (-elles)

18·3   1. Si j'avais moins de travail, je voyagerais plus.   2. S'ils attendaient, ils obtiendraient un meilleur prix pour leur appartement.   3. Si nous plantions plus de fleurs, nous aurions un plus beau jardin.   4. Si je vendais mon appartement, je pourrais acheter cette maison.   5. S'il pouvait, il déménagerait.   6. Si vous les invitiez, nous serions ravis.   7. Si ma voiture tombait en panne, je piquerais une crise.   8. Si elle avait plus d'argent, elle viendrait avec nous.   9. Si vous vous organisiez autrement, votre vie serait plus facile.   10. Si tu dormais plus, tu aurais de meilleures notes à l'école.

624   Answer key

18·4   1. Elle serait contente si tu venais ce soir.   2. Nous ferions une promenade dans le parc s'il faisait beau. 3. Ils prendraient leur retraite s'ils pouvaient.   4. Il accompagnerait Sophie à l'opéra s'il n'était pas occupé. 5. Il y aurait moins de problèmes si vous suiviez mes conseils.   6. Elles iraient au musée s'il était ouvert avant onze heures.   7. Vous finiriez plus tôt si vous travailliez plus efficacement.   8. Nous vous croirions si vous nous disiez la vérité.   9. Elle achèterait cette voiture si elle était moins chère.   10. Tu lui offrirais ce poste si tu avais confiance en lui.

18·5   1. Il irait à Paris s'il avait plus de temps.   2. Elle achèterait ce manteau s'il était moins cher.   3. Nous serions ravi(e)s si tu venais dimanche.   4. J'écrirais une lettre si tu en avais besoin.   5. Le président serait au Brésil aujourd'hui.   6. Ce serait plus joli s'il y avait plus de fleurs.   7. J'inviterais Chloé si j'allais à Paris.   8. Le directeur signerait le contrat.   9. Elle mangerait la soupe si elle avait faim.   10. Il lirait le journal ce matin s'il pouvait.

18·6   1. c   2. d   3. a   4. e   5. b

18·7   1. Nous aurions dîné avec vous si nous avions pu.   2. Elle aurait visité ce musée si elle avait eu plus de temps.   3. Elle aurait vu ce film s'il avait été sous-titré.   4. Ils auraient invité Charles s'il n'avait pas travaillé ce soir-là.   5. Il aurait fait un documentaire sur ce sujet s'il avait trouvé le financement.   6. Ils auraient vendu leur maison si leurs enfants avaient déménagé.   7. Vous seriez arrivé à temps si votre voiture n'était pas tombée en panne.   8. Le directeur aurait démissionné si les ouvriers n'avaient pas fait pression.   9. Cette pièce aurait eu du succès s'il y avait eu plus de temps pour les répétitions.   10. Nous serions venus si nous avions reçu votre invitation plus tôt.

18·8   1. S'il avait fini son projet, il n'aurait pas dû travailler le week-end.   2. Si j'avais mis mon manteau, je n'aurais pas eu si froid.   3. Si vous aviez pu témoigner au tribunal, la situation aurait été différente.   4. Si on n'avait pas guillotiné le roi, l'histoire du pays aurait pris une tournure différente.   5. S'il avait appris sa grammaire, il aurait fait moins de fautes.   6. Si elle s'était présentée aux élections, elle aurait été élue. 7. Si nous avions commandé un couscous, nous n'aurions pas eu faim plus tard.   8. Si elle avait pu, elle aurait été danseuse.   9. Si tu avais été plus pratique, nous aurions voyagé sans bagages.   10. Si j'avais su, je n'aurais pas engagé Daniel.

18·9   1. Le Premier Ministre serait allé en Chine hier.   2. Le témoin aurait donné une version différente à la police.   3. Le cyclone aurait tué deux cents personnes dans cette ville.   4. Le directeur aurait démissionné.   5. La tempête aurait détruit des centaines de maisons.   6. Le chômage baisserait l'année prochaine.   7. Le ministre de la Santé aurait signé la réforme.   8. Les pingouins ne pourraient pas se reproduire en raison du réchauffement climatique.   9. Son nouveau voisin aurait volé sa voiture.   10. Un acteur français aurait acheté une maison en Californie la semaine dernière.

18·10   1. c   2. e   3. a   4. b   5. d

19   *Could, should, would?*

19·1   1. Pourriez-vous aider à nettoyer la maison après la soirée?   2. Nous n'avons pas pu partir en vacances. 3. Je pourrais lui acheter une nouvelle flûte.   4. À cette époque-là, ils (elles) ne pouvaient pas comprendre. 5. Pourrions-nous commencer à manger?   6. Nous pourrions aller voir un film ce soir.   7. Grâce à sa tante riche, elle a pu payer ses études.   8. Je pense qu'elle pourrait mieux faire.   9. Quand vous étiez enfant, vous jouiez avec vos poupées pendant des heures.   10. Pourriez-vous m'apprendre à jouer de la guitare?

19·2   1. Vous devriez apprendre à jouer de la guitare.   2. Ils (Elles) n'auraient pas dû dire cela.   3. Je devrais écrire à Pierre.   4. J'aurais dû leur parler.   5. Pensez-vous que Julien aurait dû vous appeler avant de venir?   6. Je n'aurais pas dû vous appeler si tôt.   7. Nous ne devrions pas prendre la voiture, c'est trop dangereux.   8. Je pense que vous devriez prendre des vacances.   9. Vous devriez louer un piano pour la soirée.   10. Marie pense que son père devrait être présent pour cette occasion.

19·3   1. If he were less lazy, he would have better grades in school.   2. When we were children, our parents would take us on vacation to Morocco every year.   3. Samuel asked for a little more money. His boss would not do it (refused).   4. If Emmanuelle were available, she would come.   5. When she was a student in Paris, she would go to the movies every Sunday.   6. If Sylvie had more money, she would buy herself new shoes.   7. If they had a choice, they would not move.   8. Would you tell me what happened at that meeting?   9. Catherine wanted to turn around, but her husband would not do it (refused).   10. Could you explain to me how this works?

19·4   1. Pourrais-tu lire ce document?   2. Nous devrions acheter des billets pour le concert.   3. Valérie pourrait t'aider!   4. À cette époque-là, elle ne pouvait pas sortir souvent.   5. Pourrais-tu m'envoyer un

Answer key   **625**

double de cette lettre? 6. Je lui ai demandé de m'aider; elle n'a pas voulu. 7. Pascal jouerait du violon s'il avait plus de temps. 8. Marie n'a pas pu lui dire la vérité. 9. Quand nous étions enfants, nous jouions sur la plage pendant des heures. 10. Ne penses-tu pas que tu devrais changer de coiffure?

19·5 1. Could you open the door? 2. At that time, he should be home. 3. They could not get tickets. 4. Would you like to participate in this project? 5. I came to pick him up; he would not come with me. 6. If you were not so selfish, you would have more friends. 7. Would you be willing to show me how it works? 8. He could not leave in time. 9. When we were children, we would go to the seashore every summer. 10. He should think before talking.

19·6 1. c 2. a 3. b 4. e 5. d

20 The present subjunctive and the past subjunctive

20·1 1. soit 2. compreniez 3. ne sorte pas 4. finisse 5. gèrent 6. ne soient pas 7. ait 8. soit 9. puisse 10. dise

20·2 1. alliez 2. arriviez 3. acceptions 4. voyagions 5. soit 6. ne disions rien 7. habitent 8. vendiez 9. suive 10. emportions

20·3 1. donniez 2. ne soit pas 3. fasses 4. ne se sentent pas 5. vole 6. puissent 7. ne réponde pas 8. donnent 9. restent 10. puisse

20·4 1. est 2. fasse 3. puissent 4. a 5. fasses 6. aient 7. sont 8. obteniez 9. parliez 10. est

20·5 1. voyagions 2. vous trompez 3. trouvions 4. connaisse 5. achetions 6. ne soit pas 7. ait 8. envoyiez 9. puisse 10. soit

20·6 1. Pourvu qu'il ait raison! 2. Elle est heureuse qu'il puisse étudier le français. 3. Il est possible que vous puissiez acheter ce logiciel ici. 4. Appelez-nous avant que nous allions en France! 5. Il est étrange qu'il soit en retard. 6. Pourvu qu'il puisse venir! 7. Elle veut que vous achetiez cet ordinateur. 8. Bien qu'il soit fatigué, il lit le journal. 9. Bien qu'il fasse quelques fautes, son français est très bon. 10. C'est la plus belle ville que je connaisse.

20·7 1. aies lu 2. ayez pu 3. ait été 4. n'ayez pas vu 5. ait manqué 6. ait réussi 7. ait plagié 8. j'aie pu 9. aient lu 10. ayez dit

20·8 1. Il est content que nous soyons parti(e)s. 2. Nous sommes ravis que tu aies pu venir avec nous. 3. Je ne crois pas qu'il soit allé à l'exposition. 4. Il doute qu'elle ait réussi. 5. Elle a peur qu'il ait eu un accident de moto. 6. Ils sont contents que Laurent se soit marié. 7. Nous sommes désolés que votre sœur ait été malade. 8. Il est douteux qu'ils soient allés en Patagonie. 9. Il est regrettable que leurs enfants aient été si peu reconnaissants. 10. Il est incroyable que vous n'ayez pas su la réponse.

20·9 1. d 2. c 3. a 4. e 5. b

21 Prepositions

21·1 1. Selon lui, Julie est à Madrid. 2. Nous sommes allés au théâtre avec eux. 3. Mélanie l'attend devant la boulangerie. 4. Tes chaussures sont sous le lit. 5. Il marche vers le parc. 6. La chaise est contre le mur. 7. Il est arrivé après moi. 8. Il est sorti malgré la pluie. 9. Envoyez-moi la lettre avant mardi! 10. Le chat s'est assis entre nous.

21·2 1. chez 2. d' 3. sans 4. Chez 5. chez 6. au 7. chez 8. Chez 9. avec 10. aux

21·3 1. sur 2. sur 3. dans 4. le 5. dans 6. dans 7. sur 8. sur 9. en 10. au

21·4 1. à 2. au 3. en 4. à 5. en 6. en 7. à 8. en 9. à 10. en

21·5 1. Ils partent pour l'Irlande dans quelques jours. 2. Chez ce petit garçon, tout est pathologique. 3. Que faites-vous le dimanche? 4. La femme au chapeau de paille est une actrice célèbre. 5. Il adore la glace au chocolat. 6. Ils ont ouvert une bonne bouteille de vin pour son anniversaire. 7. Selon lui, Carole est à Hawaii. 8. Nous avons vu beaucoup de moulins en Hollande. 9. S'il te plaît, donne-moi une tasse de thé. 10. Allons chez Tante Sophie cet après-midi. 11. Simone de Beauvoir est morte en 1986. 12. Avez-vous une chambre qui donne sur la Seine? 13. Je vais au travail à pied tous les jours. 14. Leur bureau est au dixième étage. 15. Elle l'a regardé d'un air perplexe. 16. Le château donnait sur l'océan. 17. Julie ne travaille que trois jours sur sept. 18. À quelle heure commence la réunion? 19. L'écrivain a écrit ce chapitre en deux semaines. 20. Combien d'argent as-tu sur ton compte en France?

21·6　　1. Armelle est arrivée au milieu de la nuit.　2. D'après eux, elle travaille à Strasbourg.　3. Ils habitent loin de Paris.　4. À l'instar de sa mère, il est devenu chanteur.　5. J'ai laissé les valises en bas.　6. Elle est devenue célèbre en dépit d'elle-même.　7. Quant à moi, je n'ai pas de projets pour cet été.　8. Faute d'argent, il est resté chez lui.　9. Il est à notre merci.　10. Ils ont accepté de peur de les décevoir.　11. Face à de tels problèmes, il ne sait pas comment réagir.　12. Signez en bas de cette page.　13. Au lieu de perdre encore plus de temps, téléphone-lui!　14. Il a organisé un voyage à Argentine à l'insu de ses parents.　15. Il l'a appris à ses dépens.　16. Le taux du dollar est plus bas en comparaison à l'an dernier.　17. Je peux la voir à travers la vitre.　18. Cette ville a beaucoup changé à travers les siècles.　19. Carmen aime marcher le long de la rivière.　20. Il m'a donné ces fleurs en guise de remerciement.

21·7　　1. à l'instar de　2. à force de　3. en haut de　4. au bord de　5. D'après　6. faute d'　7. Au lieu de　8. à partir de　9. à l'insu de　10. loin de

21·8　　1. à même de　2. à cause de　3. grâce à　4. grâce à　5. en raison de　6. à même　7. à même de　8. à cause de　9. en raison d'　10. à même

21·9　　1. en Chine　2. au Mali　3. au Maroc　4. au Portugal　5. aux États-Unis　6. en Belgique　7. à Milan　8. en Argentine　9. en Patagonie　10. au Vietnam　11. en Hongrie　12. au Kenya　13. à Paris　14. en Sibérie　15. au Caire　16. à Madrid　17. en Inde　18. en Turquie　19. au Laos　20. au Canada

21·10　　1. Je m'appelle Christian. J'habite à Amsterdam, en Hollande.　2. Je m'appelle Paolo. J'habite à Venise, en Italie.　3. Je m'appelle Phong. J'habite à Hanoi, au Vietnam.　4. Je m'appelle Laure. J'habite à Rouen, en France.　5. Je m'appelle Christopher. J'habite à Londres, en Angleterre.　6. Je m'appelle Maria. J'habite à Mexico, au Mexique.　7. Je m'appelle Patrick. J'habite à Bruxelles, en Belgique.　8. Je m'appelle Ahmadou. J'habite à Abidjan, en Côte d'Ivoire.　9. Je m'appelle Akiko. J'habite à Tokyo, au Japon.　10. Je m'appelle Cheng. J'habite à Shanghai, en Chine.　11. Je m'appelle Vladimir. J'habite à Moscou, en Russie.　12. Je m'appelle Youssef. J'habite à Marrakech, au Maroc.　13. Je m'appelle Rachida. J'habite à Alger, en Algérie.　14. Je m'appelle Amin. J'habite à Alexandrie, en Égypte.　15. Je m'appelle Christina. J'habite à Varsovie, en Pologne.　16. Je m'appelle Karl. J'habite à Berlin, en Allemagne.　17. Je m'appelle Jean. J'habite à Genève, en Suisse.　18. Je m'appelle Hugo. J'habite à Caracas, au Venezuela.　19. Je m'appelle Pablo. J'habite à Quito, en Équateur.　20. Je m'appelle Karim. J'habite à Istanbul, en Turquie.

21·11　　1. Mon ami Julien va en Normandie et en Bretagne.　2. Nos voisins vont à Tahiti et à Hawaii.　3. Ma sœur et mon beau-frère vont au Montana et au Wyoming.　4. Corinne va en Oregon et en Alaska.　5. Nous allons en Alsace et en Auvergne.　6. Mes amis vont en Aquitaine et dans le Languedoc.　7. Je vais en Haïti et en Guadeloupe.　8. Bernard va en Lorraine et en Champagne.　9. Vous allez en Anjou et en Vendée.　10. Le camionneur va en Californie et en Arizona.

21·12　　1. en France　2. en Inde　3. au Sénégal　4. aux États-Unis　5. en Russie　6. en Italie　7. en Afrique du Sud　8. au Vietnam　9. en Allemagne　10. en Angleterre

21·13　　1. d'Inde　2. du Guatemala　3. du Chili　4. d'Espagne　5. de Norvège　6. de Suisse　7. du Colorado　8. de France　9. des Antilles　10. du Togo

21·14　　1. en Inde　2. en Grande-Bretagne　3. en Italie　4. en Chine　5. en France　6. aux États-Unis　7. au Pérou　8. en Égypte　9. en Grèce　10. au Cambodge

21·15　　1. Marc est propriétaire d'une librairie à Dublin.　2. Elle est allée en Australie l'été dernier.　3. Je suis revenu du Sénégal hier soir.　4. Léo a acheté une maison au Brésil.　5. Est-il à Tahiti?　6. Ce chanteur a une maison au Montana et une autre au Mexique.　7. Julie a perdu ses boucles d'oreille en Espagne.　8. L'appartement de Karim est au Caire.　9. Ce roi a des châteaux en Allemagne et en Autriche.　10. Ils ont ouvert une boulangerie au Vietnam.　11. Nabila va en Provence deux fois par an.　12. Théo m'a envoyé une carte postale d'Irlande.　13. Son fils a trouvé un emploi en Californie.　14. En Inde, la cuisine est délicieuse.　15. Ils importent des produits de Chine.　16. Elle a acheté ce collier au Maroc.　17. Voulez-vous aller à New York avec moi la semaine prochaine?　18. Ludovic veut travailler à Toulouse.　19. Noémie enseigne le français en Pologne.　20. Allons en Floride pour le week-end!

21·16　　1. Nous étions obligés de le faire. 2. Je suis désolé(e) de vous déranger. 3. Il est triste d'avoir oublié le rendez-vous. 4. Je suis ravi(e) de faire votre connaissance. 5. Il est interdit (défendu) de stationner ici. 6. Il est utile de connaître une langue étrangère. 7. Il est facile d'apprendre le français. 8. Il est dangereux de conduire sans ceinture de sécurité.

21·17　　1. Nous sommes prêt(e)s à partir. 2. Le taxi est lent à venir. 3. Elle est occupée à faire la lessive. 4. Je suis habitué(e) à le voir tous les jours. 5. Elle était la seule à savoir la réponse. 6. Tu es la première à me contacter. 7. Elles ne seront pas les dernières à me poser cette question. 8. Il est trop jeune pour se marier.

Answer key　**627**

21·18 1. d' 2. d', à 3. à 4. d' 5. de 6. à 7. de 8. à 9. à, à 10. de 11. à 12. à 13. à 14. à 15. de 16. à 17. à 18. à 19. de 20. à 21. de 22. à 23. de, de 24. à 25. d'

21·19 1. de 2. de 3. d' 4. de 5. d' 6. de 7. de 8. de 9. d' 10. de

21·20 Aujourd'hui, j'ai envie de vous parler de mes projets pour l'avenir immédiat.

Après avoir obtenu mon diplôme, je compte me reposer un peu. Avant de commencer à travailler, je veux m'amuser. Pour être heureux dans la vie, il faut essayer de réaliser ses rêves. Au lieu de chercher un emploi, je préfère aller à l'étranger pendant un certain temps. J'espère voir beaucoup de pays. J'ai dit à mes amis de venir avec moi, mais ils pensaient qu'il valait mieux faire des études supérieures tout de suite. C'est dommage! Pendant qu'ils écriront leurs dissertations ennuyeuses, je passerai mon temps à lire de bons livres car j'ai l'intention d'apprendre quelque chose de nouveau chaque jour. Je pourrai écouter la radio sans être obligé de faire mes devoirs. Je n'aurai plus besoin de suivre des cours obligatoires et je n'aurai plus peur de rater un examen. Je serai libre de faire ce que je veux! Je ne verrai pas le temps passer. Mes amis vont pâlir d'envie quand ils m'entendront décrire mes aventures. Je suis sûr que je garderai toujours un bon souvenir de ces vacances.

Je vais vous laisser maintenant. Avant de prendre l'avion pour l'Asie, je dois encore faire mes valises. Au revoir!
Sébastien

21·21 1. de 2. de 3. sur 4. à 5. de 6. à 7. de 8. en 9. à 10. de

21·22 1. I miss Paul. 2. My brother did not keep his word. 3. This writer lacks talent. 4. I missed the beginning of the course. 5. The boss failed to do his duty.

22   The infinitive mood

22·1 1. Écrire ce livre était un défi. 2. Étudier le français est amusant. 3. Travailler quatre jours par semaine est idéal. 4. Trouver un nouveau travail sera difficile. 5. Marcher le long de la Seine est agréable. 6. Se réveiller à cinq heures du matin est trop tôt. 7. Faire la cuisine prend beaucoup de temps. 8. Prendre ce médicament deux fois par jour. 9. Ajouter du poivre. 10. Ne pas mettre d'ail.

22·2 1. à faire la cuisine 2. à danser 3. à parler 4. à éplucher des légumes 5. à travailler pour eux 6. à chercher un autre travail 7. à lire 8. à cueillir des fleurs 9. à rêver 10. à faire les courses

22·3 1. J'ai vu Victorine manger un gâteau au chocolat dans son bureau. 2. Son cousin Grégoire passe son temps à jouer au basketball. 3. Mon voisin Carl passe son temps à regarder la télévision. 4. Je l'ai entendu parler dans le couloir. 5. Samuel passe ses vacances à visiter les bibliothèques à Paris. 6. En été, nous passons notre temps à voyager en Europe. 7. Carla l'a vu couper du bois dans le jardin. 8. Laurent passe son temps à apprendre des langues étrangères. 9. Elle les a entendu dire qu'ils vendraient leur maison. 10. Je le regardais dormir.

22·4 1. c 2. e 3. b 4. a 5. d

22·5 1. Ils sont assis dans l'herbe à regarder le coucher du soleil. 2. Le professeur est debout à lire un passage de *L'amant* de Marguerite Duras. 3. Xavier est allongé/étendu sur son lit à lire le dictionnaire. 4. Nous sommes étendus/allongés sur le canapé à regarder un nouveau film italien. 5. Yvon est accroupi dans le champ à ramasser des fraises. 6. Édouard est appuyé contre la porte du réfrigérateur à se demander ce qu'il va manger. 7. Lucien est appuyé contre le mur à regarder les gens danser. 8. Vous êtes debout sur une chaise à nettoyer les fenêtres. 9. La romancière est assise devant son ordinateur à penser/réfléchir à ce qu'elle va écrire. 10. Tu es accroupi dans la cuisine à essayer de réparer une porte.

22·6 1. avoir dormi 2. être allé 3. avoir mangé 4. s'être promené 5. avoir regardé 6. être tombé 7. s'être levé 8. avoir préparé 9. être parti 10. avoir allumé

22·7 1. Elle prend des vacances après avoir complété son projet. 2. Il écrit la lettre après avoir consulté son ami. 3. Je prépare un thé après avoir cueilli des fruits. 4. Ils rendent visite à leurs amis après être allés au théâtre. 5. Il verse le vin après avoir servi le dîner. 6. Elle se maquille après s'être habillée. 7. Nous dînons après avoir regardé le film à la télévision. 8. Ils se promènent après avoir travaillé. 9. Je réfléchis après avoir téléphoné. 10. Nous allons chez Julien après avoir choisi un cadeau.

22·8 1. déteste 2. veulent 3. devons 4. peux 5. désirons 6. veux 7. semble 8. penses 9. faut 10. allez

22·9 1. à 2. de 3. à 4. de 5. à 6. de 7. à 8. de 9. de 10. de

22·10   1. Ils (Elles) veulent voyager en France.   2. Il a passé des heures à éplucher des pommes de terre.   3. Faire la cuisine est son passe-temps favori.   4. N'oubliez pas d'ajouter du sel!   5. Il a peur de brûler la viande.   6. Ils (Elles) ont envie de manger un soufflé au chocolat.   7. Il a cessé de fumer.   8. Ils (Elles) ont refusé de sortir.   9. Elle apprend à faire la cuisine.   10. Essayez de comprendre la situation!

23   The imperative mood

23·1   1. Prends le train de neuf heures!   2. Regardez le film à la télé ce soir!   3. Dînons sur la terrasse!   4. Achète le journal!   5. Buvons à sa santé!   6. Expliquez les conditions!   7. Ne cours pas si vite!   8. Épelle ton nom!   9. Prêtez votre dictionnaire à Marie!   10. N'invite pas Denis!

23·2   1. Écoute-moi! 2. Fais-moi confiance! 3. Suivez-moi! 4. Espérons-le! 5. Demandez-lui! 6. Vas-y! 7. Aide-moi! 8. Téléphonez-leur! 9. Passe-moi le sel! 10. Achètes-en! 11. Faites-le! 12. Tiens-moi au courant! 13. Excuse-moi! 14. Attends-moi! 15. Regarde-la! 16. Essayez-le!

23·3   1. Donne-le-leur! 2. Mettez-les-y! 3. Donnez-lui-en! 4. Apportez-le-moi! 5. Montrez-la-leur! 6. Prête-m'en!

23·4   1. Ne me quitte pas! 2. Ne la croyez pas! 3. Ne nous dérangez pas! 4. Ne lui réponds pas! 5. Ne me faites pas rire! 6. Ne les écoute pas! 7. Ne me mens pas!

23·5   1. Ne les lui montre pas! 2. Ne la leur vendez pas! 3. Ne le lui offrons pas! 4. Ne m'en donne pas! 5. Ne la lui envoyons pas!

23·6   1. Lave-toi les mains!   2. Baladez-vous dans la forêt!   3. Écrivons-nous plus souvent!   4. Ne te couche pas trop tard!   5. Réveillez-vous à cinq heures!   6. Habille-toi vite!   7. Ne vous trompez pas de route!   8. Retrouvons-nous devant la Brasserie Lipp!   9. Dépêche-toi!   10. Rencontrons-nous un jour à Paris!

23·7   1. N'oublie pas ton passeport!   2. Reposons-nous sur le banc!   3. Apportez votre carte d'identité!   4. Dis-nous son prénom!   5. Prends ce médicament!   6. Ne soyez pas en retard!   7. Allons en Italie!   8. Ferme la porte!   9. Attendez-moi!   10. Écrivez votre adresse sur l'enveloppe!

24   The present participle and gerund

24·1   1. finissant   2. sachant   3. donnant   4. protégeant   5. faisant   6. ayant   7. avançant   8. étant   9. prononçant   10. vendant

24·2   1. faisant   2. prenant   3. jouant   4. faisant   5. sachant   6. allant   7. se plaignant   8. visitant   9. arrivant   10. pariant

24·3   1. Il a perdu ses clés en marchant dans le parc.   2. N'ayant pas vu le film, je ne peux pas faire de commentaires.   3. Ils (Elles) ont vu Paul en traversant la rue.   4. Sachant la vérité, elle ne pouvait pas rester silencieuse.   5. Il a gagné de l'argent en vendant des tableaux.   6. C'était un match fascinant.   7. Ayant fini le livre, il est parti.   8. Ils (Elles) écoutent de la musique en travaillant.   9. Je tricote en regardant la télévision.   10. Il est tombé en sautant par-dessus le mur.

24·4   1. en voyageant   2. en marchandant   3. en utilisant   4. en buvant   5. en rangeant   6. en riant   7. en pleurant   8. en espérant   9. En vous remerciant   10. en claquant la porte   11. en écoutant cette chanson   12. En entrant dans la maison   13. En recevant le prix   14. en déjeunant   15. en téléphonant

24·5   1. Éteignez la lumière en sortant.   2. Il ne faut pas parler en mangeant.   3. C'est en visitant la France qu'on apprend le mieux à parler français.   4. Vous avez réussi en faisant un effort.   5. Je gagne ma vie en travaillant.   6. Il est tombé en descendant l'escalier.   7. Il s'est cassé la jambe en skiant.   8. Elle a trouvé cet emploi en lisant les petites annonces.   9. J'ai maigri en faisant du sport tous les jours.   10. De nos jours, on téléphone souvent en marchant et on prend ses repas en regardant la télévision.

24·6   1. En allant au théâtre, Brice a rencontré un ami.   2. En lisant le journal, Mireille a découvert un article intéressant.   3. En regardant le journal télévisé, on se tient au courant de l'actualité.   4. En travaillant dur, nous réussirons.   5. En faisant du yoga, je me détends.   6. En s'entraînant tous les jours, les joueurs ont gagné le match.   7. En courant très vite, j'ai attrapé le bus.   8. En prenant la deuxième rue à droite, vous arriverez à la gare.

25   The simple past, the passive voice, and indirect speech

25·1   1. être   2. avoir   3. peindre   4. faire   5. venir   6. lire   7. vouloir   8. savoir   9. plaire   10. éteindre

25·2   1. fut   2. obtinrent   3. explora   4. mourut   5. peignit   6. trembla   7. introduisit   8. eut lieu   9. fit   10. devint

Answer key   **629**

25·3 1. Il vécut dix ans à Amsterdam.　2. Elle introduisit cette nouvelle méthode.　3. Ils (Elles) lurent tous ses livres.　4. Il mourut en Italie.　5. Il fut surpris.　6. Je voulus le remercier.　7. Elle naquit à Rouen.　8. Ils (Elles) achetèrent un nouveau chevalet.　9. Elle devint portraitiste.　10. Il sourit et partit.

25·4 1. fut　2. plut　3. vécurent　4. crus　5. devint　6. mangèrent　7. guéris　8. naquis　9. admira　10. crut

25·5 1. Le voleur a été attrapé par le policier.　2. Le traité a été signé par le roi.　3. Un nouveau traitement est prescrit par le médecin.　4. Le tableau a été volé par le cambrioleur.　5. L'homme au chapeau gris a été mordu par le chien.　6. L'otage a été pris par l'ennemi.　7. Le canapé a été déchiré par l'enfant.　8. Un célèbre tableau sera vendu par le marchand d'art.　9. La forteresse est prise par les envahisseurs.　10. Les étudiants sont félicités par le professeur.

25·6 1. Le chef a fait le gâteau.　2. L'artisan a conçu l'objet.　3. Le roi a érigé le château.　4. L'ambassadeur signera le document.　5. Le propriétaire a vendu le tableau.　6. Le chat griffe le fauteuil.　7. Le malfaiteur a payé l'amende.　8. L'antiquaire a volé le vase.　9. Un journaliste écrira le livre.　10. Le professeur punit les élèves.

25·7 1. Le château est construit par la reine.　2. Le tableau a été volé par un marchand d'art.　3. Un chapeau rose a été retrouvé dans le parc hier.　4. Ce verbe est suivi de l'indicatif.　5. La maison est entourée par la police.　6. Un nouveau remède sera inventé avant 2050.　7. Ce vaccin a été inventé en 1885.　8. La décision a été prise lundi.　9. La lettre a été lue par un témoin.　10. La maison est entourée d'arbres.

25·8 1. Le vaccin contre la rage a été inventé par Louis Pasteur.　2. La vedette de cinéma est suivie par les photographes.　3. Un voleur sur trois n'est jamais attrapé par la police.　4. Cinquante personnes ont été embauchées par la compagnie aérienne.　5. Ils ont été forcés de travailler.　6. En France, la peine de mort a été abolie (supprimée) en 1981.　7. Un jour, un remède contre le sida sera découvert.　8. La visite a été reportée plusieurs fois.　9. Thanksgiving est célébré le quatrième jeudi en novembre.　10. Le cours vient d'être annulé.　11. Heureusement, personne n'a été blessé dans l'accident.　12. Le distributeur de billets a été endommagé.　13. Vous êtes renvoyé(e).　14. Cela n'a jamais été fait.　15. Elle espère être invitée.

25·9 1. a. Gustave Eiffel a construit la tour Eiffel en 1889. b. La tour Eiffel a été construite par Gustave Eiffel en 1889.　2. a. Par le physicien allemand Wilhelm Röntgen a découvert les rayons X. b. Les rayons X ont été découverts par le physicien allemand Wilhelm Röntgen.　3. a. Rouget de Lisle a composé « La Marseillaise ». b. « La Marseillaise » a été composée par Rouget de Lisle.　4. a. Monet a peint le tableau « Impression, Soleil levant ». b. Le tableau « Impression, Soleil Levant », a été peint par Monet.　5. a. Lamartine a écrit le poème « Le Lac ». b. Le poème « Le Lac » a été écrit par Lamartine.

25·10 1. vrai　2. vrai　3. vrai　4. faux　5. vrai　6. vrai　7. faux　8. vrai　9. vrai　10. vrai

25·11 Lors des dernières émeutes, beaucoup de voitures ont été incendiées et de nombreuses vitrines ont été brisées par les émeutiers. Plusieurs magasins ont été pillés et des marchandises d'une valeur de plusieurs milliers d'euros ont été volées. Quand les CRS sont arrivés, une personne a été grièvement blessée par un cocktail Molotov. La victime a été transportée à l'hôpital où elle a été opérée tout de suite. Selon les médecins, elle serait dans un état critique. Quelques personnes ont été interpellées. Elles ont été condamnées à cinq mois de prison. Le jeune délinquant qui avait lancé le cocktail Molotov s'est enfui et n'a pas encore été retrouvé par la police. Aussitôt que le coupable sera attrapé, il sera arrêté et sanctionné. Le nombre précis des victimes sera connu dans les jours qui viennent.

25·12 1. Il veut savoir si le programme du parti est bien défini.　2. Il veut savoir si nous allons boycotter les prochaines élections.　3. Il veut savoir si tu vas voter dimanche.　4. Il veut savoir si le ministre de l'Éducation a proposé des réformes.　5. Il veut savoir si elle acceptera notre proposition.　6. Il veut savoir si le parti a choisi son candidat.　7. Il veut savoir si les femmes peuvent voter dans ce pays.　8. Il veut savoir si vous viendrez samedi soir.　9. Il veut savoir si elle a fini ses recherches.　10. Il veut savoir si la parité sera jamais réalisée.

25·13 1. Elle annonce qu'elle sera absente mardi.　2. Ils avouent que Paul s'est trompé.　3. La marchande dit que ses produits sont les meilleurs.　4. Tu sais bien qu'elles avaient tort.　5. On se rend compte que le candidat a peu de chance de gagner.　6. Ils ne savent pas si le musée est ouvert.　7. Tu réponds que tu n'avais rien entendu.　8. Elle nous apprend qu'il n'est jamais allé en France.　9. Il nous déclare qu'ils avaient dilapidé leur fortune.　10. Il ignore où le peintre habite.

25·14 1. J'ai entendu dire que tu avais accepté leur offre la semaine dernière.　2. J'ai entendu dire qu'elle avait vendu sa voiture hier.　3. J'ai entendu dire que tu travaillerais à Chicago l'an prochain.　4. J'ai entendu dire qu'elle irait en Asie demain.　5. J'ai entendu dire qu'ils s'étaient mariés le mois dernier.　6. J'ai entendu dire qu'il faisait froid à Moscou aujourd'hui.　7. J'ai entendu dire qu'ils s'installeraient au Canada l'an prochain.　8. J'ai entendu dire qu'il avait quitté son poste vendredi dernier.　9. J'ai entendu dire qu'elle était la candidate favorite en ce moment.   10. J'ai entendu dire que tu avais pris beaucoup de photos hier soir.

25·15   1. Ils (Elles) savent que vous habitez à Paris.   2. J'ai entendu dire que vous habitiez à Paris.   3. J'ai entendu dire que vous aviez habité à Paris en 1995.   4. J'ai entendu dire que vous iriez à Paris l'année prochaine.   5. Il dit que son chat est adorable.   6. J'ai entendu dire que vous aviez un chat.   7. J'ai entendu dire que vous aviez un chat quand vous habitiez boulevard Victor Hugo.   8. J'ai entendu dire que votre sœur vous donnerait son chat.   9. On m'a dit que vous aviez voté pour moi.   10. Nous nous rendons compte qu'elle a une chance de gagner.

26   Pronouns

26·1   1. Elle les achète.   2. Il le consulte.   3. Nous le soutenons.   4. Ils la construisent.   5. Je l'ouvre.   6. Elle la conduit.   7. Il les accepte.   8. Nous la comprenons.   9. Tu le visites.   10. Elle l'étudie.

26·2   1. Il me remercie.   2. L'écrivain les envoie.   3. Ils (Elles) nous invitent.   4. Nous l'acceptons.   5. Elle les a appelé(e)s.   6. Apportez-les!   7. Je vais l'acheter.   8. Ne le (la) vendez pas!   9. Nous devons le (la) voir.   10. La connaissez-vous?

26·3   1. La grand-mère leur a raconté une histoire.   2. Nous lui avons fait un cadeau.   3. Je lui ferai parvenir le dossier dès que possible.   4. Nous lui enverrons des fleurs.   5. Ce théâtre lui appartient.   6. Est-ce que tu lui as écrit?   7. Téléphonez-lui aussitôt que possible!   8. Ne lui mentionnez rien!   9. Il leur annoncera sa décision demain.   10. Il leur donnera le scénario en fin de journée.

26·4   1. Apporte-moi un livre!   2. Ne les appelle pas après huit heures du soir!   3. Envoie-nous ta nouvelle pièce!   4. Je lui écrirai une lettre.   5. Elle me donnera une réponse lundi.   6. Il ne m'a pas rendu les livres.   7. Ce stylo lui appartient.   8. Il ne nous parle pas.   9. Ils (Elles) nous ont raconté une bonne histoire.   10. Ils (Elles) te prêteront leur maison pour le week-end.

26·5   1. Elle s'y habitue.   2. Tu devrais y prêter attention.   3. Nous nous y intéressons.   4. Je m'y abonne.   5. Elle y tient.   6. Nous n'y croyons pas.   7. Il n'y pense jamais.   8. Ils n'y obéissent pas.   9. Elle y réfléchira.   10. Pourquoi n'y avez-vous jamais répondu?

26·6   1. J'en ai parlé.   2. Ils en ont envie.   3. Nous en avons besoin.   4. Il s'en est approché très lentement.   5. Je m'en chargerai.   6. Tu t'en sers?   7. Il en a peur.   8. Je ne m'en souviens pas.   9. Elle s'en est occupée.   10. Il ne pourra jamais s'en débarrasser.

26·7   1. e   2. d   3. a   4. c   5. b

26·8   1. Ne lui en parlez pas!   2. Elle lui en a emprunté.   3. Je le lui ferai parvenir.   4. Patrick les lui a racontées.   5. Le musicien la lui a envoyée.   6. L'ouvrier la lui a donnée.   7. Je la lui ai demandée.   8. Il la lui vendra.   9. Le médecin le lui a prescrit.   10. Je le leur recommande.

26·9   1. J'y pense.   2. Il ne s'y intéresse pas.   3. Elle s'en est occupée.   4. Je te l'ai envoyée.   5. Nous le leur avons donné.   6. Je m'en sers tous les jours.   7. Il en a parlé.   8. J'en ai besoin.   9. Elle m'en a emprunté.   10. Ils (Elles) nous en ont donné.

26·10   1. C'est lui qui a gagné...   2. C'est moi qui prendrai...   3. C'est vous qui écrirez...   4. C'est nous qui préparons...   5. C'est toi qui as fait...   6. C'est elle qui lui fait...   7. C'est moi qui vous ai invité.   8. C'est eux qui sont...   9. C'est elles qui s'occuperont...   10. C'est lui qui fait...

26·11   1. Il ira en France avec moi.   2. Moi, je déteste le café!   3. Elle travaille pour nous.   4. À qui est ce livre?   5. Fais-le toi-même!   6. Je ne peux pas prendre cette décision sans toi.   7. Il est plus grand que toi.   8. Je pense à elle.   9. Ils (Elles) ont peur de lui.   10. Elle l'a dit elle-même.

26·12   1. Moi non plus.   2. Eux aussi.   3. Elle aussi.   4. Elles aussi.   5. Nous aussi.

26·13   1. Les siens   2. Les miens   3. le mien   4. le vôtre   5. le tien   6. les leurs   7. les nôtres   8. le sien   9. le mien   10. le sien

26·14   1. Ma famille est plus grande que la vôtre.   2. Notre situation est plus difficile que la sienne.   3. Ses frères sont plus jeunes qu'elle.   4. Leur ville est plus propre que la nôtre.   5. Mon exercice est plus avancé que le leur.   6. Votre chien est plus beau que le sien.   7. Nos voisins sont plus sympathiques que les vôtres.   8. Vos hivers sont plus froids que les nôtres.   9. Leurs produits sont plus chers que les vôtres.   10. Vos enfants sont plus actifs que les miens.

26·15   1. —Quelle robe vas-tu porter? —Celle que j'ai achetée à Paris.   2. —Que pensez-vous de son nouveau roman? —C'est affreux!   3. —En quoi sont ces bagues? —Celle-ci est en or et celle-là est en argent.   4. —Que penses-tu de ma nouvelle maison? —C'est beau!   5. —Quels plats pouvons-nous préparer?

Answer key   **631**

—Nous pouvons préparer ceux que tu préfères.   6. —Ces films sont disponibles? —Celui-ci est disponible mais pas celui-là.   7. —Sont-ils sous-titrés? —Celui-ci est sous-titré en français et celui-là en allemand.   8. Leurs enfants aiment les jeux mais pas ceux qui sont difficiles.   9. Regarde ces deux livres. Penses-tu que ma mère aimerait celui-ci ou celui-là?   10. Voici deux bracelets. Celui-ci est indien. Celui-là est égyptien.

26·16   1. Celle-ci est rose. Celle-là est blanche.   2. Ceux-ci sont inconnus. Ceux-là sont célèbres.   3. Celui-ci est jeune. Celui-là est plus âgé.   4. Celui-ci est trop tôt. Celui-là est trop tard.   5. Celui-ci est un best-seller. Celui-là est épuisé.   6. Celui-ci est vieux. Celui-là est le dernier modèle.   7. Celle-ci est trop claire. Celle-là est trop foncée.   8. Ceux-ci sont bien écrits. Ceux-là sont mal écrits.   9. Celle-ci est légère. Celle-là est lourde.   10. Ceux-ci sont bons. Ceux-là sont nuls.

26·17   1. Après dix années difficiles, elle est retournée chez les siens.   2. Mon ami René n'est pas à l'aise parmi les siens.   3. Son jeune chien a encore fait des siennes!   4. Leur petite-fille a encore fait des siennes à l'école!   5. À la tienne! C'est ton anniversaire.   6. Tu vas tout perdre si tu n'y mets pas du tien!   7. S'il n'y met pas du sien, la présentation sera un désastre!

27   Relative pronouns

27·1   1. suis   2. suit   3. avons   4. peuvent   5. sait   6. ai   7. devez   8. fait   9. écris   10. veulent

27·2   1. qui   2. qu'   3. qui   4. qui   5. que   6. qui   7. que   8. qui   9. que   10. qu'

27·3   1. c   2. e   3. a   4. b   5. d

27·4   1. pour qui / pour laquelle   2. par laquelle   3. avec lequel   4. à laquelle   5. avec lesquels   6. dans lequel   7. auquel   8. chez qui / chez lesquels   9. à quoi   10. sans qui / sans laquelle

27·5   1. dont   2. que   3. dont   4. qui   5. dont   6. qui   7. dont   8. que   9. qu'   10. dont

27·6   1. Je peux me souvenir de l'année où il a ouvert son magasin (sa boutique).   2. Le lustre qu'il a acheté est pour le salon.   3. L'outil avec lequel elle travaille est très vieux.   4. C'est vous qui êtes le (la) propriétaire?   5. Le fauteuil dans lequel vous êtes assis(e) appartenait à mon grand-père.   6. La ville où ils (elles) habitent est très belle.   7. Je connais la personne dont il parle.   8. C'est le seul détail dont je me souviens.   9. Les documents dont vous avez besoin sont chez Valérie.   10. Je ne sais pas à quoi il pense.

27·7   1. Ce à quoi   2. Ce dont   3. Ce qu'   4. Ce dont   5. Ce dont   6. Ce qui   7. Ce que   8. Ce qui   9. Ce dont   10. Ce que

27·8   1. Ce qu'il veut, c'est plus de temps libre.   2. Ce dont le souffleur de verre se sert est dans l'autre atelier.   3. Ce dont je ne peux pas me souvenir, c'est de cet incident en Camargue.   4. Ce à quoi je m'attendais était différent.   5. Ce dont il a besoin, c'est de ce livre.   6. Ce dont ils (elles) parlent est intéressant.   7. Ce qu'il fait est difficile.   8. Ce à quoi elle s'intéresse, c'est à cette collection d'art.   9. Ce qu'ils (elles) aiment, c'est le chocolat.   10. Ce qui s'est passé hier soir est très triste.

27·9   1. qui   2. dont   3. laquelle   4. Ce dont   5. qui   6. ce que   7. qui   8. auxquels   9. que   10. Ce qui

28   Adjectives

28·1   1. Ta grand-mère est française? —Non, elle est italienne.   2. Ces fenêtres sont propres? —Non, ces fenêtres sont sales.   3. Sa femme est blonde? —Non, elle est rousse.   4. Il porte ses chaussures noires? —Non, il porte des chaussures bleu marine.   5. C'est une situation sérieuse? —Oui, c'est une situation très sérieuse.   6. C'est une histoire tragique? —Non, c'est une histoire amusante.   7. C'est un long voyage? —Non, c'est assez court.   8. Votre projet est ambitieux. —Non, c'est la directrice qui est ambitieuse.   9. Ses idées sont bonnes? —Oui, ses idées sont meilleures que les nôtres.   10. Ton travail est ennuyeux? —Non, mon travail est très intéressant.

28·2   1. vieilles   2. adorable   3. fascinant   4. intéressant   5. folle

28·3   1. française   2. charmante   3. amoureuse   4. belle   5. agressive   6. active   7. folle   8. généreuse   9. rousse   10. douée

28·4   1. Je suis plus optimiste que lui.   2. Cécile est aussi efficace que Carole.   3. Ce vin-ci est meilleur que ce vin-là.   4. Sa sœur est aussi intelligente qu'elle.   5. Votre chambre est moins chère que la mienne.

6. Arnaud a autant d'argent que vous? 7. Ce prix est le meilleur! 8. Marie a moins de paires de chaussures que toi. 9. Elle est plus organisée que lui. 10. Cet appartement est le plus beau de l'immeuble.

28·5 1. Charlotte est plus grande que Lucie. 2. Charles est aussi drôle que Xavier. 3. Véronique est moins optimiste que Sébastien. 4. Lucien est plus intelligent que sa sœur. 5. Élodie est aussi bronzée que Thérèse.

28·6 1. C'est une bonne idée. 2. Ils (Elles) ont acheté une vieille maison en Normandie. 3. Ce jeune homme est ambitieux. 4. Cette chemise blanche est à moi. 5. Sa tante aime les vieilles chansons françaises. 6. Je n'ai pas votre nouvelle adresse. 7. L'Angleterre est plus petite que la France. 8. Elle n'aime pas cette veste jaune. 9. Elle est aussi ambitieuse que lui. 10. Cette histoire est ennuyeuse.

28·7 1. e 2. d 3. a 4. b 5. c

28·8 1. cette 2. ce 3. cette 4. ce 5. ces 6. Cette 7. ce 8. ces 9. Cette/ce 10. Ce

28·9 1. cette pâtisserie-ci / cette pâtisserie-là 2. ce jouet-ci / ce jouet-là 3. Ce cousin-ci / ce cousin-là 4. Cette maison-ci / cette maison-là 5. Ce neveu-ci / ce neveu-là 6. cette belle-sœur-ci / cette belle-sœur-là 7. ce roman-ci / ce roman-là 8. ce jeu-ci / ce jeu-là 9. Cette poupée-ci / cette poupée-là 10. cette carte-ci / cette carte-là

28·10 1. sa 2. son 3. son 4. Sa 5. notre 6. votre 7. Votre 8. ma 9. leur 10. Leurs

28·11 1. b, d 2. e 3. b, d 4. a, c 5. a, c

29 Adverbs

29·1 1. demain / demain soir 2. la semaine prochaine / la semaine prochaine 3. aujourd'hui / aujourd'hui 4. tous les jours / tous les deux jours 5. tard 6. souvent / rarement 7. parfois / jamais 8. en ce moment / en ce moment 9. la semaine prochaine / après-demain 10. hier / avant-hier

29·2 1. Aujourd'hui, c'est le premier jour de l'hiver. 2. Elle voyage souvent. 3. Je ne suis jamais à l'heure. Je suis toujours en retard. 4. Il arrive après-demain. 5. Son rendez-vous est dans deux semaines. 6. Nous travaillons demain, mais nous ne travaillons pas après-demain. 7. Ils (Elles) ont vendu leur maison la semaine dernière. 8. Est-ce que tu vas à l'opéra ce soir? 9. Tu es en avance. Je ne suis pas prêt(e). 10. La boulangerie sera fermée la semaine prochaine.

29·3 1. Depuis quand 2. Depuis combien de temps 3. Depuis quand 4. Depuis combien de temps 5. Depuis quand 6. Depuis combien de temps / depuis 7. Depuis quand 8. Depuis quand 9. Depuis combien de temps 10. depuis

29·4 1. Je travaille pour cette agence de voyages depuis cinq ans. 2. Je cherche un nouvel appartement depuis le mois de janvier. 3. Je vais chez cet opticien depuis des années. 4. Nous sommes mariés depuis quatorze ans. 5. Nous nous connaissons depuis neuf ans. 6. Je t'attends depuis quarante-cinq minutes. 7. Je prends cette ligne de métro depuis cinq ans. 8. Le coiffeur est situé par ici depuis six mois. 9. Je ne fume plus depuis la semaine dernière. 10. Il est en vacances depuis trois semaines.

29·5 1. Il y a une demi-heure que j'attends. 2. Il y a quatre mois que Valérie a sa voiture. 3. Il y a dix jours que nous essayons de joindre le banquier. 4. Il y a deux jours qu'il est en voyage d'affaires. 5. Il y a un an que Sophie étudie le chinois. 6. Il y a cinq ans qu'elle veut adopter un enfant. 7. Il y a des semaines que nous cherchons un appartement. 8. Il y a trois mois que j'attends votre réponse. 9. Il y a longtemps que ses idées sont dénuées d'intérêt. 10. Il y a une semaine que le chien de nos voisins est perdu.

29·6 1. Ils ont souvent voyagé en Asie. 2. On a bien mangé chez eux. 3. Elle a beaucoup dépensé. 4. Il a rarement lu des romans policiers. 5. Nous n'avons pas assez travaillé. 6. J'ai trop parlé. 7. Elle a très peu écrit. 8. Tu es souvent allé(e) au théâtre. 9. Il s'est toujours très mal exprimé. 10. Nous avons bien aimé la maison.

29·7 1. Combien de 2. Comment 3. Qui 4. Que 5. Combien 6. Où 7. Quand 8. Pourquoi 9. Quand 10. Qui

29·8 1. Il a planté des fleurs partout. 2. Voulez-vous vivre ici? 3. Ma voiture est garée juste derrière la vôtre. 4. Nous irons ailleurs. 5. Il est dehors. 6. J'habite près de la rivière. 7. Vous habitez trop loin. 8. Je vois des choses bizarres çà et là. 9. Il est devant vous. 10. Venez vous asseoir près de moi.

Answer key **633**

30 Written French: Making transitions and written correspondence

30·1   1. et   2. ni   3. ou/et   4. mais   5. car   6. donc/et

30·2   1. alors que/tandis que   2. pourvu qu'   3. parce que   4. Bien que   5. pendant que/alors que/tandis que   6. parce que

30·3   1. mais   2. Puisque   3. tandis que/puisque   4. et/ainsi que   5. donc   6. bien que

30·4   1. et/ainsi que   2. et/ainsi qu'   3. Pourtant   4. En effet   5. bien que   6. En fait   7. bientôt   8. Mais actuellement

30·5   1. J'ai beaucoup appris mais il me reste encore beaucoup à apprendre.   2. Il faut que j'étudie du vocabulaire ainsi que de la grammaire.   3. Je voudrais aussi mieux comprendre la culture française.   4. Il faut être patient quand on apprend une langue, sinon c'est frustrant.   5. Bien sûr, avec un peu de diligence je vais continuer de faire des progrès, en particulier dans faire des progrès en écriture.   6. Actuellement, je sais écrire quelques phrases.   7. Mais bientôt je pourrai écrire un paragraphe entier.

30·6   1. Malheureusement   2. c'est pourquoi   3. Cependant   4. même si   5. Puisque   6. Donc

30·7   1. Il n'est pas sûr du tout   2. Il est probable   3. Il n'est pas certain   4. Il n'est pas évident   5. Il est contestable

30·8   1. À mon avis   2. Je crois   3. Je suis convaincue   4. je crois   5. je pense   6. Selon moi   7. C'est pourquoi   8. Ainsi

30·9   1. En premier lieu, je réfléchis et j'organise mes idées.   2. En deuxième lieu, je révise et je finis mon plan.   3. En troisième lieu, je commence à écrire et développer mon essai.   4. En quatrième lieu, je relis et je fais des corrections mon essai.   5. Finalement, je rends l'essai à mon prof et je quitte la salle de classe.

30·10   1. Selon moi, la politique est toujours complexe.   2. Je suis convaincu qu'il est difficile pour un politique de dire toute la vérité et rien que la vérité.   3. Il est certain que la vérité est quelque fois difficile à admettre.   4. Il va de soi que les gens n'aiment pas entendre la vérité, notamment quand elle est désagréable.   5. Étant donné que peu de les politiques ont le courage de toujours dire la vérité, il faut observer leurs actions de très près.   6. C'est pourquoi je suis les débats et les interviews.

30·11   Autrefois/Avant j'étais très timide. Je m'inquiétais beaucoup quand je devais parler, particulièrement devant un groupe de gens. De plus je rougissais toujours devant les gens. Mais bientôt j'ai appris à me calmer. Maintenant je peux même faire des interventions devant une audience. Naturellement cela ne s'est pas passé en un jour.

30·12   1. Madame Monique Meru
      12, avenue Leclerc
      59000 Lille
      France

      2. MM. Royen et Sanson
      Société Productrice d'Electricité
      10, boulevard Haussman
      75009 Paris

      3. Hôtel Le Lafayette
      5, rue de la Liberté
      97200 Fort de France
      Martinique

30·13   *Suggested answers:*
      1. Paris, le 4. 7. 2008
      Monsieur le Docteur Mason,
      Je vous prie d'agréer, monsieur le Docteur, mes sincères salutations.

      2. Metz, le 23. 5. 2009
      Chère Jeanine,
      Je t'embrasse.

30·14   *Sample note:*
   Ma chère Marie-Josée,
   Depuis que tu es partie à Cannes, je m'ennuie beaucoup. Je n'ai personne pour m'accompagner au cinéma. Tu me manques terriblement. Je me réjous à l'avance de te revoir. Je suis sûre que tu t'amuses bien en France. Cannes te plaît? Transmets mes amitiés à ta tante.
   Bons baisers,
   Tina

30·15 *Sample letter:*

Chère madame,

J'ai vu votre annonce sur l'Internet pour un appartement à louer. J'aime beaucoup la description et le prix de la location. J'espère que l'appartement est toujours disponible. J'aimerais le voir lors de ma visite le 15 juin. Est-ce que cela vous convient? J'attends votre réponse.

Veuillez agréer, Madame, mes sentiments distingués.

Georges McKaan

30·16 *Sample letter:*

Cher M. Fauchon,

Mon mari et moi sommes descendus dans votre hôtel à plusieurs occasions. Nous souhaitons faire une réservation pour les deux dernières semaines de juillet, petit déjeuner compris. Nous aimerions une chambre qui donne sur la Tour Eiffel. Puisque nous sommes des habitués, pourrions-nous bénéficier d'une remise? À l'avance, je vous remercie de votre assistance.

Cordialement,

Charlotte et James Scott

30·17 *Sample e-mail:*

1. Chère Madame Sorot,

   Je viens de recevoir le paquet contenant le courrier que vous avez eu la bonté de m'envoyer. Je n'oublierai jamais les jours passés en tant qu'invité dans votre appartement.

   Je vous remercie de m'avoir envoyé mon courrier et vous envoie mes salutations cordiales.

   Kelly Alexander

2. Cher Jonathan,

   Pourrais-tu m'envoyer ton numéro de téléphone en France? Si tu es disponible cet après-midi, je voudrais te parler. Réponds vite!

   Arnold

30·18 *Suggested answer:*

Bjr, toi. J'aime BCP ton KDO. Mr6. Tu veux aller au cine? Rdv 8 h.

31 Verb transfers and confusing verbs

31·1 1. Nous dînerons tard ce soir.   2. Jeanne, est-ce que tu peux me rendre mon stylo?   3. Il vaut mieux que vous achetiez un autre gâteau. Il y aura beaucoup d'invités à la fête.   4. J'ai si froid! Il doit y avoir une autre couverture dans l'armoire.   5. Voici le livre que tu voulais.   6. Ton frère a huit ans? Et il n'a pas peur de parler en public?   7. Il fait beau en Normandie cette semaine. Passez de bonnes vacances!   8. Combien ça coûte ? Seulement vingt euros.   9. Henri a de la chance. Il a trouvé un emploi près de son appartement. 10. Le musicien portait une casquette de base-ball bleue.

31·2 1. Bertrand ne s'est jamais remis de la mort de Paul.   2. Demain nous devons nous lever à sept heures pour prendre le petit déjeuner avec le directeur du marketing.   3. Sonia t'a emprunté beaucoup d'argent. Est-ce qu'elle te l'a rendu?   4. Il y a tant de bruit ici. Je n'ai pas entendu (compris) votre nom de famille. 5. Est-ce que vous pouvez obtenir ce roman rapidement? J'en ai vraiment besoin pour mon cours de français.   6. Descends à la station de métro du Louvre!   7. Comment est-ce que tu as attrapé la grippe en juillet sur la Côte d'Azur?   8. Nous nous réunirons une fois par mois pour parler du nouveau projet. 9. Les parents de Luc ne veulent pas qu'il rentre à la maison après 22 heures.   10. Où est-ce que le boulanger achète sa farine? Son pain est si bon.

31·3 1. Où nous emmènes-tu ce soir?   2. Il me faudra/Je mettrai/Cela me prendra deux heures pour finir cette traduction.   3. Le Grand Palais décrochera l'exposition Manet le 15 mars.   4. Prenez la première à droite!   5. Je suis sûre que Carole emportera au moins trois valises.   6. Cette place n'est pas occupée. Asseyez-vous, s'il vous plaît.   7. Enlevez vos chaussures avant d'entrer dans le temple!   8. Prends ce bracelet et mets-le dans ton sac. C'est un cadeau.   9. Les enfants aiment regarder les avions décoller à l'aéroport d'Orly.   10. Joséphine est si gentille. Elle tient de sa mère.

31·4 1. Mets ta robe rouge! Nous sortons ce soir.   2. Est-ce que vous mettrez une annonce dans le journal pour vendre votre maison?   3. Quentin a posé son ordinateur sur le bureau, puis il a déjeuné.   4. Ma collègue a mis de côté plusieurs lettres personnelles pour les lire après le travail.   5. Juliette a rangé tous les légumes dans le réfrigérateur dans un ordre parfait.   6. Mme Deville a investi tout son argent dans le nouveau magasin de sa fille.   7. Remets tout à sa place avant leur retour (avant qu'ils rentrent). 8. Jonathan a fait une demande d'aide financière.   9. Vous devez verser une caution de cinquante euros pour louer cette bicyclette.   10. J'ai mis que vous étiez employé à mi-temps.

Answer key **635**

31·5 1. Nous espérons que le temps chaud se maintiendra pendant le week-end. 2. Un policier est accusé de ne pas avoir divulgué le nom d'un complice. 3. Le mariage aura lieu dans un château du XIXe siècle. 4. Il y a plusieurs manières de tenir un crayon. 5. Pierre, comment pouvez-vous avoir de telles opinions? Vous devriez être plus objectif! 6. Tiens, tiens! Léa et Xavier à la plage! 7. Tiens l'échelle une minute! 8. Mon école a prévu une fête pour célébrer son cinquantième anniversaire. 9. Je vais essayer de trouver Madame Bernardin. Ne quittez pas! 10. Olivier gardera ces documents jusqu'à mon retour.

31·6 1. Sa famille remonte à Louis XVIII. 2. Comment est-ce que s'est passée la fête d'anniversaire de Pierre? 3. Je traversais le boulevard des Capucines quand j'ai vu Christian Lacroix! 4. Encore une assiette de cassée! 5. Louise a brûlé un feu rouge hier soir. 6. Allons à Nohant demain. Je veux visiter la maison de George Sand. 7. Nora veut retourner au Brésil l'année prochaine. Ce sera la quatrième fois. 8. Le Premier ministre de Grande-Bretagne se rendra à Dakar à la fin du mois. 9. Le bruit court que le prince a menti à sa famille. 10. Je ne peux pas enseigner aujourd'hui. Je n'ai plus de voix.

31·7 1. Je suis sûre qu'Étienne devra passer au moins une semaine à la clinique. 2. Où ranges-tu les tasses à thé? 3. Nous sommes dans un théâtre. Taisez-vous! 4. Ce pain ne se conservera pas plus de trois jours. 5. Ne me fais pas attendre! 6. Patrick ne cesse de se plaindre de tout. 7. Gardez la monnaie! 8. Tu ne peux pas l'empêcher de voir son ex-belle-mère. 9. Anne a promis de garder le secret. 10. Il oublie tout le temps d'acheter de l'huile d'olive.

31·8 1. Elle fait un chèque. 2. L'infirmière m'a fait une piqûre. 3. Cela fait trois mois que je n'ai pas rendu visite à mon grand-père. 4. Allons faire une promenade! 5. Savez-vous faire la cuisine? 6. Je ne fais que te répéter ce que j'ai entendu. 7. Son salon doit faire six mètre de large. 8. Je ne m'en fais pas. 9. Cela fait un an qu'elle n'a pas téléphoné à sa sœur. 10. Lucie voudrait faire une croisière.

31·9 1. activité artistique 2. sortie 3. dessert 4. cuisine 5. voyage 6. maison 7. études 8. problème 9. communication 10. sport

31·10 1. Demande un rendez-vous pour vendredi matin. 2. Paul veut m'emprunter ma voiture dimanche après-midi. 3. Céline a commandé une mousse au chocolat. 4. Alexandre remet sans cesse sa carrière en question. 5. Pouvez-vous me prêter les notes que vous avez prises à la conférence? 6. Le maire de Strasbourg a ordonné la fermeture d'une discothèque. 7. L'expression est sans doute (probablement) empruntée à la langue allemande. 8. Je voudrais vous poser une question délicate. 9. Inès a emprunté une robe à sa meilleure amie, Noami. 10. Le détective a interrogé Jean et son frère.

31·11 1. Nous aurons une fête à la piscine ce soir. Est-ce que tu voudrais te joindre à nous? 2. Le Premier ministre de France et de Grande-Bretagne se rencontreront à Berlin en mai. 3. Lise, est-ce que tu veux emporter ces deux énormes valises juste pour deux jours? Est-ce que tu es folle? 4. Demandez à Pierre d'être à La Perle, rue Vieille du Temple. Je vous retrouverai (rejoindrai) vers 20 heures. 5. Apportez un joli bouquet de fleurs à Léonie! 6. Rémi déménage samedi. Est-ce que tu peux venir nous aider? 7. J'ai emmené ma nièce à l'Opéra Bastille. Elle adore *Carmen*. 8. Tu emménages avec Simon! Félicitations! 9. N'amène pas ton beau-frère dimanche! Je ne l'aime pas du tout. 10. L'école de Laura sait aménager l'emploi du temps des enfants pour leur donner plus de temps pour les arts et les sports.

31·12 1. Emporte 2. J'ai rencontré 3. se sont rencontrés 4. Emmène 5. ont emporté 6. Rapporte 7. nous retrouverons/nous rejoindrons 8. vous joindre à 9. déménager 10. a aménagé

31·13 1. Mélanie rendra visite à son amie Léa à Rouen cet été. 2. Pousse cette chaise contre le mur! 3. Arrête de poser des questions! 4. L'inspecteur Clouseau est si heureux aujourd'hui. Il a arrêté Sir Charles Lytton. 5. Vous devez visiter le Futuroscope à Poitiers. 6. Mon oncle fait pousser du maïs dans son jardin. 7. Les parents de Léa m'ont fait visiter leur maison. 8. Ils se sont arrêtés dans un beau village en Corrèze. 9. Nos choux-fleurs ont refusé de pousser cette année. 10. Tu a besoin de demander une autorisation pour visiter quelqu'un dans cette prison.

31·14 1. Ils ne s'attendent pas à ce que je sache jouer du piano. 2. Ne lui en veux pas! Il est fatigué et il a oublié le rendez-vous. 3. Je n'ai pas envie de sortir ce soir. 4. —Je veux te donner des oranges. Combien en veux-tu? —J'en veux trois. 5. Je ne m'attendais pas à sa réaction. J'ai été très surpris(e). 6. Je vous envie. Vous avez de la chance! 7. Je t'attendrai devant la statue de George Sand dans le jardin du Luxembourg. 8. Marion ne parle pas à son frère. Elle lui en veut. Je ne sais pas pourquoi. 9. Charlotte a des envies de fraises. 10. Je m'attends à sa victoire en mai.

31·15 1. Il manque cinq mille euros à notre organisation pour avoir une chance de gagner. 2. Édouard ne sera pas là ce soir. Il a manqué son avion. 3. Andréa ne manque pas de talent mais elle est trop timide. 4. Ma grand-mère Victorine me manque. 5. Il manque des pages à ce roman. C'est bizarre . . . 6. Je suis si triste. J'ai manqué Amélien de trois minutes. 7. Est-ce que nous te manquons? 8. Si tu manque à ton

636 Answer key

devoir, Clara te quittera.   9. Nos voyages en Bretagne me manquent.   10. Il manque des boutons à ce cardigan.

31·16   1. Savez-vous à quelle heure ils arriveront?   2. Camille a connu la faim quand elle était jeune.   3. Savez-vous conduire?   4. Je sais qu'elle est toujours en retard.   5. Les Langlois savent organiser une soirée. 6. Je suis sûre que Jonas sait la vérité.   7. Quand saurez-vous si nous pouvons leur rendre visite en Normandie?   8. Véronique connaît une crise personnelle grave.   9. Ces enfants ne savent même pas lire! S'il vous plaît, faites quelque chose!   10. Sais-tu la nouvelle?

31·17   1. d   2. e   3. a   4. c   5. b

32   *Whatever, whenever, wherever*: French oddities and fun with prepositions

32·1   1. Quoi que tu dises...   2. Quelle que soit sa décision...   3. Qui que tu sois...   4. Où que tu ailles... 5. Qui qu'elle soit...   6. Quoi que tu penses...   7. Où qu'ils (elles) habitent...   8. Quelle que soit leur suggestion...   9. Qui que tu sois...   10. Quoi que ta mère puisse penser (Quoi que pense ta mère)...

32·2   1. Quitte à ne pas dormir, je vais avec toi à cette soirée.   2. Il démissionnera quitte à avoir des problèmes financiers.   3. Il a beau être intelligent, il est très seul.   4. Ils (Elles) ont beau être ami(e)s, ils (elles) ne peuvent pas parler politique ensemble.   5. Je prendrai deux ans de congé quitte à perdre mon poste. 6. Ils (Elles) ont eu beau essayer, ils (elles) ont échoué.   7. Cette théière a beau être magnifique, ça ne vaut pas 200 euros.   8. Tu as beau jurer de dire la vérité, j'ai toujours des doutes.   9. Quitte à t'ennuyer, j'ai besoin de te poser quelques questions.   10. Il ne quittera pas la pièce quitte à déranger tout le monde.

32·3   1. a détesté   2. sembles   3. voudrais   4. aimez   5. viendra   6. désirent   7. Laisse 8. Pourrais   9. devons   10. pensent

32·4   1. c   2. e   3. a   4. b   5. d

32·5   1. d'   2. Ø; de   3. d'; à   4. à   5. d'   6. de   7. à   8. d'   9. Ø   10. de   11. à   12. de 13. de   14. Ø   15. de   16. à   17. de; Ø   18. Ø   19. à   20. à

32·6   1. José et Julie nous ont invités à passer nos vacances avec eux.   2. Nous allons acheter un nouvel ordinateur.   3. Joël déteste faire la cuisine.   4. Sophie ne peut pas s'habituer à se lever à six heures tous les matins.   5. Ils ont réussi à rencontrer le président d'Air France.   6. Je le soupçonne de faire semblant (feindre) d'être malade ce week-end.   7. Nicolas a peur de perdre les élections.   8. Ils ont promis de nous rendre visite à la fin du mois.   9. Tu dois apprendre à jouer de la guitare.   10. J'espère que vous aimez votre nouvel appartement.

32·7   Port-au-Prince

Je suis né **à** Port-au-Prince **en** Haïti, j'ai grandi et passé mon enfance **à** Petit-Goâve. **À** Port-au-Prince, j'ai travaillé comme journaliste, puis j'ai dû quitté mon pays, exilé, pour venir **à** Montréal où j'ai travaillé **à** l'usine, **dans** différentes usines avant **d'**écrire mon premier roman.

Montréal à écrire

C'est **au** Carré Saint-Louis que j'ai commencé **à** écrire. Pour moi, Montréal, c'est la machine **à** écrire. C'est la modernité. Je n'ai jamais cru que je pourrais écrire **à** la main **à** Montréal. Montréal, c'est aussi la distance. Je suis **dans** cette petite chambre et j'écris **sur** Petit-Goâve, Port-au-Prince tout **en** sachant que les gens qui vont me lire, pour la plupart, ne connaissent pas ces villes. Ça me donne une certaine liberté. Je n'ai pas **à** fictionaliser ces villes. Elles sont déjà fictions pour mes lecteurs.

Ville en images

Quand j'ai fait un film **sur** Montréal, j'ai voulu que ce soit **en** hiver. Un hiver aussi fort que l'été du tournage de *Comment faire l'amour*. Parce que je trouvais que c'était comme si je regardais Montréal cette fois-ci pour lui-même, pour elle-même. Et **à** Montréal, il y a un hiver. Je ne peux pas passer ma vie **à** croire que Montréal est une ville du sud. Montréal, c'est aussi une ville nordique. J'ai voulu m'approcher **de** cet hiver-là et essayer **de** l'apprivoiser, essayer **de** sentir cela parce que je crois que c'est l'image fondamentale de Montréal et du Québec. D'ailleurs Gilles Vigneault, le grand poète québécois, a dit: « D'un glaçon, j'ai fait l'hiver. Mon pays, ce n'est pas un pays, c'est l'hiver ». Je ne peux pas continuer **à** ne pas voir qu'il y a un hiver dans ce pays, et j'ai voulu qu'il soit le plus fort. Et dans « Comment conquérir l'Amérique **en** une nuit », il me semblait que je devais faire quelque chose qui réconcilie les deux villes et Montréal et Port-au-Prince, deux villes qui m'habitent. J'ai pensé qu'il faudrait qu'un film montre un peu les passages successifs entre les deux villes comme s'il n'y avait même pas d'espace. Je parle **de** l'espace tendre **entre** Montréal et Port-au-Prince. Donc c'était un plaisir que je voulais me faire, de faire ce film. J'ai pas été surpris **par** la ville. Je voulais que l'image

Answer key   **637**

me fasse voir la ville sous un autre angle, d'une autre manière, et ça je l'ai voulu. Oui, tout à fait. Et je l'ai eu. J'ai voulu aussi qu'il y ait des choses que l'être humain ne peut pas voir. C'est trop minuscule, on y passe . . . On voit la ville tellement avec nos émotions quand on y passe et que je me suis dit que peut-être je, en regardant le film, je regarderai les choses que je n'ai pas vues parce que je les avais tellement absorbées rapidement en émotion et non en images.

Un petit tour de ville et puis s'ennuie

Je ne regarde pas les villes précisément. Une grande majorité de mes chroniques à l'étranger se passent **dans** une salle de bain ou **dans** une chambre d'hôtel. Mon rêve, c'est de ne jamais être un touriste. Le touriste pour moi, c'est celui qui regarde, qui cherche à savoir. Moi, je ne cherche pas **à** savoir. Je cherche à sentir. Il me faut un but. Je marche, je vais **chez** un copain dans une ville que je viens à peine **de** connaître. C'est le trajet qui m'intéresse et le désir **d'**être chez le copain. C'est beaucoup plus les intérieurs qui me plaisent, être **dans** un bar, être **dans** une libraire, être **chez** un ami, être un peu partout. Le trajet, quand je vais dans une ville généralement—comme j'y vais comme conférencier et pour mes livres—je suis reçu par quelqu'un et qui me fait toujours faire un petit tour de la ville. C'est la partie la moins agréable pour moi parce que je n'aime pas qu'on me raconte une ville et son histoire. Et je n'aime pas qu'on me montre surtout les monuments ou les endroits importants. Ce qui m'intéresse, c'est juste **de** marcher et **de** voir le peu possible qui arrive **à** attirer ma rétine. Et finalement **par** incubation, **de** finir par sentir la ville. Je veux que la ville s'amène **à** moi. Je ne veux pas la découvrir. Je veux qu'elle me découvre.

(Extrait d'un entretien de Dany Laferrière réalisé par Annie Heminway à Montréal en février 2009, pour blog *La ville est ailleurs*, aubepine.blog.lemonde.fr de Frédéric Antoine Brosson et Annie Heminway.)

33 French in conversation: Meeting people

33·1   1. F   2. F   3. F   4. T   5. F

33·2   1. Salut/Ça   2. Pas/toi   3. bien/sais/suis   4. même   5. Je pige

33·3   1. vous   2. elle   3. Toi   4. moi   5. lui

33·4   1. T   2. T   3. F   4. F   5. T

33·5   1. d   2. f   3. g   4. e   5. h   6. b   7. c   8. a

33·6   1. T   2. T   3. F   4. T   5. T

33·7   1. je peux   2. prendre   3. peut-être une autre fois   4. je peux   5. habite   6. ça se fait

33·8   1. Bonjour / Enchanté   2. monsieur / l'ami   3. madame / Je m'appelle   4. là / voilà   5. pote / va
6. Très

33·9   1. F   2. T   3. T   4. F   5. T

33·10   1. sa   2. son   3. sa   4. son   5. ses   6. ses   7. C'est le père de Didier.   8. Il est enchanté de faire la connaissance de Chris.   9. C'est sa mère. 10. Elle est affectueuse.   11. C'est sa sœur.   12. Elle est mariée.

33·11   1. Bonjour, Chris. Comment allez-vous?   2. Bien, merci. Je suis ravi de faire votre connaissance.
3. C'est bien vous, l'ami anglais de Didier?   4. Pas exactement. Je suis son copain américain.
5. Excusez-moi. Je sais bien que vous êtes son copain américain.   6. Comme c'est samedi aujourd'hui, nous avons tous deux un peu de temps libre.   7. C'est bien. Le samedi, la famille dîne toujours ensemble et on voulait tous vous rencontrer.

34 French in conversation: Making conversation and making plans

34·1   1. T   2. T   3. F   4. T   5. F

34·2   1. vous   2. moi   3. m'appelle   4. J'ai entendu parler   5. aux États-Unis   6. c'est vrai
7. exactement   8. au Colorado   9. plaît 10. Qu'est-ce qui   11. grandes villes   12. des copains
13. j'avais envie

34·3   1. T   2. F   3. T   4. F   5. T

34·4   1. b   2. f   3. h   4. d   5. g   6. a   7. e   8. c

34·5   1. T   2. T   3. F   4. F   5. T

34·6	1. a 2. d 3. e 4. b 5. f 6. c 7. a 8. d 9. f 10. b 11. e 12. c
34·7	1. F 2. T 3. F 4. T 5. F
34·8	1. a 2. e 3. g 4. f 5. b 6. h 7. c 8. d
34·9	1. profite 2. suis 3. me promener 4. quitter 5. me baigner 6. me bronzer 7. lire 8. me suffit 9. Et puis 10. tout seul
34·10	1. T 2. T 3. F 4. F 5. T
34·11	1. prêt 2. d'accord 3. Mais non, voyons 4. Ce qui est intéressant 5. C'est parce que 6. C'est gentil 7. Alors 8. si tu veux 9. Il y a mille choses à faire 10. Dommage
34·12	1. F 2. T 3. T 4. F 5. T
34·13	1. a 2. e 3. f 4. b 5. d 6. c
34·14	1. Je vais venir te chercher. 2. N'importe quand. 3. Volontiers. 4. C'est au sujet de Facebook. / Il s'agit de Facebook. Ça m'intéresse. 5. Le sujet est bon, mais le film? On verra. 6. Écoute, je serai chez toi à six heures.
34·15	1. Je suis un cours d'histoire de l'art le mercredi avec le professeur Pouce. 2. Quelle surprise! Moi aussi, je suis un cours d'histoire de l'art avec le professeur Pouce mais le lundi. 3. Mon cours n'est qu'une introduction, et le tien? 4. Mon cours est un cours de seconde année et je l'adore. 5. Tu vas régulièrement visiter les musées alors? 6. Tu penses bien! Je passe tout mon temps libre dans les musées et les galeries d'art. Tu veux me rejoindre demain à une exposition d'art moderne? 7. Volontiers! À quelle heure? 8. N'importe quand après dix-neuf heures.

35 French in conversation: Discussing current events

35·1	1. F 2. T 3. T 4. T 5. F
35·2	1. Ici 2. Quoi de neuf 3. grève 4. poisse 5. Pas de 6. Zut 7. comme ça 8. On dirait 9. Ça arrive 10. en pleine saison 11. non 12. ce sera super
35·3	1. Zut! Quelle poisse! 2. Oui, j'en ai. 3. Tu plaisantes? / Sans blague? 4. Pas de nouvelles du tout! 5. Je vois. On dirait que tu as raison! 6. Ça dépend! Pas si bien quand tu aimes ton cours / quand ton cours te plaît. 7. On verra. 8. Tu penses/trouves qu'elles sont super, ces grèves, n'est-ce pas? / non?
35·4	1. T 2. F 3. F 4. F 5. F
35·5	1. c 2. d 3. a 4. b 5. g 6. h 7. e 8. f
35·6	1. neige 2. Zut 3. On dirait que 4. être de retour 5. Veinard 6. plaisanter 7. Franchement 8. raison
35·7	1. F 2. T 3. T 4. T 5. T
35·8	1. c 2. f 3. a 4. b 5. d 6. e
35·9	1. où en est-on 2. Il paraît 3. Je me demande 4. qui circule 5. batteries 6. écologiques 7. Décidément 8. on parle 9. évident 10. tant que ça
35·10	1. Mariette, regarde la vidéo que je viens de trouver en ligne. Tu vas l'adorer! 2. Il s'agit de quoi? 3. Il s'agit du mariage de... 4. La mariée est magnifique en blanc et le marié est beau comme un dieu. 5. Je me demande combien coûte un mariage pareil? 6. Ça coûte plus que tu ne peux imaginer ou t'offrir.

36 French in conversation: Asking for help

36·1	1. T 2. F 3. F 4. T 5. F
36·2	1. reviens 2. le rayon 3. lasses 4. comme tout 5. faim 6. quelque chose 7. blagues 8. t'ai eue
36·3	1. c 2. f 3. d 4. e 5. a 6. b
36·4	1. F 2. T 3. T 4. F 5. F
36·5	1. Ce n'est pas très gentil 2. Mais je suis pressé 3. il te faut 4. J'ai besoin de / Il me faut de nouveaux pulls et de nouvelles chemises 5. il me faut 6. dès qu'on aura / aussitôt qu'on aura 7. c'est gentil/sympa de ta part 8. C'est où / Où est-ce / Où est-ce que c'est 9. c'est à cet étage / est-ce à cet étage / est-ce que c'est à cet étage? 10. suivez-moi

Answer key   **639**

36·6 1. F   2. F   3. T   4. F   5. T

36·7 1. monsieur   2. plaisir   3. déranger   4. droite   5. mauvaise   6. mademoiselle

36·8 1. T   2. F   3. F   4. F   5. T

36·9 1. F   2. F   3. T   4. T   5. F

36·10 1. Excusez-moi, madame, je cherche le rayon des vêtements de femme.   2. Ce rayon est en bas, mademoiselle.   3. Nous sommes au premier étage? / Est-ce que nous sommes au premier étage? / Sommes-nous au premier étage?   4. Oui, mademoiselle.   5. Je vous remercie, madame.   6. De rien. / Il n'y a pas de quoi. / Je vous en prie, mademoiselle.

Translations

1

Strait Is the Gate

André Gide, 1909

"Why," said she, "wasn't the door shut?"

"I knocked, but you didn't answer. Alissa, you know I'm going tomorrow?"

She answered nothing, but I laid down the necklace, which she could not succeed in fastening. The word *engagement* seemed to me too bare, too brutal; I used I know not what periphrasis in its stead. As soon as Alissa understood what I meant, I thought I saw her sway and lean against the mantelpiece for support—but I myself was trembling so much that in my fearfulness, I avoided looking at her.

I was near her, and without raising my eyes, I took her hand; she did not free herself, but bending down her face a little and raising my hand a little, she put her lips on it and murmured, as she half leant against me:

"No, Jerome, no; don't, please, let us be engaged."

"Why?"

"It's I that ought to ask you why," she said, "why change?"

I did not dare speak to her of yesterday's conversation, but no doubt she felt I was thinking of it, and as if in answer to my thought, said, as she looked at me earnestly:

"You are wrong, dear. I do not need so much happiness. Are we not happy enough as we are?"

She tried in vain to smile.

"No, since I have to leave you."

"Listen, Jerome, I can't speak to you this evening—don't let's spoil our last minutes. No, no. I'm as fond of you as ever; don't be afraid. I'll write to you; I'll explain. I promise I'll write to you—tomorrow—as soon as you have gone. Leave me now!"

32

Translation of letter

My dear granddaughter Chloé,

I commend you! I am delighted to learn that you plan to pursue a master's degree in literature at New York University. Once you begin to learn Voltaire's language, you will fall in love with the beauty of French literature. But be careful: they say that grammar is *a sweet song*–I paraphrase the title of a well-known book by the French author Érik Orsenna, I say that it is riddled with mystery, bristling with pitfalls, and spiced with magic!

For example, some prepositions are wizards, chameleons, able to completely transform the meaning of a verb. Here are a few examples:

de/par: I will celebrate my next birthday in Napa Valley, surrounded by my California clan. Mrs. Obama will celebrate her next birthday there, like me, surrounded by her clan and also by the Secret Service—protection against possible danger.

de/à/par: She holds her granddaughter by the hand; the little girl takes after her, with her blue eyes, her platinum blond hair; a booklover and Francophile, she is very fond of her collection of French books, from Gustave Flaubert to Amélie Nothomb.

There's a young man who is really irritating, boring, and annoying. He has no right to use the second person singular with my dear kitty LÉO; he is not entitled to this form of address—(it's different if *droit* is followed by a noun or by a verb). A princess can never escape her golden cage; Charles Manson will never be able to escape from prison (figurative or literal).

dans/en (général/spécifique; time): Celebrities usually fly in a private jet; I am on a plane bound for Paris, I study *French Demystified* by Annie Heminway; I must master the pitfalls and the challenges of the French language before landing. In two hours, I read "Chapter 14: All about prepositions." In four hours, I'll be in Paris, prepositions polished!

There are temperamental prepositions that flirt with verbs, no formula:

de/en: Jeanne Gonzalès began to sob when she saw the portrait of Berthe Morisot by Édouard Manet; she was foaming with rage and she burst into tears. Did her rival burst into laughter, or did she laugh her head of or until she cried when she dissected this portrait?

de/au: Édouard Manet's mother loves to play the piano; to tinkle away; she escapes from daily life; she has no desire to play golf, a useless pastime, in her opinion.

Verbs have just as much fun as prepositions do, no rule:

Gervaise, Zola's laundress, does everything: she does the dishes, she does the laundry, and she washes the linens at the washhouse. Please note, this is laundering, it is not money laundering.

I glance at the wardrobe of our dear author, Alain Mabanckou, and I give him a wink.

And there are verbs that fiddle around with their prepositions:

Keep your feet on the ground: if you are ever struck by an earthquake, you fall to the ground; we don't want to put you into the ground; we fall flat on our face; we want the ground to swallow us up (from shame); we don't want to land.

The meaning of a verb can change with the introduction of a reflexive pronoun:

Eva Gonzalès, pupil of the celebrated painter Manet, overshadows her sister Jeanne; suddenly, immediately following the master's death, she slips away and dies.

We lay ourselves bare, like Ananda Devi; we are naked as the day we were born, like Amélie Nothomb at Burning Man.

We cannot neglect the position of adjectives: before or after the noun—figurative or literal.

Charles de Gaulle was big. He was a tall man—he measured 1.93 meters. In times of crisis, he really was a great man. He will remain in the annals of History.

And how about accents, the circumflex, for example?

She returned from her stay on the Île de Ré tanned; the sailors hauled a large whale on board.

And homonyms, feminine or masculine? And euphoric homonyms?

In front of his wood-burning stove, my youngest son William finds a hair from his cat Aphrodite in the crepe pan; it's not funny.

I've had just about enough: I hide under a veil, and I head off.

In verse, she writes about the life of a green worm in a glass of rosé in Ver-sur-Mer.

At my house, in the country, the ground is covered with pines, the basket is full of bread.

Erik Orsenna told me that the sea is his mother not his mayor.

That's enough! I hope that my advice hasn't spoiled your appetite for studying French! Good luck, dear granddaughter!

With a big kiss, Lili

Lisa Ehrenkranz

(Translated by Ellen Sowchek)

Port-au-Prince

Born in Port-au-Prince, Haiti, I grew up in Petit-Goâve, my childhood home. After working, as a journalist in Port-au-Prince, I had to leave my country. Living as an exile in Montreal, I had several factory jobs before writing my first novel.

Writing Montreal

Saint Louis Square is where I started writing. To me, Montreal means the typewriter. Montreal is modernity. I never thought I could write in longhand in Montreal. Montreal is also distance. Here I am, in a small room, writing about Petit-Goâve and Port-au-Prince, realizing that most of my readers do not know these cities. This affords me a certain kind of freedom. I don't need to fictionalize these cities. For my readers, they are already fictional.

A city of images

When I decided to make a film about Montreal, I wanted it to be in wintertime. I wanted a winter as severe as the summer of filming *How to Make Love*. This would enable me to look at Montreal as if I were seeing the city as it truly was, for the very first time. Because there is a winter in Montreal. I cannot go through life experiencing Montreal as a southern city. Montreal is also a Nordic city. I wanted to step closer to that winter, in an effort to tame it, to feel it, because I believe it to be the fundamental image of Montreal and Quebec. Indeed, it was Gilles Vigneault, the great Quebec poet, who once said: "I created winter from a single icicle. My land is not a land. My land is winter." I could not continue ignoring this country's winter, and I wanted that winter to be as harsh as possible. Also, in *How to Conquer America in One Night*, it seemed to me that I needed to reconcile Montreal and Port-au-Prince, the two cities that inhabit me. I wanted the film to say something—as if there were no space—about the successive paths linking the two cities. I'm talking about the gentle space between Montreal and Port-au-Prince. Truth be told, I wanted to make this film for my own pleasure. I was not surprised by the city. I wanted the image to make me see the city from a different angle, in a different way—that's what I wanted. Yes, absolutely. And I succeeded. I also wanted to include things that elude the human eye. We pass by, it's too minute. . . . Essentially, we see a city through our emotions. In fact, these emotions are so intense that I believe that watching the film will enable me to see paths traveled with new eyes, to perceive things that initially eluded me because I hastily absorbed them as feelings and not as images.

A quick tour of the city, and then boredom

I don't really look at cities. I write almost all my travel stories in a tub or in a hotel room. Not ever having to be a tourist is my dream. A tourist, for me, is an observer, a person who wants to know. I, on the other hand, do not desire to know. I desire to feel. I need a destination. I am walking in a city that I'm just getting to know; I'm on my way to meet a close friend. What I'm focusing on is the route and my desire to be at my friend's place. What I really prefer is being indoors, in a bar, in a bookstore, at a friend's place—sort of everywhere. When there is a particular destination in a city, where I am giving a lecture or promoting my books, someone usually meets me and takes me, without fail, on a short tour of the city. That is my least favorite part of the visit, because I don't like to listen to stories about a city and its history. And I definitely don't like being shown monuments or important sites. What I really like to do is to simply stroll around, noticing only the minimum that attracts my attention. This is how, after a period of incubation, I end up getting a feel for a city. I want the city to come to me. I don't want to discover it. I want it to discover me. *Translated by Zoran Minderovic.*

(From an interview with Dany Laferrière by Annie Heminway in Montreal, Canada, in February 2009, for the blog *La ville est ailleurs*, aubepine.blog.lemonde.fr, by Frédéric Antoine Brosson and Annie Heminway.)